POWER

& RESISTANCE

POWER

& RESISTANCE

CRITICAL THINKING ABOUT CANADIAN SOCIAL ISSUES

4TH EDITION

edited by
Les Samuelson
Wayne Antony

Fernwood Publishing • Halifax

Editing: Robert Clarke
Cover Art: Jim Pringle and John van der Woude
Printed and bound in Canada by Hignell Book Printing

Published in Canada by Fernwood Publishing
Site 2A, Box 5, 32 Oceanvista Lane
Black Point, Nova Scotia, B0J 1B0
and 324 Clare Avenue, Winnipeg, Manitoba, R3L 1S3
www.fernwoodpublishing.ca

Fernwood Publishing Company Limited gratefully acknowledges the financial support
of the Government of Canada through the Book Publishing Industry Development
Program (BPDIP), the Canada Council for the Arts and the Nova Scotia
Department of Tourism and Culture for our publishing program.

Library and Archives Canada Cataloguing in Publication

Power and resistance: critical thinking about Canadian social
issues / Les Samuelson and Wayne Antony, eds. -- 4th ed.

Includes bibliographical references and index.
ISBN 978-1-55266-224-3

1. Social problems--Canada. 2. Canada--Social conditions.
I. Antony, Wayne Andrew, 1950- II. Samuelson, Leslie, 1953-

HN103.5.P68 2006   305.0971   C2006-906210-2

CONTENTS

ACKNOWLEDGEMENTS

Thank you to everyone involved in making this book happen. Thanks to all of the contributors for all your hard work, for your insights and your patience through what can be a rocky process in working with a large group — to those who revised their chapters (some now for the fourth time), to those who contributed to previous editions of *Power and Resistance*, and to those who have joined us for this fourth edition. Thank you again to Robert Clarke — your editing skills have contributed much to the success of all of the editions of *Power and Resistance*. We are grateful to all the folks at Fernwood who worked on the production of the book: Beverley Rach for designing the book, Debbie Mathers for typing the final manuscript, and Brenda Conroy for proofreading. Thanks to Jim Pringle for the cover design, which has been with us through all four editions. And, finally, thanks to all the people — individuals and groups — who continue to struggle for social justice in Canada; your dedication is an inspiration to everyone.
Wayne Antony
Les Samuelson

ABOUT THE AUTHORS

WAYNE ANTONY is a founding member of the Canadian Centre for Policy Alternatives–Manitoba (CCAP-MB) and has been on the board of directors since its inception, and taught sociology at the University of Winnipeg for eighteen years. He is co-author of three reports on the state of public services in Manitoba (for CCAP-MB) and co-editor of two other books (both with Dave Broad): *Citizens or Consumers? Social Policy in a Market Society* and *Capitalism Rebooted? Work and Welfare in the New Economy*.

PAT ARMSTRONG is a professor of Sociology and Women's Studies at York University. She is co-author or editor of many books on health care, including *Caring for/Caring About*; *Exposing Privatization: Women and Health Reform in Canada; Unhealthy Times; Heal Thyself: Managing Health Care Reform;* and *Wasting Away: The Undermining of Canadian Health Care*. She has also published on a wide variety of issues related to women's work and social policy. She chairs a working group on health reform that includes representatives from the Centres of Excellence for Women's Health and holds a CHSFR/CHIR Chair in Health Services with a focus on gender.

BRENDA AUSTIN-SMITH is an associate professor of English and Film at the University of Manitoba. She does research on film and emotion, and has published articles and essays on subjects ranging from U.S. literature to Canadian women film directors to cinematic adaptations. She has been a member of the *Canadian Dimension* editorial collective since 1990, and is very active in her local union.

BLOCK 1912 COLLECTIVE members Debra Davidson, Mike Gismondi, and Ineke Lock revised chapter 14. Ineke Lock is now writing her doctoral thesis at the University of Alberta, comparing EnCana Corporation's corporate social responsibility practices in Ecuador with its practices in Alberta. Living close to the Alberta tar sands, Deborah and Mike have started a new research project analyzing the social construction of Canada's so-called "Saudi Arabia of the North." The original Block 1912 Collective included Michelle Shari Lee, Jeji Varghese, and Angela Wilson as well as Davidson, Gismondi and Lock.

BRIAN CALLIOU is the program director of Aboriginal Leadership and Management at the Banff Centre, Banff, Alberta. Brian's research interests include Aboriginal leadership, self-government, economic development, Aboriginal and treaty rights, and legal history. He is Cree and a member of the Sucker Creek First Nation, in the Treaty No. 8 territory of North-Central Alberta.

WENDY CHAN is an associate professor in the Department of Sociology and Anthropology at Simon Fraser University. Her research examines how processes of criminalization and racialization in both the immigration and welfare system result in the marginalization of people of colour in Canada. Recent publications include *Women, Madness and the Law: A Feminist Reader* (co-edited with Robert Menzies and Dorothy Chunn) and "Crime, Deportation and the Regulation of Immigrants in Canada," in *Crime, Law and Social Change*.

JANET CONWAY teaches feminism, social movements, and democratic theory in the Politics Department at Ryerson University in Toronto. She is a long-time activist in women's and anti-poverty movements, in cross-sectoral social justice coalitions, and since 2002 in the Toronto Social Forum. She is the author of *Identity, Place, Knowledge: Social Movements Contesting Globalization*.

PARVIN GHORAYSHI is a professor in the Department of Sociology, University of Winnipeg. Her research interests include civil society organizations and community development in the countries of the South and the North. She is the author of *Women and Work in Developing Countries* and has contributed to *Gender, Race and Nation: A Global Perspective*. Her most recent research and publications focus on transformative community economic development, and the role of Canada as a recipient nation in the global diaspora.

GARY KINSMAN has been an activist in gay liberation, AIDS, anti-poverty, and anti-capitalist organizing for more than thirty years. He is a professor of sociology at Laurentian University in Sudbury and the author of *The Regulation of Desire: Homo and Hetero Sexualities* and many articles on gender and sexual politics. He is a co-editor of *Whose National Security? Canadian State Surveillance and the Creation of Enemies; Mine Mill Fights Back,* and *Sociology for Changing the World: Social Movements/Social Research.*

MURRAY KNUTTILA teaches in the Department of Sociology and Social Studies at the University of Regina, where he is also research faculty in the Saskatchewan Population Health & Evaluation Research Unit. His work ranges across issues such as state theory, Canadian agricultural policy, rural Saskatchewan, men, masculinities, and health and health services delivery. Murray is also co-author of *State Theories*, third edition, among many other publications dealing with the state.

RUTH MANN is an associate professor in the criminology program of the Department of Sociology and Anthropology at the University of Windsor. Ruth is author of *Who Owns Domestic Abuse?* and editor of *Juvenile Crime and Delinquency*. Her research includes a project focusing on "men's rights"/"fathers' rights" backlash and its policy impacts; and a larger SSHRC-funded project (with co-investigator Charlene Senn) on youth violence and youth violence interventions under the *Youth Criminal Justice Act*.

SUSAN MCDANIEL's research interests include social policy, gender, aging, population, health, family change, and social dimensions of innovation. She served as the first vice-president research of the University of Windsor (2004–06), where she is now professor of sociology, after serving on the faculty of the University of Alberta, 1989 to 2004. She is widely published and cited, is a frequent speaker at national and international conferences, advises governments in Canada, the United Kingdom, and the European Union on social policies and official data collection, and is the recipient of numerous research and teaching awards. Her research now focuses on intergenerational transfers/linkages and social engagement, social dimensions of innovation, and family/social policy challenges in globalizing Western democracies.

DANIEL MORRISON grew up in Peterborough, Ontario, Canada. In 2006 he completed an M.A. in international development studies at Dalhousie University in Halifax, Nova Scotia. His M.A. thesis was on the Intercontinental Youth Camp and World Social Forum. As a university student he did much research on social activism and was involved in social justice groups. He continues to work with others on social justice issues outside of Canada.

CLAIRE POLSTER is an associate professor in the Department of Sociology and Social Studies at the University of Regina. She has published widely on the continuing transformation of Canadian higher education and its implications for the public interest. She has also been involved in a number of campaigns aimed at resisting the corporatization of Canada's universities and reclaiming our universities as public service institutions.

LES SAMUELSON teaches sociology at the University of Saskatchewan. He has an active interest in social justice initiatives, especially at the community level. His specific research interests include justice reform, especially as it pertains to Aboriginal people, and international crime, justice, and human rights.

KRISTA SCOTT-DIXON holds a Ph.D. in women's studies. Her first book, *Doing IT,* explored the experiences of women working in information technology. She has also published a second edited book, *Trans/Forming Feminisms: Transfeminist Voices Speak Out* and manages the Gender and Work Database project at York University (http://www.genderwork.ca).

JIM SILVER is a professor in and chair of the Politics Department at the University of Winnipeg, and a founding and long-time board member of the Canadian Centre for Policy Alternatives–Manitoba. He is the author of *In Their Own Voices: Building Urban Aboriginal Communities*, co-author of *Building a Better World: An Introduction to Trade Unions in Canada*, and editor of *Solutions That Work: Fighting Poverty in Winnipeg*.

CORA VOYAGEUR teaches sociology at the University of Calgary. Her research explores the Aboriginal experience in Canada. She is the co-editor of *Hidden in Plain Sight: Contributions of Aboriginal People to Canadian Culture and Identity*, volumes I and II, and the author of *Women Chiefs in Canada*.

INTRODUCTION
Social Problems and Social Power

Wayne Antony and Les Samuelson

This book is about thinking about social issues... thinking about the pollution of our air, water, and soil, about the poverty that is increasingly widespread and seemingly impervious to all efforts to eradicate it, about the truly horrible experiences of violence between men and women, about the effects of globalization, about the glacial pace of Aboriginal economic development. It is about trying to figure out the conflicts, troubles, and dilemmas that confront us as Canadians.

In a simple but absolutely crucial sense, how we think about social problems depends on how we approach thinking about social life in general. At the risk of oversimplification, we can say that there are two basic approaches to getting below the surface of our lives in society. There is what we call the "traditional" way — some would call it the "uncritical" or perhaps the "neo-liberal" way — and there is the "critical" way. (In chapter 1 Murray Knuttila describes the theories in these two approaches in more detail.)

One way of explaining these different ways of knowing about social life is to go back to a classic statement on the nature and value of the "sociological imagination" made almost fifty years ago. In 1959 C. Wright Mills made an important distinction (despite his use of non-inclusive language) between "private troubles" and "public issues." He said:

> Troubles occur within the character of the individual and within the range of his immediate relations

"You Should Know This"

- During the free-trade era (1989–2004), the bottom 20 percent of Canadian families saw their income fall by 7.6 percent while the top 20 percent saw theirs rise by 16.8 percent.
- The wealthiest 10 percent of families in Canada control 53 percent of the wealth, and the bottom 50 percent have 5.6 percent of the wealth.
- The suicide rate for First Nations people is three times the national rate; for young First Nations people it is five to six times higher.
- At least one in four recent immigrants with a university degree and employed between 1991 and 2001 has a job requiring no more than a high-school diploma, twice the rate for native-born Canadians.
- Women on average make 71 percent of what men earn, even in female-dominated occupations; more than half of Canada's top 500 companies have no women on their boards.
- A Vector Research poll showed that most Canadians are willing to pay higher taxes for social objectives like child poverty (74 percent), publicly funded child care (57 percent), educational training (68 percent), and improving public schools (58 percent).
- The conservative think-tanks in Canada operate on large budgets: just one, the Fraser Institute, had a budget of $8.2 million in 2005. So-called left-wing think-tanks are fewer in number: the Canadian Centre for Policy Alternatives had a 2005 budget of $3.1 million.

Sources: Campbell 2006; Kersetter 2002; RCAP 1995; Statistics Canada 2004c; CRIAW 2005; Kingston 2005; Dobbin 1999; Fraser Institute 2006: 36; personal communication CCPA.

> How we think about social problems depends on how we approach thinking about social life in general.

with others; they have to do with his self and with those limited areas of social life of which he is directly and personally aware. Issues have to do with matters that transcend these local environments of the individual and the range of his inner life. They have to do with the organization of many such milieux into the institutions of an historical society as a whole, with the ways in which various milieux overlap and interpenetrate to form the larger structure of social and historical life. (Mills 1959: 8)

For some analysts, then, social problems are really about private troubles; for others, social problems involve public issues.

THE TRADITIONAL APPROACH — INDIVIDUALS AND FREEDOM

For the traditional approach, society is essentially a bundle of private troubles. In his view of troubles and issues, Mills was pointing out a profound bias in North American thinking: the tendency to see society in almost purely individual terms. For so many people, the understanding, or explanation, of how society works really comes down to the individual choices that people make. As human beings, we decide what we will eat, where we will live, what work we will do, how we will treat others, whether we will go to university or community college, what music we will listen to, who or if we will marry, and so on. We choose to do what is best for each of us. If we need to, we decide to work with others to achieve some of our goals. These choices are constrained, but only within very wide boundaries. We cannot act in ways that threaten others — their lives, their freedom, their rights; we cannot take our neighbour's new car just because driving around in it will make us feel good or because we need a car.

These constraints on freedom, the traditional approach argues, are the result of obvious and natural boundaries or at least choices on which everyone, or at least a majority of people, agrees. This is a perspective that is also preoccupied with the problem of social order, which means that it is a "set of widely shared and accepted beliefs and values" that "serve as a kind of moral cement, binding and bonding ... a social system together" (Knuttila, chapter 1).

Social theorists who call themselves pluralists share this emphasis on freedom (see chapter 1 for details). Pluralists argue that capitalist, liberal democracies are free because there are no dominant groups in society. These societies have a free press, and most people have access to the information that they need to have in order to know what is going on. Everyone is free to vote and to try to influence social and political processes. Without these kinds of individual freedoms, such a society would break down.

In its most radical form, this traditional and individualist approach can lead to the claim — made by Margaret Thatcher, prime minister of Britain from 1979 to 1990 — that there is no society, only individuals. This sense of radical individualism underlies the neo-liberal revolution, of which Thatcher was the political architect in England. Neo-liberalism, a term used mostly in political economy, proclaims the efficiency and effectiveness of the competitive market. In more general social terms, neo-liberals see society as made up of freely interacting individuals. If there is even such a thing as the common good, it is produced when freely interacting individuals are not restricted in the pursuit of their own best interests. For neo-liberals, most restrictions on individual freedom, especially in the form of government regulation, are counterproductive to a prosperous and harmonious society.

THE CRITICAL APPROACH — STRUCTURES AND POWER

In this book we look at social issues in a different way. We look at society through a critical lens. Keeping in mind Mills's distinction between public issues and private troubles, this approach begins with the observation that to understand our lives we need to examine the institutions — the social structure — of the community and society. As Mills (1959: 10–11) argues:

> What we experience in various and specific milieux... is often caused by structural changes. Accordingly, to understand the changes of many personal milieux we are required to look beyond them.... To be aware of the idea of social structure and to use it with sensibility is to be capable of tracing [the] linkages among a great variety of milieux. To be able to do that is to possess the sociological imagination.

In other words, to fully understand our lives in society we need to think within a structural or institutional framework. We need to employ a sociological imagination.

One way of getting at what this means is to return to the idea of the choices that we can and do make. If we think, even for just a minute, about how our choices — clothes, food, jobs, partners, education — work in everyday life, one of the first things we recognize is that some people have a wider range of choices than others do. Some people can choose between university and community college. Others can choose which university they will go to. But many others cannot choose either. Instead, they have to work to support themselves and others close to them.

> If we think, even for just a minute, about our choices — clothes, food, jobs, partners, education, work in everyday life... we recognize that some people have a wider range of choices than others do.

For critical thinkers, a key feature of our social structure, and the second key part of a critical approach, is inequality. In turn, inequalities are seen not just as differences in lifestyle — some people, more than others, may have and want bigger cars, the latest clothing fashions, to dine at the most elegant restaurants... more stuff. More to the point, inequality indicates a narrowing of life choices for many people — not just in what they have but also in what they can do and become.

Power resides in social relationships, and it can take many forms. Power can be exercised by virtually anyone, almost anywhere. A CEO tells the executive committee that they must devise plans to increase profits by 20 percent over the next four fiscal quarters. A software development supervisor forces a programmer, who insists on wearing a Rage Against the Machine T-shirt, to work night shifts or irregular overtime or on weekends. The big kid in Grade Six forces a smaller kid to give up a place in the cafeteria queue. In other words, there are many possible bases of power, especially when it comes to one individual pitted against another.

But even in these examples the people acting are not just individuals. Power, in the social sense, involves the ways in which people in particular social groups can force people in other social groups to act in certain ways; and these relationships tend to rest on a narrower base:

* white people expropriating land from Aboriginal people, who then find that their social and economic activities cannot conform to their own views of who they want to be and what kind of direction they want to pursue (see Cora Voyageur and Brian Calliou, chapter 5);
* men using their physical strength and capacity for violence to control women, while the surrounding culture encourages such behaviour and the society as a whole provides many women with little choice but to cope with the fallout (see Ruth Mann, chapter 2);
* business owners deciding on where, when, and under what conditions new technology will be implemented at work, with more regard for the profits and control promised by that technology than for the impact it has on the dignity of those who do the work (see Krista Scott-Dixon, chapter 10).
* heterosexual people, for so many years, deciding that society will see the lives and experiences of gay and lesbian people through the lens of deviance (see Gary Kinsman, chapter 4).

Power can also be, though not necessarily or only, enacted through the state, the government. For example, Les Samuelson (chapter 15) shows that what the state legislates as criminal offences in Canada are not always the most harmful or dangerous behaviours. Most of us at one time or another will unwillingly have money taken from us by corporations, through everything from misleading advertising to predatory pricing to violations of labour standards regulations. But most of these business activities are not defined and treated as criminal theft. Big business has enough power to ensure that the state will protect its need to maximize profits.

Relations of power also occur in other contexts. As Brenda Austin-Smith points out (chapter 3), Hollywood moviemakers tend to envision the world and human relationships in ways that produce and reinforce a particular kind of common sense — a common sense that encourages viewers to accept the social status quo. The so-called "women's films" she discusses reinforce dominant notions of female beauty, desirability, and behaviour. Similarly, as the Block 1912 Collective (chapter 14) tells us, expert scientists had the most influence in determining what was happening to the level of codfish stocks off the coast of Newfoundland. The inordinate influence of these scientists, based on "scientific" data that turned out to be wrong, ended up with inshore (small, community-based) fishers having their livelihoods completely destroyed.

Knowing that our society is characterized by inequality does not mean that we can be certain of how power will operate. In the chapter that opens this book, for example, in addition to identifying several perspectives on the state, both traditional (structural functionalism and pluralism) and critical (Marxism, neo-Marxism, and feminism), Murray Knuttila sets out a critical theory of how the state acts on behalf of the interests of powerful (class, gender, racialized) groups. But, he argues, while we know that such powerful interests dominate society, we cannot specify ahead of time the mechanisms through which power is exercised — that is, only theoretically or abstractly. An understanding of how power actually operates can come only through careful historical research, by uncovering the ways in which the powerful try to protect their interests — sometimes through the state and sometimes elsewhere, all too often successfully and sometimes not.

So, as you can see there are some basic disagreements about the nature of society and how it is organized and operates. These disagreements find their way into thinking about social issues — especially, but not only, their causes. In general terms, thinking about social issues involves trying to understand not only what comes to be seen as a social problem but also how to resolve those problems, both of which are connected to what we think causes social problems.

DEFINING OUR PROBLEMS

In thinking about social issues, we have to first consider what behaviours and conditions (in sociological terms, which groups of people) are social problems. Without getting into a long discussion of "how to define social problems" (which many social problems textbooks do), it is sufficient to say that social problems are both behaviours and conditions that (objectively) harm a significant group of people *and* behaviours and conditions that are (subjectively) defined as harmful. Both elements are part of identifying what is a social problem. Nelson and Fleras (1995: 1–9) say defining social problems involves considering conditions that both threaten and are defined as threatening by a significant segment of the population. Loseke (1999: 5–13) says that social problems involve both the actual harm caused by behaviours and conditions and what people worry about. These definitions, which are representative, are useful and accurate. But, beyond agreement at this very general level, what we will think of as a social problem turns out to be tied up with how we see society being organized.

> Social problems are behaviours and conditions that (objectively) harm a significant group of people and behaviours and conditions that are (subjectively) defined as harmful.

All too often traditional social analyses accept as self-evident the problematic nature of some set of social conditions. In this view there are behaviours that clearly, objectively, obviously disrupt the functioning of society as-it-exists. For example, of late we are constantly being told that violence is a serious problem in our society. We are constantly being warned about certain parts of the cities we live in. And there can be no doubt that violence is

> There are behaviours that clearly, objectively, obviously disrupt the functioning of society as-it-exists.

harmful and disruptive to anyone who encounters it. Yet, as Les Samuelson (chapter 15) and Ruth Mann (chapter 2) show us, we are much more likely to encounter violence at work or through people we know intimately (mainly males) than in those "certain parts of the city."

To take another example: technological innovation is usually not even a blip on the social problems radar. Technological change affects pretty well every one of us, but it is almost always discussed as progress: new technologies have created what is now referred to as "knowledge work," made housework less physically demanding, made movies more realistic; they cure illness, produce more food. Therefore, technology cannot be a problem. For many, that is the objective truth. Yet, as Krista Scott-Dixon (chapter 10) shows, many new technologies have a myriad of harmful effects on working people. Work can be overmonitored (for some workers every single keystroke they make is counted); the skills they have are not utilized or are made redundant (when certain technologies are developed and implemented workers can become little more than machine watchers); technologies can perpetuate discrimination against women (when some technologies come to be seen as "soft"). Seen in light of these conditions, through the eyes and experiences of these people, technology is a problem.

We do have to ask about and determine the objective conditions. But social conditions are actually about people's needs, so — to think this through critically — we have also to ask about whose needs are being met by the existing social set-up. And, on the other side of that coin, we have to ask about whose needs might be better met by disrupting the functioning of society as–it–exists. That is, taking some social condition as self-evidently problematic ignores who is raising the question. Some social analysts and actors — academics, bureaucrats, politicians, business people — are socially positioned so

> We have also to ask about whose needs are being met by the existing social set-up. And... whose needs might be better met by disrupting the functioning of society as-it-exists.

that our society as-it-exists functions well for them. As such, they often characterize social conditions from their standpoint and in their interests. For example, there is no doubting that hundreds of thousands of people are suffering from and dying from AIDS and AIDS-related diseases. But the problem is hardly ever stated in such simple terms. Rather, it is framed in terms of "high-risk" groups, sexual promiscuity, and debates about "responsibility" and "irresponsibility." As Gary Kinsman (in chapter 5) points out, for people living with AIDS and HIV infection, the problem is a lack of access to resources for treatment and prevention, and a lack of social support, not promiscuous sexual behaviour by gay men. In more general terms, looked at from the standpoint and experiences of lesbians and gay men and not from the standpoint of powerful state or professional agencies, and most of the mass media, "Homosexuality is no longer the problem. Rather, heterosexual hegemony and oppressive sexual regulation become the problem."

Many traditional analysts do take the step beyond seeing a social situation as self-evidently, or objectively, a problem. They go on to argue that social conditions become problems or issues when "some value cherished by publics is felt to be threatened" (Mills 1959: 8). That is, it is not "just the facts" and social harm that define what is a social problem. A condition or behaviour can become a social problem if it threatens a social value or if it is perceived by the public as being such a threat (cf. Nelson and Fleras 1995: 8; Loseke 1999: 5, 8–9). There are two interrelated issues here. Values are certainly not irrelevant in building an understanding of why some behaviours or conditions are deemed to be social problems. There is, however, a clear tendency to define problems as arising from a breakdown of an assumed value consensus within society. When we conceptualize and study issues and troubles, we must ask just what cherished values are threatened and/or supported by the characterizing trends of our time.

The case of immigration into Canada is very much about values. Wendy Chan (in chapter 6) tells us that it is the feelings of insecurity that makes immigration a problem for many Canadians. The people who see it as a problem tend to call for strict regulations and law enforcement to deal with the maladaptation of immigrants (in terms of their work skills and economic needs, and their cultural norms) and with the criminals and terrorists who enter Canada as refugees. For them, having too many immigrants and too many people who successfully immigrate represent threats to the safety, prosperity, and harmony of Canada. But as Chan demonstrates, the problem is not lax enforcement of immigration law. Lurking behind the transformation of Canadian immigration law and enforcement is racism. The new immigrants — who in recent decades have come mainly from Asia and Africa — actually threaten to upset a decades-old policy aimed at "keeping Canada white."

In a similar vein, Susan McDaniel (chapter 11) discusses the trend of seeing the family in crisis, as falling apart. Many people see the family this way because so much about the institution is "dysfunctional" — the family has less control over reproduction and over raising children, fewer and fewer members are heterosexual, more and more families are single-parent — going against a long-standing norm. But as McDaniel so carefully documents, the family is more of a problem because there are social groups and historical forces trying to push everyone into a model of the family that does not meet their needs. In this sense, the "problem" of the family, if indeed there is one, is not because of a breakdown of consensus but rather because of disagreements about what the family is and should be. Thus, in analyzing social problems we need not only to clearly identify the values that are at risk, but also, more importantly, to ask about whose values are at risk.

We cannot assume that public perceptions are freely formed. Some analysts within the traditional framework do suggest, "A problem exists when an influential group defines a social condition as threatening to its values" (see, for example, Sullivan and Thompson, 1988: 3). As the Block 1912 Collective puts it (chapter 14), a critical ap-

A critical approach analyzes definitions of the situation as shaped by powerful groups and interests in society — corporations, scientists, the media, interest groups, politicians — and the ability of each group to define reality in ways that are accepted as true.

proach analyzes "definitions of the situation as shaped by powerful groups and interests in society — corporations, scientists, the media, interest groups, politicians — and the ability of each group to define reality in ways that are accepted as true." Janet Mosher (forthcoming) refers to the ability of such "claims makers" to convince the rest of us that some condition or group is a problem and to define the problem in ways that suit their interests. She investigates how so-called welfare fraud is treated as a crime while tax evasion (which robs society of much more money) is not treated as a crime. The people who have access to the means of public debate and discourse can dominate the public agenda not only by defining what will be seen as social problems but also by framing *how* certain issues or conditions will be seen as problems. Powerful and well-off groups tend to have more access to the means of public discourse. Corporations and the wealthy people who own and control the mass media do not force all of us to think in particular ways, but they can determine what will get into the public domain. They are more likely than not to frame social issues in ways that support the status quo (see Austin-Smith, chapter 3, on this as it pertains to the cultural media).

Corporations and the wealthy also have access to think-tanks and policy networks. Organizations like the Canadian Council of Chief Executives and policy research institutes like the Fraser Institute and Conference Board of Canada were organized precisely to produce statistics and analyses that shape the social-issues and public-policy agendas in Canada. These organizations have multi-million-dollar budgets financed by donations from corporations and wealthy Canadians (most of whom are also male and white) (Brownlee 2005: chs. 4, 5).

Closer to home, Claire Polster (chapter 12) shows that through funding university research, corporations are having a huge impact on the kinds of work being done and on how the results of that work are used. As she says, this skews "the general scientific research agenda towards industry needs and interests." Thus, "The research needs of other social groups (particularly those who cannot afford to sponsor academic research) are neglected in favour of the needs of paying clients" and there is an "incentive to pursue lucrative research questions and areas, which are not always the most scientifically valuable or socially useful ones."

The chapter by the Block 1912 Collective deals with, among other things, the issues of ideology and public discourse and debate in several environmental contexts. In the case of the closure of the cod fishery on the Atlantic coast, the writers show us that small fishers knew for years that cod stocks were being overfished by the huge industrial sea harvesters owned and operated by national and transnational corporations. Their voices, however, were drowned out by those of fishery scientists and industrial fishers, who said there was no such depletion. In another case, forestry corporations have been able to hide their ecologically devastating practices behind a definition of sustainable development that privileges economic growth, by talking much about a "new paradigm" in forestry, by fostering a very restricted forum of "stakeholder" consultation, and by setting up the false dilemma of "jobs versus the environment."

For critical analysts, the issue is one of social structure and not merely social values and perceptions. The whole of Mills's *The Sociological Imagination* is taken up with examining the tendencies in sociology that led to what he terms the "cultural and political abdication" of classical (or traditional) social analysis. He castigates value-oriented theories and analyses (like those of his influential contemporary, Talcott Parsons) that are obsessed with the concept of the normative order — that norms and values are the most important element of social analysis. In the normative view, institutional structures are transformed into a sort of "moral sphere," making it "quite difficult even to raise several of the most important problems of any analysis of social structure" (Mills 1959: 36). Such an approach, says Mills, delivers the analyst from any concern with power and political relations, thereby legitimating the existing structures and social arrangements that produce major inequalities in our society. Without putting norms and values into the context of social inequality, such a view turns the values, views, and experiences of society's dominant groups into society's values, views, and experiences. To update and modify an old phrase: "What is good for Microsoft, is good for society."

RESOLVING OUR PROBLEMS — CHANGING INDIVIDUALS?

The other key aspect in thinking about social issues is trying to figure out how to resolve them. Thinking about resolving social problems is really thinking about what causes them. Even more obvious than the link between our understanding of society and what gets defined as a social problem is the connection between that understanding and the kinds of solutions proposed to resolve social problems.

Given its general social outlook, not surprisingly the traditional approach tends to see the problems of a community or society in individual, pathological terms. These analyses usually see social problems as emanating from the personal inadequacies of individuals, from their "private troubles." These personal inadequacies are, in turn, often seen as deriving from inappropriate socialization and dysfunctional behaviour choices. For example, the predominant view of violence between men and women — the so-called "family violence perspective" (see chapter 2) — is just such an individualist approach. In this view, women, it is argued, are just as violent as the men with whom they have intimate relationships. Research using the Conflict Tactics Scale finds that women use violence

> The traditional approach tends to see the problems of a community or society in individual, pathological terms... as emanating from the personal inadequacies of individuals.

as much as men. In an important sense, this violence is between two people; it is not particularly relevant that either one of them is a man or woman. Regarding a different issue, Cora Voyageur and Brian Calliou (chapter 5) discuss the long-held view that the main barrier to economic development within First Nations is their inability to adopt Western industrial values and work habits. That is, because of adherence to their traditional cultures, such as strong beliefs in collectivism and a spiritual connection to the land, they cannot or will not adapt to economic models that have been successful in capitalism. For example, it is often argued that the notion of collective land ownership acts as a barrier to bank loans to use as investment capital.

The chapter on youth and politics (Janet Conway and Dan Morrison, chapter 11) begins with an outline of what they call the mainstream understanding and prescription for the apathy of youth towards politics. Focusing on political socialization as the main cause of political behaviour, a traditional analysis points to youth motivations, acquired knowledge about the political system, and a sense of political responsibility. Without these individually acquired and desired characteristics, interest in political participation is low. While such thinking does examine and suggest changes in the role of parents, teachers, and school curriculum, the central underlying theme is individual choice and behaviour. As Conway and Morrison say, "Government initiatives like Student Vote 2004 are responses to this construction of the problem as one of ignorance and apathy, or put more nobly, civic literacy and political socialization." All of this, to put it very simply, is asking, "What is wrong with the kids?"

In recent years the traditional focus on individualism has taken a new twist. Much traditional analysis — neo-liberal in this new form — calls for using the competitive market as a model in all our social undertakings. In this view, the market or business way of doing things, as opposed to a collective approach, is seen as the solution for our economic woes and for a host of other social and political problems — not just in deregulating our economy but also in applying business principles to schooling, cultural production, assistance to the destitute, prisons, environmental protection, and so on. In a nutshell, the market is seen as being based on and promoting the individual freedom that will pave the way to a prosperous and harmonious society. In health care and education, for example, this push has taken the form of privatization.

Pat Armstrong (chapter 13) documents the trend towards

> shifting the burden of payment to individuals; opening health-service delivery to for-profit providers; moving care from public institutions to community-based organizations and private households; transferring care work from public-sector health-care workers to unpaid caregivers; and adopting the management strategies of private-sector businesses, applying market rules to health-service delivery, and treating health care as a market good.

Claire Polster (chapter12) gives us a detailed examination of the privatization of university education in Canada. In response to a number of educational issues, governments and universities are treating education as more and more a private responsibility oriented more and more to private, individual goals. This privatization is taking place through a wide range of processes and transformations. Advertising on campuses and exclusive contracts for food and beverages are growing every year. Corporations are becoming much more involved by providing university research facilities and grants.

And as universities adopt a business model of operation, collegiality and participatory governance are disappearing.

What both the health-care and education examples show is that privatization — far from resolving problems of health/health care and education — has all kinds of negative consequences. Put simply, these examples of the individual, market solutions do not solve our health and education problems because they do not address the abiding inequalities that are at the root of those problems.

RESOLVING OUR PROBLEMS — RESISTANCE AND SOCIAL CHANGE

The authors of this book's chapters use a different approach, one that sees social inequality as underlying the problems we face. Social harm, and thus social problems, arise from excesses of private power and are exacerbated when public resources are shifted to the control of elites such that benefits go to the privileged (Barlow 2005: 142). Seen in this way, the search for solutions takes a different tack. "Critical perspectives ask not only whether individual people have maintained their responsibility to the community, but also whether the community has maintained its responsibility to individuals. The approach does not focus on individual flaws; rather, it questions societal structures… inequality and disenfranchisement, abuse and victimization, classism, racism, and sexism" (Brooks 2002: 47).

In a sense, for critical observers, social problems are partly the result of behaviour choices — choices of powerful groups in society. In the case of the historical experiences of Aboriginal peoples, a critical analysis does not dispute that the dispossession of Aboriginal people is obviously a problem for them as particular individuals. But, as Voyageur and Calliou (chapter 5) so forcefully demonstrate, this dispossession has not come about because Aboriginal people, given their cultures and their values as Aboriginal people, have chosen poverty. Rather, their dispossession stems from overt and systemic racism. Canadian capitalist history is a story of the expropriation of Aboriginal land and resources to develop Canadian business and industry, along with the expropriation of generations of First Nations children to residential schools. It is the legacy of this history that is the main barrier to Aboriginal economic development. Along similar lines, Ruth Mann (chapter 3) shows that the violence between intimate partners is not just "family violence," but is, rather, "violence against women." She makes a compelling case that such violence is "male-perpetrated and male-driven." In the desire to control the women in their lives — a cultural norm so strong in our society — male violence against women is more frequent, more severe, and has more dire consequences than does women's violence directed at men. While women do engage in violence in intimate circumstances, it is most often in self-defence.

> The approach does not focus on individual flaws; rather, it questions societal structures… inequality and disenfranchisement, abuse and victimization, classism, racism, and sexism.

Thus, for a critical approach to social problems, solutions lie in resistance and action — in working to overturn the basic social inequalities of our unjust social structure. What we also see when we look carefully is that Canadians do

> Solutions lie in resistance and action — in working to overturn the basic social inequalities of our unjust social structure.

act to resist inequality, and we do this in a variety of ways. We do it as individuals and as collectivities; we do it through the state and in non-state organizations. We do not always do it intentionally, and some resistance may be more symbolic than material. But the logic of inequality forces us to reject and try to change fundamental elements of our society.

Individually, we engage in a myriad of day-to-day, small activities that are part of the long-term process of changing society. For instance, we buy what we need (as opposed to what we are told we want) from local producers and worker co-operatives; we refuse to be silent around racial slurs; and we show our children that men must be involved in caring for them and cleaning our houses. In this vein, Austin-Smith (chapter 3) shows us that women, as individual moviegoers, do not necessarily consume the patriarchal, heterosexist agenda contained in women's films. In her words, women "decode films from perspectives that are opposed to the dominant values communicated by those films." Many women viewers, she finds, actually use the content of such films to criticize gender stereotypes and oppression of women even while they are taking pleasure in watching the films. They often see these films as offering "images of themselves as heroic in their daily lives, rather than devaluing their concerns with relationships, children, work, and the domestic sphere as somehow unworthy of heroic representation."

We also join with others in resisting inequality and pursuing social change. The most obvious of these collective actions are the social movements that have already changed our world — the movements we are familiar with, including feminist or-ganizations, labour unions, anti-racist groups, gay and lesbian rights organizations, and environmentalists. In their chapter, Voyageur and Calliou tell us about the struggle for self-government and self-determination by Aboriginal bands and organizations. They leave no doubt that self-government and de-colonization are the keys to Aboriginal economic development and the central form of resistance by Canada's Aboriginal peoples, as communities. As they show us, First Nations people have never accepted the control exercised by Canada over them and their territories. An essential step is for Canada to recognize the inherent rights and land claims of Aboriginal communi-ties — their rights as a people — and live up to the treaty obligations. It is through increased control over local and regional decision-making — self-government — that First Nations people will control their own destinies.

Despite the demands and desires of some neo-liberals that government disappear from the social scene, it is clear that we cannot live in a society without some form of state. It is through the state, albeit a more participatory and democratic one, that we can make the kinds of collective decisions we must make if we are to live together and realize our collective responsibility to each other. Government is a key part of our social lives. Thus it is no surprise that collective resistance can and does also take place through the state. Parvin Ghorayshi (chapter 8) demonstrates that despite the constant chorus of business, political, and media voices telling us otherwise, corporate globalization is not inevitable — besides which it is contrary to the interests and desires of most Canadians. She shows us that because national governments have been instrumental in enforcing the new rules of corporate globalization, they can be forced to develop rules and regulations that protect citizens rather than transnational corporations. One small example is the Tobin Tax on international currency exchanges, which would slow the movement of money from one country to another, pushing capital investment towards long-term, useful investment. Moving international investments away from short-term, casino-style speculation on changes in currency valuations would be much less destructive of national economies.

This centrality of the political is taken up by Janet Conway and Dan Morrison (chapter 9). Their analysis is partly about attempts by young people to make governments act in the interests of the majority of citizens. They show us that, unlike the complaints and the traditional kinds of analysis, young people are very involved politically, in a highly collective way. It is just that they are trying not only to just present an alternative voice but also, much more importantly, to create a whole new way of doing politics. They are "problematizing" mainstream political institutions. The Intercontinental Youth Camp is not just about having a voice in the debates about, and rejecting, neo-liberal corporate globalization. It is also about experimenting with new forms of politics, forms that are much more participatory and inclusive than the current "institutions of liberal democracy, which effectively disallow any meaningful debate and rule out alternatives to the reigning order."

Still, collective action against inequality does not necessarily take place through the state, nor does it have to. At the very least, given the scale of state activities, these institutions can be insensitive to the needs of some people and, in some cases, oppressive. Jim Silver (chapter 7) shows that poverty in Canada has become seemingly intractable, in large part because most every approach that has tackled economic conditions in recent years has been market-oriented, and too often state-centred. He argues that along with some necessary changes in government social and labour-market policy, a key strategy for anti-poverty action will be found within poor communities themselves. In particular, he says, it will be found through community-based economic development (CED), which will plug the many holes through which wealth produced in poor communities "leaks out" to corporations and other groups. Just as importantly, enterprises that are developed and run locally can provide the skills development and self-confidence necessary for dispossessed people to pull themselves out of poverty.

POWER AND RESISTANCE

The title and focus of this book, then, are Power and Resistance. The chapters emphasize that — depending on class, race, gender, and sexual orientation — people face inequalities of treatment and life chances. Emphasizing power means first of all recognizing that some groups have privileged access to the resources that make life viable in our society. More importantly, a critical emphasis means revealing how those groups act to maintain and enhance their privilege, thereby creating problems for other groups of people. These inequalities — inherent in an unjust social structure — are the social problems in Canadian society. Our focus is not just on documenting existing conditions, but also on ways of generating emancipatory resistance and change.

GLOSSARY OF KEY TERMS

Structure: Social and political structures are the patterns of behavioural relationships between groups of people in society. They include how men and women, racialized people, young and old, wealthy and poor, governments and citizens, relate to one another.

Private troubles: Private troubles occur within the character of the individual and within the range of immediate relations with others; they have to do with the self and with those limited areas of social life of which we are directly and personally aware.

Public issues: Public issues have to do with matters that transcend the local environments of the individual and the range of inner life. They have to do with the organization of many such milieux into the institutions of an historical society as a whole, with the ways in which various milieux overlap and interpenetrate to form the larger structure of social and historical life.

Power: Power is the ability to set limits on the behavioural choices for ourselves and for others. Power is clearly in play when individuals and groups act in ways that contradict their desires, needs, and interests. Power has many bases and faces from the schoolyard bully to influence over public discourse.

Resistance: Resistance comes in acting to change the basic social inequalities of society. Resistance can be an individual act and can occur in collectivities; it happens through the state and in non-state organizations. It is not always intentional, and some resistance is more symbolic than material. But the logic of inequality forces us to reject and try to change fundamental elements of our society.

Inequality: Inequality refers to the more or less narrow life choices and life chances for individuals and groups of people. It refers not just to what people have; it is not just differences in lifestyle, but also what they can do and what they can become.

Objective: This is the basis in reality for whether a social condition or behaviour pattern is a problem or not. This basis involves identifying who is harmed and who benefits, and in what ways, from a social condition or behaviour pattern.

Subjective: In regard to social issues, this is often called public perception. What people perceive as real will guide their actions and their understanding of society. This aspect of social problems refers to what people think are the consequences — who is harmed and who benefits — of a social condition or pattern of behaviour.

QUESTIONS FOR DISCUSSION

1. Take an issue in the neighbourhood or city you live in, or the university you go to. What are the "facts" about it? Where do you get information about those facts? Who provides that information? Is there a debate about the facts? What individuals, groups, and organizations represent the various elements of the issue and its debate? What resources do they have to make their case known to other people and groups? To government?
2. Does a focus on structure and inequality mean that individuals bear no responsibility for social problems and their solutions?
3. How are the following private troubles? How are they public issues? Community recreation. Bank branch closure/payday loan outlets. Bullying.
4. For the issue you thought about in question 1, think about possible solutions. What government policies are involved? What changes might help? What community organizations and resources are there to help resolve the issue? What new community resources could be developed?

WEBSITES OF INTEREST

Canadian Centre for Policy Alternatives. <www.policyalternatives.ca>.
Canadian Dimension. <www.canadiandimension.mb.ca>.
Council of Canadians. <www.canadians.org>.
Democracy Now! <www.democracynow.org>.
Herizons. <www.herizons.ca>.
New Internationalist. <www.newint.org>.
Rabble — News for the Rest of Us. <www.rabble.ca>.

Chapter One

THE STATE AND SOCIAL ISSUES
Theoretical Considerations

Murray Knuttila

The study of social issues raises a number of important questions, ranging from how we define social issues to what causes them and how individuals and social institutions respond to them. Here our focus is on the state's relationship to social issues. Specifically, this means looking at some of the theoretical frameworks that have been used to analyze the role of the state in capitalist society. The chapter is based on the assumption that to explain specific state policies as they relate to various social issues, we must begin with a general understanding of how the state or polity fits into the larger structures of society.

The emphasis here tends to be on a macro or a structural approach, which means that social problems are examined and explained in terms of structural and social relations and processes. Because the state in Western capitalist societies is generally understood as the institutional order that is primarily concerned with the social organization of political, or broadly speaking social, power and the exercise of authority in the interests of social stability and order, it follows that an adequate understanding of most social problems requires an analysis of the role of the state.

"You Should Know This"
- In 1916 Saskatchewan, Manitoba, and Alberta granted women the right to vote, but it was not until 1920 that women could vote in federal elections. Aboriginal persons could not vote until 1960.
- The first elected government in Canada, Sir John A. Macdonald's Conservatives, was forced to resign after it was disclosed that Sir Hugh Allan and interests associated with the proposed Canadian Pacific Railway Company had made donations to the Conservatives in return for favours in the granting of the contract to build the transcontinental railroad.
- The Canadian Charter of Rights and Freedoms came into force on April 17, 1982. An example of its potential role came on September 9, 1999, when the Supreme Court overturned two lower court rulings against secondary picketing and leafleting as violations of workers' constitutional rights.
- On March 3l, 2006, 1,809 individuals in Ottawa were registered to lobby on behalf of 276 corporations, an increase of 847 percent in one year. At the same time the number of individuals registered to lobby for organizations increased from 266 to 2,306, or 767 percent.
- Federal government revenue sources for 2004/05: personal income tax — $89.8 billion (over 45 percent of total revenue); GST — $29.8 billion (15 percent); corporate income tax — $30 billion (15 percent); other taxes — $16.7 billion (8.5 percent); employment insurance premiums — $17.3 billion (8.7 percent).
- In 2005, bank employees working for the Royal Bank of Canada generated a profit of $56,439 per employee, while those at the Bank of Montreal generated $71,037.

Sources: Office of the Registrar of Lobbyists 2006; Canada, Department of Finance 2006a; *Globe and Mail Report on Business* 2006 (July/August): 120.

Social scientists do not all agree on the best way of theoretically approaching the study of the state in advanced capitalist or liberal-democratic society. However, over the past thirty years two major perspectives on the state have dominated Western social science: structural functionalism and Marxism. We will consider these approaches as well as more recent directions of thought.

> The state is primarily concerned with the social organization of political, or broadly speaking social, power and the exercise of authority... it follows that an adequate understanding of most social problems requires an analysis of the role of the state.

STRUCTURAL FUNCTIONALISM: THE BEGINNINGS

Throughout the modern era social scientists in general have been concerned about the "problem of social order"; for some sociologists, however, this problem has been a preoccupation.

For Emile Durkheim, the French thinker recognized as one of the founding figures in sociology, social order was a central issue. Among the questions that occupied him were: What is the basis of social order? How is social order possible in complex modern societies?

The question of order was important for Durkheim because he lived during a period of rapid industrialization and came to believe that when a society industrialized its members became more heterogeneous, differentiated, unlike each other. This is one of the themes of his book, *The Division of Labour in Society*, in which he argues that industrialization brings with it greater specialization of the tasks, jobs, or functions performed by both individuals and institutions. Durkheim believed that in pre-industrial society it was easier to establish a common set of beliefs, morals, and values that would hold society together, because people tended to share a way of life and thus beliefs, values, and morals. The emergence of a division of labour, with its attendant specialization and even fragmentation, undermines the shared experiences and concerns that facilitated the "natural" sharing of a belief system. Modern industrial society thus faces the problem of establishing a new system of beliefs and values that can serve as the basis of social order. Durkheim argues that, fortunately, some of the very characteristics of modern industrial society provide a solution to the problem of order. He maintains that as society develops and evolves, a new moral code emphasizing the interdependence of individuals and institutions also develops. As a result people come to realize that while they do different jobs, they are all part of a larger whole and all contribute to the survival of society. In the case of the political system, the state becomes responsible for making decisions on behalf of everyone in society, and it plays a role in maintaining social order by assisting in the dissemination of values, beliefs, and morals.

To understand this point about how and why the state would be able to act on behalf of society as a whole — the collectivity — we must also understand an argument that Durkheim makes about the role of corporate and occupational groups both within society as a whole and within the polity. As the division of labour develops, occupational and corporate groups become more important in terms of organizing and co-ordinating the multitude of roles in society. These different kinds of groups eventually become important conduits between individuals and the polity; they take information and concerns from the population to those in government and relay information on actions and policies back from the government to the members of society (Durkheim 1933: 27–28).

Durkheim's work is important for a number of reasons, not the least of which is his influence on the development of North American sociology. Durkheim first became known to many North American political sociologists through the writings of Talcott Parsons, who in turn became widely accepted as one of the founders of North American structural functionalist thought. This theoretical tradition had a significant impact on how the polity and state have come to be understood in this century.

TWENTIETH-CENTURY FUNCTIONALISM

As used here, structural functionalism refers to a way of understanding society developed by thinkers such as Emile Durkheim, Talcott Parsons, Robert Merton, Melvin Tumin, and Daniel Rossides. Although the theoretical ideas and systems of thought that modern functionalists produced are complicated and sophisticated, with individual themes and emphases, it is possible to distil a shared set of basic premises and assumptions that form a basis for an abstract, generic structural functionalist approach to understanding human society.

First, this perspective would suggest that human society must be understood as a system. Like all systems, every human society faces basic problems that must be solved if it is to survive. To explain this theory functionalists tend to employ an organic analogy, which is a heuristic tool, an aid to assist understanding. The analogy is designed to draw out certain features of the social system by comparing it to a living biological system such as the human body. We begin the application of the analogy by noting that if a human body is to survive, certain basic needs must be met and certain basic problems must be solved. Employing this same logic, structural functionalists argue that there are certain basic individual and species needs that must be satisfied if a human society is to survive. For example, the future of every human society depends on the development of arrangements to facilitate the production and distribution of the material goods and services necessary for biological survival. In addition, some arrangements must be established to look after spiritual needs, the enhancement and transmission of culture, biological reproduction and child care, education, and social decision-making in general.

For a structural functionalist, society is a complex unity composed of many different parts of subsystems. The functionalist approach thus explains the various parts of a social system in terms of what those parts do for the total system or, put slightly differently, in terms of their functions. The function of an organ in a biological system is to perform certain tasks or jobs for the whole system. The function of an institution or social arrangement is to solve or satisfy one or more of society's basic problems or needs.

An additional key issue in structural functionalist thought is the question of social order. The social system is composed of many complex components or parts, all presumably working in unison to solve the system's problems, and just how this system is held together has been an issue for social and political philosophers for centuries. The structural functionalist approach follows Durkheim, arguing that social systems tend to be stable and orderly as long as they possess a set of widely shared and accepted beliefs and values. Such belief and value systems serve as a kind of moral cement, binding and bonding the various components of a social system together. An additional and related assumption holds that the normal condition of a social system is one of stability. As long as each of the institutions is functioning normally and there is an accepted value system bonding the various elements together, the system exists in a condition of equilibrium, homeostasis, and order.

These, then, are some of the basic propositions common to the functionalist approach. We must now begin to focus on the polity.

Parsons maintains that the political order or the polity is an institution that functions to make decisions for the entire social system and is responsible for maintaining order in the larger social system. He argues that despite the existence of different groups and interests in society it is possible to develop a political system that operates to establish goals, policies, and priorities for the entire society. Much of the thinking and theorizing about the state in the period after the Second World War took place within a theoretical tradition closely linked to Parsons. This is the tradition we know as pluralism.

PLURALISM

When Parsons addressed the issue of how a society composed of different individuals, groups, and interests develops goals, priorities, and social policies that enjoy widespread support, he was touching on a question that had long been at the forefront of Western political thought. In the North American context the same issue has been a concern of American political thinkers for decades.

Among these thinkers was Charles Merriam. As the title of his important book *Political Power* (first published in 1934) indicates, Merriam explicitly addresses the polity in terms of power. For Merriam (1964: 32) the polity, government, and political power all have to do with the development of a decision-making process that mediates and stabilizes relations in a society divided into classes, groups, and factions.

Many of the basic assumptions that informed the work of thinkers as diverse as Durkheim, Parsons, and Merriam also influenced the growth of classical pluralism, which developed in American political sociology and political science after the middle of the twentieth century.

American pluralists tend to assume that the United States represents a social system that has successfully addressed the key question: how, within the context of a society divided into many different classes, groups, and factions, is it possible to establish a system of political decision-making that is open and democratic and capable of performing its essential functions?

In two important books, Robert Dahl (1967, 1972) lays out a series of arguments that are central to understanding a pluralist approach to the polity. According to Dahl, a complex industrial society is inevitably divided into different kinds of groups, classes, and factions based on a multitude of religious, class, occupational, regional, ethnic, and sexual differences. When understood in this context, the function of government, and indeed of the entire social decision-making process, becomes a practice of mediation and arbitration among and between these interests and factions.

After considering several options Dahl concludes that a system he refers to as polyarchy is the most appropriate. A polyarchy is different from both a simple major-ity-rule system and a pure elitist system. Among the problems associated with simple majority-rule systems is the protection of minorities. How, if the majority rules in a direct manner, can we ensure that the rights of minorities are protected at all times? Political systems based on the premises of elitism are, by definition, not democratic and are also in violation of a basic requirement that the polity be based on equality and consent.

A polyarchy is a complex system that typically involves institutional guarantees both protecting citizens from the exercise of arbitrary power and protecting basic human rights. A polyarchy has established and broadly accepted procedures defining what legal powers, rights, and privileges are to be enjoyed by both the government and citizens. Although the rights of citizens are enshrined, there is also general acceptance of the right of governments to use violence to protect the national interest. Polyarchies are typically predicated on constitutional frameworks that support legal and accepted modes of conduct determining and specifying the actual conduct of government or the selection of state officials (Dahl 1972: 40–43).

Pluralists tend to argue that what has emerged in the West — with the U.S. system being typical — is a set of structures and processes that fulfill the best possibilities for democratic political activity in an advanced industrial society. While society may be divided into different classes, factions, and interests, the electoral system with its one-person, one-vote is a great "leveller." Regardless of an individual's income, prestige in society, or authority in a particular institution, on election day every person is equal. The fact that everyone is entitled to vote once and only once means, formally at least, that all citizens potentially have the same power and opportunity to make an impact on the political process.

The political process is not, however, just about elections, and therefore individuals, groups, classes, and factions have other opportunities to influence government policies and actions. Since liberal-democratic systems are typically open societies with a free press, citizens generally have access to information about what the government is doing. When the government is about to decide on an issue, the individuals or groups interested in that issue will usually know about it and have the opportunity to present their case to the government. The opportunity to lobby is available, even if the participants did not support the particular party or individual who was victorious in the electoral process. The process of lobbying has become very important, and all members of society have the opportunity to influence the government through that process.

As society becomes more complex, the lobbying process also becomes more important and complex, and many individuals come to realize that they can be more effective if they are organized. Rather than working solely as individuals, students, farmers, and teachers have united and formed formal interest groups to press their interests with the government. Thus today governments will typically find themselves under pressure from different, formally organized pressure or interest groups, each pushing the interests of its members. Democracy may not be as direct as it was when individuals pressed their own cases, but, as we saw, even in his day Durkheim held that the intervention of organized groups would still facilitate democratic decision-making.

Based on this sort of analysis of the overall operation of the polity in Western democracies, pluralists argue that there is no single or dominant centre of power. Political power is dispersed across a multitude of centres of power that compete through the electoral and lobbying processes to influence government. That there is a plurality of centres of power in the long run means that no one of those centres is able to be dominant. The government must be willing to attempt, again over the long run, to accommodate all of the various interests, or else it runs the risk of becoming viewed as being "corrupt" and tied to one centre of power. If this happens the government will face certain electoral defeat once it becomes apparent to all the other various interests that they have become excluded from the political process. Assuming that the various excluded interests comprise the majority, they will be in a position to develop a coalition and remove the offending government from power.

The liberal-democratic polity is thus an institutional structure that facilitates social decision-making in the context of a complex and divided society. The polity is the site of mediation and "trade-offs" as the government seeks to establish policies and priorities that it sees as representing the interests of the majority (Dahl 1967: 24). No centre of power is dominant or able to consistently get its way, at least over the long haul. The phrase "You win some, you lose some" truly characterizes how different interest groups fare in the political process.

It follows that those adopting a pluralist approach tend to interpret or view the functioning of the state in liberal-democratic societies as basically democratic. In its actions, decisions, and policies the state tends to reflect the broader public or national interests; it tends to act in a manner beneficial to society as a whole. Since one of the state's main functions is the maintenance of social order and harmony, the emergence of social problems tends to produce some manner of state intervention. The precise nature of the state's actions will vary depending on the nature of the problems.

Given the logic of the general premises that inform structural functionalist thinking, those adopting this position will see some social problems as normative in origin. This means that they see those problems as the result of some breakdown or dysfunction in the society's overall system of values and norms. Under such circumstances the state is expected to actively attempt to re-establish a normative consensus or establish some new normative orientation. We might, for instance, envision a situation in which racist or sexist beliefs and ideas lead to social problems. A structural functionalist might view such problems as being rooted in the society's values and norms and would therefore advocate state actions geared towards changing those values and norms. The state's response might involve educational programs and efforts to re-educate and resocialize individuals, thus establishing a normative orientation more suited to social harmony, order, integration, and stability.

Other social problems might be explained in terms of a variety of different individual pathologies. For a functionalist, appropriate state actions to deal with individual pathologies might range from the provision of policing services to discourage the "acting out" of individual pathologies, to the provision of penal, correctional, and rehabilitative services, as well as medical facilities where appropriate. All of these actions are designed to "safeguard" the public and preserve social order by discouraging or preventing behaviour harmful to the general public, as well as by punishing, assisting, and rehabilitating those committing actions or undertaking activities that disrupt society or cause social problems.

A functionalist might also be inclined to seek the causes of certain other social problems in the dysfunction of important institutions. Ever since the seminal work of Robert Merton, the concept of dysfunction has been an integral part of functionalist thought. The possibility always exists that, for a variety of reasons, an institution may begin to dysfunction, that is, not adequately perform its allotted, socially necessary function. If this occurs there is a distinct possibility that other institutions or even the entire social structure may be affected. If the impact of such dysfunction is serious enough to threaten the entire social system, then state intervention might be necessary. Again, by way of a general example we might envision a situation in which more and more women enter the labour force and as a result the traditional nuclear family begins to change and some of its traditional functions are no longer performed as before. An orthodox functionalist might view such a situation as a case of family dysfunction and argue that the state should intervene, perhaps by providing greater funding for day cares to fill the void caused by women no longer being available to perform child-care duties in the home, or by taking action to encourage women to return to their more traditional familial roles.

> Some thinkers... of a pluralist approach suggest that the political process may not be quite this smooth.... Charles Lindblom notes that the concentration of economic power in capitalist society has significant implications for political processes.

In general this sociological perspective views the structures of liberal-democratic society as sound. Structural functionalists understand that for a variety of reasons social problems do emerge. But, they say, there are structures, including the polity, in place to address and deal with such circumstances.

Some thinkers operating within the general confines of a pluralist approach suggest that the political process may not be quite this smooth. Writers such as Charles Lindblom (1977) note that the concentration of economic power in capitalist society has significant implications for political processes. Social and political stability within capitalist socio-economic systems requires a smooth, functioning economy; therefore it is important that the state does everything in its power to see that certain economic conditions prevail. On this basis Lindblom makes an argument about business occupying a "privileged position." In addition, the enormous resources controlled by the corporate sector can give it overwhelming advantages in the competition to influence the government.

The critical questions that Lindblom and others raise might lead us to look for an alternative framework. Indeed, a reading of the sociological literature addressing the issue of the polity over the past four decades illustrates that a different framework has been emerging since the mid-1960s to late 1960s. This other framework developed out of an alternative theoretical tradition — Marxian theory.

MARXISM

Whereas structural functionalists might use an organic analogy to explain their general view of human society, a social scientist adopting a Marxian analysis will proceed by using a different set of basic assumptions, namely those associated with the materialist perspective.

For Marx there is one key defining characteristic of the species homo sapiens, and that is that we are the only life form on this planet that produces the goods and services necessary to satisfy basic material needs. Human beings are the only species that does not merely rely or depend on what is found in nature for material and physical survival. Human beings alone engage in a process of material production that is active, social, and intentional, and that relies on the cumulative development and use of knowledge, skills, and technology.

Marx's approach to human material production can be crudely, though effectively, summarized as follows: before humans can engage in any social and political activity they must ensure that their basic material needs are met; that is, they must provide themselves with food, clothing, and shelter. Further, the nature of our productive activity is of central importance in understanding our overall mode or manner of living. Marx further argues that it is the mode of material production that gives a society its general shape and character. In various places in his writing he articulates this stance in more or less forceful terms, but nevertheless it is an essential element of the Marxian position.

For Marx, then, an analysis of a society's mode of material production is the point of departure for social analysis. Marx also argues that to understand a particular mode of material production we must examine two aspects of that production: 1) the social relations of production (patterns of ownership, control, and use of society's productive resources); and 2) the forces of production (technology, knowledge, skills, or tools that aid material production). By examining the social relations of production and the forces of production we move into a position from which we can begin to understand the larger patterns of social organization. The organization of the polity, the educational system, the family, culture in its broadest meaning, and indeed the entire social structure will be fundamentally influenced by the mode of material production.

To better understand the structures and operation of capitalist society, Marx engaged in a lengthy and systematic examination of the nature of capitalist production. One of his many conclusions is that capitalist society is fractured or divided into classes. For Marx, classes are primarily determined by structural relationships to the productive forces, which means that class position is determined by whether a person owns productive property and purchases the labour power of others, or whether a person does not own productive property and is thus forced to sell the capacity to work to others who do own productive property. Although Marx recognizes that there is a class, the petite bourgeoisie, whose members own some productive property and neither buy nor sell labour power, he is mainly concerned with the relationship between those who own society's major productive resources and those who sell labour power, namely the capitalist and the working classes.

In addition, Marx concludes that the owners of productive property are in a structural position to exploit those who have to sell their labour power. Because one class exploits the other, Marx is convinced that the two major classes exist in a relationship of potential conflict, with contradictory interests. Further, the class that owns the society's productive resources and capacities possesses, by virtue of that ownership, economic power. The class with economic power is in a position to translate that economic power into other types of power, including political power.

The Marxian approach presents a radically different perspective on the treatment of social problems. Within the Marxian tradition classes are understood in structural terms, involving relations of exploitation, alienation, domination, and systemic inequalities in wealth and power. Flowing out of these systemic or structural relations is the poverty, differential educational levels, unequal access to health care and housing, unemployment and other social and economic problems that characterize advanced capitalist society. In Marxian theory the concept of class is at the centre of a critical analysis of society and the root of most social problems.

In addition the concept of contradiction is also key to the Marxian mode of analysis. Contradictions are deemed to be an inherent part of reality, especially social reality, and thus a Marxian analysis of social problems involves the analysis of the inherent contradictions found in capitalist society. Those contradictions include the workings of the economic institutions, which give rise to the recurring economic crises that characterize capitalist societies. Whether it is the tendency of capital to become concentrated and centralized, the process of the internationalization of capital with its associated transfers of capital and economic dislocations, or the tendency for rates of unemployment to grow and investment to stagnate, the implications for society as a whole, especially for the subordinate classes, can be devastating.

A Marxian analysis of capitalist society would conclude that certain kinds of social problems are normal and expected. Social conflict, change, and instability are the norm, not the exception. To the extent that one of the essential functions of the state is to provide the basis of social stability and order, the state will become an ever more important part of the social structure. There is indeed a kind of functionalist logic to this position, although Marxists would argue that the main beneficiaries of the state's actions are the members of the ruling class and not all members of society.

> To the extent that one of the essential functions of the state is to provide the basis of social stability and order, the state will become an ever more important part of the social structure... although Marxists would argue that the main beneficiaries of the state's actions are the members of the ruling class and not all members of society.

THE STATE IN CAPITALIST SOCIETY

Although there is no systematic and well-developed conception of the state in Marx's original works, for most of his life the issue of political power occupied him at both a practical and a theoretical level. At the practical level, we need only recall that Marx moved to Paris in the mid-1840s and was subsequently forced to spend the period from about 1850 to his death in 1883 in England because of state actions and repression in Europe. Even before Marx had become an especially radical thinker he felt the sting of censorship from the Prussian and French states. On a theoretical level, he first encountered the state through the writings of Hegel. Marx was quick to develop a critique of the Hegelian view that the state in modern society is an institution representing the general and social interest as opposed to the particular class interests of the members of society.

By the time Marx and Engels were writing *The German Ideology* ([1845] 1970: 80) they were becoming convinced that the state had to be understood within the context of the material basis of society. In *The German Ideology* they note that when the economic structures are predicated on class relations, the state becomes a part of the process of class domination. Marx and Engels argue that the state becomes intimately tied to the class with economic power: "The State is the form in which the individuals of a ruling class assert their common interests." Thus it comes to be an important aspect of the overall patterns of class domination that characterize capitalist society.

In the following years Marx and Engels, sometimes working alone and sometimes in collaboration, developed a series of further statements on the nature of the state in capitalist society. Because their work was done in a variety of different contexts and for different purposes, their comments lack consistency. The two writers sometimes see the state in quite simplistic terms, as in their claim that "the executive of the modern state is but a committee for managing the common affairs of the whole bourgeoisie" (Marx and Engels 1952: 44). In other works they present more complex pictures of the state (Marx 1972a, 1972b). But a constant theme is the class nature of the capitalist state — that is, the state understood as a central part of the process of class rule and class domination.

Following Marx's death, some of his ideas were reinterpreted and restated by Engels, Lenin, and others. The Russian Revolution of 1917 became an important worldwide development and resulted in the emergence of what Russell Jacoby (1971: 121) calls a "bolshevized" Marx. As some critics argue, Marxism was turned into a rigid and simplistic caricature of Marx's thinking in the form of "Soviet-style Marxism" (Marcuse 1961). Between the turn of the century and the 1960s there were few efforts to reformulate Marx's theoretical ideas in light of the continued development of capitalism, with the important exceptions of the work of Gramsci and the Frankfurt School. During the 1960s an interest in Marx re-emerged in the West, and a large number of thinkers began to re-examine Marx and disentangle his ideas and writings from their association with various political regimes that had sought to appropriate them. These thinkers — loosely referred to here as neo-Marxists — undertook the project of clarifying a Marxian perspective as it applied to an enormous number of social issues, including the state in capitalist society.

NEO-MARXIST PERSPECTIVES: STRUCTURALISM AND INSTRUMENTALISM

The development of neo-Marxist approaches to the role of the state in capitalist society must be considered in the context of the domination of the pluralist approach and the failure of Marx and Soviet-style "Marxism" to develop an adequate theory. It is not surprising, then, that the development of a systematic critique of pluralism and the articulation of a more adequate Marxian approach to the state in capitalist society were among the first projects undertaken by neo-Marxists in the late 1960s and early 1970s.

Among the first systematic neo-Marxist treatments of the state was Ralph Miliband's *The State in Capitalist Society*, first published in 1969. One of Miliband's explicit purposes in writing the book was to show the inadequacies of the pluralist model (Miliband 1973b: 6). Miliband first of all reminds his readers that a key feature of capitalist society is its class structure, and that one class overwhelmingly holds and controls economic power. Furthermore, according to Miliband, the development of large-scale corporations and the continuing concentration and centralization of capital have made the capitalist class even more powerful — indeed, so powerful that it controls political power and should thus be understood as forming a ruling elite.

> The development of neo-Marxist approaches to the role of the state in capitalist society must be considered in the context of the domination of the pluralist approach and the failure of Marx and Soviet-style "Marxism" to develop an adequate theory.

To illustrate how and why the capitalist class controls the operation of the state, Miliband breaks the state down into its various components, including the elected government, the bureaucracy and administrative apparatus, and the military. He argues that the primary decision-making positions in the major branches of the state are controlled by either representatives of the capitalist class or people sympathetic to the interests of the capitalist class. The word "sympathetic," when used in this context, refers to how those in command positions in the state generally share common ideological positions with the capitalist class. They may also share lifestyles, networks, and a general value system. These connections result in a tendency for the state to act in the interests of the capitalist class. Most of the state's actions will be geared towards facilitating the overall operation of the capitalist system and therefore the continuing control of production and wealth by the capitalist class. Miliband rejects any arguments about the state being a neutral mediator seeking to establish social policies and priorities for "the nation" in "the national interests." Indeed, he sees notions such as the "national interests" as ideological manipulations of public opinion designed to provide a façade of legitimation for the class domination that is the reality of capitalist society.

A year before the publication of Miliband's book, the French neo-Marxist Nicos Poulantzas also produced a study of the state in capitalist society. In *Political Power and Social Classes*, originally published in 1968 (but not available to English readers until 1973), Poulantzas sought to provide a different type of theoretical approach to the state in capitalist society based on insights provided by Marx. For Poulantzas the main task at hand for neo-Marxists was not to criticize pluralism, but rather to provide an alternative theoretical approach or problematic.

Poulantzas argues that it is a mistake to exert too much energy in examining the personnel and personal connections between the capitalist class and the state. What really matters is the role and function of the state in the capitalist mode of production, not the particular individuals who staff the state at any historical moment. For Poulantzas the central defining characteristic of the capitalist mode of production is its division into classes with fundamentally contradictory and conflicting interests, concerns, and structural positions. If this system is to survive, some means of alleviating class conflict must be developed, and according to Poulantzas the state emerges as the institution or set of structures that functions to stabilize the whole system. He points out: "The state is precisely the factor of cohesion of a social formation and the factor of reproduction of the conditions of production of a system" (Poulantzas 1972: 246).

What emerges in the work of Poulantzas is a form of Marxian functionalism; that is, a study of the state in terms of its functions. The essential difference between this general approach and that of North American structural functionalists is how each perspective would answer the question "In whose interests are social functions performed?" For the structural functionalists the state performs certain functions for the entire society or system. For Poulantzas the state performs its functions of stabilizing the economy and class conflicts, mediating, and facilitating equilibrium in the interests of the dominant class. The capitalist class has the most to gain from the smooth, conflict-free operation of the system, and the state tends to function in the long-term interests of that class. An important aspect of this position is the notion that the state can perform these functions only if it has a considerable degree of autonomy from the capitalist class.

Following the publication of their books, Miliband and Poulantzas engaged in a famous debate as they reviewed and commented on each other's work (Miliband 1973a; Poulantzas 1972, 1976; Laclau 1975). The eventual outcome of the process was the publication of another book on the state by Miliband (1977), in which he made it clear that the differences between him and Poulantzas were really not that significant. Poulantzas understood the state largely in terms of the functions it performed for the capitalist class. Miliband made a similar point in *Marxism and Politics*, arguing that the state in capitalist society is best understood in terms of four essential functions: 1) maintaining law and order; 2) establishing and maintaining value consensus; 3) facilitating economic stability; and 4) advancing a nation's interests in the international arena (Miliband 1977: 90). The essence of the argument is that in acting to preserve the total system the state is also acting in the interests of the class that benefits most from the maintenance of the status quo.

What emerged from the work of Miliband and Poulantzas and the debate between them was a new direction for neo-Marxist theory. This new approach is commonly referred to as *structuralism* because it directs our attention to an understanding of the structures, role, and functions of the state by examining the overall structures, dynamic, and logic of the capitalist mode of production. The general approach tended to produce some very abstract discourse (see Holloway and Picciotto 1979), which was marred by the typical functionalist tendency to utilize teleological and circular arguments. The state is assumed to be necessary for the continuance of the capitalist system, and thus it performs a set of functions that accomplish just that — the maintenance of the system. These assumed functions become the basis for subsequent explanations of state actions; thus the assumption that the state functions to promote and facilitate capitalist accumulation becomes the explanation for state actions and policies that facilitate the accumulation process.

In contrast to the structuralist tendency to explain the actions and policies of the state in capitalist society in terms of the overall logic and structures of the capitalist system, some thinkers influenced by Marx looked to more direct connections between the capitalist class and the state. The approach that has come to be called *instrumentalism* tends to explain how the state operates in the interest of the capitalist class by looking at personnel: the personal, lifestyle, interactive, and ideological similarities between the capitalist class and those in charge of the state. Although Miliband is often cited as a representative of this approach, others in England such as Sam Aaronovitch (1961) might better illustrate the logic of the approach. In the United States, G. William Domhoff (1967) has been cited as an example of this approach because he convincingly illustrates the intimate connections between the U.S. capitalist class and the state.

ALTERNATIVE DIRECTIONS IN NEO-MARXIST THEORY

While instrumentalists tend to analyze the direct connections between the ruling class and the state, and structuralists tend to utilize the abstract logic of functionalist thought, what is ultimately most important about these initial theories is their influence on other thinkers to go beyond both the structuralist and instrumentalist approaches.

Among the difficulties with many of the neo-Marxists theories of the state that developed in the 1970s and 1980s was an inability to facilitate empirical explanation and research. Within the structuralist tradition, the state is assumed to operate in the interests of the capitalist class, and this assumption turned out to be the explanation for the state's role. The instrumentalist approach has difficulty explaining those instances when there are no immediate or direct connections between the state and the capitalist class; yet it maintains that the state tends to operate so as to serve the long-term interests of capital. Several scholars, including Fred Block (1977), Theda Skocpol (1980), and Albert Szymanski (1978), argue for an alternative approach. Here we will consider Szymanski's highly developed approach, as only one example from a vast literature.

In *The Capitalist State and the Politics of Class* (1978) Szymanski offered a critique of the existing approaches while recognizing some of their strengths. He maintains that it is necessary to recognize that in liberal-democratic society the capitalist class does not absolutely control the state; however, the state does tend to act in their interests. He rejects the functionalist logic of the pure structuralist approach as the basis of an explanation of the role and operation of the state. He offers instead an analysis based on the idea that in liberal-democratic society the various classes, groups, and individuals can influence the operation, policies, actions, and decisions of the state through direct and indirect linkages or mechanisms of power.

There are three essential, direct mechanisms of power. First, as the instrumentalists argue, the operation of the state can be directly influenced by having members of a particular class in the operational and command positions, that is, running the state. Second, the state can be influenced through the lobbying process. Third, the state can be influenced through the policy-formation process. Because governments and state agencies often rely on advice to make decisions, establishing organizations to offer that advice can be a mode of influencing the state.

In addition there are several indirect linkages between the capitalist class and the state that can be utilized as mechanisms of power (Szymanski 1978: 24–25). These include the use of ideological power and economic power, and the funding of the electoral processes.

Given that the state and governments operate within a larger ideological environment, it is possible to influence the state by influencing that environment. This process includes the role of public opinion. If the capitalist class can convince the majority of the people that they all share the same interests, then the public as a whole will resist any state actions that run counter to the interests of the capitalist class. As a result the state's ability to act will be limited or constrained. Ruling classes always attempt to present their interests as the "national interest" or as the "public good," thereby ideologically constraining the actions of the state.

In terms of economic power, we know that the state and governments operate within a social environment that is dependent on the existence of a healthy and stable economy. The class that controls economic decision-making and planning is in a position to exert major influence on the state because, in the event that the state acts against their interests, they can decide not to invest or to withdraw investment or transfer investments elsewhere. All those types of actions will have a negative impact on employment, prosperity, and indeed the entire social system and political system. The actions and policies of the state are constrained by the need to maintain "business confidence."

Turning to how the political process is funded, we might begin by noting that in the simplest possible terms this mechanism refers to the commonly accepted connection between "who is paying the piper and the tune being played." Simply put, if you pay you get a chance to call the tune. At the political level this means that groups or individuals able to fund political parties and candidates can influence the policies and actions of governments when those parties are in power.

Szymanski (1978) attempts to offer an approach to the state in capitalist society that provides a way of explaining why and how, in specific instances, the state acts in the manner that it does, but he is also concerned about avoiding simplistic instrumentalist or abstract structuralist explanations. He argues that the overwhelming economic power of the capitalist class means that it is most capable of using the various mechanisms of power. In a liberal democracy those mechanisms of power are available to everyone, but because the class structure means that economic resources are unequally allocated, in reality it is the capitalist class that has the overwhelming advantage in influencing the state. There is no doubt in Szymanski's mind that the state in capitalist society operates in the interests of the capitalist class, but not for the reasons advanced by either the structuralists or the instrumentalists.

While Miliband, Poulantzas, Szymanski, and many others sought to understand the relationship between various classes and the state in capitalist society, a number of scholars were engaged in developing an approach to the state in capitalist society that went beyond merely articulating a certain degree of relative autonomy for the state. Among these thinkers were Eric A. Nordlinger and Theda Skocpol. Although it would not be appropriate to place all of these thinkers within the Marxian tradition, they all do accept that "the state is a force in its own right and does not simply reflect the dynamic of the economy and/or civil society" (Jessop 1990: 279). The "state-centred" approach directs our analytical attention to the structures and operation of the state as an independent "actor" in the complex interplay of economic, social, and political forces. Such an approach does not assume that the state is tied to or will reflect any class forces. Skocpol (1985: 9) summarizes the argument: "States conceived as organizations claiming control over territories and people may formulate and pursue goals that are not simply reflective of the demands or interests of social groups, classes or society." She goes on to note: "Bringing the state back in to a central place in analyses of policy making and social change does require a break with some of the most encompassing social-determinist assumptions of pluralism, structure-functionalist developmentalism, and various neo-Marxisms" (Skocpol 1985: 20). The question of determining whether the state is pursuing a policy objective or direction that originates within its structures and personnel, or whether it is reflecting the priorities of some class or group, is subject to historical and empirical investigation. The key point that emerges from this approach is the necessity of recognizing the possibility, and even the probability, of the state itself acting as an independent and fully autonomous actor.

Bob Jessop (1990) offers a substantial critique of the "state-centred" theorists, but he argues that the work of scholars such as Ernesto Laclau and Chantal Mouffe represents an even more serious challenge to current thinking and theorizing about the state. According to Jessop, Laclau and Mouffe do not just question the manner in which scholars operating from a variety of perspectives have understood the state; the logic of their work challenges the very existence of the state. Mouffe and Laclau represent an approach to understanding social processes that holds that "the social has an open, unsutured character and that neither its elements nor its totality have a pre-given necessity" (Jessop 1990: 289). The various relations that comprise the social, then, result in "societies that are tendentially constituted as an ensemble of totalizing effects in an open relational complex" (Jessop 1990: 290). Although Jessop is unsure as to whether this conception of human relations makes society impossible, he is clear about what this rejection of totalizing theoretical frameworks means for the study of the state. The state becomes, at most, one part of a larger set of social relations that are constantly contested, produced, and reproduced. Jessop summarizes: "Even if their approach does not require the total deconstruction of the state, it does deny states any positivity and de-privilege them as sites of political struggle" (1990: 293).

These comments do not mean that theorizing about the state during the last couple of decades leads only to postulating that the state is an autonomous social actor with interests and activities without connection to society, or that it is necessary to give up efforts to develop a systematic theory or understanding of the state because, like other social phenomena, the state is indeterminate, contested, and not subject to systematic analysis or understanding. Some of the most interesting recent thinking about the state involves an approach commonly referred to as regulation theory. While, as Jessop points out, many different, complex, and sophisticated ideas and arguments are associated with regulation theory, the approach also carries some common assumptions. A central assumption is that the social and economic structures of capitalist society are unstable and incapable of maintaining themselves in the long term without significant transformations and interventions. The theorists argue that regulatory mechanisms form the basis of the transformations and interventions that make it possible for the capitalist system and its concomitant institutional structures and arrangements to survive. Jessop states: "They all focus on the changing social forms and mechanisms in and through which the capital relation is reproduced despite its inherent economic contradictions and emergent conflictual properties" (1990: 309). Regulation theorists tend to examine both the economic and extra-economic processes and structural conditions that allow different accumulation regimes to exist and function despite the inherent contradictions and class conflicts characterizing the system. They further assume that no abstract, necessary, or typical systems of regulation work in all or even most capitalist systems. The modes of regulation that characterize a particular society or nation are the outcome of historically specific institutional arrangements, modes of conduct, and normative rules (Jessop 1990: 309).

The state is able to provide the required modes or systems of regulatory mechanisms because it is "neither an ideal collective capitalist whose functions are determined in the last instance by the imperatives of economic production nor is it a simple parallelogram of pluralist forces" (Jessop 1990: 315). The process of establishing the necessary regulatory system to facilitate continued capital accumulation is deemed to be very complex. As Jessop (1990: 315) indicates:

> Securing the conditions for capital accumulation or managing an unstable equilibrium of compromise involves not only a complex array of institutions and policies but also a continuing struggle to build consensus and back it with coercion.... The state itself can be seen as a complex ensemble of institutions, networks, procedures, modes of calculation and norms as well as their associated pattern of strategic conduct.

According to Jessop the overall approach that emerges out of the many specific thinkers associated with the regulationist perspective offers a useful antidote to the simplistic or economic reductionism arguments, conventional functionalist positions, and approaches that exaggerate the separateness of the state from the political processes that surround capital accumulation. Without succumbing to the questionable conclusion about society being impossible that flows out of Mouffe and Laclau, Jessop notes that societies are "relatively structured, sedimented or fixed," but their maintenance and continued existence require the continued co-ordination of complex individual and institutional arrangements; and this typically involves struggles for hegemony and the use of the ensemble of state institutions. Absent from this discussion is the question of how relations surrounding sex and gender are integrated into the processes.

In *Power Resource Theory and the Welfare State: A Critical Approach* Julia O'Connor and Gregg Olsen (1998: 5–6) address the problem of how functionalist logic tends to permeate Marxian and other structuralist analyses of the state. For one thing, they introduce power resource theory as an alternative approach: "Power resources theory emerged in the late 1970s and early 1980s in an attempt to redress some of the problems with existing mainstream and radical accounts of the welfare state" (1998: 6). Following the path of Gösta Esping-Anderson and Walter Korpi, O'Connor and Olsen explain that according to this approach power is neither widely dispersed nor simply concentrated. They note, rather, that "the balance of power between labour and capital was fluid, and therefore variable"; and that "while capital would always have the upper hand within a capitalist framework, labour had the potential to access political resources which could increase its power, and thereby allow it to implement social reform and alter distributional inequities to a significant degree."

In the same book Walter Korpi (1998: vii) argues that power must be conceptualized as a resource that shifts over time, and that it cannot be readily understood through the study of immediately observable behaviours. He describes an essential feature of the approach: "The power resources approach therefore focuses not only on the direct, but also the indirect consequences of power, indirect consequences mediated through various alternative strategies and actions available to the holders of power resources." According to Korpi, the exercise and distribution of power occur within a variety of institutions such as the market, the polity, and the family. Power relations are dynamic and subject to change, so that the precise configuration and operation of institutions will also change. Like regulation theory, power resource theory draws our attention to the need for historical and empirical research that is viewed through a theoretical prism providing insights into the actual mechanisms and modes of exercising power.

IS THE NATION-STATE STILL RELEVANT?

As we consider the role of the contemporary nation-state, the very question of the state's continued relevancy becomes central. For example, Thomas Courchene (1996: 45) states: "The Canada that we have come to know and love no longer exists! There is no viable status quo! We have to remake our nation and society in the light of irreversible external forces of globalization and of the knowledge/ information revolution."

Neo-conservative and neo-liberal politicians, along with elements of the mass media, have also popularized the notion that we are in a global era in which nation-states are impelled to act in a certain direction by the constraints and strictures of a global market. Writing in the *New Left Review*, Linda Weiss (1997: 4) summarizes the message of these spokespersons of inevitable and unfettered globalization: "According to this logic, states are now virtually powerless to make real policy choices; transnational markets and footloose corporations have so narrowly constrained policy options that more and more states are being forced to adopt similar fiscal, economic and social policy regimes."

Gary Teeple (2000: 74) sounds a warning about the potential political implications of globalization: "For the state the consequences of economic globalization are above all those of erosion of its functions and redefinition at the international level." Further:

> Without fear of exaggeration, it can be said that the national state has lost and continues to lose much of its sovereignty, although the degrees of independence vary with the degree of remaining integrity to national economic and military formations. It is not so much that a political state cannot act independently because of the erosion or usurpation of its powers, but that its raison d'être — the existence of a nationally defined capitalist class — has been waning. Taking its place has been the rise of an international capitalist class with global interests. (Teeple 2000: 75)

David Korten's *When Corporations Rule the World* (1995: 54) puts the matter even more starkly: "Corporations have emerged as the dominant governance institutions on the planet." For Korten (1995: 66), the relationship between economic resources and democracy is clear: "In the market, one dollar is one vote, and you get as many votes as you have dollars. No dollar, no vote." Korten (1995: 140) summarizes his point: "The greater the political power of the corporations and those aligned with them, the less the political power of the people, and the less meaningful democracy becomes."

We find ourselves in an interesting situation, then: some critics claim that the state has lost virtually all its power, some argue that it is losing power, and others maintain that it is erroneous to place too much emphasis on the new globalization and the apparent attendant loss of national state power. Vigorous proponents of the last view are often found in the pages of *Monthly Review*. William Tabb's 1997 article, "Globalization Is An Issue, The Power of Capital Is *The* Issue" (his emphasis), warns that it is defeatist for workers to accept that the power of global capital is supreme (Tabb 1997: 21). Ellen Meiksins Wood argues that although capitalism is changing, the nation-state remains essential to its continued functioning. Meiksins Wood (1998: 42) argues, "Capital now needs the state more than ever to sustain maximum profitability in a global market." Judy Fudge and Harry Glasbeek (1997: 220) make a similar point, noting: "We observe that despite repeated assertions about nation-states being outmoded political units, the very roles that governments of nation-states are asked to play on behalf of the forces that favour the development of a differently structured capitalism — a globalized one — make them a pertinent and vital site of struggle."

Several essays in Robert Boyer and Daniel Drache's *States against Markets: The Limits of Globalization* argue that we must continue to pay attention to the state. Boyer (1996: 108) points out the limitations of the free market in providing many of the goods required by the majority of the population and concludes: "The state remains the most powerful institution to channel and tame the power of the markets." Janine Brodie (1996b) argues that the state has not lost its relevance and power but, rather, states have adopted radically different policies. Her argument meshes well with Claus Offe, who points out, in "Aspects of the Regulation-Deregulation Debate," that deregulation is itself a form of state intervention. As Offe (1996: 75) reminds us, "A politics of deregulation, no less than one of regulation, has a character of massive state 'intervention.' For both cases involve a decisive change in the situations and market opportunities brought about by public policy."

> Some critics claim that the state has lost virtually all its power, some argue that it is losing power, and others maintain that it is erroneous to place too much emphasis on the new globalization and the apparent attendant loss of national state power.

B. Mitchell Evans, Stephen McBride, and John Shields (1998) have also argued that it is a mistake to underestimate the continued importance of the nation-state in the global era. To claim that the nation-state is irrelevant or has lost most of its power serves "to mask the active role the state has played in establishing the governance mechanisms and the new state form congruent with a system of neo-liberal regionalised trading and investment blocks" (Evans, McBride, and Shields 1998: 18).

Some ten years ago David Held added to his impressive contributions to state theory with a systematic and thoughtful theoretical treatise on globalization, *Democracy and the Global Order: From the Modern State to Cosmopolitan Governance*. Although Held maintains that we need to think about new models of global governance, he notes that the nation-state has not become totally irrelevant. "If the global system is marked by significant change, this is perhaps best conceived less as an end of the era of the nation-state and more as a challenge to the era of 'hegemonic states' — a challenge which is as yet far from complete" (Held 1995: 95). Held undertakes the task of examining the consequences and implications of the rise of international and intra-state entities for democratic theory and the state. He notes that his efforts are "motivated by the necessity to rethink the theory of democracy to take account of the changing nature of the polity both within pre-established borders and within the wider system of nation-state and global forces" (Held 1995: 144).

In a sense, the challenge that Held presents is as radical as the confrontation between existing theory and feminism. He suggests that we have no choice but to think our way through and around the existence of global structures and relations of power. Such centres and relations of power now exist; it is just that we do not theorize them, control them, understand them, or even realize they exist (Held 1995: 138–39). Held encourages us to engage in democratic thought experiments in order to conceive of new ways of understanding the multidimensional relations of power that characterize the contemporary era. In his final chapter he outlines what he terms a cosmopolitan model of democracy and postulates the possibility of radically new international governance structures and processes that integrate democratic governance principles into what must be termed the structures of a global polity.

MOVING BEYOND CLASS POLITICS: FEMINISM AND THE STATE

Thus far we have examined two major analytical approaches to the study of the polity in capitalist society. In the case of the pluralist and structural functionalist approaches, the polity is seen as part of a social decision-making process in which there are no dominant forces, interests, or players who consistently get their way, at least in the long run. According to the various Marxian positions, the state in capitalist society is "connected" to the capitalist class instrumentally, structurally, or through mechanisms of power, and as a result the state tends to function in the interests of that class. As a result of its ability to influence the state, the capitalist class is truly a ruling class, having both economic and political power.

Still, it has been argued that none of these positions is adequate as a basis for understanding the complexities of the role of the state in advanced capitalist society and the state's role in the emergence and unfolding of social issues.

The most important and systematic critique of the analytical and explanatory capacities of the older theoretical approaches has come from scholars and activists asso-

> Feminist theoreticians… have shown that the state plays a central role in the subordination of women and the domination of men. This has in turn led to… demands that the existing theoretical frameworks be radically rethought.

ciated with various schools of feminist thought. Feminist theoreticians have posed new questions concerning the nature and role of the state, especially as it relates to sex and gender relations, and have found the existing approaches wanting in two related, but different, aspects. First, convincing arguments, supported by overwhelming evidence, have shown that the state plays a central role in the subordination of women and the domination of men. This evidence has in turn led to the second important development, namely, demands that the existing theoretical frameworks be radically rethought to account for the role of the state in maintaining the dominant patriarchal and heterosexual relations that characterize Western society.

An early work pointing out the state's important role in sex and gender relations is Mary McIntosh's 1978 essay "The State and the Oppression of Women." McIntosh argues that the state is involved in the oppression of women through its support of the household system, which in capitalist society is intimately linked to the creation of the conditions necessary for the continuing accumulation of capital. She maintains that the household is the site of the production and reproduction of the essential commodity in the production and appropriation of surplus value in capitalist society, namely labour power. Further, she argues that the state plays a central role in the maintenance of the specific household form, the patriarchal family, in which women produce and reproduce labour power. The state thus oppresses women through various measures that serve to maintain patriarchal family relations, in part because maintaining the conditions necessary for the continuation of the system is one of the state's main functions.

Numerous feminist writers have elaborated on the themes laid out by McIntosh (1978). Michèle Barrett (1980) presents a more elaborate account of the oppression of women in which she cautions against explaining the persistence of patterns of male dominance and the patriarchal family solely in terms of economic factors; she argues that we need to consider the role of ideology as well. In a powerful essay, "Masculine Dominance and the State," Varda Burstyn (1985a) questions the value of a Marxian concept of class for addressing sex and gender oppression. Indeed, she argues that we need to develop the concept of "gender class" to understand the full extent of the oppression of women — an oppression that is not just a matter of women in capitalist society itself, but also part of a larger transhistorical pattern of sexual oppression. Burstyn suggests that the state has played a central role in both economic-class domination and gender-class domination. Further, she maintains that the state has acted to enforce these dual patterns of domination because its structures have been dominated by men.

Jane Ursel (1986) develops a somewhat different argument. She advocates the development of an analytical approach recognizing the importance of both material production and biological reproduction in determining the shape and character of human society. Ursel argues in effect that the concept of capitalism, as understood in Marxian analysis, is useful for understanding the nature of material production in Western society, while the concept of patriarchy is most appropriate for an analysis of reproduction. She notes that the state has played a central role in facilitating the continuance of the various modes of material production and biological reproduction. Thus the state has served the interests of those who benefit from the class-based relations of production in capitalist society and the sexual oppression of patriarchal society.

Two other articles, Norene Pupo's "Preserving Patriarchy: Women, the Family and the State" (1988) and Jane Jenson's "Gender and Reproduction, or Babies and the State" (1992), illustrate the complexities of the relationship between the state and sex and gender relations. Pupo examines the rise and role of what we might term "family-related" legislation in Canada, noting its contradictory nature. She writes:

> Through its vast system of laws, regulations, and the institutional structure of the welfare state, the state shapes both personal and social lives. Historically women have both welcomed and resisted the encroachment of the state in the family home. The state at once is regarded as a source of protection and justice and as the basis of inequality. Such contradictions are inherent in a state under capitalism. (Pupo 1988: 229)

She notes that while the actions and policies of the state may appear to be liberating, in the long run they work to reproduce patriarchal relations.

Jenson (1992) provides a similar analysis of the sometimes contradictory nature of state policies and actions. She reviews the efforts of feminists who have opted to use a Marxian approach to the state to understand the oppression of women, although she devotes the major portion of her article to presenting valuable comparative data drawn from the experiences of women in France and England. On the basis of this data she concludes that it is not possible to make generalized theoretical statements; however, she notes: "Beginning with the logic of the capitalist state's location in any conjuncture, and mapping the articulation of power relations such as those of class and gender in the politics of any social formation, it is possible to understand the ways in which the state contributes to the oppression of women" (Jenson 1992: 229). Jenson then makes a very important point: that within the system there is also "space for resistance" (Jenson 1992: 229). The notion that people who are oppressed have opportunities to resist is central.

Similarly, the argument that there are opportunities to use the contradictions in the system in a positive way is developed by two Canadian scholars who have contributed greatly to the advancement of feminist scholarship: Pat and Hugh Armstrong. Armstrong and Armstrong (1990: 214) note: "More and more feminists have come to realize that the state is not simply an instrument of class or male rule: that it can indeed work for the benefit of at least some women." They go on to reiterate the idea that the state remains a complex and contradictory phenomenon.

In her book *Toward a Feminist Theory of the State* (1989), Catharine MacKinnon focuses on the negative impact that many state actions have for women. In her discussion of the actions and logic of the liberal state in capitalist society, MacKinnon (1989: 169) notes: "The state, through law, institutionalizes male power over women through institutionalizing the male point of view in law. Its first state act is to see women from the standpoint of male dominance; its next act is to treat them that way." She concludes with a powerful statement: "However autonomous of class the liberal state may appear, it is not autonomous of sex. Male power is systemic. Coercive, legitimized and epistemic, it is the regime" (MacKinnon 1989: 170).

We have barely scratched the surface in terms of the available literature, but it is crystal clear that there is plenty of empirical evidence illustrating the role of the state in sex and gender oppression. Although he is referring to other evidence, R. W. Connell (1990: 54) makes an important point: "This adds up to a convincing picture of the state as an active player in gender politics. Nobody acquainted with the facts revealed in this research can any longer accept the silence about gender in the traditional state theory, whether liberal, socialist or conservative." As Connell argues, concepts of sex and gender must be included from the beginning in all theorizing about the modern state. The task of theorizing and understanding the integral connection of sex and gender relations to the polity and the state means that we must break with existing approaches. Such a task is not easy, as Mary O'Brien (1981: 5, 62) notes when she warns against the persistence of, and problems associated with, "malestream" thought and its attendant tendency to reductionism.

These concerns about gender and the state were typically developed during an era when structures and policies in most Western societies could have been described as liberal-democratic welfare or Keynesian. The political systems and policies promoted involved the provision of a limited set of social policies that provided minimal standards for health care, public education, and industrial regulation, among other things. Since the 1980s these policies and the state infrastructure to support them have been under incessant attack from the neo-liberal right. As a result even the minimalist levels of support for vital public services, including health and education, have been steadily eroded. As North America moves more and more to a new order that Janine Brodie (1996b) refers to as being driven by "market-based, self-reliant and privatizing ideals," the position of women and many others who suffer the most egregious forms of oppression in a class-based patriarchal system deteriorates even further. A powerful collection of essays edited by Brodie (1996a) explores the negative impact of the transformation of the liberal-democratic welfare state into a neo-liberal, market-oriented state that has as its main concern global competition and not the welfare or rights of its citizens.

The work of Carole Pateman provides a key critique of the inherent logic of most political theorizing. Pateman argues that the basic concepts of all Western political discourse — private, public, individual, citizen—are founded on a set of assumptions and arguments that are patriarchal and thus exclusionary for women. In an important collection of essays, *The Disorder of Women* (1989), Pateman examines a series of political themes and topics related to the theory of the polity, and in each case is forced to conclude that the core language, concepts, and discourse are flawed. While she agrees that much Western political theory and thinking about the state are predicated on patriarchal thought, Chantal Mouffe (1997) is critical of the assumptions that seem to inform Pateman's work. According to Mouffe, Pateman and others err in arguing that there is something essentially different about women that provides them with an alternate and presumably more democratic and humane conception of citizenship. Mouffe (1997: 82) explains:

> My own view is quite different. I want to argue that the limitations of the modern conception of citizenship should be remedied, not by making sexual difference politically relevant to its definition, but by constructing a new conception of citizenship where sexual difference would become effectively irrelevant. This, of course, requires a conception of the social agent of the kind I defended earlier: as the articulation of an ensemble of subject positions, corresponding to the multiplicity of social relations in which it is inscribed.

The problem might be even more difficult than it seems on the surface, especially if we consider the arguments of Diana Coole (1988), who also warns us that the conventional process of theorizing is itself part of an agenda of domination and that we thus need to rethink how it is we actually think!

In recent years feminist theory, like every other stream of social theory, has been criticized for adopting overly simplistic approaches to complex social phenomena. Some theorists utilize the label "postmodernism" to refer to these criticisms; but in the context of feminist thought the notion of "third wave feminism" is more appropriate. Leslie Heywood and Jennifer Drake's 1997 collection of essays, *Third Wave Agenda: Being Feminist, Doing Feminism*, is illustrative. While the editors acknowledge that they are building on the foundation of earlier feminisms, their intellectual and political project has a distinctly different focus. The new agenda demands a recognition and an incorporation of multiple voices representing multiple social, economic, and political positions. Patricia Madoo Lengermann and Jill Niebrugge-Brantley (1997: 332–33) explain:

> Third-wave feminism's focal concern is with differences among women. Anchored in this concern, third-wave feminisms reevaluate and extend the issues that second-wave feminists opened for general societal discourse while at the same time critically reassessing the themes and concepts of those second-wave theories. Third-wave feminism looks critically at the tendency of work done in the 1960s and 1970s to use a generalized, monolithic concept of "woman" as a generic category in stratification and focuses instead on the factual and theoretical implications of differences among women. The differences considered are those that result from an unequal distribution of socially produced goods and services on the basis of position in the global system, class, race, ethnicity, age, and affectional preference as these factors interact with gender stratification.

Third wave feminists call for an explicit acknowledgement of women's very different lived experience and a recognition of the need for what Adie Nelson and Barrie Robinson call inclusive feminism. Nelson and Robinson (2002: 96) note that inclusive feminism is critical of the apparent search by earlier feminists "for the essential experience of generic 'woman' when there were many quite different experiences." Patricia Elliot and Nancy Mandell (1995: 24) refer to the new approach as postmodern feminism — an approach that emphasizes the need to include the voices and perspectives of "women of color and women from developing countries" as well as "lesbian, disabled and working-class women." Nelson and Robinson (2002: 98) note that postmodern feminists maintain that "the theoretical claims emanating from liberal, Marxist, radical, cultural and socialist feminisms, which assert a single or even a limited plurality of causes for women's oppression, are flawed, inadequate." Any theory that claims to be "fully explanatory... is assuming a dominant oppressive stance."

Lengermann and Niebrugge-Brantley identify an additional characteristic of third wave feminism: its tendency to maintain that not all suffering is equal. They quote Lourdes Arguelles's argument that there is a "calculus of pain" that is "determined by the intersection of one's individual life of global location, class, race, ethnicity, age, affectional preference, and other dimensions of stratification" (Lengermann and Niebrugge-Brantley 1997: 334).

Third wave feminism, like the postmodernist critiques of grand theory, cannot be easily summarized. The approach addresses an unlimited number of issues and topics relating to the role, position, status, oppression, liberation, freedom, and subjugation of women everywhere. Most importantly for our purposes here, the discourse has not yet developed an approach to the study of the polity, although it does remind us that political power will remain complex and contested by multiple voices.

AN ALTERNATIVE VIEW OF THE LIBERAL STATE: STRUCTURATION THEORY

When we move from issues such as sex, gender, and class domination to issues of the environment, child development, or education, it becomes obvious that state intervention does not always seem to have a class basis. What we need is an approach that allows us to locate the structures and policies of the state within the larger and complex patterns of all of the unequal power relations that characterize liberal-democratic society.

What is needed is a new way of approaching the role and operation of the state in liberal-democratic society, a method that will facilitate empirical research, allow us to explain events in the "real world," and be theoretically consistent. A useful point of departure for the development of such an approach might be a reconsideration of how we conceptualize human society. Rather than adopting the functionalist organic analogy or the conventional materialist approach, it might be time to rethink our understanding of the very basis of society.

Such re-examination might lead us to examine how both material production and biological reproduction are organized and structured. By relating the complex institutional matrix that makes up society to these two key human processes we can move towards a more adequate understanding of all aspects of society, including the role of the state.

First of all, species homo sapiens is an intelligent creature whose very survival is dependent on developing social solutions for various needs and problems. As a species we have created, in the process of solving a variety of problems, the very social structures we are trying to figure out and understand. This means that we are, as a species, simultaneously the products and the producers of our social structures. All social structures are human products; that is, they are the arrangements or institutions that emerged historically as humans attempted to solve problems and "get things done." In turn they become the contexts and even determinants of subsequent human action. Anthony Giddens (1984) refers to this as the duality of structure.

All human societies, if they are to survive over any length of time, are dependent on some form of economic activity: their ongoing practices, activities, and institutionalized behaviour are geared towards dealing with material production and distribution. If a society is to survive over time, some arrangements and institutionalized practices for facilitating species reproduction and the care of the young must also be developed. Given these relationships, should not both the institutional practices that facilitate material production and biological reproduction be jointly understood as composing the basis or core of society? As for the other components of the social structure, in capitalist society at least it is useful to understand the state as a distinct realm of human practice, which is separate from and related to material production and species reproduction. In addition we can consider the other sorts of organized and institutionalized human practices that make up our society as composing civil society. This analytical view of society holds that all the various realms of human activity and practice are related, although a certain sense of primacy is attached to material production and species reproduction.

An additional dimension of human existence and society must be explicitly acknowledged: that is, as we have engaged in social actions and practices to solve our various problems, we have developed vast amounts of different kinds of knowledge, including both scientific learning and common sense. An integral part of the accumulation of these stocks of knowledge has been the growth of complicated and sophisticated sets of physical, verbal, and written symbols, which we use to communicate. As a species we do not seem to pass on much "knowledge" genetically or instinctually, and thus we have survived and prospered because over great periods of time we have been able to accumulate and pass on knowledge from generation to generation. The stocks of knowledge that we accumulate and the systems of symbolic communication through which we transmit that knowledge both become an integral part of the overall system of social structures and processes that make up society. Ideologies, stocks of knowledge, and systems of knowing, although grounded in the complex social workings of material production and biological reproduction, become part of the complex social structures and need to be accounted for in social analysis.

This approach, though largely undeveloped and in need of considerable refinement, nevertheless could offer a greater analytical potential than do the existing theories. If we are to examine, analyze, and understand concrete, historically specific instances of state action, intervention, and policy we must begin with an understanding of the role and location of the state in society and the roles of various actors in the determination of state policy and action. According to the alternative approach, we need to first understand that society as a whole is fundamentally influenced by how material production and species reproduction are organized. Then we can consider the impact of those practices on specific social structures, such as the state.

If we were to adopt this approach we would not assume that the state acts out its role because of some predetermined functional imperative to protect or serve capital or to ensure the maintenance of patriarchal relations. Rather, after doing the necessary empirical and historical research, we could identify specific and concrete instances in which mechanisms of power were being used by individuals, groups, and classes to influence the state. We could find out which mechanisms were effective and which were not effective. We would look at each and every one of the potential mechanisms of power to determine which ones, singularly and in combination, explain a particular state action at a particular historical moment.

An additional complicating factor that influences how we now theorize the state is the impact of globalization. Many scholars, including David Held, are attempting to develop theoretical approaches for the study of the polity that account for the ever-increasing role of non-national, non-governmental institutions that control major resources on a world scale. Held's work points the way to the development of an approach that would explain what he refers to as "cosmopolitan democracy" (Held 1995: 279). Such an approach moves our thinking about concepts such as citizenship and political power to an international level in which nation-states and their locally structured polities are components of a larger system of power relations.

In the abstract it is not possible to specify which mechanisms are more or less important, because that is a question for empirical and historical research. Still, we will make some assumptions concerning the nature of our social structure. For example, it seems safe to assume that the capitalist economic system inevitably produces class structures and, further, that in the West our system of sex and gender relations (the key relations in the reproductive sphere) is best understood and described as patriarchal. When we proceed to analytical and explanatory thinking the task will not be simple, because we will have to be aware that any one or more of a number of mechanisms of power might explain a particular outcome.

In some cases we may need to look at the overall ideological structures at a given moment in order to explain particular actions. For example, when we examine the nature of the state's interventions in issues related to sex and gender, we will have to examine patriarchal ideology to be able to explain why patriarchal legislation characterizes the statute books of most if not all Western nations. In the case of other state policies or actions, the explanation may reside in the use of economic power, lobbying, or personal connections. What this approach demands is empirical and historical research that will help us to determine which mechanisms are used by which classes and with what outcome.

If the last forty years of debate have demonstrated anything, it has been the inadequacies of functionalist and teleological approaches that merely substitute assumed function for explanation. This is, simply, not good social analysis because it fails to really explain anything. A better approach requires that we concretely locate the actors, processes, and structures in their larger social, economic, and political contexts. Our analysis of the role of the state, its actions, and its policies can then proceed to investigate the mechanisms of power and the nature of state actions, interventions, and policies. We must remind ourselves that good social analysis is not about producing theoretical schemas; rather, it is about using theoretical formulations to assist in the process of developing concrete and empirical explanations of how our society actually works or doesn't work. Our task now is to use this kind of social analysis — and if necessary build new and even better approaches—so that we can more fully understand key issues and problems in Canadian society.

THE TASK FOR CRITICAL THINKING

So much dramatic change has happened in the world of politics and state structures since the beginning of the 1990s that at times we are left wondering if past theories of the state have any relevance in an era of market hegemony, global capitalism, U.S. international domination, a so-called war on terror, and virtually countless regional, national, and international conflicts. One response to this intense realignment of forces has been the argument that we have entered a new historical epoch or era characterized by fragmentation, instability, indeterminacy, conflicting and alternate definitions of reality, and even reconsiderations of the very notion of reality (Harvey 1989).

For those who see the current era as marking the transition from what has been called modernity to the irredeemable fragmentation of the postmodern condition, the theories, arguments, and narratives set forth in this chapter

> So much has happened in the world of politics and state structures over the past decade and a half that, at times, we are left wondering if the ideas outlined above have any relevance in an era of market hegemony, global capitalism, American international domination, so-called wars on terror, and virtually countless regional, national, and international conflicts.

are not just irrelevant — they are dangerous because they provide a false picture of reality as being subject to systematic analysis, understanding, and even improvement. This is not the position I take. Whether we understand it or not, and whether it is getting more complicated or not, our lives have a material and substantial reality. Further, it is the task of critical thinkers not only to figure out what is happening in that reality but also to reflect on that reality by using a prism informed by a commitment to social justice. Neil Postman describes what happens when we lack an appropriate theoretical framework for understanding our world:

It may be said here that when people do not have a satisfactory narrative to generate a sense of purpose or continuity, a kind of psychic disorientation takes hold followed by a frantic search for something to believe in or, probably worse, a resigned conclusion that there is nothing to find. The devil-believers reclaim a fragment of the great narrative of Genesis. The alien-believers ask for deliverance from green-grey creatures whose physics has overcome the speed of light. The deconstructionists keep confusion at bay by writing books in which they tell us that there is nothing to write books about. (Postman 1999: 10)

Although there is no doubt that capitalism and the world it creates have and are changing, the task of the critical thinker remains essentially the same — analyzing and understanding our social, economic, and political world. In his book *The Condition of Postmodernism*, David Harvey (1989: 12) argues that the seeming chaotic, fragmented, and transitory dimensions of our lives today do not in themselves mean that we have passed into a new postmodern era, because these conditions have always been characteristics of capitalism. Harvey uses the core concepts associated with a Marxian critical account of capitalism to argue that what has changed is the nature of the social and political regulation of capitalism, not the fundamentals of capitalism (1989: 121–23).

In the historical era from, roughly, the Second World War to the early 1970s, a particular form of capitalism took hold. This was an era of mass production and mass consumption of consumer goods under the growing international leadership of the United States. Although, to be sure, the twentieth century was punctuated by the national and international horrors of two world wars, the Great Depression, and revolutions in Russia and China, it was an era that saw the emergence of the welfare state, underlying which was an overarching political compromise (called "corporatist") in most Western industrial nations. That compromise involved a set of social and political structures through which business/corporations, labour, and the state regulated economic, social, and political affairs more or less to everyone's agreement. In this post–Second World War social contract, it was accepted that unions would exist and would struggle to improve pay and working conditions. The state would legitimately provide a social safety net and use its resources to direct investment and economic activity (especially economic development aid for selected regions and industries). Business would be free to make most of the nation's economic decisions within these broad constraints. In particular, in key industrial sectors (autos, rubber, steel, for example) owners and managers were given a free hand with the introduction of technological change and other labour-saving innovations; and workers, through their unions, would get wage increases in line with productivity gains plus inflation. This came to be called the Fordist accumulation regime.

According to Harvey there were, however, flies in the ointment, arising from the reality that capitalism, as a system based on the necessity of continual growth and class exploitation, is prone to instability. As a result the Fordist accumulation regime broke down amid a number of interrelated crises. There were growing rivalries within and between capitalist nations. In addition, capitalists, especially big business, found themselves with large amounts of cash and increasingly fewer investment opportunities (a crisis of overaccumulation). Added to these problems were the advancing globalization of business and growing state fiscal deficits.

What emerged after the early 1970s was a new system or mode of accumulation called "flexible accumulation" (see Harvey 1989: cha. 11). According to Harvey, the world was becoming smaller in part because of advances in telecommunications and transportation, marking the end to Fordist strategies that were largely centred on particular nation-states. In this new economy there would be significant attention paid to local markets and smaller-scale production. Flexible work patterns emerged, characterized by workers needing and wanting to frequently change jobs and thus moving to different industries and different places within a lifetime. In addition consumption and cultural patterns shifted, becoming more diverse (people around the world are aware of and adopting customs — in food, dress, language, for example — from far-flung societies), with an attendant shift away from traditional Western or Northern industrial domination. Flexible accumulation also brought new roles and dynamics to the functions and operation of the nation-state.

Bob Jessop (2003) has systematically addressed the implications of flexible accumulation for the state. He concentrates on the transformation of the Keynesian welfare nation-state into what he calls the "Schumpeterian workfare state" (a term based on the work of Joseph Schumpeter, a contemporary of economist John Maynard Keynes and a critic of Keynes's political and economic ideas). Jessop (2003: 4) summarizes the essential feature of the Keynesian welfare state regime as being focused on maintaining adequate levels of consumption, general welfare, system legitimacy, and political support within the confines of national economies. He also sees the 1970s as marking the emergence of a series of crises in the Keynesian welfare state system. These crises included growing government deficits, international competition among capitalist economies, increasing regional disparities, and the growing internationalization of capital. In response to these upheavals, combined with new levels of immigration and the growth of more complex populations, many governments began to implement a series of neo-liberal, pro-market public policies (2003: 5–6). The policies included widespread and deep cuts to a wide range of social programs, from those that offered various forms of social and economic support to immigrants and refugees to public defender and legal assistance programs for those unable to hire lawyers. Cuts to Medicare, school support, day-care programs, and international aid also characterized the new era.

Whereas Harvey suggested that Fordist accumulation regimes had become transformed into the system of flexible accumulation, Jessop sees the Keynesian welfare state system as being transformed into a post-Fordist accumulation regime. In other words, a new kind of state more "suited" to flexible accumulation emerged. The key feature of this new political system is a nation-state that loses its central position; many state functions are taken over by non-government or private agents, and capital becomes fully internationalized. The end result of this process of "denationalization, destatization and internationalization" (2003: 6) is the movement to the Schumpeterian workfare state (SWS):

> The distinctive features of the Schumpeterian workfare state are: a concern to promote innovation and structural competitiveness in the field of economic policy; and a concern to promote flexibility and competitiveness in the field of social policy. Naturally the SWS will also express other concerns and perform many other functions typical of capitalist states but it is the combination of these twin concerns, together with their implications for the overall functioning of the state which differentiate it from other capitalist regimes. (Jessop 1993: 10–11)

In the Canadian context the promotion of what Jessop refers to as innovation and structural competitiveness can be seen in a range of government programs and policies, from the direct funding of research in universities to the proliferation of offices devoted to the immediate commercial application of knowledge. State spending on biotechnology, highway infrastructure, and education are all about competitive advantage. Indeed, the Canadian government now maintains a website called "Invest In Canada," which offers a number of reasons as to why investors should consider moving their funds into this country. These include: "Smart Workforce; Leading Economy; Strong Fiscal Policy; NAFTA Advantage; Cost Competitive; Sophisticated Infrastructure; A Great Place to Live; Incentives and Taxes." Absent are references to decent welfare rates and programs aimed at social justice and equity.

This shift to a SWS does "hollow out" the state in the face of the social issues plaguing society (to some it makes for an irrelevancy of the nation-state in the post-Fordist era). Although Jessop argues that some state activities are delegated to the non-government, local, or private realm (ranging across activities as diverse as the use of private police and security companies for neighbourhood patrols to food banks and private donations to foundations providing capital funds to hospitals and schools) and other activities to international agencies (such as the use of private security forces in war zones, the regulation of food quality by international trade agreements, and the prohibitions against expanding the social safety net contained in agreements such as NAFTA), he sees a continuing role for the nation-state. The major role left, according to Jessop (2003: 12), is one already identified by Poulantzas: namely the generic function of establishing and maintaining social order, consensus, and cohesion.

As was the case with the Keynesian welfare state, there are and will be many variations of the Schumpeterian workfare state found in various nations with different cultures, histories, and normative regimes. What they will share in common is a commitment to facilitating capital accumulation through supply-side policies and actions as opposed to those associated with Keynesian welfare state regimes.

POLITICS AND POWER

How, you might ask, does this litany of theories, arguments and ideas prepare us to fully understand the various issues addressed throughout this book? What does any of this have to do with welfare systems, poverty, education, health, the media, crime, sexuality, violence against women, and the complexities of racism? Although the various theories of the state and its role differ in many respects, they tend to agree that social issues are political in both the broad and narrow sense of the word. In the broad meaning of political, these issues have to do with power and human relations. In a narrow sense they are political in that they are issues often debated, discussed, and acted upon in the realm of the polity. How you analyze and understand the relationship between the activities of human social agents and the structures and dynamics of the institutions comprising the polity is therefore central to an understanding of these various issues. As you prepare to engage with the issues taken up in this book, you can begin by asking yourself some fundamental questions about how you understand the workings of power at different levels of individuals, collectivities, and major institutions of the state in capitalist society.

GLOSSARY OF KEY TERMS

Structural functionalism: An approach to social analysis that employs an organic analogy. Each component of society is assumed to have certain basic needs that must be met if society is to survive. Each social institution performs a specialized function that contributes to the maintenance of the overall system. Among the functions of the polity are the establishment of social goals, priorities, and objectives and the maintenance of social order.

Pluralism: Pluralists recognize that individuals will differ in terms of their income, social status, or authority, but liberal-democratic systems prevent these from becoming entrenched social inequalities. Pluralists maintain that democratic electoral systems, an open process of decision-making, and group lobbying ensure a democratic decision-making process because all groups and interests in society have a more or less equal opportunity to influence the government through electoral and lobbying activities.

State system/polity: All of the institutions, organizations, and agencies connected with the political processes in societies with formally organized political institutions make up the state system, or polity. In Western liberal democracies the state system or polity includes the formal elected apparatus of government, the appointed officials, the state bureaucracy, the judiciary, police and military, and national and international agencies.

Instrumentalist view of state: A particular neo-Marxist view, this approach places emphasis on personal and personnel connections between representatives of the capitalist class and the state. Instrumentalists maintain that the capitalist class is able to control and direct the activities of the state because the people operating the state either come directly from the capitalist class or share the values, ideologies, and objectives of the capitalist class.

Structuralist view of state: A version of neo–Marxist theory that draws on functionalist logic. The state's major role is seen as attempting to prevent the conflicts and contradictions from destroying the capitalist system. It is the needs and logic of the system that determine the role and function of the state and not the connections that state personnel have to the capitalist class.

Mechanisms of power: An element of an approach to the state that stresses the need to understand that there is a number of different means that can be employed to influence the state in capitalist society. A liberal-democratic system includes both direct (personnel and personal connections, lobbying, and impacting policy formation) and indirect (using economic power, ideological power, and political funding) mechanisms of power. All classes and individuals are able to use these mechanisms of power; however, the class with overwhelming economic power is better able to exercise them.

Feminism: A complex term used to describe a diverse set of beliefs, political practices, social practices, social movements, and sociological theories predicated on a set of underlying assumptions and principles that recognize the historical subordination and oppression of women. Feminists not only are committed to explaining this phenomenon, but also see alternative non-oppressive modes of social organization.

Liberal feminism: A stream of feminist thought primarily locates women's inequalities in the dysfunction of the existing social institutions. Liberal feminists argue that sexist ideas and beliefs are a central cause of women's inequalities and that these conditions can be altered through the introduction of non-sexist ideas, values, and norms and intensive resocialization without any major or radical change to the basic institutional orders.

Socialist feminism: A political approach that tends to understand the situation of women in capitalist society in terms of two forms of oppression. Women are part of the historical and overall system of class exploitation of capitalist society; and women are oppressed by the structures and dynamics of patriarchy. Rather than merely arguing that the capitalist relations of class domination and exploitation are at the root of women's oppression, socialist feminists advocate the need to confront and change all forms of patriarchal social organization.

Third wave feminism: A stream that emphasizes the necessity of recognizing the complexities of women's situations and experiences by rejecting any simple notion of women as a homogeneous category or group. Third wave feminists draw attention to issues of class, race, ethnic, age, geographic, national, and a host of other differences and divisions that combine to oppress women. Thus, there cannot be a singular, totalizing, or universal feminist theory.

QUESTIONS FOR DISCUSSION

1. Why might the polity or the state system be considered a "special institution"? What is unique about the decisions made in this institution?

2. What are the core tenets of the pluralist understanding of political power? Do these assumptions stand up to critical scrutiny given the inequality of incomes that typically characterize market society?

3. Why was Miliband's approach labelled the "instrumentalist approach"? Why in turn was Poulantzas referred to as a structuralist?

4. What, according to Szymanski, is a mechanism of power? Could it be said that his approach is merely an extension of pluralism?

5. What theory of the state informs most of the media reports that deal with the activities of the state?

6. Is the state another dimension of domination in patriarchal domination? Explain your answer.

7. What are the essential differences between a power resource approach and an approach using the notion of mechanisms of power? Are the two compatible? Explain.

8. Can the state or the polity be understood without first understanding sex/gender power relations?

9. Compare and contrast how two different theories or approaches to understanding the state would explain the decline of the welfare state over the past three decades.

10. Outline the basis of your theory of the polity. What assumptions do you make about social inequality and how to prevent social inequalities from becoming political inequalities?

WEBSITES OF INTEREST

Social Theory/Popular Culture. <www.theory.org.uk/main.htm>.
Marxists Internet Archive. <www.marxists.org>.
The Third Wave. <www.3rdwwwave.com/>.
Sociology Online. <www.sociologyonline.co.uk/politics/index.shtml>.
Government, Law and Politics. <eserver.org/govt/theory.html>.
EServer.org-Accessible Writing. <www.eserver.org/govt/theory.html>.

Chapter Two

INTIMATE VIOLENCE IN CANADA
Policy, Politics, and Research on Gender and Perpetration/Victimization

Ruth M. Mann

In Canada as in other jurisdictions, historically and today, violence is disproportionately a male crime. Especially in the case of violence resulting in serious injury or death, males are both the primary perpetrators and the primary victims (Dawson 2001). Statistics Canada data for 2004, for example, demonstrate that 90 percent of those accused of homicide and 68 percent of homicide victims were male (Dauvergne 2005). In the case of intimate violence and homicide, sexual assaults, and criminal harassment sufficient to cause a victim to fear for her safety or the safety of someone close to her, males remain the primary perpetrators while females are the primary victims.

Over the past decade (Ogrodnik 2006) and in recent Statistics Canada reports, 84 to 86 percent of police-reported victims of intimate partner assault were female (Brzozowski 2004; Patterson 2003), as were 80 to 82 percent of spousal homicide victims (Beattie 2005a; Kowalski 2006). In sexual assault cases, 98 percent of those accused

"You Should Know This"
- Men and women report being victims of intimate partner assaults at roughly equivalent rates; however, women victims reported more frequent, more serious, and more injurious violence.
- Fathers are wholly or solely responsible for exposing children to domestic violence three times more often than mothers.
- The primary difference in men's and women's use of intimate violence is that men have a greater propensity to use violence to assert control and cause fear.
- 30 percent of men who reported their partner had assaulted them stated that the assault had little or no impact on their well-being, compared to 6 percent of victimized women.
- 30 percent of victimized women compared to 5 percent of victimized men reported that violence perpetrated by their partner caused them to live in a state of generalized fear.
- Men's and fathers' rights advocates argue that intimate violence has been falsely framed as a gender issue, and that Status of Women Canada and other Family-Violence Initiative partners foster hatred against men through biased research.
- Status of Women is one of the thirteen FVI partner agencies that identify all forms of family violence as unacceptable, including violence against men.
- In the thirty-year period following 1974, police-reported spousal homicides decreased by approximately one half, to the benefit of both women and men.
- From the mid-1990s forward, the FVI has sponsored several publications relevant to male victimization, including a directory that lists governmental and nongovernmental services for abused men in Canada.

Sources: Mihorean 2005; Tutty 1999; Bala 1999; Lupri 2004; Mann 2005; F-P-T Ministries Responsible for the Status of Women 2002; Kowalski 2006; National Clearinghouse on Family Violence 2004b.

were male and 82 percent of those victimized were female (Kong et al. 2003). In the case of stalking or criminal harassment, 80 percent of those accused were male, while 76 percent of persons harassed and 87 percent of persons harassed by a current or former intimate partner were female (AuCoin 2005).

Males are also the primary perpetrators, and females the primary victims, in police-reported crimes against children and youth by family members, with 98 percent of all relatives accused of sexual assaults and 72 percent of all relatives accused of physical assaults identified as male (Beattie 2005b). In the case of family-related homicides, fathers and other male relatives outnumbered mothers and female relatives in killing children and youth at all age levels, including infants (Dauvergne 2006). Most dramatically, 97 percent of murder-suicides resulting in the death of a spouse were perpetrated by a male, as were 72 percent of murder-suicides resulting in the death of a child or children but not a spouse (Aston and Bunge 2005).

The gendered distribution of perpetration and victimization in police reports is broadly supported by self-report data on intimate partner violence generated through Statistics Canada's 1999 and 2004 General Social Survey (GSS) (Mihorean 2005, 2006). In both waves, women and men self-reported roughly equivalent rates of violence at the hands of a current or former spouse over the previous five years (7 percent women and 6 percent men in 2004). However, women reported far more repeat, chronic, and physically injurious violence, including especially violence requiring medical attention (13 percent of victimized women vs. 2 percent of men in 2004). Women also reported higher rates of a perpetrator consuming alcohol at the time of the violence (44 percent victimized women vs. 24 percent men), more generalized fear as a consequence of the violence (30 percent victimized women vs. 5 percent men), and higher rates of reporting the violence to

> A 1999 survey found that 70 percent of spousal violence witnessed by children was against mothers, with half of these mothers reporting that the children witnessed incidents in which they had feared for their lives.

the police (36 percent of victimized women vs. 17 percent of men) and of seeking a restraining order (38 percent victimized women vs. 15 percent men).

Moreover, far more women than men reported that one or more children witnessed their victimization. Indeed, in the 1999 survey a full 70 percent of spousal violence witnessed by children was against mothers, with half of these mothers reporting that children witnessed incidents in which they had feared for their lives (Dauvergne and Johnson 2001). Finally, violence rates were particularly high among separated spouses who have children with ex-spouses (reported by 27 percent, with no breakdown by gender), pointing to the need for greater policy attention to be paid to spousal violence in the contexts of child custody and access (Mihorean 2005).

> Violence rates are high among separated spouses who have children with their ex-spouses, pointing to the need for greater policy attention to be paid to spousal violence in the contexts of child custody and access.

Data from child welfare authorities on maltreatment through exposure to domestic violence show a similar gender pattern (Tonmyr, Fallon, and Trocme 2006). Overall, mothers and fathers (biological and step) appear to be roughly equally responsible for substantiated abuse and neglect (mothers at 54 percent; fathers at 60 percent). However, in the case of exposure to domestic violence, fathers are identified as wholly or solely responsible in 88 percent of cases, compared to 28 percent in which mothers are deemed responsible. Also revealingly, domestic violence victimization is a principal stressor for mothers across child maltreatment categories (occurring in 51 percent of substantiated cases), followed by lack of social support (40 percent), mental heath issues (27 percent), and having themselves been maltreated as a child (25 percent). In contrast, for fathers the correspondingly prevalent stressors are having an alcohol, drug, or solvent abuse problem (47 percent), followed by a lack of social supports (33 percent), mental health issues (18 percent), and having themselves been maltreated as children (18 percent). These differences aside, male and female children who witness spousal violence exhibit a common set of negative impacts including increased aggression, mental health problems, learning difficulties, and school problems (Dauvergne and Johnson 2001).[1]

THE FAMILY-VIOLENCE INITIATIVE (FVI)

Statistics Canada data on the gendered dynamics and impacts of intimate partner violence on all who experience and witness it are part of the evidence base that informs Canada's Family-Violence Initiative (FVI), within which Statistics Canada and twelve other agencies of the federal government partner.[2] Through these agencies the FVI helps to fund a host of intimate violence prevention and intervention efforts through a strategy that co-situates federal and provincial-territorial governments, community-based organizations, and citizens as stakeholders who share responsibility for the problem and its solution (Family-Violence Prevention Unit 2002; Jamieson 2004).[3] Mindful that intimate violence affects people in all social categories, both genders, and all ages, but that women and children — especially young and marginalized women and children — are the principal victims of serious violence, the FVI employs a dual strategy aimed at preventing and over the long term "eliminating" intimate violence (Family-Violence Prevention Unit 2002; Jamieson 2004). On the one hand, FVI agencies sponsor research and services for virtually all victim constituencies, including not only abused women and children (National Clearinghouse on Family Violence [NCFV] 2004a), but also abused men (Lupri and Grandin 2004; NCFV 2004b; Tutty 1999), older adults (McDonald and Collins 2000; NCFV 2004c), people with disabilities (Sobsey 2002), Aboriginal people (Green 1996), parents abused by teen children (Cottrell 2003), immigrant and refugee women (MacLeod and Shin 1992), lesbian women (Chesley, MacAulay, and Ristock 1998), and gay men (Kirkland 2004). On the other hand, the FVI recognizes that in the case of spousal violence, the problem "remains predominantly an issue of male violence against women" (Federal-Provincial-Territorial (F-P-T) Ministries Responsible for Justice 2006: v).[4]

> Intimate violence affects people in all social categories, but women and children are the principal victims of serious violence.

The FVI focuses on violence against women as a core component of a "serious and complex issue with multiple dimensions and causes" (F-P-T Ministries Responsible for Justice 2006: 1). This focus responds to the of-

> Status of Women has succeeded in locating physical, sexual, and psychological violence against women as a key concern linking male abuse of women with gender inequality.

ficial data on the gendered dynamics and distribution of perpetration and victimization. The FVI's interpretation of these data is shaped, however, by the controversial influence of FVI partner Status of Women Canada (hereafter Status of Women), the federal agency responsible for monitoring and promoting the social, economic, and political advancement of women in Canada and internationally (Dobrowolsky and Jenson 2004; Morrow, Hankivsky, and Varcoe 2004; Shaw and Andrew 2005). As a funded FVI partner, Status of Women has succeeded in locating the physical, sexual, and psychological abuse of women as a key concern within the FVI, in linking male abuse of women in public and private contexts with gender inequality, and in promoting research predicated on the feminist position that domestic or family violence is first and foremost *violence against women* (Shaw and Andrew 2005; Walker 1990). At the same time, Status of Women has succeeded in focusing the FVI on serious violence or battering, defined as violence and abuse that aims to or results in the degradation, diminishment, control, or terrorizing of another person, especially a person disadvantaged due to gender, youth, age, ethnicity, immigrant status, poverty, sexual orientation, physical disadvantage, or racism (see Canadian Panel on Violence Against Women 1993; Harder 1994; see also definitions of family violence in Family-Violence Prevention Unit 2002; F-P-T Ministries Responsible for Justice 2006; Jamieson 2004).

A Status of Women assessment of Statistics Canada data on police-reported and self-reported intimate violence captures Status of Women's, and by implication the FVI's, "feminist-sociological" (Harder 1994) stance on violence.[5] According to this assessment, the social and historical roots of violence against women situate it as a unique aspect of the larger violence problem:

> Violence against anyone is unacceptable whether it is directed against children, women, men, seniors, people with disabilities, visible minorities or anyone else.... Violence against anyone is unacceptable. Violence experienced by women, however, particularly intimate partner violence and sexual assault, represents a unique aspect of the wider social problem of violence, and requires specific attention and solutions. Individual experiences of violence against women must be assessed against the backdrop of historical, social, political, cultural and economic inequality of women. (F-P-T Ministries Responsible for the Status of Women 2002: i–2)

FVI INTERVENTIONS AND IMPACTS

FVI strategies to prevent and eliminate violence against women and other forms of intimate violence include federal, provincial, territorial, and municipal governments' and community-based agencies' co-involvement in a range of support, prevention, and criminal justice efforts. Prominent among these are governments' and community agencies' co-sponsorship of Canada's extensive and internationally acclaimed but still inadequate network of shelters and related supports for abused women and their children (Taylor-Butts 2005; Tutty 2006).[6] Just as important is their co-sponsorship of education to enhance public awareness of the serious impacts of violence on all who experience and witness it, including especially children (for example, Dauvergne and Johnson 2001; see also Dobrowolsky and Jenson 2004); and their co-sponsorship of research to assess public attitudes (for example, EKOS 2002) and advance knowledge on the effectiveness of government-sponsored support services and criminal justice sanctions (for example, F-P-T Ministries Responsible for Justice 2006; Tutty 2006).

Criminal justice interventions include a range of mechanisms designed to address unique aspects of domestic or family violence that draw upon three decades of innovation and evaluation (F-P-T Ministries Responsible for Justice 2006). Prominent among these are dedicated domestic violence courts staffed by specially trained judges, prosecutors, and victim advocates; civil legislation for victims seeking protective orders; court-mandated abuse-intervention programs for convicted domestic offenders, and intersectoral co-coordinating strategies that link government and community-based initiatives. In addition, jurisdictions across the country employ special mechanisms to facilitate prosecution of domestic cases, including pro-charge and pro-prosecution policies that make the laying of a charge a police responsibility and the decision to act on this charge a Crown responsibility, and the admission into court of enhanced evidence such as 911 tapes and taped victim and witness statements so prosecution can proceed even when a victim is unable or unwilling to testify. Finally, jurisdictions across Canada are developing, piloting, and implementing risk assessment tools designed to better identify dangerousness and potential lethality, which allows authorities to "triage" (Campbell 2005) cases for more and less intrusive intervention; establish supervised parental access programs for children who are at risk due to family violence; and enact Domestic Violence Death Review Committees that investigate and report on intimate homicides on an annual basis (see also Patterson 2003; Roberts 2002; Tutty 2006).

> Spousal homicides declined from 16.5 per million female spouses in 1974 to 7.1 in 2004, and from 4.4 per million male spouses in 1974 to 1.4 in 2004.

By the late 1990s, this combination of victim supports, research and education, and criminal justice strategies appeared to be working, evidenced by widespread condemnation of all forms of intimate violence by surveyed publics (EKOS 2002), modest declines in self-reported spousal violence (Mihorean 2005), and significant declines in police-reported domestic assaults and homicides (F-P-T Ministries Responsible for

Justice 2006; Kowalski 2006; Ogrodnik 2006). Indeed, in the thirty-year period follow-ing 1974, when data collection began, police-reported spousal homicides decreased by about one half, to the benefit of both women and men. Specifically, spousal homicides declined from 16.5 per million female spouses in 1974 to 7.1 in 2004, and from 4.4 per million male spouses in 1974 to 1.4 in 2004 (Kowalski 2006: 53). Men appear, then, to have benefited as much or arguably even more than have women from the FVI's focus on violence against women as a unique and particularly problematic aspect of the larger problem of violence and abuse in intimate relationships.[7]

AN OPPOSITIONAL VOICE — MEN'S/FATHERS' RIGHTS

In Canada and across Anglo-American/European jurisdictions (Jaffe and Crooks 2004), men's rights lobbyists are an increasingly vocal, visible, and organized presence in policy debates on the regulation of intimate and family relations (Bala 1999; Gavanas 2004; Heath 2003; Laing 1999; Mann 2005; Smart 2004). Most prominent in Canada are in-dividuals and groups championing or affiliated with fathers' rights, an "overt and angry anti-feminist backlash" (Messner 1998: 266) movement committed to reversing feminist influence on social policies, including policies designed to protect women and children from domestic or family violence. In testimony before legislative bodies (Bala 1999; Boyd and Young 2002; Laing 1999; Mann 2005), in the mainstream and alternative press (for example, Brown 2001a, 2001b, 2001c, 2001d, 2001e, 2002; Evenson and Milstone 1999; LaFramboise 1999, 2000; McElroy 2003), in popular magazines (Berns 2001, 2004), in academic books, papers, and conference presentations (for example, Fekete 1994; George 1994; Lupri 2004; Mandell 2002; McNeely and Robinson-Simpson 1987; Miller and Sharif 1995), and across a host of internationally linked websites (Bouchard, Boily, and Proulx 2003; Mann 2005) fathers' advocates situate women as equally or more violent than men, and frame feminism and feminist-endorsed victim services as panic-driven, greed-inciting adversaries of men and families (see also Bertoia and Drakich 1993; Coltrane and Hickman 1992; Crean 1988; DeKeseredy 1999; Kimmel 2002; Lucal 1995; Messner 1998; Saunders 2002; Schwartz and DeKeseredy 1993).

In Canada the argument that men are equal or even principal intimate violence victims moved into centre stage during the 1998 Special Joint Committee Hearings on Child Custody and Access (Canada, SJC 1998), at which over 500 Canadians testified, including 281 who advanced various pro-men's arguments on intimate violence and child custody issues (Mann 2005). Witness after witness blamed feminists for fostering a false and gender-discriminatory construction of the intimate violence problem, and Status of Women and Statistics Canada for sponsoring biased research that supports this false construction. Some argued that anti-male bias must be redressed through affirmative action to restore to men their natural and indeed their "primordial right" (Canada, SJC 1998: Rock Turcotte, April 2). Others argued that women's shelters are sites of "indoctrination of gender feminism" (Canada, SJC 1998: Gus Sleiman, April 29), and that they are the source of women's "weapon of choice" (Bala 1999; Laing 1999; Mann

2005) — false allegations.[8] Many referred policy-makers to studies conducted from a *family-violence* perspective, which men's advocates maintain proves men are equally or even more victimized than are women in intimate contexts. Several referred to or cited studies from Martin Fiebert's Internet-disseminated and constantly updated annotated bibliography, which lists 175 "investigations" that purportedly prove intimate violence is gender-symmetrical (Fiebert 2005):

> This bibliography examines 175 scholarly investigations: 139 empirical studies and 36 reviews and/or analyses, which demonstrate that women are as physically aggressive, or more aggressive, than men in their relationships with their spouses or male partners. The aggregate sample size in the reviewed studies exceeds 164,600. (Fiebert 2005)

Many men's advocates relate personal anecdotes of their victimization at the hands of violent women. One example is the frequently cited 1998 Special Joint Committee testimony of Grant Wilson, a father active in the Toronto-area fathers' rights movement who lost custody of his daughters in 1996 following a lengthy court battle. Wilson's testimony, which he repeated almost verbatim before the Ontario legislature in 2000 (Bill 117 Hearings, October 30, 2000), includes a graphic account of a "bloody" assault perpetrated by his ex-wife. Wilson's story is noteworthy because his ex-wife and teenage daughter exposed his domestic assault conviction history in *The Globe and Mail* (McIlroy 1998), as well as that the assault described in Wilson's testimony took place after his daughter phoned her mother in "physical fear" of what he might do. In Wilson's account, however, he is a restrained and even a chivalrous victim of an irrational or possibly jealous attack, who the police and courts refused to believe and protect:

> *Grant Wilson, Men's rights activist*: I am a victim of domestic violence. After we split up, my ex-wife broke into my house. I was assaulted in a bloody battle. She was convicted of assaulting me. She received no sentence, by the way. My tooth was damaged. My face was bleeding from the nose and on the cheek. My wrist was cut. I was badly bruised all over. The police came and took her out of the house. This was three weeks after my fiancée moved in with me and the children. She's much smaller than I am, and I used a very minimal amount of force to try to subdue her. It's very difficult to explain to people that this happened, because many people say that because I played college football and hockey, I could destroy this woman. They said that a couple of shots to the face could probably rearrange her face for the rest of her life.

It is in the context of these passionate claims and counterclaims on the extent, nature, context, and credibility of men's claims of victimization that FVI partner Health Canada commissioned two reports on the intimate abuse of men. The first, *Husband Abuse* by Leslie Tutty (1999), addresses men's advocates' claims that the abuse of husbands and boyfriends is serious and widespread, and that social policy needs to be revised to address this problem. Noting that domestic violence policies are shaped by evidence rooted in opposing *violence-against-women* and *family-violence* research perspectives and methodologies, and by social advocacy that draws on this research, Tutty reviews the evidence, implicitly from a *violence-against-women* perspective. In addition to Statistics Canada data on police-reported assaults and homicides, 1999 General Social Survey data on gender disparities in the severity and consequence of self-reported spousal victimization, and findings from victimization surveys from other jurisdictions, Tutty reviews an emerging literature on treatment programs for both male and female batterers, material that examines similarities and differences in men and women mandated to counselling for domestic assault. Based on this evidence, Tutty concludes that abuse is unacceptable regardless of the gender of the perpetrator, and that services for men appropriate to their needs should be more available. She argues, however, that the Government of Canada must continue to prioritize funding for services that address the needs of the principal victims of intimate assault and homicide, women and children.

The second report, *Intimate Partner Violence Against Men* by Eugen Lupri and Elaine Grandin (2004), is far more sympathetic to men's advocates' claims of victimization and demands for services (2004). As is common in family-violence research, Lupri and Grandin focused on aggregate counts of abuse as measured in the 1999 GSS, in particular the finding that in 1999 19 percent of women and 18 percent of men reported that they had been victims of one or more acts of psychological abuse, which is to say name-calling, jealousy, monitoring of contacts with friends and family, financial control, and intimidation. Except for a token acknowledgement that women report more serious physical victimization, Lupri and Grandin do not examine gender differences in injury, chronicity, or psychological terror. Nor do they discuss how self-reported victimization data fit with police, hospital, and treatment data on female and male victims and perpetrators. Rather, they emphasize that male and female victimization rates are roughly equivalent. They cite family-violence research in the U.S. and Canada that yields similar findings, and direct readers to Fiebert's bibliography on this body of research. To contextualize these findings Lupri and Grandin cite a small "in-depth narrative study" of twelve abused men to demonstrate how being abused undermines a man's confidence in his masculinity, leaving him feeling "emasculated and marginalized" (2004: 6). They conclude that the abuse of male partners is a "complex social problem that warrants close attention" (7), and direct men who are abused to the *Directory of Services and Programs for Abused Men in Canada* (NCFV 2004b).

THE VIOLENCE AGAINST WOMEN/FAMILY-VIOLENCE DIVIDE

As emphasized by Tutty (1999) and other commentators from the 1980s forward (for example, Breines and Gordon 1983; Dobash and Dobash 1992, 1998, 2004; Gelles and Loseke 1993; Mann 2000, 2003; Tutty 1999) violence-against-women and family-violence researchers employ different conceptualizations and methodologies. Feminist-influenced violence-against-women conceptualizations and research efforts focus on the serious problem of battering, defined as a persistent pattern of willed physical, sexual, and emotional behaviours, intentions, and self-perceptions centred on and resulting in the control, denigration, and terrorism of an intimate partner (Ferraro 2001; Jacobson and Gottman 1998; Johnson 1995). They argue that evidence from a variety of sources conclusively demonstrates that battering is gendered, which is to say it is overwhelmingly both male-perpetrated and male-driven, including police, court and homicide statistics, hospital emergency reports, national victimization surveys, and the body of qualitative findings generated through the testimony of abused and abusive women and men. Importantly, violence-against-women researchers do not deny that women are also violent; rather, they argue that male and female violence are qualitatively and quantitatively different and that to equate them increases women's and children's vulnerability to battering (see also Anderson and Umberson 2001; Dobash and Dobash 1979, 1992, 1998, 2004; Dobash et al. 998; Ferree 2004; Gadd 2000; Hamberger et al. 1997; Hamberger, Lohr, and Bonge 1994; Hamberger and Potente 1996; Johnson 1998; Kimmel 2002; MacLeod 1987; Mann 2000, 2003; Miller, Gregory, and Iovanni 2005; Miller and Meloy 2006; Osthoff 2002; Pollack, Battaglia, and Allspach 2005; Schwartz 2000; Saunders 2002; Swan and Snow 2002, 2003; Umberson et al. 1998).

In contrast, family-violence conceptualizations are rooted in a sociological paradigm that privileges quantitative methodologies, which produce findings through statistical analysis of data generated through original and modified versions of Murray Straus's Conflict Tactics Scale (CTS, see Straus 1979; Straus et al. 1996; see also Gelles and Straus 1988). This act-based instrument defines and measures intimate violence in terms of acts, which range from pushing, shoving, and slaps to beatings and assaults with weapons, perpetrated by and against intimate partners in the course of "spats and fights" that occur "no matter how well a couple gets along."[9] CTS-based research consistently finds that while women suffer greater injury, women and men perpetrate and indeed instigate violence at equivalent rates. Moreover, the same psycho-social risks (for example, poverty, substance abuse, child exposure to family violence, emotional problems) predict violence perpetration across genders. Based on these findings, Straus and other family-violence researchers argue that violence by wives or women is also a major social problem, emphasizing the point that the assault of a partner is morally and criminally wrong (Straus 1993, 1999, 2006; see also Dutton and Nicholls 2005; McFarlane et al. 2000; McNeely and Robinson-Simpson 1987; Moffitt, Robins, and Caspi 2001; Smith and Straus 1995; Steinmetz, 1977–78; Straus, Gelles, and Steinmetz 1980).

Violence-against-women researchers attribute this decontextualized portrait of domestic violence to the family-violence researchers' reliance on a methodology that addresses acts independent of consequences, meanings, and motives. As a number of violence-against-women critics have observed, family-violence findings are generated by practices that include, for example, coding a single punch or kick by a female as "severe" violence, and a push that results in a woman falling down the stairs as "minor," while sexual abuse, social isolation, stalking, financial control, and other features of battering remained outside the analysis. In his influential article "Patriarchal Terrorism and Common Couple Violence: Two Forms of Violence Against Women," Michael Johnson (1995) captures the violence-against-women argument succinctly. While women and men both express or perpetrate acts of violence against intimate partners, these cannot, especially from the perspective of social policy, be conflated. The truly terrorizing battering by males, captured in studies of women's shelter clients and other "clinical" (for example, counselling, offender) populations is qualitatively different from the characteristically minor physical explosions of male and female partners captured in social surveys. Differences in these two (in more elaborated versions, four) violence types reflect the different consequences and the different meanings of male and female violence to participants (see also Hamberger et al. 1997; Swan and Snow 2002, 2003).

VICTIMIZATION SURVEYS

In the early 1990s, violence-against-women researchers began designing and conducting social surveys that employ original and modified versions of Straus's CTS in combination with measures of injuries, coercive control, intimidation, fear, and other salient features of battering as revealed in violence-against-women research (Schwartz 2000). The first nationally sponsored survey to use a feminist-modified CTS was Statistic's Canada's "groundbreaking" (Dobash and Dobash 1995) Violence-Against-Women Survey (VAWS), administered by telephone to 12,300 Canadian women in 1993 (Johnson 1998; Rodgers 1994). Major modifications include the recontextualization or reframing of questions on spousal or partner violence to emphasize that the research issue is "the serious problem of violence in the home" as opposed to Straus's "spats and fights." This reframing coincides with an emphasis on violence as something that does or can result in harm, and the inclusion of sexual assault as a violent act — indeed, as the most serious violent act. Most importantly, however, Statistics Canada constructed an emotional abuse module to better capture contextual features of battering relationships, namely coercive control, jealousy, intimidation, and fear, which replace Straus's measures of insults, sulking, spite, stomping out, and crying.

Internationally prominent violence-against-women researchers heralded the 1993 VAWS as a watershed, as groundbreaking, and as a model for other nations (Dobash and Dobash 1995, 1998; Ferraro 2001). Family-violence researchers and men's advocates, however, continue to critique the 1993 VAWS and its U.S. counterpart, the 1994–95 National Violence-Against-Women survey (NVAW) (Bunge 2000), for

> The decision to measure only violence against women impedes efforts to test or refute family-violence claims that male and female violence are equivalent in terms of meanings, motives, and impacts.

addressing only violence against women and not also violence by women (for example, Fekete 1994; Lupri 2004; Straus 2006; see also Evenson and Milstone 1999; LaFramboise 1999, 2000). There are sound theoretical and even methodological justifications for the decision to measure only female victimization, including, for example, widely replicated evidence that men underreport violence, especially their own serious violence (DeKeseredy 1999; Doob 2005). This methodological choice makes it difficult, however, to compare VAWS and NVAW findings with the findings of surveys conducted by Straus and other family-violence researchers. In particular, the decision to measure only violence against women impedes efforts to test or refute family-violence claims that male and female violence are equivalent in terms of meanings, motives, and impacts.

These considerations influenced Statistics Canada to administer its redesigned CTS to both sexes in the 1999 and 2004 GSS, each of which assessed domestic violence victimization by a current or ex-spouse over the previous twelve months and previous five years; and in both the 1999 and the 2004 waves the aggregate rates of intimate violence victimization were roughly equivalent for women and men (Mihorean 2005), which some interpret as support for a gender-symmetrical family-violence perspective on the problem (for example, Fiebert 2005; Lupri and Grandin 2004; Lupri 2004). However, the gendered distribution of severity and chronicity of violence, degree and severity of injury, threats to harm or kill, generalized and lethal fear, and the nature and extent of violence witnessed by children reveal significant gender differences that support a violence-against-women perspective (see Tutty 1999). Equally salient to this perspective is the finding that close to a third (30 percent in 2004) of victimized men view violence perpetrated by their partner as having little or no impact on their well-being, compared to 6 percent of victimized women (Mihorean 2005).

Canada's GSS and other victimization studies provide compelling support for the violence-against-women argument that women's and men's violence is both qualitatively and quantitatively different, with women unequivocally the principal victims of severe violence, injury, and forms of coercive control marked by intimidation and terrorizing. At the same time, victimization data confirm victim and offender profiles that are consistent with police data. Intimate violence cuts across all social categories, but the most serious and chronic patterns of perpetration and victimization are concentrated at "the margins" (Hall 2002), where Aboriginality, substance abuse, common-law marital status, and youth interact to exacerbate violent propensities and vulnerabilities (Mihorean 2005). While victimization research provides data on the dynamics of this violence, it does not yield answers to questions about whether men's and women's violence is rooted in similar or dissimilar propensities and motives. As Johnson (1995) observed, differences between violent types have as much to do with the meanings and motives of violence to perpetrators and victims, as with the nature of violent acts.

PERPETRATOR MOTIVES AND PROPENSITIES —
CLINICAL AND POPULATION-BASED STUDIES

Family-violence research (for example, Dutton and Nicholls 2005; Moffitt et al. 2001; Straus 1993, 1999, 2006), police reports (Ogrodnik 2006), and victimization surveys (Mihorean 2005) are in agreement that women and men who perpetrate intimate violence manifest similar risks — including poverty, family of origin violence, substance abuse, jealousy, sexist and pro-violent attitudes, and criminal or delinquent involvement. To assess how these risks intersect to foster violence and especially battering, violence-against-women researchers have turned to scientifically designed clinical studies that assess motivations of court-identified male and female domestic offenders (Anderson and Umberson 2001; Dobash et al. 1998; Hamberger et al. 1994; Hamberger et al. 1997; Hamberger and Potente 1996; Gadd 2000; Jacobson and Gottman 1998; Miller and Meloy 2006; Swan and Snow 2002, 2003). This body of research finds that violence by women that comes to the attention of authorities is, in the majority of cases, primarily a defensive or retaliatory response to male-perpetrated psychological, physical, and sexual abuse and control (see also McMahon and Pence 2003; Pollack et al. 2005). This is not to say that women who face domestic assault charges are without anger or malice. Both women and men clearly use violence in frustration, anger, retaliation, and revenge (Anderson and Umberson 2001; Dobash et al. 1998; Hamberger et al. 1997; Swan and Snow 2002, 2003; see also McFarlane et al. 2000; Miller et al. 2005). The primary gender difference is that male perpetrators assessed through these studies demonstrate a greater propensity to use violence as a mechanism for asserting control. Moreover, men have a far greater likelihood of achieving control through violence. As Swan and Snow (2002) observe, even when a woman wishes to dominate her partner, rarely, for cultural and physical reasons, is she able to socially and geographically isolate, intimidate, and terrorize in the ways in which male batterers do. Violence-against-women researchers conclude, therefore, that even in jurisdictions in which a sizable minority of domestic violence charges are laid against women, only 5 percent or at the most 10 percent of true batterers are female, as only 5 percent to 10 percent of charged women appear to use violence to dominate or terrorize their partners (see also Tutty 1999).[10]

In contrast, family-violence research focuses on perpetrator propensities as evidenced in population-based studies large enough to produce data that can be assessed statistically. Moffitt, Robins, and Caspi (2001), for example, used a representative sample of 360 New Zealand married, cohabiting, and dating couples, with both partners in a couple

> Only 5 percent to 10 percent of charged women appear to use violence to dominate or terrorize their partners.

participating in the study, to test and refute Johnson's (1995) hypothesis that terrorizing or severe violence is more gendered than is common-couple violence. Their stated aim is to challenge "the long-standing claim that only males commit abuse, with its accompanying view that women's abuse is nonexistent or inconsequential" (6).[11] Their analysis reveals that regardless of whether violence is male-perpetrated, female-perpetrated, or mutual, people who inflict violence, serious violence in particular, rate high for "negative emotionality." That is, women and men who perpetrate violence tend to describe themselves as feeling tense, nervous, vulnerable, worried, fearful, hostile, angry, callous, suspicious, revengeful, and remorseless. Though Moffitt and colleagues do not assess whether and how male- versus female-perpetrated violence operates to achieve or resist control or dominance, they conclude that since statistical differences between violence perpetration and negative emotionality by sex of respondent are non-significant, a male-dominance model of domestic violence is not supported (for a similar argument against alleged non-evidence-based feminist claims that female-perpetrated intimate violence is non-existent or exclusively defensive, see Dutton and Nicholls 2005).

VICTIM AND PERPETRATOR VOICES

Ethnographic and interview-based qualitative research on how abused and abusive women and men experience and view intimate partner violence is part of a long-standing effort by violence-against-women researchers to squarely face and conscientiously listen to the voices of victimized and violent women and men, and to incorporate these voices into policy (MacLeod 1987). When we consider the findings that emerge from this effort, we need to recognize that all data are problematic, whether generated through police reports, social surveys, clinical studies, ethnographies, or public testimonials. In interviews research participants narrate experiences as they see them at the moment, and as they choose to present them, as evidenced in Grant Wilson's testimony to the 1998 SJC and his ex-wife's and daughter's countertestimony in the press. As David Gadd (2000) observes, the selves displayed and produced through self-narratives are "defended selves" who "hide the truth," not only from researchers, but also, not uncommonly, from themselves (see also Comack 1999). Moreover, rather than being unmediated or natural accounts of lived experiences, self-narratives are shaped by the discourses available at the moment, whether through street talk, movies, video games, music, newspapers, psycho-educational counselling, or the anti-feminist rhetoric of men's rights advocacy (Bhatia 2006; Wodak 2006).

A number of interview excerpts capture experiences with and views on intimate partner violence as related to me (Mann 2000, 2003; Mann et al. 2007) and other researchers (Totten 2000, 2003; see also Artz 1998) in a variety of interview contexts. They highlight the complexities and contradictions of masculinity, femininity, and power as situated social accomplishments, shaped by the contingencies not only of gender but also of ethnicity, class, popular discourse, and personal experience (Messerschmidt 1993, 1999, 2000). As these excerpts demonstrate, intimate violence is not just an act; it is a socially and historically situated site through which and in which female and male intimate partners "do gender" (West and Zimmerman 1987; see also Boonzaier and De La Rey 2003; Gadd 2000; Hall 2002; Mandell 2002; Mann 2000, 2003; Miller 2001; Totten, 2000, 2003; Towns and Adams 2000; Varcoe and Irwin 2004; West and Fenstermaker 1995). In other words, gender is produced through intimate violence; it is not just a characteristic that allows researchers to sort women from men.

My own study on domestic abuse and efforts to address this problem in an un-named Ontario community captures adult perspectives on intimate partner violence as related in twenty in-depth interviews with female and male victims and perpetrators recruited in abuse intervention, activist, and related social contexts (Mann 2000: 278, endnote 1). "Keith" (172–79), an abuse intervention client in his mid-thirties, described his violence against a series of spousal and dating partners, which he understood as a response to his childhood experiences of father-perpetrated child and spouse abuse, and his ongoing struggles with substance abuse and jealousy. When his first wife decided to end their marriage, he "pushed her head into the wall," "booted her ass," "popped her in the nose," and "drug her down the stairs and threw her out the door," telling her, "go to your lover." At the time of the interview his second wife had fled to a shelter to escape emotional and sexual abuse, including what Keith referred to as "forced sex," which he knew was not right. When asked if any of his partners had also been violent, Keith answered that he had only known one woman who was violent, a girlfriend he "was lucky" not to have killed. As Anderson and Umberson (2001) maintain is typical, in Keith's account of a mutually violent exchange with this ex-girlfriend her violence comes across as irrational and ineffectual, and Keith's response as explosive, dangerous, primal, potentially lethal. Indeed, he stated that his fear in this relationship was not at what his girlfriend might do to him, but of what he might do to her.

> When I was living with this one girlfriend, Nadene, this one (pointing to a tattoo on his forearm), I ended up getting real sick [while out drinking].... Nadine come over to me [after they got home from the bar] and started kicking me in the face while I was bent over. I told her I wasn't in the mood for this. She was physically violent all the time. She grew up that way. If she drank she was nuts, total nuts. You couldn't reason with her, talk to her at all.... She was kicking me in the head, two or three times.... Then she was grabbing me by the hair, trying to lift me up to punch me. I come right up, I grab her behind the throat and I just went pow. I drove her so hard she flew over the couch, knocked the whole couch over and slid under our dining room table and she was like this, knocked out cold. I couldn't believe I hit her that hard.... I probably could have killed her that night if I kept going, but one punch was enough. I was lucky I didn't kill her.

"Sam," another abuse intervention client (Mann 2000: 179–85), also described recurrent jealousy and severe violence in a series of dating and spousal relationships. In his own words, Sam, in his late twenties, had been "seriously dangerously violent" with both his current wife and his high-school ex-girlfriend, whom he still passionately loved, and neither of the women were violent in return. Sam said he had thrown both women around, assaulted their family members, came after them with a gun, and threatened both with homicide and suicide. He also reported that he regularly went on a "rampage" that resulted in extensive property destruction. Sam described the intoxicating sense of power he experienced when perpetrating violence, and also his intense need for respect at any cost. In Sam's words, he was a man looking for control, and violence temporarily met this need, producing a rush of power that was "super difficult to control," and in the moment of violence was its own reward.

> I lost the love of my life [ex-girlfriend].... The two years we were together [I]

was very violent and very abusive and very controlling, with temper, choking....
I get super violent, very dangerous. I throw Florence [wife].... I always felt that
if I punched her, she doesn't stand a chance.... You [that is, men] are violent
mainly just to relieve that pain — someone is hurting you, they are not listening,
they are not understanding you. Then you're violent, wham, now everybody
understands, Sam is upset.... The rush while you are doing it is unbelievable
adrenaline and power you know.... It's super hard to control. The depression
comes immediately after, but at the time, at the instant, it's the rush.... You are
letting yourself go and getting the control you are looking for... just standing
your ground and holding your honour and pride — you stand up for your
style, nobody screws around in my own house, no matter what the cost. I guess
I am fortunate to realize the, holy cow, I am going to shoot myself one night
because I am going to have to follow through.

The stories of women who reported reciprocating and even instigating violence in
this same study capture how some adult women manage, or attempt to manage, relationships with men like Keith and Sam, and also how violence from a past relationship
can spill over into a new relationship. One woman, "Elaine" (Mann 2003), a waitress
and single mother in her mid-thirties, said she was tired of "feeling like a victim" at
the hands of belligerent and violent partners. Another, "Tracy" (Mann 2000, 145–56), a
single mother on social assistance, in her early twenties, had struggled to survive child
sexual abuse and intimate partner violence in a series of adolescent and adult relationships. In contrast to Keith and Sam, neither of these women indicated that she was
impressed with the power that violence produced. Rather, they described engaging in
violence with reluctance and guilt, feeling that they were beyond their limit for physical, emotional, and sexual violence and abuse.

Elaine: I quite frankly said to him [live-in boyfriend], have I provoked you
enough [verbal argument in which her male partner became violent]. Take
another swing at me and I'll really finish the job. I was mad.... I don't believe
in violence. I am a very non violent person by nature. I was at my limit....
Quite frankly, the way I did it, the way I did it was that I was tired of feeling
like a victim and I thought, I am going to fight back for once. I am going to
in essence, get even. I am not going to sit here and be the victim again. I will
make him deal with his consequences.

Tracy: The one time that my boyfriend Tommy hit me I was pounding him
and left scratches on his face, and then he slapped me. You shouldn't be violent when you're provoked, but when he provoked me I just started hitting
him. You see red.... He plays mind games, lies to me [and] says I love you, I
want you, and then he goes to see her [his ex-wife]. It was the same in a past
relationship [cheating, lying, mind games].... I'm used to guys beating me up.

One held a gun to my head.... I was made to do sexual things that made me sick.... Frank [who still stalked her] was very, very abusive. He used to punch the crap out of me all the time.... He held a gun to my head and said if I ever fooled around on him he would shoot me.... One night we were lying in bed with a pocket knife out.... He said, I know you want to kill me, just go ahead and stab me. I said, if I really wanted to kill you I would take this knife and slice your throat.... So I took as much of his nattering as I could take, and rolled over and grabbed the knife and heaved it out of his hand and sliced his hand open, and he should have gone to the hospital and got stitches but at that point in time I wouldn't care if he had bled to death.

In another interview, "Kim" (Mann 2000: 165–72), a university student in her early twenties, spoke of how she had survived being "not really a street kid" while completing high school. During that time she had survived not only a relationship with a physically and sexually abusive drug dealer, but also gang rape, two miscarriages, and other terrors that commonly beset young women on the streets, or not quite on the streets (see Mann et al. 2007). Similar to some female youths interviewed in Artz's (1998) violent school girl study, Kim reported that violence actually made her feel good, or in control. In Kim's words, she had "adopted the male attitude" and was now ready and willing to fight anyone, especially any male who affronted her dignity through an unwelcome sexual advance.

I have adopted the male attitude. You know, the egotistical, me-first kind of attitude, the, I'm-not-taking-any-shit attitude.... I don't take shit from any living creature.... When I really beat someone up (it's) when I'm provoked. Like when I fell asleep after another party and I woke up with this jerk trying to take my pants down. I pounded him good.... He [drug dealer boyfriend] was obsessive.... He would follow me and quit jobs on me.... I worked in the dining room at the country club, and he walked in reeking of alcohol and picked me up by my hair, right out of my seat, and dragged me out by my hair in front of everybody I worked with.... One time he broke three fingers.... He liked to push me up against walls.... He said that sometimes a woman deserves it, but I don't buy that at all.... I know with a lot of stuff going on now is, well I know there is a lot of reciprocal violence among young people. I think as time goes on you're less likely to take it. And I think that in a second violent relationship the woman is less likely to be passive from the start. She realizes she doesn't have to stand for it.

Another set of interviews focused on community-based and justice-affiliated efforts to prevent and intervene into various aspects of youth violence in a Southern Ontario urban community.[12] In these interviews youths responded to questions on whether they had ever witnessed, knew of, or experienced violence perpetrated in the context of a boyfriend-girlfriend relationship, by either a male or female. Some thirty-two youths (44 percent) responded that they did (fifteen female; seventeen male). Of these, twenty-six described instances of male-perpetrated violence against a female partner (81 percent), three described mutual or reciprocal violence between dating youths (9.5 percent), and three described female-perpetrated violence against a male partner (9.5 percent). While many female and especially male youths described physical and verbal fights with other female or male youths, none admitted to having themselves assaulted a partner. However, six of them did report that a dating partner had assaulted them (four female; two male).

All four young women who identified themselves as the victims of intimate partners reported serious violence. These young women, all high-school students, reported being choked, dragged, thrown, hospitalized, raped, and threatened with death — which are more severe acts than the majority of domestic assaults captured in police reports (Ogrodnik 2006; Mihorean 2006), victimization surveys (Mihorean 2005), or family-violence research (for example, Moffitt et al. 2001; Straus et al. 1980; Gelles and Straus 1988). None of them described provoking their assailant. Rather, the assaults occurred after breaking up (Veronica), when trying to leave (Jane), after seeking help to deal with a rape (Connie), and in the context of chronic, severe battering (Evelyn).

> *Veronica*: One of my ex-boyfriends, he came up to me [on the street after she broke up] and he like choked me right. That was before I, I received the black eye from him. Yeah, this was before. He choked me, after then he gave me the black eye. Then that was it. That was it, never ever. I haven't been with him since.

> *Jane*: He [drunken ex-boyfriend] like picked me up, held me up against the wall again [after dragging her back up the stairs when she tried to leave]. He's like "what are you going to do? What are you going to do?" And all that was going through my head was okay you know, you got to do something. Whether it's kicking him in his (inaudible) or whatever, you got to do something. And I just, I froze. I couldn't do anything.

> *Connie*: And he attacked me [male youth who raped her on their first date, and subsequently stalked and threatened to kill her]. Like he was choking me; throwing me around. He was trying to kiss me as he was attacking me. Like just to taunt me, like, like, like oh man, like it was bad.

> *Evelyn*: I started dating this guy [ex-boyfriend] who abused me and so I ended up in the hospital because of him. ...The first time he was violent we got into this argument (and) he hit me and I went falling down the stairs. And I cracked my head open. That was the first time, and after that he got into the regular thing. ...I got pregnant by him and he told me that if I did not get an abortion that he would kill me. So I had to have an abortion.

In contrast, the two male youths who identified themselves as victims of intimate partners described slaps and punches that elicited neither fear nor, it would seem, distress. Like 30 percent of the men who reported intimate partner victimization in the 2004 GSS (Mihorean 2005), and as clinical studies also find is common (Anderson and Umberson 2001; Gadd 2000), these young men, both in the correctional system at the time, stated that they did not really care about the violence. One said that he just let his partner "beat the shit" out of him and then he "just walked away." Both indicated that their partners were violent "for a good reason," which is to say both viewed their partners' violence as warranted by their own cheating, disrespect, or general bad behaviour.

> *Andy*: Like my girlfriend, she's hit me before. . . . But it started for a good reason, like me cheating on her, or, me like, messing around or something. Or like me getting arrested, I know I'm getting a slap when I get out. . . . No she'll slap me [slapping noise] a couple times and call me a loser and make me feel bad.

> *Researcher Probe:* Now how do you react to that?

> *Andy*: I smoke a joint. . . . Like, I love her at the end so, I don't really care.

> *Lyle*: I've, actually yes I have [experienced/seen dating violence]. My ex-girl-friend beat the shit out of me, but I let her and I walked away. . . . And I told her, like I told her I was cheating on her with her sister, ha ha ha. And, I don't know, she punched me like ten times in the face and I just walked away.

In this investigation, male youths — even a few whose files documented a domestic assault charge — tended to deny that they would ever hit a girl. In contrast, Mark Totten (2000: 65) elicited self-narratives of female partner abuse from male street youths who he recruited through youth centres, a youth shelter, and a local mall in the Ottawa area. A number of excerpts from Totten's work capture the subjectivities and perspectives of young males on the margins of Canadian society, demonstrating how sexist and pro-violent attitudes and anti-feminist sentiments fuel or justify violence against female partners. At the same time, these statements demonstrate the ambivalence, hostility, and despair of male street youths who draw on these cultural resources.

> *Colin*: My Mom and Dad always told me not to hit girls. Girls are weaker and they can't defend themselves. It's different for guys. It's sad to hit girls. But they want all this equal rights bullshit. And we can't lay a hand on them. They've got all the fuckin' rights they need. It's time to give some back.

> *Steve*: Give her a bitch-slap if she mouths off or hits you first. But it's only if she's only your girlfriend. I mean, they [male friends] joke all the time. If she disses you, smack her. If she gets drunk and makes an idiot of herself, smack her. If she fucks around on you — you know, talks to other guys, give her a bitch-slap.

> *Serge*: She's [speaking of an ex-girlfriend] pissed me off, and she won't stop. I've grabbed her arm, squeezed her, and slapped her. I've punched her after she put me down in front of my friends.... I'll tell her to "Shut up bitch," or I'll call her a slut.... I don't know what to do. It's like I know what I should be as a man, I mean — strong, lots of money, a good job, and a beautiful wife. But my life isn't like that.... She makes me so angry when she won't do what I want her to do. It's not supposed to be that way. A girl is supposed to get along with a man. She's supposed to respect him and listen to him. But that never happens to me.

These victim and perpetrator narratives (Mann 2000; Totten 2000) suggest that rather than inhabiting "distinct and intersecting realities" (Dobash et al. 1998), men and women inhabit overlapping realities shaped by influences that have been identified in both family-violence and violence-against-women research. In these three studies, interviewees routinely reported that they themselves, and/or their partners, struggled with emotional or psychological issues and problems, including in many instances alcohol or substance abuse. Moreover, in case after case these personal issues coincided with childhood experiences of abuse, neglect, and/or deprivation. These risks arguably foster propensities to inflict or tolerate violence, as family-violence researchers argue.

But, as violence-against-women researchers argue, men's and women's motives for perpetrating violence, and the consequence of violence for victims, also appear to be decidedly gendered. Men and women agree that men perpetrate violence to control their female partners, punish them, and get the respect, or sex, that they believe they need and deserve as men. They agree that to achieve these aims men denigrate, intimidate, and slap their female partners, that men throw their partners around, drag them up stairs and out doors, slam them against walls, blacken their eyes, break their bones, knock them unconscious, rape them, threaten to kill them, and in some instances almost do kill them. They agree that these actions terrorize. In contrast, women slap, punch, scratch, and sometimes wound with weapons — when they can't, or won't, take any more emotional, physical, or sexual violence and abuse, and to assert and uphold their equality, dignity, and autonomy as women. In most instances, this violence by women does not seriously wound or terrorize. Male victims "just walk away" — although at times they retaliate in fear that if they're not "lucky" enough to exercise a modicum of self-restraint, they might actually end up killing their partners.

> Male perpetrators and female victims agree that men denigrate, intimidate, and slap female partners, or throw them around, drag them up stairs and out doors, slam them against walls, blacken their eyes, break their bones, knock them unconscious, rape them, threaten to kill them, and in some instances almost do kill them.

CONCLUSION

Statistics Canada findings on the gendered nature and distribution of intimate partner perpetration and victimization have shaped intervention efforts under the Family-Violence Initiative, a broad-based multisectoral governmental and community-based partnership that aims to eliminate all forms of intimate violence, whether against women, children, men, seniors, disabled persons, Aboriginal people, new immigrants, parents of abusive teens, gays and lesbians, or anyone else. This broad aim coincides, however, with a prioritization of protections for the predominant victims of serious intimate violence: women victimized by male partners and the children who witness their victimization. This focus is informed by Statistics Canada data on intimate partner assaults, sexual assaults, criminal harassment, and intimate homicide, and by the broad feminist-sociological or indeed violence-against-women lens that FVI partner Status of Women Canada brings to the research and support efforts that it helps to sponsor. This lens situates gender and other markers of inequality and exclusion as root causes of intimate battering, and assigns to all governmental and non-governmental partners responsibility to ameliorate and eventually eliminate these root causes.

In second half of the 1990s, men's rights advocates intensified their lobbying aimed at exposing and discrediting an alleged feminist anti-male bias at the heart of FVI research and interventions. Across a variety of forums, men's advocates argue that men are equally victimized in intimate partner contexts, and that the Government of Canada refuses to heed the body of family-violence research that proves this. Statistics Canada, Health Canada, Status of Women Canada, and other FVI partners responded by clarifying the FVI position that all victims deserve support and protection, including men victimized by female partners, and through intensified efforts to generate better data on the extent, nature, and consequences of female and male victimization. This response led to the inclusion of spousal violence measures in the General Social Survey, administered in two waves to over 20,000 women and men. Based on their self-reports, men and women alike experience violence at the hands of intimate partners, as family-violence research has long demonstrated. However, as clinical and ethnographic research confirms, men's and women's reports back up the violence-against-women argument that women suffer significantly more severe and chronic violence, more injury, and

> It is important to resist revising social policy to "degender" the intimate violence problem not because men are never victims… but because serious intimate violence is rooted in the history and continuing dynamics of our gendered social existence.

more fear or terror than do men. Moreover, as child maltreatment data also confirm, when children are exposed to intimate partner violence they overwhelmingly witness violence against their mother, including in a disturbingly high proportion of cases violence that causes their mother to fear for her life. It is, then, overwhelmingly women who are the victims of intimate battery. Moreover, it is increasingly evident that this aspect of the larger violence problem fuels increased aggression, mental health problems, learning difficulties, and related problems among children.

This body of evidence demonstrates how important it is to resist lobbying aimed at revising social policy to "degender" the intimate violence problem (Berns 2001, 2003), not because men are never victims, or because women's violence against men is always defensive or never consequential, but because serious intimate violence is rooted in the history and continuing dynamics of our gendered social existence. Anyone whose partner subjects them to terrorizing violence and control deserves support, assistance, and protection, including men who are battered by their partners. Most victims of battering, however, like most victims of intimate homicide, are women. Official statistics, social surveys, clinical studies, and the testimonies of abused and abusive women *and men* confirm this finding.

If FVI partners truly aim to eliminate intimate violence, existing policies do require revision, or at least expansion. The elimination of intimate violence is only possible if we target structural conditions that foster not only gender inequality, but also inequalities rooted in race and ethnicity, sexual orientation, and other exclusions and injustices that overlap with poverty and the deprivations, neglect, abuse, and humiliation accompanying this injustice in Canada and across the globe. Horrifying displays of visceral violence that bring disproportionate numbers of marginalized men and women before the courts are fostered by sexist and pro-violent norms, unquestionably. Structural inequalities other than gender, however, are also root causes of this problem. Conditions of structural inequality foster not only violence against wives and girlfriends, but also violence against male peers, visible minorities, immigrants, gays and lesbians, and children.

The kinder world that violence-against-women and family-violence researchers both envision (Schwartz and DeKeseredy 1993) depends on a fundamental transformation of our world. In the meantime, policy-makers need to stay the course and continue to prioritize protections for women within a larger effort that has helped to reduce the rates at which intimate partners of both sexes — but the majority of them women — are assaulted and killed in Canada.

GLOSSARY OF KEY TERMS

Family-Violence Initiative: A horizontally organized multisectoral entity founded in 1988 to co-ordinate and enhance prevention and intervention efforts aimed at the elimination of all forms of family violence, in co-operation with provincial-territorial governments and local communities, within which Status of Women Canada, Statistics Canada, Health Canada, the Department of Justice Canada, and nine other federal agencies work together as partners.

Gender: Not a mere physical attribute (being male or female), but rather the discursively mediated and structurally situated, contingent and contradictory social accomplishment of femininity and masculinity, an accomplishment shaped in part by the dynamics and consequences of intimate partner violence.

Feminism: A social movement committed to advancing the position of women in society and at eliminating sources of women's inequality, including intimate partner violence and other forms of violence against women, and committed more generally to eliminating all structurally constituted inequities and injustices.

Men's rights: A social movement aimed at revising social policies that recognize and seek to redress women's inequality and victimization, in part by promoting a "degendered" family violence rather than a "gendered" violence-against-women conceptualization of domestic violence.

Violence-against-women research: Feminist research aimed at documenting, explaining, and eliminating emotional, physical, and sexual battering of female partners and other forms of violence and abuse of women by men, and the gender inequality that lies at the root of this problem.

Family-violence research: Social-scientific research associated with the finding, appropriated by men's rights advocates, that women and men are equally violent in domestic or intimate contexts, generated through population-based surveys in which domestic violence is operationalized through Murray Straus's Conflict Tactics Scale (CTS).

QUESTIONS FOR DISCUSSION

1. What is the relevance of official data (police reports, victimization surveys, child maltreatment reports) to efforts to eliminate intimate partner violence through the federal Family-Violence Initiative? Do official data better support a gender-sensitive or a gender-neutral intervention strategy? Are these data biased?
2. How do violence-against-women and family-violence research traditions fit with feminist and men's rights arguments on the relevance of gender to intimate partner victimization and perpetration? To what extent do these research traditions rely on similar and dissimilar methodologies?
3. Why are the findings of population-based and clinical studies on the motives and propensities of male and female intimate partner violence perpetrators so dissimilar? To what extent are the findings shaped by the political sensitivities of researchers?
4. How do men's and women's "voices" on intimate partner violence, as captured in ethnographic research, fit with violence-against-women and family-violence perspectives on the intimate partner problem? Are men's rights advocates likely to find this body of evidence convincing? Why or why not?
5. To what extent have the FVI's gender-sensitive strategies worked to eliminate (or reduce) intimate partner violence in Canada? Is a major policy reorientation needed to better address the needs of all victims, including especially male victims? Why or why not?

WEBSITES OF INTEREST

Family-Violence Initiative. <www.phac-aspc.gc.ca/ncfv-cnivf/familyviolence/initiative_e.html>.

Family Violence in Canada. <dsp-psd.communication.gc.ca/Collection/Statcan/85-224-X/85-224-XIE.html>.

Status of Women Canada. <www.swc-cfc.gc.ca/index_e.html>.

NOTES

1. The 2003 Canadian Incidence Study of Reported Child Abuse and Neglect identifies about half (49 percent) of investigated child maltreatment cases as substantiated; that is, welfare authorities concluded that the evidence indicated that abuse or neglect had taken place. Neglect was the most common substantiated category (principal or most serious form of abuse, at 30 percent) followed by exposure to domestic violence (28 percent), physical maltreatment (24 percent), emotional maltreatment (15 percent), and sexual abuse (3 percent) (Tonmyr, Fallon, and Trocme 2006: 35). In the case of domestic violence, responsibility is assigned to one or both parents for failing to protect a child or children from exposure to spousal violence, a measure that overlaps with but is not equivalent to identification of the primary perpetrator. On intentionally false allegations and their gendered distribution, see Trocme and Bala 2005.

2. The thirteen federal agencies within the FVI are Canada Mortgage and Housing Corporation, Citizenship and Immigration Canada, Correctional Service of Canada, Department of Canadian Heritage, Department of Justice Canada, Department of National Defence, Health Canada, Human Resources Development Canada, Indian and Northern Affairs Canada, Public Health Agency of Canada, Royal Canadian Mounted Police, Statistics Canada, and Status of Women Canada. For the mandates and activities of these department agencies, see description and department agency links at <http://www.phac-aspc.gc.ca/ncfv-cnivf/familyviolence/initiative_e.html#fvidepartments>.

3. Dedicated FVI funding, as reported in 2004, stands at $7M (Jamieson 2004), down from a 1991 high of $136M (Morrow, Hankivsky, and Varcoe 2004: 362). However, "The FVI is not to be equated only with the $7M allocation [as] FVI member departments [also] fund family-violence activities through their regular departmental budgets" (National Clearinghouse, email, April 11, 2006).

4. The Public Health Agency of Canada website posts about 150 downloadable reports and resources on various aspects of family violence, organized under six links: Family Violence (n=35), Abuse of Older Adults (n=14), Child Abuse and Neglect (n=31), Child Sexual Abuse (n=27), Intimate Partner Abuse Against Women (n =32), and Intimate Partner Abuse Against Men (n=9). See <http://www.phac-aspc.gc.ca/ncfv-cnivf/familyviolence/archives/archives_e.html>. More reports and resources are posted on the websites of other FVI department agencies. See <http://www.phac-aspc.gc.ca/ncfv-cnivf/familyviolence/initiative_e.html#fvidepartments>.

5. Status of Women is not officially feminist. It is, however, a site through which feminist and feminist-sympathetic individuals and groups network and strategize to enhance supports for women in need, conduct research, inform the public, and pressure government on social issues that have particular salience to and for women (Dobrowolsky and Jenson 2004;

Morrow, Hankivsky, and Varcoe 2004; Shaw and Andrew 2005; Walker 1990).

6. As documented by Taylor-Butts (2005), in the fiscal year ending March 31, 2004, a total of 58,486 women and 36,840 children were admitted to 473 shelters and transition houses. On April 14 of that year, 93 of these shelters turned 221 women and 112 children away, either because the shelter was full (six out of ten cases) or because another shelter or service was deemed more suitable to the woman's needs (see also Jamieson 2004). The majority of women admitted to shelters were fleeing intimate abuse (76 percent). The rest sought shelter due to homelessness, drug problems, or mental health problems. All of these latter reasons for seeking shelter have increased since 2000 (up 11 percent), while the numbers of women fleeing abuse have remained largely unchanged (up 1 percent).

7. In Canada, the numbers of women and men killed by domestic partners have decreased at roughly equivalent rates since 1974 (unlike the United States, where male rates have decreased far more than female rates, leading some analysts to conclude that battered women's shelters protect men more than women (see discussion in Dawson 2001). As Dawson (2001, 2004) and various Statistics Canada authors (for example, Ogrodnik 2006) note, declines in intimate assaults and homicides against both women and men are a consequence of many interrelated factors. In addition to targeted criminal justice sanctions and enhanced victim supports, probable contributors are changes in public attitudes, a strong economy that affords employment opportunities for men and women alike, and increased levels of female workforce participation that decrease women's dependency and vulnerability to abuse.

8. The 1998 Canadian Incidence Study of Reported Child Abuse and Neglect is the first national study to document the rate of intentionally false allegations of abuse and neglect as identified by investigating child welfare authorities. These data do not substantiate fathers' advocates' claims. Rather, they indicate that while false allegations are elevated in child custody dispute contexts, it is non-custodial parents, mostly fathers, who most frequently make false allegations. The rate of intentionally false allegations by non-custodial parents was seven times the rate of intentionally false allegations by custodial parents (15 percent versus 2 percent). See Trocme and Bala 2005: 1341.

9. The introduction to the CTS (Gelles and Straus 1988: 277), reads: "No matter how well a couple gets along, there are times when they disagree, get annoyed with the other person, or just have spats or fights because they're in a bad mood or tired or for some other reason. They also use many different ways of trying to settle their differences. I'm going to read you some of the things that you or your partner might do when you have an argument. I would like you to tell me how many times in the past 12 months you [19 items from 'discussed an issue calmly' to 'used a knife or fired a gun'].... Thinking back over the past 12 months you've been together, was there ever an occasion when (your spouse/partner) [the same 19-item list]?" When a respondent chooses "never" or "don't know" for an item, the interviewer asks, "Has it ever happened?"

10. In Canada, 16 percent of domestic violence charges are laid against women (Ogrodnik 2006). That is, men are charged five times as often as women, compared to six years earlier, when men were charged seven times as often as women. In contrast, in some U.S. jurisdictions women constitute 35 percent of all charged domestic offenders, due largely to the greater prevalence of charging both partners when violence is mutual, as opposed to charging only the primary perpetrator when one partner appears most responsible (McMahon and Pence 2003; Pollack, Battaglia, and Allspach 2005; Swan and Snow 2002; Tutty 1999). For

a family-violence perspective on dual charging versus primary perpetrator policies, see Straus 2006.

11. Moffitt, Robins, and Caspi (2001) is among the 175 scholarly investigations listed in Fiebert's (2005) annotated bibliography, as is Dutton and Nicholls (2005). It should be noted that violence-against-women researchers do not claim that only males commit abuse, or that violence by women is non-existent, non-consequential, or always defensive.

12. Ruth Mann and Charlene Senn's ongoing research on community partnering in interventions for violent and at-risk youth in an unnamed Ontario community combines participant observation in intervention sites, content analysis of youth correctional files, and semi-structured interviews with youths. Interviewees are recruited from correctional facilities and high schools that provide specialized services and programs for violent and "at-risk" adolescents in co-operation with community-based service agencies. The excerpts here are selected from a preliminary set of seventy-three interviews with young women and men aged sixteen and older recruited in high schools (twenty-six female; twenty-four male) and correctional facilities (three female; twenty male). As of May 2006, 73 youth interviews (target 100) and 47 interviews with professionals (target 50) were transcribed and coded. Names and details of all participating agencies and individuals are changed to safeguard confidentiality. The research is funded through the Social Sciences and Humanities Council of Canada (SSHRC). See also Mann et al. 2007.

Chapter Three

FEELING FRAMED
Emotion and the Hollywood Woman's Film

Brenda Austin-Smith

Lisa (49): I think there's value in them. It shows you a perspective. If you're looking at, say, *Now, Voyager* you would never see a movie like that now where everybody gives up everything. People are just too selfish. It's showing you that there is another way of looking at things, not just the way they're portrayed in movies now, and not just the way you think of them yourself.

> **"You Should Know This"**
> - The first public screening of a film in Canada took place in Montreal, on June 28, 1896.
> - Screen Actors Guild formed in 1933 to improve working conditions for film actors. Its motto: "He best serves himself who serves others."
> - About 30 percent of the feature-length films made in Canada are released directly to television and video-DVD markets.
> - English-Canadian cinema accounts for only 2–3 percent of the commercial film market in Canada.
> - In Quebec, domestically produced films account for 4 percent of the market.
> - 75 percent of Canadian theatrical screens are controlled by Cineplex Odeon/Famous Players. In the United States, this corporation controls 20 percent of the theatrical screens.
> - Canada is the second-largest export market for U.S. film productions, following only Japan.

In a little more than one hundred years since its invention in 1895, film, and in particular Hollywood film, has become an astonishingly significant cultural form. Although going to the movies is not the special occasion it was early in the twentieth century, when viewers dressed up to see a feature film at grand movie theatres filled with plush seats, the new season's releases still attract crowds to downtown and suburban multiplexes. Films are significant not only for their stories, and their representation of ideas and themes, but also for how they communicate messages to viewers. This communication can take obvious and not so obvious forms. Commercial products are now placed strategically in front of the camera to make sure that brand names are clearly visible to spectators — all in the hopes that viewers will be influenced to go out and make the appropriate purchases.

More subtly, film communicates to its spectators by offering them visions of the world and of human relationships that tend to reinforce so-called "common-sense" views of gender, race, and class. Hollywood films typically present serious social inequalities in terms of individual problems. They offer the solution to an individual crisis as a substitute for profound and collective social change. So, for example, they may dramatize racism not as a deeply rooted system of inequality but as a misunderstanding that can be overcome through friendship and affection. Similarly, they may romanticize class differences in screen images of the poor but happy working-class family, and obscure the realities of poverty through the story of a hard-working hero who rises from rags to riches according to the dictates of the American Dream. Then, too, in most Hollywood films romance is a heterosexual affair, with marriage and conventional family structures presented as the goals of "normal" men and women.

Given the association of Hollywood film with images that encourage viewers to accept the social status quo, for people interested in the connections between art, politics, and power, film becomes part of the "problem of culture." The problem is this:

> Can critical resistance to some of Hollywood's persuasions be combined with an enjoyment of its images?

within a capitalist, patriarchal, racist culture, how are we to understand and interpret the artistic and cultural products of that culture? Is film merely a mechanical reflection of all that is politically negative in the culture from which it arises? Does film have the power to lull viewers into a passive acceptance of its messages? Can critical resistance to some of Hollywood's persuasions be combined with an enjoyment of its images?

For decades critics have pursued answers to these questions. Mainstream views of culture tend to regard film as either a mirror or a model: it reflects situations, events, and attitudes as they currently exist (the liberal view), or it urges viewers to adopt the behaviours and attitudes dramatized onscreen (conservative views). According to liberal perspectives, film is yet another example of the marketplace — in this case, a marketplace of images — in which the viewer can choose freely. Those who hold this view might, for instance, say that spectators who object to or criticize the way in which ethnic groups or women or seniors are presented in a particular film can always go to another film and see a different set of images. Their position is that film, like other cultural products, merely presents what is already there in the world. The liberal "mirror" view tends to downplay the subtle effects of representation on spectator attitudes, and ignores the extent to which most commercial films come from the same corporate sources and so tend to be shaped by similar perspectives. So even if you travelled here and there and saw several different films showing at different multiplexes, chances are good that the stories told onscreen would be similar, and the characters would play similar social roles.

Conservative views of film often express concern over the potential for film to inspire behaviour that may be somehow subversive of various social and moral orders. Those who hold these views tend to overstate the effects of representation on spectators, often arguing that a simple imitative relationship exists between what people see, and what they do. Conservative positions are sometimes expressed in calls for more control over screen images that challenge patriarchal or capitalist or heterosexist attitudes. These positions are often the source of censorship campaigns intended to limit sexually explicit imagery in films, or objections over the portrayal of gay, lesbian, bisexual, or transgendered characters in storylines.

In contrast to the liberal or conservative perspectives, a cultural studies approach to film offers a different way of studying the power of film to shape our views of the social world that we inhabit. "Cultural studies" is defined most simply as the critical study of contemporary culture in its social, historical, economic, and even personal contexts. A cultural studies approach to film explores how and in what ways film becomes part of culture. One writer defines this process as "the text of our lives, the ultimately coherent pattern of beliefs, acts, responses, and artifacts that we produce and comprehend every day" (Kolker 2002: 116).

People interested in cultural studies are often critical of both the liberal and conservative perspectives on the grounds that they tend to oversimplify our relationships to cultural artifacts such as books, television, and film. A cultural studies view would argue that we are neither completely uninfluenced nor completely controlled by film images. Similarly, cultural studies scholars contend that film is neither just a mirror of society nor a powerful model that somehow dictates or controls viewer behaviour. Instead, a cultural studies approach promotes the careful examination of connections between people, cultural products (such as films), and the social situations in which the two come together. Scholars interested in cultural studies might, for example, be interested in why some young female viewers are attracted to horror films, and try to figure out what these films mean to their viewers. The point is not to applaud or condemn the practice of watching horror films, or to criticize the content of such films, but to arrive at a more complex understanding of the place of this aspect of popular culture in relation to the social self.

> A cultural studies approach promotes the careful examination of connections between people, cultural products (such as films), and the social situations in which the two come together.

Popular culture is important to cultural studies because the sheer ubiquity of the popular — the saturation of everyday life by popular media such as music, video, television, and film — testifies to its influence. Most of us listen to commercial radio, watch popular commercial television programs, and read popular fiction or magazines. We sing along with our favourite pop songs. We buy T-shirts advertising the tours of our favourite bands. To ignore the effects that these popular activities and products have on our thinking, or the very real pleasures that we receive from them, is to overlook a considerable part of our daily lives. It is to say that these everyday experiences are somehow not as important as what we do at work or at school. For these reasons popular film has attracted the attention of people interested not only in artistic form and content, but also in the effects a movie has on its various audiences and how it takes on meaning for them. Even as it analyzes everyday interactions between people and cultural artifacts, though, cultural studies maintains a critical stance informed by knowledge about the commodification of culture (for example, the transformation of cultural identities, activities, and practices into objects that can be sold to someone, like going to a festival where you pay to eat "exotic" food, or dress up like someone from another culture).

For many of these analysts the importance of popular culture is also related to

American cultural imperialism, that is, the global dominance of American culture. For instance, when people refer generally to "popular culture," they are usually talking about American popular culture. Most of the commercial films and television shows we see are made in the United States. Even television shows made in Canada often imitate successful U.S. programs in concept or content; *Canadian Idol* is just one example. In this way even locally produced pop cultural products, such as films, novels, music, and television shows, become homogenized. Cultural producers tend to understand that for their work to achieve commercial success — which is often equated with popularity — it must resemble other familiar instances of that work, and those instances are usually American in origin. Interestingly, several U.S. production companies, such as Warner and Disney, which started out in the movie business, diversified and expanded their businesses over the years and became involved in television and radio broadcasting, book publishing, and the Internet, among other broad cultural activities. The export of American popular culture has been assisted and accompanied by a remarkable corporatization and monopolization of outlets for the production and spread of popular culture products.

While the analysis of film by viewers committed to a cultural studies approach does not take the form of necessarily judging films as "good" or "bad" for people, this view of film is indeed interested in the relationship between movies and moviegoers, and examines power as an inevitable aspect of that relationship. This approach has led to intense debates about the relative influence of film over its spectators versus the ability of spectators to resist the values and attitudes communicated to them by film.

Debates within the left over the value of the popular have taken two general forms. One is the criticism of mass culture and the "culture industry" of Hollywood and the media as manipulative, and of the audience for mass culture as passive. The other side of the debate insists on the value of the popular in understanding what culture means to people who have little interest in non-commercial or "high" culture, such as ballet, modern dance, or opera, but who prefer movies, comic books, and television.[1] Though recognizing the implication of cultural industries such as film production in capitalism, this second perspective stresses the opportunities that viewers have to decode films from perspectives that are opposed to the dominant values communicated by those films (Hall 1990). Stuart Hall's influential work on cultural studies and media suggests three ways in which viewers "decode" or interpret material. One is from a position that accepts the dominant values of the transmitted material. Another is from a "negotiated" position: the viewer accepts some of but not all of the "messages" communicated by the material. The third is from an oppositional position: the viewer interprets the media material in a way that is contrary to what its producers intended. In the years since the publication of Hall's essay, cultural studies critics of television and film have concluded that most audiences operate from a negotiated position: that is, most viewers interpret media by agreeing with some of its messages and claims and resisting or rejecting others.

One result of this emphasis on film as culture rather than on film as art is a challenge to established ways of distinguishing between "high" and "low" forms of film production. No longer are we directed to pay attention only to those film texts deemed artistic by virtue of their seriousness of theme or subject. On the contrary, attention to film as a cultural practice invites us to consider examples of popular films that have been hitherto regarded as unworthy of sustained critical interest. Horror films, gangster films, westerns, and even pornographic films have been analyzed from the vantage point provided by cultural studies, which instead of treating viewers as cultural dupes — that is, as unsophisticated and gullible, completely vulnerable to manipulation by mass culture — sees them as agents. This idea of viewer "agency" in relation to film is key because it involves recognizing the complicated interaction of power and resistance. According to a cultural studies view, a movie spectator is never completely hypnotized by a film to the extent that he or she believes or accepts as "right" everything the film depicts on screen. But the movie spectator is also never completely "free," in the liberal sense of the word, to make a film mean anything he or she wants to. Hollywood films are clearly the products of an industry with a certain allegiance to capitalism and corporate success, and spectators just as clearly come to the movie theatre with opinions and attitudes formed by class, race, and gender. The limited but important amount of power possessed by the movie spectator to create meanings from the film on the big screen is what cultural studies theorists mean by "viewer agency."

> This idea of viewer "agency" in relation to film is key because it involves recognizing the complicated interaction of power and resistance.

Theorized most famously by John Fiske, this theory of "cultural populism" (During 1994) investigates commercial culture as a place in which consumers play with and create their cultural identities—imagining different lives for themselves while watching a film, for example. Fiske's claim is that popular culture is created by people from the choices provided by commercial cultural industries. This process of creation is active, not passive. However, just as "the people" do not exist as an objective, stable category of beings that can be adequately described by referring only to sociological facts (Fiske 1989: 24), so too is the popular culture forged by this energy shifting and contradictory in its forms and effects. To understand how people use and make sense of popular culture means paying attention to how they feel about themselves and not just to how they can be described as belonging to a particular social or ethnic group. Just as people's feelings about themselves are contradictory and changeable, so too will be their interpretations of popular culture products, and people's gender or class identity is not a reliable predictor of what they will absorb from a film. Essential to explanations of how popular culture emerges from the agency of those who engage with commercial texts and artifacts such as Hollywood film is a recognition of the inevitability of this contradiction.

> Popular culture is always situated in a complex relation to power, in opposition to some forms of it and in alliance with others.

Popular culture, then, is never a complete escape from the social realities of life outside the movie theatre, nor is it just another form of opium for the masses, hopelessly contaminated by the forces of industrial capitalism. Rather, popular culture is always situated in a complex relation to power, in opposition to some forms of it and in alliance with others. Fiske's argument is that for a text such as a film to become truly popular, it must represent these opposing forces. That is, it must depict or represent both the power that oppresses and the chances for that power to be subverted or opposed, even if the opposition is limited in its effects and those who oppose it are not completely triumphant in the end (Fiske 1989).

Based on this perspective of "cultural populism," my subject here is specifically the responses of Canadian women viewers to the emotional content of Hollywood "woman's films" of the 1930s and 1940s. Rather than see emotional responses to films as a sign of the social problem of media control over audiences, I argue that these viewers perform a more interesting and complex act of cultural negotiation with movies (Gledhill 1988). Cultural negotiation is a form of bargaining or exchange that takes place between a person and a particular element of culture. The phrase suggests that film viewers, for example, are not empty glasses into which the political views of the film are poured; rather, they are active viewers who often question what they see. Through their emotional engagement with the content of film, the women viewers of my study display resistance not only to the ways in which Hollywood represents gender relations, but also to the ways in which some academic film theory tends to characterize viewer pleasure as naïve, or as proof of Hollywood's power to brainwash its spectators.

Looking at how women spectators respond to the "woman's film" allows us to see examples of "viewer agency" in action. Women who watch and enjoy the Hollywood woman's film are not cultural dupes hoodwinked into accepting stereotyped views of sex and gender. Rather, they are active, creative viewers whose responses to films demonstrate that film spectators can be critical of popular culture products even as they enjoy them. These women provide evidence that taking pleasure in popular culture can still involve resistance to the sexism, racism, and patriarchy expressed in the films themselves and reinforced in the social world outside the film.

> Looking at how women spectators respond to the "woman's film" allows us to see examples of "viewer agency" in action.

THE HOLLYWOOD WOMAN'S FILM: HISTORY, ECONOMICS AND THEORY

The "woman's film" is a term that refers to a subgenre of melodramatic film produced by several Hollywood studios from the 1930s to the late 1950s. Melodramatic films typically present extreme emotions, stereotypically good and evil characters, and co-incidences as plot devices. They tend to centre on pitiful or heart-rending situations. The woman's film used all of these elements in its depiction of romance, domestic relationships, child-rearing, and female friendship from a woman's point of view. An early form was the short serial melodrama, such as *The Perils of Pauline* (1914), and its descendants are contemporary films known as "chick flicks": *Terms of Endearment* (1983), *Beaches* (1988), *Stepmom* (1998), and *Divine Secrets of the Ya-Ya Sisterhood* (2002), for example. Its heyday, though, was in the middle years of Hollywood's classic period (1930–66), represented by such films as *Stella Dallas* (1937), *Now, Voyager* (1942), and *Imitation of Life* (1959). Although these films can be, and are, criticized for their conventional representations of patriarchal family structures and exclusively heterosexual gender roles, they also played an important role in the history of Hollywood film as a film genre made for and marketed to female audiences.

Reviewers and film scholars alike criticized woman's films for their extreme sentimentality. The films became known as "weepies" or "tear-jerkers" and were marginalized as irrelevant to the larger audience of filmgoers. Though the critics were often male viewers who responded in a sexist and condescending way to the emotional content of the films, female critics and scholars also reacted negatively to what they perceived as stereotypical material. These films typically featured a female protagonist, often a mother, beset by difficulties that demanded some kind of personal sacrifice or surrender: most often of her marriage or her child, but sometimes of her very life. The musical score was often lush with violins, the dialogue laden with the language of intense feeling, and the plot vulnerable to wild coincidence and strange and sudden twists of fate.

These films were, however, immensely popular with their female target audiences, and their stars — most notably Bette Davis, Barbara Stanwyck, Joan Crawford, and Lana Turner — became screen idols whose love lives and fashion styles filled the pages of contemporary fan magazines. In turn the woman's film was one aspect of a larger, integrated marketing strategy aimed at female consumers, and thus one of capitalism's attempts to sell women mass-produced fantasies of glamour that reinforced dominant cultural notions of female beauty and desirability (Stacey 1994).

The political economy in which the woman's film was produced was part of what industrial historians of film call the classical period of Hollywood studio production. This phase of film production, which lasted roughly from 1930 to 1948, was an oligopoly (Gomery 1998) controlled by five major film studios, all of them vertically integrated corporations. A studio such as Paramount, for example, not only made films and distributed them but also owned the theatres in which the films were screened, guaranteeing an audience for the product. Actors, writers, and directors signed contracts with a particular studio for a number of pictures over a number of years, becoming permanent staff. Films were made according to the mass-production model (Staiger 2000) with filmmaking duties distributed among specialized practitioners in plotting, dialogue, and editing (Thompson and Bordwell 1994). Although the studios lost control of their theatres as a result of U.S. anti-trust legislation passed in 1948, it was years before the distribution practices of the old studio system changed (Cook 1996), taking with it the old star system. For decades, then, studios were film factories, each one churning out a film a week, and genre films such as westerns and the woman's film lent themselves well to this kind of assembly-line production method.

The very lack of originality in its production contributed to the bad critical reputation of the woman's film among reviewers, critics, and film scholars. In the past twenty years, however, scholars interested in the history and effect of popular culture have turned to the formerly despised woman's film as a genre worthy of serious study.[2] The influence of feminism and cultural studies in work by Janice Radway (1984) and Janet Staiger (1992) on audience reception has also contributed to the attention paid to a popular genre that places female characters and conventionally female concerns at the centre of the filmed action. The woman's film has claimed this critical attention precisely because of its lowly status as a commercial product aimed at a particular market. Scholars have become interested in how and why this highly unoriginal film genre managed to capture the loyalty — and the tears — of its audiences for so many years.

Critical and theoretical literature on the woman's film has been largely ahistorical in its emphasis. Mary Ann Doane (1987), Tania Modleski (1984), and Linda Williams (1984) tend to discuss the woman's film from a psychoanalytic perspective, examining how film addresses the unconscious of its viewers and encourages them to identify with the portraits of female sacrifice and suffering they see onscreen. Critical work influenced by psychoanalysis focuses on the theoretical concept of the "cinema spectator" formed in the process of watching a film. The cinema spectator is not a flesh and blood individual, but rather an effect of the way in which films are organized. Films, by virtue of how they represent the world and its power relations, communicate to viewers by offering them a point of view from which these representations make perfect sense. Encouraging viewers to sympathize with a character, for example, may make it easier for viewers to defend or make excuses for that character's opinions, even if those opinions differ from those the spectator holds in "real life" outside the theatre. Many of the feminist film scholars regard the woman's film as a conservative genre that tends to punish female characters for their attempts at independence, and that presents self-sacrifice and suffering (particularly of a mother) as the inevitable fate of the heroine. This critical approach to the woman's film also stresses the masochism of female spectators who are persuaded by the film's rhetoric to identify emotionally with these films (Doane 1987). Though it has yielded rich interpretations of individual films, this reliance on psychoanalytic theories of film viewing ignores the specificities of individual viewers, and the historical, social, and cultural forces that shape responses to these emotionally powerful films. The focus of psychoanalytic scholars is on the power of these films to enforce dominant ideologies of sex, gender, and sexuality, and on the vulnerability of female audience viewers to these ideologies.

Related to this concentration on the powerlessness of female viewers to resist the messages communicated to them by film is a suspicion of pleasure. The pleasure that viewers take in watching films has been central to a feminist critique of Hollywood film associated with Laura Mulvey (1975) and to a strand of analysis of culture in capitalist patriarchy.[3] This attitude to pleasure — that it is politically suspect in some way — influences how critics see the viewers of the woman's film. They implicitly construct audiences who take pleasure in melodrama as being complicit with the dominant social order, as cultural dupes who have learned to love their oppression.

The opposing critical view is that the woman's film, in dramatizing woman's domestic and emotional lives onscreen, can provide female audiences with a positive source of pleasure and self-regard. Critics who study the woman's film from this perspective stress the difference between the idea of the spectator as it is used in psychoanalytic film theory and the "social audience" in its historical and economic specificity (Kuhn 1987). Feminist film scholars who value the woman's film point out that because it was one of the only film genres produced especially for women viewers, it avoids the standard Hollywood treatment of sexualizing female characters for the erotic viewing pleasure of the presumably male heterosexual spectator (Doane 1987). In opposition to the gangster and western genres, populated with heroes who exemplify dominant cultural norms of rugged heterosexual masculinity, including an emphasis on physical strength, violence, and emotional reserve, the woman's film turns its female protagonists into heroes by focusing on their emotional struggles. The genre thus offers its female viewers images of themselves as heroic in their daily lives, rather than devaluing their concerns with relationships, children, work, and the domestic sphere as somehow unworthy of heroic representation. The woman's film "raises the possibility of female desire and female point-of-view" (Kuhn 1987: 348).

Part of this, too, is that female viewers are active consumers of popular culture rather than passive sponges. They are capable of constructing alternative and often resistant meanings from the most conventional or conservative texts. This focus on the woman's film is related to research on other forms of women's cultural consumption, such as reading romance novels and watching soap operas (Radway 1985; Ang 1985), and it seeks "to rescue the female sub-cultural activity, resistance and pleasure that may be embedded in popular, mainstream culture" (Gledhill 1987). This is not to argue that viewers are not influenced by the politically regressive content of some popular films. Rather, it is to qualify extreme statements about the helplessness of spectators to resist ideological content in films with which they become emotionally involved.

The idea of "cultural negotiation," that film spectators engage in a give-and-take activity with film when they watch and interpret it, is thus central to this analysis. "It allows space to the subjectivities, identities and pleasures of audiences" (Gledhill 1987: 72) while still acknowledging the power of cultural forms such as films to attempt to impose dominant political meanings upon viewers.

VIEWER RESPONSES TO THE WOMAN'S FILM

Although the woman's film has come under close scrutiny for the ways in which it perpetuates women's gender oppression by representing images of women in highly stereotypical situations, little attention has been paid to the responses of real spectators to these films. This avoidance is surprising given that the genre was produced specifically with women audiences in mind and given the popularity of the films with those target audiences. How, for example, do female viewers respond to the woman's film and its emotional content? Are viewers who cry while they watch these films aware of how the films use emotional manipulation to communicate ideological material about the nature of the family, women's roles, and "appropriate" sexualities? Does an emotional response to such a film indicate an uncritical acceptance of the film's dominant ideology?

To answer these questions I conducted a study of women viewers, gathering and analyzing their responses to examples of the Hollywood woman's film. To begin, I placed ads in local papers, asking viewers and fans of the woman's film to contact me. The eventual ten respondents were somewhat diverse in terms of class and ethnic identities, and all of them presented themselves as heterosexual. They ranged in age from forty-eight to eighty-three. Most of them had been married at one time, and most had children. The project began with individual home viewings of *Stella Dallas, Now, Voyager, Mildred Pierce* or *Dark Victory*, followed by one-on-one interviews carried out from November 1999 to April 2000. The audiotaped interviews took place on campus, in participants' homes, and in one case in the food court of a shopping mall. In each case they lasted about an hour and consisted of responses to a loosely structured series of questions focusing on film-viewing history and practice; emotional responses to the film; forms of identification with film protagonists; responses to elements such as plot, theme, character, and music, and, finally, the meaning and value of women's films to the viewer.

As for the movies: in *Stella Dallas*, a working-class woman eventually surrenders her daughter to her divorced husband's new upper-class wife; in *Now, Voyager*, an ugly duckling under the thumb of an oppressive mother gains independence, falls in love, and gives up her married lover in order to maintain a relationship with his daughter; in *Mildred Pierce* a working mother loses one child to disease and another to a faithless lover; and in *Dark Victory* a rich and snobbish woman is transformed by love and disease into the nobly suffering wife of the doctor who attempts unsuccessfully to cure her.

In addition to the interviews, in March and April 2000 I arranged on-campus screenings of *Stella Dallas, Now, Voyager,* and *Imitation of Life* (a film about a relationship between a white and a Black woman and their daughters, one of whom is of mixed-race identity) for sixteen women between the ages of thirty-five and seventy. We had five viewing groups: one screening each for women in their thirties, forties, fifties, sixties, and sixties and seventies. Each film screening was followed by a semi-structured discussion in which I asked questions and also contributed information about the film under discussion. A research assistant acted as an observer, making notes on threads and themes of the discussion.

The interviews and focus group discussions with these film viewers uncovered a range of responses that argues against the model of the gullible female viewer who consumes popular culture material in an unquestioning fashion. The complexity and contradictions in some of these responses support arguments that viewers use popular culture to negotiate conflicting and often painful social identities and to make sense of difficult personal and social histories. The viewers were drawn to some and resisted other elements of the same popular work because of their

> Viewers use popular culture to negotiate conflicting and often painful social identities and to make sense of difficult personal and social histories.

contradictory feelings and views about their social positions in a world that values certain aspects of their identity (as wives or mothers) but devalues others (as working-class women, for example).

Emotionality

The women in the study had strong but varied responses to the emotionality of the films, ranging from complete emotional engagement with, to detachment from, the film, its characters, and its events. Some cried during the movies they watched, and some, though they didn't cry, recalled or described crying in viewing other examples of the woman's film. Women are regarded as particularly susceptible to the power of images (Doane 1987), and popular ageist assumptions are that older women are more vulnerable to emotional material than younger women are. However, several viewers in their thirties and forties were deeply moved by the films, while some of the older women found the films so unrealistic and sentimental that they couldn't identify closely with them. Our eighty-three-year-old viewer said, "I'm such a realist; I can't help but think, they're drowning, the cameraman's right there, you know. I just never completely lose myself." Another viewer, in her seventies, agreed: "It's just the acting. I didn't notice it so much in this film, but some of the old movies were so stupid, you know, it's the way they acted then, and it bothers me enough that I can't get into the story." Still, one forty-six-year-old viewer reported, "I got tears in my eyes about halfway through. I thought I was going to burst out sobbing," while another viewer, in her late forties, commented, "They're sad, the self-sacrifice, all the way around, nobody saying anything about what they wouldn't want, nobody forcing any issue."

There were, in short, more similarities than differences across age groups, even though not all of the viewers found these particular examples of the woman's film touching. For some of the older women, the films had lost their emotional power. For many of the women under fifty years of age, however, the films were still moving, because for all that had changed in women's lives, the films depicted situations that were still common and familiar: separation, divorce, single motherhood, illness, death, and women's struggles for recognition and independence.

Critical Viewing

Interestingly, some of the women's emotional responses consisted of anger or frustration at the female characters and the limited choices they were given as part of the film. In these responses, the viewers actively named and criticized, as part of the film's political ideology, the insistence on women's self-denial and silence. In some instances, the emotional response was mixed — a combination of sadness and anger, or a response that had shifted over the years since the viewer had last seen the film. These examples of critical viewing, which resemble those described by Jackie Stacey (1994) in her study of women and film stars, are a function of the viewer's critical reflection on the difference between a past and a present viewing self. The mixed emotional responses also suggest the degree to which weeping at a woman's film is itself a form of critical viewing rather than a surrender to uncritical feeling. Women who watched these "weepies" often cried as much in anger as in pity at the plots that trapped the female protagonist in hopeless relationships, or that forced her to give up her child. Viewers often judged the heroines of the films according to contemporary gender roles, expressing dismay at what they saw as these heroines' weaknesses and at their own past acceptance of such filmic images as somehow appropriate or attractive.

> *Pam* (46): Yes, I did [get angry at them] but then I got emotionally hooked on it over and over and over again.... However, I thought that I wouldn't have made those same choices in that way and I thought, "Oh, my God, what a fool!"

> *Priscilla* (65): I think that women nowadays would put up a much better fight. And I get even to the point when I see some of those old movies I get even a little bit disgusted. I think "Oh, gosh, were we really that naïve and stupid?"

Some viewers criticized the films outright as forms of gender propaganda written and produced by men, as representing what men think women are, or should be. They often connected these thoughts to the way in which the woman's film represented motherhood and the female protagonist's attachment to her children. Viewers were particularly critical about the woman's films' portrayal of sacrificial motherhood as the essence of a woman's identity, suggesting their resistance to this particular social message.

> *Kate* (65): I would tend to think these are men's perceptions of women. As these tigresses doing anything for their children.... And the women are manipulative. The men are self-sacrificing and kind in temper and good, but the women are degraded. I didn't find them strong women, I found them weak and degraded.

While these responses lend support to a description of the woman's film as a genre capitalizing on images of women's suffering and sacrifice to an unrealistic degree, the ease with which many of these viewers moved back and forth from a criticism of the films' portrayal of women to an emotional connection with the films contradicts claims that women — and in particular senior women — are likely to be "taken in" and held in the grip of an emotional film, unable to resist its power to make them cry. On the contrary, the life experiences of many of the senior women I talked to had made them more, not less, critical of the images of women's lives on the silver screen, and more inclined to mix whatever tears they shed with judgment. This finding echoes observations made by Christine Gledhill and Janice Radway about the "culinary fallacy" of the reader/viewer as consumer: "One who, meeting with the media product as a discrete object, swallows

The life experiences of many of the senior women had made them more, not less, critical of the images of women's lives on the silver screen, and more inclined to mix whatever tears they shed with judgment.

it whole" (Gledhill 1988:73). Rather, these viewers accepted and rejected different elements of these films as they shifted their alliances with the characters and situations depicted in the films. This shifting was influenced by the life experiences of the viewer herself, and by how convincing she felt the film was in capturing the particular stresses and challenges of women's lives that she recognized as her own.

Weeping

In comments about the particular pleasures of crying at the movies, and why viewers thought "weepies" appealed to women in particular, many viewers saw emotionalism in response to films as a particularly "feminine" quality, something that women take pleasure in without self-consciousness. "I think that we females are just emotional human beings," said one viewer. Although this link between sex and emotional capacity is consistent with dominant sexist attitudes, viewers who subscribed to this view saw it as a positive marker of women's identity, something that made women "special" and somewhat superior to men. These viewers took an association regarded by the dominant culture as a sign of women's weakness and reinterpreted it as an asset.

Several women saw weeping at the movies a form of escape from daily pressure and stress. The film gave a woman permission to express emotion, providing her with, as one woman put it, "an emotional bath." Weeping at films is a kind of emotional recreation, a way of blowing off excess feeling or of channelling emotion into a harmless activity in a safe place, rather than holding it in.

> *Priscilla* (65): I think that women go to movies as a form of escapism, and the tears are incidental. I don't believe that they go to see a sad movie because they feel like crying. I think they just get all wrapped up in the movie, and it's just part of it, is these tears…. I think the sadness tells you more about your own personality than it does about the movie.

> *Margaret* (66): I think we all need to cry every once in a while. It relieves tension, you know. It's good for us to cry. We're meant to cry once in a while. If you're like myself right now, living alone, if you don't cry from — I find myself if I don't watch a weepie movie I put a comedy on so that I have a good laugh and cry.

There is in some of these responses a melancholy sense of films providing viewers with permission to release emotions that might otherwise be experienced as overwhelming, emotions that have their source in loneliness, isolation, and depression. One woman saw her responses to the woman's film as an explicit sign of emotional health and evidence of her ability to make emotional connections.

> *Cathy* (43): I think it's part of being alive. Like when you stop having those responses…. I've been at times in my life, I've been so depressed that I wasn't moved by anything, you know? Instead of being someone who was crying all

the time I was dead and cold and not feeling anything, just totally not caring.... But I think normally you go to a movie or you read a book and you want to be involved.

This response credits the scenes of emotional anguish with the power to enable the viewer to feel moved again after a period of depression and detachment. This positive vision of the emotional power of the woman's film stands in vivid contrast to the negative portrayal of the "weepie's" effects on its viewers. Instead of seeing the emotional response as a sign of weakness, or of infantilization, this approach sees it as the sign of health and human connection with others.

For others who took part in the project, the response of crying at the movies was a reaction linked to the stress of traumatic historical events such as war, and its effects on the family. The woman's film, with its focus on the family as a source of sorrow and difficulty, was a complex and contradictory reflection of women's experiences outside the theatre, a reflection that validated the worth of their efforts to keep things going during the war effort.

> *Harriet* (72): The movies was an outlet, especially during the war, for the women because the men folk had gone. They were bringing up their children and, you know, "Where's Daddy?"... So I think, when you saw these sad movies, that was another thing to let it out. You know, because you had to be strong for the next person. That was the way you could let yourself go.

The very act of going to the theatre became, then, a limited and specific example of escape from the realities of war and the "blitz" bombing of England. Watching a woman's film, with its story of romance and heartbreak, provided an opportunity for women to express their feelings of stress, fear, and grief in a place removed from those areas of life in which they were expected to "be strong for the next person." The viewer could connect the self-sacrifice depicted onscreen to the demand for sacrifice in her own circumstance; the tears she shed for the heroine could indirectly be those she shed for herself.

Loss and Escape

One emotional thread linking many of the responses of women who had lived through the later years of the Depression or the Second World War was the theme of loss. Both Flo Leibowitz (1996) and Jackie Stacey (1994) discuss the significance of loss in the responses of women viewers to film. Leibowitz in particular argues that the pleasure that audiences take in women's films is located precisely in the films' depictions of loss or near loss. The stories stress the meaning and value of what is lost or almost lost: a lover, a child, a marriage. Complicating audience response is the mixture of sorrow and admiration for the heroine who must face these losses. Audiences admire her strength and yet feel sadness that she must endure these challenges (Leibowitz 1996). This was very much the case for the viewers in my study. They responded emotionally to the films by connecting their own losses, often of parents or of a sense of their own carefree childhoods, to the losses experienced by the mothers and daughters in the films.

> *Harriet* (72): I was working in a lace factory, making lace. And I was in a clerical position and then I went to work in guns and ammunition. We only wanted to see happy movies you know. Well, there's so much sad, the war was on, there's so much sadness, that you didn't want to dwell on the bad things. Because my father was always talking about if the Germans came over what he would do, he would kill his girls. So we was frightened of that, you know….That's why we went to those pictures… and if you wanted a good cry that was allowed but, you know, because my father used to say, "You don't cry. You're strong." But that [crying at movies] was allowed.

> *Margaret* (66): I felt abandoned at the time. My mother had been onto the army reserve during the war, and of course when war was declared, she was gone. About a year later, they took my father as well….He said, "What do I do with my children?" And they said "Oh well you can put them in an orphanage until you come back." And it was my grandmother stepped in at that time… "No, those children are not going to an orphanage, as long as I'm alive, they'll live with me." So we did that. And I think that had a lot do to with me, how I felt about these movies… feeling abandoned. I didn't think of it as that at the time, but now I do, looking back… looking for love and care. Somebody to watch out for me.

These responses are striking for the way in which they connect watching films about women's domestic tribulations and finding an outlet for one's fears of emotional and physical harm. Understanding the pleasure that woman took in watching these films thus means taking into consideration not just what fantasies audiences might be escaping into, but what they are escaping from (Stacey 1994; Dyer 1985). Significant here are the patriarchal and bureaucratic threats these women see themselves escaping by going to the movies: in one instance a father's warnings of rape by invading armies (or death at the hands of that same father), and in the other the intervention of the state in the family.

In these two instances the woman's film functions again in a complicated way. It provides viewers with a dramatic analogue of their own lives that both allows them to give in to their feelings and offers them comfort by presenting them with self-sacrificing but strong women onscreen. Viewers can be consoled by the screen image of an all-loving mother who may be missing in real life. They can be inspired to make sense of their own difficulties by witnessing the noble suffering of the heroine onscreen. While there is nothing remotely revolutionary about the ideological content of the films themselves, the ways in which these women use the films to make sense of their situations and to comfort themselves for the loss of other more tangible forms of emotional security testify to their agency in constructing points of relevance between the films and their own lives. Their social identities are those of relatively disempowered working-class females who nevertheless create something personal and significant from the mass-produced fictions of Hollywood. In Michel de Certeau's (1984: 18) terms, they "make do with what they have."

For some participants, the films *Stella Dallas* and *Now, Voyager* resonated emotionally because of specific and recent losses in their own lives. One woman said that she wanted to participate in this project to honour the memory of her daughter. Another participant spoke movingly of how the films had captured her grief at the deaths of her parents. More specifically, the theme of female self-sacrifice and renunciation in both of these films had triggered both sorrow and anger when the viewer recognized similarities between the lives of the female heroines and that of her own mother.

> *Elizabeth* (56): Mum and Dad both died last fall. Dad died of cancer of the prostate; Mum died six weeks later. She decided not to eat. She decided not to eat, my sense is, because she didn't think she was of value. I never saw my mother's signature on any official document until I saw her will.

This response combines grief at a mother's death with an analysis of the reasons for that death, connecting the sorrow and suffering of the female protagonist of the woman's film to the quiet suffering of a real woman. This viewer's anger at what she saw as her mother's acceptance of a subordinate identity expressed itself in tears while she watched the films. It was as if she were watching her mother's life and understanding it for the first time.

Identity and Belonging

One of the significant themes that Stacey analyzed in her study of women and film stars related to belonging. The women in Stacey's study reported that going to the cinema provided them with a "shared group identity" that was pleasurable particularly during wartime (Stacey 1994: 100). Stacey (1994: 101) notes how the sense of community fostered by going to the movies and being part of a common audience "clearly broke down feelings of isolation and offered a sense of self with a collective meaning." The women I talked to reported similar feelings with some important differences. These women identified themselves not as belonging to a historically specific audience that had once attended movie theatres, but rather as part of a larger, generalized community of women who shared in the recognition of their common social, economic, and emotional circumstances.

> *Mary* (55): These movies tell universal women's stories. You've been there and can identify, or a friend has been there. We cry because women do the weeping for the world....The universal nature of these films makes me feel included; it gives me a sense of belonging, which is what I am searching for.

The romantic terms of this response are in keeping with dominant social assumptions about the connections between sex, gender, and emotion, what Fiske (1989: 118) calls "the common sense of patriarchal capitalism." This common sense is replicated in the content of the woman's film itself. It can thus be argued that the woman's film encourages its viewers to accept dominant definitions of femininity (as forgiving, sacrificial, and above all emotional) that circulate in the culture at large. However, when asked about the significance and value of the woman's film to them, viewers countered judgments of the woman's film's negative effects by pointing to

> Viewers countered judgments of the woman's film's negative effects by pointing to what they saw as its role in promoting generosity and tolerance.

what they saw as its role in promoting generosity and tolerance. One viewer spoke of the slow pacing of the films as one of their attractions for her. Another viewer spoke of the films as preserving a sense of beauty in the world. Other participants made connections between the films and the influence of other women in their lives; how watching such films could lead to the cultivation of empathy, a recognition of shared experiences, the development of generosity, and a sense of ethics.

> *Margaret* (66): Those kind of movies sort of reinforce what my grandmother was teaching me. That you get back what you give type of thing and that you always feel better if you gave what you expected.... If you watch these kind of movies it sort of reinforces that. They are love movies. They're love stories. But they're also tragedies in a way.... How many of us would be able to be so unselfish to say "well I would rather look after your little girl than have you because I can't have you but I'll take very good care of your little girl." I mean, how many people would do that?

The strong attachment of some viewers to the woman's film and the values they find in it are examples of the relevance and productivity that Fiske sees as marking popular culture. For these viewers the depiction of domestic and emotional crises as the stuff of high drama is relevant to their lives; and in their emotional engagement with the films they produce meanings from

> They see the films as portraits of gender roles long out of date yet still annoyingly persistent and compelling, and thus as spurs to anger and criticism.

these texts that can help them negotiate the demands of their own social lives. They see themselves as partaking of the female protagonist's emotional heroism and the films themselves as testimonies to the endurance of women. They see the films as portraits of gender roles long out of date yet still annoyingly persistent and compelling, and thus as spurs to anger and criticism. They also see these films as instructive, as demonstrations of love and sacrifice that they themselves value and imitate in their daily lives.

> *Linda* (61): I think sometimes when you look at something like that and there's pain, but there's also out of that comes joy sometimes too, and I think sometimes

you identify with maybe some of your pain and you survived and it's okay, and you've felt like that and you've lost like that, and we move on. It's life… it's also a way of looking at where we were, where we are, and where we're going. So it does show there has been change, where my grandmother was, where my mother was, and where I'm going. There is transition there. You can connect up, and sometimes we need to know where our grandmothers came from.

CONCLUSION

These constellations of meanings are contradictory and at first glance perhaps seem even absurd, for we expect that a person's response to a film will be consistent in either its criticism or its celebration of it. Yet viewers of the woman's film express a contradictory pleasure in their emotional responses to these films: they deplore the circumstances that bring about the heroine's suffering and social martyrdom, but enjoy participating in the cathartic weeping that accompanies their witnessing of that suffering. And it is that pervasive sense of pleasure, even joy in the experience of emotion, that makes these viewers creators of alternative meanings rather than mere victims of media power. The experience turns their tears of recognition, anger, and grief into potential resistance.

While the responses of these women to silver-screen images of the self-sacrificing wife, mother, and lover challenge claims about the unqualified power of Hollywood film to shape and direct our opinions about the social world, we must acknowledge the local and limited nature and effect of this resistance. Popular films are still commodities designed in the first instance to turn a profit. Even though they may watch critically, these women are still contributing to a capitalist patriarchy that benefits from their pleasure in ways that do not immediately or obviously improve their own concrete situations. These viewing activities are an example of what Fiske (1989) describes as "progressive" rather than "radical" politics. In Fiske's terms, progressive politics are "micropolitical," concerned with "the day-to-day negotiations of unequal power relations" within existing social structures, rather than with the radical alteration of those social structures at the macropolitical level.

The meanings produced by these viewers of the Hollywood woman's film may or may not lead them to abandon these films in favour of other films with more obviously feminist content, or encourage them to translate their critical viewing skills into more public forms of political action. Then again, why should they give up this source of pleasure? In his book *The Practice of Everyday Life*, theorist Michel de Certeau writes, "Where there is pleasure, there is agency," arguing that the creation of pleasurable experiences from the consumption of popular culture is a social practice. His observation allows those with an interest in cultural studies to revisit assumptions about the role and effect of popular culture, especially persistent and negative assumptions about the consumption of popular culture as a waste of time, or as a distraction from "real" political activity. Why would we assume that if these women did not watch Hollywood movies they would inevitably fill their time with something more truly "political"?

And just who is defining what counts as political?

Questions like these — and especially this re-fusal to condescend to spectators, readers, and other consumers of popular culture — are what distinguish cultural studies from other approaches to the study of popular culture. Cultural studies scholars take popular

> Popular film may be one of the sources that people draw on for comfort, inspiration, and self-understanding, though in itself the act of watching film will never change the world.

culture very seriously, but at the same time they resist romanticizing it, or crediting it with more liberatory potential than it could possibly possess. Popular film, for example, is an important element in the leisure activities of many people, and it may be one of the sources that people draw on for comfort, inspiration, and self-understanding as they conduct their social and political lives, though in itself the act of watching film will never change the world. This approach is very different from both liberal and conservative views, which regard popular culture as completely irrelevant to political practice or warn against it as dangerous.

What we need to recognize from this particular analysis of how spectators respond to Hollywood film is that forms of resistance to capitalist patriarchy are indeed possible, no matter how limited in scope or temporary in duration. If this local, limited ambivalence can be detected in responses to conservative cultural products such as the woman's film, we can only ask, and wonder: in what other surprising situations is the complex dance of pleasure, power and resistance taking place?

GLOSSARY OF KEY TERMS

Cultural studies: The interdisciplinary study of contemporary culture that examines cultural products (books, comics, films, music videos, for example) and cultural activities (playing hockey, dating, going on spring break, for example) in several contexts. Cultural studies looks at how these products or activities are created by economic and historical forces, and also at how they are experienced and understood by those who use them or engage in them.

Culture industry: Negative term for corporations that mass-produce entertainment products; for Adorno and Horkheimer, the culture industry is a sign of capitalist totalitarianism.

Cultural populism: The celebration of commercial culture as the place where subordinate social groups engage with cultural products and remake them to suit their own needs and interests.

Cultural negotiation: Term for the give-and-take relationship existing between individuals and the cultural products or practices they interact with.

Melodrama: Originally a play with music; now used to describe any over-the-top story,

93

play, or film that typically features scenes of intense emotion, overacting, and unrealistic plots, as in many soap operas.

The woman's film: A subcategory of film melodrama made for women audiences that centred on a female protagonist's domestic trials and tribulations, infamous for its emotional manipulation.

Ethnography: In anthropology, the observation of a particular group over an extended period of time; in cultural studies research, the analysis of group or individual responses to cultural products or practices.

QUESTIONS FOR DISCUSSION

1. What distinguishes a cultural studies approach from other ways of regarding popular culture?
2. What is it about the "woman's film" that these viewers find so valuable?
3. How does this chapter try to explain the paradox of pleasurable weeping that some of these viewers report? Can you think of explanations for this phenomenon that are not mentioned here?
4. Were you surprised at any of the responses reported in this chapter? Which ones, and why?
5. Do you know of other cultural activities or leisure pastimes (such as skateboarding) that have been unfairly criticized as either wasteful or dangerously influential and might also be analyzed in a similar fashion?

WEBSITES OF INTEREST

Images: A Journal of Film and Popular Culture. <www.imagesjournal.com>.
Cultural Studies Central. <www.culturalstudies.net>.
Communications, Cultural and Media Studies. <www.cultsock.ndirect.co.uk>.
Sarah Zupko's Cultural Studies Centre. <www.popcultures.com>.

NOTES

* I gratefully acknowledge the support of the University of Manitoba Centre on Aging for the fellowship award that enabled me to carry out research for this chapter. Thanks also to the anonymous reviewer as well as to Wayne Antony and Les Samuelson for their helpful comments on an earlier version of this chapter.
1. The view of mass culture as powerfully manipulative can be found in works by Richard Hoggart (1957), by Theodor Adorno and Max Horkheimer of the Frankfurt school (Adorno and Horkheimer 1972) and to a certain extent in the early work of the Birmingham Centre for Contemporary Cultural Studies established in England in the 1960s (During 1994: 4). According to this view Hollywood, for example, was a "culture monopoly" whose commercial film products "stunt" the viewer's capacity for "imagination and spontaneity" (Adorno and Horkheimer 1972). The other side of this debate, to be found in work by

Raymond Williams, Stanley Aronowitz, Frederic Jameson, and Noam Chomsky, and in left journals such as *Jump Cut* and *TABLOID*, sought recognition that audiences of popular culture were more than passive receptors of capitalist ideology.

2. Book-length studies by Doane (1987), Byars (1991), Klinger (1994), Cavell (1996), and Basinger (1993), as well as collections of essays on melodrama (Gledhill 1987; Bratton, Cook, and Gledhill (1994), and articles on the woman's film by Kaplan (1983), Butler (1990), Jacobs (1993), and Leibowitz (1996) testify to this genre's newfound importance to film scholars.

3. The most important feminist attack on film pleasure was launched with the publication of Mulvey's 1975 essay "Narrative Film and Visual Pleasure," which popularized the idea of "the gaze" and "looking relations." According to this critique, most feature-length Hollywood films are structured according to a system of "looks": that of the camera, of a male character in the film, and of the spectator in the audience (who is assumed to be male and heterosexual). Mulvey's argument is that all three of these looks construct a set of "looking relations" that are gendered as masculine, and that subject the woman onscreen to the sadistic power of the gaze. Her conclusion is that to restore gender equality to film, viewer pleasure needs to be destroyed by replacing conventional mainstream film with avant-garde film.

Chapter Four

CONSTRUCTING SEXUAL PROBLEMS
"These Things May Lead to the Tragedy of Our Species"

Gary Kinsman

Writing in the *Canadian Journal of Medicine and Surgery* in 1898, Ezra Hurlburt Stafford defined female prostitution and male same-gender sex ("homosexuality" was not yet mentioned) as "perversions." "These things may lead to the tragedy of our species," he stated. In Canadian medical and psychiatric circles Stafford popularized the work of the Italian criminal anthropologist Cesare Lombroso and the German forensic psychiatrist Dr. Richard von Krafft-Ebing (a "founding father" of sexual science). Lombroso and Krafft-Ebing were in the vanguard of the movement to classify certain types of sexuality as abnormal and perverse.

Stafford's paper contributed to the construction of prostitution and male same-gender sexuality as social problems in a specific historical and social context. These "perversions" were linked as part of an "insidious process of degeneration which is taking place in the inmost structure of modern civilization." In the late nineteenth century in Canada prostitution and "homosexuality" were defined increasingly as "social problems" in medical, psychiatric, legal, and governmental practice. This association of prostitution and "ho-

"You Should Know This"
- The Kinsey Report of 1948 finds that 50 percent of the white males report erotic response to other males, and that 37 percent of men admit at least one homosexual experience to the point of orgasm.
- The Hutt Decision (1978) requires that prostitution had to be "pressing and persistent" in order to be a criminal offence, striking down vagrancy as a major provision used against prostitutes. In 1985, "communication for the purposes of prostitution" is added to the Canadian Criminal Code.
- In 1965, Everett George Klippert is sentenced to indefinite detention as a "dangerous sexual offender" for participation in consensual sexual activities with other males. In 1967, the Supreme Court upholds the sentencing.
- In the 1960s the Canadian government tries to develop a "fruit machine" to "scientifically" identify gay men and lesbians so they could be purged from and denied jobs in the public service and military. It is a pupillary response test using same and different sex semi-naked images.
- Within the psychiatric profession it is common practice until the early 1970s to try to "cure" gay men and lesbians with aversion and electro-shock "therapy."
- In 1988 the age of consent for "anal sex" is lowered to eighteen for two individuals in private. "Gross indecency" is abolished as an offence and the age of consent for sexual activity other than anal sex becomes fourteen in general unless involving people in positions of "trust and responsibility."
- Representations of same-gender sex are still considered under the law, policing practices, and forms of social censorship to be more "obscene" than similar heterosexual portrayals. This is one of the reasons why you never see explicit same-gender sex (especially between men) on mainstream TV.

mosexuality" in the construction of sexual problems continues today in some circles.

How is it that sexual relations are made into "social problems"? In our everyday lives we often experience not only the pleasures but also the dangers and contradictions of sexual activities and relationships (Vance 1984). But this personal experience is not usually about the social generation of "sexual problems." We might experience problems in sexual practice or relationships that lead us to talk to friends and search out sexual advice literature. We might go to therapists (if we are middle class), or be tempted to use Viagra and other drugs to enhance our sexual "performance." If we are women who are raped or battered, we might contact a rape crisis centre, a battered women's shelter, or the police. But the "social problem" frameworks — such as "homosexuals are a major social danger" or "street prostitutes are a big social problem" — tend to be located somewhere else, outside our everyday lives. Most often they pop up in mass media coverage and the official discourse of the law, police work, government commissions, and parliamentary debates — in what are the authorized social languages and ways of naming and defining social problems.

> The knowledges produced by professional sexual experts are not neutral, value-free, or simply "objective."

These "sexual problem" frameworks are constructed in power/knowledge relations — in connections between state agencies, professional groups, and the mass media.[1] The frameworks are part of the social organization of knowledge. The knowledges produced by professional sexual experts are not neutral, value-free, or simply "objective." They embody specific social positions and social standpoints. This knowledge has clear class, gender, race, and sexual dimensions.

The official sexual "problems" are indeed often not problems for people outside the ruling relations of state agencies and professional groups.[2] The world looks very different to a gay man, or a female prostitute, than it does to the police officer arresting them for a "criminal" sexual offence. To the gay man, his

> The world looks very different to a gay man, or a female prostitute, than it does to the police officer arresting them for a "criminal" sexual offence.

sexual encounter, or to the prostitute, her work, is not the "crime" that it becomes in sexual policing. There is a real rupture in experience between the everyday lives and experiences of gay men and prostitutes and the language of sexual regulation that criminalizes them and their activities. We must, then, always ask: Who is defining sexual problems? Who is being defined? Who are the definers silencing or opposing? We need, especially, to investigate where the definitions have historically and socially come from. If we can grasp where they have come from, and how they have been put in place, we can act to challenge and transform them.

THE EMERGENCE OF "SEXUAL PROBLEMS"

There was not always a distinct realm of "sexual" problems. Sexuality was not always distinguished as a separate area of social concern, and erotic relationships were often subject to other forms of ethical, community, and church regulations (Foucault 1980a, 1980b, 1985, 1988). Particular historical and social conditions were required before sexuality could emerge as a distinct realm of discourse (or social language) and regulation.

The specific demarcation of the "sexual" occurred as part of a protracted social process that accelerated in the nineteenth century. Sexuality began to appear as an area distinct from gender relations and the social relations of biological reproduction — as a distinct and essential human instinct or drive. Its emergence was rooted in the new industrial capitalist societies, which organized profound transformations in family, generational, class, and erotic relations (Kinsman 1996a: 48–81). Capitalism continually transforms social relations and generates crises for some people. State and professional agencies attempt to manage these broad social changes by regulating sexual activities and cultures. By the nineteenth century new "social problems" had appeared in the expanding urban centres. This led to the growth of new social sciences and professions such as sociology and eventually sexology — the science of sexuality (Weir 1986; Bland and Doan 1998a, 1998b). New disciplines emerged to study and classify these "problems" in capitalist urban settings and to suggest solutions to authorities.

In these social conditions sexuality became an area for the production of "scientific" knowledge and "truth" in the hands, especially, of "professional" researchers and "experts." The power of the knowledge produced rested on the claim to objectivity, which, in turn, rested on two particular approaches to the subject matter. First, those engaged in particular sexual practices — in this case gay men, lesbians, and prostitutes — were rarely involved in producing knowledge about their own experiences. Second, the professional experts tended to ignore their own social positions of privilege and power over those very people about whom they compile "facts." These approaches ignore the social standpoints and power relationships involved in producing knowledge. As such they are characteristic of ruling forms of knowledge in society in general (D. Smith 1987: 71–78, 1990a, 1999, 2005).

Sexuality, then, became a terrain for medicalization by professional groups: the new medical, psychiatric, and scientific professions became the new definers of sexual "identities" and "norms" in a shift away from previous religious and local community forms of regulation. Of course, religious regulations did not disappear — far from it. Religious definitions of social norms conditioned and shaped how the new secular "scientific" knowledge emerged and also reappeared as an organizing ideology for moral conservatives.

In his 1846 book *Psychopathia Sexualis* Heinrich Kaan demarcated a specific sexual instinct, which then became an object to be categorized and managed. Various "irregular" forms of sexual behaviour were studied and classified. The sexual sciences established themselves as a regime of sexual categories and definitions composed of forensic psychiatry with its relation to the courts and police, sex psychology, and later sexology. Sexuality became an especially problematic terrain (Weir 1986; Foucault 1980a; Bland and Doan 1998a, 1998b). The sexual sciences investigated and labelled the "sexual perversions," separating them from acceptable behaviour, before returning to outline in more detail the norm of male-dominated heterosexuality itself. Sexual scientists classified sex between men and between women as a "gender inversion" (for men a female soul or personality trapped in a male body, for women a male personality trapped in a female body) or a "perversion." They used the knowledge they produced to justify new criminal, social, psychiatric, and psychological penalties against such practices and the people who engaged in them.

This sexual science had a specific, gendered character. It was linked to the social organization of a male-dominated, two-gender binary "opposite-sex" way of socially accomplishing gender (Kessler and McKenna 1978) with associated male/female sexual characteristics. This way of doing gender participates in the oppression not only of those who would come to be called and to name themselves as lesbians and gay men but also of transsexuals, transgender, and intersexed people (Kessler and McKenna 1978; Kessler 1998; Namaste 2000) and of women more generally.

In the nineteenth century white middle-class women came to be increasingly defined (and to define themselves) as "passionless," as lacking in any active erotic desire. Working-class, Black, and other women of colour came to be seen as being more sexually available to elite and middle-class men — although at the same time women who expressed an active interest in sexuality or women who sold sex for money were defined as "social problems" (Kinsman 1996a: 59–60; Walkowitz 1980a).

This social process included the construction of racism. During the nineteenth and into the twentieth centuries, dominant discourses defined whites as more sexually "respectable" and Blacks as driven by "sex" and being "promiscuous" (Valverde 1992; hooks 1992). We are still living with the legacy of this sexual racism, exemplified in how the Western media and Western white-dominated "popular" culture cover and portray AIDS among people of colour and in Africa (Watney 1988; Patton 1990:77–97; Treichler 1999; Miller 2005).

The regime of sexual sciences and disciplines that formed in the late nineteenth century carried two-sided implications for sexual experience. According to Stafford (1898), Krafft-Ebing's work (which was also called *Psychopathia Sexualis*) was the "bible of the bawdy house." On the one hand, the "perversions" are named so that they can be identified and contained. On the other, the very naming of these distinct perversions provided the opportunity for some people to develop resistance to oppressive sexual regulation. A number of the early sex scientists were also sex reformers of one persuasion or another. They created possibilities for categories like homosexual or lesbian to be taken up as a basis for opposition; but they also participated in constructing oppressive sexual norms that were used to police sexual life.

The development of these sexual sciences, then, was contradictory and uneven. Capitalist development not only opened up new work spaces, public spaces, and personal social spaces, but also regulated these spaces and closed off others (D'Emilio 1983; Kinsman 1996a: 48–53, 2004a). Regardless of the intentions of early sex researchers, their work became part of an oppressive regime of sexual regulation. Scientific sex knowledge was and is used to mandate police action, to assist parliaments, judges, and courts in the formation of Criminal Code offences, and to help organize psychiatric, medical, media, and social practices for dealing with sexual "problems." The categorization of different sexual "types," "deviations," "perversions," and norms was entered into administrative regulations, mandating action for the containment of sex "deviants." This process has been a crucial part of making these groups into "social problems." This work is grounded in specific institutions whether they be forensic psychiatry, asylums, prisons, the courts, the police, social work, or government discussions. There is no free-floating "sexology" outside these institutional settings (see Weeks 1985, 1986; Kinsman 1989, 1996a: 30–34, 58–59).

The work of sexual science also shapes the ideological[3] categories and knowledge used in mass media coverage and enters into "popular culture." Through what Dorothy Smith describes as an "ideological circle," the media and popular culture rely on the knowledge of official and bureaucratic agencies as the only means of interpreting particular social issues (Smith 1974, 1983, 1990a, 1990b, 1999). This phenomenon is a crucial part of how prostitutes, homosexuals, and other sexually "deviant" groups are socially made into individual and collective "problems." Dominant attitudes towards these groups are not simply based on prejudiced, bigoted, backward, or uninformed ideas, but are the results of active organizing by professionals, state agencies, the mass media, and moral conservative groups, all of which lead to laws and policies that criminalize or problematize sexual "deviance."

SEXUAL REGULATION

Sexual regulation is the complex of relations of the various institutions and practices that define and manage our sexual lives. Sexual regulation in some form exists in all societies. All societies have to make collective ethical decisions regarding erotic activity. The question becomes how to move away from the oppressive forms we now experience and towards non-oppressive forms of sexual regulation.

> Sexual regulation ranges from the law and police activity to social and family policies, the school system, the mass media, the church, sexual advice literature, the medical and psychiatric professions, and peer group pressures.

The practices of sexual regulation range from the law and police activity to social and family policies, the school system, the mass media, the church, sexual advice literature, the medical and psychiatric professions, peer group pressures, and many others. My focus here is on sexual regulation centred in state relations — with the state being not a "thing," but a social relation, a process of organizing consent, legitimacy, exploitation, and repression (Corrigan and Sayer 1985: 1–13; Holloway 2002). These relations are part of a broader network combining state and professional relations with corporate relations to make up the social organization of ruling (D. Smith 1987: 3, 67, 1999: 73–95, 2005).

The practices are also part of a broader shift from local communities and the church to more "trans-local" forms of social regulation. Social regulation is more and more the combined work of several state and professional bureaucracies and agencies. These bureaucracies co-ordinate their work (though not always successfully) on the basis of written and textual policies that mandate courses of action or proper procedures for dealing with "sexual problems" (Smith 1990a, 1990b, 1999, 2005). For instance, the policing and criminalization of sex between men have been organized through the Criminal Code. Using offences such as "gross indecency," "buggery," "anal sex," and "acts of indecency/indecent act," the Criminal Code has mandated police and legal action against sexual activities between men.[4] Thus, police, lawyers, court officials, and judges co-ordinating their activities through the text of the Criminal Code organize the criminalization of male homosexual activity (G. Smith 1988, 2006; Kinsman 1995b).

Sexual regulation does not simply take place through the criminal law. Lesbian activities and cultures, for instance, are not regulated as much by the criminalization of sexual activities as they are by the social, family, corporate, and professional policies that deny social, economic, and sexual autonomy to women (Stone 1990; Khayatt 1992; Ross 1995). Lesbians, who are less visible than gay men, are also oppressed through the dominant images of femininity in the mainstream media, in the advertising and fashion industries, and within a "popular" culture that still largely excludes them (D. Smith 1990c; Hennessy 2000: 175–202). Today when lesbians are represented in popular culture it is often in a very "de-dyked" fashion through the imagery of "lesbian chic" (Giese 1994). For instance, in 1997, after Ellen DeGeneres finally came out on her sitcom *Ellen*, she was subsequently never shown as having a significant sexual relationship with another woman. The show was cancelled a year or so later. While the "L word" is available to a more select audience on cable and has greater diversity in terms of its lesbian representations, lesbians are portrayed as largely stylish, middle class, and into consumer capitalism (Sycamore 2004). We need to always ask, who controls and defines these images? Why are only images of respectable middle-class lesbians who don't directly challenge gender relations acceptable?

The sphere of gay men has also seen a shift towards increased visibility for certain types of representations.[5] While greater visibility for gay men and lesbians in popular culture is a reflection of the expansion and growth of gay/lesbian communities and movements, we also have to be critical of the forms of representation that have been developed. In *Will and Grace* (1998–2006), Will was portrayed throughout most of the program's run as existing without a significant male partner, and when he did have one it was never in a very sexually explicit fashion. The program often portrayed Grace in a sexist fashion, and in general gay men were portrayed as white and aspiring to be middle class and highly fashion-conscious and commercialized.

This form of representation has been carried further in *Queer Eye for the Straight Guy* (now just called *Queer Eye*), which has advertising content that seems to be mostly directed to heterosexual-identified women. In this show, at least initially, fashion-conscious and very commercialized gay men are mobilized to try to improve the appearance and commercialized fashion-consciousness of heterosexual-identified

Queer Nation activists in the early 1990s used to chant at demonstrations against anti-queer bigotry that "We're here, we're queer, and we're not going shopping."

men. These gay men are enlisted to save heterosexuality through imparting to the heterosexual-identified men a fashion and commercialized consciousness that will make them more attractive to heterosexual women. Gay men are called upon to modernize this new hetero-masculinity. In part, this is also part of the extension of consumer capitalist relations to men's personal care and fashion in a more extensive way than ever before. This representation of gay men as largely white and middle class, and as being attuned to fashion trends and consumer capitalism, exists not only in the mainstream mass media and popular culture but also in much of the gay media. As such, it operates to cut out or marginalize non-white, poor, and working-class queers, and often trans-people and young queers, who are not able to participate in these worlds of commodities and commercialization in the same way as in this construction of "gay" and "queer" (Sycamore 2004). In response to this worship of commodities, Queer Nation activists in the early 1990s used to chant at demonstrations against anti-queer bigotry that "We're here, we're queer, and we're not going shopping."

In sexual regulation (as in other matters), state relations, which continue to be key, are dominated by a particular class, gender, and race: white, capitalist, and middle-class men. This same group dominates various professions, including medicine, psychiatry, criminology, sociology, and the mass media, which interconnect with state organizations to regulate sexuality and the social world. At the same time, through a limited focus on "diversity" and "multiculturalism,"[6] openings in the elite have been created for some women, some people of colour, and some lesbians and gay men based on feminist, anti-racist, and queer struggles. The knowledge produced by the professions and academic disciplines is a vital part of ruling relations.

Professional and state agencies share, among other similarities, an administrative or managerial standpoint. The goal is to regulate sexual activity, which they assume is problematic, and together these interconnected groups produce the concepts or language used for the regulation of sexuality. For instance, through the Criminal Code the police can transform consensual sexual activity between two men, or involving the exchange of money, into a legal offence. In the distinction between "public" and "private," for instance, if two people engage in an activity behind closed bedroom doors it is not a crime; but if that same activity takes place in a situation of intimacy in a legally defined "public" place (like a park), it is a criminal offence (Kinsman 1989: 315–480, 1996a: 264–78, 397–98; G. Smith 1988). In late 2005 a Supreme Court decision regarding "swingers" sex clubs in Montreal modified the interpretation of "indecency" under the Criminal Code to focus on the question of "harm." The decision argued that if these actions were consensual, took place in a "private" club, and were not causing any "harm" to people, then they should not be crimes under the Criminal Code (Crossman 2006). It is not clear whether this ruling will extend to cover sex between men in bars or bathhouses, given the greater "indecency" constructed legally and socially around same-gender erotic acts, and the decision certainly will not cover consensual erotic acts in a park, which remains defined legally as a "public" place.

Contemporary practices of sexual and moral regulation set up a contradictory situation for gay men and lesbians. On the one hand the development of neo-liberalism and capitalist globalization (Sears 1999, 2003; McNally 2002) has shifted and weakened the centrality of the heterosexual family in the social organization of capitalist relations, leading to a lessening of the moral regulation of some sex-related questions; the expansion of consumer capitalism into new areas has also opened up space for the construction of a gay or "pink market" (Sears 1999, 2000; Maynard 1994; Kinsman 1996a: 295–302). On the other hand, despite major gains in human rights, there are still profound forms of heterosexist discrimination and bigotry against queers rooted in state formation, the Criminal Code, social policy, popular culture, and moral conservative organizing (Kinsman 1996a). While queers (especially white middle-class gay men) are tolerated in certain areas, criminalization and censorship of our consensual sexualities continue, and hatred is continually mobilized against queers, including manifestations of heterosexist violence (Janoff 2005) and the ideologies of "fag" and "dyke" that continue to be pervasive in many high schools (Khayatt 1995; G. Smith 1998).

Coupled with these contradictions, the oppressive sexual regulation of our lives is not automatic or self-generating. These practices are actively accomplished and fought for by people in state and professional agencies, in the popular culture industries and elsewhere — people who also face resistance from gay men, lesbians, prostitutes, and many others. They are therefore always open to subversion and transformation.

Sexual regulation is an integral part of the hegemonic rule of white, heterosexual-identified, middle-class men within capitalist, patriarchal society. Hegemony, the term of analysis developed by Antonio Gramsci (1971), combines force and coercion with legitimacy and consent in the social organization of ruling.[7] Gramsci argued that the power of the capitalist class does not rest solely on the use of various forms of repression or in its direct control of the means of production (offices and factories). The hegemonic rule of the capitalists requires the consent or at least acquiescence of the working class and other subordinated groups, a consent that must be actively won and maintained. Subordinated social groups must feel that the existing relations of power are "legitimate." Moreover, this consent must extend beyond the legitimacy of capitalist control of the means of production and work to broader social practices. The emergence of this hegemonic rule has generated a series of "common sense," "respectable," "responsible," and "proper" attitudes to sexuality — sexual practices that, again, are bound up with class, gender, race, and state relations.

Developing sexual "norms" were both forced upon and taken up by the working class and poor in what Michel Foucault describes as the "moralization of the poorer classes" (Foucault 1980a: 122). This was a major part of the bourgeois "cultural revolution" of the last few centuries (Corrigan and Sayer 1985). Class struggles were not only fought in factories, but also fought over gender, sexual, racial, state, and moral relations. Sexuality came to play an important part in state policies, providing access both to the life of the species and the life of the individual (Foucault 1980a). The emergence of the "problem" of sexuality was grounded in the new politics of population, which was centrally concerned with sexual and reproductive life as the population became a resource and form of power to be harnessed by governments and professions. Consent to bourgeois norms was resisted, negotiated, and accepted by the male-dominated organizations of the working class, which eventually took up notions of sexual "respectability," thus excluding homosexuals, prostitutes, and others from "respectable" working-class culture (Walkowitz 1980a, 1992). This makeover was a central part of the construction of patriarchal (or male-dominated) relations.

An important aspect of these class, gender, and social struggles was the social purity movement in a number of countries in the late nineteenth and early twentieth centuries. Examining the English experience, Judith Walkowitz (1980b: 130) points out:

> Social purity, which called on men to protect and control their women, served as the ideological corollary of the family wage (where the "family" wage was paid to the male "breadwinner"), morally legitimating the prerogatives of patriarchy inside and outside the family. Thus social purity served to undermine working-class solidarity, while tightening definitions of gender among respectable working men and working women.

Notions of "social purity" and "sexual respectability" played important roles in uniting the middle class and the "respectable" working class against aristocratic "decadence," lust, and selfishness, and at the same time against the "pariah" sexual practices of the outcast poor, including casual forms of prostitution and same-gender sexualities. The idea of "respectability," then, helped to establish a broad social bloc of different class, gender, and social groups under the hegemony of moral conservative political and religious forces. This social bloc played an important role in shaping state and social policy and the regime of sexual regulation (Kinsman 1996a: 59–60, 114–20; Valverde 1991).

HETEROSEXUAL HEGEMONY

A key and integral aspect of sexual regulation in our society is heterosexual hegemony — the practices that make heterosexuality "normal," "natural," and "healthy" while making homosexuality/lesbianism sick, abnormal, deviant, and dangerous (Kinsman 1996a: 23–40; Frank 1987). Heterosexual hegemony necessarily involves lesbian/gay subordination. As Rachel Harrison and Frank Mort (1980: 106) note, in reference to much of the scientific "work" on homosexuality and lesbianism: "The 'deviant' subject is not absent from the discourse but she/he is only permitted to speak from a subordinate position: as 'patient,' as 'pervert' etc." Similar remarks could be made about the experiences of prostitutes, people living with AIDS and HIV infection (PLWA/HIVs), and other groups defined in ruling discourses as having "sexual problems."

Canadian state formation established heterosexual hegemony in the Criminal Code and in the assumptions built into social and family policies and popular culture that institutionalize and privilege a particular form of heterosexuality as the social norm. For example, in 1892 the offence of "gross indecency," which could only be applied to acts between men, was added to the Canadian Criminal Code. This offence served to criminalize and to specify homosexual practices, mandating the police to arrest men for having sex with each other (Kinsman 1996a: 128–33, 243–47).

In various ways, then, certain forms of "deviant" consensual sex are policed and denied, while other "normal" non-consensual sexual and gender relations that can include violence, coercion, and harassment are often ignored. Regulation often focuses on "deviant" or unorthodox sex such as homosexuality and prostitution. Official discourse constructs these as the "sexual problems."

In the 1950s in Canada homosexuals could be defined as "criminal sexual psychopaths" in the Criminal Code and therefore as a sexual danger to "society." Constructing homosexuality as a "national" and "social" as well as a "sexual" danger took place within a broader right-wing political project during those years. Lesbians and gay men were purged from the military as "sex deviates" and from the civil service as "national security risks" (Robinson and Kimmel 1994; Kinsman 1995a, 1996a: 171–83, 2000, 2003a, 2004b; Kinsman and Gentile 1998; Jackson 2004). Lesbians and gay men were prohibited from immigrating to Canada. In the 1960s the Canadian national security regime developed a "fruit machine" to detect gay men and lesbians so that they could be rejected as applicants for, or could be purged from, government service (Kinsman 1995a, 1996a: 177–81; Kinsman and Gentile 1998: 106–16).

During Second World War mobilizations, sex/gender relations had been disrupted as many women entered the wage labour force, child-care centres were established, and many men and women found themselves far from their families and thus able to explore their same-gender sexual desires (Berube 1990; Kinsman 1996a: 148–57; Jackson 2004). After the war there was a reconstruction of patriarchal and heterosexual hegemonies. Extending criminalization and social sanctions against homosexuality worked to re-establish these hegemonies by constructing sexual danger as being in the "public" realm and associated with "deviant" sex such as homosexuality, and not in the "private" realm of the "normal" patriarchal family, where most sexual violence was taking place (Kinsman 1989: 55–307, 1993b, 1996a: 183–200; Freedman 1987).

Government commissions have since transformed feminist concerns over sexual violence against women and children into proposals for new strategies of oppressive sexual regulation. The 1984 federal Badgley Commission (Canada 1984) report on sexual offences against children and young people grouped together a series of consensual and unconsensual activities, labelling them all as "sexual abuse." It also avoided the social roots of sexual violence and harassment against young people. In the end grassroots feminist concerns tend to disappear. New forms of regulation do not get at the root of the problem in patriarchal social relations and the social construction of hegemonic masculinity, which associates masculinity with violence and aggression towards women (Brock and Kinsman 1986; Walker 1990).[8]

In another context, "child sexual abuse" has been transformed in significant ways into a problem of "deviant" homosexual sex. In Newfoundland the 1989/90 royal commission inquiry into why the police did not prosecute Christian Brothers for physical and sexual assaults on boys in the 1970s (the Hughes Commission), along with media coverage, associated "child sexual abuse" with "deviant" homosexual sex (Kinsman 1992a, 1993). One of the central pieces of police evidence that the commission relied on was the 1975 police report "Child Abuse and Homosexual Acts at Mount Cashel Orphanage," which the authorities suppressed. Rather than exploring the social and institutional power relations that led to the harassment of these boys and young men, the commission often focused on homosexuality as the problem.

Out of this commission work and media coverage emerged a new "framing" of "child sexual abuse" that views it as largely affecting boys, as often being "homosexual" in character, and as occurring in institutional contexts like orphanages, training schools, and sometimes day-care centres rather than in family contexts. The award-winning film *The Boys of St. Vincent* (National Film Board and Tele-Action 1992) also accomplishes this transformation. In 1997 the mass media turned their focus on hockey coaches (for a particular anti-gay framing of this, see Sillars 1997) and on Maple Leaf Gardens in Toronto as a site of "sexual abuse." These cases have served to obscure the gendered character of sexual violence and harassment, which still most often take place in the private, family realm against girls and young women. They also shift attention away from the pervasive physical abuse and corporal punishment that was, for instance, part of the disciplinarian regime at Mount Cashel orphanage, and moves the focus towards the "sexualization" of abuse.

The new context is remobilizing elements from earlier campaigns that associated sexual danger with "deviant" men outside the family realm. In the accounts of the horrific cultural, physical, and sexual harassment that many young First Nations people faced in the residential school system, which was part of a racist attempt to "assimilate" them to "white" culture, there has also been a tendency to reduce the issue to problems of "sexual abuse," which makes the broader racist context disappear.

Often media coverage regarding "child sexual abuse" now focuses on the problem as a matter of "pedophiles," often referring to this term as if it were itself a criminal classification. Instead, pedophilia is a sexological and psychological classification of a "deviant" erotic interest in prepubescent young people, even though in relation to males it is often used to cover sexual activities involving postpubescent adolescents (Kinsman: 1996a: 192–200). The portrayal of "pedophiles" as individual deviants who are often coded as "homosexual" locates sexual danger for young people as again coming from "deviant" men who are strangers, and it constructs the site of the abuse as being outside the familial "private" realm. This approach avoids the very real sexual dangers that exist for young people in families, from fathers, brothers, and other relatives. It also avoids the social and gendered processes that organize sexual violence against young people and the aggressive masculine sexualities that are in some ways rooted in the social relations of "normality" and not "deviancy." Instead this conceptualization locates the problem as one of "sexual deviancy."

Meanwhile the danger is often much closer to home. The very concept of "sexual abuse" tends to collect together and confuse various sex-related activities, ranging from sexual assaults to consensual sexual activities (see Brock and Kinsman 1986; Brock 1991;

Kinsman 1992a, 1993a). In this sense "sexual abuse" has the features of an administrative "collecting category" in a similar fashion to "deviance."[9] Statistics vary, but most studies indicate that 80 to 90 percent or more of sexual harassment and assault of children and young people are inflicted by men upon girls and young women. Most cases occur within family and domestic settings and involve someone whom the young person knows.[10]

In June 2006 the new federal Conservative (minority) government tabled a bill as one of its first Criminal Code initiatives to raise the basic age of consent for sexual activity from fourteen to sixteen (Weber 2006; Bailey 2006). At the same time it was not proposing to lower the higher age of consent for "anal sex" (often identified as a homosexual sexual act) from eighteen. The government argued that raising the basic age of consent would "protect" young people from "sexual abuse." In contrast the new law would make it even more difficult to do safe-sex and sexuality education with young people — making it difficult for young people to get the sexual knowledge they need. It could also lead to the criminalization of young people for engaging in consensual sexual activity with other people despite the inclusion of a "near-age exemption" that will allow fourteen- and fifteen-year-olds to engage in sexual activity with a partner who is less than five years older than them (Kirkby 2006; Kirkby and Rau 2006; Black 2006). There are major problems with "protective legislation" that constructs incapacities among those who are supposedly being protected. This raising of the age of consent will do little to get at the social roots of adult sexual violence and harassment against young people, which are located in familial and patriarchal relations and in the social organization of hegemonic masculine sexualities.

Sexual-orientation protection providing limited human rights protection for lesbians and gay men has now been enacted across all Canadian provinces and territories. In Alberta this change only occurred in 1998 because of a Supreme Court decision in the case of Delwin Vriend, a teacher at a private college who was fired because he was gay. Sexual orientation was finally enacted at the federal level in 1996 through the struggles of lesbians, gay men, feminists, unionists, and human rights supporters. But sexual orientation has not provided for full social equality for lesbians and gay men. Human rights protection is an important but also very limited form of protection, and violence and discrimination against lesbians and gay men continues.[11]

After winning basic human rights protection, many lesbian and gay activists, and supportive lawyers, found that this victory did not end the oppression of, or establish the social equality of, lesbians and gay men. In this context lesbians and gay men in many jurisdictions began to fight for the same spousal and family recognition rights granted to heterosexual common-law couples, a battle that required challenging legal and social policy definitions of "spouse" and "family" as exclusively heterosexual in character. In most jurisdictions the law denied lesbians and gay men the right to adopt and even the right to visit their partners in the hospital. A series of social and legal battles challenged these exclusions.

In 1994 the Ontario legislature debated Bill 167, a wide-ranging piece of legislation that would have granted formal equality with common-law heterosexual relationships to lesbian and gay spousal and family relationships in many areas. An opposition of moral conservatives, the Tories, most of the Liberals, and a number of New Democrats defeated the bill in a "free vote" (Kinsman 1996a: 313–16, 1996b: 401–3; Nicol 1995). Successful struggles for adoption rights for same-sex couples took place in a number of provinces in the 1990s.[12] While many lesbian and gay activists affirm that "We Are Family!" moral conservative groups have mobilized to defend the heterosexual character of spouse, family, and marriage.

In spring 1999 the Supreme Court of Canada handed down a landmark decision in the *M v. H* spousal support case. After her relationship with H. ended, M. attempted to seek support under the Ontario *Family Law Act*. She was denied the right to do so due to the exclusively heterosexual definition of "spouse" in the Act. The Supreme Court found, in an 8–1 judgment, that the Ontario *Family Law Act* violates the rights of lesbians and gay men by defining "spouse" as someone only of the "opposite sex." The decision made it clear that governments could not continue to deny spousal rights to same-gender couples (Barnholden 1999). In response the Ontario Conservative government reluctantly passed Bill 5, which amended Ontario statutes to include same-gender partners, granting them the same rights as common-law heterosexual spouses in a number of areas — but, significantly, without defining same-gender partners as spouses or as members of families. While the changes were an important step forward in the battle for spousal benefits and family recognition rights, many lesbian and gay activists were critical of the legislation for establishing lesbian and gay couples as separate from heterosexual spousal and family relations (T. Warner 1999).

In June 2000 the federal government finally passed legislation ensuring a series of same-gender spousal rights. At the same time the legislation added a definition of marriage that defined marriage as being only heterosexual in character — "the union of one man and one woman to the exclusion of all others." What was supposed to be an affirmation of lesbian and gay rights became legislation setting limits on these rights.

> Some activists also believe that simply affirming "we are family" divides "normalized' lesbians and gay men from "irresponsible" lesbians and gays.

While there is support for equality with heterosexuals in regards to spousal, family recognition rights, and marriage, important discussions have also taken place among lesbian, gay, and feminist activists over how to fight for recognition and support for lesbian and gay relationships and how to provide social support for relationships outside institutionalized heterosexuality. Existing forms of spousal benefits do little to redistribute income and resources to those who most need them, and they allocate benefits on the basis of what type of relationship it is (and what type of plan a partner has at work) rather than on the basis of need. The benefits are also generally only available to a limited stratum of the population – with no benefit to people living in poverty. Some activists also believe that simply affirming "we are family" — just like "respectable" and "responsible" heterosexual families — allows for "responsible" lesbian and gay couples to be "normalized" — to be just like, or almost like, heterosexual families. The tendency divides these "normalized" lesbians and gay men from "irresponsible" lesbians and gays who make no such claims to spousal or family status (Kinsman 1996a: 311–16, 398–99, 1996b: 401–405). Rather than trying to invent and develop new, more egalitarian and liberatory social ways of living, this strategy leads to demands for simple integration into and acceptance of existing, often oppressive, social forms.

MARRIAGE STRUGGLES: IS THERE SEX AFTER MARRIAGE?

The struggles over the right to same-gender marriage intensify these problems.[13] As long as state legislation and moral conservatives deny lesbians and gay couples the right to marry, that denial represents a social practice of discrimination, and lesbians and gay men need to work to secure this right. At the same time, privileging marriage in state policy over and above all the other relationships people live in and with is also a social practice of discrimination (Kinsman 2003c; Law Commission of Canada 2001; Warner 2004).

The focus on marriage and becoming part of "normality" can also shift attention away from the continuing and vital erotic dimensions of the lesbian and gay liberation struggles (Sears 2005). This shift is a major problem, because sexual oppression remains the central material

> Denying lesbians and gay couples the right to marry is discrimination... privileging marriage above all the other relationships people live in and with is also discrimination.

and social basis of queer oppression. Even more disturbingly, some mainstream lesbian and gay rights supporters have often come to see the securing of lesbian and gay marriage as the end point of our struggle, as *the* way of establishing integration and securing "respectability" in society. It is as if when this right is won, all the other forms of hatred and discrimination that gays and lesbians continue to face will somehow magically disappear. Some have argued that winning same-gender marriage rights will mean that the situation for young lesbians, gay men, bisexuals, and trans-persons will dramatically improve, when this has not at all been the case and when the sources of queer youth oppression have very little to do with the denial of same-gender marriage. The forms of hate, denial, and oppression that young lesbians and gay men continue to experience include the 2002 decision of the Catholic School Board in Durham County, Ontario, to deny Marc Hall the right to take his boyfriend to the school prom, a decision challenged and ultimately overturned in court (Sinopoli 2002; Wheeler 2002).

More radical lesbian and gay activists view marriage as a patriarchal institution that has historically and socially contributed to the oppression of women.[14] They argue therefore for the ending of the institutionalization of marriage as a state-sanctioned relationship that sets these relationships between people above other forms of social relationships (Kinsman 2003c). More egalitarian and democratic ways of living will necessarily take diverse forms. Asking simply to be included in the heterosexual and patriarchal institution of marriage will not accomplish queer liberation (Sears 2001,

2005; M. Warner 1999; Lehr 1999).

In using the equality rights section of the Charter, the struggle for same-sex marriage was remarkably successful, building on the gains won in earlier spousal and family recognition struggles. In 2001 the Supreme Court of British Columbia ruled that excluding same-gender couples from marriage was discrimination, but that this discrimination was "justifiable in a free and democratic society." But in the very next year, in July 2002, the Divisional Court of Ontario ruled that same-gender marriage must be allowed in that province before July 2004. In response to this and other legal and social pressures, the House of Commons Standing Committee on Justice and Human Rights began hearings on same-sex marriage in fall 2002. The hearings took place in ten cities across the Canadian state (Kinsman 2003c), and the Committee finally voted with a majority of one vote in favour of same-gender marriage. On May 1, 2003, the B.C. Court of Appeal ruled that same-sex marriage must be allowed in the province before July 2004. On June 10, 2003, as a result of the Ontario Court of Appeal's judgment, marriage was immediately established as a right for same-gender couples in the province (Lahey and Alderson 2004; Larocque 2006).

This decision, and subsequent legal decisions in British Columbia and Quebec, provoked a wave of mobilization of moral conservative forces against same-gender marriage and lesbian and gay rights more generally, with major backing from some of the major churches, especially the Roman Catholic Church. Unfortunately those groups most pushing same-gender marriage as the end point of queer struggle were often not prepared to undertake the activism and popular education necessary to respond to the moral conservative right-wing, leaving it to more radical queer groups to mobilize in response. In September 2003, by a vote of only 137 to 132, the House of Commons defeated a Canadian Alliance Party motion to reaffirm the "traditional" definition of marriage. But rather than proceeding to then introduce legislation supporting same-gender marriage, the Liberal government referred the question to the Supreme Court of Canada for a legal opinion — which continued the basic response of the Liberal government to lesbian and gay rights struggles. Rather than taking the lead in pushing forward human rights, the Liberals only move after the courts have made a clear decision, which allows them to construct lesbian and gay rights as having some sort of special troubling or "moral" character. It also means they can argue that they had no choice but to enact these rights since the courts have spoken. This position does not decisively challenge heterosexism.

On December 9, 2004, the Supreme Court confirmed that same-gender marriage, "far from violating the Charter, flows from it." On June 28, 2005, the House of Commons, by a vote of 158–133, finally passed legislation establishing that same-gender couples can get married (Larocque 2006).

Many thought the issue was finally settled. But in January 2006 the new Conservative Party was elected to a minority government position. Its campaign platform promised to hold a free vote on the definition of marriage in the House of Commons and to then introduce legislation restoring the "traditional" definition of marriage. By June

2006 it became clear that the Harper government planned to hold a vote in the House of Commons in the fall of 2006 to see if members wanted to reopen the same-gender marriage debate. In a minority government situation this approach had little likelihood of success — and in the end the motion, on December 7, 2006, was defeated by a vote of 175 to 123 — but at least it allowed the Tories to shore up their moral conservative support (along with the proposal to raise the age of consent to sixteen) and allowed for the extension of moral conservative organizing against same-sex marriage — a process that continued to stir up hatred and bigotry against lesbians and gay men. The response to this continuing moral conservative organizing requires a grassroots coalition-building approach focusing on activism and popular education.

The legal situation facing lesbians and gay men in Canada now has an ambiguous and contradictory character. Since 1985 people have been able to use section 15 of the Charter of Rights (the equality rights section) to push forward lesbian and gay legal struggles for limited formal equality with heterosexuals, while more substantive forms of social inequality have not been addressed (Herman 1994; Lahey 1999). On an abstract and individual basis our rights are recognized, but not always in the context of our actual and substantive relationships and sexualities. While we may be abstractly and formally "equal," our relationships can still be stigmatized in popular culture and social interaction, we continue to face heterosexist violence, and our sexualities are still criminalized and censored (Kinsman 1996a: 288–374). Clearly, a male-dominated form of heterosexuality is still constructed as the hegemonic form of sexuality in Canada, and when it comes to progress on lesbian and gay human rights we may have reached the end of the space opened up by section 15 with same-gender marriage rights. Further advances may require more militant struggles and alliances with other oppressed groups.

PROBLEMS OF DEVIANCY — OR JUST WHOM ARE YOU CALLING A DEVIANT?

Since the 1960s liberals within sociology and other disciplines have been advancing deviancy theory as a way of explaining what they see as "social problems." This approach is far superior to the biological determinism (reducing social relations to biological causes) of pathological approaches (Pfohl 1985: 83–130) — that "deviants" are sick or genetically backward. But it also participates in constructing a number of groups as "deviants." Indeed, at least until the last twenty years and still in some areas, the only way in which the topics of lesbianism and homosexuality, or the experiences of prostitutes, could be legitimately raised in academic circles was under the heading of "deviance" (see Adam 1986: 398–411).

Deviancy theory, in its many variants, attempts to explore how an individual comes to be labelled as deviant by social agencies and significant others, and the perspective has informed some very useful work. For lesbians, gay men, prostitutes, and others the approach can mark an improvement over earlier theories of gender inversion, perversion, degeneration, and criminality. But deviancy theory is not a form of knowledge produced from the standpoints of lesbians and gay men, prostitutes, or others defined as "deviant." Even critical approaches within deviancy studies can become part of "doing" deviance — participating in the social accomplishment of some groups as deviant.

Deviancy theory often groups together, as "deviants," gays, lesbians, prostitutes, hustlers, women seeking abortions, "juvenile delinquents," and people in prison, along with rapists and sexual mass murderers — even though these groups have qualitatively different social experiences. Deviancy is an administrative "collecting category" that includes people who engage in unorthodox forms of consensual sex-related activities as well as those who engage in sexual violence and harassment. This common conceptualization makes it hard to disentangle different activities and groups. While deviancy studies have been able to make visible some of the social processes that ruling institutions use to label people as deviant, they continue to maintain the standpoint of heterosexual hegemony and features of oppressive sex regulation.[15] It is still the homosexual or the prostitute who is some sort of "problem" in need of explanation. This result is part of the social power mobilized through the conceptualization, or "framing up," of deviance.

In my experience this standpoint comes to the fore in teaching deviancy courses, no matter how critical you are or no matter how much you stress the social construction of deviancy and "normality." Many students still come away thinking that there is something really wrong with gays, lesbians, prostitutes, and others who are socially made into "deviants." There is something fundamentally wrong with the very powerful concept of "deviancy" that prevents those who operate within its boundaries from taking up the standpoints of the oppressed.

The conceptualization of deviance implies that as gay men, for instance, we are somehow different from the norm. We are transformed into an object of study. Similar questions are not posed about the social process through which heterosexuality is organized as the social norm. Whatever breaks it makes from dominant thought, deviance theory still produces lesbians, gays, and prostitutes as social problems. In deviance theory the tables are never turned in the same ways on sexual "normality" (Brock 2003; Kinsman 2003b). We need courses instead on the social construction of normality.[16]

> The conceptualization of deviance implies that as gay men we are somehow different. Similar questions are not posed about the social process through which heterosexuality is organized as the social norm.

So if deviancy theory is not the answer, what is? Undertaking historical sociological inquiries into the social relations through which "sexual problems" have been constructed provides us with a much more rewarding approach.

TO WHOM IS HOMOSEXUALITY/LESBIANISM A PROBLEM?

Homosexuality, as we have seen, is constructed as a "social problem" through a social and historical process of sexual and state regulation, backed by dominant "traditions" within the professions and academic disciplines. In turn these definitions have entered into the Criminal Code, social and family policy, popular culture, and mass media coverage.

Lesbianism is constructed as a distinct social problem, but through a different, if related, social process that also includes the denial and social invisibility of sexual desires between women (Khayatt 1992; Stone 1990, Kennedy and Davis 1993; Ferguson 1989: 188–208; Hennessy 2000: 175–202). There were major gender differences in the impact of sexual regulation on those who would come to be called lesbians as compared to homosexual men. At first in capitalist social relations, more social spaces opened up that men could seize to develop their own same-gender erotic cultures, while women's dependence on men was reinforced (Kinsman 1996a: 48–71). The distinct sexual-scientific classification of "lesbian" was articulated later than that of "homosexual." When it came it was in response to the emergence of feminism and of networks of women able to begin to earn their own incomes and live apart from men. While previously romantic and passionate attachments between girls and between women were not seen as a problem, in response to the emergence of networks of women who were erotically interested in other women and who were living apart from men the disciplines of sexology and psychology constructed the "morbidity" and "perversion" of lesbianism (Faderman 1981, 1991; Ferguson 1989: 188–208; Kinsman 1996a: 69–71, 134–37). The marginalization that lesbians face is organized differently than is the social oppression faced by homosexual men, and it is bound up with the relations of oppression facing women in patriarchal societies. Lesbians generally have less access to social space than do gay men. They have less access to financial resources than do most gay men, and they face the sexism not only of men generally but also of gay men.

At the same time as they were constructing the perversions of homosexuality and lesbianism, ruling disciplines were also constructing the relations of heterosexual hegemony — the "naturalness," "normality," "health," and "necessity" of heterosexual relations for women and men (Kinsman 1996a: 69–71; Katz 1990, 1995; Adams 1997). Anyone not attracted to the "opposite sex" was defined as a social problem, as someone suffering from some sort of perversion or inversion. The "naturalness" of heterosexuality was actively opposed to the lesbian and homosexual "threat." Jonathan Katz (1983: 661), referring to the U.S. experience, writes: "The word and concept 'heterosexual' was produced and distributed in late nineteenth and early twentieth century America to express and to idealize qualitatively new relationships between men and women in which eroticism was defined as central and legitimate." This "necessity" of an intrinsic and essential heterosexual desire was quite different from previous forms of the regulation of different-gender and reproductive relations.

According to Magnus Hirschfeld, an early sex psychologist and homosexual rights reformer, most of the thousand or so works on homosexuality that appeared between 1898 and 1908 were addressed to the legal profession (see Nungessar 1983: 55). Many early works by medical and legal experts "were chiefly concerned with whether the disgusting breed of perverts could be physically identified for the courts, and whether they should be held legally responsible for their acts" (Karlen 1971: 185). Men and women engaging in same-gender desire and love have been labelled "deviants," "perverts," "gender inverts," "criminal sexual psychopaths," and "dangerous sexual offenders."[17] They have been called "promiscuous" and "grossly indecent" and accused of engaging in "anonymous sex." They have been the subjects of the distinction between "public" and "private" sex. These sexual classifications are used for the policing, criminalization, and psychiatrization of gay men and lesbians in specific historical contexts.

The entry of heterosexual hegemony into public "common-sense" attitudes involves many variants of heterosexist discourse. These include homosexuality as sin (in religious discourse, currently being remobilized by moral conservatives); as unnatural (in both religious and secular discourse); as illness (in medicine and psychiatry and in a new sense with the AIDS crisis); as a congenital disorder or inversion (in forensic psychiatry, sex-psychology, sexology, and in a new form in recent biological claims to have uncovered the "cause" of homosexuality) (see Kinsman 1996a: 32–33, 310; Kinsman 2003b); as deviance (in sociology); as child molesters, seducers, and "pedophiles" (in certain sexological studies, by the police, and in the work of government inquiries like the Hughes royal commission in Newfoundland and in media representations); as a symptom of social degeneration (in social Darwinist and eugenic discourse); as communists, "pinkos," and national security risks (rooted in McCarthyism, military organizations, the Cold War, and the national security campaigns in Canada); as tolerated only when practised between consenting adults in "private" as in the 1969 Criminal Code reform (the Wolfenden Report strategy of "privatization") (Kinsman 1996a: 213–87, 1989: 315–58); as a criminal offence or social menace (in police campaigns, "moral panics,"[18] and the mass media); as only to be tolerated when practised in "respectable" and "responsible" forms that do not challenge hegemonic gender and sexual relations (current assimilationist, liberal, and social-democratic perspectives); and, finally, as in the sense that queers are only to be accepted if they are fashion-conscious and fully immersed in the worship of commodities and consumer capitalism (a current mode of representation of gay men in popular culture and constructed through the social organization of the "pink market") (See Sears 2000).

For lesbians the variants also include the constructions of women-loving-women as "man-haters" and "radical feminists" (in anti-feminist moral conservative organizing and in some mass media coverage), as leading to a "manless horror world" when they raise children without men (in some psychological work and some media coverage) (Hemmings 1980), and also in depictions of sex between women as "foreplay" before the entry of the man and his penis in pornography made for heterosexual men (Valverde 1985: 89, 95–99).

Each of these variants merits its own specific social and historical investigation. Each constructs lesbians and gay men as a particular type of "problem."

Heterosexist ideas about the naturalness of heterosexuality and the sickness of homosexuality and lesbianism are not simply backward ideas. They are a key social means of constructing heterosexual hegemony. The term "homophobia" — "dread of being in close quarters with homosexuals" (Weinberg 1973) — has often been used not only to describe the panic reaction that some heterosexuals display when confronted by visible lesbians and gay men but also to try to explain homosexual oppression in general. As such "homophobia" tends to simply reverse psychological definitions of homosexuality as a mental illness, turning them back onto heterosexuals who have difficulty dealing with "queers." This approach individualizes and privatizes gay oppression. The problem becomes one of particular heterosexuals who have problems with "queers" — rather than the social relations that construct only heterosexuality as the "normal," "natural" sexuality.

The term homophobia continues to be taken up even in the new work in "queer theory" to describe lesbian and gay oppression (Kinsman 1996a: 13–14, 33–34; Sedgwick 1990). Queer theory challenges the binary opposition between heterosexual and homosexual that it finds at the heart of Western culture, although it does this largely on a literary and cultural terrain (Jagose 1996; Turner 2000). "Homophobia" is used in some queer theory to separate out analysis of sexual oppression from that of gender oppression (Sedgwick 1990) and tends to break some of the connections between sexual and gender relations that we experience in our everyday lives. I prefer to use the term "heterosexism," relating the practices of heterosexual hegemony to institutional and social settings and to sex and gender relations. In this context homophobia can be seen as a particularly virulent personal response organized by heterosexist discourse and practice.

Powerful state and professional agencies and popular culture industries have constructed lesbians and gay men in different ways as a social threat and danger. Some queers, however, are now to be tolerated and integrated in limited ways. Looking at this process from the standpoints of lesbians and gay men, we can see that the problem is not homosexuality or lesbianism, but the state, professional and cultural practices that create problems for lesbians and gay men in our lives.

PROSTITUTES: "OFFENDING PUBLIC ORDER AND DECENCY"

Much that has been written here so far regarding lesbians and gay men could also be said regarding the rather different experiences of prostitutes.[19] The Italian anthropologist Lombroso viewed prostitutes as biological "throwbacks." Lombroso saw prostitutes, like "homosexuals," as either physical or moral "degenerates" (Gould 1981; Pfohl 1985: 85–89).

Walkowitz, in her pioneering studies of prostitution in nineteenth-century England, points out that originally prostitution was one of the occasional forms of activities that working-class and poor women engaged in to survive (Walkowitz 1977, 1980a, 1983, 1992; Weir 1986). One woman brought before the courts on prostitution-related charges during that period declared, "We are not beasts of the field" — a class and gender statement of defiance (Walkowitz and Walkowitz 1973). Walkowitz (1980a) tells us about the struggle against the British *Contagious Diseases Acts*. In the second half of the nineteenth century there was a focus on venereal disease in the military and the threat that this disease presented to the health of the imperial armed forces (Davin 1978). Under the *Contagious Diseases Act* any woman in selected districts could be identified as a "common prostitute" and required to have a compulsory medical examination every two weeks. If she was found to be "infected" she could be interned in a "lock hospital" for a period not exceeding nine months.

In response to this legislation a feminist mobilization occurred, largely among middle-class women, alongside the initiation of a social purity campaign. As Walkowitz (1980a) points out, the social-purity mobilization eventually succeeded in subsuming feminist-inspired agitation, which had been protesting the sexual double standard between men and women and trying to develop some solidarity with working-class and poor women who worked as prostitutes. In social-purity discourse, prostitution became the "social evil" and "the white-slave trade."

Social purists defined the question of prostitution not as a gender or class question but as a highly "moral" issue (Valverde 1991). They constructed prostitution as a particular kind of "social problem." They did not examine (and far too often commentators today still do not examine) the social and economic realities of the lives of women who work as prostitutes. They did not look at prostitution as a work relation (Brock 1998). If they had they might have realized that prostitution was possibly one of the best options for these women, given the circumstances of their lives. The social-purity movement ignored women's reasons for involvement in the trade, simply calling for state "protection" from prostitution. If movement members had started from the standpoints of the women involved in the sex trade, they would have come to very different conclusions.

Canadian social purists associated prostitution with "feeble-mindedness" and "immigrants." They saw prostitutes as especially abhorrent, since women were not supposed to be lustful and instead were supposed to be asexual mothers. Social-purity agitation led to the growing criminalization of prostitution-related activities.

Prostitutes were also defined as the "spreaders" of sexually transmitted diseases (STDs), even though they were only ever very marginally the cause. In the late nineteenth and into the twentieth centuries the focus was always on prostitutes when official agencies talked about STDs. There was a quarantine of 18,000 suspected prostitutes in the United States in 1918–20 in an ostensible attempt to control STDs (Brandt 1985: 89). The focus of regulation was always on the "loose" women who spread infection — never on the men who might have infected the women — and the goal was to quarantine infected women rather than educate men in sexual responsibility and safety.

In Canada in the late nineteenth and early twentieth centuries a whole series of measures, often social-purity inspired, tried to wipe out the "social evil." In 1918 the Canadian government moved to further regulate prostitution. It stipulated, "No woman who is suffering from Venereal Disease in a communicable form shall have sexual intercourse with any member of His Majesty's forces or solicit or invite any member of the said forces to have sexual intercourse with her" (Cassell 1987: 141). Notice that the order placed no responsibility on the men involved. Government educational pamphlets during these years included statements such as "Practically all prostitutes and loose women are diseased" and "Prostitution cannot be made safe" (Cassell 1987: 216). Prostitutes and "loose" women were constructed as the "problem." Clearly embedded in this professional and official discourse were sexist double standards. The regulatory focus was on the women and not the men, as women's "sexual deviance" came increasingly to be defined as "promiscuity" and prostitution.

A series of "public-health" practices and regulations that are still with us and are being redeployed in the context of the AIDS crisis came out of this state and professional response to prostitution. These measures include mandatory reporting of HIV infection (the virus assumed to lead to the development of AIDS) to medical officers of health and the government, which has led to serious cases of discrimination; contact-tracing of the sexual partners of those affected, which violates people's rights to confidentiality and anonymity; and possible quarantine measures. Rather than addressing health concerns, the measures often have more to do with state and professional moralities and the extension of forms of social and moral regulation (Corrigan 1981: 313–37; Valverde and Weir 1988: 31–34; Canadian AIDS Society 1991; Patton 1990, 1996; Kinsman 1996b; Worth, Patton, Goldstein, 2005) and surveillance of some people's lives. If health concerns were central there would be much more emphasis on popular and effective education regarding safe sex and needle use.

In the practices of "public health" it is always wise to ask which "public" is being referred to and whose health is being protected. Often it is the health of the white middle class being "protected" at the expense of prostitutes, people of colour, PLWA/HIVs, gays, and others. Often "public health" mobilizes a series of practices designed to protect the "general population" (in the context of AIDS coded as white, heterosexual, and middle class) from those defined as the "infected" groups.

It was through these processes of criminalization, "public health," and the legal and "expert" definition of prostitutes as a "social problem" that the working-class and poor women who had engaged in prostitution as part of their survival strategies became separated from their poor and working-class communities. They were actively made into a "problem." For instance, they came to be viewed as "disruptive" to working-class communities because they were seen as bringing in the police, the law, and middle-class moral reformers. As a result prostitutes became a distinct outcast group, which resulted in a series of problems for prostitutes in their everyday lives.

Anti-prostitution legislation hit women the hardest. As Sylvia Pankhurst, an English feminist responding to the passage of an anti-white-slave trade act in 1912, commented, "It is a strange thing that the latest Criminal Amendment Act, which was passed ostensibly to protect women, is being used almost exclusively to punish women" (quoted in Walkowitz 1983: 433). I would add that it was mostly working-class and poor women who were punished and this continues to this day. In many situations this criminalization led to a dependence on male pimps for protection, which in turn also led to the restructuring of the trade so that it became much less female-organized than it was in the nineteenth century. The trade also became far more likely to be a "professional" activity than the occasional money-earning activity it often was more than a century earlier.

In the 1990s legislation ostensibly designed to protect young people from "child pornography" was used in London and Toronto against young people themselves, especially against young male prostitutes (hustlers) (Kinsman 1996a: 256–358; Bell 1997). In a broader sense this legislation can be used to deny young people access to the explicit safe-sex materials and sexuality education materials that they need, denying young people access to knowledge about their bodies and eroticism. This tendency will be intensified if the basic age of consent is raised to sixteen as proposed. The youth porn legislation also constructs the problem of sexual violence against young people as being rooted in images and representations of sexual activity involving younger people. This law was challenged by Robin Sharpe, who was charged with possessing "child pornography" after the seizure of stories he had written and a collection of photos of younger males. In response the Supreme Court reaffirmed most of the "child pornography" law but also stated that people can't be prosecuted for producing written or visual materials that are works of their own imagination for their own use. Sharpe was found not guilty of possessing written "child pornography," but he was found guilty of two counts of possessing "pornographic" photos of young males (O'Malley and Wood 2001; Persky and Dixon 2001; Perelle 2002; Doyle and Lacombe 2003).

Prostitution itself is not criminalized in Canada, but every activity associated with it is, which makes it extremely difficult for someone to work as a prostitute (Brock 1998). The laws include "living off the avails of prostitution," "bawdy-house" legislation, "soliciting," "communication for the purposes of prostitution," and the criminal enterprises bill, which potentially criminalizes any income earned from prostitution-related activities.[20]

Even "liberal" official discourse, like that of the British Wolfenden Report (1962), constructed street prostitutes as the "problem" regarding prostitution (Kinsman 1996a: 219–20, 1989: 354–55). The Wolfenden Report took the visibility of streetwalkers as an affront to "public order and decency." Again, this category of "the public" is socially constructed; it excludes as much as it includes. The "public," defined as "decent," "respectable" citizens, excludes street prostitutes as being inherently against "public" interests. The Wolfenden Report argued, "The simple fact is that prostitutes do parade themselves more habitually and openly than their prospective clients" (Report of the Committee on Homosexual Offenses and Prostitution 1962: 87). The standpoint constructed is that of the "normal decent citizen" and of "public decency" and not that of the prostitute herself. Intrinsic to the public/private distinction that the Wolfenden Report argued for in the regulation of prostitution and homosexuality is the social organization of gender inequality, patriarchal relations, and a number of sexist assumptions. The woman is assigned to the "private" realm, and any transgression of the boundaries into the "public" realm calls for legal and police regulation. The report called for clearing the streets of "public" prostitutes.[21]

From the 1970s to today in Canada the police themselves have actually organized the problems surrounding street prostitution (Brock 1998). In Vancouver, through clampdowns and arrests in bars and hotels, the police drove hookers onto the streets. This was before the Hutt legal decision in 1978, which stated that street soliciting had to be "pressing and persistent" before the police could lay charges (Lowman 1986a). In Toronto the "clean up Yonge Street campaign" of the late 1970s had a similar impact and, with the closing of massage parlours, also drove women working in the sex trade onto the streets. Police, through their own arrest patterns, create street prostitution as a "public nuisance problem" in some urban zones. When street prostitution becomes a noise or harassment problem in some neighbourhoods the police and some conservative residents' groups (also extremely concerned about their property values) campaign for tougher laws against street prostitutes (Brock 1989a, 1998; Kinsman 1996b: 387, 395–96; Lowman 1986a).

In 1985 Bill C-49 — passed over the opposition of prostitutes' rights and feminist groups — criminalized "communication" for the purposes of prostitution. Some critics argued that the legislation would mean the arrests of more customers, but the provision continues to be largely and more severely used against prostitutes (Brock 1989a; Canadian HIV/AIDS Legal Network 2005). As a diversion program many of the male clients charged are sent to "John" schools, where they hear presentations on why they should not use prostitutes and thereby can avoid any criminal sanctions. This offence has made the lives and work of street prostitutes more difficult, increasing possibilities for violence against them because it has also curtailed their ability to communicate with each other regarding safety concerns. Before this legislation, prostitutes would have been able to talk to each other about where they and a customer were going in case they didn't return soon. After Bill C-49 any such conversation could become evidence of "communication

> Prostitutes' rights activists want the decriminalization of all prostitution-related activities, which would allow prostitutes to gain more control over their lives.

for the purposes of prostitution" and used against them. This tendency creates even more problems for sex-trade workers in their everyday lives. Despite a series of legal challenges the constitutionality of this addition to the Criminal Code has been upheld, and the police and some politicians continue to push for even tougher legislation.

The police and federal officials have come out strongly against municipal proposals for the limited legal regulation of prostitutes. At the same time, prostitutes' rights activists are opposed to legal regulation, which, they argue, would make the state their pimp; instead they want the decriminalization of all prostitution-related activities, which would allow prostitutes to gain more control over their lives (Brock 1998; Brock and Scott 1999; Canadian HIV/AIDS Legal Network 2005). Proposals for the decriminalization of prostitution-related offences (like that of Canadian HIV/AIDS Legal Network in 2005) continue to be adamantly opposed by the police and are dismissed by government officials.

The sex trade, like other trades or professions, is also stratified along class, racial, and ethnic lines. Those who work the streets are more likely to be working-class and poor women and women of colour, including Aboriginal women. Women from mid-dle-class backgrounds are more likely to work in "private" and for escort services.

Recently there have been a number of "expert" attempts to construct prostitution as a "problem" or special form of deviancy related to "sexual abuse" at an early age (Brock 1991). As Valerie Scott of the Canadian Organization for the Rights of Prostitutes (personal conversation) puts it, responding to this association given the pervasiveness of sexual harassment and assault against girls and women: "Why don't they spend as much time and money seeing if there is any connection between women lawyers and earlier experiences of sexual abuse? Why is it always the whores who are focused on in these studies?" (See also Brock and Scott 1999.)

In recent years in Canada there has also been a police and media focus on pimps and younger prostitutes, with various proposals in Alberta and Ontario for seizing young prostitutes off the streets (Sinopoli 2001; Martin 2001). Often this coverage, in a racist fashion, has portrayed the pimp as a Black man, associating Black men with criminal activity. It has also not investigated why girls and young women sometimes find them-selves on the streets fleeing from hostile families, with a lack of non-stigmatizing social services to turn to for support (Lowman 1986b; Brock 1998). In many cities the police continue to conduct regular anti-prostitute sweeps.

Violence against women working in the sex trade has been ignored and greatly facilitated by the criminalization of prostitution (Canadian HIV/AIDS Legal Network 2005: 31–35; Lowman 2000). In 2002, after years of organizing by community activ-ists and family members, the police in Vancouver finally started to take seriously the disappearance and murder of more than sixty women who worked in the sex trade in Vancouver's Downtown East Side. A joint task force was formed between the RCMP and the Vancouver Police, and murder charges have been laid in only a minority of these cases. An RCMP task force was also set up to review the cases of missing Edmonton-area women, many of whom were sex workers. In January 2005 the RCMP added the eighty-fourth woman's name to the Edmonton list (Canadian HIV/AIDS Legal Network 2005: 33). The highest risk of violence for sex workers is among Aboriginal women and transgender sex workers (Canadian HIV/AIDS Legal Network 2005: 33).

> In 2002 the police in Vancouver finally started to take seriously the disappearance and murder of more than sixty women who worked in the sex trade in Vancouver's Downtown East Side.

Prostitutes have also been portrayed in the mass media and by some medical professionals as "vectors of transmission" for the HIV virus. This is done even though studies have shown that most prostitutes in North America practise safe sex with their "tricks" and that prostitutes have a very low rate of HIV infection because of their work (Brock 1989b, 1998; Alexander 1987: 248–63). Recently a number of prostitutes' rights groups in North America have moved into the forefront of safe-sex education as the most experienced sex educators.

The law, the mass media, politicians, and even some feminists construct prostitutes as "problems" (and often simply as passive "victims") rather than examining the social world from the standpoints of prostitutes themselves. From those standpoints the problem is not prostitutes, but rather how prostitution is socially organized and criminalized (Delacoste and Alexander 1987; Bell 1987; McClintock 1993; Brock 1998).

"AIDS FIEND STRIKES AGAIN": MAKING PEOPLE LIVING WITH AIDS/HIV INTO THE PROBLEM

A number of social groups have long tried to portray the AIDS crisis as a problem of deviancy, especially sexual deviancy. The AIDS crisis was used by the mass media, the right wing, and state officials to reconstruct homosexuality as a social problem and a sexual danger at a time when lesbian and gay liberation movements had started to gain ground. Initial Western media coverage of AIDS "homosexualized" the syndrome as the "Gay Plague," building on the medical profession's early category of "Gay Related Immune Deficiency" (Treichler 1999; Kinsman 1996b). Professional, media, and state practices saw the remobilization of notions of homosexual illness and sickness. Gay sex once again became constructed as a contagion and social danger.

An important racist construction of AIDS has also occurred (Watney 1988; Patton 1990: 77–97; Treichler 1999; Miller 2005). Early on, the medical profession and much of the mass media associated Haitians as a group with AIDS. When I worked for the AIDS Committee of Toronto in 1983 I received calls from people asking if they should fire their Haitian housekeepers. Other Haitians reported that they did not get jobs they applied for after the potential employers determined that they were Haitians.

Many of these mistaken ideas come from the media's use of the medical term "high-risk groups," which associates Haitians, gays, prostitutes, and others with the "transmission of AIDS." These groups then come to be seen as a threat to "public health." The term "high-risk groups" was used to blame particular groups for AIDS and to organize discrimination against them. This categorization helps to construct people living with AIDS and HIV infection as "other," and this process of "otherization" needs to be resisted (Treichler 1999). As AIDS activists stress, there are no "high-risk groups": only high-risk activities that anyone can engage in.

PLWA/HIVs have also been made into a "social problem." For one thing, they have been portrayed as irresponsible individuals who are a sexual danger to others. In Nova Scotia, for instance, Scott Wentzell — a person living with HIV infection — had his HIV status leaked by public-health personnel to the police and the media, and the police organized a nationwide "manhunt" for him. Referring to Wentzell, the daily newspaper in Halifax used the headline "AIDS Fiend Strikes Again" (Weatherbee 1989; Petty, 2005). The media/police campaign creates a framework of interpretation for the AIDS crisis that portrays "irresponsible" PLWA/HIVs as the problem.

Similarly, Randy Shilts constructed and popularized the "Patient Zero" story in his book *And the Band Played On* (1987). "Patient Zero" was supposedly the single "promiscuous" gay man who was responsible for the spread of AIDS throughout North America. The mass media gave this story considerable publicity, once again constructing PLWAs as the problem.[22] AIDS thereby becomes a problem of sexual and other forms of deviance.

There have also been attempts to focus on HIV transmission as being the fault of "deviant" HIV-infected individuals. For example, in 1991 the media described an HIV-infected male prostitute in Saint John, N.B., as a "social danger" even though he engaged only in safe sex. In 1991 police also charged an HIV-infected woman with "sexual assault" for allegedly having unprotected sex with two men. The charge was dropped after outrage from feminist and other groups. In 2005 a major media "panic" produced concern at a number of military bases over an HIV-infected woman who was accused of having unprotected sex with a man at Canadian Forces Base Borden. She pleaded guilty to a charge of "aggravated sexual assault" and was sentenced to a twelve-month conditional sentence, to be served under house arrest, and three years' probation (Franklin 2005).

Public-health measures and Criminal Code sections (ranging from "sexual assault," to "aggravated assault" to "being a common nuisance" and "criminal negligence caus-ing bodily harm") have been used against PLWA/HIVs accused of having "spread" HIV infection (Kinsman 1996b: 396–99; HIV/AIDS Legal Network 2004). Often these charges have been directed against female and male prostitutes, "street people," and/or injection drug users. Criminal charges have most often been laid in cases of HIV transmission, or the threat of HIV transmission, to women from men, but this approach is starting to change.

In the first HIV transmission case to make it to the Supreme Court, in the 1998 *Cuerrier* decision, the Court decided that a person who knows that he or she is HIV-positive and has unprotected sexual intercourse with someone who is HIV-negative without disclosing their HIV status can be convicted of "aggravated assault" (Canadian HIV-AIDS Legal Network 2004). This ruling was often understood as imposing a legal duty on the PLWA/HIV to disclose their HIV status before engaging in sexual activity — which interpreted by some AIDS organizations as meaning not only that they must tell PLWA/HIVs that they have to disclose their HIV status to sexual partners but also that if support workers for the AIDS group knew about unsafe sex taking place they also had to report this to authorities. These types of developments are also taking place in other countries (Worth, Patton, and McGehee 2005). This approach begins to incorporate AIDS groups into the practices of regulating and policing the sexual lives of PLWA/HIVs. In 2003 in the *Williams* case the Supreme Court decided that an HIV-positive person cannot be convicted of "aggravated assault" for having unprotected sexual intercourse without disclosing their status if there is a reasonable doubt about whether the other person was HIV-positive at they time they had unsafe sex. Despite what many AIDS groups believe, legal experts point out that these decisions do not impose on AIDS workers and counsellors any legal responsibility to report unsafe activities by individual PLWA/HIVs to the police (Canadian HIV-AIDS Legal Network 2004).

In the spread of HIV the focus of official attention has been on those who are already infected. There has not been the same focus on the need for everyone to take responsibility and to engage in safe practices. This framing of the problem constructs PLWA/HIVs as the risk and the problem. The framing sees it as their responsibility not to engage in "risk" activities. At the same time attention does not focus on the lack of responsibility of governments, public-health officials, and medical professionals in ensuring good AIDS and safe activity education and the necessary social supports and access to treatments. Most HIV infection comes from people who have no knowledge that they are HIV–infected or from those who are ignorant of its means of transmission. These interpretive frameworks divert attention away from the need for everyone to engage in safe sex (and safe needle use) to prevent the spread of HIV. Focusing on the problem as being sexually deviant PLWA/HIVs shifts attention away from the lack of good government-funded safe-sex education (Kinsman 1996b: 393–401).

> There has not been the same focus on the need for everyone to take responsibility and to engage in safe practices. This framing of the problem constructs PLWA/HIVs as the risk and the problem.

In an effort to use the AIDS crisis to try to reverse some of the progressive sexual changes of the last few decades, state agencies and some religious groups have focused their solutions on demanding "abstinence"[23] and "monogamy." This is the official position of the George W. Bush administration in the United States. Since people are not likely to give up on sex (nor should they), this type of anti-sex AIDS "education" does not allow people to learn about positive forms of safe-sex interaction (much of which has been pioneered in the gay community's response to AIDS). Nor, as portrayed in more liberal AIDS education, is monogamy per se necessarily safe, especially given that most people understand monogamy as including serial monogamy, in which HIV transmission can occur if unsafe sex is practised (Kinsman 1991). The crucial aspect of HIV transmission is not the number of sexual partners you have, but the types of activities you engage in. Anti-sex AIDS education actually gets in the way of dealing with an important health issue. Promoting abstinence or monogamy has far more to do with the moral and conservative sexual agenda of particular groups than it does with real health education (Patton 1986, 1990, 1996; Crimp 1988).

> Anti-sex AIDS education actually gets in the way of dealing with an important health issue.

Focusing on PLWA/HIVs as the problem also deflects attention away from the many problems that state agencies and pharmaceutical corporations create for PLWA/HIVs who need to get access to treatments that could extend or save their lives. Often state regulations, the ideologies of scientific research, or the profit concerns of drug companies stand in the way of people getting access to the drugs and therapies they need (G. Smith 1990; Kinsman 1991b, 1992b, 1996b: 393–401, 1997; Epstein 1996). Since 1996 in North America, access to the new "drug cocktails" for dealing with HIV and the opportunistic infections that actually kill people has extended the lives of many PLWAs even though these drugs are no lasting solution to the health problem. At the same time the treatments are generally denied to people in Third World countries, especially in Africa. To really deal with the global AIDS crisis requires not only making these treatments freely available in Third World countries but also a massive transfer of resources to those countries to address health and poverty concerns. Constructing PLWA/HIVs as the problem also deflects attention away from the problems that people face in gaining access to social support and social services that are crucial to maintaining their levels of nutrition and health. This raises important questions of poverty and class relations and the health work that PLWA/HIVs must engage in (Mykhalovskiy and Smith 1994).

The media continue to elaborate on their earlier distinctions between "innocent" and "guilty" PLWA/HIVs. Financial assistance packages have been announced for those infected through the blood supply and blood products in Canada and other countries, in part as a result of the struggles of hemophiliacs and others infected through the blood supply. While this is a move forward and the funding is badly needed, it also leads to the construction of divisions between different groups of PLWA/HIVs — dividing people on the basis of how they were infected — and poses the danger of reconstructing the distinction between "innocent" (infected through the blood supply) and "guilty" (infected through gay sexual activities or injection drug use). This time the distinction carries with it important financial implications, which can also lead to the privileging of the stories of those deemed to be innocent and responsible over those deemed to be guilty and irresponsible.

This issue is closely related to divisions between "responsible" and "irresponsible" PLWA/HIVs (Kinsman 1996b: 393–401, 1997). The "responsible" are those who do not challenge medical hegemony, or social policies regarding AIDS, and who are self-regulating or "compliant" in response to HIV/AIDS. They basically follow the advice of the medical "experts." The "irresponsible" are those who do act up against problems with access to treatments, social support, and even against the priorities of the medical research establishment. Some of them are designated to be "non-compliant" by medical authorities (Mykhalovskiy, McCoy, and Bresalier 2004). These "irresponsible" PLAW/HIVs often point to the need for clear and explicit safe-sex education that does not push abstinence or monogamy. This strategy of regulating and dividing PLWA/HIVs into responsible and irresponsible is not based on giving them the necessary resources, access to treatments, knowledge, or control that would allow them to take more control over their own health care and lives. The focus is shifted from the actions or inactions of powerful social institutions onto the individual capacities and incapacities of PLWA/HIVs (Kinsman 1996b: 393–401, 1997).

Looking at the world from the standpoints of people living with AIDS, we see that many problems in their lives are organized through state and social policies that define them as deviant and deny people adequate care, education, support, and treatment. For PLWA/HIVs, the problem is state, professional, corporate, and social support practices that do not meet their needs.

RESISTANCE

The varied experiences of sexual oppression give rise to progressive movements and struggles to transform sexual regulation in all these areas. This is a relational process in which forms of sexual resistance meet with various responses from official and professional agencies. The experiences of resistance — from the lesbian/gay liberation movements to prostitutes and sex-trade workers to AIDS activists and PLWA/HIVs — all bring into view many aspects of the social construction of "sexual problems." What we begin to see is that these groups are not the problem. Instead they have been made into "social problems" by powerful state and professional agencies.

Their experiences and the sexual resistance based on them provide us with a social basis for shifting standpoints in exploring sexuality and sexual regulation. Beginning from the experiences of those facing sexual oppression, we can see the making of oppressive sexual regulation from a very different place. From that place we can see much more about the social making and regulation of our diverse sexualities than is apparent in looking only from the standpoint of those who have been doing the sexual defining and regulating.

The social problems facing these varied groups do not lie in their erotic activities themselves, but in the social organization of sexual policing and regulation — in broader state and professional social relations. Taking up these alternative standpoints allows us to focus on the actual social relations and practices that organize problems for oppressed groups. We can then see the social practices and relations that need to be transformed.

In looking at "sexual problems" critically we need to shift social standpoints. We cannot rely on knowledge that constructs lesbians/gays, prostitutes, PLWA/HIVs, and others as "social problems." Feminism has posed this shifting of social standpoint so that we can begin, for instance, from the experiences of women outside ruling discourses (D. Smith 1987, 1999, 2005; G. Smith 2006). We must also take up this approach in our critical perspectives on sexuality and sexual regulation.

BEYOND LIBERAL PLURALISM — FOR A RADICAL PLURALIST, ANTI-RACIST SOCIALIST FEMINISM

Radical pluralism shifts our attention to the character of sexual relations between people rather than focusing on sexual acts themselves. It emphasizes the social practices engaged in by people in sexual relationships, including the social meaning and context of sexual relations for the participants and the amount of choice involved.

Radical pluralism is counterposed to the absolutist perspectives of moral conservatives — who represent a single "right" male-dominated heterosexuality — and to naturalist or biological determinist notions of any single "natural" or "normal" sexuality (Weeks 1985, 1995). Central to this perspective are the ideas that sexual difference in and of itself is not a social problem and that there can be numerous consensual and ethical sexual choices (Kinsman and Champagne 1986).

I suggest taking this much further than Jeffrey Weeks does in his work — to move beyond liberal pluralism and to link the approach much more clearly to broader socialist-feminist and anti-racist perspectives of social transformation. The perspective must not be reduced simply to liberal tolerance and pluralism, a reduction that sometimes seems implied in Weeks's writing (1985, 1995). Pluralism in and of itself is not enough. In the wrong hands, if the social relations that organize inequality and discrimination are not challenged and transformed, it can lead to new ways of marginalizing, ghettoizing, and containing unorthodox sexualities. Pluralism is a necessary defence against moral conservatives, but in and of itself it does not get at the need to transform social relations and uproot oppression. It is an inadequate basis from which to build a transformative response to the politics of "respectability" and its relation to class formation. Radical pluralism must therefore be linked to the transformation of social relations based on the standpoints of those oppressed by sexual regulation. In turn, the transformation of sexual relations based on the standpoints of those oppressed by sexual regulation must be linked to the elimination of class inequality and exploitation as central to projects of progressive social transformation. With regard to gender oppression, Mariana Valverde (1989: 247–48) suggests:

> Weeks' concept of "radical pluralism" may be the necessary starting point for a nonabsolutist sexual ethics, and it may give us a defence against the rising tide of conservatism that one can detect in the AIDS panic. However, it has to be admitted (at least among feminists) that the notion of "pluralism" cannot provide any content for a feminist sexual ethic.

This is why I stress the *radical* in "radical pluralism." In my view this transformative "radical pluralism" must become an important part of challenging state policies and of pointing us towards the making of a democratic and erotic-positive socialist-feminist anti-racist society in which people will have far more control over their bodies, sexualities, and lives.

We must also move beyond the important but also limiting focus on "difference" in postmodernist and poststructuralist work, including much "queer theory" (Jagose 1996; Turner 2000). While a focus on the affirmation and celebration of difference allows more space for marginalized people to speak about their experiences, it does not get at the social roots of oppression and marginalization. As the anti-racist Marxist-feminist Himani Bannerji (1995a: 71–72) suggests, we also need to problematize the notion of difference itself:

> Where does such "difference" reside? Who are we "different" from? Upon reflection it becomes clear that the "difference" which is significant is not a benign cultural form. The "difference" which is making us "different" is not something inherent or intrinsic to us but is constructed on the basis of our divergence from the norm…. It remains a question as to why white middle-class heterosexual feminists do not need to use the "difference" argument for their own theory or politics.

We need to ask, who gets defined as different and who does not? For instance, a focus on difference can allow for people of colour to be allowed their "differences," but it could also maintain white hegemony in the centre, because whites would not be defined as different in the same way. Lesbians, gay men, bisexuals, and others could also be allowed our "differences," but this would not challenge heterosexual hegemony in the centre.

To move beyond liberal pluralism and a simple affirmation and celebration of difference requires a transformation of the law and social regulations, in which ruling moral/political perspectives are embodied. We can perhaps best think of this in relation to some of the "problems" associated with street prostitution, such as noise and street harassment. A radical pluralist approach, which would be supported by prostitutes' rights activists and most feminists, would lead towards repealing the laws that criminalize prostitutes. This would get rid of a number of the "nuisance" problems associated with street prostitution, which are created by policing and denying prostitutes access to working indoors. But radical pluralism is limited in not addressing some of the underlying relations of class, gender, and sexual inequality that shape how male/female prostitution is institutionalized in this society. A socialist-feminist approach would go further, through focusing on sex work as work and posing the need for social and economic equality for women and the profound social changes required to make this a reality. This approach would begin to undermine the sexist ways in which prostitution is organized in this society, while empowering those who work as prostitutes to gain more control over their lives (Brock 1998).

Once these kinds of social changes have begun, and outside the present framework of the criminal law, we could then begin to imagine the possibilities of getting different parts of the community together to discuss, debate, and negotiate how to deal with the common social space in their area. This approach has to be based on the recognition that all people working and living in an area have needs and interests that must be addressed. In this new context people would be able to come to a new consensus on their common use of this social space.

In our present society, however, with the criminal law, police policies, real estate interests, and moral and class prejudices against prostitutes (including the sexist double standard) organizing "deviance" and oppression against prostitutes, it is impossible even to contemplate this radically different scenario. Elaborating a radical, pluralist, socialist-feminist perspective requires thinking through how to create new social conditions in which sexual disputes and problems could be resolved very differently.

With a shift in standpoint to starting from the experiences of the oppressed, the problem becomes the oppressive strategies of sexual regulation, and this focus directly engages us in the struggle to transform sexual regulation in an emancipatory direction. The point, as Marx suggested, is not only to understand the world but to change it. Beginning outside official discourse (in which gays and prostitutes are prepackaged as social problems), we start instead with the experiences of gay men and prostitutes to see how sexual policing and oppressive sexual regulation are the problems.

More generally this project opens up inquiry for the development of a radically different basis for sexual regulation. This approach would not be based on administrative categories standing over and against people's lives, but on the transformation of social relations, including the law and policing, which would empower gays, prostitutes, and other oppressed people. This requires a different kind of oppositional discourse organizing very different kinds of social and political relations between movements of sexual resistance and other movements for progressive social transformation.

Dealing with progressive sexual change also involves us with class, gender, and anti-racist politics, because sexual relations are bound up historically with these social relations. Sexual relations are not simply autonomous from or independent of other social relations, as some queer theorists contend (Sedgwick 1990). They are constructed in and through relations of class, gender, race, and state relations just as these social relations are also in part constructed through sexual relations (Hennessy 2000). Sexual relations therefore have a mediated social character (Bannerji 1995a, 1995b).

Today, as we've seen, a number of sites of sexual and social regulation are deploying the distinction between the "responsible" and the "irresponsible" as a key part of an oppressive regulatory strategy. As in the last century, when a social bloc was constructed in defence of "respectable" sexuality against prostitutes and homosexuals — part of the class struggle between the new ruling class and the emerging working class — such distinctions are now also part of the terrain of class struggles. In this decade the attempts to construct and defend "responsible" against "irresponsible" sexualities are also part of the reconstruction of hegemonic class relations to manage and deal with social transformations while at the same time preserving class and social power and weakening the composition of working-class and social movement struggle. Capitalist globalization, neo-liberalism, and social program cutbacks are creating serious social conflicts and tensions. Dividing people between the "responsible" and the "irresponsible" is one way of maintaining ruling hegemonies.

To deal with these shifting strategies of oppressive regulation we need to move beyond liberal strategies of sexual regulation (including deviance theory, the public/private regulatory strategy, limited human rights protection, and queers as only acceptable when worshiping commodities) and engage in projects of socialist, feminist, and anti-racist social transformation. The movements for sexual emancipation are contributing ideas for this engagement, and the strategies will become even clearer through further struggles and discussions within and between our various movements.

> An emphasis on choice, relationships, context, social equality, pleasure, consent, and a process of decommodification could provide us with the initial basis for alternative sexual policies.

Already these experiences indicate the need to focus on ending violence and transforming social power relations and not on policing "deviant" or unorthodox sex. There is no need to code difference as disadvantage or deviance, or to divide consensual sexualities into deviant and normal forms. The necessary shift requires challenging patriarchal, heterosexist, class, racist, and state relations. The aim of this kind of socialist-feminist radical pluralism is to democratize sexuality by expanding the possibilities for non-exploitative sexual choices, by collectively clarifying the criteria for building our sexual communities and lives. An emphasis on choice, relationships, context, social equality, pleasure, consent, and a process of decommodification could provide us with the initial basis for alternative sexual policies. These priorities could become part of a broader socialist-feminist transformation of social relations, which would overturn the public/private, adult/youth, normal/deviant, monogamous/promiscuous, good girl/bad girl, responsible/irresponsible dichotomies and act-specific categories that now dominate and organize sexual rule.

The alternative policies would focus not on regulating acts themselves, or on location (whether it was in public or private), or on whether it was deviant sex or not, but rather on questions related to the actual character of the social relations. For instance, the act of two men engaged in oral sex with each other would not in itself be defined as deviant or abnormal. But if one of the men engaged in violence with or harassment of the other, that would be grounds for social action. If a consensual sexual activity took place in a park, disturbing no one, it would not be considered a problem. If a different-gender relationship involved coercive sex, the act would not be categorized as being more "normal" sex because it was heterosexual in character. Instead, the violence and coercion would be seen as the problem, and various social efforts would be mobilized to deal with the situation. These alternative policies could become a basis for social and sexual transformation.

This struggle to transform sexual regulation means that people themselves — as individuals, groups, and communities — must gain control over the institutions that regulate and confine eroticism and gender relations so that we can remake for ourselves our pleasures, desires, and loves. Such a vision of the future is grounded in the struggles that we are engaged in today, including the struggles for lesbian and gay liberation, for prostitutes' rights, for women's reproductive freedom, and for the rights of PLWA/HIVs. All of these are struggles to take our destiny into our own hands and away from the doctors, sexologists, state agencies, police, legal system, and mass media, who have for far too long defined and regulated our lives.

The institutions that regulate our erotic lives have not been around for all time — they have developed as part of a social and historical process. We, too, are part of that process. These institutions and relations can be transformed. We can then make the pleasures and desires of the future and build a world free of sexual danger.

GLOSSARY OF KEY TERMS

Discourse: A social language. Official discourses are the authorized social languages through which social problems are named and defined. When we enter into the doctor's office as a "patient" we are only allowed to speak about symptoms, while the doctor is mandated through medical discourse to diagnose and prescribe treatment. Discourse is linked to social power relations and the organization of social courses of action.

Hegemony: A term of analysis developed by Antonio Gramsci (1971), which combines force and coercion with legitimacy and consent in the social organization of ruling. Gramsci argued that the power of the capitalist class does not rest solely on the use of various forms of repression or just in their control of the means of production (offices and factories). The hegemonic rule of the capitalists requires the consent or at least acquiescence of the working class and other subordinated groups, and this consent must be actively won and maintained. That is, subordinated social groups must feel that the existing relations of power are legitimate. The emergence of this hegemonic rule has generated a series of "common sense," "respectable," "responsible," and "proper" attitudes that are just taken for granted. This is a useful critical analytical perspective, but it can be too state-focused in its proposals for social transformation (Day 2005).

Heterosexual hegemony: The practices and ideologies that make heterosexuality "normal," "natural," and "healthy" while making homosexuality/lesbianism sick, abnormal, deviant, and dangerous. Heterosexual hegemony necessarily involves lesbian/gay subordination.

Heterosexism: The ideologies and practices that justify heterosexuality as "natural" while invalidating lesbian and gay sexualities.

Ideology: A social form of knowledge production that produces knowledge for the ruling and management of people's lives. This form of knowledge is separated from the social practices and relations through which it is produced.

Power/knowledge relations: Drawn from the work of Michel Foucault, this linking of power and knowledge clarifies that claims to knowledge are always simultaneously claims to power and that power relations are justified through forms of "expert" and professional knowledge.

Sexual regulation: Refers to the various institutions and practices that define and manage our sexual lives. The practices of sexual regulation in this society range from the law and police activity to social and family policies, the school system, the mass media, popular culture, the church, sexual advice literature, the medical and psychiatric professions, peer group pressures, and many others.

QUESTIONS FOR DISCUSSION

1. How have sexual problems been constructed?
2. How have homosexuality and prostitution been socially and historically linked as "sexual problems"?
3. What are the limitations of the concept of sexual "deviance"?
4. Why has there been such opposition to same-sex marriage from moral conservatives?

Why do more radical queer activists have major concerns about the strategic focus on same-sex marriage as the end point of the lesbian and gay liberation struggle?

5.   How can non-oppressive forms of sexual regulation be developed?

WEBSITES OF INTEREST

Canadian HIV/AIDS Legal Network. <www.aidslaw.ca>.

Coalition for Lesbian and Gay Rights in Ontario (CLGRO). <www.web.ca/clgro/>.

Equality for Gays and Lesbians Everywhere (EGALE). <www.egale.ca/index.asp?lang=E>.

NOTES

This chapter is drawn from my past and current work on sexual regulation in Canada. It has been revised and updated for this edition. I thank Kaili Beck, Patrick Barnholden, Barbara Marshall, Les Samuelson, Christine Burr, Brian Conway, Deborah Brock, and Wayne Antony (Fernwood Publishing) for their comments on the various versions. Thanks to Tracy Gregory for her help on this version. And, thanks to the students who have challenged and taught me at Nipissing University, Ryerson, Memorial University of Newfoundland in St. John's, Acadia University, and Laurentian University. The quote from Ezra Hurlburt Stafford was used in the title of a paper by Geoffrey Egan given in 1980.

1.   On power/knowledge relations see Michel Foucault, *Power/Knowledge* (1980b); and Foucault's other work. Unfortunately, valuable insights in Foucault's work such as power/knowledge relations are limited by a lack of attention to both social standpoint and active subjects in his discourse analysis. See D. Smith 1990a: 70, 79–80; see also Kinsman 1996a: 71–72, note 7.

2.   Ruling relations is a term that brings together the various state, professional, and corporate agencies and institutions that are involved in ruling contemporary capitalist societies. It is broader than state relations and includes the important work of the professions in the social organization of ruling. See D. Smith 1987: 3–6, 1999: 73–95, 2005.

3.   I use "ideology" to refer "to all forms of knowledge that are divorced from their conditions of production [their grounds]" (Bologh 1979: 19). These ideological forms are characteristic of ruling forms of knowledge in our society. Ideology is not a "thing," but a relation that embodies ruling relations. On this see also the work of D. Smith, especially 1990a, 1990b, 1999, 2005; Bannerji 1995a, 1995b, 1994; and Hennessy 2000: 18–22.

4.   The offence of "gross indecency" in Canada was abolished in a series of Criminal Code reforms on January 1, 1988. It can still be laid for "offences" prior to that date. It has been used in many of the charges against the priests and Christian Brothers in Newfoundland for sex-related offences, where it has participated in the "homosexualization" of the problem of "child sexual abuse." The age of consent for anal sex is set at eighteen, which is much higher than for other sexual activities. This is because it continues to be a "homosexualized" offence. This discriminatory age of consent provision has now been successfully challenged on constitutional grounds in Ontario, Quebec, and British Columbia. The Federal Court of Canada upheld the Ontario decision and the Crown did not appeal the decision to the Supreme Court of Canada. In 2006 the federal Conservative government attempted to raise the basic age of consent from fourteen to sixteen and was not proposing lowering the age

of consent for anal sex (Kirkby and Rau 2006). Under the Criminal Code same-gender sex between men (and sometimes between women) can still be considered to be "indecent acts" and "acts of indecency" in relation to the provisions of the bawdy house legislation (see note 20).

5. For interesting commentary on shifting representations of homosexuality in TV programs, see O'Brien and Szemen 2004: 181–84.

6. "Multiculturalism" can be seen in the Canadian context as a particular strategy of state formation attempting to handle the expansion of non-white communities and anti-racist movements through allowing for the expression of differences on the "cultural" level but without challenging the social roots of racism in social and class relations. See Ng (1995), (Bannerjee 1995b and 2000b).

7. While continuing to view hegemony as a useful analytical tool for critical social analysis, I also recognize that the conceptualization of hegemony often carries with it a state-centred notion of social power and social transformation. On this see Day 2005.

8. Hegemonic masculinity in this society is generally coded as heterosexual, white, and middle-class. Other forms of Black and gay masculinities are generally subordinated to this hegemonic masculinity. See Frank 1987, 1992; Connell 1995; Mercer and Julien 1988.

9. "Collecting device" is a term used by Philip Corrigan (see Corrigan 1981: 313–16) to describe the grouping together of different activities under common administrative procedures so that they can be dealt with by state and social agencies.

10. For instance, Wini Brienes and Linda Gordon write that "approximately 92 per cent of the victims are female and 97 per cent of the assailants are male" (1983: 522; see also Wilson 1983: 117–34). The July 1994 issue of *Pediatrics* (41–44) reports that of 269 cases of child sexual abuse studied, only two offenders were identifiable as gay or lesbian. A young person's chances of being molested by a heterosexual partner or a relative are more than one hundred times greater than the chances of being molested by an identifiable gay man, lesbian, or bisexual.

11. For instance, while working at a Loeb grocery store in Sudbury in the mid-1990s Mary Ross experienced discrimination because she is a lesbian, even though discrimination on the basis of sexual orientation is prohibited in Ontario. Ross's initial human rights complaint was not pursued by the Ontario Human Rights Commission (OHRC) on arbitrary, technical grounds: it was officially received by the Commission more than six months after the discrimination had led her to go on disability leave. Later, even though Ross reached a settlement with the corporation owning the store, OHRC refused to address this discrimination.

12. In 1995 a limited legal victory supported the adoption rights of non-biological lesbian mothers in Ontario (Kinsman 1996a: 5), and a number of provinces, including British Columbia, Ontario, and Quebec, established adoption rights for lesbian and gay couples. A significant legal victory came in the 1998 Rosenberg case, involving two employees of the Canadian Union of Public Employees (CUPE) who challenged the federal income tax regulations that only recognize opposite-gender spouses for survivor benefits. The court ruled that the federal *Income Tax Act* is unconstitutional and must be read to include coverage for same-gender partners. The federal government finally accepted this ruling and was forced to amend its legislation.

13. The subhead for this section comes from the title of Alan Sears's insightful 2005 article.

14. Judy Rebick argues convincingly for reclaiming the word radical (getting to the root of

the problem) in her book *Imagine Democracy* (2000). The social and historical struggles over marriage relations are covered for the U.S. context in Chauncey 2004. At the same time, Chauncey exaggerates the egalitarian changes that have taken place in marriage law and relations over the last few decades and does not significantly address the radical queer critique of marriage.

15. Even critical thinkers who accept aspects of the "deviance" framework do not seem able to break free of it. See David Greenberg 1988, and my review of that book in Kinsman 1990.

16. I avoided these problems in teaching "deviance" at Acadia University in 1992 by renaming the course "the social construction of deviant/normal relations," which focused on the relational and social/political character of these classifications. I also focused on institutional sites like the mass media and the criminal justice systems, which are constantly constructing both "deviance" and "normality." I have tried to maintain this perspective in my teaching in these areas since then.

17. On "criminal sexual psychopaths" and "dangerous sexual offenders," see Kinsman 1989, 1996a: 183–87.

18. "Moral panics" are defined by Stan Cohen 1972: 9. In my view it is important to avoid an overly expansive usage of "moral panics." I also do not want to use "moral panics" as an ideological sociological "concept" that automatically explains events in the world. Instead we have to specifically locate and ground "moral panics" in social and institutional relations that get actively organized between the mass media and "citizen's groups" and the police, courts, professional experts, and state agencies. These relations are combined differently in different "moral panics." Moral panics in this sense enter into the organization of relations of ruling as well as being organized through these relations. They are often only attempted or intended projects of different groups or agencies that never achieve official success. See Kinsman 1996a: 336–39.

19. The quote in the subhead is from the Report of the Committee on Homosexual Offenses and Prostitution (Wolfenden Report) 1957, 1962: 80.

20. The "bawdy-house" legislation has also been used against gay men for "acts of indecency," for instance during the raids on the gay baths in Toronto in 1981, at Katacombes in Montreal in 1994, and at Remington's in Toronto in 1996. The Canadian bawdy-house legislation had originally been drafted to deal with houses of prostitution. As part of social-purity agitation and "in defence of marriage," in 1917 the law was broadened to include any place existing "for the practice of acts of indecency," putting massage parlours on the same footing as houses of prostitution. The Criminal Code defines a bawdy-house as "a place that is kept or occupied or resorted to by one or more persons for the purposes of prostitution or the practices of acts of indecency." See Russell 1982; G. Smith 1988. In 1999 the Bijou club in Toronto was raided and a number of charges were laid by police, with nineteen men arrested for engaging in "indecent acts" (consensual gay sex). After extensive community mobilizations the charges were dropped (Pavelich 1999). In 2000 the police used liquor regulations to raid and lay charges against a woman's bathhouse night in Toronto. In 2002 the charges against the organizers of this event were defeated in court (Gallant 2002a, 2002b; Valverde 2002).

21. This recommendation has not stopped the police from continuing to go after prostitutes who work in "private" as well.

22. There are many critical reviews of *And the Band Played On*. See especially Douglas Crimp,

"How to Have Promiscuity in an Epidemic," in Crimp 1988: 238–47. As a useful musical antidote to the "Patient Zero" mythology, see John Greyson's film *Zero Patience* (1993).

23. For a useful critical analysis of the "abstinence" movement in the United States, see Lerner 2003.

Chapter Five

ABORIGINAL ECONOMIC DEVELOPMENT AND THE STRUGGLE FOR SELF-GOVERNMENT

Cora J. Voyageur and Brian Calliou

Provincial government policy statements these days strike something of a new chord in the relationship between the state and Canada's Aboriginal peoples.[1] The policies require all the regional and district staff who are planning industrial management activities to examine whether those actions infringe upon Aboriginal or treaty rights; if so, the staff must consult with affected Aboriginal communities before proceeding (Alberta 2005; British Columbia 1997; RCAP 1996b).

This consultation requirement is significant because it demonstrates a new and better way of doing business in the Aboriginal community. It casts Aboriginal peoples as partners and benefactors in development. The procedure respects Aboriginal community governments by giving them more input into projects on their traditional territories, and it reflects the new postcolonial relationship between Aboriginal and non-Aboriginal people. Aboriginal communities are given an opportunity to negotiate the much-needed political and economic benefits from development activities.

> **"You Should Know This"**
> - First Nations people in Canada were not granted the right to vote in both provincial and federal elections until 1960.
> - Aboriginal tourism contributes more than $250 million to the Canadian economy annually.
> - Artifacts show that Aboriginal people have inhabited the land known as Canada for more than 12,000 years.
> - Aboriginal labour force participation rates are 66 percent while the non-Aboriginal participation is a mere 3 percentage points higher at 69 percent.
> - The tar/oil sands are located on traditional Aboriginal territory.
> - Aboriginal business has created 49,000 new jobs for Aboriginal and non-Aboriginals.
> - The vast majority of Aboriginal people pay taxes in Canada. Only First Nations people who live and work for an Aboriginal-owned business or organization with its head office on a reserve are exempt from paying taxes.
> - Treaty 8 commissioners' notes show that First Nations people were promised tax-exempt status by the government representatives. This promise was the basis of R. v. Benoit.

It is no secret that in the past little, if any, of the vast economic wealth derived from the exploitation of the land and resources found its way to Canada's Aboriginal peoples. One analyst argues that in all liberal democracies Aboriginal peoples are transformed into "politically weak, economically marginal and culturally stigmatized members of national societies" (Dyck 1985: 1). Another maintains that liberal lawyers who apply liberal laws to protect American "Indian" rights have actually contributed to the loss of indigenous culture (Medcalf 1978). By failing to examine the structural inequities inherent in Canadian Indian legislation and policies, some social scientists mistakenly characterize Native-white relations as "the Aboriginal Problem" (Frideres 1988). On the contrary, the Canadian state's institutionalized and oppressive economic and legal structures have played a key role in Aboriginal community underdevelopment, which has resulted in the increasing dependency of some Aboriginal peoples on the state. Institutional structures have had a profound impact on Aboriginal peoples. The constraints imposed by those structures need to be overcome in the new relationship between Aboriginal peoples and Canadian society.

Although First Nations people in Canada remain subject to unilaterally imposed state regulations and policies, they have never passively accepted the Canadian state's domination. They have long resisted both overtly and covertly, yet much has changed in recent years. First Nations peoples are gaining control over their lives and their communities. The current struggle for self-government plays a part in the First Nations peoples' resistance to the control exercised over them by the Canadian state and its institutions. They see the key to economic development in self-government — not in the sense of achieving a nation-state but in achieving official recognition of their inherent rights, treaty obligations, and land claims — and by gaining increased control over local and regional decision-making. Ironically, the struggle for self-government has produced a new form of resistance: now the Canadian state and various interest groups are resisting the attempts by Aboriginal peoples to control their own destinies.

> It is no secret that in the past little, if any, of the vast economic wealth derived from the exploitation of the land and resources found its way to Canada's Aboriginal peoples.

If self-government can be achieved, a new social order for Aboriginal peoples and for all Canadians may truly be at hand. In the meantime, by examining Canada's institutional structures — as opposed to the standard focus on the shortcomings of First Nations peoples — we can come to a better understanding of the dispossession of Canada's First Nations peoples and their marginalization from the economy.

BARRIERS TO NATIVE ECONOMIC DEVELOPMENT

Barriers to Aboriginal economic development have had negative consequences that have resulted in Aboriginal peoples being collectively located at the lowest rung of the socio-economic ladder. Quite simply, the experiences of Aboriginal peoples are notably distinct from those of non-Aboriginals. Despite strides in educational attainment and the growing number of Aboriginal peoples in positions of power and prestige as a group, they remain among the country's poorest and least educated. The median Aboriginal income in 2000 was $13,593, while the median non-Aboriginal income was $22,431 (Treasury Board of Canada Secretariat 2006: 8). Some 61.3 percent of Aboriginal people between the ages of twenty-five and sixty-four years complete high school, compared to 71.0 percent of non-Aboriginals in this same age group (Statistics Canada 2006: 1). Fewer Aboriginals, at 38.4 percent, complete some form of post-secondary education, compared to the non-Aboriginal community at 48.3 percent (ibid.). This distinct Aboriginal experience is the result of cultural, legal-political, and economic barriers.

Cultural Barriers: Difference, "Race," and Racism

Cultural differences can both directly and indirectly result in barriers to development. The different values and beliefs of non-Aboriginal people often conflict with Aboriginal worldviews. A Western, non-Aboriginal worldview often includes a strong belief in the basic principles of liberalism: individualism, the notion of land as a commodity, the private ownership of property, and human control over nature. An Aboriginal world-view usually includes a strong belief in collectivism and stresses a spiritual connection to the land — of living with, rather than controlling, nature, and sharing rather than owning land. These historical-cultural differences set Aboriginal people apart from the Eurocentric notions upon which Canada's institutions are based.

Socio-cultural differences can create barriers to economic development. For example, collectively, Aboriginal people may not want to encourage development that requires mass destruction of the landscape, such as mining or clear-cutting forests. This point of view could restrict economic opportunities for those pursuing environmentally unsustainable projects.

Problems arise particularly when racism and racist attitudes use cultural differences to treat Aboriginal peoples and their cultural practices as unworthy of respect. A belief in "racial separateness" or "racial difference" justified the undertaking by which settler populations took Aboriginal peoples' lands and resources. Race, as a socio-political concept, entails "an ideology of inherent White superiority [used] to justify White dominance and exploitation" (Frideres 1988: 378).

> Problems arise particularly when racism and racist attitudes use cultural differences to treat Aboriginal peoples and their cultural practices as unworthy of respect.

By characterizing "others" as inferior, Western Europeans gave themselves leave to move in and take over the lands and lives of the indigenous peoples, avoiding or lessening their guilt.

Western religious doctrines served to further the Euro-Canadian aim of private land ownership. The Aboriginal peoples' supposed animalistic state was, in the eyes of colonial Euro-Canadians, clearly evidenced by the indigenous peoples' lack of legal and individual title to the land on which they lived. In early Euro-Canadian society, as Sidney Willhelm (1969: 3) points out:

> The White races, in the final analysis, never felt superior in an absolute sense since they yielded to the Christian Bible and to Nature's demand in command-ing the inferior races. When the Indian and Negro were in the animalistic state, they were heathens; Whites fulfilled obligations to the Almighty in defending racists' feelings against the non-believers and would suffer no sense of loss should they even exterminate the non-White.

Because of this belief — that the Aboriginal occupants were not human beings, and were thus incapable of being legal land titleholders — Euro-Canadians viewed Aboriginal peoples as having neither legal nor moral claim to the land. Laws regulating land in non-Aboriginal North America are based in this racism and religious intolerance. Thus, as Aboriginal legal scholar Robert Williams Jr. (1990: 8) puts it: "Law and legal discourse were the perfect instruments of empire for the European colonizers of [North] America and served a legitimating function for the taking of Indian land." Europeans justified taking the New World's land and resources by characterizing its original inhabitants as "savages." When the removal of Aboriginal peoples from the land and resources resulted in an inability to make ends meet through their traditional means of livelihood, they became dependent upon transfers.

For the most part Canadians do not question the underlying racist notions or actions that played an integral role in establishing our country. Our society appears to have little problem accepting the legal and political domination of Aboriginal peoples. The reality that Aboriginal people have been denied a fair share of Canada's wealth, resources, and land does not seem to disturb our collective conscience to any great degree. A covert or subtle form of racism occurs, for instance, when social scientists explain what is "wrong" with Aboriginal people by focusing attention on the values and traditions of "those" people.

> For the most part, Canadians do not question the underlying racist notions or actions that played an integral role in establishing our country.

The view that Aboriginal people must shed their "Indianness" to make it in today's society barely masks the still-lingering racist ethos of Aboriginal inferiority. In this view, the Aboriginal notion of collective land ownership is not only outmoded but also restricts First Nations peoples' access to, for example, bank loans for development projects. But as we shall see in the realm of legal barriers, the restricted access to capital is more a function of the *Indian Act* than of differing cultural ideas about land tenure.

Systemic Barriers: Discrimination

In theory, institutions in liberal societies promote the equality of all citizens, but in reality certain groups continue to suffer from systemic discrimination — practices firmly set in place at all levels in society's structure. By examining societal structures we can better understand problems that have their roots in the institutional rather than the individual level. Systemic discrimination, for example, can have a negative impact on Aboriginal peoples' abilities to gain stable and worthwhile employment. David Stymeist (1975) studied ethnic relations in a small Northern Ontario community and found that the non-Aboriginal townspeople's discriminatory and prejudicial views caused Aboriginal people to be excluded from the town's social and economic life. Overt and covert discrimination meant that Aboriginals were unable to obtain jobs in the community, thereby leaving them marginalized from the economy.

Educational institutions play a role in systemic discrimination. Aboriginal people have long been, more often than not, unable to obtain extensive schooling. The last residential school closed only in the mid-1990s. Under that system Aboriginal children were forced to leave their homes and go to residential schools, where they were subject to strong assimilation efforts by the church and state, and often punished simply for speaking their own languages. These conditions represent systemic discrimination: barriers to learning built into the institution of education.

Anthropologist Alan McMillan (1988: 305–306) points out that as early as 1972 Aboriginal communities recognized the need "for increased community control of education, more native teachers, the development of curricula relevant to modern natives and increased instruction in native languages and culture." McMillan (1988: 306) found that in the late 1980s "more than three-quarters of Canada's Indian bands" were administering "all or part of their educational programs." Most of them had "instituted some form of native language instruction. The number of native teachers and administrators [had] greatly increased." According to the Department of Indian Affairs' *Overview of DIAND Program Education Data*, the number of band-operated schools in Canada increased from 312 in the 1990–91 school year to 481 in 1999–2000, an increase of 54 percent (Indian Affairs and Northern Development 2001: 16).

At one time Aboriginal people had very low levels of education and job-related experience, but academic achievement and work experience levels have now increased significantly in the Aboriginal community. Nevertheless, Aboriginal persons are still often incorrectly labelled as unskilled labour. Helmar Drost (1995), in his study of Aboriginal unemployment, found that often the problem of high unemployment rates was linked to the lack of job opportunities and the willingness of business and industry to hire Aboriginal employees and not to the Aboriginal people's lack of skills or job-related experience. He found that there were more qualified Aboriginal workers than there were available jobs.

Legal Barriers

Perhaps the most significant barrier to economic development for First Nations is a legal one: the lack of legal control over land and resources. The Canadian state, through its federal and provincial jurisdictions, often legislates access to land and resources that benefits corporate interests and is detrimental to Aboriginal peoples.

The *Constitution Act 1867* set out the legislative powers for federal and provincial governments, giving the federal government responsibility for "Indians, and Land reserved for Indians" (McMillan 1988: 287). The Canadian Parliament exercised its authority by creating the *Indian Act* (1876). An Indian Affairs representative once stated, "Probably there is no other legislation which deals with so many and varied subjects in a single act. It may be said indeed to deal with the whole life of a people" (MacInnes 1946: 388). The *Indian Act's* extensive regulation, in addition to fish and game laws and other legislation that restricts access to traditional resources, has had a detrimental effect on Aboriginal economies. The Canadian government has used the *Indian Act* to deny First Nations peoples their basic rights, such as freedom of association and the right to representation in the judicial system. A 1927 amendment made it illegal for anyone to raise money for an Indian band to bring claims against the government (Kellough

1980). Over the years, amendments to the *Indian Act* have outlawed social, cultural, and religious gatherings such as the sun dance on the Plains and the potlatch on the West Coast.

One of the most restrictive legal-political regulations was the banning of First Nations peoples from universal participation in Canada's democratic system. At various times in Canadian history voting

One of the most restrictive legal-political regulations was the banning of First Nations peoples from universal participation in Canada's democratic system.

rights were given to Indians and then taken away. The *Electoral Franchise Act* (1885) gave "Indians" in Eastern Canada the right to vote in federal elections, but not "Indians" in Western Canada. At the end of the nineteenth century the ruling Liberal Party strongly resisted giving the vote to Indians, and after an Ontario Conservative Party member was elected with strong support from Indian voters, the Liberals enacted the *Franchise Act* (1898), which stopped Indians from voting. Provincial laws prohibited Indians from voting provincially (Krauter and Davis 1978). Although on-reserve Indians were given the right to vote federally and provincially in Newfoundland and British Columbia in 1949, it was not until 1960 that all reserve Indians were allowed to vote in federal elections (Johnston 1993; Krauter and Davis 1978). As a result, historically, Indians were virtually without representation in either Parliament or provincial legislatures, and until recently Aboriginal peoples' interests and rights were not officially or adequately represented in the drafting of legislation.

The political and legal structures that impose economic restrictions on Aboriginal peoples represent the state's attempts to control them. State laws and policies set out many legislative restrictions that act as barriers to Native economic development. Government policies again express the values of liberalism, which supports individual freedom, a free-market economy, private ownership, and the accumulation of wealth. Critics of liberalism argue that liberal law protects elite property interests and does not recognize Aboriginal peoples' rights to the land and resources (Loo 1994).

A lack of financing for on-reserve ventures is a major problem in Aboriginal communities, stifling economic development. Financial institutions, situated in the metropolitan financial centres, generally do not lend to persons who do not have property as collateral. The *Indian Act* exempts land and property situated on a reserve from seizure. Banks cannot seize an Indian's property if that Indian defaults on loan payments. Thus major banks tend to avoid giving loans to Aboriginal people because of the risk involved. Still, some changes are now making Indian ventures more viable. Governments give loan guarantees to banks, which are then more willing to lend to First Nations individuals. Aboriginal-owned and administered financing institutions are emerging. Federal funding, as well as procurement contracts, has aided in the establishment of Aboriginal businesses. In 2000 there were about 20,000 businesses owned and operated by Aboriginal people in Canada (Aboriginal Business Canada 2000: K1). According to the 2001 Census of Canada, 27,195 Aboriginal people (18 percent of all Aboriginal people in the labour force) were self-employed (Industry Canada 2004).

Economic Barriers

As an economic system, capitalism emphasizes private ownership and the accumulation of wealth. Indeed, as Ted Parnell (1976: 171) argues, the capitalist economic system has exploited Aboriginal peoples by destroying their economies and making them dependent on the state. Aboriginal people became an internal colony. Comparing this colonial structure to a feudal system, Gail Kellough (1980: 347) argues:

> These feudal-like features, however, are not due to a lack of incorporation of Indians into the Canadian economy. On the contrary... they are due to, and reflect precisely, the incorporation of Indians into the capitalist system. The institutions conceived in the Indian Act have functioned as mechanisms in the expansion of the capitalist system.

The Canadian state is in a conflict of interest situation because it has a trust-like duty to ensure the best interests of First Nations peoples, but at the same time promotes the exploitation of traditional Aboriginal lands by privately owned corporations. Aboriginal peoples become disempowered when their rights to traditional lands and resources are not respected and when the state acts more as a protector of capital (Mann 2000: 530).

> The Canadian state is in a conflict of interest... it has a duty to ensure the best interests of First Nations peoples, but at the same time, promotes the exploitation of traditional Aboriginal lands by privately owned corporations.

EXPLAINING BARRIERS TO ECONOMIC DEVELOPMENT

Debate about the lack of Aboriginal participation in the Canadian economy involves, in general, assimilationist and anti-assimilationist approaches. Assimilationists argue that the cultural differences of Aboriginal peoples and mainstream society place Aboriginals at a clear disadvantage. This stance does not account for the barriers created by the racism and systemic discrimination experienced by Aboriginal peoples. Meanwhile, human capital theory argues that Aboriginal peoples would be more "successful" if they only accepted and attained education along Euro-Canadian lines. This approach does not account for those many Aboriginal people who have acquired education and skills and are still unemployed.

Modernization theory, a dominant theory within the assimilationist stream, views industrialization and technological change as part of a "progress" that is both inevitable and desirable. Modernists further state that traditional economies that fail to undergo industrialization will remain underdeveloped. Thus the lack of economic development within a region or amongst a particular population is linked to outmoded economic organization and ideas. The region or people are responsible for their own economic underdevelopment due to their inability or unwillingness to "change with the times." This approach does not consider factors such as geographic isolation, lack of access to capital, or small economies of scale that might inhibit profitability as significant impediments to development. Modernization theory, in the final analysis, really "blames the victim."

Anti-assimilationist perspectives use an amalgam of theories to explain barriers to economic development. They include, among others, the metropolis-hinterland interaction, colonialism, and dependency theories that serve to underline the overt and systemic structures that explain the frequent economic marginalization of Aboriginal peoples.

The metropolis-hinterland and colonialist theories examine the root of legal and political barriers. In the metropolis-hinterland paradigm, the political and economic elite of metropolitan centres are the decision-makers who exploit the hinterland's raw materials and sell the finished products back to the outlying areas. Hinterland communities have little or no say in choices made for them and their regions. Local interests have little priority in relation to large-scale capitalist interests. Thus, First Nations reserves, most of them located in rural areas, had no input in decisions made on their behalf in distant locales. Critics of the Canadian state's approach to economic development argue that development must proceed under local control to meet local needs and aspirations rather than serve only the goals of multinational corporations (Frideres 1988). Colonialist theory argues that Aboriginal communities are internal colonies exploited for economic gain by the dominant society for cheap, unskilled labour.

Dependency theory emerges as a critique of modernization theory. According to dependency theorists, underdevelopment can only be understood through an analysis of the economic relationships between developed and undeveloped economies. Hinterland populations become dependent upon the productive relationships established by the capitalist metropolis (McArthur 1989). James Frideres (1991) argues that reserve Indians occupy a position of "domestic dependency." In other words, major decisions affecting their socio-economic progress are made by individuals and institutions outside their communities. Aboriginal peoples, originally self-sufficient, became dependent over time. Although they enjoyed the convenience of European goods during the early days of the fur trade, historically those goods had not been essential to their survival. They soon became more dependent upon trade goods such as guns and ammunition, and their dependence greatly increased when European immigrants settled their traditional lands and they found themselves limited to reserves. Because of the newly restricted land base, their traditional economies suffered and some of the peoples became more dependent on government transfer payments for support. The economic system creates a relationship and structure of inequality and ultimately, dependency.

ABORIGINAL PEOPLES' PARTICIPATION IN THE ECONOMY

Aboriginal peoples were by no means passive figures in Canada's history and economy. Rather, Canada's Aboriginal peoples were active participants in events and relations before and after the coming of the Europeans, and they made valuable contributions to the economic development of Canada. To begin with, they played an enormous role in European explorations and in the fur trade (Ray 1974; Friesen 1987; Miller 1989). Frank Tough (1985) found that in the post-treaty period in Northern Manitoba, many Aboriginals voluntarily left the fur trade to pursue wage labour in lumbering and fishing. They geared their diversified economy to seasonal changes. Peter Douglas Elias (1990) found that Aboriginal peoples' participation in the wage labour market occurred as early as the mid-nineteenth century. He noted that wage labour was only one component of a complex regional economy, which included market and domestic production components.

> Aboriginal peoples were by no means passive figures in Canada's history and economy.

Steven High (1996: 244) argues that Aboriginal people did not enter an "era of irrelevance" after the decline of the fur trade, but rather:

> Aboriginal peoples not only participated in the capitalist economy during this [period] but did so selectively to strengthen their traditional way of life. Native efforts to incorporate aspects of the capitalist economy into their seasonal round and their resistance to the government's assimilation policy laid the groundwork for the future construction of the non-proletarian Amer-Indian worker.

Rolf Knight's (1996) study *Indians at Work* indicates that Aboriginal peoples in British Columbia and elsewhere in Canada have had a long history as both wage-workers and independent producers — people who quickly adjusted to the industrial world. Knight argues that the farming, trapping, and other methods of independent production undertaken by Aboriginal peoples were an integral part of the capitalist economy. Aboriginal people on reserves adapted quickly to farming, with many of them becoming quite successful. Eventually, however, the government sabotaged successful Aboriginal farming operations by imposing strict regulations prohibiting the commercial sale of the agricultural products from reserves. Government policy prohibiting reserve farmers from using mechanized farming equipment further impeded their farming attempts (Carter 1990). Aboriginal participation in wage labour in Northern Manitoba continued to climb until the 1920s, after which it gradually declined (Tough 1992).

The Royal Commission on Aboriginal Peoples (1996a), in its comprehensive study of Native economic development, found that Aboriginal peoples long coped with social and economic changes in Canada as the land became increasingly settled and industrialization began. The commissioners found that even in the early twentieth century Aboriginal people participated in many new industries, finding employment in farm labour, house construction, building municipal infrastructures, road construction, and railroad construction. Native people also worked at logging, milling, mining, shipping, and longshoring. They pursued their own ventures in farming, freighting, and arts and crafts production. Throughout this adaptation to the capitalist economy, most Aboriginals continued traditional pursuits and independent production year-round. Their marginalization from the economic development of Canada, then, is a relatively recent phenomenon brought about by systemic barriers.

RESISTANCE AND THE STRUGGLE FOR INDEPENDENCE

Aboriginal peoples resisted control by the Canadian state in many different ways. They made — and continue to make — persistent attempts to exercise independence through political, economic, and self-governing initiatives. They protested the *Indian Act* from the beginning. John Milloy (1983: 59) writes:

> Immediately upon publication of the act, tribal councils recognized its intent and rejected it. Surely, one tribal leader noted accurately, it was an attempt "to break them to pieces." It did not, he continued, "meet their views" since it was inconsistent with their desire to maintain tribal integrity within customary forms most recently expressed by their insistence on group rather than individual tenure of reserve land.

They also long opposed the government's assimilation program. Laurie Barron (1984: 31) summarizes:

> The very idea that their reserves should be used to transform them into "brown Whiteman" was completely unacceptable and their reaction was immediate. Lacking either political or military power, they responded the only way they could — through passive resistance. To protest restrictions on their economic activities, many cut back on agricultural production, while some abandoned farming altogether. Despite the law, parents refused to send their children to school, both because of the appalling rate of disease there and because it was a system that taught children to be ashamed of their parents and their traditions. And most importantly, tribesmen reacted to government measures by consciously persisting in their traditional institutions, and in some cases, by devising or adopting counter-innovative techniques as an assertion of Indianness.

Vic Satzewich (1996) notes that in the 1890s Blood Indians in Southern Alberta killed cattle belonging to ranchers. They did this not only out of hunger but also as an act of political defiance aimed at the Department of Indian Affairs, which had cut their rations — and they became dependent upon those rations since their traditional lands were taken up by settlers as private property for farming, logging, mining, and settlements. Various Aboriginal peoples joined the Métis resistance to the federal government's surveying of homesteads, protesting the government's cutback on rations and farming assistance (Krauter and Davis 1978). In 1885 the state brought down its full force against the Métis and Indians, sending the military to Batoche to crush the resistance. Eight Indian chiefs and the Métis leader, Louis Riel, were arrested, charged, convicted, and hanged for asserting their rights and standing up to the state.

During the late nineteenth and early twentieth centuries, Aboriginal people "were actors who pursued their interests and struggled to preserve their identity and their interests. They resisted, evaded, and defied efforts to control their decision making, limit their traditional rites, and deprive them of their children" (Miller 1991: 340).

More recently, Aboriginal people who entered treaties with the Crown vehemently expressed the sacredness of treaties and the importance of protecting their treaty rights. Any attempts by the state to infringe upon or reduce treaty rights were met with strong opposition, as evidenced by the reaction of chiefs across Canada to the 1969 *Statement of the Government of Canada on Indian Policy* (also known as the White Paper).

Using Courts to Protect Aboriginal Rights

Aboriginal peoples have also used the courts to resist the dispossession of their land and resources. For example, Chief Frank Calder, on behalf of the Nishga people, launched a court challenge against the province of British Columbia over the development of traditional land (*Calder v. A. G. British Columbia* 1973). The challenge wound its way to the Supreme Court of Canada, where it became the first case to recognize Aboriginal title. The Nishga lost on a technicality, but six of seven justices held that there was a notion of Aboriginal title — although three of those six justices held that those rights were extinguished and therefore no longer existed. This case had a dramatic impact on Aboriginal law and prompted the federal government to change its stance and move towards settling Aboriginal land claims. First Nations won a significant victory and wrestled power away from the federal government, which had previously refused to negotiate Aboriginal land claims. More importantly, the Calder case spawned a series of Aboriginal rights litigation in the Canadian courts.

In 1985 the Supreme Court of Canada made a significant ruling in the Guerin case, giving legal recognition to the Aboriginal peoples' view of their "inherent rights" and thereby rejecting the state's notion that Aboriginal rights were "derivative rights" (rights derived from the state's recognition of them). The case also stands as authority for the principle of fiduciary duty, which means that because First Nations people are in a trust-like position vis-à-vis the federal government, the federal government must always act in their best interests. The court held that the Crown breached its fiduciary duty to act in the best interests of the First Nations when it leased surrendered lands to a golf club on terms that were not agreed to by the chief and council. It awarded a multi-million-dollar damage award against the Department of Indian Affairs.

Taking Political Action

Aboriginal peoples have also expressed their resistance in the political arena. A growing number of Aboriginal lawyers, judges, doctors, and academic professors have become politically active in the last decade or so. An emerging group of Aboriginal professionals often takes leadership roles in the struggle for Aboriginal rights and Aboriginal peoples' share of Canada's wealth.

Aboriginal political organizations have played a central organizing role in attempts to influence government policy. Indeed, political scientist Paul Tennant has explored Aboriginal political activity from as early as 1900 (Tennant 1982). In 1969

Aboriginal political organizations have played a central organizing role in attempts to influence government policy.

the National Indian Brotherhood (now the Assembly of First Nations), in responding to Indian Affairs Minister Jean Chrétien's White Paper on Indian policy, reflected the tenor of Aboriginal political organizations:

> The policy proposals put forward by the Minister of Indian Affairs are not acceptable to the Indian people of Canada. We view this as a policy designed to divest us of our Aboriginal, residual and statutory rights. If we accept this policy, and in the process lose our rights and our lands, we become willing partners in cultural genocide. This we cannot do. (Krauter and Davis 1978: 12)

The strong opposition to the 1969 *Statement of the Government of Canada on Indian Policy* led to amendments to the *Indian Act*, giving Aboriginal people more control over self-governing policies. In the 1960s the federal government introduced a policy of devolution of powers to band councils (Frideres 1988). Perhaps partly in response to Aboriginal peoples' agitation, more control and responsibility were shifted onto the Aboriginal communities. The National Indian Brotherhood used various tactics to express Aboriginal peoples' interests, including intense lobbying of Parliament, international forums, and the education of Canadian society and its political leadership (Riley 1984). In the 1980s the Assembly of First Nations pressed for a seat at the first ministers' conferences on the Constitution and on the Quebec question. Aboriginal peoples have also used the existing political structures to achieve their goals. In 1990 Elijah Harper, a member of Manitoba's Legislative Assembly, used his power to withhold consent to halt the passage of the Meech Lake Accord constitutional amendments. Harper's objection was based on Canada's refusal to deal adequately with Aboriginal rights.

Sykes Powderface (1984: 166) expressed a prerequisite for independence for Aboriginal peoples:

> If we are going to be strong, if we are going to develop independent Indian government, we must first declare our financial independence. So long as we are financially dependent upon the federal government, we cannot chart our own paths and set our own goals. We must not be afraid to bite the hand that feeds us.

Aboriginal resistance has also led to violent confrontations. In 1990 a highly publicized and violent crisis occurred when Mohawk warriors barricaded a road to protect land from being developed into a golf course near the town of Oka, Quebec. The Mohawks maintained that the land was the site of traditional burial grounds. Gunfire was exchanged and a police officer, Marcel Lemay, was killed in the mêlée. In 1996 another armed conflict, known as the Gustafson Lake incident, occurred in British Columbia when Native people claimed privately owned land as sacred ground and would not vacate. An armed standoff resulted and a heavy exchange of gunfire ensued. Subsequently the protesters were taken into custody, charged, and sentenced.

The summer of 1995 saw unarmed Aboriginal people using civil disobedience tactics to protest the provincial government's failure to settle an outstanding land claim at Ipperwash, Ontario. Provincial government leaders refused to negotiate and instead obtained a court injunction. When heavily armed police were sent in to deal with the Aboriginal protesters, an Indian man, Anthony "Dudley" George, was killed by gunfire. A police officer was eventually convicted of the murder. An even more recent example is the 2006 Six Nations protests against a new housing development at Caledonia, Ontario, based on land claims, which has resulted in numerous clashes and some violent confrontations.

In general, then, Aboriginal peoples have struggled to gain more control over local matters and have reacted to the erosion of their treaty and Aboriginal rights. They have organized to gain greater control of their natural resources — fighting against hunting and fishing regulations that have had the effect of criminalizing their traditional economy. They have pushed for the retention of their independent means of production, openly defying regulation by continuing to hunt and fish out of season (Gulig 1994).

Although Aboriginal people have won occasional victories, some commentators argue that such victories are exceptions rather than the rule and are meant only to pacify the dispossessed (Havemann 1989). Whether these victories are truly significant or merely anomalous pacifiers, Aboriginal peoples have no choice but to compete for their share of economic development and self-sufficiency in what is clearly a continuing struggle (Wotherspoon and Satzewich 1993).

Successes over jurisdiction include the case of the Cree of Northern Quebec, who halted the Quebec government's plans to develop a huge hydroelectric project by obtaining a court injunction. This victory eventually led to the James Bay and Northern Quebec Agreement, which reserved land, hunting, and fishing rights and gave monetary compensation to the Cree in return for the extinguishment of rights to traditional territories.

The experience of the Dene of the Mackenzie Valley is similar. Community members, elders, and community leaders who testified before the Berger inquiry (which examined the socio-economic impact of an oil pipeline) emphasized the importance of the rights set out in Treaty 8 — in the area of the Southern Northwest Territories — and of land claims in the other areas not settled by treaty. Indeed, the July 1975 Dene Declaration expressed the need for a land settlement, a relatively high degree of self-government, and Dene control of Northern development (Krauter and Davis 1978; Watkins 1977). The James Bay Cree and the Dene of the Mackenzie Valley are examples of success, because governments and industry took their claims seriously. Aboriginal resistance produced results.

The 1990 *Sparrow* decision is touted as the high-water mark in Aboriginal rights jurisprudence. Sparrow, a First Nations man, successfully challenged the federal fisheries regulations, with the court holding that fishing regulations could not apply to him because he had an existing Aboriginal right to fish and that the regulations could not infringe upon that right. The case was significant not only because it was the first case in which the Supreme Court of Canada considered Aboriginal and treaty rights entrenched under section 35(1) of the Constitution but also because it provided extensive discussion of the protection of Aboriginal and treaty rights. The court created a strict test for state regulations (which could potentially infringe upon existing Aboriginal or treaty rights) to meet before they can be validated. The Supreme Court of Canada's *Sparrow* decision (1990: 180) stated:

> Our history has shown, unfortunately all too well, that Canada's Aboriginal peoples are justified in worrying about government objectives that may be superficially neutral but which constitute de facto threats to the existence of Aboriginal rights and interests. By giving Aboriginal rights constitutional status and priority, Parliament and the provinces have sanctioned challenges to social and economic policy objectives embodied in legislation to the extent that Aboriginal rights are affected.

The case declared that the constitutional status of Aboriginal and treaty rights takes priority over the state's economic and social policies, a determination deemed necessary because governments had continually disregarded Aboriginal peoples' interests and rights. It was also significant because the Supreme Court of Canada expanded the scope of the fiduciary duty by recognizing it as a general guiding principle for section 35(1). Thus, legislation must respect the "special trust relationship" between the state and Aboriginal peoples in order to meet the justification test (*R. v. Sparrow* 1990).

In recent years, having become more assertive about their inherent rights to be self-governing on their own territories, Aboriginal peoples have devised, analyzed, and implemented initiatives in their communities. They have taken control of local issues, arguing that imposed Canadian government structures have continually failed them. The federal relationship with the First Nations began as a nation-to-nation partnership, and many First Nations leaders continue to regard it in this way. This approach gives credence to the notion of self-government in international law. Sally Weaver (1990: 13) argues that the Department of Indian Affairs' new way of thinking about its relationship with Aboriginal peoples must rest on the "principles of the Aboriginal and democratic self-government, and the need for aboriginal-designed and legitimated political institutions" if co-existence and self-determination are to prevail.

Self-Government

At the heart of the changes being pursued by First Nations people and their political organizations is the principle of self-government: the necessary step towards co-existence, self-determination, and actual economic development.

> A necessarily fluid political concept: self-government will take different forms in different communities and at different times.

The strategy of self-government is based on the "special relationship" between Canada and First Nations, but the term cannot be rigidly defined. It is a necessarily fluid political concept: self-government will take different forms in different communities and at different times. Although the concept aims at a broad set of powers over local matters, under some circumstances the form adopted can resemble a provincial structure; under other circumstances the form could be that of a municipality. Self-governing forms could include "self-administration" but ultimately must be more than that. Indeed, self-government could involve a devolution of powers from the Department of Indian Affairs, an approach attempted in Manitoba. The key is that the particular form must be defined by the community so that traditional practices and traditional forms of government can be accommodated and traditional values can underpin the more European-based forms of self-government. As Del Riley (1984: 159) puts it:

> I have said that Indian people in Canada are experiencing a reawakening. They have come of age. Indian people are saying that we are not satisfied with someone else shaping our future and running our affairs. Instead, we want a future that will take into account our spirituality and our traditional forms of government, that will allow us to live the kind of lives we desire.

In a self-governing system, parallel systems of governance could be established with bilateral agreements or tripartite agreements negotiated between the various governments; or co-management agreements could be established in which First Nations people become partners in the planning and management of lands and resources.

Over time First Nations' relationship with the federal government has changed. Before 1982 Aboriginal peoples dealt only with the Department of Indian Affairs. Since the repatriation of the Constitution that relationship has now expanded beyond a single federal ministry. First Nations leaders and political organizations now deal face-to-face with first ministers on constitutional issues. They deal with various federal and provincial cabinet ministers and high-ranking bureaucrats and corporate managers on a range of issues. They wield more power and authority than they did in early Aboriginal-white relations.

Weaver (1990) argues that in the 1980s the Department of Indian Affairs moved into a transitional stage of thinking, which led to a "new paradigm" in the early 1990s. The Penner (1983) and Coolican (1986) reports outlined many Aboriginal peoples' political thoughts and ideas, including: parallel political entities in a permanent organic relationship, evolving state-sanctioned rights of Aboriginal people, evolving Aboriginal cultures, honourable dealing by the state with First Nations people, and consultation with First Nations people to create jointly formulated policies. These ideas represented a shift from the old assimilationist paradigm. Weaver (1990: 15) states: "In terms of the overall ethos of the two paradigms, the old one is characterized by a preoccupation with law, formality, and control over Aboriginal peoples; while the new one is more concerned with justice, adaptation, and workable inter-cultural relations."

Generally, governments now consult Aboriginal people before passing legislation that would infringe upon their constitutionally protected inherent or treaty rights. As well, there is a growing trend for industry to consult First Nations about development projects planned in their traditional territories (British Columbia 1997; RCAP 1996b).

Taking control of services such as health, education, and policing on their own initiative represents a key step towards self-government (Delisle 1984).

Weaver (1990) suggests that another form of self-government is found in the "idea of joint management systems." Co-management agreements enable First Nations people to exercise a measure of control over the use and conservation of natural resources. Aboriginal communities can, and do, play an important partnership role in the planning and implementation of natural-resource management policies and development programs. Indeed, wildlife management programs can and ought to incorporate Aboriginal knowledge of the flora and fauna (Usher 1987). Thus, as the key to Aboriginal economic development, self-government will evolve as Aboriginal peoples and the Canadian state negotiate the details.

NON-ABORIGINAL RESISTANCE TO ABORIGINAL INDEPENDENCE

While federal and provincial governments have recognized Aboriginal rights, negotiating the details of self-government has produced new forms of resistance, this time from non-Aboriginals. With their growing control of land and resources through land claims, treaty land entitlements, and co-management agreements, First Nations people are encountering social and political obstacles. State agencies and various interest groups frequently complain about the growing power and control of First Nations. Looking at the role of senior bureaucrats in the Department of Indian Affairs, Weaver (1990: 16) notes a persistent "resistance to fundamental change" regarding new ideas that would give First Nations more power. The resistance, for example, sometimes takes the form of departmental rejection of *Indian Act* bylaw proposals made by local bands.

Non-Aboriginals' resistance to First Nations peoples' increasing self-determination reflects the essence of the Aboriginal struggle. Control of land and resources is the foundation of Canada's economy. Many non-Aboriginals view the Aboriginals' push for control of resources and land as a zero-sum game. If someone (the Aboriginals) wins, then someone (the non-Aboriginals) must necessarily lose. Aboriginal peoples and the state must work to convince non-Aboriginal Canadians that increased Aboriginal powers can be a win-win situation. If Aboriginal people can gain control over their territories and resources, their communities can prosper and make larger contributions to Canada's economic and social well-being. By improving their socio-economic conditions, Aboriginal peoples could brighten Canada's tarnished international image with regard to its treatment of First Nations.

In an article outlining the preparations made by the Saskatchewan First Nations peoples to work towards "Indian government," Sol Sanderson (1984: 154) points out that in pursuing their objective — to take control over their communities and lives — the local Aboriginal people "have encountered opposition from non-Indian people because the movement towards self-control by Indians is impacting on them." The anxiety among non-Aboriginals is understandable, especially when jobs and livelihoods appear to be at stake. All too often, though, resource corporations have exploited these anxieties. It is far too easy to blame job loss on treaty and land-claims settlements or negotiations — despite the disappearance of resource-sector jobs through runaway plants, downsizing, and technological change.

Industries, such as the forestry, fisheries, and other non-renewable resource areas, have expressed concern about First Nations people gaining control of land or resources that private businesses seek to exploit. Academics have discussed anti-Aboriginal stances and actions taken by non-Aboriginals over fishing rights (Hudson 1990; Cleland 1990). In the 1999 Supreme Court of Canada *Marshall* decision, for instance, the Court held that First Nations citizens have the right to earn a "modest" living under the treaty signed with the Micmac in 1760 (*R. v. Marshall* 1999). Non-Aboriginal fishing people reacted violently to the decision. In certain cases environmentalists, although often allies of Aboriginal peoples on industrial development issues, have also resisted Aboriginal peoples' push for control over resources and land (Clairman 1993). Not surprisingly, then, a 1997 Insight Canada survey showed that public support for increased Aboriginal control was slipping (Aubry 1997: A7).

> Industries, such as the forestry, fisheries, and other non-renewable resource areas, have expressed concern about First Nations people gaining control of land or resources that private businesses seek to exploit.

In the political realm, the former Canadian Alliance Party, now part of the federal Conservative Party, took an anti-treaty and anti-Aboriginal rights stance, asserting that no group in Canada should receive special rights. Right-wing academics such as Mel Smith (1995) and writers for the Fraser Institute and the Canadian Taxpayers Federation also argue against Aboriginal rights. They tend to use economic arguments about the amount of Canadian taxpayers' dollars allotted to Aboriginal people and the amount of land under Aboriginal peoples' control. Although concerns over the spending of taxpayers' dollars are understandable, these critics tend not to look at the overall picture: spending on Aboriginal peoples is, at the very least, no higher than spending on non-Aboriginals. For example, Assembly of First Nations statistics indicate that in 1993 government spending on Native health care was $2,318 per capita compared to $2,476 for non-Aboriginal Canadians (Kenny 1996). Right-wing critics generally ignore the reality of inequality and discrimination inherent in the institutions of Canadian society and the unique historical and constitutional relationship of First Nations and the Crown. The right-wing ideologues argue that no group, Aboriginal peoples or Québécois, should have special rights despite the unique constitutional history of Canada. They fail to understand that the historical relationships have great symbolic and cultural meaning for these groups. Resistance to collective rights is a stance taken by advocates of classical liberalism.

An issue for Aboriginal peoples in liberal democracies is that, because the individual is the basic moral agent, problems can arise when policy-makers or advocates try to apply liberal principles to protect group rights such as Aboriginal or treaty rights. Liberal theorists tend to silence alternative views because they define communities bound by ties of race, religion, language, culture, and lifestyle out of political existence (Svensson

1979). Liberalism believes that only individual rights should be taken seriously. It sees group rights as "derivative" or as deriving from an individual's membership in a particular group (Kapashesit and Klippenstein 1991). Without minority rights, vulnerable groups like Aboriginal peoples would suffer from the tyranny of the majority of nation-states. Liberal states, such as Canada, have trouble accepting "group rights" because they do not view a group as having intrinsic moral worth (Kapashesit and Klippenstein 1991; Weaver 1985). However, some liberal theorists have argued that there is room within liberal theory for Aboriginal group rights (Kymlicka 1989).

Right-wing critics argue that special treatment for some groups at the expense of others is unfair. However, Aboriginal peoples are unique in their relationship with Canada. After all, they were here on these lands before European immigrants began to settle and displace them and assert sovereignty over Aboriginal lands. Furthermore, non-Aboriginal groups have essentially "consented to the liberal individualist political model or ideal, while Aboriginal groups have not" (Kapashesit and Klippenstein 1991). It may be argued that giving special rights to a specific race of people creates a racist society. Will Kymlicka (1989: 241), who has worked on a liberal defence for Aboriginal rights, has stated:

> The main difference, I've argued, is that Aboriginal peoples of Canada, unlike the racists, face unequal circumstances even before they make their choices about which projects to pursue. Unlike White-Canadians, the very existence of their cultural communities is vulnerable to the decisions of the non-Aboriginal majority around them.

Despite the continuing debate, the collective rights of Aboriginal people have been recognized in law with the constitutional entrenchment of Aboriginal and treaty rights in section 35(1) of the *Constitution Act 1982*. These collective rights of Aboriginal people have led to conflict with the individual rights protected in the Charter of Rights and Freedoms. In the case of *Thomas v. Norris*, after members of a First Nations group forcibly took a member of their band to a healing ceremony to help him overcome his addictions, they were ordered to pay compensation by the court. The court found that Aboriginal peoples' collective Aboriginal rights took a secondary position to the individual rights of the individual member (Denis 1996). The case illustrates the strength of the underlying liberal values of individual freedom in our Canadian laws and how they prevail over collective rights.

Critics who ignore the unique historical and constitutional relationship existing between Aboriginal peoples and the Canadian state necessarily begin with a misunderstanding. They fail to recognize that Aboriginal peoples are the founding peoples of this land called Canada, and that they had their autonomy restricted by the imposition of laws based on racism and religious intolerance — a failure that gives a distorted picture of the existing relationship. The prevailing fears of increased powers of self-government for Canada's Aboriginal peoples are unwarranted because such powers would merely give back to Aboriginal peoples powers and rights destroyed for them by colonialism and yet enjoyed by other Canadians. Furthermore, no segment of society should be left behind in this land of opportunity, and when Aboriginal peoples prosper, all Canadians receive the benefits.

NATIVE ECONOMIC DEVELOPMENT IN THE NEW MILLENNIUM

In these early years of the twenty-first century, we seem to have the potential to re-vitalize Aboriginal communities, something that in turn would benefit the country as a whole. But as the Royal Commission on Aboriginal Peoples argues, this potential hinges on a historic reversal: Aboriginal peoples must gain more control over their lives, territories, and resources; they must become self-govern-

> The three factors required for successful economic development are external opportunities, internal assets, and development strategy.

ing. In Aboriginal economic development, any strategies must take account of three types of Aboriginal economies: Indian/Métis land economies, urban economies, and Northern economies (RCAP 1996a). In addition, RCAP (1996a) outlined three factors required for successful economic development on reserves. Based on case studies of reserves in the United States, the three factors are: 1) "external opportunities," which refers to political control over reserve decision-making, access to capital financing, unique economic niches or markets based on the band's strengths and resources, and short distances to markets; 2) "internal assets," which refers to a band's natural resources and lands, human capital, and institutions of governance and culture; and 3) "development strategy," which refers to the choice of plans and approaches to development activity (Cornell and Kalt 1990; RCAP 1996a).

Progress has been made on the first set of factors. First Nations have asserted local sovereignty and now make their own decisions, and many of them have leveraged their strengths and assets to establish successful local economies. For example, the Osooyoos First Nation in southern British Columbia has developed its own economy by building a resort, golf course, cultural interpretive museum, and winery. The Membertou First Nation in Nova Scotia has taken advantage of partnerships in a variety of economic ventures with Georgia Pacific, Sodhexho Marriott Services Canada, and Clearwater Fine Foods. Financial institutions have recently begun to increase services to Aboriginal people. Banks have been set up on reserves. Native newspapers carry many advertise-ments from Canada's leading banks as they compete for First Nations business. The numbers of Aboriginal entrepreneurs are steadily increasing, with Aboriginal businesses numbering 20,000 and Aboriginal tourism generating $270 million annually while employing more than 14,000 people (Voyageur 2005).

With regard to internal assets, various joint Aboriginal-government initiatives hold promise. National Aboriginal organizations have entered into agreements with the federal government to gain local control of training and education programs. Priorities might include short-term skills training or longer-term education within an individual's career plan. Criteria might be based on need or a proven track record. Nevertheless, planning and implementation are in the hands of local Aboriginal people.

The institutional capacity for Native economic development has also grown. Again, largely through the creation of joint Aboriginal-government organizations, Aboriginal peoples have increased their influence over the development process and related government policy. These planning groups include: National Indian Socio-Economic Development Committee; joint Assembly of First Nations/Department of Indian Affairs and Northern Development committees; Aboriginal economic development loan boards; the Native Economic Development Program (NEDP) advisory board, the Native Economic Development Program committees; and Canadian Aboriginal Economic Development Strategy (CAEDS) boards (RCAP 1996a). Many First Nations are focusing greater efforts on developing or strengthening institutions of good governance, such as the West Bank First Nation in the B.C. interior, which has an elaborate and formalized system of its own constitution and laws. In Alberta the Tsuu T'ina First Nation has, located within its reserve lands, its own provincial court, which utilizes a traditional peacemaker process.

This third set of factors may be the most important to Native economic development. Within these choices lie the dangers of assimilation and co-optation. New Aboriginal economic organizations will, necessarily, operate within the context of a global capitalist structure. Entering this economic arena will require developing knowledge about and understanding of capitalist development. Such understanding does not mean accepting or reproducing the capitalist way of doing business (Hosmer and O'Neill 2004). To avoid the political, social, and cultural assimilation that would follow such economic assimilation, Aboriginal organizations must be selective, adapting and modifying existing capitalist business practices to meet their cultural beliefs and needs. Indeed, some writers have argued that this is already the case (Newhouse 1993). As Ian Chapman, Don McCaskill, and David Newhouse (1991) point out, the management of Aboriginal organizations differs from the capitalist norm in that those bodies are based on the values of consensus-making, elders, advisory boards, and holistic employee development. Contemporary literature now argues that a strong indigenous cultural identity is necessary for successful Aboriginal economic development (Smith 2000; Wuttunee 2004). Aboriginal communities are increasingly planning for long-term development and are doing strategic plans or community plans.

Another development strategy could follow the more traditional path of licensing non-Aboriginal corporations to develop resources on traditional lands. But, as the Royal Commission on Aboriginal Peoples (1996a) argues, the licences must include strict performance requirements that benefit Aboriginal communities. In the context of self-government, these requirements would include preferential training and employment at all levels of operations; preferential access to supply contracts; respect for traditional uses of the territories; acceptance of Aboriginal environmental standards; and union participation in these policies (RCAP 1996a). Similarly, joint ventures and partnerships with non-Aboriginal people and corporations could be made to provide economic benefits to Aboriginal communities (Anderson 1995). The key is that Aboriginal peoples, as partners, must play an active role in the economic venture in order to gain the knowledge and experience of running businesses.

Even with full control over their reserve lands and resources, some First Nations will not gain independence, at least in part because most reserves are very small. A land base must include reserve expansion and benefits from industrial development on traditional territories, even where title has been given up. There is an increasing trend of the negotiation of lands bordering or within municipalities being designated as urban reserves, which First Nation leaders view as instruments that can contribute to economic development, where they set up businesses, buildings, and lease space (Barron and Garcea 1999). Co-management agreements with the federal government occurring in the North, for example, do provide some measure of control in determining how and when development will occur and who will benefit from the jobs and wealth created. One example is the Nisga'a Nation, which entered into a modern treaty that includes self-government and some control over traditional lands outside their immediate community lands. As the RCAP (1996a: 799) states, "Aboriginal people must participate in federal, provincial and local economic planning mechanisms (such as economic development commissions, economic planning boards, and local economic task forces). The establishment of genuine partnerships with the non-Aboriginal private sector should also be encouraged."

Joint ventures and partnerships with corporations and governments have been linked historically to the dispossession of Aboriginal peoples and thus may be a new path to cultural genocide. To avoid this new form of assimilation, those involved must continually push government and industry into the "new paradigm" that fully accepts the validation of Aboriginal rights, including the right to self-government.

These development strategies are long-term, and they will lead towards greater financial independence. In the meantime, the need remains for the state to make transfer payments to First Nations peoples, similar to the equalization payments made to Canada's poorest provinces. These payments are part of the treaty obligations that First Nations negotiated and which allowed open access to the settler population to traditional lands and resources. The Royal Commission on Aboriginal Peoples (1996a) recommends that federal, provincial, and territorial governments enter into long-term agreements with First Nations and organizations to provide multi-year funding commitments to support economic development.

A recurrent theme in the reports of the Royal Commission on Aboriginal Peoples (1996a) was the rejection of externally imposed models and approaches to development. Aboriginal peoples want autonomy to build their economies according to their own cultural visions. Aboriginal organizations expressed this same viewpoint through a series of reports critical of the federal approach. Generally, Aboriginal peoples call for a more holistic approach to economic development, centrality of local control and self-government, and recognition of Aboriginal and treaty rights. They call for a collective or community emphasis while allowing for individualism. They want approaches that reflect a basic compatibility with the Aboriginal culture and identity, the support of traditional economies, a transfer from social assistance to economic development assist- ance, and a recognition that the influence of Aboriginal culture on business development is not uniform (RCAP 1996a).

> Aboriginal peoples call for a more holistic approach to economic development, centrality of local control and self-government, and recognition of Aboriginal and treaty rights. They call for a collective or community emphasis.

Aboriginal peoples require more control over on-reserve activities and businesses. They have made moves towards increasing jurisdictional control over reserve lands and resources. The *First Nations Gazette* (1997) provides a list of First Nations communities from across the country that have passed and implemented band bylaws on various aspects of regulation of reserve lands. Frideres (1991) argues that Aboriginal people need to gain control of jurisdictional, financial, managerial, and tribal matters.

The heavy price tag causes some onlookers and participants to withhold support for federal and provincial legislatures entering into long-term funding for Aboriginal economic development. But as the Royal Commission clearly pointed out, the failure to adopt this long-term strategy will carry an equally heavy burden in the form of social service provisions necessary to provide for the rapidly growing number of Aboriginal people who would be without employment. The partnership approach is most desir- able because it enables the First Nations to be more involved in governance, develop- ment, and sharing the wealth of Canada. It is a win-win situation and recognizes the "new relationship" between Aboriginal peoples and the Canadian state. Rejecting the partnership approach could perpetuate Aboriginal poverty and continued conflict.

CONCLUSION

Aboriginal peoples were once distinct and sovereign nations on the land that is now recognized as Canada. They had their own systems of laws, religion, and other institu- tions, all of which supported self-governance. Long after contact with Europeans they remained sovereign — so much so that they were not only partners in the fur trade economy but also participated in the wars between the European powers in North America. As European settlement in North America grew, the Europeans' desire for more lands and resources became insatiable. The newcomers justified taking First Nations' land by characterizing Aboriginal peoples — their former benefactors and allies — as being less than human. The Europeans created laws based on racist and religious intolerance designed to dispossess Aboriginal peoples of their land, resources, and cultures.

Over time, Aboriginal peoples' numbers were depleted by disease and epidemics. Non-Aboriginals saw them as a dying race. The First Nations increasingly came under the control of the state and its institutions and were subjugated by a foreign set of im- posed laws. Many academics have explained this loss of control by applying the tenets of "dependency theory," arguing that Aboriginal peoples were controlled by outside institutions and individuals and thus became dependent on the state, particularly the

Department of Indian Affairs. The theory explains how Aboriginal peoples became dependent, but it does not adequately explain how Aboriginal people continually resisted the domination and control by outsiders. This resistance took many forms, from passive resistance to armed conflict; it was used to exercise their independence and, recently, to increase their control over their lives. The state and interest groups have met this increased control, however, with their own resistance, often based on the argument that no group should have special rights. Liberal ideology, with its dislike for collective rights, lends support, and the courts have given primacy to individual rights over collective rights.

Right-wing, neo-conservatives' resistance to increased Aboriginal control relies on classical liberal notions and tends to ignore the constitutional and historical relationship between Aboriginal peoples and the non-Aboriginals who settled Canada. The classical liberal notions of equality and neutrality in the law ignore how liberal laws promote and protect certain Western European values such as individualism and capitalism, which necessarily lead to race and class stratification and inequality. They also ignore the tendency, in practice, of our liberal laws and institutions to systemically discriminate against certain ethnic groups, including Aboriginal peoples.

Aboriginal peoples have struggled within the structures of Canadian society and are regaining control over and management of substantial tracts of land through comprehensive and specific land claims settlements. Pamela Sloan and Roger Hill (1995) point out that corporate Canada "has come courting" Aboriginal communities because of the changing power base within the communities. They view power as moving from the Canadian government to the communities.

It makes sense for Canadian citizens to embrace the growing control of land and resources, and increasing powers of self-government for Aboriginal peoples. In this new millennium, Aboriginal peoples should be viewed more as partners in Canadian society and recognized for the important contributions they make, and have made, to Canadian society and its immense wealth. Their voices must be heard, respected, and accommodated in discussions and planning for resource development in their traditional territories. They still have important interests and rights to those lands, whether the territories have been ceded or not. They must receive a share in the economic and employment benefits that flow from development of the land and resources. They must not be left behind.

Co-management agreements can make Aboriginal peoples partners in land and resource extraction in their traditional territories. The Aboriginal worldview, which respects nature, can be used to help build the ethic of sustainable development that protects the environment. The time is favourable for First Nations to regain control over their economies and an increased role over their traditional territories. With increased power and control come increased responsibilities, accountability, and the potential for abuse of powers. Aboriginal leaders and their emerging professional and business elite must be responsible to their communities. Aboriginal communities may combine traditional government with mainstream notions of accountability and must make the professional development of their leaders a priority so they have the competencies necessary to manage their governments, institutions, and businesses effectively and efficiently (Calliou 2005). The use of elders as advisors and of consensus decision-making can help to make the leaders and elite in the communities accountable.

To reflect their increased control, Aboriginal peoples should approach their relationships with federal and provincial governments as partnerships. They must work to obtain solutions that require compromise and reconciliation. They must argue that their goals are similar to those of Canadian society and that all Canadians should share in the benefits of the land and resources. Sharing the wealth is not a zero-sum game in which one side loses if the other wins. First Nations people want to be treated as equals by the Canadian state — as partners in a common purpose in which everybody can win. However, they want to maintain their distinct cultures, and they desire that Canadian society respects their difference. It is our hope that Canadian citizens can picture a scenario in which Aboriginal men and women work alongside non-Aboriginal persons in a partnership aimed at giving all Canadians the chance at the good life.

GLOSSARY OF KEY TERMS

Aboriginal peoples: Those who have a special historical and constitutional relationship with the Crown because they are the original peoples to this land (that is, they were living in what is now called Canada before the arrival of the Europeans).

Aboriginal rights: Refers to the rights that Aboriginal peoples (defined by the *Constitution Act* 1982, s. 35(2), as Indians, Inuit, and Métis) have due to their prior use and occupation of North America as self-governing, sovereign nations before the arrival of Europeans. These rights include the right to land, hunting, fishing, gathering, and self-government.

Colonialism: Refers to a specific relationship between countries where one intrudes on the other and formally dominates it politically and economically, and exploits its human and natural resources, including land. The invaded country, the colony, is exploited to enrich the colonial power, the mother country.

Dependency theory: A way of explaining the exploitative relationship between countries. A colonial power, through imperialism (spreading its control and exploitation throughout the world), establishes certain relations that place the colonized society in a state of dependence for income and support.

Indians: Those peoples who inhabited North America before the arrival of Europeans and are now referred to as First Nations; people who fall within the legal definition imposed by the *Indian Act* and for whom the federal government is willing to assume responsibility — often referred to as "Registered Indians" or "Status Indians."

Land claims: Made by Aboriginal peoples to the traditional lands they historically oc-cupied and used. There are two general categories: (1) comprehensive claims are based on the assertion of continuing Aboriginal title to lands and resources in areas where treaties were not entered; (2) specific claims deal with specific actions or omissions by government where treaties were entered but government promises were not kept, or where First Nations assets were unlawfully surrendered.

Metropolis/hinterland theory: Emphasizes how important economic, political, or social decisions made by the elite, who live in a metropolitan centre, have an impact on popu-lations living in the hinterland (rural regions). The metropolitan centre's political and economic elite exploits hinterland raw materials and sells finished products back to these outlying areas. Local hinterland communities are the most affected by the metropolitan elite's decisions for large-scale capitalist developments, yet have little or no voice.

Modernization theory: Views societies as advancing through stages from primitive to highly advanced technical and industrialized "civilized" societies. Technological progress and industrialization are inevitable, and traditional economies must modernize. Traditional societies must shed their cultural beliefs and practices and gain the skills and knowledge necessary for participation in a modern capitalist economy.

Potlatch: A Pacific Coast First Nations traditional social and religious ceremony, dur-ing which a host entertains guests with feasts, songs, and stories and distributes gifts. It has many purposes, including establishing rank among members, confirming rank, or celebrating an important event. The Canadian government outlawed the potlatch through an amendment to the *Indian Act* in 1884.

Self-government: A political tool by which First Nations or Aboriginal groups make their own decisions regarding the allocation of scarce resources, without answering to a higher authority. The concept involves law-making decisions regarding membership, land, and resources within reserve land or traditional territories. Self-government is an Aboriginal right preceding the assertion of European sovereignty.

Sun dance: A traditional social and religious ceremony of Plains Indians in which par-ticipants (dancers) fast for four days while praying, singing, and dancing within a circular dance lodge constructed around a centre pole. The dance is meant to appease the sun and other spirits through prayers and rituals and to gain individual strength.

QUESTIONS FOR DISCUSSION

1. What impact has racism had on Aboriginal life in Canada?
2. Do you agree or disagree that Aboriginals must shed their culture and traditions to "make it" in mainstream society. Why?

3. Discuss the differences between the liberalism and collectivism worldviews.
4. How has Aboriginal peoples' participation in the Canadian economy changed over time?
5. Will Aboriginal self-government aid or deter resource development in their traditional territories?
6. How have the courts helped Aboriginal peoples in their quest for social, economic, and political justice in Canada?
7. How have Aboriginal economic ventures contributed to the Canadian economy?

WEBSITES OF INTEREST

Turtle Island. <www.turtleisland.org>.
Canadian and International Indigenous Peoples. <www.bloorstreet.com>.
Aboriginal Business Canada. <www.abc-eac.ic.gc.ca>.
Aboriginal Connections. <www.aboriginalconnections.com>.
Aboriginal Multi-Media Society of Alberta. <www.ammsa.com>.
Indian and Northern Affairs Canada. <www.inac-ainc.gc.ca>.

NOTE

1. We use the terms Aboriginal and Native interchangeably throughout this chapter. The terms include First Nations, Métis, and Inuit. The term Indian or First Nations speaks exclusively of those individuals or communities governed by the *Indian Act*.

Chapter Six

KEEPING CANADA WHITE
Immigration Enforcement in Canada

Wendy Chan

In the spring of 2006, hundreds of protesters went out onto the streets of Canada's major cities to march against what many regard as Canada's overly restrictive and unfair immigration policies (*Globe and Mail* 2006a). Supporters argued that immigration enforcement officers were too heavy-handed in their approach with immigrants. They said that the deportation of undocumented immigrant workers must stop, and that a full regularization program should be set in place. According to various news accounts, undocumented immigrants and their families spoke of the inhumane treatment they had received at the hands of the Canadian Border Services Agency, now the primary institution for immigration enforcement in Canada.

In the same week that these protests took place, newspapers in Canada were also reporting on a growing public concern about how refugees, particularly failed refugee claimants, were fuelling a crime wave. Questions were being raised about the adequacy of Canada's immigration enforcement policies. A series of high-profile criminal cases committed by recent immigrants had led critics (Campbell 2000; Bauer 1999) to argue that Canada's immigration system was "too soft" and was allowing the "wrong" type of immigrants into the country.

> **"You Should Know This"**
> - In 2005 Canada admitted 262,236 immigrants as permanent residents.
> - In 2004 and 2005 the top source countries for immigrants to Canada were China, India, Philippines, Pakistan and the United States. In 2005, of 262,236 immigrants, 75,291 came from China and India.
> - In 2005 Canada had 19,624 refugee claims. The previous lowest number of claims since the implementation of the current refugee system in 1989 was 1989, when there were 20,056 claims. In 2005, 63 percent of claims were inland, 20 percent at the land border, and 17 percent at the airport.
> - Under the *Immigration and Refugee Protection Act*, detention reviews for refugee protection claimants are held in-camera. This process recognizes the need to protect the confidentiality of the claimant.
> - The IRPA permits the arrest of people in Canada who are uncooperative and fail to establish their identities, provided that they are not permanent residents or protected persons.
> - As of January 2004, permanent residents are required to carry the Permanent Residents Card for re-entry into Canada.
>
> Sources: Citizenship and Immigration Canada 2005; Globe and Mail Oct. 18: A7; Citizenship and Immigration Canada 2006; Canadian Council for Refugees listserve, January, 2006.; IRPA 2002.

What are we to think about Canada's approach to immigration enforcement? Is it too harsh and racist, as many immigrants argue? Or is it not harsh enough because it permits immigrants and refugees who commit crimes to enter into Canada?

Many immigration scholars agree that successive reforms to immigration policies in Canada have resulted in increasingly harsh and punitive measures, particularly as related to the enforcement provisions of the *Immigration Act*. Both the language used and the substantive changes contained in various amendments construct negative images of immigrants as "abusers" of Canada's "generous" immigration system, as "bogus" refugee claimants, and as "criminals" who "cheat" their way into Canada. The latest immigration act, the *Immigration and Refugee Protection Act* (IRPA), exemplifies the criminalizing and retributive tone that is now commonplace in immigration policy-making. The convergence of criminal justice strategies with concerns regarding immigration control found in the IRPA, the most comprehensive set of amendments since the introduction of the *Immigration Act* in 1975, marks an important direction in Canadian immigration policy-making.

Yet immigration critics continue to argue that not enough is being done to ensure that the best immigrants are allowed entry while potential immigrants who pose a threat are screened out. Critics also argue that the rules must be the same for everyone, and therefore undocumented immigrants should not be given "special" treatment. A letter to the editor published in the *Toronto Star* (2006b) is typical:

> Our illegal immigrants have paraded through the streets of Toronto demanding their rights, which obviously includes the right to ignore our laws and just do as they please. This is a criminal act and should be viewed as one. Demanding your rights does not include ignoring the law of any country, including this one. Therefore, I believe immediate expulsion is in order in spite of all the overzealous lawyers who have in the past encouraged disregard for these laws.

Ironically, after being elected in early 2006, Stephen Harper's minority Conservative government — many of whose members were once among Canada's harshest immigration critics — recognized that these issues are more complex and difficult than newspapers would suggest.

Untangling the myths and controversies around immigration enforcement requires a critical examination of enforcement provisions in the IRPA. Taking a critical approach involves asking how immigration laws and policies acknowledge issues of gender, race, and class differences in the development, interpretation, and application of the country's approaches. The allegations of an effort to keep Canada "white" by excluding immigrants of colour call for a close consideration of how well (or not) immigrants of colour fare under the new immigration act. As we shall see, the trend towards criminalizing and demonizing immigrants is nothing new, and race and racism have played an important role in organizing racial identities and enforcing a specific racial reality in Canada. Then too, the enforcement provisions of the *Immigration and Refugee Protection Act* seek to address public concerns over "problem" immigrants, which means that it is important to consider the rationale for these provisions, as well as the responses and criticisms to them. Is there an adequate balance between enforcement and protection for immigrants? The new act appears to mark racialized immigrants as criminals and outsiders, with enforcement provisions driven by the need to scapegoat and punish immigrants for a range of fears and insecurities, an approach legitimized by racist ideologies and practices. Immigrants of colour pay the price for Canadians' need to be reassured that their established way of life will not be lost and that immigrants are not "taking over" their country. The result is that many immigrants will continue to be marginalized and excluded as full participants in Canadian society.

CANADIAN IMMIGRATION POLICY: RECENT

Canada, like many Western democratic countries, experienced a continued decline in births after the 1960s, combined with a relatively low level of immigration. The implications of this demographic raised concerns about whether there would be enough people to keep the country afloat. In the 1980s Brian Mulroney's Progressive Conservative government sought to address these problems, and boost the economy, by increasing levels of immigration, targeting both young people, particularly those of child-bearing age, and skilled immigrant workers. In particular, the Business Immigration Program added a new category of immigrants, investors, to boost the number of educated and skilled immigrants entering Canada (Li 2003: 27). The result was a significant increase in immigration levels during the late 1980s and early 1990s. Between 1980 and 2000, immigration accounted for almost half of the country's population growth, with over 3.7 million immigrants admitted (Li 2003: 32). In comparison, between 1955 and 1970 Canada had admitted just over 1.6 million immigrants, accounting for 30 percent of total population growth.

The composition of immigrants was also shifting. Whereas in the postwar period immigrants came mainly from Britain and continental Europe (87 percent of immigrants from 1946 to 1955), by the 1980s and 1990s Asia and the Pacific region had become the key source continent for immigrants (53.8 percent from 1970 to 2000). By 1998–2000 the top four source countries were China, India, Pakistan, and the Philippines (CIC 2001a: 8). Much of this shift can be attributed to alterations in immigration policies in the 1960s. The changes allowed Canada to abandon national origin as a selection criterion, and admit immigrants from all over the world. The implementation of the point system[1] in 1967 and, subsequently, the *Immigration Act of 1976* removed the explicit racial and ethnic discrimination found in previous policies, with the effect that many more immigrants from non-European countries were now being admitted into Canada (Li 2003: 33).

Throughout the 1980s and 1990s, the public debate about immigration was also heating up. The increasing numbers of non-white immigrants had not gone unnoticed and had contributed to an immigrant backlash, promoting views that Canada could not absorb all this "diversity" (Li 2001) and that the "quality" of immigrants was threatening the destruction of the nation (Thobani 2000). While immigration was on the increase, so too were unemployment rates. Public-opinion polls highlighted immigration as a hot-button issue — primarily, many pollsters believed, because the public associated high unemployment rates with too much immigration (Palmer 1996; Economic Council of Canada 1991). Opinion polls recorded between 1988 and 1993 found that 30–45 percent of the Canadian population believed the country had too many immigrants, and indicated that hostility towards immigrants was on the rise (Palmer 1996). The polls expressed fears and anxieties about immigrants not assimilating sufficiently and creating social problems. Clearly, the issue of immigration had become highly charged, with pro-immigration and anti-immigration sentiments being strongly asserted in all types of public forums.

The issue, however, was not so black and white. While immigration was increasing, only certain types of immigrants were gaining access to Canada. The gender, class, and race dynamics of the immigration system were not lost on many critics of the recent reforms. Although the point system appeared to be neutral in terms of how it evaluated potential immigrants, the resources provided to immigration offices abroad were having an impact on who actually got their applications processed in a timely manner. The United States, Britain, and Western Europe had reasonably adequate immigration services, but in non-traditional source areas, such as Africa and parts of South Asia, immigration services were few and far between, resulting in administrative delays and long waiting periods. As well, the professional qualifications of potential immigrants from countries in the Northern Hemisphere were given greater weight than the qualifications of immigrants trained in the South (CCR 2000: 12). Wealthier applicants were also given preferential treatment in that they were not assessed on all criteria of the points system if they met the criteria of the investors program.[2] These hidden biases resulted in continued racial and ethnic as well as class-based discrimination by favouring potential immigrants from countries more similar to Canada than not.

Gender biases also played a role, particularly in the types of categories that immigrants slotted themselves into when they applied for entry into Canada. Typically, men are the primary or main applicant, and women are in the category of dependent spouse. Although many women who come to Canada are skilled, they may not have had access to a traditional education, which is recognized through the point system and which in turn makes it difficult for them to succeed as the main applicant. Abu-Laban and Gabriel (2002: 49) also point out that how skills are constructed relies on a sexual division of labour. Women's work, both paid and unpaid — for example, cleaning, caring, cooking — is devalued in the point system because it is classified as unskilled or semi-skilled, and offers few if any points. Furthermore, patriarchal attitudes continue to cast women into the role of being dependent on men, and Canadian immigration policies and practices rely on these assumptions in the processing of applications. The net effect is that potential female immigrants have the best chances of entering into

> Although the point system appeared to be neutral in terms of how it evaluated potential immigrants, it was the resources provided to immigration offices abroad that had an impact on who actually got their applications processed in a timely manner.

Canada by assuming the role of dependent spouse regardless of whether they fit that category or not. For women who do not have male applicants to support their immigration applications, the chances of successfully immigrating are greatly diminished. The only category in which women's applications have been largely successful is when they are able to enter Canada through the Live-In Caregivers Program (LCP). This program allows women to migrate to Canada and work for three years as a live-in caregiver, after which they can apply for permanent residence status.[3] Yet the relationship of these women to Canada is still precarious, because upon entering Canada they are not given landed status, but a temporary permit only. They have to satisfy the contractual agreement with their employers before they become eligible for landed status and possibly citizenship.[4]

The worry over illegal immigration to Canada and the high numbers of refugee applications further intensified the debate about the effectiveness of Canada's immigration system. Although the problem of "illegal" entry is an accepted problem in any immigration system, a number of high-profile cases of immigrants and refugees (for example, Chinese boat people) seeking entry led the public to conclude that Canada's immigration system was no longer effective and that more reform was necessary. What the public wasn't aware of, however, was that most "illegal" immigrants were not in fact cases of people seeking entry, but of people whose visas had expired and who had not yet left the country. Furthermore, governments have never regarded the problem of "illegal" entry into Canada to be a major immigration issue. Indeed, over the years a number of amnesty programs had been implemented to regularize immigrants who lacked proper documentation (Robinson 1983). If a "crisis" situation did exist, it was that the media and political opportunists permitted the public's imagination on this issue to run unchecked, resulting in uninformed speculation about Canada's immigration system.

Controlling Immigration and Immigrants

A key element of many Western countries' immigration programs includes determining who is denied access. In Canada the perceived need to control the flow of immigrants resulted in a marked resurgence of strictures in Canadian policy in the 1980s, a trend that peaked in the 1990s and coincided with the politicization of immigration. Beginning with the *Immigration Act of 1975*, numerous reforms and amendments led to more strict and exclusionary requirements. Search and seizure provisions were expanded, and refugee claimants would be photographed and fingerprinted upon arrival. Fines and penalties were increased for transportation companies that brought in individuals who lacked appropriate documentation (Kelley and Trebilcock 1998).

Various explanations have been offered for why these changes occurred. Many authors cite the breakdown in Canada's refugee system combined with the rise in requests for asylum as a major contribut-

These conditions paved the way for independent immigrants (typically male, business class) to be viewed as more desirable than dependent immigrants (typically women and children, family class).

ing factor (Creese 1992; Matas 1989). The backlog of applications, the cumbersome administrative process, and allegations that the refugee system was being abused challenged the legitimacy of the system. Other explanations included the lack of consensus amongst the political parties over what is an acceptable level of immigration, along with the belief that immigrants applying to Canada should be more self-reliant. These conditions paved the way for independent immigrants (typically male, business class) to be viewed as more desirable than dependent immigrants (typically women and children, family class). Racist beliefs — to the effect that different racial and ethnic backgrounds of immigrants were eroding Canadian values and traditions — shaped the contours of the debates around these issues (Frideres 1996).

In 1987 the federal government introduced two major policy reforms, Bill C-55 and Bill C-84, in response to unanticipated high levels of refugee claims, which were placing a major strain on the immigration system. The *Refugee Reform Act* (Bill C-55) created the Immigration and Refugee Board of Canada (previously the Immigration Appeal Board) and restructured the refugee determination process to respond to the problem of unfounded refugee claims. Refugees were now required to undergo a screening hearing to determine the credibility of their claims. *The Refugee Deterrents and Detention Act* (Bill C-84) gave immigration officers and agents more power to detain and remove refugee arrivals, particularly those considered criminals or a security threat (Kelley and Trebilcock 1998: 386). Both of these reforms led to heated debates, with many critics arguing that the changes proposed were not well-thought-out pieces of legislation but, rather, a reactionary and knee-jerk response to an alleged refugee "crisis" that had been created by the media (Creese 1992: 140–41). Due to these intense debates, the implementation of these bills did not occur until January 1989. Interestingly, the procedure of screening refugees at the beginning of the refugee determination process was eventually eliminated when it was discovered that 95 percent of refugee claims were legitimate (Garcia y Griego 1994: 128). In other words, the speculation that many refugees were "bogus" was unwarranted; the process of forcing refugees to undergo a screening was eventually removed in 1992.

Attempts to curtail and control immigration continued into the 1990s, when two more pieces of legislation were introduced to address security concerns and the growing belief that illegal immigrants rather than legitimate refugees were infiltrating Canada's borders. Introduced in June 1992, Bill C-86 proposed primarily restrictive revisions to the refugee determination system. The restrictions included fingerprinting refugee claimants, harsher detention provisions, making refugee hearings open to the public, and requiring Convention Refugees[5] applying for landing in Canada to have a passport, valid travel document, or "other satisfactory identity document" (CCR 2000). In addition, individuals with criminal or terrorist links would no longer be admissible. In July 1995 the government introduced Bill C-44, better known as the "Just Desserts" bill because it was enacted in response to the killing of a Toronto police officer by a landed immigrant with a long criminal record. Sergio Marchi, the immigration minister, reminded Canadians that immigration is a privilege and not a right and proposed changes that would "go a long way to stopping the tyranny of a minority criminal element" (Marchi 1995). Bill C-44 made it easier to remove from Canada permanent residents who were deemed by the minister to be a "danger to the public." This would be done by restricting their ability to appeal their deportation orders or submit a refugee claim. The bill included additional measures to address fraud and multiple refugee claims.

Like the earlier reforms, these two bills were equally divisive and resulted in intense public and political debates. The most controversial change implemented was the discretionary power given to the immigration minister to deport a permanent resident. Widespread academic and public discussions ensued, with legal scholars arguing that returning discretionary power to the minister was "a throwback to a less enlightened era" (Haigh and Smith 1998: 291) and advocates for a fairer immigration policy arguing that the new provisions were racist and would have the result of increasing the criminalization of non-European individuals in Canada (Hassan-Gordon 1996; Noorani and Wright 1995). Yet some critics believed that Bill C-44 had not gone far enough in tightening up the system against false claimants and criminals. The Reform Party argued that a "criminal is a criminal" and that it was not sufficient to define "serious criminality" as offences carrying a ten-year sentence or longer (Kelley and Trebilcock 1998: 434). That party's position highlights how, despite the lack of research demonstrating any links between immigrants and high crime rates, public fear about crime, based only on several high-profile cases, could be easily manipulated to argue for tighter immigration controls.

These debates highlight how immigration had, by the mid-1990s, become a hot-button issue for politicians and policy-makers as the Canadian public became more involved in shaping Canada's immigration system. Teitelbaum and Winter (1998: 188) attribute this change to the presence of the Reform Party, and that party's calls in the 1993 election for an abandonment of the policy of multiculturalism and significant reductions in Canada's annual immigration levels. The right-wing populist movement in Canada, as elsewhere, recognized that immigration and immigrants were easy targets in placing blame for the economic decline of the time. Furthermore, such views coincided neatly with the shift to neo-liberal approaches in public-policy development — approaches that fostered a belief in how the more vulnerable sectors of society, such as single mothers and immigrants, were to blame for the lack of jobs or high crime rate (Abu-Laban 1998: 194). Good immigrants, it was understood, were those who could look after themselves and their families. With this came the "common-sense" view that strong immigration controls were a necessary component of any effective immigration system. The harsh government reforms of the 1980s and 1990s delivered the message that security and enforcement were now key priorities in immigration policy-making.

> The right-wing populist movement in Canada, as elsewhere, recognized that immigration and immigrants were easy targets in placing blame for the economic decline of the time.

THE IMMIGRATION AND REFUGEE PROTECTION ACT 2002

Crepeau and Nakache (2006: 4) note that while immigration controls emerged years before 9/11, those attacks gave authorities more incentive to radically overhaul policies and make them harsher towards unwanted migrants. Canada, like many other states affected by aspects of globalization, transformed immigration from a policy issue into a security issue. The introduction of the *Immigration and Refugee Protection Act* in 2002 thus marks an important shift in Canadian immigration policy-making. As the Standing Committee on Citizenship and Immigration (2001) affirmed, "The *Immigration and Refugee Protection Act* represents a significant step in addressing current security concerns. Even though drafted before September 11th, the legislation was clearly created with the threat of terrorism in mind." The Canadian government's response in deterring these activities and individuals is to impose tighter sanctions and increase levels of scrutiny and authority for immigration officers.

According to Citizenship and Immigration Canada (CIC), the IRPA is intended to serve a number of different immigration goals, such as attracting skilled workers, protecting refugees, allowing family reunification, and deterring traffickers. The aim, according to the Liberal government of the time, was to accomplish these goals by simplifying the legislation and striking the necessary balance between efficiency, fairness, and security. CIC asserts that there is a need to "simplify," "strengthen," "modernize," and "streamline" the immigration system. A key priority in this set of policy reforms was to close "the back door to criminals and others who would abuse Canada's openness and generosity." This would be achieved by including in the act the necessary provisions to "better ensure serious criminals and individuals who are threats to public safety are kept out of Canada, and, if they have entered the country, that they are removed as quickly as possible" (CIC 2001b).

> As the Maytree Foundation stated, IRPA "is much more about who cannot come to Canada and how they will be removed, than it is about who we will welcome, who we will protect, and how we will do that."

The new legislation would have a significant impact on controlling immigration to Canada. While some immigrant and refugee groups applauded the changes to the family reunification and sponsorship requirements, immigrant supporting organizations pointed to growing concerns and trepidation about an act that was overly reactive and too "obsessed" with security issues. As the Maytree Foundation[6] (2001: 3) stated, IRPA "is much more about who cannot come to Canada and how they will be removed, than it is about who we will welcome, who we will protect, and how we will do that." Many organizations expressed an uneasiness that racialized immigrants would suffer the consequences of immigration officers' concerns about the need to maintain border security. Moreover, women refugees and immigrants would be likely to shoulder the burden of the many changes that encompassed racist and sexist practices.

Targeting Traffickers and Smugglers

Within the IRPA, the crime of human smuggling and trafficking involves several types of activities. It is an offence to organize, induce, aid, or abet immigrants to Canada who do not have the necessary travel documents (s. 117). The trafficking of persons through abduction, fraud, deception, the use or threat of force or coercion (s. 118), and leaving a person or persons at sea for the purposes of helping them come to Canada (s. 119) are also offences subject to criminal penalties. The difference between trafficking and human smuggling rests in the distinction between coerced and consensual irregular migrants. People who are trafficked (usually into forced labour or prostitution) are assumed not to have given their consent and are considered "victims," whereas migrants who are smuggled are considered to have willingly engaged in the enterprise (Bhabha 2005).

The penalty for organizing the smuggling of less than ten people is a maximum of ten years imprisonment or a $500,000 fine, or both, for the first offence, or a maximum of fourteen years imprisonment or a $1 million fine, or both, for subsequent offences. When ten persons or more are involved, the penalty is a maximum of life imprisonment or a $1 million fine, or both. Trafficking persons or leaving them at sea carries a maximum penalty of life imprisonment, a fine of $1 million, or both (s. 120). Aggravating factors (s. 121) such as the occurrence of harm or death during the offence or the association of the offence with a criminal organization will be considered in determining the penalty imposed.

The Canadian Council for Refugees (CCR) argues that the effect of attempting to deter the activities of human smuggling and trafficking can have the unintended consequence of criminalizing family members who help refugees escape from their home countries (given that the law does not distinguish between smugglers for profit and others who are just trying to help). While the claimants can escape prosecution if they are found to be refugees (s. 133), their family members are not equally protected because they can be denied an asylum hearing or lose permanent residence without the possibility of an appeal (Crepeau and Jimenez 2004). Nor are individuals who apply for asylum in good faith but are rejected adequately protected. Given the lack of differentiation, both categories of individuals — those who engage in human smuggling for profit and those who are motivated by humanitarian concerns — will suffer the same penalties.

Moreover, while these provisions are intended to bring Canadian immigration policy in line with international protocols such as the U.N. Convention against Transnational Organized Crime, and thus have included strong enforcement measures to curtail and deter human smuggling and trafficking in persons, the bill has no provisions for protection of those being smuggled or trafficked, even though Canada is also a signatory to the U.N. Convention on the Status of Refugees. It would seem that while Canada has sought to meet some of its international obligations, in other agreements that Canada has undertaken it has yet to fully realize compliance. As the CCR points out, "The migrant protocol states that the criminalization measures are not to apply to people who are smuggled into a country, whereas Bill C-11 [now the IRPA] gives an exemption only to those recognized as refugees." As a result, protection from prosecution is limited only to those who can make a successful refugee claim.

Yet obtaining refugee status is a political process, and as the Vancouver Association of Chinese Canadians noted in the government's treatment of the Chinese boat refugees in the summer of 1999, over one hundred people were prevented from making a refugee claim. Morrison and Crosland (2001) argue that the deterrent effect of such grossly exaggerated penalties is doubtful since entry into the "Western fortress" necessitates that irregular migrants and refugees use some kind of help to enter Western countries for any reason.

Interdiction and Detention

Attempts to prevent and deter irregular migrants from entering Canada have resulted in a number of measures that were initiated or retooled in the IRPA either to stop migrants from setting foot in Canada or to swiftly remove them. Interdiction measures include the Smart Border Agreement between Canada and the United States. In that agreement Canada increased the number of countries for which it requires visas to be held by foreign nationals to enter the country (DFAIT 2004). Coupled with this are penalties (up to $3,200 per traveller) against airlines, railways, and shipping companies that fail in advance to check their passengers for adequate documentation (IRPA, s. 148[1][a] and s. 279[1]). Finally, immigration officers are also stationed at various countries of origin or of transit with the aim of stopping migrants before they reach Canada (DFAIT 2004).

With the IRPA, immigration detention and the power to detain have been fortified. Sections 55 and 56 of the new act state that someone can be detained if there are reasonable grounds to believe that the person would be inadmissible to Canada, a danger to the public, or unlikely to appear for future proceedings. Enhanced powers have also been given to immigration officers at ports of entry to detain people on the basis of administrative convenience, suspicion of inadmissibility on the grounds of security or human rights violations, and failure to establish identity for any immigration procedure under the act. Immigration officers also have wider discretion to arrest and detain a foreign national but not a protected person without a warrant, even in cases where they are not being removed (s. 55[2]). The length of detention is not specified for any of these grounds. Thus, someone who fails to provide adequate identification can be detained for the same length of time as can a person who is considered a danger to the public (s. 58[1]). Children can be detained, but only as a measure of last resort (s. 60).

Many concerns have been raised about the nature of the detention provisions and the manner in which they will be executed. The fear amongst most immigrant and refugee organizations is that conferring greater powers to individual immigration officers will result in racial profiling and that a high proportion of racialized migrants will end up being detained (CCR 2001; Getting Landed Project 2002). Other worries include the broad arbitrary use of power by immigration officers, the possibility of long-term detention of migrants who fail to establish their identities, the criminalization of trafficked or smuggled migrants who will be detained for the purpose of deterring human traffickers, and the use of detention on the basis of group status rather than on the particular circumstances of the person involved.

The UNHCR (United Nations High Commission for Refugees) states that it opposes any detention policy that is fashioned to deter asylum seekers or to discourage them from pursuing their refugee claims. Moreover, it cautions against establishing a policy that detains migrants on the basis of being "unlikely to appear" at an immigration hearing because of their "*mode of arrival*" to Canada, because many refugees are forced to use smugglers in order to reach safety (UNHCR 2001: 29). Finally, it argues that the act of detaining a person for failing to establish their identity, which includes making determinations about the person's level of co-operation with authorities, calls for a recognition of the difference between a willful intention to deceive and the inability to provide documentation (UNHCR 2001: 30). The UNHCR joins the voices of others (CCR 2001; Maytree Foundation 2001) who also recommend that the government needs to establish clear guidelines and criteria as to what constitutes a refusal to co-operate.

The drift towards the use of preventative detention to deal with migrants perpetuates the mistaken and prejudiced perceptions that those being detained are a threat to public safety and are behaving illegally rather than being people who actually need safety from danger (CCR 2001). Indeed, the culture of criminalization within the present immigration system points to disturbing trends. Unlike convicted offenders, migrants can face indefinite lengths of detention as they wait for the arrival of their identity documents, and they can be detained on the basis of suspicion or convenience. Statistics published since the implementation of the IRPA note that the use of detention has increased, both in the number of non-citizens held and the length of time people have been detained (Crepeau and Nakache 2006: 16). For example, 2003–04 saw a 16 percent increase in the number of people detained compared to the previous year (13,413), a 40 percent increase compared to 2001–02 (9,542), and a 68 percent increase compared to 1999–2000 (7,968) (Crepeau and Nakache 2006: 16). Somewhat ironically, the increased federal spending in this area has resulted in detention being used not for people who are considered threats to security, but instead to detain migrants who arrive without adequate documentation (Dench 2004).

> The drift towards the use of preventative detention to deal with migrants perpetuates the mistaken and prejudiced perceptions that those being detained are a threat to public safety and are behaving illegally rather than being people who actually need safety from danger.

Loss of Appeal Rights

The elimination of immigration appeals in Canada, particularly in cases where "serious criminality" is involved, is a measure that many other countries have not implemented to the same extent. Section 64 of the new act states that individuals found to be inadmissible on considerations of security, violating human rights, serious criminality, or organized criminality, or individuals convicted of a crime and given a term of imprisonment of two years or more may not be allowed to appeal to the Immigration Appeal Division. Although judicial review remains available, applicants who lose their right to appeal can apply to the federal courts but only with leave from the court and only if there is a purely legal issue that needs to be dealt with. Therefore, if a factual mistake is made, or if all the evidence was reasonably considered by the original decision-maker (even if that person reached the wrong conclusion), the federal court will not intervene. The effect of this change is to disallow any of the discretion formerly exercised in determining whether an individual should or should not be removed based on the circumstances of their case. While these changes may make the system more efficient, they do so at the cost of diminishing the rights of immigrants. As one commentator notes, such an approach illustrates a move towards a "mechanical application of the rules," which is the antithesis of the just administration of the law (Dent 2002: 762).

The introduction of the new act also included provisions for the establishment of a Refugee Appeal Division (RAD), where refugee determinations could be reviewed. However, although the number of Immigration and Refugee Board (IRB) members was reduced from a panel of two to one to balance the right to an appeal for refugees, by 2006 RAD had yet to be implemented (Crepeau and Nakache 2006: 15). When refugees and immigrants do have the right to an appeal, their access to the process is made all the more difficult because of reduced funding in legal aid. Depending on the province where the appeal takes place, some appellants may never see the inside of a hearing room because some provinces do not have any funding available to migrants.

Protecting Immigrants' Rights

Many critics of the new immigration act note the erosion of immigrant rights in the legislation. The emphasis on security and terrorism has clearly overshadowed migrants' rights and the need for a more balanced approach. Kent Roach (2005) observes that governments have taken advantage of concerns around security to reconfigure immigration law to bypass the human rights of migrants. He states, "Immigration law has been attractive to the authorities because it allows procedural shortcuts and a degree of secrecy that would not be tolerated under even an expanded criminal law" (Roach 2005: 2).

Critics argue that the IRPA will have a detrimental effect on racialized individuals, groups, and communities. For example, the attempts by government to combat human smuggling and trafficking should not occur at the expense of further victimization of the migrants smuggled or trafficked. The National Association of Women and the Law (NAWL) and the United Nations High Commission for Refugees (UNHCR) assert that by failing to include adequate protection for trafficked or smuggled migrants, the Canadian government is reneging on its responsibility to international protocols. The UNHCR notes that many reasons exist as to why migrants resort to smugglers and traffickers. While many migrants are people searching for better economic opportunities, many migrants are refugees whose only option for escape is with the smugglers or traffickers. NAWL believes that this new category of immigration enforcement will result in smugglers and traffickers charging migrants higher prices to escape. For women and children, who are less likely to have the financial resources to pay, the possibilities of fleeing persecution, conflict, and human rights abuses will become even more remote unless they are willing to pay the costs in the form of enforced prostitution and sexual violations (NAWL 2001). It has been strongly recommended that the Canadian government provide protection to migrants by granting them immigration relief, access to permanent residency, or the opportunity to submit applications to stay on humanitarian and compassionate grounds (see briefs by NAWL 2001; CCR 2001; and UNHCR 2001). Affording migrants the necessary protection would help to alleviate their vulnerability to the smugglers and traffickers.

Racialized women migrants in particular will experience the impact of the new act in harsh and uncompromising terms because they are typically more vulnerable to the effects of migration. For example, a third of all women who immigrate to Canada do so through the family class category, which means that they are sponsored by a Canadian citizen or permanent resident who agrees to ensure that their essential needs are met so that the sponsored person will not resort to social assistance (NAWL 2001). In its brief to the Standing Committee on Citizenship and Immigration, NAWL (2001) recommended that family reunification be recognized as a fundamental human right, and specifically that people who are being reunited with their families in Canada be given the right to obtain permanent residence in Canada in order to avoid the development of exploitative or abusive relationships. In its review of the first several years of the IRPA, NAWL points out that neither this recommendation nor any of the others it submitted has been implemented, although cursory attention to the issue of gender in immigration has been paid. It notes, "Almost four years after the adoption of the new legislation, the only tangible result of the legislative commitment to gender based analysis of the Act is the sex-disaggregated data in the Annual Report 2005" (NAWL 2006).

> Racialized women migrants in particular will experience the impact of the new act in harsh and uncompromising terms because they are typically more vulnerable to the effects of migration.

The decrepit state of detention centres in Canada and the now increased potential for long-term detention of migrants add to the growing list of concerns that detainees' civil liberties will be violated, particularly when the majority of the detainees are racialized migrants. Indeed, many organizations believe that the heightened powers of detention in the new act are a racist and reactionary response to the arrival of four boatloads of Chinese migrants on the shores of British Columbia in the summer of 1999 — primarily economic migrants seeking a new life in Canada.[7] That their arrival resulted in their immediate detention without much public outcry highlights how racism, through the practice of racial profiling, was used to gain legitimacy for the government's practices. The assumption was that if one boatload of migrants were "bogus" refugee claimants, then all Chinese migrants would be as well, which justified the government's "tough" stance on "illegal" immigrants (CBC Online 1999a, 1999b).[8] Not surprisingly, issues of due process and other human rights abuses surfaced in a

United Nations Human Rights Commission report over the treatment of the Chinese migrants (Canadian Press, April 12, 2001; CBC Online 1999c). The U.N. investigator said that Canada "needed to avoid criminalizing the victims." Her report pointed to the poor psychological state of some of the Chinese women who were detained, and how mistreatment by penitentiary guards had led one woman to attempt suicide. In her report, the U.N. investigator reminded Canadian authorities that the migrants had been doubly victimized because they were also the victims of the traffickers.

For many activists and scholars involved in debating and discussing the new act, the government's recognition of the importance of human rights does indeed appear to be either non-existent or timid at best. Crepeau and Nakache (2006) argue that governments need to recognize that the principle of territorial sovereignty is not incompatible with protecting individual rights and freedoms. One way of recognizing this principle is to clearly identify and justify all security exceptions to the recognition of human rights that are normally conferred by the state to migrants (Crepeau and Nakache 2006: 25). The extent to which Canada and other Western nations will give priority to human rights while pursuing an immigration agenda focused on security and control remains to be seen. As Catharine Davergne (2004: 613) observes:

> The proliferation of human rights norms over the last half century has not markedly increased rights entitlements at the moment of border crossing, nor has it significantly increased access to human rights for those with no legal status, those "illegals" beyond the reach of the law but at the centre of present rhetoric.

As a result, the approach taken continues to reinforce the unequal distribution of rights on the basis of birthplace, and it leaves those who are unprotected vulnerable and open to intimidation and exploitation.

RACE AND NATION
National Fears and Immigrant Scapegoating

As the successor to the 1975 *Immigration Act*, the IRPA represents a different era of immigration policy-making. The 1975 act was born out of a perceived need for "race-neutral" categories of eligibility and non-discriminatory treatment of immigrants and is considered to be liberal in its approach.[9] The IRPA emerged out of the continuing racialization[10] of immigration, whereby immigrants of colour have come to be viewed not only as threats to the social, cultural, and linguistic order of the nation, but also as threats to the security of the nation. Martin Rudner (2002: 24), for example, blames Canada's immigration policy for the presence of "large, identifiable homeland communities from societies in conflict," communities that presumably became an attractive arena for fostering international terrorist networks. These anti-immigrant sentiments are not new and were present in various forms during previous immigration debates. However, in recent times they occupy a greater role in framing immigration debates as a result of the negative representation of immigrants of colour by the media in Canada and the realignment of immigration policy-making towards a conservative agenda (Abu-Laban 1998; Teitelbaum and Winter 1998).

It would seem that public concerns and anxiety about immigrants and national security are linked to "perceived immigrant desirability and legitimacy," as Buchignani and Indra (1999: 416) remark, rather than to any real threat to Canada's borders or sovereignty. Garcia y Griego (1994: 120) concurs, stating, "Canada has never lost control over its borders, but it has, on more than one occasion, lost control over its own admission process." This state of affairs has been made possible through the belief that it is the "outsider," the migrant or foreign national, that poses the greatest threat, and that this threat can only be contained by retaining a tighter control over the criteria for determining who can immigrate to Canada. This view is evident in statements made by Public Safety and Emergency Preparedness Canada (2004), which notes that "many of the real and direct threats to Canada originate from far beyond our borders."

The implication is that problems are imported into the country via immigrants, and that only through the adoption of a security-driven, regulatory agenda will those problems be contained. Indeed, the flurry of immigration reforms post-9/11 is perhaps more a reflection of the government of the time demonstrating that it has matters under control than it is a proportionate response to security issues. What this allows for, as Maggie Ibrahim (2005: 169) points out, is the legitimization of new racist fears. Instead of focusing on how to support immigrants who are at risk, a security-driven approach emphasizes the need to protect citizens because the incorporation of immigrants will result in an unstable host state (Ibrahim 2005: 169). Of significant concern is that these sentiments are no longer being echoed by conservative, right-wing political parties and organizations only. They are also being legitimized by more liberal, humanitarian-focused groups such as the U.N. and liberal-minded academics (Ibrahim 2005).

Immigrants who do not fit into the predefined mould of what constitutes a "good immigrant" will increasingly become the target of the new security-focused state. It is no surprise that hate crimes have risen dramatically since 9/11 (Statistics Canada 2004) and that many people of colour speak of experiencing racial profiling on a daily basis at the hands of various law enforcement agents (Bahdi 2003). The public acceptance of racist treatment towards people of colour is evident in the way in which the Canadian mainstream media described

> Immigrants who do not fit into the predefined mould of what constitutes a "good immigrant" will increasingly become the target of the new security-focused state.

Muslims during the June 2006 arrest of seventeen Muslim men in Canada. The *Globe and Mail's* (2006b) front-page story noted, "Parked directly outside his... office was a large, gray, cube-shaped truck and, on the ground nearby, he recognized one of the two brown-skinned young men who had taken possession of the next door rented unit." As Robert Fisk points out, "What is 'brown-skinned' suppose to mean — if it is not just a revolting attempt to isolate Muslims as the 'other' in Canada's highly multicultural society?" (Fisk 2006). Backed into a corner, Muslim groups and organizations have no choice but to join this process of "othering" by distancing themselves from the men arrested and attempting to calm an increasingly hostile public through reinforcing the idea of peace as the centrepiece of their religion (*Globe and Mail* 2006c). Good Muslims, they argue, are not violent and do not engage in terrorist activities. Within all these discussions, it is clear that in a climate of fear, suspicion, and hostility produced by the association between Muslims and terrorist activities, homogeneity becomes the default security blanket, now made all the more possible by the new immigration act.

A close look at the enforcement provisions of the IRPA shows that the process of blaming and punishing immigrants allows for a "suitable enemy" to blame for the problems of society (Christie 1986). Few strategies are as effective as processes of criminalization for reinforcing an ideology of "us" and "them," with the immigrant, usually understood as non-white, poor, and/or female, occupying the status of the outsider (Bannerji 2000a). The racialized, gendered, and class nature of this marking ensures that in the construction and definition of who is Canadian, access to this identity is far from

> Few strategies are as effective as processes of criminalization for reinforcing an ideology of "us" and "them," with the immigrant, usually understood as non-white, poor, and/or female, occupying the status of the outsider.

equal. Casting immigrants into the role of the "other" has been beneficial in suppressing public fears and insecurities about immigrants "terrorizing" Canadians, taking jobs away from Canadians, and overtaxing the welfare system.

As immigration authorities seek to reclaim their ability to secure Canada's borders, and to argue that the integrity of the immigration system has not been compromised by "illegal" migrants, an increase in the degree of punishment to offenders allows governments to demonstrate their power through the use of force. Such has been the case in the European Union, where resolutions and legislation were brought in to counter a broad range of terrorist activities (these include not just terrorist organizations, but also anti-globalization protests, animal rights activism, and youth subcultures), resulting in the use of deportation and detention without trial against foreign nationals suspected of posing a security risk (Fekete 2004: 6).

Keeping Canada White

Historically, immigration control linked the decline of the nation with the sexual excesses and mental and moral degeneration of Native peoples and people of colour (Valverde 1991: 105). Racist ideas determined which groups of people would be regarded as having more character, and thus be considered more "civilized." People of British descent were viewed as morally superior for their ability to self-regulate and exercise self-control (Valverde 1991: 105). Importantly, this position was not contested, but rather taken for granted by moral reformers at the turn of the century in Canada (Valverde 1991: 106). The historical studies on immigration of Barbara Roberts (1988) and Donald Avery (1995) confirm the presence of these beliefs. The Canadian government sought to attract the most desirable immigrants, which it had identified — not surprisingly — as white, British, English-speaking, and Protestant. As Strange and Loo (1997: 117) note,

"Determining who could become or remain Canadian was one more way to shape the moral character of the nation." Immigrants identified as "low quality" or morally degenerate would find themselves subjected to various forms of regulation, with deportation being the most drastic measure imposed. Here, gendered and racialized ideologies shaped the circumstances that would be defined as undesirable. For men, unemployment or left-wing affiliation were sufficient to warrant deportation, while for women, having children out of wedlock, carrying a disease like VD or tuberculosis, or appearing to court more than one man would bring them to the attention of immigration officials (Strange and Loo 1997: 119). In terms of racial exclusions, simply being non-white was sufficient to be classified as undesirable. The exclusion of Black and Chinese people from Canada was made on the belief that they posed a moral threat that could not be overcome by any means, and therefore special measures needed to be taken to ensure that they did not corrupt the moral integrity of the nation (Bashi 2004; Strange and Loo 1997). Examples of measures taken included the *Chinese Immigration Act, 1923*, which excluded anyone of Chinese descent from immigrating to Canada, prohibiting the employment of white women by Asian employers, and preventing Chinese people from forming families in Canada (Strange and Loo 1997: 120–21).

An overarching feature of immigration policies in Canada, both historically and at present, is to build a nation of people who fulfill the highest moral standards. As Strange and Loo (1997: 145) observe, ideals of purity, industry, piety, and self-discipline were regarded as essential features of Canadianness. Few would argue that these standards continue to characterize and shape present-day immigration policies, often to the detriment of non-white immigrants seeking to come to Canada. Vukov (2003) points out how contemporary public articulations about desirable and undesirable immigrants in both the news media and governmental policy with respect to sexuality and security issues reinforce the long-standing fears that sexually deviant immigrants and criminals continue to threaten the process of replenishing and sustaining a secure population base. Likewise, Angel-Ajani (2003: 435) argues that this climate of anti-immigrant rhetoric relies on the dual discourses of criminalization and cultural difference. Within this climate of insecurity, a wide range of screening practices have been enacted to ensure that people belonging to designated groups are properly filtered out. The construction of Middle Eastern, West Asian, and Muslim peoples as security threats to the nation since September 11 and the introduction of new policy measures to secure our border underscore the ways in which definitions of undesirable immigrants are highly racialized (Vukov 2003: 345).

The narrative that emerges from the new immigration act supports this vision of Canada, with the good immigrant reaffirming Canada's essential goodness and "the bad immigrant forcing otherwise generous people into taking stern disciplinary measures" (Razack 1999: 174). A critical component of this ongoing story is that "good" is equated with whiteness and with being Canadian, while "bad" is associated with being an immigrant, an outsider to the nation. Thobani's (2000) study of the Immigration Policy Review in 1994 highlights this most clearly. She found that throughout the public consultation process, Canadians expressed concerns that their national values were being eroded and degraded by immigrants who did not share these values (Thobani 2000: 44). While Canadians saw themselves as respectful, honest, and hard-working, immigrants were consistently represented as criminal, disease-ridden, and lazy. Thobani notes that by placing immigrant values in the context of social and cultural diversity, definitions of immigrants and Canadians are reproduced in racialized terms. Audrey Kobayashi (1995: 71) sums up the situation in asserting that immigration law is a central site for articulating how Canada imagines itself:

> Immigration law is in Canada one of the most significant cultural arenas, a contested territory wherein people's relations with one another and with the places they designate as home are expressed. To aid them in that expression, people have faith in the law; it establishes a moral landscape and it codifies our myths about ourselves. It is our recourse to defining ourselves and others, as well as a means of systematically reproducing our imagined reality.

These comments highlight why the harsh treatment of immigrants, particularly immigrants of colour, is so uncontroversial. For to question how immigration practices are carried out within Canada would not just be a challenge to the fairness of the system, it would also call into question how Canada envisions itself. Such a challenge would be neither lightly accepted nor welcomed.

CONCLUSION

As the boundaries between insider and outsider become more ambivalent and converge with nostalgia for a bygone period of immigration, immigrants of colour are the ones classified and defined as inauthentic, "illegal," or outsiders. Anti-racists allege that racial identity remains a key marker of those who are not perceived as belonging, as "legitimate" immigrants of the nation. Even though Canada moved away from blatant forms of discrimination in its immigration policies in the 1960s and 1970s, racism and patriarchy continued to define spatial and/or social margins in portrayals of the dominant vision of the nation (Simmons 1998; Kobayashi 1995).

Even though Canada moved away from blatant forms of discrimination in its immigration policies in the 1960s and 1970s, racism and patriarchy continued to define spatial and/or social margins in portrayals of the dominant vision of the nation.

The racialization of immigration, which focuses on the process of constructing racial identities and meanings, enables ideas about "race" to proliferate. Now, cultural differences, rather than racial inferiority, become the distinguishing markers between us and them. Avtar Brah (1996: 165) writes that this form of racism is "a racism that combined a disavowal of biological superiority or inferiority with a focus on 'a way of life,' of cultural difference as the 'natural' basis for feelings of antagonism towards outsiders." This tendency has made it possible, for example, for recurring themes to continue to characterize immigration debates — themes alleging that too much racial diversity will lead to conflict, that immigrants have large families that expect to be supported by the welfare state, that immigrants are criminals with no respect for the law, or that immigrant workers take jobs away because they are willing to work for low wages (Hintjens 1992). In Canada and other Western nations, immigrants are now required to speak the official languages as proof of their adequate assimilation into mainstream culture (Fekete 2004: 22). As Thobani (2000: 293) observes, such demands elevate Europeanness/whiteness over other cultures and ethnicities, and clearly redefine the national Canadian identity as being "white" while seemingly appearing to be race-neutral.

The lack of public outcry over the treatment of immigrants in the new act suggests that the public's imagination has been captured in such a way that immigration is understood as a sign of Canada's decline. While Canada cannot do without immigrants, those who are admitted are expected to adhere to Canadian values and adopt a "Canadian" way of life. Non-compliance is not an option, because the failure to assimilate has become a sign of being someone who is a potential contributor to uprisings and terrorist activities. While Canada has always been distrustful of racialized immigrants, IRPA highlights how we need to find a "suitable enemy" for whom we can blame all our failures and insecurities.

Racialized immigrants have been, and continue to be, the scapegoat containers for a variety of economic and cultural insecurities (Beisel 1994). One consequence of this is that any benefits that immigrants provide to host societies like Canada are drowned out by the discourse of exclusion (*Toronto Star*, March 30, 2006a). This is the new Canada.

GLOSSARY OF KEY TERMS

Immigrant: A person who comes to live permanently in a foreign country.

Refugee: A person in flight who seeks to escape conditions or personal circumstances found to be intolerable.

Discrimination: The unjust or prejudicial treatment of different categories of people or things.

Criminalize: Turning an activity into a criminal offence by making it illegal.

Deportation: The act of expelling a non-citizen from a country, usually on the grounds of illegal status or for having committed a crime.

QUESTIONS FOR DISCUSSION

1. Do you think immigration control is possible without engaging in racist or discriminatory behaviour?

2. Should multiculturalism be abandoned for the sake of national security? Can and should these issues be prioritized?
3. How can we create a more inclusive society in light of the culture of fear of the "other" that now exists?

WEBSITES OF INTEREST

Citizenship and Immigration Canada. <www.cic.gc.ca/english/index.html>.
Canada Border Services Agency. <www.cbsa-asfc.gc.ca/menu-e.html>.
Canadian Heritage. <www.pch.gc.ca/index_e.cfm>.
No One Is Illegal Vancouver. <noii-van.resist.ca/>.
Status Campaign. <www.ocasi.org/STATUS/index.asp>.
Noborder network. <www.noborder.org/news_index.php>.
Canadian Council for Refugees. <www.web.net/~ccr/fronteng.htm>.
Stop Racial Profiling. <www.stopracialprofiling.ca/news.html>.

NOTES

This chapter is a revised and shortened version of Wendy Chan, 2002, "Illegal Immigrants and Bill C-11: The Criminalization of Race." In Law Commission of Canada (ed.), *What Is a Crime?* Vancouver: UBC Press.

1. With the point system, immigrants would be assessed on the basis of age, education, language skills and economic characteristics and be assigned points for each of these categories. Applicants who had a sufficient number of points would be eligible for entry (Boyd and Vickers 2000).
2. For more details about the Investor's program, see Citizenship and Immigration Canada website <http: //www.cic.gc.ca/english/business/invest-1.html> (accessed September 8, 2006).
3. See Citizenship and Immigration Canada (CIC) website for information about the program. <http: //www.cic.gc.ca/english/pub/caregiver/index.html> (accessed September 8, 2006).
4. Critics of this program have pointed out how many women are exploited and ill-treated by their employers. See Martinez, Hanley, and Cheung 2004; and Langevin and Belleau 2000.
5. A Convention Refugee is anyone who holds a well-founded fear of persecution based on one or more of five grounds as defined in the U.N. Convention Relating to the Status of Refugees: reasons of race, religion, nationality, membership in a particular social group, or political opinion. See Galloway 1997.
6. According to its website <www.maytree.com>, "The Maytree Foundation is a Canadian charitable foundation established in 1982. Maytree believes that there are three fundamental issues that threaten political and social stability: wealth disparities between and within nations; mass migration of people because of war, oppression and environmental disasters, and the degradation of the environment."
7. The public reaction to the Chinese migrants was generally one of hostility; they tended to be regarded as "bogus" refugees. Many of them were detained and eventually deported

back to China. See briefs by Coalition for a Just Immigration and Refugee Policy 2001; NAWL 2001; the Getting Landed Project 2002; African Canadian Legal Clinic 2001; UNHCR 2001.

8. Supporters of the migrants argued the government had overreacted in this situation, while critics contended that the government needed to take harsher measures.

9. This view of the 1975 *Immigration Act* has been challenged by critical immigration scholars who contend that, while the act did not directly discriminate against particular racial and ethnic groups, the outcome of the point system nonetheless resulted in differential access to immigration. See Thobani 2000; Jakubowski 1997.

10. Racialization "refers to the historical emergence of the idea of 'race' and to its subsequent reproduction and application" (Miles 1989: 76). This suggests that the criminalization of certain racialized groups within the Canadian context can be understood, first, in light of the ways in which white, majority groups have been constructed as race-less, and, second, within the context of historical relations between First Nations peoples, early settlers, and recent immigrants and migrants.

Chapter Seven

PERSISTENT POVERTY AND THE PROMISE OF COMMUNITY SOLUTIONS

Jim Silver

For two decades or more, poverty rates in Canada remained persistently high and, for the most part, climbing. They began to turn down in 1998 and continued to decline in the following years, though they remain very high. In 1980 the Canadian poverty rate[1] was calculated at 16.0 percent of the population. In 2003 the rate was 15.9 percent — that is, where it had been two decades earlier (see Table 7-1). For most of the 1980s and 1990s, poverty rates moved in lockstep with broad economic trends. They rose during the recession of the early 1980s, declined during the ensuing economic recovery, and rose again during the recession of the early 1990s (to peak at 20.6 percent in 1996). Rates then declined again steadily to 2001 (15.5 percent), turning up slightly to 15.9 percent in 2003, almost exactly where they had been twenty-three years earlier. That most recent figure represents about one in seven Canadians, and it can be expected to begin to climb again when the next economic downturn arrives, as it inevitably will.

This pattern shows that, although poverty rates in Canada move up and down with the overall health of the economy, they also move at levels that are persistently high, even in relatively good economic times. Canada's record in fighting these persistently high levels

"You Should Know This"
- Although declining, the child poverty rate of 17.6 percent in 2003 is higher than the 1989 rate of 15.1 percent, the year the House of Commons passed a unanimous resolution to end child poverty by the year 2000.
- Out of 26 high-income OECD countries, Canada's child poverty rate ranks 17th worst. Canada's 14.9 percent compares to Norway's 3.4 percent, Finland's 2.8 percent, and Denmark's 2.4 percent.
- By 2001, the poverty rate was approximately 40 percent for Aboriginal children, more than double the rate for all children.
- In 2003, 48.9 percent of single-parent mothers were living in poverty, while the rate was only 20 percent for single-parent fathers.
- The average income of female lone-parent families is 43 percent of the average income of two-parent families, and 71 percent of the average income of male lone-parent families.
- In March 2004, 841,640 people in Canada used food banks — more than the population of large cities such as Winnipeg, Hamilton, or Quebec City, and more than double the 378,000 who had used food banks in 1989.
- Government spending in Canada as a share of GDP has dropped below the average of the G7 industrial economies, and now ranks ahead of only Japan and the United States.
- While 74 percent of unemployed Canadians received UI benefits in 1990, only 39 percent of unemployed Canadians received EI benefits in 2001.

Sources: National Council of Welfare 2006; United Nations Children's Fund 2005; Campaign 2000 2005; Drover 2004: 6; Canadian Association of Food Banks 2004: 9; Canada, Department of Finance 2005; Canadian Labour Congress 2003.

Table 7-1 Poverty Trends, 1980–2003

Year	Poor People (millions)	Total Population (millions)	Poverty Rate %
1980	3,852	24,107	16.0
1981	3,872	24,389	15.9
1982	4,251	24,654	17.2
1983	4,631	24,890	18.6
1984	4,704	25,128	18.7
1985	4,447	25,358	17.5
1986	4,202	25,612	16.4
1987	4,145	25,921	16.0
1988	3,953	26,253	15.1
1989	3,719	26,620	14.0
1990	4,369	27,014	16.2
1991	4,781	27,367	17.5
1992	5,062	27,715	18.3
1993	5,416	28,031	19.3
1994	5,271	28,351	18.6
1995	5,530	28,662	19.3
1996	5,970	28,967	20.6
1997	5,867	29,227	20.1
1998	5,466	29,443	18.6
1999	5,151	29,694	17.3
2000	4,917	29,988	6.4
2001	4,711	30,321	15.5
2002	4,963	30,611	16.2
2003	4,917	30,893	15.9

Source: National Council of Welfare, *Poverty Profile 2002 and 2003,* Table 1.1.

of poverty, much less doing away with poverty, is not an impressive one for such a rich country. Some eleven other liberal-democratic industrialized countries, with the notable exception of the United States, are finding ways of achieving more success on this front. Indeed, Canada's international ranking on poverty indicators (though it varies according to the measures used) is low to middling. The United Nations Human Poverty

What the lower rates of poverty in other industrialized countries suggest is that Canada's high rates are by no means inevitable: they could be lowered.

Index 2003, which takes into account the percentage of the population not expected to live to age sixty, the level of functional illiteracy, the incidence of income poverty, and the incidence of long-term unemployment, ranks Canada twelfth from the top among seventeen industrialized countries in its treatment of the poor (UNDP 2001).

What the lower rates of poverty in other industrialized countries suggest is that Canada's high rates are by no means inevitable: they could be lowered if the country made different policy decisions.

PEOPLE AT RISK OF POVERTY

In Canada, particular groups of people are more likely than others to be poor. One important determinant of the risk of poverty is family type: single-parent mothers and unattached individuals are much more likely to be poor than are couples. In 2001, 42.4 percent of single mothers had incomes below the poverty line. Unattached individuals experienced poverty rates ranging from almost 30 percent to just over 40 percent, depending upon the sex and age of the individuals. Rates for couples, by contrast, ranged from 6.3 percent to 9.5 percent. (See Figure 7-1.)

Gender and age are also determinants. Women are more likely than men to be poor. Since 1980, poverty rates for women have consistently been one-quarter higher than poverty rates for men. In all age categories except ages 45–54, where the rates are equal, the incidence of poverty is higher for women than for men, and the spread by gender is especially wide for older (65+ years) and younger (18–34 years) women (NCW 2001: 107–10).

Young people, both women and men, no matter the family types, also have a relatively high incidence of poverty. For single-parent mothers, couples with children, childless couples, unattached women, and unattached men, those under the age of twenty-five years have a much higher incidence of poverty than do those twenty-five years of age and over. The rate of poverty for the relatively small number of single mothers under the age of twenty-five, for instance, is an astonishing 74 percent (NCW 2001: 44).

Incidences of poverty also correlate with the number and age of children. The greater the number and the younger the age of children in a family, whether in a two-parent or single-parent family, the greater is the likelihood of poverty. (Figures 7.2 and 7.3.)

Members of racialized groups also have a much greater chance of being poor, according to the statistics. For our purposes, racialized groups are people (other than Aboriginal peoples) who are non-Caucasian in race or non-white in colour (Galabuzi 2001: 7). According to 1996 Census Canada data, the incidence of poverty for members of racialized groups is double that for the Canadian population at large (Galabuzi 2006: 183, 186). For Aboriginal peoples, rates of poverty are even higher. For exam-

Figure 7-1 Poverty Rates by Family Type, 2003

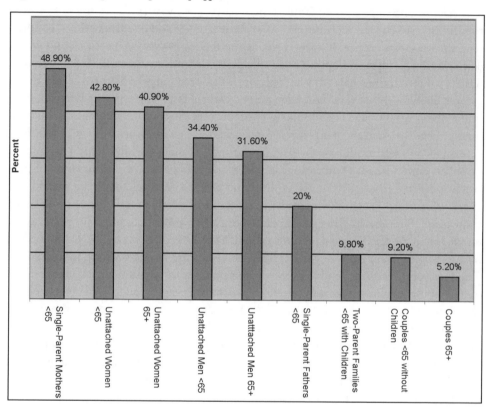

ple, according to 1996 Census Canada data, almost two-thirds — 64.7 percent — of Aboriginal households in Winnipeg had incomes below the poverty line (Lezubski, Silver, and Black 2000: 39). In 2001 this number had declined to 54.7 percent — still over one-half of Aboriginal households in the city as a whole — while 71.3 percent of Aboriginal households in Winnipeg's inner city had incomes below the poverty line (Statistics Canada, customized data, Social Planning Council of Winnipeg 2001).

Food bank usage reflects both the growth of poverty and the relationship of children to poverty. In March 2004, 841,640 people in Canada used food banks — more than the population of large cities such as Winnipeg, Hamilton, or Quebec City, and more than double the 378,000 who had used food banks fifteen years earlier, in March 1989. At the beginning of the 1980s there was no such thing as a food bank in Canada. In 2004, almost 40 percent of the food-bank users were children under the age of eighteen, although that age group makes up just over one-quarter of Canada's population (Canadian Association of Food Banks 2004: 9).

POVERTY AND THE LABOUR MARKET

The relationship of poverty to family type is based in large part on varying positions in the labour market. Not surprisingly, two-parent families and couples without children have the lowest incidence of poverty, mainly because they tend to have a second wage-earner in the family — an option not available, by definition, to unattached individuals. Single-parent families have the highest rate of poverty, largely because of the much greater likelihood that they will have no wage-earners. A single parent with children under seven years of age is more likely to be poor because of the obvious difficulty of going out to work in the paid labour force when the children are not yet in school.

A person's relationship to the paid labour force is the most important determinant of poverty, and Canada's "precarious labour market" has been "the main cause of persistent poverty" (Battle 1996: 1). As the Ecumenical Coalition for Economic Justice (1996: 9) puts it, "Unemployment is the single most reliable predictor of poverty for those aged 18 to 65." In other words, employment is a poverty fighter. But not just any employment. As the National Council of Welfare (1996: 37) observes, "A *good* job is the best insurance against poverty for Canadians under the age of 65" (emphasis added). The level of poverty depends as well on the number of weeks of work you can put in. Generally speaking, the more weeks of work that a family puts in, the less likely its members are to be poor (see Figure 7-2). This, again, is another factor in the persistence of poverty: the number of weeks worked by working poor families has declined dramatically since the 1970s. For those with earned incomes in the lowest 10 percent of working families, the average number of weeks worked per year fell by almost half by the mid-1990s, from 43.3 to 23.5 (Yalnizyan 1998: 41, 46).

Type of work is yet another factor (see Table 7-2). The incidence of poverty is

Figure 7-2 Poverty Rates by Weeks of Work for Families under 65, 2003

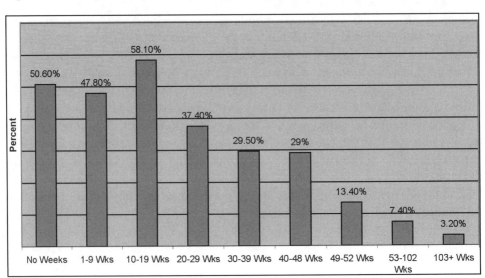

Table 7-2 Poverty Rates by Occupation, 1997

Occupational Group	Family Heads %	Unattached Individuals %
Managerial	3.5	10.6
Processing and Machining	6.1	10.5
Professional	8.0	17.1
Transport	8.5	20.1
Construction	8.9	27.8
Product Fabrication	9.5	18.5
Farming, Fishing, Forestry	10.8	33.5
Sales	11.2	28.5
Clerical	14.5	24.6
Services	19.4	41.6

Source: National Council of Welfare, *Poverty Profile 1997,* Table 9.

particularly high for people working in primary industries and the service and retail sectors. Again, just being in the paid labour force and earning wages are no guarantee against poverty: an important category of people in poverty are the working poor — people who might have jobs but not the *good* jobs that the National Council of Welfare refers to. Growing numbers of jobs are either part-time or low-wage positions, or both; even though people are working, their earnings may be so low that they are still below the poverty line.

> Growing numbers of jobs are either part-time or low-wage positions, or both; even though people are working, their earnings may be so low that they are still below the poverty line.

The majority of heads of poor families, 60 percent, were in the paid labour force. In 1998 less than one-half — 40 percent — of heads of all poor families under sixty-five years of age had no employment, while 34 percent worked part-time and 26 percent — just over one in four — worked full-time. For unattached individuals under sixty-five years of age, the situation was similar: 52 percent of those who were poor in 1998 were among the working poor. The majority of the poor, then, fall under the heading of working poor.

Part-Time and Low-Wage Jobs

The growth of part-time jobs as a proportion of the total number of jobs in Canada is an important factor in explaining high rates of poverty. The proportion of jobs that are part-time grew steadily from under 5 percent in the 1950s to over 19 percent in 1996 and 1997, and was still at 18.5 percent in 2004 (see Table 7-3).

As economist Jim Stanford (1996: 132–33) observes: "Fully one-half of the new jobs created in Canada during the 1980s were non-standard: that is, jobs that were not full-time, were not year round, or involved working for more than a single employer." By 2004 part-time jobs were making up almost one in five job opportunities (see Table 7-3), compared to one in ten in the mid-1970s (Yalnizyan 1998: 26). In clerical, sales, and service occupations, six of every ten workers are part-time, a fact contributing to the relatively high proportion of people in those occupations who have incomes below the poverty line (see Table 7-2).

Part-time workers are usually paid lower wages than full-time workers. In 1995, 43 percent of part-time workers earned less than $7.50 per hour; fewer than 10 percent of full-time workers earned less than $7.50 per hour. While 60 to 70 percent of full-time workers had access to benefits packages — pensions, medical/dental, paid sick leave — fewer than 20 percent of part-time workers had such benefits. Members of racialized groups, and especially women, are overrepresented in part-time, low-wage jobs, which is a major factor in their higher incidence of poverty (Galabuzi 2006: xii, 125).

Taking a part-time job is often a matter of choice; but still the percentage of part-time workers who wanted but could not find full-time jobs tripled between 1975 and 1994, from 11 to 35 percent (Schellenberg 1997: 39). In 2005 just over one-quarter (25.6 percent) of those working part-time did so because they were unable to find full-time work (Statistics Canada 2006d). The end result, as Grant Schellenberg (1997: 2) has put it, is an increasing "polarization of the work force — with one group of workers receiving good wages, benefits and job security, and another group, including most part-time workers, receiving poor wages, no benefits and little security."

Another consequence of changes in the structure of the Canadian economy and changes in government economic policy has been a drift to self-employment. The downsizing of large corporations, cutbacks in government spending and in the numbers of government employees, and high rates of unemployment more generally have made self-employment not just an option but often a necessity for more people. From 1977 to 2004 the number of self-employed Canadians doubled, from 1.2 million to 2.4 million; their share of the total numbers employed grew from 12.2 percent to 15.4 percent (see Table 7-4).

On average, self-employed workers earn less than paid employees. This is especially the case for what Statistics Canada calls "own-account" self-employment — that is, when the self-employed person works on his or her own and has no employees. In the 1990s, 90 percent of the growth in self-employment was own-account self-employment; and own-account self-employment amounted to about 60 percent of the total self-employed. In 1995 the average earnings of own-account self-employed persons was $22,900, or two-thirds the average earnings of paid employees (Stanford 1999: 132; see also Yalnizyan 1998: 30). While some self-employed persons do have high incomes — in 1995 almost 5 percent of the self-employed earned over $100,000, while only

Table 7-3 Growth in Part-Time Work as a Percentage of Total Employment, 1977–2004

Year	Part–time Employed (millions)	Total Number Employed (millions)	Part–time Employed as a Percentage of Total Number Employed
1977	1,291	9,917	13.0
1978	1,349	10,220	13.2
1979	1,467	10,669	13.8
1980	1,569	10,984	14.3
1981	1,674	11,305	14.8
1982	1,741	10,944	15.9
1983	1,849	11,022	16.8
1984	1,892	11,302	16.7
1985	1,986	11,627	17.1
1986	2,030	11,987	16.9
1987	2,054	12,334	16.7
1988	2,136	12,708	16.8
1989	2,159	12,986	16.6
1990	2,219	13,079	17.0
1991	2,333	12,851	18.2
1992	2,359	12,720	18.5
1993	2,457	12,782	19.2
1994	2,475	13,044	19.0
1995	2,496	13,271	18.8
1996	2,560	13,392	19.1
1997	2,616	13,676	19.1
1998	2,641	14,019	18.8
1999	2,648	14,390	18.4
2000	2,671	14,759	18.1
2001	2,706	14,947	18.1
2002	2,871	15,308	18.8
2003	2,964	15,665	18.9
2004	2,950	15,950	18.5

Source: Statistics Canada 2005d, *Canadian Economic Observer Historical Statistical Supplement* 2004/05 (11–210–XIB), Table 8.

Table 7-4 Self-Employment, 1977–2004

Year	Number of Self-Employed (millions)	Total Number Employed (millions)	Self-Employed as a Percentage of Total-Employed %
1977	1,210	9,917	12.2
1978	1,263	10,220	12.4
1979	1,325	10,669	12.4
1980	1,364	10,984	12.4
1981	1,425	11,305	12.6
1982	1,483	10,944	13.6
1983	1,543	11,022	14.0
1984	1,570	11,302	13.9
1985	1,726	11,627	14.8
1986	1,674	11,987	14.0
1987	1,713	12,334	13.9
1988	1,780	12,708	14.0
1989	1,791	12,986	13.8
1990	1,842	13,079	14.1
1991	1,896	12,851	14.8
1992	1,929	12,720	15.2
1993	2,033	12,782	15.8
1994	2,038	13,044	15.6
1995	2,079	13,271	15.7
1996	2,173	13,392	16.2
1997	2,353	13,676	17.2
1998	2,419	14,019	17.3
1999	2,452	14,390	17.0
2000	2,385	14,759	16.2
2001	2,278	14,987	15.2
2002	2,319	15,308	15.1
2003	2,400	15,665	15.3
2004	2,452	15,950	15.4

Source: Statistics Canada 2005d, *Canadian Economic Observer Historical Statistical Supplement* 2004/05 (11-210-XIB), Table 8.

1 percent of paid employees reached the same level — a higher proportion have low earnings. Over 35 percent of all self-employed individuals earned less than $15,000 in 1995, compared to just 17 percent of paid workers (Stanford 1999: 132). These trends were relatively unchanged according to data for 1999 (Delage 2002: 20). What is more, the average earnings of the self-employed are probably even lower than these numbers suggest. According to Stanford (1999: 421, n6): "These averages exclude individuals with negative income from self-employment, and those who have been operating their businesses for less than 16 months."

Low wages are an important contributing factor in the persistently high rates of poverty in Canada. This appears to be particularly so on the Prairies, where poor families were more likely to be fully employed than in other regions, "indicating that low wages were a major contributor to their market poverty" (Schellenberg and Ross 1997: 38). In the twenty-year period from 1976 to 1995, the annual earnings of a full-year, full-time worker employed at the minimum wage declined by 25 to 30 percent in almost every Canadian province (Battle 1999a: 4; see also Black and Shaw 2000).

This combination — the rise in part-time jobs and self-employment and a drop in the real value of minimum (and near-minimum) wages — directly relates to the anomaly that occurred in the mid-1990s: the break in the long-term correlation between rates of poverty and of unemployment. Historically, when unemployment has declined, the rate of poverty has declined; when unemployment has risen, the rate of poverty has risen. For instance, the rate of unemployment rose in 1982 and again in 1983, and the poverty rate rose in each of those years. The unemployment rate declined in each year from 1984 to 1989, and the poverty rate declined in each of those years except 1984. The unemployment rate rose from 1990 to 1993, and so did the poverty rate. Unemployment dropped in 1994, and so did the poverty rate. However, this pattern was temporarily broken in the mid-1990s: unemployment declined from 1994 to 1996, while poverty rates rose significantly from

> The rise in part-time jobs and self-employment and a drop in the real value of minimum wages directly relate to the anomaly that occurred in the mid-1990s: the break in the long-term correlation between rates of poverty and of unemployment.

1994 to 1996, reaching a peak of 18.5 percent that year. In 1997 the traditional pattern resumed: both unemployment and poverty rates declined to 2001, although poverty rates continued to be very high (see Table 7-5).

It is likely that the "anomaly" from 1994 to 1996, when unemployment declined but poverty rates did not, occurred because so many of the jobs in which people were employed were "contingent" jobs — part-time, low-wages, no benefits, no security. To the extent that this is the case, "official" unemployment rates can be misleading. People may be employed, but in jobs that do not lift them above the poverty line. "Official" unemployment rates do not, for example, indicate what percentage of those who are working are part-time workers who want but cannot find full-time employment — that is, they do not tell us how many people are underemployed. Statistics Canada does gather such information, and when the unemployed and "discouraged" workers

Table 7-5 Unemployment and Poverty Rates, 1980–2003

Year	Unemployment Rate %	Poverty Rate %
1980	7.5	16.0
1981	7.6	15.9
1982	11.0	17.2
1983	11.9	18.6
1984	11.3	18.7
1985	10.7	17.5
1986	9.6	16.4
1987	8.8	16.0
1988	7.8	15.1
1989	7.5	14.0
1990	8.1	16.2
1991	10.3	17.5
1992	11.2	18.3
1993	11.4	19.3
1994	10.4	18.6
1995	9.4	19.3
1996	9.6	20.6
1997	9.1	20.1
1998	8.3	18.6
1999	7.6	17.3
2000	6.8	16.4
2001	7.2	15.5
2002	7.7	16.2
2003	7.6	15.9

Source: Statistics Canada 2005d, *Canadian Economic Observer* (11-210-XPB), 2000/2001, Table 8; National Council of Welfare, *Poverty Profile 2002 and 2003,* Table 1.1.

— that is, those who have given up actively looking for work — are taken into account, the real unemployment rate is much higher than the official rate: from 1993 to 2001 the real unemployment rate — which includes people who have given up actively searching for work and part-time workers who want full-time jobs — was

18.9 percent, more than double the 8.7 percent official rate (Silver, Wilson, and Shields 2004:8).

For these reasons — together with the enormous amounts of money taken out of social programs, especially after the 1995 federal budget, the recent declines in unemployment rates have not solved the long-term problem of persistently high poverty rates. Further, recent economic growth has dramatically widened the gap between rich and poor in Canada. Yalnizyan (1998: 45) documents this gap: "In 1973, the top 10 percent of families with children under 18 earned an average income 21 times higher than those at the bottom.... By 1996... the top 10 percent made 314 times as much as the families in the bottom 10 percent." Young people, those under thirty-five years of age, appear to have suffered most from economic restructuring. As Yalnizyan (1998: 24) observes:

> People under 35 years of age are evidently worth less than workers of the same age before the recession of 1981–82. But it is the young men whose hourly rates of pay have been most sharply and consistently eroded over the past 15 years. Virtually every data source, from Census to special surveys, documents this same trend. Study after study shows that we are devaluing our young.

CHILD POVERTY

A particularly troubling aspect of Canada's persistently high poverty rate is the growth of child poverty. In 1980 just over a million children under eighteen years of age were living in poverty — a poverty rate of 15.7 percent. By 1989 the number and proportion of children living in poverty had declined. But in the early-mid 1990s child poverty showed a dramatic growth. By 1996 the number of children under eighteen living in poverty had grown to 1,484,000, an increase of more than 400,000 children since 1980, and the poverty rate had risen by more than five full percentage points, to 21.1 percent (see Table 7-6). In the mid-1990s the poverty rate for children was higher than the overall poverty rate, and the poverty rate for Aboriginal children was higher still. By 2001 the poverty rate was about 40 percent for Aboriginal children, more than double the rate for all children (Campaign 2000, 2005).

There is an important sense in which the notion of "child poverty" is misleading. As the National Council of Welfare (1996: 13) quite rightly observes, "Children are poor because their parents are poor." Growing up in a poor family can severely harm a child's life chances. Researchers David P. Ross and Paul Roberts examined the correlation between family income and twenty-seven indicators of child development: a child's family, community, behaviour, health, cultural and recreational participation, and education. They found that for each of these aspects of development, children living in low-income families were "at a greater risk of experiencing negative outcomes and poor living conditions than those in higher-income families. It is also evident from these data that child outcomes and living conditions improve gradually as family incomes rise" (Ross and Roberts 1999: 3).

Table 7-6 Poverty Trends, Children under 18 Years of Age, 1980–2003

Year	Poor Children (millions)	All Children (millions)	Poverty Rate %
1980	1,098	6,778	16.2
1981	1,110	6,787	16.6
1982	1,272	6,625	19.2
1983	1,306	6,563	19.9
1984	1,358	6,529	20.8
1985	1,253	6,492	19.3
1986	1,142	6,526	17.5
1987	1,131	6,538	17.3
1988	1,032	6,573	15.7
1989	1,002	6,636	15.1
1990	1,227	6,705	18.3
1991	1,325	6,795	19.5
1992	1,361	6,874	19.8
1993	1,541	6,910	22.3
1994	1,435	6,966	20.6
1995	1,546	6,995	22.1
1996	1,654	7,008	23.6
1997	1,548	7,005	22.1
1998	1,436	6,971	20.6
1999	1,343	6,959	19.3
2000	1,251	6,912	18.1
2001	1,191	6,924	17.2
2002	1,238	6,878	18.0
2003	1,201	6,824	17.6

Source: National Council of Welfare, *Poverty Profile 2002, 2003*.

Some of these correlations are striking. For example, delayed vocabulary development occurs four times more frequently among children from low-income families than among children from high-income families; and "about one in six teens from low-income families is neither employed nor in school, compared to only one teen in twenty-five from middle- and high-income families." The result is what Ross and Roberts call "poverty of opportunity." Children who grow up in poor families are, on average, less likely to do well in life than are children who grow up in non-poor families (Ross and Roberts 1999: 8, 25, 34, 36).

Campaign 2000, which describes itself as "a national movement to build awareness and support for the 1989 all-party House of Commons resolution 'to seek to achieve the goal of eliminating poverty among Canadian children by the year 2000,'" describes the lasting effects of child poverty: "child poverty is associated with poor health and hygiene, a lack of a nutritious diet, absenteeism from school and low scholastic achievement, behavioural and mental problems, low housing standards, and in later years, few employment opportunities and a persistently low economic status" (CCSD 1994: 1). A quarter-century ago, in its 1975 study *Poor Kids*, the National Council of Welfare (1975: 1) made much the same argument:

> To be born poor is to face a lesser likelihood that you will finish high school, lesser still that you will attend university. To be born poor is to face a greater likelihood that you will be judged a delinquent in adolescence and, if so, a greater likelihood that you will be sent to a "correctional institution." To be born poor is to have the deck stacked against you at birth, to find life an uphill struggle ever after.

Figure 7.3 Poverty Rates by Family Type and Level of Education, 2003

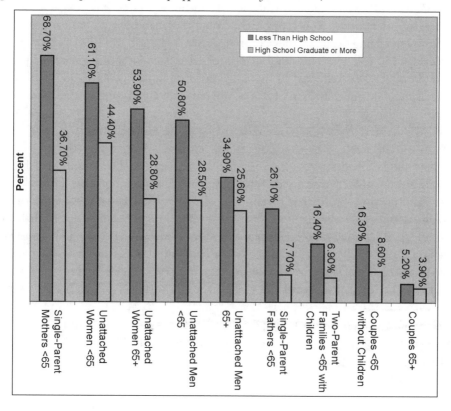

The relationship between poverty and educational attainment is a crucial factor in the reproduction of poverty. The lower the level of educational attainment, the higher is the risk of poverty (see Figure 7-3). A vicious cycle is created: poor children are less likely to do well in school; those who do less well in school are more likely to experience poverty as adults; their children, in turn, will probably do less well in school, and thus poverty is reproduced. The growth of child poverty is, then, a particularly serious aspect of a larger Canadian problem — our persistently high overall rates of poverty.

THE ECONOMY

The high levels of poverty throughout the 1980s and into the mid-1990s were associated with the relatively weak economy during that period. As measured by almost any indicator, the Canadian economy — like virtually all economies in the industrialized world — was much weaker in the 1980s and first half of the 1990s than it had been during the long, postwar economic boom. The average annual rate of growth in both Gross Domestic Product (GDP) and employment from 1950 to 1980 was about double the rate from 1981 to 1997 and about triple the rate from 1990 to 1997. In 1998 to 2003, the rate of growth in GDP and employment returned to levels almost as high as those from 1950 to 1980 (see Table 7-7). Unemployment rates from 1981 to 1997 were almost double the rates from 1950 to 1980, and remained half again as high from 1998 to 2003. In the 1981–97 period real short-term interest rates were six times higher, and real long-term rates four times higher, than they had been in the earlier period, and although having declined, they continued to be higher in the 1998 to 2003 period than from 1950 to 1980. This combination of relative economic stagnation and high real interest rates was reflected in the emergence of annual deficits and a buildup of accumulated debt from 1981 to 1997, a problem contained only in the most recent period.

Why did the Canadian economy experience such a decline in the twenty-five years or so to the late 1990s? The character of the global economy is a partial explanation. The prevailing capitalist system has certain intrinsic features, chief among which is the constant, competitive drive of individual business firms to earn profits. This relentless drive for ever more profits has certain inevitable results. One of them is a constant revolutionizing of the means of production, leading to rapid technological change, as firms relentlessly innovate in attempts to find ways of producing goods and services less expensively and thus gain an advantage over their competitors. Another is the constant drive to expand, which results in both ever-larger firms and geographic expansion, as transnational corporations scour the globe in search of lower wages, bigger markets, and cheaper raw materials in order to maximize their profits. These two phenomena — globalization and the constant revolutionizing of the means of production — are important parts of the reason for the economic downturn that has only recently (and perhaps temporarily?) been reversed.

While economic activity has become much more global in the past quarter-century,

Table 7-7 Economic Performance Indicators, 1950–2003

	Golden Age	Era of Permanent Recession		Resumption of Growth
	1950–80	1981–97	1990–97	1998–2003
	%	%	%	%
Average Annual Growth Real GDP	4.7	2.4	1.8	4.6
Average Annual Growth Real GDP per capita	2.8	1.1	0.5	2.6
Average Annual Growth Total Employment	2.6	1.4	0.8	2
Average Unemployment	5.4	9.8	10.0	7.6
Real Short-Term Interest Rates	0.9	5.6	5.1	4.2
Real Long-Term Interest Rates	1.6	6.5	6.8	5.6
Changes in Government Program Spending (as a % of GDP)	+16.3	+1.1	-2.5	-0.5

	1950–80	1981–96	1997–2003
Annual Federal Deficit (% GDP)	0.0	4.2	0.9
Closing Federal Debt (% GDP)	23.0	73.0	53

Source: Jim Stanford, *Paper Boom* (1999), Table 9-2; Stanford, "The Rise and Fall of Deficit Mania" (1998), Table 2; Statistics Canada 2005d, *Canadian Economic Observer Historical Statistical Supplement* 2004–05 (11-210-XIB), Tables 7, 8, & 34; Department of Finance, *Budget 2005 — Budget Plan* (Annex 1); Jean Dupuis, "The Evolution of Federal Government Finances, 1983–2003 *Library of Parliament* (2005).

globalization is not a new phenomenon. Rather, it is an accentuation of the drive to expand that is intrinsic to capitalism. In the past few decades, trade between nations and investment across national borders have increased dramatically. Companies no longer confine their production to their home nations. They can, and do, set up production facilities anywhere in the world, choosing to locate wherever they are most likely to be able to maximize profits. Moreover, Gary Teeple (2000: 91) states. "as transnational entities, corporations can play one nation off against another by moving to where the concessions and incentives are greatest, the relative labour costs lowest... and environmental and employment standards the most limited." This response also often means locating production to where government regulations of corporate activities are weakest and wages are lower. The trend has been accelerated by international trade agreements, such as the Canada-U.S. Free Trade Agreement and the North American Free Trade Agreement, which significantly reduce the capacity of elected governments to interfere with the profit-seeking activities of transnational corporations (TNCs). They free these corporations from many of the obstacles such as environmental regulations and labour standards formerly placed in their way by governments. The changes increase the freedom of TNCs to search the globe for the most profitable production sites, making it more likely that the corporations will set up shop wherever they can maximize their profits. This is especially the case for heavily unionized, relatively high-wage, mass-production industries. According to Teeple (2000: 67), "The effects of this emerging global labour market began to become visible from the early 1970s on with a general downward pressure on wages in the industrial world."

In the face of the intensified competition created by globalization, companies have sought not only to reduce wage levels, but also to create what the corporate sector calls more "flexible" workforces. Corporations have sought to move away from the relatively fixed and permanent high-wage regime characteristic of the mass-production industries of the 1950s and 1960s — sometimes referred to as "Fordism," after the mass-production, relatively high-wage system introduced early in the century by Henry Ford — to a more flexible labour force, increasingly characterized by the use of part-time and lower-waged work. The resultant increase in part-time work and decrease in wages at the lower end of the income scale have been significant factors in creating persistently high levels of poverty.

The increased degree of globalization, and the problems that the phenomenon creates for many working people, especially those with relatively little formal education and relatively few skills, have been facilitated by the particularly rapid technological change associated with the microelectronics revolution,

> Most of the jobs open to relatively unskilled school-leavers in the 1950s and 1960s, jobs that could support a family, have relocated elsewhere or been eliminated by technology, replaced by low-wage and often part-time work.

and more particularly the widespread use of computers. By the mid-1970s computers were beginning to be widely employed in industry, with dramatic results. Not only has their use facilitated the increased globalization of economic activity, including an acceleration of the ease and rapidity by which investments can be moved around the globe, but their use in industry — in both factories and offices — has often resulted in massive job losses. The loss of jobs has exerted downward pressure on wage levels at the lower end of the wage scale, and it has contributed to the growth of (generally low-paid) self-employment. Most of the jobs open to relatively unskilled school-leavers in the 1950s and 1960s — jobs that could support a family — have now disappeared. These jobs have relocated elsewhere or been eliminated by technology, only to be replaced by low-wage and often part-time work in the service sector.

Government policy also played an important part in the economic downturn to the late 1990s. Of particular importance was the shift to a high interest rate policy. Real interest rates in Canada were dramatically higher in the two decades after 1980 than they had been in the three decades before (see Table 7-7).

The ostensible purpose of the high interest rate policy was to reduce inflation; the more important purpose was to keep levels of unemployment from falling too low (higher real interest rates impede borrowing for productive investment, with the result that fewer jobs are created). The reasoning behind this perverse policy — a policy clearly articulated and aggressively carried out by the Bank of Canada — is that when unemployment is low, workers feel emboldened to demand higher wages; and higher wages impinge upon corporate profits and contribute to inflation. By contrast, when unemployment is higher, and especially when social benefits for those not employed are weak, the fear and insecurity created by the risk of job loss reduce the upward pressure on wage levels and inflation. The fear and insecurity created by higher levels of unemployment and reduced social benefits are therefore functional in a capitalist economy.

SOCIAL POLICY

A second major contributor to the high poverty levels of the 1980s and 1990s was the dismantling, during that period, of the many social policy mechanisms put in place during the post–Second World War boom as a means of protecting individuals from the hazards of the inevitable ups and downs of the capitalist economy. Overall government spending — particularly government spending on social programs — was dramatically reduced during the 1980s and 1990s. Unemployment insurance was restructured to the disadvantage of unemployed workers. The universality of social programs was largely abandoned, and the social safety net was significantly weakened.

These changes in social policy were directly related to the dramatic changes in the economy. The social policy initiatives from the 1950s to the early 1970s were funded out of the proceeds of the long postwar economic boom. Sustained economic growth and relatively low levels of unemployment generated the government revenue, the "fiscal dividend," needed to pay for new social programs. With the end of the postwar boom in the early 1970s and its replacement with a long period of relative economic stagnation, the fiscal dividend disappeared, replaced by government deficits and the buildup of accumulated debt (see Table 7-7).

Although social spending did not cause the deficit/debt problem (Mimoto and Cross 1991) — stagnation and the associated high interest rate/high unemployment strategy were the culprits there — most governments chose to respond to the problem by cutting social spending, which had become a large and obvious target. Social spending was, in certain minds at least, too effective by far in reducing the fear and anxiety that forces workers to pull back on their wage demands and accept jobs of lesser quality. The various elements of the welfare state had provided at least a semblance of security, however limited. To some degree the much-lauded safety net removed the fear of unemployment and poverty that made people anxious to work at whatever wages and under whatever conditions were on offer. As early as 1975 advocates of unfettered free enterprise were expressing concerns about the perceived consequences of the redistributive character of the welfare state in advanced capitalist economies. As the 1975 Trilateral Commission put it, Western states had too much democracy — an "excess" of democracy — and the solution was to attack "big government" (Crozier, Huntington, and Watanuki 1975). If profitability was to be fully restored, the relative security created by the welfare state had to be eroded, especially because, as time went by, an increasingly competitive global economy and global labour market were making strong demands for the creation of a more "flexible" labour force.

In Canada, federal program spending as a share of GDP began to decline after 1975. By 1995, even before Finance Minister Paul Martin had announced massive spending cuts in that year's federal budget, "Government in Canada was already smaller as a share of our economy than it had been two decades earlier" (Stanford 1998: 31). Federal program spending in the 1996/97 fiscal year was 13 percent of GDP, the lowest level as a share of the Canadian economy since 1950/51

> Government spending in Canada as a share of GDP has also dropped by international standards: we are below the average of the seven largest industrial economies, and now rank ahead of only Japan and the United States.

(Yalnizyan 1998: 64). Federal program spending continued to decline, to 11.6 percent of GDP for fiscal year 2003/04 (Canada 2005). Government spending in Canada as a share of GDP also dropped by international standards: we are below the average of the seven largest industrial economies (often known as the G-7 economies), and now rank ahead of only Japan and the United States (Canada 2005).

Government spending was shrinking even relative to U.S. spending: "In 1992 total government program spending as a share of GDP was two-thirds higher in Canada than in the U.S., but by 1998 this 'social advantage' would shrink to barely one-quarter." As Stanford (1998: 45) observed, given this dramatic decline in public spending, "It is hard to imagine how Canada's reputation as a 'kinder, gentler' society will be sustained."

The cuts in social programs initially took the form of reductions in the rate of increase of federal government spending on transfer payments to the provinces for health, education, and social assistance, and the abandonment, in 1977, of the federal government's open-ended commitment to pay 50 percent of provincial government expenditures on health and post-secondary education. Federal government contributions to Established Programs Financing (EPF) — the 1977 program by which federal funds were transferred to the provinces for health and post-secondary education — were tied to the rate of growth of per capita GDP. From the early to mid-1980s, and especially after the 1984 election of the Conservatives under Brian Mulroney, the government further reduced the rate of growth in federal transfers, primarily by limiting that growth to a rate that was less than the rate of growth in the GDP (Silver 1992: 233).

The results of these seemingly innocuous changes, often called "de-indexing," were dramatic. They "saved" the federal government an estimated $150 billion over a fifteen-year period — money that was not available to provincial governments for social spending (Silver 1992: 234). Provincial governments had to either make up these costs or, as was generally the case, cut their spending on these services. In addition, in 1991, Bill C-69 placed a 5 percent limit on the growth in federal contributions to Ontario, Alberta, and British Columbia under the Canada Assistance Plan (CAP) — the cost-shared, federal-provincial program under which welfare and social assistance services were financed — even though the costs to these provinces under CAP were increasing at the time at about 7 percent per annum (Silver 1992: 234).

The biggest change to, and the biggest reduction in, the federal transfer payment system came five years later, in 1996. The EPF and CAP were rolled into a new program, the Canadian Health and Social Transfer (CHST). In its first two years of operation (1996/97 and 1997/98), in its payments to the provinces for health, post-secondary education, and social assistance, the CHST transferred an amount that was $7 billion less than what would have been the case under the previous arrangements (Pulkingham and Ternowetsky 1999: 93; Yalnizyan 1998: 56). Further, the CHST is a block transfer, which means that the provinces get a single amount for health, education, and social assistance, and it is then up to each province to determine how to divide up this fund in its allocations for the various purposes. Under the previous system, by means of the CAP, the federal government had transferred a specific amount for social assistance. The result of the change, according to Jane Pulkingham and Gordon Ternowetsky (1999: 93), is that dollars traditionally spent on supporting the safety net came into direct competition with the spending needs of health and education: "If we compare the political clout of the health and education sectors with that of social assistance, there are grounds for assuming that welfare dollars will be further squeezed as the competition for scarce resources heats up." In other words, middle-class Canadians demanding more spending on health and education are almost certain to have more success than social assistance recipients calling for greater spending for their needs.

Another alteration made matters worse for social assistance recipients: under the CHST the standards that had existed under the CAP were eliminated; certain forms of assistance were "no longer mandated by legislation or directly supported by cost-shared transfers" (Pulkingham and Ternowetsky 1999: 94). Under CAP, in order to receive federal funds for social assistance the provinces were required to ensure that all people judged to be in need received funding; that benefit levels met basic needs; that an appeal procedure existed, enabling people to challenge welfare decisions; and that no work requirement was imposed as a condition of receiving social assistance. The removal of these standards, critics warned, would almost certainly lead to reduced levels of social assistance. As the Canadian Council on Social Development (1996) pointed out, the CHST "opens the way for jurisdictions to provide little or no assistance to those in need."

Indeed, that is precisely what happened in the years after 1995. One by one the provinces of British Columbia, Alberta, Manitoba, Ontario, Quebec, Nova Scotia, Prince Edward Island, and Newfoundland cut back their benefit rates and/or shelter allowances and altered the rules of eligibility to programs of assistance (Yalnizyan 1998: 57). The Ontario government, for example, cut welfare rates by 21.6 percent in 1995. Several provinces introduced provincial workfare programs (MacKinnon 2000). Social assistance recipients experienced a greater degree of financial insecurity and became subject to a variety of forces that pushed them into the paid labour force, usually at the low-wage end of the job market.

> One by one the provinces of British Columbia, Alberta, Manitoba, Ontario, Quebec, Nova Scotia, Prince Edward Island, and Newfoundland cut back their benefit rates and/or shelter allowances and altered the rules of eligibility to programs of assistance.

Following the Romanow Commission's recommendations, in 2004 the CHST was eliminated and replaced with two new funds: the Canada Health Transfer (CHT) and Canada Social Transfer (CST). Supplied in the form of cash and tax points, the CST is a block transfer to provinces and territories, which came to about $15.7 billion in 2006–07. The fund supports post-secondary education, social assistance, and social programs such as early childhood development (Canada 2006a). Much like with the CHST, the CST is funded at levels much lower than what was allotted for the CAP and EPF. During the 1995–98 period, the federal government reduced the CHST by some $7 billion, $2.8 billion of which would have been dedicated to social and post-secondary education spending. By 2007–08, the CST is slated to rise to $16.9 billion, representing merely a 2 percent per year increase of the cash portion, which is actually below the rate of inflation (CCPA 2005). Despite the new contributions, the total social transfer will still be below the pre-1995 period.

The desire to push people on social assistance into the paid workforce also drove other social policy changes. In 1985 the Family Allowance was partially de-indexed; that is, annual increases were pegged at a level less than the rate of increase in the cost of living. In 1989 the Family Allowance benefits of those above a certain income threshold were clawed back, thus changing what had been a universal social program to an income-contingent program. The abandonment of the principle of universality had wide repercussions, because universal benefits are more likely to enjoy broadly based support — and the support of middle-class recipients — than are income-contingent benefits, which are more likely to be supported only by that lower-income segment of the population that receives the benefits. In 1992 the federal government abandoned the Family Allowance entirely, replacing it with the Child Tax Benefit. The stated purpose of the change was to better target low-income families with children. "With this action," Pulkingham and Ternowetsky (1999: 88) pointed out, "the government made absolutely clear its rejection of the principle of universality." Significantly, the shift to the Child Tax Benefit and the introduction of the Working Income Supplement meant that only parents in the paid labour force were eligible for additional benefits; low-income parents on welfare and employment insurance received the same benefits as before. This policy had the perverse effect of reinforcing — in much the same way as workfare did — one of the primary structural mechanisms that maintains a persistently high rate of poverty — namely, low wages:

> Because of these policies, low wages became more attractive even if remuneration levels were unable to meet basic needs. In this context the Working Income Supplement acted as a low-wage subsidy, making low-wage jobs more tolerable, enlarging the pool of people willing to take up low-wage jobs, and thereby intensifying a downward pressure on wages. (Pulkingham and Ternowetsky 1999: 89)

The adopted policies were consistent with the desire to respond to a more competitive global economy by creating a more "flexible," more "competitive" labour force.

In 1997/98 the federal government replaced the Child Tax Benefit with the new National Child Benefit (NCB). The result was an increase in federal child benefits paid to all low-income families, both the working poor and people on social assistance. However, the federal government encouraged the provinces to claw back a portion of the NCB from social assistance recipients. Two provinces, New Brunswick and Newfoundland, chose not to do so; they left the money in the hands of families on social assistance. Manitoba eliminated the clawback in a staged fashion. All other provinces reduced their payments to social assistance recipients, reinvesting the "savings" in programs and services for all low-income families with children.

The new initiative sparked considerable debate. Social policy analyst Ken Battle of the Caledon Institute suggested that, whatever its limitations, the National Child Benefit had the potential to be "the most important social policy innovation since medicare." It could provide the basis on which governments could "wage a real war on family poverty." He admitted, though, that "as of now" the policy is "only a downpayment" and "much work remains to be done" (Battle 1999b: 38, 60). The National Council of Welfare more guardedly called the new National Child Benefit "promising" and "a small step forward" (NCW 1997: 12). A study by the Canadian Policy Research Network observed that while the NCB "is an important new program and might be a useful anti-poverty measure, it will only be truly effective if the amount of the benefit is increased significantly" (Jenson and Stroick 1999: 22).

Other, more hostile, critics pointed to a variety of perceived weaknesses, including the absence of national standards for the provincial reinvestment programs; the fear that the provinces may use the money simply to offset costs that they would have incurred anyway; and the only partially indexed nature of the program. What is more, the National Child Benefit claws back a portion of the benefits of low-income families on social assistance, but not of low-income families whose members are working for wages (Pulkingham and Ternowetsky 1999: 90). The purpose, again, is "to improve work incentives." The danger is that provinces might use the National Child Benefit as a justification for pushing social assistance recipients into workfare programs (Battle 1999b: 53), a concern that is not without foundation. After all, the determination to push people into the paid labour force has characterized many of the social policy changes of the 1980s and 1990s — irrespective of how growing numbers of jobs are part-time and low-wage and will not drive workers' incomes above the poverty line.

That is certainly the case with Unemployment Insurance. In 1989/90 the federal government effectively privatized Unemployment Insurance. As the result of Bill C-21 the government withdrew from its previous role as financial contributor to this crucial program, leaving its financing completely in the hands of employees and employers. There followed a series of changes to UI in the early to mid-1990s, each making the provision of UI more restrictive: stricter qualifying requirements and reductions in the level and duration of benefits, for example (Pulkingham and Ternowetsky 1999: 86). These trends were intensified with the introduction in 1996 of Bill C-12, creating the new Employment Insurance (EI) system. The more restrictive provisions applying to EI served to accelerate the downward trend in the proportion of unemployed Canadians receiving benefits. While 74 percent of unemployed Canadians received UI benefits in 1990, only 39 percent of unemployed Canadians received EI benefits in 2001 (Canadian Labour Congress 2003).

Over the past decade and a half these changes to Employment Insurance only helped to make employment even more precarious, with the result that wage demands were reduced. This is no accident, since the purpose, according to Stanford (1996: 144), is to "harmonize Canada's labour market outcomes with those of our trading partners (especially the U.S.)." The goal of the reforms — "to enhance the international competitiveness of Canada's economy on a low-wage basis" — was to be achieved by "deliberately increasing the economic insecurity facing Canadian workers, hence moderating their wage demands and disciplining their behaviour in the workplace." This purpose, again, is entirely consistent with many of the changes made to Canadian social programs throughout the 1980s and especially the 1990s.

The cuts to and redesign of social programs in Canada during the past two decades were not necessary for fiscal reasons. As necessary as it was for the country to bring recurrent deficits under control, the problem could have been addressed without making cuts to social spending — as demonstrated repeatedly in the alternative federal budgets prepared annually since 1995 by Cho!ces and the Canadian Centre for Policy Alternatives. Stanford (1998: 46–47) observes:

Just as it was high interest rates and slow growth that lit the fuse on Canada's fiscal explosion earlier in the 1980s and 1990s, it was the post-1995 decline in interest rates and improving economic growth prospects that laid the foundation for the recovery of public-sector finances. Spending cuts accelerated the elimination of deficits; *but those deficits would have disappeared anyway*, at a slower pace, thanks to lower interest rates and stronger economic growth.

The cuts in social spending and redesign of programs were the result of conscious government policy. The social policy changes were, at least in part, an attempt to create a more flexible, competitive labour force in Canada in response to the increased global competitiveness

> The social policy changes were, at least in part, an attempt to create a more flexible, competitive labour force in Canada arising from global economic shifts. But from start to finish those economic changes and changes in social policy have together resulted in the country's persistently high poverty levels.

arising from economic changes. But from start to finish those economic changes and cuts to and changes in social policy have together resulted in the country's persistently high poverty levels.

SOLUTIONS TO POVERTY

Persistently high levels of poverty are not inevitable. Nations are fully capable of achieving lower levels of poverty, as we have seen in the case of other advanced capitalist societies. But the problem of poverty has no *single* solution. Any effective response will have to be multifaceted.

The creation of more good jobs and the construction of a stronger set of social policies will have to be at the heart of an effective anti-poverty strategy, and the policies that comprise our social welfare system have an important part to play in this. They may not in themselves solve the problem of poverty, but they are crucial to any efforts at narrowing the gap between rich and poor. Additional measures would include higher minimum wages, together with strengthened trade unions and especially an expansion of the benefits of trade unionism to the retail and service sectors, which would help push up wage levels at the lower end of the income scale and thus address the problems of the "working poor." We also need public investment to increase the availability and accessibility of child-care facilities, which would create significantly improved opportunities for young parents, especially young women. We need investment in early childhood educational initiatives; strong evidence indicates that such public investment produces a financial return far beyond the initial investment.

> Each of these responses implies a more activist and interventionist state, governing directly in the interests of those at the lower end of the income scale.

We need investment in education more generally, given strong evidence that levels of educational attainment are correlated to success in finding jobs and to lifetime earnings. We need a much more serious approach to the development of a range of anti-racism initiatives; the evidence is clear that poverty in Canada has increasingly been racialized (Galabuzi 2006).

Each of these responses implies a more activist and interventionist state, governing directly in the interests of those at the lower end of the income scale. The prevailing ideology in Canada over the past twenty-five years has shifted the distribution of power in exactly the opposite direction. Government policies have disproportionately benefited people at the upper end of the income scale. Turning this direction around will require more effective political action by low-income and working-class people.

An additional and especially important element in an anti-poverty strategy is work done at the community level by community-based organizations. This kind of work is sometimes called community development, or community economic development (CED), which is an economic and social strategy based on the idea that, given some supports, people can organize themselves to act collectively as communities in order to meet their economic and social needs. The case for a CED strategy follows from the twofold observation that neither a reliance on the free market by itself nor top-down government programs will provide a solution to poverty. With some supports, people working collectively can develop the community-based solutions to enable them to solve their own economic and social problems.

It comes as a response not only to the ravages of poverty, but also to frustrations with top-down bureaucratic programs designed by distant policy-makers and delivered by those who have no stake in the community.

In Winnipeg's inner city, to give just one example, a wide variety of innovative and effective community-based initiatives have been put in place over the past twenty years. This community development approach has emerged from those who are themselves living in poverty. It comes as a response not only to the ravages of poverty, but also to frustrations with top-down bureaucratic programs designed by distant policy-makers and delivered by those who have no stake in the community. In 1990 the Community Inquiry into Inner City Revitalization, a public inquiry initiated and run by Winnipeg's inner-city community, criticized the inner-city development initiatives of the previous decade, including two multi-million-dollar tri-level Core Area Initiatives, for not being sufficiently participatory, for not involving inner-city residents themselves to the extent that was possible and desirable. The inquiry concluded that the inner-city community should play a larger and more direct role in planning and program delivery. In a summary of the May 9, 1990, hearings, the inquiry co-ordinator presented the rationale for this conclusion:

> Inner city residents hold the key to sustained revitalization efforts. In principle, they have the most at stake, and their needs and aspirations — not those of outside institutions or investors — should prevail. In practice, a number of organizations and projects have demonstrated that residents can assume effective decision-making and administrative control over local issues and initiatives, given appropriate development support. If public sector intervention is to be preventive rather than remedial in nature, resources should be allocated to community and self-help, grassroots projects/groups that foster local ownership and responsibility. (Community Inquiry into Inner City Revitalization 1990)

This is an approach that has a great deal of potential. Once this kind of process begins, a positive culture can emerge: people living and working in inner cities or rural communities suffering from poverty can best under-

> People living and working in inner cities or rural communities suffering from poverty can best understand the needs of their communities, and are in the best position to develop innovative ideas to meet those needs, and design and implement community-based responses.

stand the needs of their communities, and are in the best position to develop innovative ideas to meet those needs, and design and implement community-based responses.

At the Andrews Street Family Centre in Winnipeg's inner city, for instance, an entire program has been built upon the central CED principles of hiring locally, purchasing locally, and working to meet local needs (Silver 2000: 139). The Centre emerged in the 1990s in response to concerns expressed by community members about the needs of children and families in the area. Community members carried out a survey to identify the needs and the skills of neighbourhood people. Although the Centre would initially be professionally staffed, the plan called for the professionals to work themselves out of a job on a fixed schedule. The Centre would hire local people and mentor them to take over. Community people come to Andrews Street to use the facilities, as often as not to use the most basic things, like washing machines and telephones. Frequently adults come just to talk to someone, especially another adult. They may begin to build a relationship with others, and with staff, and out of that relationship sometimes a clearer sense of their circumstances and their needs emerges. Sometimes they end up volunteering at the Centre. Those who demonstrate ability may be hired. The philosophical foundation of Andrews Street includes a commitment to identifying and building on people's strengths, not their weaknesses. Volunteer opportunities are plentiful: in the food-buying club, the clothing exchange, the community kitchen, the children's and teens' programs, the moms-helping-moms program, and others. Andrews Street has started a catering co-operative that provides casual and part-time employment to as many as ten people. The Centre has trained and hired people for home renovations and repairs, and also employs local staff in the moms-helping-moms program, among others. These opportunities give local residents not only much-needed income, but also equally needed confidence and self-esteem.

Aboriginal people working in Winnipeg's inner city, to offer another example, have developed their own, highly effective approach to community development. It is a holistic approach that starts by working to heal individuals from the many adverse effects of the colonization to which they have been and continue to be subjected. But individuals cannot heal unless they are a part of strong communities, so community-building is a central part of the Aboriginal approach to community development. Building stronger and healthier communities requires organizational capacity, and Aboriginal people have built Aboriginal organizations — organizations run by and for Aboriginal people — to work to this end. This entire approach is rooted in the belief that the problems experienced by many Aboriginal people are not a product of personal failings, but a product of Aboriginal peoples' history of subjection to colonization — a process that continues to this day. So Aboriginal community development in Winnipeg's inner city is rooted in the ideology of de-colonization. The result of this holistic approach — working at the personal, community, organizational, and ideological levels — is a distinctive and highly effective form of community development (Silver 2006, especially cha. 5).

If reasonable levels of funding are provided to such community-based initiatives, neighbourhoods and communities ravaged by high levels of poverty can begin to turn themselves around. A recent study of Winnipeg's inner city found:

> Different neighbourhoods are at different stages in the process of beginning to solve their own problems. Some have deteriorated very dramatically, some have not deteriorated quite so much, and others are beginning to show some genuine signs of improvement. A major variable, we believe the major variable, is the extent to which solid community-based organizations have emerged and are being funded. (Silver 2002: 12)

Community economic development is not an easy or a quick solution to the problem of poverty, but its participatory, community-based approach and its commitment to being inclusive have great potential as an important element, perhaps even a central element, in fighting persistent poverty in Canada.

Successful community economic development initiatives, like most of the other anti-poverty initiatives — job creation, strong social policies, higher minimum wages, adequate child care and early childhood initiatives, the unionization of service-sector jobs, strong anti-racism initiatives — require an active and supportive role on the part of the state. This role will only come about through a massive effort at the political level — when poor and working-class people organize themselves to ensure that the state advances their interests, and not simply, as usual, the interests of the corporate sector and the well-to-do.

GLOSSARY OF KEY TERMS

Canada Social Transfer (CST): A federal block transfer to provinces and territories in support of post-secondary education, social assistance, and social services. The CST is made up of both a cash transfer and tax transfer component. The CST was created in 2004 when the Canada Health and Social Transfer (CHST) was eliminated, and the CST and Canada Health Transfer (CHT) were created. Because of the cuts to social transfers in the post-1995 period, the CST is currently set up with levels of funding far less than what was provided under the CAP and EPF programs.

Community economic development (CED): An economic and social strategy based on the idea that, given some supports, people can organize themselves to act collectively as communities in order to meet their economic and social needs. CED is an approach to economic and social development that is intended to be participatory. It is rooted in ideas such as local control and local decision-making, and seeks to operate on the basis of principles such as hiring, purchasing, and investing locally and producing to meet local needs.

De-indexing: Limiting the growth of something — government transfer payments of various kinds, for example — to a rate less than the rate of growth of the economy, so that it declines as a proportion of total economic activity.

Low-income cut-off (LICO): Most Canadian social policy groups use Statistics Canada's low-income cut-offs as a poverty line, although Statistics Canada does not call the LICO a poverty line. The LICO is established by using Statistics Canada data on family expenditures to determine what proportion of its total income the average Canadian household spends on food, clothing, and shelter. Any household whose expenditures on these necessities is twenty percentage points or more higher than the average household is considered to have an income below the LICO. The reasoning is that any household spending such a high proportion of its income on these three essentials has too little money left for other necessary expenditures.

Own-account self-employment: When a self-employed person works on his or her own and has no employees.

Workfare: A program in which government forces people on social assistance to work in order to qualify for social assistance benefits. It is rooted in the assumption — many believe a false assumption — that people are not working because they do not have the incentive to work, and therefore must be forced.

Working poor: People who are employed, but whose employment earnings generate incomes that are below the LICO.

QUESTIONS FOR DISCUSSION

1. Discuss the relationship between poverty and family type. How are changes in the structure of the family over the past twenty-five years related to poverty? What kinds of solutions to poverty could be designed in response to changes in family type?
2. What relationship does poverty have to jobs? How are changes in the structure of the labour market over the past twenty-five years related to poverty? What kinds of solutions to poverty could be designed in response to changes in the labour market?
3. How are changes to Canada's social welfare system over the past twenty-five years related to poverty? What kinds of solutions to poverty could be designed in response to changes in the social welfare system?
4. What is CED? How and why could it be useful in combating poverty?

5. Consider the debate about poverty lines in Canada. Do you think the LICO is a useful measure of poverty? Do you think a market-basket approach would be better? Why?

6. Why are poverty levels so high in Canada compared to many European countries? Why have governments failed to institute policies that are known to reduce poverty levels? What might be done to encourage governments to introduce such policies?

WEBSITES OF INTEREST

Canadian Centre for Policy Alternatives. <www.policyalternatives.ca>.
National Council of Welfare. <www.newenbes.net/>.
Caledon Institute of Social Policy. <www.caledoninst.org/>.
Canadian CED Network. <www.canadiancednetwork.org/>.
Centre for Social Justice. <www.socialjustice.org>.
Canadian Association of Food Banks. <www.cafb–acba.ca/>.

NOTES

I am grateful to Matthew Rogers for his assistance in preparing the tables and figures and for much additional assistance in revising this chapter, to Tara Rudy of the Social Planning Council of Winnipeg for providing us with customized data, and to Wayne Antony, Shauna MacKinnon, Todd Scarth, and Lisa Shaw for contributions to earlier versions.

1. Statistics Canada's low-income cut-offs (LICO) are used to determine poverty rates. See the appendix to this chapter, "The Debate about Poverty Lines."

APPENDIX: THE DEBATE ABOUT POVERTY LINES

In Canada today the question of how to measure and therefore to define poverty is a matter of considerable debate. The most commonly used measurement is the Statistics Canada low-income cut-off (LICO), which is used as a poverty line by most social policy groups in Canada. However, the government bureau itself does not see the LICO as a poverty line. A Statistics Canada paper (Wolfson and Evans 1989) described some of the limitations of the LICO. As well, recent objections — perhaps most notably from the Fraser Institute (Sarlo 1996) — have been expressed regarding this "relative" approach to defining and measuring poverty. As a result, in 1997 the federal, provincial, and territorial governments began considering the merits of an alternative measurement of poverty based on the market costs of a "basket" of goods and services deemed to be "essential" (Human Resources Development Canada 1998).

The LICO

The LICO is a relative approach to poverty based on using Statistics Canada family expenditures data to determine what proportion of its total income the average Canadian household spends on food, clothing, and shelter. Any household whose expenditures on these necessities is twenty percentage points or more higher than the average household has, by definition, an income below the LICO. The reasoning is that any household spending such a high proportion of its income on these three essentials has too little money left for such other necessary expenditures as such transport, personal care, household supplies, recreation, health, and insurance.

The Statistics Canada researchers have established thirty-five separate LICOs in Canada. These are the result of dividing the population into seven different household types, based on the size of household, and establishing five different types of geographic area, based on the size of the community in which people live. Thus a family of four in a large centre like Vancouver would have a different LICO than a single person in Portage la Prairie, who in turn would have a different LICO than a single-parent with two children in Kingston.

Those who object to the LICO as a poverty line advance several arguments. One is that choosing to establish a LICO at twenty percentage points above what the average household spends on food, clothing, and shelter is arbitrary. All poverty lines, including those based on absolute measures, have an arbitrary element to them. More importantly, those opposed to the LICO as a poverty line argue that it is a relative as opposed to an absolute measure. They argue that it measures not poverty, but income inequality, because it is based on a given family's expenditures relative to an average Canadian figure. A more meaningful measurement, these critics argue, would be to determine the cost of the basic necessities of life for any Canadian household. The cost of a "basket" of such necessities then becomes the poverty line; those with incomes below that amount are below the poverty line. This is the argument advanced by Christopher Sarlo, whose work on poverty has been published and promoted by the Fraser Institute (Sarlo 1996). This absolute approach, though, raises as many problems as it solves.

The Fraser Institute Approach

The main problem with the absolute approach is the difficulty of determining what should be included in the basket of basic necessities of life and what should be excluded. Beyond a basic agreement about food, clothing, and shelter, reasonable people can legitimately differ about the important details that make up "necessities." The determination of what those basic necessities are becomes, at least in part, arbitrary. Sarlo defines basic necessities narrowly. He argues, for example, that the cost of health services and products not covered by Medicare and the cost of newspapers are not to be included in a basket of basic necessities. He calls those items "social comforts" or "social amenities" (Sarlo 1996: xvii, 28, 46). Basic necessities by his definition include only the physical necessities of life: "People are poor if they cannot afford all basic physical necessities — items the absence of which is likely to compromise long term physical well-being" (Sarlo 1996: 196). As a result, his poverty line is far below all other Canadian-designed poverty lines (Ross et al. 1994: 12–25); by his definition, then, far fewer Canadians live in poverty than is the case when, for example, the LICO is used. Sarlo found that one million Canadians were below his absolute poverty line in 1988, which led him to conclude, "Poverty, as it has been traditionally understood, has been virtually eliminated. It is simply not a major problem in Canada" (Sarlo 1996: 2).

A different but reasonable conclusion might be that the presence in Canada of one million people whose incomes are "too low to afford all of the basic requirements of living" (Sarlo 1996: 193) is indeed a problem. Sarlo thinks otherwise, arguing that existing government programs are sufficient to lift all of these people above his poverty line, so that "everyone is able to acquire all the basic necessities of life" (Sarlo 1996: 193). By this means, he makes poverty disappear entirely.

Sarlo's absolute approach to poverty constructs a definition of poverty that some critics have called "mean-spirited" (NCW 1998/99: 27). A definition that has the result of reducing the number of those for whom some form of public expenditure might be required is consistent with the ideological orientation of the Fraser Institute, an organization strongly in favour of reduced government expenditures. The National Council of Welfare's biggest complaint with the very low poverty lines supported by the Fraser Institute is that the Institute's only apparent interest in poverty lines is to show that poverty is not a problem in Canada and does not warrant action by government (NCW 1998/99: 5).

A strong case can be made that the Sarlo approach is too narrow and that the basic necessities of life in Canada include more than simply what is needed to avoid compromising long-term physical well-being. For example, why would health and dental costs that are excluded by Medicare not be included in a "basket" of necessities? What about school supplies and school outings for children? Do these kinds of expenditures have a crucial impact on the quality of life? Reasonable people may well disagree about exactly what items to include in a market basket of necessities, but most would conclude that for a healthy and reasonably equitable society the basket should not be as small as the one Sarlo advocates.

An innovative experiment in Winnipeg in 1997 provided that larger viewpoint. The Social Planning Council of Winnipeg and Winnipeg Harvest recruited seven low-income Winnipeggers to determine what should be included in a basket of goods and services that would provide an acceptable living level — what they described as "a reasonable but not extravagant expectation of living costs." Using a hypothetical family of three that included a single mother who neither smoked nor owned a car, plus a girl under six and a boy of fifteen years, they concluded that the cost of a basket of goods and services necessary to produce an acceptable living level required an annual income of $26,945.60 — a figure very close to the LICO of $27,672 (Social Planning Council of Winnipeg and Winnipeg Harvest 1997: iii). As the National Council of Welfare (1998/99: 37) put it: "That led them to the view that the market basket and statistical approaches validate each other and make both approaches more credible."

Human Resources Development Canada has also been attempting to develop market-basket measures of poverty. The HRDC market-basket method calculates costs for food, clothing, and shelter; and then, rather than itemizing and costing each of the additional items that would have to be in a market basket, as the "acceptable living level" calculation did, adds an "other" category equal to 60 percent of the cost of food and clothing (NCW 1998/99: 23). This approach is consistent with the idea that any measure of poverty must, of necessity, include assumptions that are relatively arbitrary.

The Statistics Canada LICO not only avoids many of these problems, but also has certain advantages. Although it is, in part, arbitrary, so too is the basic necessities approach, because someone must determine what is a basic necessity and what is not. Furthermore, although the LICO is a relative as opposed to an absolute measurement, poverty itself is a phenomenon having much to do with a particular person's relative position in society. For example, it may be true, as Sarlo argues, that school supplies and money for school outings are not necessities of life. Their absence does not "compromise long-term physical well-being." Still, the focus on those kinds of items indicates why it is best to think of poverty in relative terms. In Canada today most children live in families that are able to afford school supplies and money for school outings. The child whose family cannot afford these purchases or outings is, in a very real sense, a child who is living in poverty. In other words, poverty in Canada has a social and psychological component as well as simply a physical component. Sarlo can say, as he does, "I am not at all offended by inequality. I have no problem with large variations of income and wealth. I do not regard it as unjust or unfair that Wayne Gretzky earns one hundred times as much as most men his age" (Sarlo 1996: 3). But most Canadians find it both unjust and unfair that some families cannot purchase school supplies or pay for school outings while others earn six-figure incomes. In a society of material affluence, there is more to poverty than simply the absence of the material means to meet bare physical needs.

In their study, David P. Ross and Paul Roberts (1999: 37) ask: what if we set the poverty line at a level that would provide all children roughly equal chances of full development? They examined twenty-seven elements of child development, including such variables as children's behaviour, health, learning outcomes, and participation in sports and clubs. They found that for 80 percent of these twenty-seven variables, the risks of negative outcomes for children were noticeably higher in families with incomes below $30,000; and for 50 percent of the variables, children in families earning less than $40,000 did noticeably less well. They concluded that an appropriate child poverty line is between $30,000 and $40,000 for a family of four: "If healthier child development is considered to be an important objective of our society, it seems that at the very least, the LICO is defensible as a measure of poverty."

Whatever its limitations as a measurement of poverty, the Statistics Canada LICO is a useful measurement for research purposes. It enables us to determine, for instance, that poverty is higher in Winnipeg than in most other Canadian centres, that it is higher in Winnipeg's inner city than in Winnipeg as a whole, and that it has been growing steadily in Winnipeg's inner city for many years and rapidly in recent years. It enables us to determine that poverty in Canada has been persistently high in recent decades, and that certain categories of people — those in particular family arrangements and those with a particular relationship to the labour market — are more likely than others to be poor. These useful research findings are made possible by the use of the Statistics Canada LICO; and they are confirmed by innovative approaches such as the Social Planning Council/Winnipeg Harvest market-basket study, which established acceptable living levels roughly equivalent to the Statistics Canada LICO. Sarlo's claim that poverty "is simply not a major problem" in Canada has a hollow ring, and it throws into doubt the merits of his alternative approach to the measurement of poverty.

Chapter Eight

UNHOLY ALLIANCES
The Discourse of Globalization and Our Global Future

Parvin Ghorayshi

We need to urgently bring the planet and people back into our picture of the world. — Vandana Shiva 2000

Perhaps the greatest threat to freedom and democracy in the world today comes from the formation of unholy alliances between government and business. This is not a new phenomenon. It used to be called fascism....The outward appearances of the democratic process are observed, but the powers of the state are diverted to the benefit of private interests. — George Soros 2000

Our house is burning and we're blind to it... the earth and humankind are in danger and we are all responsible. It is time to open our eyes. Alarms are sounding across all the continents.... We cannot say that we did not know!... Climate warming is still reversible. Heavy would be the responsibility of those who refused to fight it. — French President, Jacque Chirac, 2002.

In the past decade or so, "globalization" has emerged as a popular, seemingly inescapable concept and buzzword. The term readily appears in the sound bites of politicians

"You Should Know This"
- 70 percent of the 1.5 billion people living on 1$ a day or less are women.
- Nike shoes that sell in the United States or Europe for $73 to $135 are produced for about $5.60 by girls and young women paid as little as 15 cents an hour.
- Amount of money owed by the world's 47 poorest and most indebted nations: $422 billion. Amount of money spent by Western industrialized nations on weapons and soldiers every year: $422 billion.
- In 2005 more than $2.1 trillion was spent on corporate mergers and acquisitions, 19 percent more than in 2004. In telecommunications, the ten largest corporations control 86 percent of the world market.
- In six of the eight years from 1990 to 1997, developing countries paid out more in debt payments than they received in new loans — a total transfer from the poor South to the rich North of $77 billion.
- More than $1.9 trillion ($1,900 billion) changes hands daily on global currency markets, compared to $80 billion in 1980. Almost all exchanges are short-term speculation: more than 80 percent are completed in less than a week and 40 percent in less than two days.
- More than 700 social movements from 122 different countries, represented by 4,700 delegates and more than 15,000 participants, went to a meeting in Porto Alegre, Brazil, in early 2001 to reaffirm that human life has a greater value than profit.

Sources: Van der Gaag 2004: 44; Korten 2001: 115; Steger 2003: 43; Ellwood 2006: 55, 63, 85; Houtart and Polet 2001: vi.

and the critiques of environmentalists. Every business guru talks about it. No political speech is complete without reference to it (Giddens 1999; Annan 2000). There are people in favour of it (often economists and business journalists) and people against it (sometimes called "anti-globalization activists"). The concept seemingly knows no boundaries. It pops up constantly in the media in both the industrialized and the so-called developing countries. In France the word is *mondialisation*. In Spain and Latin America, it is *globalizacion*. The Germans say *globalisierung*. Still, despite this ubiquitous existence, as Anthony Giddens states, few key terms are as frequently used and as poorly conceptualized (cited in Richter 2001: 1; see also Soros 2000; Starr 2000). Although globalization as a process is by no means new, as a term it made its appearance in the *Oxford Dictionary* only in 1992 (Kaldor 2000: 12). Social scientists and various schools of thought — from politicians to economists, and postmodernists to Marxists — use the concept to refer not just to different processes but also to different states of existence (Sklair 1991; Castells 1996; Annan 2000; Held and McGrew 2000).

Despite a lack of agreement on definition, the concept of globalization has a number of interrelated dimensions — economic, political, cultural, and social — that need to be distinguished (Teeple 2000; Murphy 1994; Chase-Dunn 1994; Harvey 1989; Meyer 1996; Markoff 1996; Giddens 1996; Petras and Veltmeyer 2001, 2005). Here I focus on the economic dimension of globalization, the growing push for the deregulation of the market and the free movement of investment capital, and especially as these concerns relate to Canada. Globalization has deep roots in history and has now found contemporary expression as a process within capitalism (Nayar 2003; Steger 2003; Ellwood 2002). Part of the process involves the growing financial power of large corporations and how they have been pushing for a free market as the best way of building and governing modern societies. Part of it, too, is the way in which capital has recaptured the state by implementing neo-liberal policies of free-market capitalism. Today a growing tension exists between the demands of corporate globalization and the basic needs of democratic, sustainable, and equitable economies. The clash is between two opposing views of society: on the one side are people who seek open borders for increasing the mobility of their investment, trade, and money flows with minimal government intervention; and on the other are those who make social justice their priority and call for globalization from below, attempting to build a shared international sense of how best to meet societal needs around the world (Gindin 2002; Kung 1998; Robinson 2002). The first vision is called corporate globalization, and it is encouraged by big business and politicians who stress the efficiency of the market in promoting rapid growth. But although free-market capitalism benefits large corporations, it damages people's lives and creates deep cleavages — both within societies and

> The clash is between two opposing views of society: on the one side are people who seek open borders for increasing the mobility of their investment, trade, and money flows with minimal government intervention; and on the other are those who make social justice their priority and call for globalization from below, attempting to build a shared international sense of how best to meet societal needs around the world.

between the North and South (McNally 2002; Mandle 2003; Khor 1996). In this sense, globalization, as Henry Kissinger, secretary of state under President Richard Nixon, once candidly stated, is another term for U.S. domination (Gindin 2002: 1, 11).

Globalization is not compatible with social justice. It undermines the power of the welfare state and raises important questions regarding the role of democratically elected governments. The restructuring of economies and business under the banner of globalization has changed how labour markets operate and has harmful impacts on workers, particularly women (Mandle 2003; Marchand 2000; Pettman 1996; Rege 2003). Kofi Annan, Secretary General of the United Nations, in speaking about the global turmoil, economic crisis, and political challenges and conflict throughout the world, reminds us:

> If globalization is to succeed, it must succeed for poor and rich alike. It must deliver rights no less than riches. It must provide social justice and equity no less than economic prosperity and enhanced communication. It must be harnessed to the cause not of capital alone, but of development and prosperity for the poorest of the world. (Annan 2000: 129)

The challenges and changes fostered by globalization have not gone unnoticed. Informed and organized citizens around the world have been fighting against the rising social costs of ever-expanding global capitalism. Social justice activists, people from all walks of life, continue to question neo-liberal trade policies. Despite the repressive forces of police and lawmakers, concerned citizens demand that globalization be tied to democratic reforms, gender equity, labour rights, and environmental protections. These demands lead to questions about the possible shape of post-corporate society (Dodds 2002; Harriss 2001; Gelbspan 2004; Balaam and Veseth 2005a; Rege 2003).

There is no doubt that we live in a global society, but the question to be asked is what kind of global economy do we want to live in? The question is not whether globalization is good or bad, but whether we can reconcile the creation of a mutually beneficial system of global trade with the accommodation of a plural world (Winthrop 2000; Boyer and Drache 1996; Shiva 2000; Shiva and Holla-Bar 1996). Contrary to the official discourse, corporate globalization is not "natural" or "inevitable" — it does not have a will-of-God dimension to it. Alternative directions are possible. Politically conscious citizens have enormous power in exposing the role of corporations in society and have a chance to join with others in the creation of truly human communities (Harriss 2001; Brownlee 2005; Gelbspan 2004; Balaam and Veseth 2005a; Cavanagh and Manders 2004).

WHAT IS GLOBALIZATION? IS IT NEW?

The recent political discourse focusing on economic globalization implies that significant changes in the areas of technology and economic competitiveness have occurred. We are told that our economic competitiveness has to be assessed within the global or regional, rather than national, markets. It is said that the trade, capital flow, and technological advances in the last two or three decades have been more intensive and extensive than in earlier periods (Teeple 2000). Globalization is presented as being at once all-powerful, incomprehensible, impossibly complex, seemingly unchallengeable, and, on top of all that, unprecedented (Dobbin 1998).

Based on these assumptions, governments and other public and private institutions all over the world have changed the rules of policy-making, putting economic decisions at the mercy of market forces. They have adopted new policies and practices to alter the political balances among states, firms, unions, and various groups in society (Teeple 2000; Kolko 1988). The discourse of globalization has generated a new social contract in which many people are excluded or left in the margin (Bello 1996; Mandle 2003; Harriss 2001).

Despite the presence of this seemingly new discourse, global economic integration has been a long-term trend over the past six hundred years. It has long been part of the capitalist intersocietal system of Europe and its expansion internationally. Trading activities date from the earliest civilizations, but it was in the Middle Ages in Europe that institutions of a private corporate nature initiated systematic cross-border trading operations. Beginning in 1241, for instance, the Hanseatic League organized German merchants in the conduct of their Western European commerce (Hirst and Thompson 1999), and by the fourteenth century, various states had formed important economic and political/military links (Wallerstein 1974; Frank 1978). By the end of the fourteenth century as many as 150 Italian companies were already operating multinationally (Hirst and Thompson 1999). During the seventeenth and eighteenth centuries the great colonial companies were established: the Dutch and British East India companies, the Muscovy Company, the Royal Africa Company, and the Hudson's Bay Company (Arrighi 1994; Taylor 1996). The closest precursor to modern-day transnational corporations (TNCs) appeared with the development of international manufacturing as the Industrial Revolution took hold.

Globalization, then, has been around for a long time, and the most recent technological, cultural, economic, and political changes are part of a long-term phenomenon (Harvey 1995; Steger 2003; Ellwood 2002). Except perhaps for their scale and complexity, the present transformations are by no means novel (Arrighi 1997). Still, although not new, globalization is an accentuation of a newly felt drive to expand and make the best of a necessary adjustment in a system of international finance (Harvey 1995: 8); it is closely related to the recent major expansion in the foreign exchange market (Arrighi 1997). Powerful financial interests have been putting pressure on national governments to restructure their economies. Corporate globalization means the free movement of capital and the increasing domination of national economies by global financial markets and TNCs. My argument is not that things have remained unchanged: fundamental reorganizations are going on in the international economy to which an imaginative

> Powerful financial interests have been putting pressure on national governments to restructure their economies.

response is desperately needed. As Mary Kaldor (2000: 14) rightly states, "So it is really that globalization rules. It is that the rules of globalization are set by the powerful and imposed on the rest of us, who, if we do not like these rules, have to be serious about mobilizing the broad support." The key questions to be asked are: Who sets the rules and in whose interest? How do the recent changes compare with the long-run trend of capitalism? What are the important continuities and differences? And what we can do about it?

The discourse of globalization should not blind us to how, while the world economy continues to integrate economically, in political-economic terms it appears to be breaking up into three blocs: the United States, with its North and South American peripheries; Japan, with its Asian peripheries; and Western Europe, with its East European, Middle Eastern, and African peripheries (Magdoff 1992). A good deal of economic exchange is between regions, rather than being truly worldwide. The countries of the European Union (EU), for example, mostly trade among themselves. The same is true of the other main trading blocs, such as those of North America or the Asia-Pacific. Globalization for the most part is limited to the core of industrialized countries: Europe, North America, and Japan. For instance, 85 percent of foreign investment flow is between the members of this triad. Thus, intense "triadization" of financial markets is more apparent and likely than full-scale globalization.

Despite the pressure for economic globalization, local economies and national states continue to play an important role. The law of the single price everywhere for the same good is far from reality. Big Macs are available all over the world, but prices differ according to local conditions (Boyer and Drache 1996: 2). State activity has been internationalized to an unprecedented degree in all industrial countries, but production methods, industrial relations, taxation, and many other economic matters remain specific to each national state (Boyer and Drache 1996: 13). For instance, Canada, since its colonization by European settlers, has always been a "globalized" economy. But more than 80 percent of its total economic output is produced by Canadians, for Canadians, without ever crossing its border (Stanford 2001: 16). Its foreign trade has grown dramatically, but it is not larger, as a share of Gross Domestic Product (GDP), than it was a century earlier (Stanford 2001). Foreign direct investment, even after the recent wave of foreign takeovers, accounts for a much smaller proportion of the Canadian economy than it did thirty years ago.

At the same time, though, the reality is that the shocking powers of the international and regional trade agreements, such as the World Trade Organization (WTO) and North American Free Trade Agreement (NAFTA), have put a dangerous and anti-democratic twist on economic integration (Brownlee 2005; Petras and Veltmeyer 2005). These new dimensions of the global economy have truly changed how the world economy operates and, as a result, have rightly sparked great concern. But, again, the underlying forces of international trade and investment are neither new nor notably more important than they were in the past (Stanford 2001). Although the Canadian state is in a difficult transition period, it does and should play a major role in managing the economy (Brownlee 2005: 127–41). Indeed, whether it works alone or as part of international institutions for world governance, the state remains the only institution ultimately powerful enough to challenge corporate rule (Dobbin 1998: 284; Brownlee 2005; Weiss 1997). Governments can stand up to the interests of big business. They can turn things around and promote democracy.

GLOBAL CAPITALISM AND GLOBAL PLAYERS: THE NEW LEVIATHAN

Canadians find themselves in a world dominated at every turn by large corporations — banks, trust companies, companies involved in currency speculation, firms that buy and sell government bonds, large agribusinesses, and bond-rating companies that pronounce on government polices. Corporations have exploded in terms of growth, profit, and power. Wal-Mart, Shell, General Motors, Ford, and Nike are household names. Of the one hundred largest economies in the world, fifty-one are corporations. Wal-Mart, the number twelve corporation (forty-two on the overall list) is larger in its corporate sales than 161 countries are in GDP; including Israel, Poland, and Greece. Mitsubishi is larger than the fourth-most populous nation on Earth, Indonesia. General Motors is bigger than Denmark. Ford is bigger than South Africa. Toyota is bigger than Norway (Centre for Social Justice Team 1998; Anderson and Cavanagh 1996; Balaam and Veseth 2005b: 376–402).

These huge transnational corporations shape virtually every aspect of our lives, and the extent of their economic power is alarming (Ritzer 2006). In the food industry, for example, the corner-store grocer has been replaced by 7-Elevens and Mac's Convenience stores. The local drugstore is gone, replaced by huge chains. George Weston owns Loblaws, Loeb, Valu-Mart, The Real Canadian Superstore, and the largest bakery chain in the country. The Weston empire shares domination of the retail food business with the U.S.-owned Safeway corporation. The monopolization of retail is not as obvious. Not many shoppers have heard of Dylex, unless they are investors. Yet any given mall in Canada and other countries might have as many as ten outlets owned by this transnational giant — shops such as Tip Top, Harry Rosen, Big Steel, Fairweather, Suzy Shier, Town and Country, Club Monaco, Alfred Sung, Biway, and Thriftys (Dobbin 1998: 11). The powerful corporations exercise tremendous power over the lives of individuals as both workers and consumers. For example:

> Nike, a major footwear company, employs 8,000 people in management, design, sales and promotion and leaves production in the hands of 75,000 workers hired by independent contractors. Most of the outsourced production takes place in Indonesia, where a pair of Nike that sells in the U.S. or Europe for $73 to $135 is produced for about $5.60 by girls and young women paid as little as 15 cents an hour. The workers are housed in a company barracks, there are no unions, overtime is often mandatory, and if there is a strike, the military may be called to break it up. The $20 million that basketball star Michael Jordan reportedly received in 1992 for promoting Nike shoes ex-

ceeded the entire annual payroll of the Indonesian factories that made them. (Korten 2001: 115)

The Nike case is a striking example of the distortion of an economic system that shifts rewards away from those who produce real value to those whose primary function is to create marketing illusions to convince consumers to buy products they do not need, at inflated prices.

The combined sales of the world's top two hundred corporations amount to more than a quarter of the world's economic activity. The top two hundred corporations in the world have almost twice as much economic influence as the poorest four-fifths of humanity (Banks and Gerlach 2001), which means that they alone have the resources to be global players. This incredible concentration of economic power, and control of markets, nationally and internationally raises serious questions regarding the existence of competitive markets, the free market, and the free-enterprise system. When General Motors trades with itself, is it free trade? One-third of world trade consists simply of transactions among various units of the same corporation (Centre for Social Justice Team 1998). Despite their economic wealth, the top two hundred corporations provide employment to less than a third of 1 percent of the world's population. Critics argue that TNCs have excessive power and that the expected benefits of financial globalization have not materialized (Boyer and Drache 1996: 15). In September 2000 *Business Week* magazine reported, in a cover story on public perceptions about the dangers of growing corporate power, that 72 percent of Americans believed that big business had too much power over people's daily lives, and 95 percent believed that corporations were responsible for the well-being of their employees, not just for making profit (Clarke 2001: 30).

> The top two hundred corporations in the world have almost twice as much economic influence as the poorest four-fifths of humanity.

TNCs, of course, favour the internationalization of business. They seek, as always, the gradual elimination of restrictions on capital investment and of claims on the profits on that investment. They are strong supporters of an unregulated market that enables them to minimize costs by moving from one country to another; they aim to enhance their competitive edge and their profit margins. The explosion of information and other technological and transportation innovations has helped make possible the internationalization of production processes and expansion of transnational conglomerate firms. As a result, during the past two decades the growth of trade and investment has been surpassed by the even more phenomenal growth of international financial flows, aided by the progressive extensive liberalization of financial control (Khor 2001). This growth has largely taken the form of short-term investments, mostly in foreign-exchange currency, derivatives, securities, and equities markets, resulting in the most globalized sector of the economy — an international financial market. For instance, in 1996 some $93 billion in private capital flowed into Indonesia, Malaysia, South Korea, Thailand, and the Philippines. The next year, when problems developed in Thailand, foreign investors suddenly became nervous, started pulling out their money, and a panic quickly developed. By 1997 the huge capital inflows of the previous year had turned into a net outflow of $12 billion (McQuaig 1998: 4). The international flow of short-term investment, the so-called "hot money," has grown to an incredible $2 trillion U.S. worth of international transactions in currencies, stocks, and derivatives every business day (Stanford 2001).

It is not hard to imagine how destabilizing such a movement of financial capital can be for an economy. The most dramatic example of how large-scale speculation can affect a country's currency involved the British pound. As Murray Dobbin explained, "Currency speculator George Soros actually caused the British pound to fall 41% against the Japanese Yen, and in effect sabotaged the system of fixed exchange rates planned for the European Union, eliminating a major threat to speculators who depend on a floating rate" (Dobbin 1998: 68). Although often the interests of national governments and international capital markets would seem to be clearly opposed, many governments fear going against financial markets and passively accept the push for globalization. Robert Boyer and Daniel Drache (1996: 16) conclude: "Not only do they determine the direction of foreign investment flows, but they have more control over governments than even democratically elected bodies. The most powerful governments in the world today — the U.S., Japan and Germany — seem unable to dampen the speculative fever of international bankers. Financial markets have won by default."

NEO-LIBERAL POLICIES: LET THE MARKET RULE

The resurgence of neo-liberal economic policy — which advocates that unfettered markets deliver goods and services most efficiently and are therefore best left alone — has been a strong driving force behind the power of TNCs and economic globalization. Embodied in the politics of Reagan in the United States, Thatcher in Great Britain, and Mulroney in Canada, a surging emphasis on the unique power of the market as the most efficient allocator of resources resulted in the introduction of pro-market policies in the late 1970s and 1980s. Increasingly, many world leaders unambiguously endorsed pro-market policies, arguing that they provided the key to global prosperity (De Santa Ana 1998). For example, Pierre Pettigrew, minister for international trade under Jean Chrétien, clearly expressed the Liberal government's pro-market position: "The government of Canada is committed to bringing down barriers in key markets and securing predictable access to the world for Canadian traders and investors. Enhanced market access is the path to continued prosperity for Canadians" (Canada, Department of Foreign Affairs 2001: i). The Conservative minority government of Stephen Harper, elected in early 2006, also clearly endorsed the supremacy of market and the ideology of "laissez faire" economy. The emphasis on market-based growth and efficiency has replaced the 1960s and 1970s goals of promoting social welfare through equity and redistributive policies.

In general, market deregulation, government budget cuts, privatization of public services, and devolution/decentralization increased in countries across the globe. In Western countries the 1989 events that ended the Cold War (the dismantling of the U.S.S.R. and the destruction of the Berlin Wall) reinforced these tendencies and paved the way in the early 1990s for the speedy development of globalization. International trade and foreign direct investment intensified at the global level via the General Agreement on Tariffs and Trade (GATT) and the World Trade Organization (WTO), which in 1995 supplanted GATT, a post–Second World War institution. The change represented the institutionalization of a truly global organization overseeing new aspects of world exchange. This implied the inclusion of new sectors, such as services, in free-trade schemes and the establishment of an international court to settle trade disputes. Regional trade agreements and organizations such as NAFTA, the European Union, and similar organizations in Africa and Asia complemented the international trade deals. At the country level, the International Monetary Fund (IMF) for years encouraged or forced what came to be known as Structural Adjustment Programs (SAPs), seen by many governments as the only path to economic growth. SAPs were adopted to balance budgets and increase competitiveness through trade liberalization, privatization of social services, open-door foreign investment, and export-oriented policies stressing a "flexible" labour process (Sparr 1994; Bello 1996).

The original, and controversial, Canada-U.S. Free Trade Agreement (FTA) was renegotiated in the early 1990s, extended to Mexico, and renamed NAFTA. Under the mantle of these trade agreements came a dramatic Canada-U.S. "social harmonization" and "corporate restructuring" (Campbell 1990, 2001). The FTA was enacted in Canada in a way that sets this international treaty above all other laws in the country.[1] NAFTA, together with a broad range of anti-government and deregulation policies, has been transforming national economies and restructuring the roles and relationships among governments, markets, and citizens in the push to create an integrated global market economy. As a cornerstone of this well-known neo-liberal family of policies — privatization, deregulation, investment and trade liberalization, public-sector cutbacks, tax cuts, and monetary austerity — NAFTA has made it easier for Canadian policy-makers to bring about a "structural adjustment" of the economy in line with the dominant U.S. model (Campbell 2001: 25). As Donald Johnston, former Liberal government minister and head of the Organization for Economic Co-operation and Development (OECD), stated: "Free trade agreements are designed to force adjustments on our societies," (quoted in Campbell 2001: 21), and no doubt major adjustments have taken place in the Canadian economic and social landscape. The provincial and federal governments are also looking to expand upon the existing Agreement on International Trade (AIT) to promote freer trade amongst the provinces. The idea is that the fewer barriers there are between provinces, the more attractive Canada will be to corporations and free-trade partners (Banks and Gerlach 2001: 32).

Significantly, these treaties are not principally about trade. They are more about investment and production; they are agreements that aim to restrict the capacity of governments to act contrary to market forces. NAFTA and policies such as the move towards a single European currency are designed to override national political decision-making. Such agreements contain explicit clauses making all participating members accept free competition, capital mobility, and minimal state intervention as their only option (Boyer and Drache 1996: 19). Kaldor (2000: 19) rightly suggests that global organizations such as the WTO, World Bank, and IMF have taken on qualities of "stateness" — they decide what is and is not allowed, and they settle disputes between and among nations in a host of vital areas. They are not accountable to the United Nations, but were established as separate, competing, and parallel institutions (Jawara and Kwa 2003; Petras and Veltmeyer 2005). They set forth an increasingly wide range of policies that were traditionally under the jurisdiction of national governments (Khor 2001). The WTO can force an individual nation to change its laws and regulations by declaring that those rules or regulations are violating WTO rules (Wulwik 1999). With both legislative and judicial powers, it can trump the sovereignty of the national governments that make up its membership. It can negate a government's ability to deliver services.[2] WTO rules cover the environment,[3] copyright law, cultural industries, food safety, and agricultural policy. The institution can also impinge on human rights legislation, minimum-wage laws, health and safety laws, and the ability of local businesses to succeed (Wulwik 1999). For the institutions and TNCs, barriers to corporate activity can include labour laws and human and social rights protections, as well as environmental regulations.

For instance, the French government had imposed an important ban on U.S. beef because it contains residues of drugs and growth hormones. The U.S. government sued the French government at the WTO, complaining that the French ban was a "barrier to free trade." The court agreed, warning France to repeal the ban or face trade sanctions in an amount equivalent to lost sales claimed by the U.S. beef industry. France had no choice but to conform to the ruling. When outraged French citizens demanded a strict labelling law so that they could continue to avoid buying U.S. beef, once again the U.S. government took France to court, insisting that labelling interfered with the industry's ability to compete in the French market and was a "barrier to free trade." Again, the court agreed, denying the French citizens' right to know what they are eating. The entire European Union went on to repeat this battle, fighting for their right to choose what to eat (Starr 2000: vii). People's struggle for their rights over profit abounds around the globe (Shiva and Holla-Bar 1996). → brings efficiencies

THE DOWNSIDE OF FREE-MARKET CAPITALISM

Since the implementation of NAFTA on January 1, 1994, officials in Canada, Mexico, and the United States have regularly declared the agreement to be an unqualified success. Given that it was designed to bring extraordinary government protections to a specified sets of interests — investors and financiers in all three countries who search for cheaper labour and production costs — NAFTA clearly has been a success. Increased volumes of trade and financial flows in themselves testify to NAFTA's achievements. The hitch is that the overwhelming majority of people in North America do not support

themselves on their investments. They work for a living. NAFTA, while extending protections for investors, explicitly excluded any protections for working people in the
form of labour standards, working rights, and bargaining power; and it has had nothing
to do with finding a way of redistributing the benefits of any resulting growth. This
imbalance inevitably undercut the bargaining power of the working people in all three
nations (Faux 2001: 1) and has raised serious concerns regarding the role of the state,
the harm done to labour, and the widening of inequalities within and among nations
(Barndt 1999; Weiss 1997; Bello 1996; Mandle 2003; Harriss 2001; Robinson 2002).

Supporters of free trade stress the benefits that come in shifting resources from
protected industries to those with an international comparative advantage (Hufbauer
and Elliott 1994; Krueger 1990). But, as many others remind us, the free market cannot be the key mechanism governing modern societies, and a global-free-trade-for-all
is not the best means of promoting international co-operation and strong economic
performance (Faux 2001; Scott 2001) As Bruce Campbell (2006: 1) states, "Not only
has NAFTA failed to deliver the goods it promised, but its cumulative effect on the
well-being of most Canadians has been negative. Inequality has been widened, income
growth stifled, unions undermined, social programs eroded. At its core, NAFTA is about
shifting power in the economy from governments and workers to corporations." Along
the same line, Ed Finn (2006: 4) argues that NAFTA is not about trade. It was and is "a
legal bill of rights for TNCs to make profit without having to pay fair wages and taxes
or to pay for the damages they cause to the environment."

The Welfare State under Attack

After the Second World War, most industrialized countries adopted what came to be
called the welfare state. For the first time in the history of the modern world, most
citizens gained access to services such as health care and education and had at least a
minimum of financial security. In the past those conditions were reserved for a society's
elite; now they became broadly available to a large number of citizens — in a period
that Linda McQuaig (1999: 9) refers to as "good globalization."

The recent waves of globalization changed this. Welfare states came under attack,
and governments, at various levels, willingly or
by force, accepted the doctrine of the supremacy
of market forces. Business saw government social
services as an obstacle to growth and productive
innovation, and a source of investment and profit-
making. Globalization redefined the nation-state
as an ineffective manager of the national economy
(Boyer and Drache 1996). Powerful international

> The Canadian state increasingly
> acquiesced to the demands of big
> business and put less emphasis on
> the provision of concrete benefits to
> citizens, such as full employment and
> social services, instead transferring
> many of its activities to the market.

interests came to monitor major aspects of state spending, making very clear their preferences for broad policy goals with respect to employment, social welfare, taxation, and
the like.

In Canada the push to reduce government debt and cut spending was led by business interests and their supporters, such as the Canadian Council of Chief Executives, composed of the CEOs of Canada's businesses, the C.D. Howe Institute, the Fraser Institute, the National Citizens Coalition, and the Canadian Taxpayers Federation. The explanations for the contemporary "restructuring" or "downsizing" focused on the need to battle the recession and ensure international competition. The restructuring of government services (Coburn 1999: 844) and undermining of the political process took many avenues, including the abrogation of the right to strike for various categories of workers; wage freezes or rollbacks for public employees; and reduction in the number of workers in the public sector (Coburn 1999: 845). The Canadian state increasingly acquiesced to the demands of big business and put less emphasis on the provision of concrete benefits to citizens, such as full employment and social services, instead transferring many of its activities to the market (McBride 1992: 214, 218; Brownlee 2005: cha. 1).

The full-scale attack in Canada included the erosion of Canadian social insurance and regional development benefits; of federally subsidized communication services such as Via Rail and the CBC; and of various social service programs and federal transfer payments (Campbell 1990: 27; see also chapter 7 here). Yet reducing the role of the state has jeopardized the general welfare and living standards of Canadians in terms of health, education, and social welfare services, as well as undermining Canada's political-economic independence (Campbell 1990; Coburn 1999; McBride 1992; Broad 1995; Carroll and Beaton 2000). Neo-liberal policies have transformed public institutions — working to integrate universities, for example, into the corporate world (Carroll and Beaton 2000: 92; Tudiver 1999; Turk 2000). Similar changes are taking place in the Canadian health-care system, where global expenditure caps were placed on medical services, personal restrictions were implemented, new regulations governing the health professions were put in place, and the use of various types of advanced medical equipment was restricted (Coburn 1999: 845; Flood et al. 2006; see also chapter 13 here).

Undermining the Power of Labour

Globalization has also altered how labour markets operate. The restructuring of capital entailed takeovers, mergers, downsizing, rationalization, production shifts, buybacks, bankruptcies, adjustments, closures, layoffs, and wage cuts. It also involved public-sector adjustments such as privatization, deregulation, contracting out, and other measures that have a direct impact on labour. The stiff competition among leading firms to enhance market share, together with the drastic effects of monetary policies, has significantly weakened the collective bargaining power of labour. Workplace restructuring has called for "labour flexibility" and competitive wage-bargaining across national boundaries. Firms have used a variety of strategies to lower wages and cut social benefits. In the world of global capitalism, with the increasing mobility of business, trade unions in the industrial countries have been put on the defensive, often simply by the business threat to run away (Scott 2001), and, in many instances, they have been forced to make concessions.

The drive to compete globally means that thousands of companies based in Canada have relocated, most of them transferring operations to the Southern United States or the Mexican *maquiladora* zone close to the U.S. border, where the labour force is less unionized and wages are low (Broad 1995; Boyer and Drache 1996: 17). Publicly owned enterprises in strategic sectors such as energy and transportation have been transferred to the private sector, a move that goes hand in hand with the decline in public-sector spending and employment (Campbell 2001: 21). These changes have hurt workers, both men and women, who are not, for the most part, as mobile as capital (Broad and Antony 2006). Mass-production industries have seen an unprecedented job shedding. The economy as a whole has seen a record high number of business failures, falling family incomes, and an unparalleled growth in food banks.

> The richest 10 percent of Canadian families own between 49 and 56 percent of personal wealth. Between 92 and 95 percent of the wealth is owned by the top 50 percent of family units in Canada.

The promise of increased "good" employment and high-skill, high-wage jobs — in the so-called New Economy — did not materialize. On the contrary, Campbell argues that displaced workers in the trade sectors moved to the service sector, in which jobs are associated with low skills and low wages. Indeed, during the past fifteen years Canadians have experienced a growing inequality in wealth and income. The bottom 20 percent of families saw their income fall by 77.6 percent from 1989 to 2004, while the income of the top 20 percent of families rose by 16.8 percent. The income gap in Canada is widening. The top 1 percent of Canadian taxpayers increased their share of the total taxable income from 9.3 percent to 13.6 percent from 1990 to 2000. The top 0.1 percent of the taxpayers had a larger increase, from 3 percent to 5 percent. During 1999–2000 the average Canadian wage increased by 8 percent, but those in the top 1 percent and 0.1 percent experienced a 64 percent and 100 percent increase in their earnings respectively (Campbell 2006: 8–9; see also Broad 2006). While the impacts of these changes have been uneven on Canadian families, people in the low-income category definitely felt the pressure.

Globalization and Gender Inequality

To generate profit and gain a competitive edge, capitalist economies rely on creating divisions among workers based on gender, class, and ethnicity, among other factors. Women's work, for example, in all its forms and in all sectors of the economy — paid or unpaid, formal or informal, private or public — has been crucial for both the local and global expansion of capitalism. Indeed, the "feminization" of the labour force[4] has been an outcome of the increasing globalization of production (Standing 1989). The big-business search for cheaper workers and fewer labour restrictions has been particularly important for women's work (Carr, Alter Chen, and Tate 2000: 125; Barndt 1999; Marchand 2000; Pettman 1996). No doubt a minority of women have benefited from globalization, but in general women have remained disadvantaged in terms of pay and types of work that they do (Ghorayshi 2002).

Women's labour, paid or unpaid, as part of the global assembly line continues to be central to national economic growth and therefore to the creation of the global economy. The heavy promotion of export-oriented growth in particular has led TNCs to rely heavily on women's labour. Nike is a classic example. The company began operating in the 1970s in Taiwan and South Korea but has since moved to Indonesia, China, Vietnam, and El Salvador. Testimonies from women working in a factory producing for Nike in El Salvador reveal a scenario of excessive overtime, below-survival wages, violence, humiliation, and intimidation. In Australia Nike has been in the Federal Court for breaches of its labour contract (Nolan 2000: 32). With the growth of world markets, more and more women have been drawn into labour-intensive and low-wage industries such as garment, electronics, and pharmaceuticals. Women have become a main source of cheap labour for the growing transnational corporations (Nash and Fernandez-Kelly 1983; Lim 1985; Pearson 1992; Barndt 1999).

Female labour force participation has consistently increased over the past hundred years, from 14.4 percent in 1901 to 22.9 percent in 1941, and then to 59.9 percent in 1991 and 61.6 percent in 2003 (Nelson: 2006: 215). In the past quarter-century a particularly a sharp growth in the employment rate of women with children has occurred. As well, the proportion of employed lone mothers has increased substantially since the mid-1990s. Despite the growing presence of women in the public sphere of paid work, though, gender inequality persists — evidenced by occupational segregation, the wage gap, and the overrepresentation of women in part-time and non-standard work. Women's participation in the paid labour force has also not resulted in their liberation from the unpaid work (Boyd 2004: Nelson 2006: 217–62)

The dismantling and redefinition of the welfare state have particularly undermined women. Prior to the 1970s, many feminist programs and services were funded through government initiatives. With the neo-liberal policies starting in the mid-1970s, government funding for feminist organizations began to dry up. In the 1990s the federal government cut funding programs in eighty women's centres and also cut subsidies to many women's publications. It significantly cut funds to the National Action Committee on the Status of Women (NAC) (Vickers, Rankin, and Appelle 1993: 22). Women also often depend on — and work — in services such as health, education, and family benefits, programs cut back in the attack on the welfare state. The concomitant privatization of elder care, health care, and child care has placed a growing burden on women in Canadian families (Briskin 1999: 548).

Then, too, women tend to be concentrated at the bottom end of the economic ladder (Ghorayshi 2002). According to Langford Parks (2005: 9), "2.8 million Canadian women live in poverty, or nearly one in five (19 percent compared to 16 percent men). That includes one in four immigrant women (27 percent) and possibly two in five aboriginal women (43 percent)." Cutbacks in education and universal programs, such as Medicare, hurt women disproportionately. People at the upper end of the economic ladder can just pay the difference when health-care services are cut or the costs of services are raised (McQuaig 1999: 9), but those at the bottom cannot afford to pay.

Similarly, tax cuts do not help people who are at the bottom of the income group. For instance, federal corporate income taxes were cut by 7 percentage points between 2001 and 2005, saving companies at least $10 million a year (Stanford 2006: 5). By the time all of the 2005 federal budget measures are fully implemented in 2009, "about 40 percent of the value of new commitments will be in the form of tax cuts" (Russell 2005: 16). By 2009 the current corporate income tax rate of 22.1 percent will be reduced to19 percent — making Canada's corporate tax 4.5 percent lower than that of the United States. Tax cuts do not help low-income and moderate-income Canadians. When an increase in basic personal exemption is fully phased in by 2009, "it will provide $192 per year — still less than $4 a week. *Only an estimated 3% of the value of this tax measure will go to low-income Canadians"* (Russell 2005: 16). Such policies widen the income gap between men and women. The United Nation's *Human Development Report* continues to show the existence of a severe income gap between men and women (UNDP 1995; Van der Gaag 2004).[5]

WORKING TOWARDS POST-CORPORATE SOCIETY: THE CONTEXT

Today, along with ecological risk, expanding inequality is the most serious problem facing world society (Bradshaw and Wallace 1996). Ever-expanding global capitalism has imposed social costs on the most vulnerable groups of people in our society (Annan 2000; Mandle 2003; Khor 1996; Buckman 2004). The statistics are daunting — so much so that the situation has been referred to as "global pillage." The world is increasingly divided between those who enjoy affluence and those who live in poverty and economic insecurity. The Human Development Report sees the state of progress towards realizing the millennium development goals as "depressing," with the majority of countries falling behind most of the goals. The promise to the world's poor is being broken (Martens 2005: 3). According to current trends, 827 million people will live in extreme poverty in 2015. According to researcher Jen Martens (2005: 3): "The richest 50 individuals in the world have a combined income greater than that of the poorest 416 million. The 2.5 million people living on less than $2 a day — 40% of the world's population — receive only 5% of global income, while 54% of global income goes to the richest 10% of the world's population." In general, the income gap between the rich and poor is growing, and at current income growth rates it will take over a hundred years — until 2112 — for the people of sub-Saharan Africa to restore average incomes to the level they were at in 1980 (Ellwood 2006: 117; see also Korten 2001; Giddens 1999; Sutcliffe 2001; Ellwood 2002). The disparity is not confined to remote areas of the world: in the United States forty-seven million people have no health insurance (Polet 2001: 5). In many less developed countries, safety and environmental regulations are low or virtually non-existent. Some transnational companies sell goods in less developed countries that are controlled or banned in the industrial countries — poor-quality medical drugs, destructive pesticides, or cigarettes with high tar and nicotine content (Giddens 1999; Braun 1991; Chossudovsky 1998; George and Sabelli

1994; Cornia, Jolly, and Stewart 1987; Da Gama Santos 1985).

There is both an increasing awareness of the dangers of growing corporate power (Clarke 2001: 30; Balaam and Veseth 2005a; Robinson 2002; Annan 2000) and a recognition that in the realm of multinational agreements it is not just the ordinary citizens who are kept in the dark, but also the leaders of the poorest countries (Steger 2003; Ellwood 2002). Too often poor countries are excluded from negotiations and are left without the required knowledge and participation when it comes to agreements signed by major industrial countries (Dobbin 1998: 102). Public-opinion polls reveal a growing sense of personal insecurity and loss of faith in major institutions all around the world. As Kaldor (2000: 19) puts it, "People fear job loss, condemn the use of child labor and exploitative working conditions in foreign factories that supply brand-name products we consume, and worry about the environmental impact of the corporations and business, and thus they want regulation of business behavior in these and other respects."

In the United States, the country that defines for many of the world's population their vision of prosperity and democracy, polls indicate that the real dream of Americans is not for fast sports cars, fancy clothes, and country estates, as the popular media might lead us to believe. Rather, it is for a decent and secure life (Korten 2001). More and more people everywhere have begun to question the policies and policy-makers that are undermining the democratic basis of society (Sparr 1994; Elson 1991; Campbell 2001; McQuaig 1999, 1998; Boyer and Drache 1996; Annan 2000; Gelbspan 2004; Kung 1998).

THE GROWING VOICE OF DISSENT

The voice of protest is broad-based and comes from various countries and a variety of groups such as the Canadian Labour Congress (representing labour); NAC (representing women); the Sierra Club; Global Exchange; Direct Action Network; People for the Ethical Treatment of Animals (PETA); Rainforest Action Network; Earth First; Jubilee 2000; Ralph Nader's Group (a consumer advocate group); Global Trade Watch; Reclaim the Streets (a U.K.-based initiative); and the Calgary-based Co-Motion Action. The result is the most internationally focused, globally linked movement the world has ever seen (Welton and Wolf 2001; Brownlee 2005: 142–52; Steger 2003: 113–30).

Social justice activist groups from North and South have been calling the world's attention to the destructive environmental consequences of market forces, the problems of uncontrolled growth, and the lack of transparency and accountability in the decision-making processes of global institutions such as the WTO and IMF. The coalition, using various media, is organized and has gained momentum and popularity in addressing issues from NAFTA to the Multilateral Agreement on Investment (MAI) and the WTO's role in the global economy (for a discussion of the role of youth in the anti-corporate movement, see chapter 9 here).

In December 1999 tens of thousands of demonstrators — trade unionists, environmentalists, human rights activists, church groups, AIDS activists, family farmers, and grassroots organizations from around the world — gathered in Seattle, Washington, at the WTO's third ministerial meeting. More than fifty thousand people and seven hundred organizations took part (Welton and Wolf 2001: xi). They held workshops and forums (in a week-long "Festival of Resistance"), staged marches, occupied streets, and blocked the entrances to WTO gatherings. Demonstrators called for "fair trade, not free trade." For many people around the world the WTO had come to symbolize the tremendous damage being done by globalization. In Seattle, U.S. and Canadian farmers along with South Korean rice growers and Caribbean banana farmers demanded an end to the trade regime that squeezes out small producers while favouring large agribusiness firms. Environmentalists of all stripes adamantly opposed the big resource-extraction companies that are destroying the world's old-growth and rain forests while drastically reducing or killing off thousands of species (Burbach 2001).

The events of Seattle showed the tremendous buildup of criticism that the WTO has drawn from different segments of the international community. In particular, the Seattle events illustrated a now-widespread perception: that the WTO represents the interests of the large multinational corporations at the expense of workers and average citizens. As Kaldor (2000) accurately notes, Seattle was the first time that the political presence of a variety of new actors was taken seriously. It was the first time that those inside the talks had to acknowledge and accept the role of those outside.

> Thousands chanted, "The world is not for sale, neither am I."

The Seattle meeting was followed by protests at the spring meetings of the World Bank and IMF in April 2000. Next came the demonstrations at the World Economic Forum's gathering in Melbourne on September 11, 2000, and, the following week, in Prague, at the main annual meeting of the World Bank and IMF. Meetings and demonstrations continued in Windsor, Calgary, Quebec City, Genova, and other places (*Economist* 2000; Clarke 2001). Social justice activists turned up in thousands wherever there was an important meeting of the heads of states and international agencies. Activists also worked to build international solidarity. A gathering of over 100,000 people in Millau, France, against the WTO's ruling and in support of French farmer José Bové became a global symbol of resistance. At a rock concert in support of this event thousands chanted, "The world is not for sale, neither am I" (Clarke 2001: 30). The spectacular growth of the Vía Campesina, which has direct links to the National Farmers' Union in Canada, epitomizes this kind of movement. Loosely, but deeply, connected, organizations from around the world are working together to protect the "family farm" and promote sustainable agriculture by halting the spread of corporatized farming (Desmarais 2007).

It is all too easy to dismiss the protesters as radicals with "sixties envy," or to accuse them of not following the law, not knowing what they are doing. Michael Moore, head of the WTO, described his opponents as being nothing more than protectionists launching an assault on internationalism (Klein 1999). The media portray the protesters as a "backlash against globalization," "flat earthers," and, at best, sadly misguided (*Economist*

2000; Kite 2001). But the protest movement is essentially anti-corporate rather than anti-globalist, and its roots are in the anti-sweatshop campaigns that take aim at corporations like Nike, in the human rights campaign focusing on Royal Dutch/Shell in Nigeria, and in the backlash against Monsanto's genetically engineered foods in Europe (Klein 1999). They are a "movement for globalization," a movement resisting neo-liberal trade and corporate policies that put the needs of profit before people (Dominick 2001; Shiva and Holla-Bar 1996; Gelbspan 2004). When protesters shout about the evils of globalization, most of them are not calling for a return to narrow nationalism, but rather for an expansion of the borders of globalization, for trade to be linked to democratic reforms, higher wages, labour rights, gender equity, and environmental protections. They are demanding that national governments be free to exercise their authority without interference from the WTO, and they are asking for stricter international rules governing labour standards, environmental protection, and scientific research (Klein 1999; Gelbspan 2004; Marchand 2000). They are demanding more generally that the rules by which the global future unfolds should be set not by TNCs, but by democratic participation (Kung 1998; Swift 2002).

Some observers have pointed out that this is a youth-led protest and the participants are members of the first generation to experience what it means to "grow up corporate" (Klein 2000). This is the generation that has been the focus of the corporate push in creating a global consumer culture that includes every individual, worldwide, with enough income to take part. While the world middle-class adult population is still by far the largest segment of the consumer market, the commercial focus is carefully and deliberately on teenagers everywhere (Dobbin 1998: 56). Ironically, then, what we are witnessing is a new generation of activists who challenge corporate globalization and the powerful financial institutions that stand behind it (Burbach 2001). Within this group the creative leadership comes not from conventional power-holders, but from ordinary people who are doing extraordinary things around the goal of building democratic and sustainable communities (Korten 2001; Barndt 1999: 193–260). Some of the participants within this coalition, such as women's groups and organized labour, have long histories of activism, both at national and international levels, and have played critical parts in the recent protest movement. In Canada NAC has been involved in the Pan Canadian Coordinating Committee of the World March of Women 2000, along with several other national groups such as the Canadian Labour Congress, the Canadian Research Institute for the Advancement of Women, the National Anti-Poverty Organization, and the Women's Inter-Church Council of Canada. The World March was initiated by the Fédération des Femmes du Québec (FFQ), based on its highly successful 1995 women's March Against Poverty. As well, many international women's groups and prominent feminists participated in the November 1999 WTO ministerial talks. The International Women Workers' Forum featured participants from Mexico, Brazil, and Bangladesh. A panel entitled "Women Say No to WTO" brought women from Malaysia, India, and the Philippines together. The International Forum on Globalization hosted two teach-ins: "The Multiple Impacts of Economic

Globalization," which included Vandana Shiva, Maude Barlow, and Lori Wallach; and "Views from the South."

Seattle's "Festival of Resistance" was a highly successful demonstration of the international coalition-building that characterizes the feminist agenda for change. The "Women, Democracy and Development Day" was held in Seattle on the day following the huge protest. Speakers from Mexico, Tanzania, and St. Lucia highlighted issues like the *maquiladoras* and the impact of privatization on land. Also included in the day's events were workshops on "Developing WTO Alternatives," "Community Perspectives and Global Actions," and "A Feminist Critique of Current Trade Negotiations." One presentation, "Voices from the South: Building Cross-Border Resistance from the South to the North," featured workers and organizers from the South sharing their stories of resistance to the WTO and globalization. Jubilee 2000, a broad-based alliance of religious organizations, including Christians, Buddhists, First Nations, Jews, Muslim, Hindus, and Baha'is, called for the erasure of Third World debt. In addition to workshops and panels, the meeting included a showing of the 1998 film *Globalization in India* as part of a teach-in exposing the impacts of privatization and market liberalization. The Raging Grannies (from Canada) and Sweet Honey in the Rock (from the United States) entertained people with their political lyrics.

> The police shot a plastic bullet at one of the protesters, Eric Laferriere, who was standing near the walls. The bullet "hammered into his throat," crushing his larynx and trachea.

Beginning with Seattle and moving on from there, the global activism attracted the serious attention of institutions, governments, lawmakers, and local authorities (Stewart 2001: 25; Welton and Wolf 2001). The response was excessive and at times fierce. In April 2001 the air in Quebec City, with its new, temporary walls designed to keep demonstrators away from the site of the Summit of the Americas meetings, was heavy with the smell of tear gas (George 2001). The police shot a plastic bullet at one of the protesters, Eric Laferriere, who was standing near the walls. The bullet "hammered into his throat," crushing his larynx and trachea (Gomberg 2001). In Europe, too, the use of force and manipulation in response to protests reached new extremes. The July 2001 meeting in Genoa ended with beatings, six hundred injuries, an unwarranted death, and great frustration.

It wasn't long before, in the name of security, the meetings of the heads of the states were taking place in guarded, if luxurious, compounds or isolated (and still well-guarded) places: in the middle of a desert, on a cruise ship, or (in the case of the 2002 G8 summit) in a remote spot in the Canadian Rockies (George 2001). The activities and meetings of the international institutions and government leaders became marked by conspicuous surveillance, pre-emptive detentions, militarized security perimeters around public spaces, intimidation, border closings, infiltration of activists' meetings, indiscriminate police brutality, and mass arrests of peaceful demonstrators.[6] Think-tanks and organizations that support the activists' cause or are critical of the practices of globalization are beginning to be denied resources; electronic surveillance has become a powerful weapon (George 2001). Police forces from city to city, across national boundaries — from Washington, D.C., to Philadelphia and Los Angeles to Quebec City, Montreal, Windsor, and Calgary, to Prague and Genova and other places — no matter where — are sharing intelligence reports on activists, regardless of their level of involvement in the meetings or demonstrations, or their method of political activity (Stewart 2001: 25; George 2001).[7]

Still, all the power of repressive state force has apparently had little effect. Ever since Seattle hundreds of thousands of people have continued to mobilize around the world. More than 700 social movements from 122 different countries, represented by 4,700 delegates and more than 15,000 participants, went to a meeting in Porto Alegre, Brazil, in early 2001 to reaffirm that human life has a greater value than profit. The meeting, organized by the World Social Forum, marked an important step in the convergence of the resistance struggle (Houtart and Polet 2001: vi). The World Social Forum (WSF) continued to meet and push for social justice around the globe.[8] The 2004 meetings in Mumbai marked a major step in the global advance of the process, with the participation of about 100,000 delegates. It was followed, in January 2005, by another gathering in Porto Alegre. Clearly the WSF process has grown over the years and is able to attract increasingly larger participation each year. There is also no doubt that the movement for global justice — which joins the movements led by women, environmentalists, and labour activists, to name a few — has had its major successes. Public attention, public involvement, and popular mobilization around an issue bring results: the corporate elites do not always get their way, and governments become more inclined to listen to the counterarguments (Shiva and Holla-Bar 1999).

The successful campaign against the Multilateral Agreement on Investment (MAI) is a case in point: massive demonstrations, consciousness-raising, and community organizing, both in Canada and elsewhere, led to the defeat of the agreement (Kite 2001; Wulwik 1999).[9] Much the same thing happened around the matter of bank mergers in Canada. The financial elite were certain that the public would favour the merger of the Bank of Montreal with the Royal Bank and the Toronto Dominion Bank with the Canadian Imperial Bank of Commerce. After public concern with the mergers spread, the finance minister would not allow the deals to go through (McQuaig 1999). The growing public awareness of the dangers of genetically engineered food sources also illustrates the power of individual and collective action. The spillover effect has given considerable pause to North American farmers, as well as corporate agriculture, in their seeding choices.[10]

The coalition that formed Jubilee 2000 applied enormous political pressure for debt write-downs. Global Exchange, based in San Francisco, pressured Starbucks into promising to seek fair trade coffee beans (*Economist* 2000). As a result of the pressure brought on it by various groups, the IMF now runs seminars to teach non-governmental organizations (NGOs) the basics of the country programs where they plan to work. The World Bank has introduced a Grassroots Immersion Program (GRIP) to provide introductory teachings to private-sector associates and partner NGOs before they start their programs in the Third World. A raised awareness, collective resistance, and the power of civil society generally are not easy to ignore.

THERE IS AN ALTERNATIVE: A POST-CORPORATE SOCIETY

Contrary to all the globalization hype, the problems we now confront are neither new nor insoluble. The present time has many striking parallels with the interwar period. Then, as today, finance and competition set the agenda for national economic policies (Boyer and Drache 1996: 8). The dominant ideology of both periods was an extreme version of free-market theory (McQuaig 1998: 2). But one key aspect of managing a national economy is to regulate the flow of investment and capital. Only direct or indirect state intervention can end a recession and put the economy back on track towards full employment (Boyer and Drache 1996: 9). From the immediate postwar period until the mid-1970s, the Canadian economy, among others, was highly regulated to defend the public interests, and "the rights of society as a whole were given precedence over the rights of investors" (McQuaig 1999: 9). At that time, financial elites resisted capital controls all the way, but government stood up to them. For almost three decades after the Second World War, governments in general were relatively free from the constant threat of capital withdrawal (McQuaig 1998: 3).

This system came apart in the early to mid-1970s, and was replaced by a global economy that rejects the notion that governments should be able to control their economies and the flow of capital. George Soros (2000: 2) outlines the historical shift: "At the end of WWII most countries strictly controlled international capital transactions. The Bretton Woods Institutions (IMF, and GATT [now the WTO]) were designed to facilitate international trade and investment in an environment of restricted capital flows. Controls on financial capital movements were gradually removed. International capital movement accelerated in the 1980s... and became truly global in the 1990s."

> The slogan TINA serves the interests of big business, but more and more it is being challenged.

These days, political and economic leaders sell a view that "there is no alternative" (TINA) to the political and economic packages of reform. The new global institutions have immense power. The conventional argument is, "We cannot because technology has changed everything." We have computers, we are told, and with these computers, money can move around the world quickly — in a flash of an eye it's halfway across the world. How could government possibly control the movement of capital and govern this situation (McQuaig 1999: 10)? But computers also give us enormous power to record and track the movement of money. What has changed is "the political willingness of governments to stand up to financial markets" (McQuaig 1999:10).

The slogan TINA serves the interests of big business, but more and more it is being challenged. As John Harriss (2001: 2034) rightly states,

> Globalization is an extremely powerful ideology being projected as having no alternative. There is resistance, even if not coherent as yet. The practical basis

for an alternative is to be seen in the progress being made in different parts of the world, often by left parties, to make a reality of deliberative democracy, as in the experiments with people's planning in Kerala or with participative budgeting in Porto Alegre in Brazil.

The economic rules of our times are not written in stone. We can change them. The notion that certain conditions are inevitable is, of course, a convenient rule of thumb for those who want to maintain a profitable (for them) system that leads to ever greater levels of inequality. The real task for the future is to find ways of democratizing nations so that they, on behalf of people, can insist on a basic tolerance for variations in social and economic policy between nations. We have an opportunity to develop a culture of resistance, to energize the constituencies of our own civil society organizations, to decolonize ourselves, and to learn what it means to be self-governing peoples, which is the hallmark of democracy. We need sustainable local communities, and participatory democracy. Above all, we need legislative initiatives to restructure the nature and role of corporations (Clarke 2001: 32).

Certainly, the nation-state cannot be replaced by the market for any significant period, because it is the only institution that society can use to organize itself, protect the social solidarity of its citizens, and safeguard social values (Boyer and Drache 1996: 13). The state, whatever its faults, is still the only human organization ultimately powerful enough to challenge corporate rule. Globalization offers new opportunities, but it also requires the regulations necessary to provide a framework for responsible behaviour (Annan 2000; Gelbspan 2004; Kung 1998). Corporate globalization can be opposed, regulated, or reversed by political action. Indeed, governments should recognize that the "free" market has never been unregulated (Richter 2001), and markets work best when the state is a strong regulator. For instance, the market-driven societies of Canada, the United States, Great Britain, Australia, and New Zealand have experienced mediocre economic performances along with deepening social inequalities. The more social-democratic countries, such as Germany, France, and Sweden, have faced equally severe adjustment problems and rising unemployment levels without sacrificing, to the same extent, their social entitlements (Boyer and Drache 1996: 5). As long as governments are powerless — or, more accurately, the public believes that they are powerless — to stand up to financial markets, we have little chance of turning things around. Governments can make a difference, and they have a responsibility to do so.

A number of proposals have been put forth for regulating capital in various areas: economic (tax of corporations), ecological (protection of non-renewable resources), social (labour legislation), political (reconstruction of the power of the state) and cultural (creation of new cultural consumer models) (Houtart 2001: 57). Various civil society groups have advocated the need to restructure capital; moreover, former Finance Minister Paul Martin went so far as to advocate the use of emergency capital controls in certain situations. Temporary controls are a good idea, but they do not solve the problem. Other workable solutions have more merit. For example, the Noble-prize-winning economist

James Tobin has suggested imposing a small worldwide tariff on money every time it is exchanged from one currency into another. The net result of this "Tobin Tax" would be to discourage short-term capital movements and encourage more beneficial long-term investments (McQuaig 1998: 5). The financial markets, offering considerable resistance to the Tobin Tax, argue that it is technologically unfeasible — but, again, this is a matter of will, especially given that computers allow us to record and track the movement of money (McQuaig 1999).

The World Health Organization's Commission on Macroeconomics and Health, led by Harvard economist Jeffrey Sachs, has proposed that rich countries spend an extra one-tenth of 1 percent of their economies on the health of the poor. Commenting on this proposal, Mary Robinson (2002: 6) points out:

> If all wealthy countries cooperated, it would add $38 billion a year to health spending by 2015. The commission argues that if that money went to poor nations that also spent more and improved their health care systems, these countries would see that at least $360 billion a year in economic gains, lifting millions of people out of poverty and saving an estimated 8 million lives a year.

Civil society organizations, despite their diversity, also put forth alternative proposals. For instance, Canadian unions have noted that the negotiations for the European Union include a social charter that stipulates conditions for labour standards throughout the European Community. Such rights do not exist in NAFTA. The fight for improved labour standards is perhaps the best way of protecting Canadian labour against the ravages of the new global capitalism (Black and Silver 2001; Broad 1995: 31). Common Frontiers, a Toronto-based organization, promotes alternatives to recent trade agreements. Its booklet, "Alternatives for the Americas: Building People's Hemispheric Agreement," co-published by the Canadian Centre for Policy Alternatives (Wulwik 1999), argues, "Human rights and environmental rights must be given more importance than commercial interests." Democracy Watch has put forward a twenty-step agenda pointing out changes "that all governments in Canada should enact (in accordance with their respective powers)" to ensure that the country's "stakeholders" will have "a greater and more meaningful role in government and business decision-making." Similarly, at the international level, there is recognition that the rich G8 nations should be displaced by an organization that reflects global democracy (Monbiot 2001: 23).

What Can We Do?

A definite hazard in becoming aware of major problems — and it always seems to be just one problem after another — is a feeling of powerlessness. But we need to keep in mind that socially conscious citizens of other eras have achieved major victories for human progress in the face of seemingly impossible odds, and we can achieve victories too. As we look to the formidable task ahead, we should remember that there was once a

> Corrupt and unjust regimes have a way of falling once ordinary people decide their turn has come.

Roman Empire, and that slavery was once legal in the United States — and so too was discrimination based on race. As recently as 1989 there was a Berlin Wall; and until the 1990s there was apartheid in South Africa. Corrupt and unjust regimes have a way of falling once ordinary people decide their turn has come.

One of the first things we can do is to take charge of our lives. Becoming conscious citizens requires a different way of thinking and behaving. It means challenging political ignorance whenever we encounter it. It means incorporating our political convictions into our daily lives. David Balaam and Michael Veseth (2005a) draw our attention to the increasing role of non-governmental organizations as actors in the international political economy. Many people can make contributions to the solution of the problems they care about by becoming active in a local, regional, national, or international NGO. Idealist.Org is an excellent website for those who want to find out how they can become active, or possibly even have a career in this line of work.

> "You are what you read.... Fresh ideas, critical thinking and the energy to actively pursue them working with others of like mind. That is what you can do."

We can, among other things, take aim at the barrage of propaganda directed at influencing values and implanting corporate priorities. An important side of taking charge of our lives is seeking alternative information in books, journals, magazines, films, and websites. "You are what you read.... Fresh ideas, critical thinking and the energy to actively pursue them working with others of like mind. That is what you can do" (Balaam and Veseth 2005b: 493). As politically conscious citizens we can identify our parts in the mass consumer culture and use our consumer power to challenge and expose the role of corporations in society. We can and must exercise our political franchise, hold our governments responsible, and realize that governments have a major role to play in making sure that the rights of society as a whole gain precedence over the rights of investors. As individual citizens we can initiate our own ethical boycotts. The time has come to accept and use our power of responsible freedom to create economies and societies dedicated to the service of life — our own lives included.

Obviously, we are not going to bring down capitalism just by buying a locally grown head of organic lettuce, although this can be a useful start. We must work in many ways and intervene at many levels: buy small and local, simplify our lives, keep informed, get political, use our political franchise, get active in advocacy groups, start our own groups (Korten 1999, 2001; Dobbin 1998). We can choose to join a growing number of people who are saying no to the forces of corporate globalization — people who are reclaiming their spaces, taking back responsibility for their lives, and working to create participatory communities. As we begin to see the world as conscious citizens, the very quest for what we can do will begin to provide the necessary answers. *There are alternatives*: what we need is the political will that will allow us to implement those alternatives.

GLOSSARY OF KEY TERMS

Capital controls: When governments use their power to introduce rules and regulations to control the free movement of large sums of money by individual investors.

European Union: A political and economic alliance with roots that go back to the early 1950s and the formation of the European Coal and Steel Community (with six original members: France, Belgium, West Germany, Italy, Luxembourg, and the Netherlands) and later (1957) the European Economic Community, popularly called the Common Market. Today the EU has fifteen member states and is preparing for the accession of thirteen Eastern and Southern European nations. The EU works to defend the joint interests of its member states; all decisions and procedures are derived from the basic treaties ratified by the member states.

Free Trade Agreement (FTA): Between Canada and the United States, it was designed to promote market deregulation and, through removing tariff and non-tariff trade barriers, to facilitate the transnational movements of corporate structures and investment. Like NAFTA, it largely protects large businesses.

General Agreement on Tariffs and Trade (GATT): A treaty to promote international trade in goods, originally signed in 1948. The eighth round of GATT talks, begun in Uruguay in 1986, eventually led to the 1995 establishment of the WTO as the successor to GATT.

International Monetary Fund (IMF): An organization of 184 member countries. It was established to promote international monetary co-operation, currency exchange stability, and orderly exchange arrangements; to foster economic growth and provide temporary financial assistance to countries to help ease balance of payments adjustment.

North American Free Trade Agreement (NAFTA): Signed by Canada, the United States, and Mexico, the agreement came into effect in 1994, removing barriers to trade between the three countries for a period of ten years.

Neo-liberal policy: Based on the belief that unregulated markets deliver goods and services most efficiently when left alone without the intervention of the government. Privatization, deregulation of trade and investment, tax cuts, and monetary austerity are part of this family of policies.

Structural Adjustment Programs (SAPs): Economic policies that countries must follow to qualify for World Bank and IMF loans and help them make debt repayments on the older debts owed to commercial banks, governments, and the World Bank. SAPs are designed for individual countries but have common guiding principles and features, which include export-led growth; privatization and liberalization; and the efficiency of the free market. SAPs generally require countries to devalue their currencies against the dollar; lift import and export restrictions; balance their budgets and not overspend; and remove price controls and state subsidies.

The World Trade Organization (WTO): The only global international organization dealing with the rules of trade between nations. Under the rules of the WTO a law that hinders international commerce can be considered a "barrier to trade." This new expansive view of trade implemented by a non-elected body puts democracy at risk.

QUESTIONS FOR DISCUSSION

1. What is globalization? Is globalization new?
2. What are transnational corporations (TNCs) and how are they different from other business firms? Why should we be concerned about the power of TNCs?
3. Is globalization a positive or a negative force in the world today? Why?
4. What is right and what is wrong with the following statement: "Most TNCs invest in the 'less developed' countries because of the low wages that they can pay there."
5. Globalization creates deep cleavages not only between the social classes in advanced industrial countries but also, and just as importantly, between the North and South. Discuss.
6. Can markets be the key mechanism governing modern societies? What future, if any, is there for the nation-state?
7. Is economic globalization compatible with social justice?
8. Why does the WTO matter?
9. If there is to be a stable global order, countries need to find ways of making TNCs and all the institutions created under the mantra of globalization accountable. Discuss.
10. Who are the protesters? What do they want?
11. Is there an alternative to the current direction of globalization? How can we work towards a post-corporate society?
12. Gender, class, and ethnic inequality is an integral part of global restructuring. Discuss.
13. Compare and contrast different visions of the future. Which do you think is the most likely? Why does it matter which of these scenarios actually occurs?
14. What items would you add to the list of things that you can do as an individual to make the world a more livable place?

WEBSITES OF INTEREST

Citizen activism. <www.idealist.org>.
Coalition for the International Criminal Court. <www.iccnow.org>.
Independent Media Center. <www.indymedia.org>.

Z Magazine. <www.zmag.org>.
Monthly Review Magazine. <www.monthlyreview.org>.
RedPepper Magazine. <www.redpepper.org.uk>.
Centre for Social Justice. <www.socialjustice.org>.
Common Frontiers. <www.web.net/comfront>.
Corporate Watch. <corpwatch.org>.
Democracy Watch. <www.dwatch.ca>.
Adbuster Culture Jammers. <www.adbuster.org>.
WTO Watch. <www.wtowatch.org>.
Global Trade Watch. <www.tradewatch.org>.
International Forum on Globalization. <www.ifg.org>.
Economic Policy Institute: Research for Broadly Shared Prosperity. <www.epinet.org>.
The Socialist Project. <www.socialistproject.ca>.
United for Fair Economy. <www.faireconomy.org>.
Coalition of Labor Union Women. <www.cluw.org>.
Institute for Women's Policy Research. <www.iwpr.org>.
Sweatshop Watch. <www.sweatshopwatch.org>.
Women's Environment and Development Organization. <www.wedo.org>.
Public Leadership Education Network. <www.plen.org>.
Centre for Women's Global Leadership. <www.cwgl.rutgers.edu>.
Guerrilla Girls, Inc. <www.guerillagirls.com>.

NOTES

I am grateful to Jim Silver and an anonymous reviewer for their suggestions on an earlier version of this chapter. My special thanks go to Wayne Antony for his excellent comments and detailed editorial contributions. Thanks also to Robert Clarke for his editing and other comments.

1. This is not the case for the United States, for which it was just another piece of trade legislation that could be constrained by other domestic laws (Griffin Cohen 1996: 401).
2. As critics note, these trading agreements grant unprecedented rights to corporations, with the main aim being the facilitation of capital mobility. The ability of states to act individually is critically weakened, and the limits imposed on social policy by the trade agreements undermine the redistributive goals of disadvantaged groups. The supremacy of this law has profound implications for Canada as a nation-state.
3. The U.S. negotiator at the Rio Earth Summit announced that 80 percent of U.S. environmental agreements are subject to challenge through the WTO (Starr 2000: vii).
4. This "feminization" is seen as an increase in the number of women in the labour force and a deterioration of their working conditions. The International Labour Organization reported in 1996 that the feminization of international labour migration was "one of the most striking economic and social phenomena of recent time" (Kempadoo and Doezema 1998: 17).
5. As borders become more fluid with the globalization of capitalism and ethnic strife, the

flow of women as immigrants, refugees, migrant labour, sex-trade workers, and marriage partners increases (Bulbeck 1998).

6. Activist Jaggi Singh is uniquely qualified to talk about the rapid evolution of political policing in Canada. He was virtually kidnapped by plainclothes RCMP officers on the University of British Columbia campus during the infamous meeting of the Asia Pacific Economic Cooperation forum in late 1997. At border crossings, customs agents are now equipped with computerized records, listing activists to be turned back (Stewart 2001: 26).

7. On the day of the big demonstration in Quebec, FBI and U.S. secret service agents appeared at the Indymedia office in Seattle with court orders requiring it to disclose the names and email addresses of everyone who had visited the site in the previous forty-eight hours. This was in flagrant breach of rights guaranteed under the U.S. Constitution (George 2001). Also, *The Economist* (2000) reported that the Czech police had been co-operating with the FBI and British police.

8. Thematic Forum, Crisis of the Neo-liberal Model, at Buenos Aires, Argentina, August 2002; European Social Forum, Florence, Italy, November 2002; Thematic Forum, Negotiated Solutions for Conflicts, Ramallah, Palestine, December 2002; Asian Social Forum, Hyderabad, India, January 2003; African Social Forum, Addis-Ababa, Ethiopia, January 2003; Panamazonic Social Forum, Belam, Paraj (Brazil), January 2003; Thematic Forum, Democracy, Human Rights, Wars and Drug Trafficking, Cartagena de Indias, Colombia, June 2003; European Social Forum, Paris, France, November 2003; Pan-Amazon Social Forum, Ciudad Guayana, Venezuela, February 2004; Social Forum of the Americas, Quito, Ecuador, July 2004; European Social Forum, London, U.K., October 2004; Pan-Amazon Social Forum, Manaus, Brazil, January 2005; Mediterranean Social Forum, Barcelona, Spain, June, 2005; European Social Forum, Athens, Greece, May 2006.

9. The MAI would have limited government's ability to effectively regulate corporate activities because foreign investors would be given the right under the agreement to sue governments. The MAI would also have guaranteed corporations unlimited access to all markets. Under the MAI, TNCs would have gained a legal status with the same amount of political rights as the nation-state (Wulwik 1999).

10. See <www.saskorganic.com>.

Chapter 9

A NEW POLITICAL GENERATION?
Youth Engagement in Canada and Beyond

Janet Conway and Daniel Morrison

When people use the terms "political participation" and "youth" in the same breath, they are often naming a problem: young people are not voting; youth are not joining political parties; youth are not interested in matters of public debate or in public service as a vocation. Anxious questions follow. What will become of "democracy" if these trends continue? How should we (adults, experts, "policy wonks," political scientists) understand the problem of youth political participation in order to fix it and secure our liberal–democratic future? Similar anxieties are increasingly being voiced in all the "advanced democracies."

This chapter takes these discussions as its starting point but departs sharply on the contours of the question. We see many young people in Canada and beyond deeply engaged in struggles over the future, profoundly critical of their parents' democracy, and enacting new democratic practices and discourses that are flourishing under the radar of most political observers. Our aim is to make some of the visions, projects, and experiments of a new political generation visible and to reflect on their meaning, even if they seem, at the moment, remote from the institutions and practices of liberal and representative democracy.

In the worldwide anti–globalization movement and in the emergence of the Intercontinental Youth Camp associated with the World Social Forum, many

"You Should Know This"
- Only 5 percent of Canadians under the age of thirty belong to a political party. The average age of membership of all of Canada's political parties is sixty-three.
- Only 18 percent of Canadians identify "very strongly" with a political party — down from 37 percent in 1980.
- Almost the entire decline in voting rates over the past two decades (61 percent in 2004, down from 70 percent in 1993) is the result of low rates of voter participation by youth.
- Voter turnout in Canada hit an all-time low in 2004 at 60.9 percent. Interestingly, voter turnout among youth (eighteen to thirty years old) actually increased in that election.
- Rates of voting among first-time voters (age eighteen to twenty-four years old) in Canada are lower than those of the United States (42 percent in 2004) and just below those of the United Kingdom and most other developed democracies.
- The five Intercontinental Youth Camps involved roughly 80,000 people, the vast majority of whom were younger than thirty.
- The World Social Forum, since its inception in 2001, has directly involved more than half a million people; as many more have been involved in regional social forums.
- Over 70,000 people, the majority of them young people, mobilized in Quebec City in 2001 to demonstrate resistance against the Free Trade Area of the Americas.

Sources: Green Party of Canada n.d.; The Democracy Project.

commentators posit the appearance of a new political generation.[1] Richard and Margaret Braungart (1989) define "political generation" as "an historical age group that has mobilized itself to effect

> Many young people in Canada are deeply engaged in struggles over the future, profoundly critical of their parents' democracy, and enacting new democratic practices... under the radar of most political observers.

social and political change" (quoted by Gauthier 2003: 267). When we speak here of a new political generation, we are not referring to a particular age cohort. We are following the practices of young activist writers who reject the category "youth" but do see themselves as carriers of new ways of doing politics, embodying a horizontal networking logic opposed to a vertical command logic and embracing an ethos of direct action and participatory democracy (Juris 2005; Nunes 2005: 287).

Through a study of the Intercontinental Youth Camp and its position in the anti-globalization movement, we examine the character of and claims about this new political generation, its appearance on the world stage, and its expressions in Canada. We also raise questions about who is left out of this discourse and what kinds of activism are rendered invisible. Throughout we argue for broader understandings of "the political" and for concrete attention to be paid to the emergent practices of young activists as essential starting points in any contemporary discussion of youth political engagement. We are both activists who identify with movements for global justice and sympathize with the projects described here, even as we seek to critically analyze them. Janet Conway is a long-time feminist and anti-poverty activist, active in cross-movement coalitions for social justice and an organizer of the Toronto Social Forum. Daniel Morrison has been active in several social justice groups, working with young people, refugees, and popular education. As white, urban, anglophone Canadians from different activist generations, we try to be aware of the specificity of our identities and our angles of vision.

MAINSTREAM UNDERSTANDINGS OF YOUTH POLITICAL ENGAGEMENT

Voter turnout in Canadian elections is declining, and much of that decline has been attributed to young people. According to Elections Canada, less than 40 percent of eligible voters between the ages of eighteen and twenty-one voted in the 2004 federal election. This is down from an estimated 70 percent turnout by those between the

> Voter turnout in Canadian elections is declining, and much of that decline has been attributed to young people.

ages of eighteen and twenty-four in the 1970s (Adsett 2003: 247). The overall voting turnout in 2004 was just under 61 percent. What has people talking about youth is that voter turnout has risen steadily with age to a high of 75 percent among people in the fifty-eight to sixty-seven age bracket, so there was a point spread of thirty-five between the youngest and oldest voters in the 2004 vote (Kingley 2004).[2] Furthermore, research indicates that political habits formed in youth continue throughout life, so that non-voting among today's youth is expected to continue, causing the overall voter turnout to decline precipitously as the current youth cohort ages (Adsett 2003, citing O'Neill

2001). This finding accounts for the growing anxiety among scholars and policy-makers about projected catastrophic effects on the state of Canadian democracy. They are desperate to understand what accounts for youth alienation from electoral politics and what might be done to address it. Most are seeking generational rather than life-cycle explanations (O'Neill 2004: 2).

Many social-scientific explanations focus on the question of political socialization — that is, how do people acquire knowledge of the political system and both the sense of responsibility and the habit of acting on that knowledge in the regular exercise of voting? For example, in her overview of the current state of research on youth political participation, Brenda O'Neil (2004) identifies ability, opportunity, and motivation as key elements in the decision to vote. This focus on individual attitudes and behaviour orients scholars to looking at families or schooling as primary sources of the problem. How are children's attitudes and behaviours shaped by those of their parents? Is youth disengagement really a failure of parents? Or if knowledge of the political system and an ethic of civic responsibility should be cultivated primarily through the school system, does the problem lie with the civics curriculum, or the lack thereof? Government initiatives like Student Vote 2004 are responses to this construction of the problem as one of ignorance and apathy or, put more nobly, civic literacy and political socialization.

Other constructions of the problem suggest that many people are alienated from Canada's political system, which, since the 1940s, has been producing majority governments with less than 50 percent of the popular vote. Proposals for electoral reform in the direction of proportional representation are responses to this understanding of the problem.

Margaret Adsett (2003) proposes a different way of understanding the phenomenon of a growing political disengagement that begins in youth. She argues that it is a "period effect," that is, a result and reflection of a particular political era. Under the prevailing conditions of neo-liberal globalization, which she dates for Canada from the 1984 election of the Progressive Conservatives under Brian Mulroney, liberal-democratic governments have embraced free trade, privatization, and a radically reduced role for governments in managing economic life and guaranteeing social welfare and equality. This approach has narrowed the scope of public debate as more and more domains of life are relegated to the market and beyond the reach of either political parties or citizen advocacy.

Studies that focus more on what youth are actually doing, rather than on what they're not doing (such as not voting), argue that young people are very politically active but in different ways than older people. According to the 2003 General Social Survey, when political participation is defined more broadly to include volunteering, participation in community organizations, membership in public-interest groups, or participation in protests, young people in Canada are actually more politically engaged than seniors are (Milan 2005).

Scholarship in this vein in both Canada and the United States is concerned about countering dominant views of youth as apathetic (for example, Pancer and Pratt 1999;

Camino and Zeldin 2002; Youniss et al. 2002). It valorizes youth civic engagement as expressing an ethic of social responsibility and broad political interest, as something that builds civic competence, enhances political socialization, and can provide youth with ways of reconnecting with mainstream channels of political representation, notably parties and elections. While broader definitions of what counts as "political" are welcome and essential, such studies leave mainstream political institutions unproblematized. They imagine a largely seamless evolutionary continuity, from a wide variety of community involvement and social activism to electoral participation. Insofar as there is a problem of electoral non-participation by young people, the problem continues to lie with youth, or how families and communities are working (in)effectively with youth, not with the political system or even less with the larger social or world order from which they are alienated. Such studies preserve actually-existing liberal democracy (and its unspoken capitalist character) as the centre and norm of social life and construct the future as the continuous present. These views of the political engagement or disengagement of youth have persisted in the face of the massive eruptions of the anti-globalization movement, in which young people have been key protagonists.

THE ANTI-GLOBALIZATION MOVEMENT: THE APPEARANCE OF A NEW POLITICAL GENERATION

With the November 1999 demonstrations against the World Trade Organization meetings in Seattle, the anti-globalization movement erupted onto the world stage. The epicentre of the Seattle protests was non-violent direct action in the downtown intersections by fifteen thousand protesters. Most of them were young, white, and profoundly alienated from political and corporate elites, cynical about institutionalized channels of representation, and impatient with protest practices that had shown no results. They were intent on preventing the WTO from meeting and largely uninterested in how the elites might negotiate social and environmental clauses that would legitimate the global free-trade regime while moderating its worse effects. Their direct action, coupled with the mass demonstrations of fifty thousand others and the decisions by key developing country trade negotiators, effectively shut down the WTO negotiations. Seattle is rightfully identified as a turning point, perhaps the May '68 of the present generation, not least because of its location in the heartland of global capitalism (Yuen 2001).[3]

The anti-globalization movement is more accurately understood as a "movement of movements," a broad convergence of diverse activisms, North and South, challenging the imposition of a neo-liberal world order through free-trade agreements and the structural adjustment programs of the IMF and World Bank. We do not want to reduce the worldwide anti-globalization movement, in its many diverse expressions, to the mass demonstrations that took place in the cities of the North around elite summits from 1999 through 2001; but in a discussion of young people's political engagement and claims about a new political generation, those demonstrations are of undeniable importance.

More confrontational forms of political protest, with young people as key protagonists, were on the rise in Canada before the events of Seattle. The mid- to late 1990s saw the emergence of radicalized student and anti-poverty movements in many regions of Canada, especially in Quebec (Conway 2003). New forms of direct action were also evident in radical environmentalism, protecting stands of old-growth forest in Temagami, Ontario, and Clayoquot Sound, British Columbia. Aboriginal communities forcefully asserted their treaty rights to hunt and fish. In 1990 Mohawk people maintained an armed standoff in Oka, Quebec, over a proposed development project on ancestral lands. In 1995 indigenous people occupied a provincial park to protect a burial ground, and during that occupation Dudley George, an unarmed member of Stoney Point First Nation, was shot and killed by the Ontario Provincial Police (Edwards 2003). In 2006, young Aboriginal people organized a long-term blockade at Grassy Narrows to prevent clear-cutting and to force governments and Abitibi Consolidated to negotiate with their nation.[4]

The Zapatista uprising of 1994, in which indigenous peoples in Chiapas, Mexico, declared their opposition to the North American Free Trade Agreement, provoked an outpouring of solidarity in Canada as elsewhere. *Zapatismo* became a global political force, generated by the power of the Internet, effectively forcing the Mexican government into peace negotiations. The autonomist[5] politics of the Zapatistas, demanding a world with the space for many worlds and patently disinterested in contesting power through parties and states, inspired political debate and innovation worldwide and resonated especially among young people organized in small grassroots groups advocating horizontal, networked-based organizations

> The autonomist politics of the Zapatistas, demanding a world with the space for many worlds and patently disinterested in parties and states, inspired political debate and innovation worldwide and resonated especially among the young.

(Nunes 2005:278). Community-based direct action by Aboriginal peoples to protect and reclaim land from colonial governments and rapacious resource corporations is grounded in processes of communal, consensus-based decision-making and the reassertion of traditional forms of governance. Histories of Aboriginal resistance to capitalist colonialism, neo-liberal or otherwise, are an important reminder that autonomist and participatory traditions have multiple cultural and geographic origins.[6]

In the 1990s in Canada and elsewhere in the North, young activists increasingly identified transnational corporations as primary targets. They organized boycotts, buycotts, petitions, and demonstrations in new "political consumerism" movements (Micheletti and Stolle 2005). The shift away from state-centred politics reflected both the contraction of democratic space under neo-liberalism, the growing power of corporations in a new regulatory and technological environment, and the increasing visibility of that power to Northern publics.[7]

Somewhat convergent with these developments was a new student movement contesting the corporate incursion into universities through the funding of research and infrastructure, exclusive food and beverage contracts, and contracting out of janitorial and other support services. North American campuses became hotbeds of the new anti-sweatshop movement when students researched the conditions under which their university apparel was produced and proceeded to educate, demonstrate, and occupy presidents' offices in support of alternative labour codes.

In a climate of intensifying global crises, a deep sense of urgency felt most intensely by the young propelled the development of new modes of organization and action and new codes of solidarity. The most marked features of the new mass movements in North America, especially among young people, were an emphasis on direct democracy and an embrace of affinity groups as the preferred organizational form.[8] In the cycle of global protest following Seattle, the new practices embodied a critique of prevailing forms of organization, participation, representation, and action: in NGOs, unions, political parties, and governments. In the lead-up to massive protests against the Free Trade Agreement of the Americas in Quebec City in April 2001, for example, militant youth movements posed challenging critiques to long-standing traditions of "non-violence" among activists as being moralistic and authoritarian. In the name of creativity, resistance, and democracy, many anti-globalization activists advocated "respect for diversity of tactics" as a non-negotiable basis of unity (Conway 2003).

Throughout the summer of 2001, massive protests continued across Europe and North America wherever international institutions or heads of state or their delegates gathered. Tens of thousands of young people organized in a seemingly infinite array of self-organized affinity groups. Hosting groups housed and fed tens of thousands of activists converging on their cities. They organized communal kitchens, medical facilities, and independent media centres. By night, thousands danced and drummed. By day, they confronted police, stood their ground, and were beaten, tear-gassed, and jailed. In August 2001, 300,000 protesters converged on the G8 in Genoa. A young Italian protester, Carlo Guiliani, was shot and killed, and subsequent protests rocked the Italian government.[9]

The events of September 11, 2001, and the subsequent "global war on terror" changed the terrain of anti-globalization politics, especially of mass demonstrations. The protests did not end, but the conditions changed. Gatherings of global elites now take place in ever-more remote places, behind barricades and walls of riot police. Anti-terrorism laws mean that demonstrations can be shut down before they get going. In the new geopolitical context, the new political generation in Canada has turned to community-based struggles on their home terrain, particularly the struggles of immigrants and refugees, the homeless and poor, and Aboriginal peoples. At the same time, an explosion of interest and participation in new forms of global convergence has occurred. The most important of these are the World Social Forum (WSF) and the Intercontinental Youth Camp, which has grown up within, beside, and sometimes against the WSF.

THE WORLD SOCIAL FORUM AND INTERCONTINENTAL YOUTH CAMP: PRACTISING THE POLITICS OF A NEW GENERATION?

Originally conceived as an alternative to the World Economic Forum held annually in Davos, Switzerland,[10] the World Social Forum was initiated by a group of Brazilian organizations to convene, from around the world, groups and movements of civil society opposed to neo-liberalism. The idea was to create a forum for the free and horizontal exchange of ideas, experiences, and strategies oriented to enacting and generating alternatives to neo-liberalism. The gathering was conceived of as being thoroughly international but anchored geographically and experientially in the global South. The first WSF, held in Porto Alegre, Brazil, in January 2001, attracted fifteen thousand participants. Its astounding success led organizers to commit to the WSF as a permanent process. The event has taken place each January since then, growing exponentially in size, diversity, complexity, and importance so that it is now regularly attracting over a hundred thousand people.

After three years in Porto Alegre, Brazil, the WSF moved to Mumbai, India, in 2004, and the 2007 Forum was in Nairobi, Kenya. Brazil remains the homeplace of the WSF, but there is a widespread commitment to moving the world event geographically to other sites in the global South. This is a strategy for expanding and deepening the Forum's international character. In a related move, at the second WSF in Porto Alegre in 2002, organizers called on participants to organize similar processes in their own countries and regions, defined by their own priorities, and at whatever scale made sense to them. Inspired by the world event and organized in accordance with the WSF's Charter of Principles, hundred of social forums are appearing worldwide, on every continent and at every scale.

According to Ana Paula De Carli, an organizer of the Intercontinental Youth Camps of 2001–03 and 2005, youth activist groups based mainly in Porto Alegre were dismayed when they learned that only established non-governmental organizations were invited to the initial World Social Forum (Morrison 2006).[11] She added that these activists demanded a right to participate in the WSF. Instead, a decision was taken by the Municipality of Porto Alegre to set up big television screens in public spaces so that the youth could watch the inaugural WSF proceedings. By late December 2000, just one month before the WSF, the screens had not yet been provided, and many young people who wanted to be present at the Forum did not yet have places to sleep. At that stage, some of the excluded groups were already initiating alternative activities. They ended up setting up a camp of their own.

From these inauspicious origins, the Intercontinental Youth Camp (IYC) emerged as an annual experiment in co-management and shared living for a wide range of campers who are interested in practical ways of making social change. Camps were assembled each year in Porto Alegre's Parque de Harmonia alongside Lake Guaiba in late January to coincide with the World Social Forum. When WSF 2004 moved to Mumbai, the fourth IYC took place on the grounds of the Don Bosco Catholic High School on the outskirts of that Indian metropolis.

The camps lasted from six to ten days and over the years hosted some 80,000 resident campers from dozens of countries. Participation in the four camps in Porto Alegre grew steadily from about 3,200 in 2001 to 35,000 in 2005, roughly paralleling the expansion of the WSF and comprising about one-quarter of its numbers. The vast majority of campers came from the host country and region, but with a consistent presence of youth from North America and Europe, reflecting their greater access to resources. Men and women in all age groups, especially those aged sixteen to thirty-five, have participated in roughly equal numbers.

In its first year the IYC was a hastily organized undertaking, conceived largely as a low-cost camping ground to enable youth from outside the city to participate in the inaugural Forum. The organizing committee comprised youth members of leftist Brazilian political parties, especially from the Workers Party (PT) (see Nunes 2005: 282; Oliveira 2005: 319). The PT was the governing party of both Porto Alegre and its home state, Rio Grande Do Sul. The major initial task of the Camp's organizing committee was to negotiate with the state and the municipality for financial and infrastructural support.

A broader Camp Organizing Committee (COA) was set up for IYC 2002, which included not just youth members of left-wing political parties, but also new sets of actors from "the student movement, street children's movement, hip-hop movement, community radio stations, black movement, and the free sexual orientation movement" (Oliveira 2005: 320). Another group that was to provide extremely valuable input was the Free Metropolitan Council of Architecture Students. Its members "brought with them the concept of the Youth Camp as a city" (Nunes 2005: 283). De Carli said that the establishment by the COA of Camp organizational commissions to work on the second Camp marked a commitment to practise horizontal decision-making in both the organizational process and the Camp itself. Each commission practised consensus decision-making, and each member of the COA could contribute equally in meetings.

The IYC 2002 was conceived by organizers as a "laboratory of practices." (IYC 2003 Camp Organizing Committee — hereafter COA 2003: 1). Potira Preiss explained that the conception of the Camp as a practical laboratory embodied a critique of the World Social Forum, which IYC organizers perceived as being limited to debating, rather than enacting, alternatives to neo-liberalism. The Youth Camp, in contrast, would encompass social spaces and activities of collective experimentation that ideally would have a minimal ecological footprint (IYC 2004 and 2005 websites — hereafter IYC 2004, 2005). De Carli underscored that for IYC 2003 the Camp Organizing Committee sought to broaden outreach to youth cross-continentally and to expand the range of issues and forms of social activism informing the program of activities. The principle of self-management, coupled with the concept of the Camp as a laboratory of practices, defined the approach to organizational planning for later camps.

The notion of "intercontinental" youth has been synonymous with "transnational" and has denoted an openness to youth, from any geographic origin, who are willing to approach politics in new ways and — since IYC 2002 — to *live* alternatives to neo-liberalism. The overarching vision of the IYC has been to foster alternative social practices that will be carried beyond the time-space of the camp to challenge global systems of neo-liberal

Creating the Intercontinental Youth Camp (IYC) as a lived alternative to neo-liberal capitalism has meant paying concrete attention to the practices of everyday life, promoting ethical exchange and consumption, fostering a safe and respectful environment, and practising forms of governance based on consensus.

capitalism that privilege economic growth, mass consumerism, and corporate domination and exploitation over people and the environment (IYC 2004, 2005). Creating the IYC as a lived alternative to neo-liberal capitalism has meant paying concrete attention to the practices of everyday life involved in constructing the built environment, planning and sharing physical space, providing food and water, managing waste, promoting ethical exchange and consumption, fostering a safe and respectful environment for all participants, and practising forms of management and governance based on consensus. The approach also rejected hierarchy and encompassed an expectation of participation by all in both decision-making and camp chores.

Campers brought their own tents, but organizers planned logistics. Working with volunteer campers who arrived early, they built infrastructures, including activity spaces, communal kitchens, and stages. They negotiated with local authorities for water and sewage services, and in turn government workers built open-air showers and portable toilets, all with an eye to minimal ecological damage. Each Camp has featured biodegradable constructions ("bio-constructions") built by organizers and volunteers using bamboo, straw, mud, and recyclable materials such as plastic bottles and milk cartons. These activity spaces or "action centres," used mainly for participatory workshops, proved to be whirlwinds of social life, cultural exchange, and creative expression.

Some campers prepared food collectively in communal kitchens. Others bought food from family-based providers on site or local merchants. Based on the concept of "solidarity economy," organizers aimed to maximize fair trade possibilities by looking, as much as possible, to local organic farmer co-operatives as a source of food. This type of practice extended to many forms of exchange and consumption inside the camps as people engaged extensively in barter and boycotts of multinational corporate commodities.

Other regular features of the camps included free software exchanges, independent media outlets, a Camp broadcast system, documentary films, art exhibits, protest marches, cross-cultural forms of music and dance, and countless campfires and social interactions. In Brazil many distinctive perspectives were shared with campers by locally based farmers, artisans, small-scale vendors, and activists from movements of unemployed peoples, street kids, and indigenous groups (IYC 2004, 2005).

For those committed to the IYC, the key to fostering alternative social practices was the resident campers' engagement with non-hierarchical, horizontal self-management. Concretely, this approach involved everyone in sharing responsibility for the day-to-day functioning of the Camp. The approach included a co-operative division of labour and collective stewardship of the public environment; and it reflected an underlying ethical commitment to participatory decision-making within a decentralized system of campsites. The IYC aimed to generate critical self-reflection among campers on their daily life practices in the hope that youth campers would henceforward embrace habits that reinforced living in co-operatively respectful and ecologically sustainable ways.

The IYC's conception of self-management seeks to question daily life under capitalism. But how can such an objective be realized when it is practised on a temporary basis in an intercontinental space of youth activism? One way that this has occurred is through the decentralization of the Intercontinental Youth Camp. After IYC 2002, the organizers of that Camp and later on youth activists in numerous places around the world organized local and regional youth camps in a process of dissemination and regionalization paralleling that of the WSF. The Youth Camp experience in Quebec is one successful example of this process. Established in August 2003, it was developed as a direct consequence of IYC 2003, where many young people from Quebec were inspired by their experiences in Parque de Harmonia.

INTERCONTINENTAL YOUTH CAMP 2003: A CASE STUDY

After originally planning for an influx of thirteen thousand people, the Camp Organizing Committee began to anticipate the arrival of upwards of thirty thousand campers as the start of the third Camp, scheduled for January 19 to 28, 2003, approached. Some thirty-four hectares were set aside, including annexed land that the Municipality officially declared as part of Parque de Harmonia (Nunes 2005: 288–89). The huge number of expected campers required logistical management systems of epic proportions, at least in comparison to IYC 2001. The organizers had to build fifteen pavilions for workshop activities. These were designed out of "light adobe," consisting of water, sawdust, and mud. Five large tents set up next to Lake Guaiba were designated for various social movements to conduct activities. Workshops in the action centres focused on the five WSF themes: Media, Culture and Counter-Hegemony; Political Power, Civil Society and Democracy; Global Democratic Order, Fight Against Militarized Combat and Peace Promotion; Sustainable and Democratic Development, Principles and Values; Human Rights, Diversity and Equality (COA 2003: 1–2). The activities explicitly linked the WSF 2003 themes with participatory education and low-impact ecology.

A "Communication Factory" was designed to include spaces for dialogue and eighty computers with Internet access for both accredited media representatives and alternative radio broadcasts. A speaker system was set up to disseminate information on activities to the entire camping population (COA 2003: 2). There were 150 portable bathrooms and 150 shower stalls designed to recycle much of the organic waste. The IYC Environmental Work Group planned to distribute organic soap and information on ethical consumption of water to campers (COA 2003: 1–2; Oliveira 2005: 324).

Meanwhile, the COA's Culture Subcommittee made plans for two stages on the riverbank to welcome established independent artists, as well as lesser-known bands, theatrical groups, and dance troupes. "Free Spaces" were built for artisans to improvise poetry, music, or other kinds of creative expression. A reading room and spaces for testimonials were also established on the lakefront (COA 2003: 2). Whether or not campers were engaged in political struggles, the sharing of creativity opened possibilities of interlinking identities and human expressions with a forging of new friendships.

The COA dubbed this third camp "the City of cities" (COA 2003: 1). Estimates of the camping population ranged from between 23,500 (Nunes 2005: 288) and 30,000 (Oliveira 2005: 324). Inside Parque de Harmonia, there was a serious attempt to practise self-management. Each of the fifty residential campsites (known as barrios or neighbourhoods) had a co-ordinator responsible for tent placement, monitoring cleanups, and resolving internal conflicts (COA 2003: 1). The barrio system established a management council based on campsite representation, which decided how to allocate activity spaces between the various social groups represented. A similarly comprised board of representatives from barrios and the COA tried to ensure that services and information were distributed equally throughout the campsites and park. Decisions made in daily meetings and information were disseminated by members of the management council, posted on billboards, and transmitted through the speaker systems (see Oliveira 2005: 323–24).

Ana Paula De Carli noticed as the camp evolved, however, that only about 10 percent of the massive camper population became actively engaged in self-management. That finding still translates to an estimated two to three thousand people. According to Rodrigo Nunes, many people remained passive observers unnoticed by organizers. He also reported that program planning failed in many regards because activities did not occur as scheduled, and there was confusion about the allocation of spaces for seminars and workshops (Nunes 2005: 290–91). Nevertheless, even without everybody's direct involvement in self-management, IYC 2003 did exhibit a well-developed system of representation based on barrios, campsites, and groups.

Júlia Coelho de Souza helped to ensure that food provisioning was based on a local solidarity economy. Most of the food in the park was provided and sold through fair trade markets at designated vendor outposts by movements such as the Landless Workers Movement (MST) and small-scale self-organized agricultural networks.[12] Organizers also arranged meal deals at nearby restaurants. However, while another objective had been to ensure that food in the Camp would be organic, genetically modified organisms (GMOs) and chemically produced products were sold in the park. De Souza added that these were cheaper and reflected the daily reality of much of the export-oriented, monoculture agriculture produced in Brazil. This contradiction prompted widespread reflection and discussion on consumption habits and alternatives to large-scale chemical production.

De Souza also pointed out that a special medium of exchange was used inside the park and just outside its perimeters, which was convertible one to one with the Brazilian currency. Its use integrated resident involvement in solidarity economies. Direct market systems of exchange run by and for family food co-operatives exemplified how the

Camp attempted to practise the ideals of fair trade and to make a real (if short-term) difference in supporting the livelihoods of solidarity networks. However, the alternative currency had no viability in the larger neo-liberal economy after the ten-day Camp ended.

Another significant innovation unfolded in a white tent put up at the outer edge of the Camp to house the Intergalaktica Laboratory of Global Resistance, later known as the Caracol. The action centre hosted self-identified anarchists, Marxists, and fellow activists who were influenced by the Zapatistas. They put together participatory workshops aimed at strategizing for political change through self-organization (Osterwil 2004: 185, 190). De Carli said that the Intergalaktica Laboratory was also the site where the Global Resistance Network (RRGN) was founded. The RRGN was conceived as a network to link young people from different countries in self-managed spaces and Youth Camps worldwide, with the Intercontinental Youth Camp as a blueprint. It would come to rely on Internet-based communication for its members to post information on protests and other events against the neo-liberal order (Bartholl 2005). The RRGN could form only at a site such as the IYC, where people from different parts of the world met and discussed their ideas together.

There were also critical social problems. Romualdo Olivieri (2005: 324) notes that the negative impact of Porto Alegre's urban violence and theft infiltrated the Camp. A resident of Porto Alegre and participant at the third Camp, Eduardo Sanchez, heard much local gossip about the IYC in 2003, and the media in Porto Alegre referred to it as a place used mainly for parties. Roberto Soares Francisco recounted that some organizers and activist groups were upset by campers who seemingly partied to the exclusion of all else.

The achievements in experimenting with collective self-management at the third Camp were moderated by the reality that only a minority of campers actively participated in that facet. This condition concretely demonstrated the challenges of realizing collaborative alternatives and equal divisions of labour. The time was short, and thousands of people were in the park. Most residents did not share either the knowledge or the motivation needed to take part. In addition, despite a strong rhetorical commitment to the goal of self-management, members of the COA themselves had difficulty in abiding by its practical application. Their responsibilities far outweighed the contributions of many other campers.

Despite the limits and frustrations, this ambitious attempt at self-management within the IYC reinforced the commitments of the organizers to develop programs of solidarity and promote alternative daily practices related to agriculture, ecology, and cross-cultural creative expression. Moreover, even though the Camp was largely put together by youth living in the state of Rio Grande Do Sul, the laboratory of practices did facilitate the emergence of a transnational youth activist network to carry forward the IYC's objectives. Indeed, some campers from Quebec were so inspired by IYC 2003 that they returned home to establish a youth camp there later that same year.

FROM PORTO ALEGRE TO QUEBEC

Colin Perreault was among hundreds of activists from Quebec at the Intercontinental Youth Camp in Porto Alegre in 2003 and 2005. He spent considerable time at the Caracol Intergalaktica action centre.[13] Based on his experience at IYC 2003, Perreault came to believe that youth camps should take place anywhere in the world at various times, and not just on an annual basis at one global convergence. He was not alone in this thinking.

Eugénie Pelletier, an organizer of the Campement Québécois de la Jeunesse (CQJ), explained that those involved were mainly "white francophone middle-class youth" connected through a francophone network of non-governmental organizations based in Quebec. These NGOs worked in the field of international development, which provided them with government-funded internships and, in turn, avenues to engage in World Social Forums and protest events around the world. Pelletier also explained that many connections between francophones and Brazilians were forged in Parque de Harmonia during January 2003. Some of the youth from Quebec became part of the Global Resistance Network. Email communications between them and their counterparts located outside of Canada were important in developing the youth camp model in their home province. Between thirty and forty organizers worked hard on the new initiative.

Based on the IYC's vision, le Campement Jeunesses du Québec — renamed le Campement Québécois de la Jeunesse a year later — was intended for youth activists to practise alternatives to contemporary capitalism in a shared living space premised on collective experimentation. Participants were expected to engage politically in a dynamic learning environment of social activism and camping. Committed to consensus decision-making, the organizers prioritized participatory debating in their planning process. In their open discussions, two members filled the roles of facilitator and secretary to keep the dialogue moving and to maintain a record of it. Voting was used in early meetings simply to decide if an item needed more discussion or if sufficient agreement had been reached (Campement Jeunesses du Québec 2003a: 1–2).

In conceiving what became le Campement Québécois de la Jeunesse as a self-managed village of solidarity patterned on the IYC, the organizers extended a welcome to all people young and old who were interested in horizontal political activism (Campement Jeunesses du Québec 2003b: 1). The organizers of the CQJ established themselves as a collective group with one voice and a committee- or commission-based division of labour. To make the Youth Camp model viable, they incorporated broader activist networks in the organizing. Organizers sought to promote concrete social practices and associated direct actions to move beyond the left politics of political parties, labour unions, and mainstream non-governmental organizations in Quebec and elsewhere, which they saw as paralyzed by intellectual debate. In their own organizing, they refused to see themselves as leaders. Instead, they were committed to horizontal decision-making for three main reasons: to decentralize and share organizing responsibilities; to reject hierarchy; and to facilitate a socially inclusive open process. They also formed commissions devoted to infrastructure/financing, programming, and communication/mobilization (Campement Jeunesses du Québec 2003b: 2, 4).

The first camp took place on Perreault's father's land in a rural area south of Ville de Québec near St-Malachie, Comté de Bellechasse. It ran from August 11 to August 20, 2003 (Campement Jeunesses du Québec 2003b: 1). Perreault noticed a substantial level of support for the initiative given that other people also offered host sites to the cash-strapped organizers. Campers were mobilized on the basis of existing activist networks from Montreal, Quebec City, Sherbrooke, and surrounding areas (CQJ 2004b: 1). Despite limited financial resources, the organizers successfully attracted over two hundred participants (CQJ 2004a: 1). Activities included music around campfires, improvised theatre, book exchanges, circus arts, independent film screenings, and creative onsite spaces for children (CQJ 2003a: 3).

The second Campement Québec de la Jeunesse took place for ten days, August 13–23, 2004, in Durham-Sud (CQJ 2004c: 1–2). Perreault recalled that organizers numbered 60 to 70 of the eventual 200 to 250 participants. The camp was hosted by a theatre group of seven or eight people and held on the group's organic farm. More creativity flourished in the form of arts, theatre, and painting. Andrea Browning arrived at a time when residents had just completed the set-up for most activities to get underway. She was the only anglophone. She saw only one other non-French speaker, a Mexican who came to give a workshop. Browning also noticed that the vast majority of resident campers were white and middle-class, and that many already knew one another socially. She saw more women than men, some families and a few children. Most of the campers were in their twenties or thirties.

Browning recounted that there were usually two meetings per day where decisions about running the camp were made through consensus. Collective kitchens were run effectively. There was a workshop period during the day and at night. Typically four workshops were run simultaneously. A generator was used for music at the stage. Otherwise, there was very little electricity. There were also many casual meetings and activities around the fire.

The third Campement Québec de la Jeunesse took place from August 15 to 29, 2005, at one of North America's largest ecovillage projects, at Mount Radar, located between Quebec City and the Eastern Townships. Low-impact ecology was prioritized in situating the third camp there. Ecovillages are primarily rural, typically numbering five hundred or fewer people who attempt to sustain community life on a permanent basis in ways that avoid exploiting the environment. Since 1996 ecovillages have taken root in five continents (see Global Ecovillage Network 2005; Jackson 2004: 25–27). Perreault explained that activists involved in this ecovillage had purchased Mount Radar, named for a base operated by the Canadian military during the Cold War. In extending the invitation, the residents expressed particular interest in seeing how the Youth Camp functioned. The site proved to be a bonus for the sixty to seventy organizers, who did not have to build bathrooms and kitchens. Less work spent on infrastructure meant more time for discussions. Some four hundred people participated in this third CQJ. A media room was established onsite. The focus on ecology was coupled with mutual learning not only between campers, but also between the youth camp itself and the residents of the ecovillage. A collectively written book project was launched and remains in process.

Over the first three years, an impressive number of people were involved in CQJ organizing. While the main issue for key organizers has been how to run the camps collectively, political differences and transient and unequal participation have challenged the practice of horizontal self-management, just as they have in the larger IYCs in Brazil and India. Various ideological perspectives and competing visions about Quebec's future inside and outside of Canada and urban-rural divides have been relevant issues to many campers. Nevertheless, the Campement Québec de la Jeunesse has served as an effective point of convergence for activists.

The camp has been a venue for building knowledge and initiating new collaborative projects. Eugénie Pelletier has seen many networks of solidarity forge and expand in Quebec because of the youth camp, especially in the cities of Montreal, Sherbrooke, and Quebec. Hundreds of activists have advanced campaigns against poverty, racism, and discrimination against women. The camp has been an important space for environmental groups, artists, and youth-led initiatives in the province and has fostered extensive experimentation with various forms of collective self-management. Perreault pointed out that while not much priority has been placed on media outreach, the organizers provided information to local media, and some media groups willingly covered the camps. Word of mouth was crucial. Many people in Quebec in their twenties and thirties have a "six degrees of separation" relationship with the youth camp. They know people or know people who know people who have taken part in some capacity. Most of the key activists, though, have been part of the inner circles of the Porto Alegre camps.

Perreault — making a point that reflected in part the distance between the political cultures of Quebec and the rest of Canada — remarked that there had as yet been little contact with fellow activists elsewhere in the country. For example, hardly any cross-participation had taken place between the CQJ and the Regional Social Forum (RSF) in London, Ontario. According to Pelletier, informal networking in the Campement Québec de la Jeunesse had led, however, to mobilizing support for refugees, migrants, and immigrants with counterparts in Ontario. Still, much remained to be done in developing linkages and promoting the youth camp process elsewhere.

The establishing of the Forum Social de Québec, organized for June 2007, raises new possibilities and dynamics for the future trajectory of the Campement Québec de la Jeunesse. Unlike the IYC, which emerged as a response to the WSF, the youth camp in Quebec preceded a Social Forum. The possibility that these initiatives may connect with the RSF of London, Ontario — which took place in June in both 2005 and 2006 — or other Social Forum endeavours in Ontario, Alberta, and elsewhere would mark an important step in building such alternative spaces into dynamic processes across the country. If this scenario unfolds, the question of who takes part raises a fundamental set of issues about political engagement. Whose alternatives are being imagined, developed, and practised?

A NEW POLITICAL GENERATION (AND ITS "OTHERS")

The massive anti-globalization demonstrations of the turn of the century were spectacular occasions of convergence for a great range of movements focused on different issues, working in different modes, at a variety of scales and rooted in different parts of the world. Especially in their North American and European variants, the demonstrations were also specific forms of activism in the North. The priority given to direct action and autonomist forms of organizing must be further situated within the predominantly white student and youth movements. While this was a very significant element of the street mobilizations, it remains one demographic in a much broader, more politically and culturally diverse reality in the movement of movements. In particular, the practices and discourses of the youth movement were influenced by much older traditions and debates about anarchism.

Some commentators argue that the global political space created by the mass demonstrations and which made the World Social Forum and the IYC possible, was the fruit of a new political culture created by new network- and web-based forms of organization. These are transnational and horizontal, and depart from the "old" nationally oriented and vertically organized politics carried on by parties and unions, which is criticized for being bureaucratic, hierarchical, and authoritarian (for example, Nunes 2005). This analysis may be too simplistic in its binary opposition; but attempting to name what is new (or specific) about the actors and cultures of politics in these contemporary forms of mobilization is important.

> The young people who have been key protagonists in the mass anti-globalization demonstrations and the Intercontinental Youth Camp value concrete and direct action. They want to act to change the world, not just talk about it.

The young people who have been key protagonists in the mass anti-globalization demonstrations and Intercontinental Youth Camp value concrete and direct action. They want to act to change the world, not just talk about it. They pay attention to the practices of everyday life, to patterns of relating, working, and consuming, to embeddedness in their local communities, and to living in an ecologically sustainable way. Commitment to the local, especially in the North, is heavily inflected with a global consciousness, an awareness of the effects that their choices have elsewhere, and a capacity and interest in transnational and cross-cultural networking.

> Despite the limits and contradictions of the Youth Camp, tens of thousands of young people have clearly been inspired to experiment with new ways of life, to reflect critically on their practice, and to constantly innovate.

Affinity groups as an organizational form express the new political ethic as one of self-organization, collective action, participatory decision-making, and personal and direct involvement in keeping with personal codes and values.

Despite the limits and contradictions of the Youth Camp, tens of thousands of young people in different parts of the world have clearly been inspired to experiment with new ways of life, to reflect critically on their practice, and to constantly innovate as they take the IYC model up in their local places. Many share and enact this new political culture, although it is not yet clear how class- and culturally-specific it may be or whether, indeed, it can be characterized as a single culture. The young activists may well be disproportionately urban, middle-class, and wired and reflect a particular geography, primarily of Latin worlds (Brazil, France, Italy, Quebec). What is evident is that the practices of the IYC have inspired others beyond Brazil, including in Canada and especially in Quebec.

Recent studies of youth political participation in Quebec converge with the arguments about the appearance of a new political generation. These studies have argued for a new definition of participation, more accurately labelled *civic participation*, which allows for involvement in civil society organizations and popular mobilizations, and pays explicit attention to anti-globalization activism in Quebec in studying contemporary political engagement among Quebec youth (for example, Gauthier 2003). These studies conclude that young people are intensely involved, but not in parties or unions. They are more comfortably active in an eclectic mix of popular organizations and initiatives where they can act directly on specific issues in ways consistent with their values and concerns (Quéniart and Jacques 2004: 188). They actively resist political or ideological labelling. This tendency holds true particularly for women, who have long been observed as being prominent in community-based organizing while remaining underrepresented in formal politics. In a study focused on young women, Anne Quéniart and Julie Jacques (2004: 188) found, "They want to defend their convictions, not the party line," and they "refuse to accept a single and only way of thinking." The authors concluded that their respondents were enacting an active citizenship, not reducible to electoral or political party involvements, that is, "a way of being, a lifestyle that requires them to act consistently in all aspects of daily life and therefore implies living in accordance with one's ideals… a 'search for ethical consistency'" (191).

Those arguing that the anti-globalization demonstrations and the IYC are expressions of the emergence of a new political generation are silent on the race and class composition of that generation. Likewise, the studies of the political participation of youth in Quebec, and in Canada, do not specify the race and class of the youth activists (for example, Juris 2005; Nunes 2005; Quéniart and Jacques 2004; Gauthier 2003). There is also a lack of data with respect to the camper populations of the IYC in Porto Alegre and of the Campement Québec de la Jeunesse in terms of race and class, although we have reported the perceptions of some organizers and participants. These omissions raise questions about the class- and race-specificity of the putative "new political generation" being posited by these commentators. It therefore seems important to also inquire about political engagement among economically and racially marginalized youth, to be open to the possibility that new and generationally distinct activisms may be emerging among them, and to explore the relations, such as they are, with the predominantly white anti-globalization and youth camp activisms.

In her discussion of the anti-WTO protests in Seattle, Kristine Wong (2001) argues that the way in which the anti-globalization politics of the demonstration were "framed" by the white-dominated, national-scale, and more institutionalized organizations marginalized the more grassroots, community-based activisms of people of colour in Seattle.[14] The organizing efforts of a low-income neighbourhood to oppose a hospital incinerator were not viewed as relevant to the kind of "global" environmental politics being put forward by the big activist coalitions opposing the WTO, so the perspectives and approaches of local people of colour were not incorporated. This is an example of how the discourses of culturally dominant groups can be projected as "global" or "universal," even in a radical social movement that aims to be egalitarian and inclusive. The dominant discourses make invisible the presence and specificity of more marginalized groups and of their political agency. We must be alert to this possibility in considering the Youth Camp and the claims about a new political generation emanating from it, both in Porto Alegre and Quebec.

In the wake of critiques from activists of colour about racism in the anti-globalization movement, activist self-critiques about summit-hopping and activist jet setting, and the changed context following 9/11 and the U.S. invasion of Iraq, anti-globalization activism in Europe and North America took a more clearly anti-racist and anti-imperialist turn. Many young activists who had been radicalized in the anti-globalization movement began to reconceptualize movement politics to recognize a wide range of critical activisms, many of them localized, rooted in the survival and rights struggles of specific communities, as broadly convergent. Anti-globalization activists took up the struggles of refugees, immigrants, and guest workers in campaigns like the Montreal-based "No one is illegal," Vancouver-based "Open the borders," and Toronto-based STATUS (Sharma 2002; Nadeau 2002–03: 54, note 4; Sharma 2003; Wright 2006). Solidarity with close-to-home Aboriginal struggles for sovereignty has also gained greater prominence among non-Aboriginal activists and contributed to more explicitly anti-colonial understandings of anti-globalization politics in Canada and beyond.

The Intercontinental Youth Camp process is politically and culturally specific. It is one expression among many of a new political generation responding politically to its historical conditions. It is, however, a particularly rich action with enormous potential for encounter and dialogue across geographic, cultural, and political difference. The IYC has linked many youth-led social movements from many civil society arenas and alternative political/social practices from around the world. There are contradictions inherent in self-organizing in public spaces that are marked by unequal power relations among organizers, resident campers, and a variety of social movement actors. However, the IYC offers both a conceptual and a practical model of transnational youth activism oriented to alternative ways of learning and living. By creating opportunities for transnational networking among youth activist movements, the IYC has bolstered youth activism in the early twenty-first century, particularly through the proliferation of smaller local and regional youth camps. Localization and regionalization were the keys to becoming more globally inclusive and locally effective.

Potential outcomes rest with countless reverberations from social experiences developed among thousands of campers who came to the IYCs and returned to different parts of the planet. Some of them, such as the organizers of the Campement Québécois de la Jeunesse, are imagining alternative ways of doing politics in Canada. Their contributions, alongside other social struggles across Canada and around the world to define and develop alternative pathways, are necessary in a world consumed by money and exploitation, and with so few powerful voices. Alternatives must be imagined and practised if a world of diversity and of hope for future generations is to survive.

Certainly, many young people are deeply concerned about the state of the world, injustices at home and abroad, and deepening ecological disruption. They are, in our view, rightly cynical about the institutions of liberal democracy, which effectively disallow any meaningful debate and rule out alternatives to the reigning order. Why do Aboriginal land claims go unresolved? Why do poverty and homelessness continue to grow in the midst of wealth? How can species continue to disappear, food, water, and air quality deteriorate, and cancer rates rise while the Kyoto Accord is dismissed? How can the U.S. invade Iraq and plunder its resources in the name of democracy?

We do see a new political generation in formation, but in order to perceive its presence we need a broad and open understanding of the political. We need to observe what young people are actually doing in acting politically in the world and listen to what they are saying about it. We need to be open to the radical nature of their critiques and the depth of their hope that other ways of living in peace with justice, with people and the planet, are possible.

> We do see a new political generation in formation, but we need to observe what young people are actually doing in acting politically in the world and listen to what they are saying about it.

Every political practice is culturally specific, and no practice is perfect and without contradiction. One important feature of the Youth Camp is the premium placed on practice oriented to ecological and horizontal modes of life, and on sustaining and improving in the light of critical and collective reflection. Struggles for participatory and non-hierarchical modes of organizing life are difficult, messy, and rife with conflict and contradiction. The path is made by walking, as the Zapatistas say, because there is no map to another world. A new generation is on the move. It is many-hued and working on many fronts. It is hungry for new forms of democracy. Through its practices, it may yet change the world. Our future depends on it.

GLOSSARY OF KEY TERMS

Activism: Participation in activities and groups that aim to protest or change some existing situation in ways that can include but extend beyond institutionalized channels of participation and representation.

Anti-globalization movement: A "movement of movements," a broad convergence of diverse activisms, North and South, that appeared in the late 1990s and challenges the imposition of a neo-liberal world order.

Direct action: A form of activism that seeks to address, directly and immediately, an unjust situation by physically intervening to cause or prevent something from occurring without appealing to, relying on, or waiting for "official" or institutionalized channels of change.

Horizontal politics: Co-operative, consensual, and non-hierarchical forms of organizing and practising social activism.

Neo-liberalism: A bundle of policies oriented to reducing the role of governments in managing economic matters in favour of "free markets" through privatization, deregulation, reduced government spending, and free trade.

Neo-liberal globalization: The global spread of neo-liberal policy orientations, often through coercion by the richest countries and international institutions like the IMF, World Bank, and World Trade Organization through mechanisms like Structural Adjustment Programs and free-trade agreements.

New political generation: A particular age cohort that is politically active in a specific way, whose new ways of doing politics embody a horizontal networking logic that embraces an ethos of direct action and participatory democracy.

Political engagement: Narrowly understood, this often refers strictly to participation in electoral processes through the act of voting; more broadly, it refers to a range of activities by citizens interacting with their governments, through lobbying, public-policy consultations, public hearings, and the like; more broadly still, it can refer to any kind of participation in civic or voluntary organizations oriented to some social good; a few authors include participation in demonstrations and activist groups as forms of political engagement.

QUESTIONS FOR DISCUSSION

1. Do you vote? Why or why not? Why do you think other young people are not voting?
2. Are you attracted to the Intercontinental Youth Camp, its aims and activities? Why or why not?
3. Is activism in the anti-globalization movement or in the Intercontinental Youth Camp a replacement for voting or participation in political parties as a means of social change?

4. What are the main kinds of political engagement in our society? What is the relationship among the different forms of political engagement in fostering a healthy democracy? In creating a more just society?

WEBSITES OF INTEREST

World Social Forum — Brazil. <www.forumsocialmundial.org.br/>.
World Social Forum — India. <www.wsfindia.org>.
World Social Forum — Kenya. <www.wsf2007.org>.
Toronto Social Forum. <www.ryerson.ca/tsf/>.
Student Vote 2004. <www.studentvote2004.ca/>.
World Trade Organization. <www.wto.org/>.
International Monetary Fund. <www.imf.org/>.
World Bank. <www.worldbank.org/>.
World Economic Forum. <www.weforum.org/>.
EZLN (Zapatistas). <www.ezln.org/>.
Workers Party Brazil (PT). <www.pt.org.br/>.
Movimento Sem Terra. <www.mstbrazil.org/>.
No One Is Illegal. <nooneisillegal.org/>.

NOTES

The research for this chapter was funded by the Social Sciences and Humanities Research Council of Canada.

1. We use the term "anti-globalization" because it is recognizable, but it is contentious among activists, many of whom refer to themselves as committed to global justice or alternative (alter-) globalization. See Conway 2004, cha. 1, for discussion of the difficulties of conceptualizing the "movement of movements."
2. Drawing on a different set of data from the 2003 General Social Survey, Gauthier (2003) notes that youth voter turnout is higher in Quebec than elsewhere in Canada. Quebec respondents named pressure groups and anti-globalization demonstrations as important aspects of their political involvement (Gauthier 2003, cited by Milan 2005: 5).
3. May '68 refers to the massive strikes and protests against the postwar order that took place on the streets of Paris, France, in May 1968. It has come to symbolize the multifaceted worldwide revolutions of the 1960s. See Ali and Watkins 1998. For a compelling account of the events in Seattle, see *This Is What Democracy Looks Like*, Indymedia and Big Noise productions.
4. See the documentary film *As Long as the Rivers Flow* (directed by Dave Clement) for an account of the organizing at Grassy Narrows.
5. "Autonomist" refers to a political orientation that values direct participation in decision-making, self-organizing, and self-management by groups asserting the power of their own agency to change their conditions of existence over against centralized bureaucracies of states, parties, or social movements that they view as authoritarian, remote, and undemocratic.
6. Many narratives of the anti-globalization movement are Eurocentric in their overwhelming focus on the mass demonstrations in the North, autonomist organizing, direct action

by (mostly white) youth, and an accompanying celebration of European anarchism as the philosophical backbone of "new politics." These narratives erase or marginalize long-standing struggles in the South against structural adjustment, megadevelopment projects, and debt, indigenous struggles for sovereignty worldwide, feminist, queer, and other equality-seeking movements, many expressions of which have converged in the anti-globalization movement.

7. Klein (2000) documents this proliferation of new activisms opposing corporatization of life.

8. Affinity groups are small, autonomous self-organized groups that operate according to consensus decision-making by those participating directly in any given action and independent of any centralized movement authority, although they voluntarily network with other affinity groups to produce large-scale actions. Affinity group organizing was also a hallmark of feminist and anti-nuclear movements in the 1970s and 1980s. See Conway 2003: 510–11 for further discussion.

9. For testimonies of this new generation of activists and of this movement from the events of Seattle through the post-9/11 period, see Yuen, Katsiaficas, and Rose 2001; Chang et al. 2001; Welton and Wolf 2001; Shepard and Hayduk 2002; Prokosch and Raymond 2002; Starr 2006; Solnit 2004; Yuen, Katsiaficas, and Rose 2004. For an account of the Genoa protests, see Neale 2001, 2002.

10. The World Economic Forum has been a conference of and for the world's political and economic elites since the 1970s. It has been an important place for business and state leaders to define capitalist agendas for the global political economy.

11. Unless otherwise noted, all information on the Intercontinental Youth Camp in this chapter derives from Morrison 2006. For this thesis Daniel Morrison did field work at the fifth Intercontinental Youth Camp, where he interviewed twenty-three people, including eleven organizers. Those interviewed are identified by name in the text.

12. The MST (Brazil's Landless Workers Movement or Movimento dos Trabalhadores Rurais Sem Terra) officially began as a national movement struggling for land reform in Brazil early in 1984. The MST has supported the livelihood-based struggles of peasants and small-scale farming families, including through large-scale land occupations (see Morrison 2006).

13. To date, there is no academic literature and very limited information on the Campement Québécois de la Jeunesse. This section relies on internal organization documents and interviews with Colin Perreault (March 6, 2006), Eugénie Pelletier (June 13, 2006), and Andrea Browning (June 6, 2006).

14. There are further important gender and race dimensions of the mass mobilizations that we do not have the space to explore here. See Wong 2001; Parrish 2001; Lamble 2001; Hwang 2001; Hewitt-White 2001a, 2001b; and Starhawk 2002.

Chapter 10

"WAYS OF DOING SOMETHING"
The Social Relations of Technology and Work

Krista Scott-Dixon

Technology and work are intimately connected. Both are forces, institutions, practices, and processes that are in some way central to most people's lives. Both work and technology are socially organized. They shape and are shaped by existing and emergent social, political, and economic forces, as well as by relations of power and inequality. All work, paid or unpaid, skilled or rudimentary, has been altered to some degree by technology. Work typically requires the completion of some task, and participation in some process; technology provides the means to do so.

Technology's role in work, though, is rarely accidental or simply a matter of executing a particular function. Rather, it reflects human needs and values, such as speed, greater employee control, or precision. Thus, human interests determine both the "problem" and the "solution." Technology and work can also resist control and regimentation: technological tools and labour processes can be sabotaged, slowed down, or stopped, and pre-empted for other purposes (such as union organizing via phones and the Internet). Technology's implementation in a workplace can be contradictory, with unintended consequences and opportunities for both workers and employers to exert control, to expand their creativity and autonomy, to gain or lose flexibility and autonomy. The same technology can be applied for different reasons or used in disparate ways.

This chapter explores work and tech-

"You Should Know This"
- Some 77 percent of Canadians between the ages of fifteen and sixty-four are part of the paid labour force.
- Among people between twenty-five and forty-four, 92 percent of men and 82 percent of women are in the paid labour force.
- About 90 percent of Canadians reported in 2001 that they engaged in some form of unpaid work.
- In the year 2000, women made up only 15 percent of all university graduates in the engineering and applied sciences field, and only 10 percent in applied science technologies and trades.
- In 2001, more than 91 percent of Canadian homes had a VCR; more than 48 percent had cell phones.
- In 2005, 61 percent of Canadian households were connected to the Internet. Some 68 percent of adult Canadians surfed the Internet for personal non-business reasons, mostly to read news or sports, or to bank online.
- Internet use is affected by income, education, age, and having children in the household. Canadians who were richer, more educated, younger, and/or who had children were more likely to use the Internet. There was no clear difference between men and women.
- Some 4 percent of total Canadian employment in 2001 was in the information and communications technology sector. The sector contributed 6 percent to Canada's Gross Domestic Product.

Sources: Statistics Canada 2006e; Statistics Canada 2003.

nology as social practices, structures, and
processes that intersect with one another
as well as relations of power and inequality.
Although I refer mostly to Canadian trends,

> All work, paid or unpaid, skilled or
> rudimentary, has been altered to some
> degree by technology.

it is essential to think about work and technology as part of global, interconnected practices. To understand people's work with and in technology, we need to understand how their positions within these social structures shape their experiences.

WORK

Work is an activity that fundamentally shapes human experiences and personal and political consciousness, as well as an activity that is organized around occupational and social identities (such as gender, race-ethnicity, and class), structures (such as the labour market), and institutions (such as unions). Work has individual dimensions, such as a worker's unique experience or choice to engage in particular pursuits; but work also occurs within a broader context of global shifts in labour patterns, social norms, and economic and political forces.

In Canada, nearly every adult does some form of work. About 77 percent of Canadians between the ages of fifteen and sixty-four are part of the paid labour force.[1] Among people between twenty-five and forty-four, this number rises to 92 percent of men and 82 percent of women. Canadians work in hundreds of occupations and industries, from agriculture to zookeeping. About 90 percent of Canadians reported in 2001 that they also engaged in some form of unpaid work, such as housework or child care and other forms of caregiving.[2] Work thus forms a central part of most people's lives.

Although some form of labour is a human constant, the nature of work in Canada has changed significantly over the last several decades. Originally built on fur, fish, and forests, Canada's economy now depends heavily on services. Enabled by worldwide networks of transportation and communication, both capital and the global workforce are more mobile (virtually or physically) than ever before. For many groups of workers, employment is becoming increasingly unstable and precarious, with relatively lower wages in jobs that are less secure, offer fewer benefits and worker protections, and carry higher risks to workers' health (Vosko 2006). Secure full-time employment is declining in favour of temporary, contract, and part-time jobs along with solo or "own account" self-employment.[3] This phenomenon depends on social relations such as gender, race-ethnicity, immigrant status, and age. For example, more men than women continue to hold full-time permanent jobs; women's income in solo self-employment is among the lowest; women make up about 85 percent of part-time workers and the majority of casual temporary workers; and young people are less likely to find secure, well-paying jobs (Vosko 2006).[4] Union coverage, one of the best sources of worker protections, is declining: in 1984, about 42 percent of Canadian workers were covered by a union, dropping to about 32 percent by 2002 (Jackson and Schetagne 2003). While highly skilled immigrant workers make up an increasing proportion of the Canadian work-force, their wages are lower and job prospects poorer. Workers who arrived in Canada from the mid-1990s or so went on to earn about 75 percent of the workforce average.[5] So-called "visible minorities" earned between 86 and 72 percent.[6]

Along with changes to work as a whole, so-called "knowledge work" has emerged in the last several decades. Definitions of knowledge work vary, but it is generally agreed that it involves some significant interaction with information and communications technologies (ICTs). Indeed, today many more Canadians are likely to earn a living manipulating symbols, machines, and ideas than manipulating raw materials. In the past ten to fifteen years, a number of new occupations and fields of work have appeared, such as web designers and e-commerce developers, and old jobs are continually being redefined.

Since the mid-1970s, two other processes have shaped changes in technologically based work. The first is economic restructuring, often accompanied by privatization. In Canada, for example, public services and public infrastructure have been eroded in many areas (Armstrong and Armstrong 2001) and replaced by private, generally for-profit ownership and management. This process is both material and ideological (Noble 1995). In other words, technology serves both as a practical means or tool by which to achieve goals of privatization and restructuring, and as a justification for these goals. For example, in the last decade in Ontario, online "telehealth" services were introduced as a way of defraying demand on the health-care system at the same time as health-care services, such as home care, were cut (Browne 2000). As the state provides fewer and fewer services such as health care, individuals are required to perform a greater number of tasks, many of them facilitated by technology, such as phoning a telehealth line, or searching on the Internet for health-care information. "Digital restructuring," therefore, rather than offering new opportunities for many workers, has accompanied, enabled, and often justified state restructuring of public services and infrastructure, perpetuating existing inequalities (Crow and Longford 2000; Longford and Crow 2003). The aim is to create a "culture of compliance" that accepts the deployment of particular technologies as natural and inevitable, without critically examining who benefits from technological change (Franklin 1999).

The second process relates to the emergence, inflation, and subsequent downturn of a technologically based "new economy" centred on the production and use of ICTs. Ideas about this "new economy" were based on a number of assumptions: that technological change was inevitable, value-neutral, and necessary; that the "new economy" represented a major break from the old, and that wealth would be abundant and easily produced through the suitable application of technologies; and that information, skills, and knowledge could be a new form of capital and currency (Millar 1998). These assumptions obscure persistent inequalities in the ICT labour market (Menzies 1997) as well as the growth of precarious employment and the "new" norms of long hours, stock options in lieu of salaries and benefits, and temporary employment in ICT professional and paraprofessional work (Scott-Dixon 2004). Despite the dramatic downturn in fortunes in the late 1990s and early 2000s, including accounting scandals at ICT companies and massive layoffs, the ideologies of the "new economy" continue to inform the way in which ICT work is understood by the public as well as by policy-makers (Scott-Dixon 2004).

TECHNOLOGY

What is technology? We are used to thinking of technology as including only objects, machines, or tools that enable human beings to solve particular problems. We are also used to thinking of some of these things, such as fighter jets or satellites, as "hard technology" or "high-tech." Other things, such as blenders or telephones, we might consider "appliances" or "soft technology." The difference between these things is not necessarily in their complexity or their components, but in their context, use, and implied users. The more a given object is associated with pure or applied science, the more likely it is to be considered "technical," and thereby associated with so-called men's work (Berner 1997). Conversely, the more a given object is associated with daily life and/or the household, the less likely it is to be considered "technical," and the more likely it is to be associated with so-called women's work (Leonard 2003). The same objects may take on different meanings and cultural characteristics through their history. For example, during the first few decades of the twentieth century, the radio was transformed from a masculine-oriented hobby item that technically minded men would tinker with in their workshops to a familiar living-room object around which the family would gather (Carlat 1998). This shift required advertisers to promote a new use for the radio, cultural ideas about radio technology to change, and consumers to alter their behaviour. A hundred years ago, radio was the exclusive province of scientific and military users; now radio is a fixture of daily domestic life.

In addition, each technological item has its own unique character: a tractor is different in its conception and use from a photocopier. We should think, then, about "technologies" in the same way we think about work: rather than assuming that technology is all the same, we must also look at the diversity of technology and how it is experienced in different ways.

Other assumptions about technological objects circulate in our culture: first, that technology alone (rather than people) causes social change; second, that technological change is generally positive for everyone; and third, that technological objects are "objective" and neutral tools that are developed outside of political and social concerns (Leonard 2003). Technological objects are linked to "progress"; progress is assumed to be inevitable, and indeed, it is often assumed that technology *itself* equals progress (Leonard 2003). That is, society's development can be measured by how much technology (and what kind) is present. We feel that technology is what brings us "into the future."

Clearly, technology is more than just objects or tools. Technology is also a series of *processes* and *practices* that are embedded in and organized by social, material, and ideological relations of power and privilege. This is what Ursula Franklin (1999) calls "ways of doing something," or what Eileen Leonard (2003) calls "practical know-how." How technologies are used, for what purpose, by whom, and how the users view themselves (as well as how they are viewed by others) are as important for understanding technology as the objects themselves. Technologies themselves don't determine their own use. Rather, people and ideas shape how technologies are created and experienced by various users. For example, the introduction of computers in a workplace can mean that workers will lose their jobs and/or find their skills downgraded. Or it could mean that workers will find their jobs enhanced. The computers are the same; what shapes their use is the intent of the employer and the culture of the workplace. Looking at relationships of power and privilege can help explain why certain technologies and not others are developed, how they are implemented and used (often in contradictory ways), and by whom.

SKILL, KNOWLEDGE, AND CREDENTIALS

In the opening scene of Monty Python's comedic film *The Meaning of Life* (1983), a woman in labour is wheeled into a hospital delivery room. Attendants bring in all kinds of impressive-looking machinery, which temporarily obscure the mother, until one of the nurses locates her hidden behind a monitor. The hospital administrator visits, and the equipment is fired up, with the proud announcement that the "machine that goes *bing*" is the most expensive piece of machinery in the hospital. The administrator inquires about what procedure is taking place.

"It's a birth," responds one of the obstetricians.

"Wonderful what you can do nowadays," the administrator enthuses. Understandably in some distress, the mother asks the obstetrician, "What do I do?" He replies, "Nothing, dear. You're not qualified."

As this satirical example illustrates, skill is socially constructed. In other words, who is viewed as having skills and "expertise," what skills are valued, and who has access to acquiring new skills depend on social relations. In the (admittedly tongue-in-cheek) Monty Python example, the two male doctors are perceived as skilled by virtue of medical credentials, surgical uniforms, and pricey machinery, even if they are apparently not certain as to what any of the machines actually do. The administrator is proud of his technology acquisition and appears to believe that "birth" is a new medical development. Finally, the woman who is in labour is not seen as having any skill at all. The scene closes with the newborn baby being quickly encased in another mechanical contraption. All the medical personnel depart, leaving the bewildered mother alone in the room with the machine that goes *bing*.

Like commodities or currencies that have no inherent value until they are given meaning within a market system, both workplace and technical skills are evaluated through a contextual web of systemic dynamics of power and privilege. Which skills are considered valuable can change depending on scarcity as well as who possesses them. For instance, in studies testing people's perception of scientists, respondents across a range of contexts imagine a "stereotypical scientist" as a white, middle-aged male who is intelligent but a socially awkward loner, who wears a lab coat and glasses, and who prefers to work alone with data rather than with people (Parsons 1998). Responses are similar when people are asked to imagine technological professionals. Technical skills, sometimes known as "hard skills," are usually seen as the opposite of people skills, which are often known as "soft skills." "Hard skills" associated with "expert knowledge" are typically viewed as masculine and associated with men's work, and tend to be given a higher value. Conversely, "soft skills" associated with women's work often fall into two categories: they are seen as "natural" extensions of women's abilities (for example, we assume that caregiving is a "natural" feminine skill); or they are not given much value (for example, although "soft skills" of interpersonal interaction and communication are critical to many jobs, including technical jobs, they are not always judged to be as important as academic degrees or knowing certain forms of software).

Technical skill and expertise are associated with certain types of affluent, Northern, educated masculinity — though not all men. Things that are associated with masculinity tend to have a greater value in our culture, and technological skills are no exception to this. Patterns that shape social inequalities in workplaces shape our understanding of what constitutes valuable skills. These patterns also shape how a wide variety of technologies are created, implemented, and used. For example, as Lisa Saugeres' (2002) work on farmers illustrates, hierarchies of value and gendered divisions of labour within farming households result in even tractors being assigned traditionally "masculine" characteristics, such as physical strength and power; in her study, women were typically restricted to "menial" and "non-mechanical" tasks, and actively discouraged from tractor use.

Ursula Franklin's (1999) idea of technology as "ways of doing something" provides a useful way of thinking about how technology is organized by social relations and how technology operates within workplaces. Technological practice often involves the formation of a *knowledge community*, or a group of people who are seen to be appropriate designers, creators, and users of certain technologies, as well as "experts." Knowledge communities share knowledge among themselves and may control and/or restrict outsiders' access to it. Access to privileged forms of technological knowledge, such as engineering and computer science, has historically been restricted to groups with social and economic status. For instance, women were not even permitted to attend many technical and scientific universities until the early twentieth century. Even in the year 2000, only 15 percent of all university graduates in the engineering and applied sciences field, and only 10 percent in the applied science technologies and trades, were female (Statistics Canada 2001a). The field remains male-dominated, and in its social and educational organization, and professional technological work, it often functions as a closed group that restricts access (Margolis and Fisher 2001).

Traditionally male-dominated technical fields such as engineering have often defined themselves as knowledge communities not only in terms of *who* does the work, but *how*. Hardship and arduous forms of work have typically been central to male workers' understanding of their labour process as well as their occupational and gender identities (Johnston and McIvor 2004; Evetts 1994), even though many traditionally female professions such as sex work, factory work, and care work can also be difficult, dirty, and dangerous.[7] Historically, a defining feature of technical masculinity was a gruelling work regime that was physically and intellectually demanding (Berner and Mellström 1997). This regime was intended to exclude not only women (whose access to public spaces was traditionally restricted), but also working-class and non-white men who could not measure up, either ideologically or practically, to its rigorous norm. Professional male workers sought to distance themselves from men of the working class (who were viewed as emasculated because of their subordinate relationship to capital), and increasing numbers of female office workers, even as the organization of their work was growing more similar.

Thus, forms of technology and technological knowledge that are socially valued continue to be associated with men and masculinity, particularly highly educated and affluent men in the global North. Despite some value given to craft workers' skill, women and working-class men have traditionally been viewed as "just" users, rather than creators or designers, of technology (for example, in the factory or household). Technology is "imposed" on these marginalized groups either by companies looking to expand their consumer base, or by employers looking to control workers (Noble 1995; Schenk and Anderson 1995). While marginalized groups may possess other forms of technological knowledge, such as indigenous craft practices, because of the group's lower social status, this knowledge is often discounted.

> Forms of technology and technological knowledge that are socially valued continue to be associated with men and masculinity, particularly highly educated and affluent men in the global North.

A "technocentric" (as opposed to humancentric) view of knowledge assumes that all knowledge can be quantified and stored in a machine; that there is little difference between information (what Franklin calls "knowing that") and skill (what she calls "knowing how"); and that knowledgeable people are only needed in the production process to "fill the gaps" that workplace automation cannot yet address (Chapin 1995). This view effectively separates workers from their knowledge and views them as units that are interchangeable not only with each other, but also with machinery. Still, this process is not uniformly distributed throughout the workplace. Some workers' knowledge and skills may be perceived as being more easily automated than others' knowledge and skills. What this looks like in practice depends on social relations of power and privilege — workplaces and labour markets are still profoundly differentiated and stratified by social relations of inequality, and this affects *who* develops work-related technologies, *what* these technologies are, and *why* and *how* they are developed. For example, why are people with

> Workplaces and labour markets are still profoundly differentiated and stratified by social relations of inequality, and this affects who develops work-related technologies, what these technologies are, and why and how they are developed.

disabilities still underrepresented in the labour market despite assistive technological tools such as telework and screen readers? Why do technologies of worker surveillance and monitoring continue to be a major area of development, and in this regard, which workers are most closely monitored?

DIVISIONS OF LABOUR

The persistence of work inequality is particularly interesting given the promise of technologically facilitated work. Today, very few jobs are limited by requirements for physical strength. Technology enables people to perform work with the assistance of machinery, which decreases the need for the human body to shoulder the loads. Yet notions of "men's work" and "women's work" persist. For instance, in her study of electronics manufacturing in Mexico, Leslie Salzinger (2003) observes rigid gender differences based on such notions. In one particular factory, she notes that men and women perform separate tasks in electronics assembly, and are differentiated by elements such as where they are placed physically (men stand at the end of the assembly line; women sit along the line); their uniform types; and how management deals with them. If male workers in this factory step out of line, they are "punished" by demotion to the women's work area. Work designated as "detail" work, such as inserting electronic components, is assigned to women, and work designated as "heavy" is assigned to men, regardless of what *actual* abilities such work might involve, and regardless of how, prior to labour shortages in the 1980s, all of the jobs, heavy or not, were done by women. Divisions such as gender shape occupational status as well as how workers are positioned (often literally) in relation to workplace technologies.

With the availability of female workers, who can be paid lower wages than male workers, many previously male-dominated jobs, such as clerical work, have become sex-typed as female. In the late nineteenth century, nearly all clerks and secretaries were men (Huws 2003). By the mid-twentieth century most clerical work was done by women and considered to be "women's work." When innovations in office technology such as the adding machine began to be more widespread in the 1950s and 1960s, there was some debate about whether they were properly masculine (because of their computing power) or feminine (because they routinized work). But such technologies eventually aligned themselves with notions of women's work, and the innovations were generally intended to make the work more routine rather than more creative (van Oost 1998). Employers began to feel that women's "intrinsic qualities," such as "nimble fingers," interpersonal skills, and tolerance for tedium, made them ideally suited to work with this office technology in these clerical jobs (although interestingly, women's nimble fingers did not especially qualify them to become surgeons, nor did their interpersonal skills qualify them to become politicians). Thus particular stereotypical characteristics of gender became associated with particular occupations and tasks (and vice versa).

This example of office technologies demonstrates the shifting meanings attached to technologies, unlike other approaches that see technology as neutral, eternal, and universal in its meaning. The implementation of workplace technologies shapes and is shaped by labour force inequalities and divisions. The meaning of office technologies shifted as the gender makeup of offices shifted, and there was often debate about how best to understand the technologies — a debate framed in terms of gender and occupational status. Thus ideologies and practices of technology and the workplace reinforce one another; they change over time, and with social, political, and economic forces.

TECHNOLOGY AND UNPAID WORK

Some people imagined that household technologies might alleviate women's unequal burden of unpaid domestic work, and reduce much of the dirt and drudgery. However, contrary to what many women anticipated (and appliance companies promised), household technologies did not really decrease the amount of time that women spent on household tasks. They merely increased expectations of the speed and quality of the work. For instance, tasks that might be done twice yearly (such as large-scale cleaning) could now be done weekly or daily. Instead of just removing visible dirt, surfaces could be disinfected. Meals could be more elaborate. Standards for cleanliness, food production, and so forth thus rapidly increased, as did expectations of the pace and frequency of household work.

The development of household technologies in the twentieth century was largely intended to produce a consumer base for electricity and goods consumption. Which technologies were produced, and how they were intended to be used, reflected prevailing social attitudes about how work was to be done in the home. As Judy Wajcman (2004: 28) notes, household technologies "reflect the sexual division of domestic activities and the social organization of the family."

Another assumption about household technologies is that they would "simplify" work. Electricity in the early twentieth century was linked to progress and cultural modernity. As such, its management and promotion were largely a male preserve. Yet the home was a female sphere, and thus attempts to place electricity within the home had to combine both notions of progress and efficiency as well as domestic comfort. Managing a household in the pre-industrial or early industrial eras required a large foundation of knowledge and skill. To encourage women working in households to consume new domestic technologies, manufacturers had to persuade them not only that their homemaking skills were outdated, but also that the technologies would improve their daily lives. Although technological skill was generally regarded as the bastion of men, promoters of domestic technology tried hard to show that domestic technology required little skill to operate (or, if it did require skill, these skills were not valued as real technical expertise). For instance, instead of finicky wood stoves that required loading, lighting, stoking, and monitoring to ensure correct temperature, electric or gas stoves were advertised as providing perfect conditions with the mere touch of a button. Manufacturers assumed that although women did not possess technical proficiency, they were "compliant, pliable, and willing to learn to use any new domestic appliance" (Williams 1998: 103).

Women did not always respond positively to these messages, and refused to purchase items that male engineers designed without understanding how work was actually done. For example, male engineers at the Southern California Edison Company in 1915 assumed that it would be more efficient if all cooking was actually done at the table, "saving many steps to and from the kitchen" (quoted in Williams 1998: 103). This assumption proved incorrect, because women preferred to keep the smell and mess of cooking separate from the eating area. Once the electrical and household technology industries realized that no amount of scientific management principles would work unless they incorporated the needs of housewives into their creations, they were much more successful.

The effect of this was that despite the hours of work remaining the same, many household management and production skills were lost, and housework became deskilled. Few of us now know how to produce our own food or make our own clothing from start to finish. A woman in the mid-twentieth century might describe her occupation as "just a housewife."

Another type of unpaid work facilitated by technology has been called "shadow work," although it might also be termed "self-serve consumerism" (Menzies 1997; see also Illich 1981). For example, people are now able to shop and bank online, check out their own groceries, and pump their own gas while paying for it with a swipe of their credit cards. Although these features appear to enhance consumer choice, shadow work may limit choice and promote Franklin's "culture of compliance." For example, when calling automated helplines for assistance in everything from insurance claims to telephone banking to technical assistance for home computers, callers may have to sit through an array of menus with options that do not match their concerns. Interestingly, shadow work is often promoted as increasing consumer or leisure choice — which obscures the element of unpaid shadow work, as well as its role in perpetuating technological consumption. Shadow work not only replaces paid with unpaid work, but reproduces a cycle of dependency on digital products, such as computers that are needed to perform online transactions because a bank teller is no longer available. It also has a dual relationship to skill: it increases the skill demand on the user (for instance, people need to be computer-literate to bank online) but simultaneously decreases the skill demand on service providers, often reducing them to "user babysitters," or eliminates the service provision job entirely.

UPSKILLING AND DOWNSKILLING

A central debate about technology and work (among theorists of work as well as workers themselves) is whether technology "upskills," increasing the challenge and expertise level of a job, or "downskills" (or "deskills"), rendering the job more routinized and rote.

One group of theorists in favour of the "upskilling" hypothesis believed that technology would enhance creativity and worker autonomy, as well as "improve the quality of work, reducing drudgery and promoting more integrated work processes" (Wajcman 2004: 24; Toffler 1980). With dirty, dangerous, and tedious tasks performed by machines, workers would be free of menial toil, which would result in both more interesting paid work and more leisure time.

Technology would also provide opportunities for interesting new forms of work. Emergent forms of technological work often combine "technical" and "non-technical" elements, or they may be offshoots of industries and occupations not previously considered to be technologically based. For example, software and video-game production now includes computer artists, animators, and writers along with coders and developers. Labour processes in the "new" economy demonstrate increasing boundary-crossing in their task and skill demands at the same time as calling for new industrial and occupational classification. Technology enables workers to synthesize apparently unrelated occupational demands and, as a result, to create new occupations (Scott-Dixon 2004).

A second group of theorists and workers was hesitant to embrace technology as an intellectually liberating force for workers. This group argued that workplace technologies were largely intended to fragment labour processes into tiny, easily managed, and controlled pieces, removing craft knowledge from the worker's repertoire and subjecting the worker to greater monitoring (Braverman 1974; Franklin 1999; Menzies 1996). They referred to this process as "downskilling." In addition to changes in the content of tasks and skills, theorists also pointed to workers' decreased autonomy and control. Technological innovations increase the capacity for employers to monitor workers at the workplace, which often transfers control of the labour process from the employee to the employer in conjunction with the technologies used.

Although the goods-producing industrial sector also focuses on worker surveillance, the service sector has been particularly receptive to technologically based worker monitoring. For example, many fast-food restaurants monitor the speed at which food is prepared and delivered. Reminders may pop up on cash-register displays ensuring that workers ask customers whether they want to use their discount card or increase the size of their fast-food meal. At a donut store near my office, workers prepare food under the watchful eye of an enormous computer monitor that indicates the exact time that workers should spend buttering bagels and provides an ominous countdown. Although it is hard to quantify service work in the same way as manufacturing work, because service work involves many things that are intangible and unexpected, employers nevertheless attempt to do so through technology in order to monitor workers and standardize the service process (McLaughlin 1999; Bain and Taylor 2000).

When I worked as a cashier as a teenager in the 1980s, many smaller supermarkets had not yet installed automatic bar-code scanners. Cashiers inputted prices into the cash register by hand, using a basic numeric keypad. To move a line of customers through smoothly, a cashier needed to be fast and accurate in her typing and have a wide-ranging memory for price idiosyncrasies, products that were inevitably not marked with price tags, weekly specials, and the like. Eventually, most cashiers had an intuitive grasp of the prices (and their fluctuations) of just about every item in the store, even the most obscure products. Beyond having to balance our till so that the register's account of the day's sales matched the amount of money in the cash drawer, and having to watch out for the occasional manager's stroll past our stations, we found that our work was not monitored much. Now, twenty years later, workers in retail rarely have to know the price of anything: they either scan it or simply hunt for the button marked with the product's name on the cash register. To complete a sale they swipe cards or type in elaborate passwords. If they work for Holt Renfrew, they now put in their fingerprint. I often think back to my cashier days when I stand in front of a clerk who reacts with great puzzlement when I attempt to buy an item not "on the list," or who spends minutes painstakingly searching for the name of what I am purchasing. Skills have changed, and workers are now trained to use elaborate technological processes, but it is not yet apparent that this has increased job mastery.

Thus, the effect of technology on skill is ambivalent. Indeed, the relationship between technology and skill is complex, and depends heavily on underlying social relations of power and privilege. Workers may learn a new skill, such as a software package or machine, but their job status may not increase as a result. Rather, this new skill simply becomes incorporated into their existing work. Whether the skill is seen as "technical" depends on the pre-existing nature of the job. Jobs that are already considered lower-status work are rarely given a higher status by virtue of the worker having acquired more skills; rather, the skills are simply absorbed into the way the job is already understood. For example, clerical office workers are now responsible for a wide array of computer skills, and yet their jobs are not seen as technical. While the skills may change, the job status may not.

Ursula Franklin (1999) argues that technology is developed in two ways: work-related technologies, which enable the actual practice of completing a task; and control-related technologies, which are geared towards increasing control over the operation. She also identifies two forms of technological development that are derived from the relationship of the maker/user to the technology: holistic technologies, which allow the creator/user to be in control of the process of making/doing; and prescriptive technologies, which confine each user to a particular function in the process of making/using technology. An example of a holistic technology is a power tool that has multiple uses, such as a drill with many attachments ranging from drill bit to power sander (or, in the case of a handy relative of mine, an eggbeater attachment when the blender broke down) and allows users to build anything they like. An example of a prescriptive technology is an assembly machine that only performs a single function as part of a larger process of manufacturing.

When work becomes broken down into a linear progression of codified steps, control of the work shifts from individual creators to a central organizer. The shift of control from creator to overseer ensures that the workforce is both interchangeable and compliant, and that technological practices become codified and static. Prescriptive forms of technological practice have some distinct advantages. For example, they yield predictably quantifiable results. However, according to Franklin, they also "eliminate the occasions for decision-making and judgement in general and especially for the making of principled decisions. Any goal of the technology is incorporated a priori into the design and is not negotiable." Thus, as Franklin proposes, "technology itself becomes an agent of ordering and structuring," which "has now moved from ordering at work and the ordering of work, to the *prescriptive ordering of people* in a wide variety of social situations" (Franklin 1999: 25; emphasis added).

Technology's implementation in the workplace, and consequently how skills change and are evaluated, varies according to employer interests. For example, in auto manu-facturing in the 1980s, employers believed that large automated machines provided the best competitive advantage in production; by the mid-1990s, "lean production" emphasized the reorganization of labour, and low-cost technology strategies sought to implement machinery that was cheaper, lighter, more flexible, and more mobile (Roberts 1995). While enhanced production and "competitiveness" were cited as key objectives, the system also entailed increased employer control over workers, especially skilled tradespeople, as well as an intensifica-tion and speed-up of work (Roberts 1995). Whether technology changes the skill level of jobs, and how it changes it, is not always clear or straightforward. Technologies often have

> Technology's implementation in the workplace, and consequently how skills change and are evaluated, varies according to employer interests.

unintended effects, or different effects on different groups of workers. For instance, in the construction industry, the introduction of automated processes such as the prefabrication of building components has resulted in the elimination of many skilled construction trades jobs (Sobel 1995). Conversely, according to David Sobel (1995: 53), labourers, "once the work horses of the construction industry, have absorbed growing areas of construction work which have lost their 'craft' status, partly as a result of the technological change."

The social value attached to technologically based work is intimately connected to ideologies about the acquisition of knowledge and skill, and how these processes intersect with social location and social context. Interestingly, unlike many professions, IT employers often privilege youth in assessing skill level. Older workers, who might enjoy a premium linked to experience and seniority in other sectors, are often viewed as not "cutting edge" enough, or not able to assimilate rapidly changing skill demands (Scott-Dixon 2004). Thus, technology skill alone does not tend to change the fun-damental character of work that is already structured along lines of gender and other social inequalities. Additionally, gender, class, occupational status, and other divisions of labour shape how technology will be experienced, and whether it will be a deskilling or upskilling force.

WORKING TIME

Many types of technologies, particularly ICTs, have enabled us to change our notions and practices of working time (Franklin 1999). Technology has altered the arrangements and boundaries between paid and unpaid work as well as leisure time (Bryce 2001). ICTs enable work to be done asynchronously, constantly, rapidly, under close surveillance, and in a regimented fashion. ICTs have increased the possibilities for non-standard working time, and the demands for speed and pace of work, as well as employee availability through electronic devices. It has the potential to expand and contract employment and leisure time through telework. For example, a worker may save time commuting or set his or her own hours, but may also be expected to do work at any time of the day. As with skill, analysts of technology and work typically suggested that one of two things would occur when technology was introduced into a workplace: first, that the technology would give employers greater control over worker time (Zuboff 1988); or second, that the technology would provide workers with more opportunities for autonomy, creativity, and leisure (Toffler 1980). Both of these scenarios now appear to co-exist, and the relationship is more complex than such a simple binary would imply.

There is no doubt that the majority of employed Canadians experience time stress as a result of their paid and unpaid work (Statistics Canada 1998a). However, much of the earlier research on the role of technology assigned technology a greater responsibility for work-time changes than it deserved. Technologies alone cannot accomplish effects on work time and work arrangements without the aid of human intervention. Changes in working time serve primarily social and economic, rather than technological, objectives. Although technological innovations increase what *can* be done, it is employment practices and employer expectations that dictate what *should* be done. Thus, as with skill, rather than the technology it is the expectations and cultures of workplaces, along with labour market trends, that shape norms of working time.

With industrialization and mechanization of labour processes in capitalist economies, working time ceased to be organized around the completion of craft or tasks, or the agricultural seasons, and began to be framed by the precise meter of the clock. Once work is broken into prescriptive chunks, it can also be monitored and measured (Franklin 1999). In practice, this has also meant increasing the speed at which work is performed. New information technologies such as the Internet and the home PC enabled working time to expand past the physical and temporal boundaries of the employer's work site. Speaking of this "diffusion" of technological work that has "abandoned the factory," Nick Dyer-Witheford (1999: 80) notes, "Wage labour is deconcentrated, spatially and temporally dispersed throughout society, and interleaved[8] with unpaid time in new and irregular rhythms."

Although all forms of work have been in some way altered by the introduction of technology, occupational structure also plays a role in the organization of working time. Some industries are characterized by highly regimented schedules where the pace of work is organized around set, often regular, shifts and the pace of the assembly line. However, in manufacturing, working time may also be determined by a "project time" consisting of cycles of intensification and escalation combined with shifts in the task demand as workers develop a product to be released. For instance, in video-game production, workers such as artists and software developers may experience increasingly urgent demands on their time as a game nears its publication deadline, and may be expected to participate in a "crunch time" work regimen that eventually resembles all-out panic as the company scrambles to get the product out.

Other industries, such as service industries, are often characterized by more flexible time frameworks and precarious work practices such as part-time, temporary, on-call, and other contingent work arrangements. Service work also tends to resist the strictly controlled time and task structure of manufacturing work; it is harder to organize care and service work into prescriptive types of tasks. The time of salaried professional and managerial occupations is typically more expansive than that of other occupations, such as blue-collar occupations, where there is a close link between time and value, as exemplified by the hourly wage (Kalleberg and Epstein 2001). However, a small proportion of technical professionals are now likely to work as contractors, and as a result, they organize their work habits around the exchange of time for money (Evans, Kunda, and Barley 2004; Kunda, Barley, and Evans 2002).

Thus, not only can hours of work expand, but they can also become denser, more irregular, more contingent, and more demanding. Technology not only enables work to be done over a longer period of time and enables the intensification and speed-up of work, but also requires a desire to do so. Chronologies of work are technologically restructured in conjunction with norms of economic production that favour work speed-up and intensity. Where the rhythms of the assembly line cannot dictate worker behaviour, as in the case of post-industrial professional work, pressure to conform to an ideal of working time tends to be expressed in the form of group and managerial coercion (Evans, Kunda, and Barley 2004). In short, the technology enables work to be done; workplace practices dictate that it *should* be done. The technology makes it possible; workplace practices make it normal and desirable.

In practice, what this has meant is that along with the application of information technologies, working time also sits at the intersection of shifts in economic production, gender norms of paid and unpaid labour responsibilities, the emergence of post-industrial types of jobs, and occupation types and status. Although ICTs offer great potential for work flexibility and individualization of work schedules based on need, this promise has failed to materialize for workers.

DOES TECHNOLOGY CHANGE WORK OR WORK CHANGE TECHNOLOGY?

Work in Canada is changing. It is growing more precarious, with greater numbers of jobs characterized by insecurity, instability, irregular work hours, low pay, few benefits, and higher risks to worker health (Vosko 2006). Many theorists predicted similar negative consequences for the nature of work with the introduction of technology. For example, David Noble (1995: xi) writes, "In the wake of five decades of information revolution, people are now working longer hours, under worsening conditions, with greater anxiety and stress, less skills, less security, less power, less benefits, and less pay." Noble also suggests that the purpose of information technology is to "deskill, discipline, and displace human labour in a global speed-up of unprecedented proportions." In this he echoes Christopher Schenk and John Anderson (1995: 15), who write that the implementation of workplace technologies results in job loss, "social isolation" as workers "are pushed back into the home," the elimination of collective representation, and generally "devastating" effects on workers.

But is the technology alone responsible for such changes? Much analysis has concerned itself with the "effects" of technology, and has often implied that technologies themselves were responsible for large-scale social and political changes. As Daniel Miller (2003: 9) writes, schoolchildren in the United Kingdom were typically taught that "new technologies caused the industrial revolution and that in turn caused capitalism, under which people became subject to the determinants of commerce and capital as in effect commodified wage labour." It is this emphasis on the directive properties of technology, argues Miller, that contributed to losses in the dot.com crash, as investors imagined that information technologies alone would revise the basic rules of capitalist exchange.

Yet focusing solely on technology's "effects" does not consider how technology and work may be mutually constitutive. In other words, work may shape technologies as much as technologies shape work. Forms of social and economic organization in place before the introduction of a technology tend to remain in place after the technology has become embedded. As Eileen Leonard (2003: 6) points out, "Technology is typically envisioned and implemented *within* the parameters of inequality that fracture our society. In this way, it reflects and even reproduces prevailing social relations, extending rather than eradicating the inequality associated with gender, race, or class." Social, economic, and political inequalities that existed *before* the introduction of a particular technology tend to continue to exist *after* that technology has been implemented. Thus, technology's social construction is shaped by "structural and ideological constraints" (Leonard 2003: 6). For example, although household technologies (such as washing machines or microwaves) were often intended to reduce the time spent on particular tasks that were introduced throughout the twentieth century, they did not fundamentally change the idea that

> Social, economic, and political inequalities that existed before the introduction of a particular technology tend to continue to exist after that technology has been implemented.

women were responsible for doing the housework. Although such technologies changed the kinds of skills required to do the work, they did not necessarily alter the gendered way in which the work was performed, nor did they improve the value given to house-work — indeed, their effect was often to *de*skill the tasks and reduce the importance of "women's work" even further.

WORKER RESISTANCE

Although technologies are often imagined to be "imposed" on workers with little argument, workers are active agents who respond to workplace technologies. Perhaps because such actions are often more surreptitious, stories of worker resistance to technologies are heard less frequently than are stories of employer oppression. Although it may seem that there has been little concerted resistance to technology itself, history is replete with accounts of worker sabotage, machine-breaking, slowdown, and subterfuge. For instance, as Noble (1995: 7) explains, the term "Luddite," which originally referred to groups of weavers who deliberately smashed weaving machines in the early nine-teenth century, is now used to refer to those who irrationally fear or avoid technology. However, he argues, Luddites were in fact protesting the cheapening of their labour, and machine-breaking, though of great symbolic significance as an attack on capitalist notions of "progress," was only one of many strategies used. The workers, states Noble, were not against the technology itself, but rather in a historical moment of economic instability and precarious employment, "they were struggling against the efforts of capital, using technology as a vehicle, to restructure social relations and the patterns of production at their expense." More recently, white-collar workers may appear to be diligently tapping on their computer keyboards for company business when they are really sending personal emails, playing video games, looking up their labour rights, or perhaps contributing to badbossology.com (Kurtz 2000).

On an individual level, workers can resist the domination of their time and space by technology: they can choose to turn off the pager, set limits on email correspondence, and identify other ways in which they themselves collude in workplace technology's negative effects (Menzies 2005). For example, although professional workers are often in charge of setting their own hours, many find technologically-enabled workaholism an addictive lure. Other workers, finding themselves snowed under by emails and alienated by virtual work teams, have returned to good old-fashioned in-person conversations. Employers, too, can participate in setting limits on workplace technology use, and question their own assumptions that technology always makes things more efficient. For instance, recognizing the detrimental effects of overwork and time pressures, the pharmaceutical company Pfizer has established "Freedom 6 to 6," which means that employees are prohibited from sending emails between 6 p.m. and 6 a.m. on weekdays, and completely on weekends (Galt 2005).

Collectively, labour and social justice groups are finding that many technologies can be used for organizing and activism as well as they can be used for surveillance and deskilling. For instance, as Arthur Shostak writes, "Labor now understands the internet is an instrument of social revolution, one that has 'put power in different people's hands and connected people who have never been connected before'" (Shostak 2002: 4; citing Gadiesh in Friedman 2001). During the Canadian Broadcasting Corporation strike in 2005, a number of CBC picketers kept blogs that updated readers and other union members on the progress of labour negotiations, allowed an "insider look" into life on the picket line, and provided insight into worker struggles that would not otherwise have been publicly available.

> Workers who labour in technical fields such as information technology are showing renewed signs of interest in collective organization in the wake of major downturns in the industry.

Additionally, workers who labour in technical fields such as information technology are showing renewed signs of interest in collective organization in the wake of major downturns in the industry. Groups such as the Communications, Energy, and Paperworkers Union of Canada (CEP) or, in the United States, the Washington Alliance of Technology Workers (Communications Workers of America) are involved in negotiating collective agreements to guarantee decent working conditions, hours, and wages.

CONCLUSION

Those of us born in the last few decades have never known any other world than this. There have always been microwave ovens, TVs have always had remote controls, and relatively fewer daily-life tasks now involve the back-breaking manual labour of humans and animals. Because of our ease with technological objects and processes, we find it easy to become complacent about their use, and to see them as relatively benign and harmless. Yet we should always ask, as workers and as citizens: Who truly benefits from the creation and use of these technologies? In whose interests is this "way of doing things"? This is a particularly salient question in a time when parts of the world are consumed with the "war on terrorism" and intent on solving political problems with the application of technologies designed for surveillance, domination, and obliteration of opposition. It is also relevant when we realize that our work processes are increasingly fragmented, standardized, and controlled by bodies that are not necessarily concerned with improving the quality of our work but often the manageability and cheapness of our labour power. Technologies have the potential to make labour rewarding, autonomous, and creative; but this promise has yet to be kept for the majority of the world's workers.

GLOSSARY OF KEY TERMS

Luddite: Workers in nineteenth-century England who destroyed machinery as a form of protest against poor working conditions and unemployment. The term has since come to mean any opponent of technology.

ICTs: Information and communications technologies, such as computers and telecommunications equipment.

Knowledge work: Work that is primarily concerned with the manipulation of ideas and information.

Technology: Tools, processes, and a set of social relations generally aimed at solving a problem.

Upskilling: An improvement to the skill and knowledge demands of particular tasks and jobs, often enhancing opportunities for autonomy and creativity in performing the work.

Downskilling/deskilling: Work skills, aptitudes, and capacities no longer used or outdated, usually due to technological change. Can often be improved by retraining.

Knowledge community: "Ways of doing something" (Franklin 1999), that is, the social recognition of a set of skills, processes, and/or methods for accomplishing tasks. A knowledge community can have a shared language and set of rules, not only about who is included or excluded (and on what basis), but also about how things should be done.

Self-serve consumerism: The downloading of the work associated with consumption and purchasing on to the consumer, such as self-serve gas or self-checkouts. It is also sometimes called shadow work.

Technocentric: Placing technology "at the centre" of knowledge production. A technocentric view assumes that all knowledge can be quantified and stored in a machine; that there is little difference between information and skill; and that knowledgeable people are only needed in the production process to "fill the gaps" that workplace automation cannot yet address.

QUESTIONS FOR DISCUSSION

1. How is work changing in Canada? What role do you think technology plays in enabling or shaping these changes? Why?
2. What are some common ideas about the role of technology in the workplace? What assumptions inform these ideas?
3. What does it mean to say that technology is organized by social relations? Can you think of examples of how this works in practice?
4. Make a list of all the workplace technologies you can think of. Which ones are "masculine" and which ones are "feminine"? Why?

WEBSITES OF INTEREST

Association for Progressive Communications. <www.apc.org/>.

Centre for Women and Information Technology. <www.umbc.edu/cwit/>.

Center for Work, Technology and Society. <repositories.cdlib.org/iir/cwts/>.

Institute for Work and Technology. <www.iatge.de/>.

International Game Developers Organization. <www.igda.org/>.

Women in Global Science and Technology. <www.wigsat.org/>.

NOTES

1. Statistics Canada, CANSIM, table 282-0002.
2. This participation is also divided by gender. In 1998, the General Social Survey (Statistics Canada 1998a) reported that 86.8 percent of Canadian men and 95.8 percent of Canadian women were engaged in unpaid work.
3. Vosko (2006) defines solo self-employment "as an arrangement where the self-employed person has no employees"; Statistics Canada terms this "own account self-employment." See also chapter 7 here.
4. See also Jackson 2005.
5. Jackson (2005: 105), citing 2001 Census data, indicates that among immigrants who arrived after 1994, average annual employment income is 75.2 percent of the workforce's earnings as a whole.
6. Cited in Jackson 2005: 105; Canadian-born visible minorities fare worse than all visible minorities.
7. For an interesting discussion of how male-dominated white-collar work is interpreted using this "masculinist" framework, see, for example, Jones 1998.
8. "Interleaved" is a term describing a book structure in which printed pages alternate with blank pages.

Chapter 11

FAMILIES, FEMINISM, AND THE STATE
Canada in the Twenty-First Century

Susan A. McDaniel

Families are both havens from social changes and springboards of change. They are both power and resistance. Family, once thought to be no one's concern but your own, and possibly the parish priest's, continues to be a basic element in Canada's social policy agenda. Reproductive rights, child care, new legislation on reproductive technologies, Quebec's initiative to raise birthrates, tax changes for the divorced and separated, legal marriage and family rights for gay and lesbian couples, and the downloading of more care onto families through cuts to health care and social services: these are all recent family-related policy initiatives. Family as both an idea and a lived reality is changing profoundly, and yet the ideologies connected to family may be changing less rapidly, and some seem to be going backwards. The concept of family is mythologized by ideologies of what it should be, could be, or was thought to be in the past or in various religions, with every interest group having its own ideal.

There are three apparent explanations for why concerns about the family have increased, and they are interconnected. The widely acknowledged neo-liberal political agendas of many Western countries see families as the primary means by which society functions, as the basic social institution of individualism. Individual freedoms are thought to be maximized by strong families, a condition that allows the state to shrink (DeGoede 1996; McDaniel 2002). This rationale could be a motivation for the mainstream media endorsement of gay and lesbian marriage, now legal in Canada.

"You Should Know This"
- The proportion of married couples in Canada declined to 70 percent in 2001 from 84 percent in 1981.
- Common-law unions rose from 6 percent in 1981 to 14 percent of all unions in 2001.
- Some 50 percent of stepfamilies include only the woman's biological children; 10 percent have only the husband's biological children; 32 percent of stepfamilies consist of blended families; 8 percent have only children from previous unions.
- In 2002, 49.5 percent of custody disputes that went to court were awarded to the mother (down from 75.8 percent in 1988); 41.8 percent of cases were granted joint custody; in 8.5 percent, custody was awarded to the father.
- 42 percent of women and 54 percent of men move into second unions five years after a disruption to their previous relationship.
- In a 1993 national survey, 2 percent of the men surveyed had physically forced women into sexual activities, 19 percent had been emotionally abusive, and 4 percent had been physically abusive. Some 4 percent of women reported having been forced into sexual activities, 24 percent had been emotionally hurt, and 7.2 percent had been physically abused.

Sources: Department of Justice 2005; Statistics Canada 2002b, 2002c, 2004d, 2004e; Wu and Schimmele 2005.

> Neo-liberal political agendas of many Western countries see families as the primary means by which society functions, as the basic social institution of individualism.

The second explanation is the long-standing tendency to account for social problems in the manner least costly to the society. When we say that the causes of "social unrest" are found in families rather than in an economic system, government policies, or spending cuts or priorities, we not only privatize the problems that people experience but also redefine those problems as being of people's own making, rather than the doing of governments, big business, or massive historical changes (Luxton 1997; McDaniel 1992b, 1995, 1997a; Sorensen 1999). We can find parallels to this state of affairs in nineteenth-century Canada (Gaffield 1988: 29), when the "instability of the family" during urban growth and industrial development led to concern among public leaders. Out of that concern grew new ideals for women, whose centre of social worth was shifted deliberately, by policy, to home and family, to the "cult of the true womanhood." Compulsory education made school the dominant experience of growing up, and schools became a way of dealing with the "idle youth" of the time.

The third explanation is paradoxical. Feminism has made visible both the problems and the power of contemporary families (Albanese 2006; McDaniel 1996; Peters 1997; Pringle 1997) and the families of the past (McDaniel and Mitchinson 1987). In calling attention to child poverty, family violence, inequalities in families,

> Feminism has made visible both the problems and the power of contemporary families and the families of the past.

pensions for homemakers, and the caregiving crunch that many women experience as their relatives get older (McDaniel 1992a; McDaniel and Tepperman 2006; Walker 1991), and in saying that all is not well with the family, the women's movement has called for a pact between families and the state (Baker 2005; Brodie 2001; Pringle 1997). The change that feminists envision is profoundly different from that espoused by many politicians, particularly neo-liberal politicians such as Stephen Harper and many others in the federal Conservative Party.

SOCIAL SCIENCE, SOCIAL PROBLEMS, AND FAMILY POLICY

Sociologists and policy-makers do not always agree on what constitutes a problem in or for society. When advising policy-makers on issues of public importance, sociologists tend to ask whether a specific problem is, in fact, a problem for society and, if it is, for whom is it a problem. Given the shrinking governments of the past few decades, government actions — in sharp deficit-reduction, for example — and inaction in poverty reduction, particularly in the sphere of children and Aboriginal people, often leave policy-makers shrugging their shoulders about problems that they increasingly see as not theirs.

But just what is a social problem? In the broadest sense, any policy issue is problem-focused. The concept of social policy is to improve people's lives by redistributing a scarce social resource (money, power, or skills). Without a problem, argue order-based,

Keynes-influenced policy-makers, social policy is not needed (see McDaniel and Agger 1982: 7–28; and chapter 1 here). Based on these assumptions, policy-makers work towards solving what they see as problems and returning society back to "normality," which usually means the status quo. Of course, the status quo has always been detrimental to some groups, such as women, gays and lesbians, children, and the elderly (Fraser 1987; McDaniel and Tepperman 2006).

Yet policy issues are not always social problems. Take, for example, the concerns about "lone-parent families" — a misnomer from the outset, because these families are overwhelmingly headed by women (Baker 1990; Ferri 1992; Peters 1997; McDaniel 1997b). In Canada in 2001, lone-parent families headed by women outnumbered those headed by men by more than four to one (Statistics Canada 2006a). Even though there are now more male-headed lone parents, the gender imbalance has actually increased since 1996 (Statistics Canada 1997). A policy-maker might see lone parents as an economic problem, as a case of increasing numbers of women living with dependent children on social assistance or with low incomes. The "solution," then, is to get them off social assistance or out of poverty. Seen through a different lens, the problem is not the mothers but fathers who renege on child support, or courts that do not order child support (both of which cases reinforce a patriarchal, nuclear-family model), and a society that offers few child-care options to families and promotes inequities in work for women, making it difficult for women to support themselves and their families.

Sociologists most often locate the causes of social problems in the structure of social life rather than in, or with, individuals, an approach that contrasts sharply with neo-liberal political approaches. Their models of social structure are the lenses through which they see social problems and explore solutions. Despite criticisms, the perspective of *functionalism* (also known as the *sociology of order*), remains a dominant perspective in sociology (McDaniel and Tepperman 2006; Pulkingham and Ternowetsky 1997), particularly in the sociology of families (Baker 1990; Janz 2000; Mann et al. 1997; McDaniel and Tepperman 2006). Society, according to the sociology of order, operates on a consensus achieved by competing interest groups (stakeholders), working in a co-ordinated division of labour. Rewards may not be distributed equitably, so social policy becomes the means of redistribution of rewards to keep the system going, and to keep order.

Policy-makers work to reduce both the economic and ideological costs of various "dysfunctions." In functionalist terms, policy "fine-tunes" the systemic inefficiencies generated by the normal operation of an otherwise efficient socio-economic system. Under welfare state capitalism, social policy interventions aimed to address issues of inequitable health and welfare before they cast a blight on the system. In the case of family policy the purposes are no different: to bring families back to "normalcy." The "marriage movement" in the United States in the mid-2000s is an example of "solving" the problem of poor lone-mother families by having them remarry. Studies have revealed the extent to which these approaches work against the interests of women, because they aim to re-establish a "functional" family defined by structure (traditional nuclear family) rather than by how a particular family operates effectively and in the interests of all its members (Baker 2005; Duffy 1988; Fraser 1987; Janz 2000).

A contrasting sociological perspective, and one that is growing in popularity in Canada, is a power and resistance perspective (Kitchen 1981; McDaniel 1996; Pulkingham and Ternowetsky 1997). Solving social problems, according to this perspective, requires addressing the fundamental underlying structural inequities that caused the problems in the first place. This view sees social problems as being both caused by powerful groups in our society and defined, for social policy purposes, in ways that protect the privilege of those same powerful groups. In the long run society will become more equitable, and social problems less intractable, through the efforts of disadvantaged groups and their allies. Focusing only on welfare/resource redistribution schemes may make problems worse.

Rather than fixing "dysfunctional" families, for example, social programs need to remedy the factors that cause trouble in families and create disadvantage. As Anthony Giddens and Ulrich Beck argue, family must

> Families are not only acted upon by larger social forces; they are also active agents shaping social change.

be seen as a part of the wider social, cultural, political, and economic world (Luxton 2005; Smart 1997). This wider world might include a lack of adequate income (Smart 2000), discrimination against disadvantaged minorities (Boyd and McDaniel 1996; Crawley 1988; Peters 1997; Pringle 1997), sexist treatment of women, or the imposition of an outdated and unrealistic model of the family (Baker 1990; McDaniel and Tepperman 2002). Family policy, according to this perspective, could facilitate choices after basic structural inequities are eliminated or reduced (Baker 1995, 2005; McDaniel 1997b).

My writing and research have been guided by a power and resistance stance on family and family change, acknowledging that families are sites of political struggle and resistance. Families are not only acted upon by larger social forces; they are also active agents shaping social change.

FAMILY POLICY IN SOCIAL CONTEXT: WHAT IS KNOWN?

Assessing what is known is a useful place to begin thinking about the future of family policies for Canadians. Of course, any such assessment is as much a statement of what is *not* known.

Biases in Family Research

Much of what is known, and not known, about Canadian families is filtered through biases, myths, and misconceptions about what "family" is and what it should be. (See, for instance, Eichler 1997, 2005; Luxton 2005.) Much, if not most, research on the family is still done from the vantage point of men, which results in an incomplete picture of family, both as a resource and as a prison (Luxton 2005). Adding to this bias is the tendency of family research to be carried out with "traditional" families, or by assuming that non-traditional families are deficient, deviant, abnormal, or in the process of becoming traditional (Eichler 2005). Lone-parent families are seen, then, as either having just emerged from a "normal" family or being in the process of becoming "normal" again (Baker 1995, 2005; Ferri 1992; McDaniel 1992b). Ethnic

> Much of what is known, and not known, about Canadian families is filtered through biases, myths, and misconceptions about what "family" is and what it should be.

families might be seen as becoming "Canadianized" (Albanese 2005), or studied in comparison to "Canadian" families that are implicitly seen as "normal." Poor families are often seen as struggling out of poverty so that they won't be "deviant" or "deficient" (Baker 2005; Sorensen 1999). And HIV/AIDS families are seen as mimicking the nuclear family (Wong-Wylie and Doherty-Poirier 1997).

Researchers make assumptions, sometimes without conscious awareness that they are doing so, about the nature of family and what is "normal" (Luxton 2005). Indeed, the seemingly solid beliefs about what makes up a "normal" family can lead to preposterous statements — like a conference paper that opened by stating that more and more children were now being born *outside of families*. What the writer meant was that more children were being born outside of traditional marriages. A 1997 "position" (not policy, argues the Alberta government) on gay/lesbian foster parents offers another example:

> It is the position of the Director of Child Welfare that if a child is under temporary or permanent guardianship, the Director will not place a child in a family living in a non-traditional arrangement or with a single person when it is known within the community that they are a practicing gay or lesbian. (Quoted in *Globe and Mail* 1997b: A2)

The concept of being a practising gay or lesbian is a curious one. Are there practising and non-practising heterosexual couples?

Another bias is the belief that family should not stand in the way of individual opportunity or mobility, either geographical or social. This bias is apparent in workplace policies that forbid hiring relatives (so-called anti-nepotism rules), or when workers are discouraged from taking time away from work for anything but personal illness — presuming, in essence, that they do not have family responsibilities or that there is someone else they can get to look after their families. These assumptions overlook the fact that more than two-thirds of family caregivers work outside the home in Canada (Armstrong and Armstrong 2002; Statistics Canada 2006b). A Conference Board of Canada study (MacBride-King and Bachman 1999) found that significant proportions of workers, both male and female, face challenges in balancing work and family responsibilities. The study, a nationally representative survey of 1,500 Canadian employees, found that 63 percent agreed with the following statement: "In my organization, you are expected to leave your personal problems at the door."

Private vs. Public Family

Another common misconception is that family is private. Although the church and welfare agencies have always had strong public interests in, and connections to, the family, many researchers and policy-makers resist the notion that the family itself is a public institution that is both shaped and controlled by other social institutions. When university students are introduced to this reality for the first time, they often see it as a cynical interpretation of the family. To suggest, for instance, that the family form that we know so intimately has emerged and is perpetuated to suit the interests of capitalism (Luxton 2005; Pupo 1988; Young 1987) or is the terrain of political struggle and resistance (Luxton 2005; Peters 1997) is seen as heresy. We are carefully taught that what we experience on intimate frontiers cannot work in anyone's interest but our own.

Iris Young (1987: 73–75), among others, argues that the distinction between family as private and public is artificial and thus excludes many groups, particularly women and others, who are resisting traditional structures, ideologies, and constraints. Moreover, defining the family as private ignores its many social functions, and the social forces acting on it (McDaniel and Tepperman 2006). On the other side, the powerful define the public realm (the non-family world of work and economic and political organizations) as being rational and universal, as a world not subject to individual whims, desires, and objectives. Defining non-family institutions as public also implies an openness and accessibility — a meritocracy — conditions often belied by social institutions as now structured, particularly when they are seen from women's vantage points. What might be considered private is that which an individual has a right to exclude others from, rather than only what is not public. Women on social assistance, for instance, whose every purchase and action are scrutinized, lead the least private of family lives (Baker 2005). Definitions of private and public need rethinking.

FAMILY AS A SOCIAL INSTITUTION

Social science theory and research, particularly feminist theory, can be extremely useful in providing insights on what is known about family as a social institution. Essentially, family as an institution has four central, interrelated purposes: service to the economy, the socialization of children, social control, and reproduction. In all of these purposes, family serves a distinctly public function.

In *servicing the economy*, family provides new workers who are ready and able to begin work and take on citizenship responsibilities. It provides a place where, as Dorothy Smith (1977) suggests, workers are stored and restored when they are not at work. Family, further, tends to be a conservative influence on workers who might want to organize against the injustices of society or of the workplace. For many men, because of the traditional division of labour by gender, family provides a cheap and efficient source of domestic labour and sexual services (Duffy 1988; Luxton 2005; Wilson 1996). These ideas remain largely unchallenged (Pilcher 2000) because families exist within societies and adopt their socially constructed gender norms (Doucet 2000).

> Family as an institution has four central, interrelated purposes: service to the economy, the socialization of children, social control, and reproduction.

Family is, in addition to schools, the primary agent for socializing young people. As such, it is vital to society as the carrier of cultural heritage (Abu-Laban and McDaniel 1997; Albanese 2005) and gender expectations (McDaniel and Tepperman 2006) — as well as being vital to the economy (Luxton 2005; Wilson 1996). Most importantly, in socializing children and adults, the family creates the social harmony needed for the economy (Baker 1995; Wall 2005). Dominant groups in society view any threats to this fundamental family function with apprehension and concern. This, of course, is precisely what is occurring now with the public-policy spotlight on families in Canada, but especially in the United States.

The family is also an agent of *social control*. But not only do families control children in the interests of society — making sure they go off to school and, sometimes, church, and making sure they "behave" — but they also control adult men and women. For example, a man with a family is often seen as a better risk in the labour market because of the assumption that he will be willing to work harder and more steadily. The concept is that a man will compromise his own needs and interests for those of his family. A woman with a family is seen as being more solid, sexually less threatening, and protected, although she is also seen as a greater risk for absenteeism in the workplace. The presumption is that she will be caught in the conflict between family and work, and she will be the one "on call" for family emergencies; thus she is seen more often as a less serious worker. The family is where private satisfactions and consumerism are expected to compensate for the deprivation and alienation of the workplace (Ranson 2006). The notion of man's home as his castle may stem from the societal granting of power to men at home in compensation for the loss of power in an alienated capitalist work world. This understanding of family as a place of social control leads, in part, to the fear of increased individualism (Lewis 2001). If people prioritize personal growth, if women are increasingly attached to the labour force rather than to families, what impetus is there for conformity and submission to familial control?

Reproduction, biological as well as social and cultural, may be the family's most essential social function. Families reproduce themselves each day in the work they do for themselves and for society. Each family also reproduces itself in its children's opportunities or lack of them. Despite our Canadian belief in rewards based on merit, the family of origin remains the single most important determinant of a child's life chances (Kitchen 1981: 186). Children from poor families seldom become the powerbrokers of the next generation, while children from rich families often do. Economic reproduction

> Families are called on in these times of shrinking public services to do more and more work for the public good.

has an obvious impact on the growth of inheritances and transfers from parents to adult children (including the parental funding of education), which has been identified as one of the central factors in the growing difference between the less wealthy and wealthy families in Canada (Statistics Canada 2002b).

Family is thus among the most public of social institutions, serving the economy and society in vital, yet thankless, ways. It is not surprising, then, that families are called on in these times of shrinking public services to do more and more work for the public good.

Family Policy in Social Context

From what we know about family, then, we can draw several inferences about family policy. When policy-makers direct their attention to family, they do so often because family, in their eyes, no longer serves the needs of society as well as they think it should; or because they expect families to pick up responsibilities that the state has dropped. Often family policies in Canada and elsewhere have focused on getting more out of the family. After the Second World War, for example, authorities showed an interest in encouraging a higher birthrate to boost recovery and encourage consumerism. The "baby bonus," or "family allowance," which has since disappeared, was thus instituted in Canada and paid specifically to women. The birthrate did rise — although there is now a general understanding that the baby bonus was not responsible for the baby boom.

> When policy-makers direct their attention to family, they do so often because family, in their eyes, no longer serves the needs of society as well as they think it should; or because they expect families to pick up responsibilities that the state has dropped.

A second important point about family policy is that it is not likely to be effective if it is out of step with contemporary trends and realities. Policies will be ignored, will be worked around, or will generally have deleterious effects on people if they go against social or historical trends or the felt interests of families or individuals. For example, policies based on the model of a nuclear family with a male breadwinner have had negative effects on African-American households that are female-headed and involve an extended family (Sudarkasa 1999). The same can be said of Aboriginal families or female lone-parent families. Resistance by women to policies that are not in their interests is long-standing (Baker 2005; Peters 1997).

Third, policies can either be responsive to what people want and are doing anyway, or they can lead them in new directions. Policy can enable people to do what they would like to do but lack the resources and/or supports to do. But even social interventionist policies that strive to empower can work against empowerment if they simply make people dependent on artificial or temporary resources.

FEMINIST SOCIOLOGICAL PERSPECTIVES AND FAMILY POLICY

Feminist theorists have shown how much of the social world, as we understand it, is based on the experience of men and male ideologies (Luxton 2005; Pringle 1997; Smith 1987) — how social significance relates to the power to discover, to name, and to give authority to social problems and understandings (Wajcman 1991). Social science has largely been a male science, peopled by men and steeped in a masculinist outlook on the world. Much may have been lost in seeing family largely in male terms (Mann et al. 1997). For instance, from a male standpoint family can be a haven from the stresses of today's insecure workplace and of society. Yet for women, the family can entail the responsibilities of an increasingly stressful second job with no holiday pay, no backup, no pensions, a great deal of insecurity (the risks of divorce and widowhood), and few tangible rewards. Additional stresses of family work for women stem from the

> From a male standpoint family can be a haven from the stresses of today's insecure workplace and society; for women, the family can entail an increasingly stressful second job, a great deal of insecurity, and few tangible rewards.

downloading of health, social services, and child care to women in families (Luxton 2005; McDaniel 1995, 1997a, 1997b, 2002; Peters 1997). The growing number of women who report being time-stressed reflects the impact of the increased expectations for women to provide care to elders and other family members, who are increasingly recovering from medical interventions for which, in the past, they would have been in hospitals. According to Statistics Canada's 1998 General Social Survey, 21 percent of adult Canadian women felt time-stressed, an increase from 16 percent six years earlier. Some 22 percent of women aged forty-five to fifty-four reported that they felt time-stressed (Statistics Canada 1999). There are no more recent national data on time stress.

A disjuncture is apparent between the world women live in and experience every day, and the world of family as written about largely by male social scientists (Eichler 2005; Duffy 1988; Pringle 1997). Family problems such as the feminization and juvenilization of poverty (Bianchi 1999; Boyd and McDaniel 1996; Eichler 1988), inadequate day care (Baker 1995; Fillion 1989; Human Resources Development Canada 2000; National Action Committee on the Status of Women 1988), and violence against women and children tend to be underemphasized because male-dominated policy circles and social science have still not sanctioned their legitimacy as social problems (Baker 2005)

Similarly, male-dominated social science has also overlooked women's degradation at the hands of the welfare state (Baker 2005; Fraser 1987; McDaniel 1996, 1997a; Ruspini 2001). The welfare state depends on the perpetuation of poverty to justify its huge expenditures from the public purse. The usually invisible gender subtext of the welfare state forced women into being familial at the cost of being self-respecting (Fraser 1987). Caroline Andrew (1984) argued that gender was an essential concept to the functioning and understanding of the social assistance system, because women who work in it are divided against women clients, who they realize could be themselves if they lost their jobs or divorced. She pointed out the profound political importance of this dividing of women against other women because of the potential power of an alliance between welfare recipients and public-sector workers.

Today poverty and welfare services for women continue to create an enforced dependency on a patriarchal state, and they shape women's self-identities as caregivers (Baker 2005; McDaniel 1992a, 1992b, 1996). To understand women's poverty, and the disproportionate vulnerability of women to poverty, we must take up perspectives that move beyond seeing poverty as a gender-neutral phenomenon and work to identify the economic disadvantages that women face in the labour market, domestic circumstances, and welfare systems (Ruspini 2001).

COMPETING PERSPECTIVES ON FAMILY AND FAMILY POLICY

In seeing families as problematic in Canada now and in the years ahead, I would argue that the family is a terrain of power and resistance resulting from differences in social expectations and ideology. While more than two perspectives on the family are clearly possible, competing perspectives in Canada tend to come down to two profoundly different images of family in society.

One perspective is that of the family in crisis. In various ways this perspective expresses concern that the family is "falling apart." Often, but not always, the family in crisis perspective takes the view that "family" is (or should be) the traditional 1950s form of nuclear family, with the father working and the mother at home with the children. Neo-liberals see changes in the family, such as high divorce and cohabitation rates, as manifestations of the disintegration of society and threats to social order and conformity (Smart 2000). So-called pro-family, conservative groups such as REAL Women (Realistic, Equal, Active, and for Life) on both sides of the 49th parallel have succeeded in undermining sex education programs, reducing access to abortion (McDaniel 1985), changing definitions of what constitutes abuse of spouses and children, and restricting the rights of gays and lesbians in many states and in several provinces in Canada (*Globe and Mail* 1997b), despite the legalization of same-sex marriage in Canada.

Those who adhere to the family in crisis perspective are not of one mind. Some see the challenge in primarily moral terms, or as the "decline," "disarray," or even "demise" of the traditional patriarchal family. Others see the problem in ostensibly economic terms, focusing on the increasing numbers of single mothers, the declining birthrate, or the aging of the population. These concerns relate to demands on the public purse, unpaid caring for both young and old, and future labour force supply. Still others emphasize specific social problems, defined in both economic and moral terms (Sorensen 1999). Many analysts agree, for example, that family dissolution places extra burdens on the taxpayer with the court costs, child welfare costs, and many other costs that shift from the private to the public realm (Baker 2005; Eichler 2005). Margaret Brinig (2000), for example, argues that the adoption of no-fault divorce creates an increase in the divorce rate, because it reduces the social and economic costs of divorce to men. People divorce too easily, according to her analysis, and then rather than being responsible for themselves they rely upon the state for support. The policy solution has been to minimally support the reinforcement of court-ordered child-support payments from so-called "deadbeat dads"— an essentially private family approach, and one that reinforces rather than contests the patriarchal family.

Despite the differences, those who adhere to the family in crisis perspective share common concerns, which taken together form the tenets of this approach:

- family change is not welcomed;
- families are not diverse in either form or function;
- families that diverge from the acceptable form of family (the "traditional" nuclear

family) tend to be dysfunctional or deviant;
- women's changing roles are generally deleterious to family;
- the history of family and family change goes back only to the 1950s in North America (a generally ahistorical perspective);
- family is essential to society's overall functioning, and families should take on more and more previously public responsibilities; and
- family is basically private, but in need of public policy to strengthen its traditional social roles and structures.

The second perspective on family — progressive and largely feminist — contrasts sharply with the family in crisis perspective. The progressive perspective sees family as taking diverse forms. At the core of this perspective is the belief that men and women should have equal or comparable opportunities in families as well as in the workplace. Analysts taking this approach see advantages in having alternative kinds of families to suit the needs of different kinds of people and to accommodate people's different life circumstances (see Luxton 2005; McDaniel and Tepperman 2006).

Like the adherents of the family in crisis perspective, those taking a feminist perspective are not of one mind. Generally, they link family to wider societal forces, including women's and other oppressed minorities' social and political circumstances. Some of them see families as being in need of greater social supports. Others see less need for policies and programs to support families generally, except on a casualty basis for those families experiencing economic or social deprivation. Still other feminists call for a radical redefinition of the family to encompass other kinds of caring relationships. Indeed, there is a clear increase in the acceptance of diverse definitions of the family in Canada, including of gay marriage (Ambert 2005). The emergence of new family forms out of the monolithic traditional nuclear family of the 1950s becomes a sign of progress rather than crisis.

Feminist perspectives have some common guiding beliefs:

- family change is welcomed as a sign of progress and evolution;
- families are diverse in both form and function, and should not be expected, or forced, to conform to any single model;
- men and women should be treated equitably and have comparable opportunities both in families and in society;
- family change has always occurred, and recent changes in families do not constitute a crisis;
- family is central to most individuals' lives and is not likely to pass out of existence;
- family is a social institution and, as such, articulates with other social and economic institutions — sometimes in ways not apparent to us; and
- families, as social institutions, are not private, but the diversity of family needs must be respected.

Still, even these two profoundly different perspectives on family are not diametrically opposed. They have in common an interest in the family as a social institution that could benefit from increased public-policy attention. However, each of them would like to see very different kinds of public interventions in family. It is wise to keep in mind H.G. Well's caution, as quoted by Hilary Land and Roy Parker (1978: 360): "Many are fearful that in seeking to save the family, they should seem to threaten its existence."

Policy formation is itself a process of political and social struggle and resistance. With respect to policies and programs that support and enable family caring and sharing, the political struggles are immense. The continuing "welfare wars" and neo-liberal political agendas are "wars" about women and families — and about how both women and families relate to society and the economy. The terrain on which Canada's postwar welfare state has been dismantled is a terrain of families, women, and often elders and the sick and disabled as well.

CANADIAN FAMILIES IN CHANGE OVER TIME

Myths about the families of the past abound. A common belief is that Canadians, in times past, lived in large, self-sufficient, stable, and happy extended families. Family change is perceived as something new, a jarring shift from the past. The realities of family in Canada's past, however, are quite different, as recent social histories show. A proliferation of studies have focused on families of the past (Gaffield 1988; McDaniel and Mitchinson 1987; McDaniel and Tepperman 2006; Nett 1981), with fascinating findings. The work has shown us that the family, contrary to popular belief about its stability, has altered its form and function dramatically over time and under changing socio-economic conditions.

There is now little doubt that Canadian pioneers and colonists for the most part lived in two-generation nuclear families (Nett 1981: 242–43). Considerable family instability was characteristic of families past, most often occasioned by the death of the father while the children were still dependent (McDaniel and Mitchinson 1987) but also resulting from poverty and need, which caused families to send their children away to work as domestic servants or to work the streets. Illegitimacy, premarital and extramarital relationships, incest, alcoholism, marital rape, and wife and child abuse were common, even though they were seldom spoken about. These conditions left the victims to suffer in silence and without support. Most often the persons who experienced the problems were held accountable for them, adding guilt to injustice.

Marriage in Canada in the past was virtually compulsory for women, with religious vocations serving as an important alternative (Danylewycz 1987). Interestingly, even this alternative was couched in terms of "marriage," symbolized by "wedding" rings worn by nuns. Procreation in marriage was more important than love or passion, especially for the better-off, for whom inheritance was very important. Despite current conceptions that marriages of the past occurred at a very young age, research indicates that, on average, people in the early twentieth century married in their mid- to late twenties, and it was common for women to spend time spent in the labour force before marriage (Burkie 2001). For wage-workers in Canada's early industrial economy, children were either sources of cheap labour or drains on the family's resources (Gaffield 1988). The law saw women in all classes as their husbands' possessions, and husbands could do what they pleased with them, including disciplining them by physical force.

Family size was considerably smaller, too, largely due to the high rates of infant mortality (McDaniel and Mitchinson 1987). Family size was also smaller among the poor than among the better-off because of the combined effects of higher rates of mortality and because the children of the poor were often sent, or taken, away. Images of large happy families disappear quickly in light of the grim reality experienced by many families, particularly of having one child after another die.

People today also idealize the treatment of older people by families in the past, with images of loving familial care until death, when the large family gathered around the bed to bid good-bye. But older people were often shabbily treated by their children, who may not have had enough to get by themselves or might have been eager to inherit the family farm or home. It was common in the nineteenth century for grown children to turn out their widowed mother to live on her own, with a servant or as a servant, depending on the family's status and circumstances. Most older women in nineteenth-century Canada lived on their own or with people unrelated to them (Nett 1981). Many older women became homeless.

History teaches us other important lessons as well. There is apparently nothing new in seeing the family as being in crisis. Chad Gaffield (1988: 29) points out that the rapid changes related to industrialization and urbanization in mid-nineteenth-century Canada caused "considerable concern among politicians and other public leaders, who feared that widespread social disorder would result from the rapid pace of social change." In response, the authorities promoted new ideals of family. Women came to be defined more in terms of their responsibilities in the home, and especially for looking after children. For the children themselves, schooling came to be seen as the dominant fact of life in growing up (Gaffield 1988: 29). Family policy issues that became prominent during the nineteenth century's "family crisis," interestingly, reflect close parallels to the issues of today: fears of substance abuse, family values, the reproductive behaviour of young women, and family stability (Garbarino 1996).

This narrowing of the female role resulted from socio-economic changes that required more to be done by the family, even as the family was being transformed from a unit of production to one of consumption. Authorities saw women's familial roles as being essential to the transition. The cult of "true womanhood" was born: being a woman entailed constant work, the consumption of goods, care for others, and submission to the needs of men and family.

During the Second World War women were brought into the Canadian labour force to fill positions left vacant by the men called to war. Then, following the war, women were systematically drawn out of the labour force to enable men to resume working to support families (Wilson 1996). The postwar period was also a time when the instability of the family again became an issue. The social priority moved away from physical well-being and towards the mental and emotional well-being of the child, which could only be achieved through the "normalcy" (a white, patriarchal normalcy) of the family (Gleason 1999). Women thus served as a reserve army of labour, called out of the home when the economy warranted, but hidden in the household once again when the economic need for their labour disappeared (Fox 1988). In today's restructuring economy, women's concentration in part-time work suggests that their role as a reserve army of labour is not just a thing of the past.

FAMILY POLICIES ELSEWHERE

My intent here is to assess existing research and theory rather than undertake a comprehensive analysis of family policies in Canada, which has been done elsewhere (Baker 1995, 2005; Garbarino 1996). In addition I want to draw attention, however briefly, to the family policy experiences in other countries. Those experiences can be invaluable in considering Canadian policy.

While modelling policies and social programs on the experiences of other countries may be acceptable, even commonplace, it is not without problems (Baker 1995: 10–12; Steiner 1981: 177). Cultural contexts, socio-economic circumstances, and basic definitions vary from country to country. Yet much can be learned from the experiences of others. Sheila Kamerman and Alfred Kahn (1978: 15) refer to "an international transmission of social policies" and note that family policy is central to the international diffusion of social policies. Maureen Baker (1995: 371) emphasizes, as part of comparative analysis, that "family policy is part of social and economic policy and should not be viewed as a separate entity."

Many countries, most notably those of Western Europe, are far ahead of Canada and the United States in recognizing the importance of family policy in creating a balance between caring and earning (Baker 1995; Gornick and Meyers 2001; McDaniel 2002; Steiner 1981: 178–79; Tyyska 1995). France, for example, has had its Code de la Famille since 1939. The Code outlines the legal position of French families, focusing specifically on raising the French birthrate (Baker 1995: 6; Lefaucheur and Martin 1992). Great Britain's long-standing policy concerns with early childhood have strong family policy implications (Ferri 1992), although the model is clearly one of private responsibility in which women are institutionalized as the primary caregivers (Baker 1995: 223–27; McKie, Bowlby, and Gregory 2001). Sweden's policy (dating from the 1930s) of promoting equality between women and men on the family front as well as in the workplace is family policy as part of labour-market policy and has much in common with other Western European countries (Baker 1995: 345, 1997; Kamerman and Kahn 1978: 480–81; Steiner 1981: 188–90). Germany has had a long, but decidedly mixed, experience with family policy, from the Hitler era of "Kinder, Kirche, Kuche" (Family, Church, and Home — a slogan used by the Nazis to promote domestic allegiance) to its present-day subsidized day-care system (Baker 1995: 215). Based on extensive interviews with Western European social scientists and policy-makers, Gilbert Steiner (1981:179) notes, "Respondents in western Europe are puzzled by the sudden American anxiety over family policy" — not surprisingly, because their experiences, both good and bad, with family and policy have a much longer history. Louis Roussel and Irene Thery's (1988) review of French family policies comes to a similar conclusion.

The 1980s and 1990s witnessed additional developments in family policy in Western Europe. In the 1980s France developed family policies focused on income maintenance. Previous policies, which had been pro-natalist (encouraging births), assuming a traditional patriarchal family, had been widely acknowledged as unsuccessful by the late 1970s (Lefaucheur and Martin 1992; Roussel and Thery 1988: 347–51). French women now have more realistic choices available. They can choose between full-time homemaking and child care or full-time labour force participation, guided by the principles of equality and neutrality (Roussel and Thery 1988: 347; Steiner 1981: 185–88). Yet France by the mid-1980s was sufficiently concerned about its low birthrate to provide incentives to encourage childbearing to counter the aging of the population. These efforts included subsidized day care to any child over two and a half years of age. The belief was that this policy would enable women to adopt the male model of career progression, yet a study by Rosemary Crompton and Nicola Le Feuvre (1996) challenges this belief. They found that, despite the equalized opportunities, there were still significant differences between occupational achievement and that "traditional assumptions relating to the gender division of labour are remarkably persistent" (Crompton and Le Feuvre 1996: 441).

Great Britain's Margaret Thatcher put forward a discussion paper that stressed family policy as a central aspect of social policy (Baker 1995: 223–27), yet the policy trend under her Conservative government of the 1980s placed a traditional focus on early childhood and male work incentives rather than on family per se (Baker 1995: 223–27; Ferri 1992). The Labour government, which gained power in 1997, greatly improved the levels of publicly subsidized child care and introduced unpaid paternity leave. This change has in part come about through improved potential for parents (especially mothers) to enter or increase their participation in the workforce. Yet, as Linda McKie, Sophia Bowlby, and Susan Gregory (2001) argue, as positive as these changes are, they mask the policies' ideological connection of women and caring. The very manner of the policies, the unpaid paternal leave (which is unlikely to promote change among low-income people), and the avoidance of addressing the low pay of caregivers, ensure the maintenance of traditional notions of "the family" (McKie, Bowlby, and Gregory 2001: 234).

Germany's recent efforts in family policy have emphasized the home rather than the workplace. Kindergartens, for example, are ostensibly aimed at facilitating the labour force participation of mothers of preschoolers at the same time as providing early childhood education by trained private and public staff (Baker 1995: 215). Yet the lack of full-day programs and the absence of school meals (to which parents contribute) militate against mothers working (Baker 1995: 215; Steiner 1981: 180–81). Similarly, the "day mothers" experimental program in Canada, whereby day care is provided on a rotating basis by stay-at-home mothers, helps with the child-care problem but works against the possibility of mothers seeking full-time employment. The declining birthrate in Germany, of concern to policy-makers, had led to the "young family" program in which families of children born after July 1, 1989, could claim a one-time payment (Baker 1995: 101–2).

The United States, with its individualistic, minimalist welfare state, has been reluctant to develop a family policy per se (Baker 1995: 40; Sorensen 1999; Steiner 1981: 191–92; Spakes 1983: 12–13), and came to the family policy scene much later than did Western Europe. It might be argued, however, that many precursors of family policy exist in the United States, including Roosevelt's "New Deal," the 1960s "War on Poverty," welfare reforms ad infinitum, and various policies on child development (Baker 1995: 111–12; McLanahan and Garfinkel 1992; Steiner 1981: 193). Walter Mondale, in 1983, chaired a congressional committee on the state of the American family, which gave both family and family policy a new saliency. At the same time Mondale's committee found that many proposed family policies might be more harmful than helpful to the family (Spakes 1983: 12). The U.S. attempt at family policy since has been characterized as a "muddled one that lumps together concerns about child development, about day care… about changes in family structure… about cohabitation, about abortion, and about the implications of the women's movement for family life" (Steiner 1981: 191). In the twenty-first century, neo-liberal agendas have been brought to the fore, espousing values of either non-intervention to oppose any family policies (Baker 1995: 334) or aggressive intervention to favour the "traditional" heterosexual nuclear family. Employment and welfare policies that do exist, according to Angela O'Rand and John Henretta (1999), benefit families that best fit the traditional model, leading to a situation in which, although there are greater commonalities between the life courses of men and women, the well-being of women has dropped significantly in relation to men.

In considering family policy in Canada, we should examine the longer experiences of Western Europe for lessons. Maureen Baker (1995: 371–72) concludes that countries with traditions of social democracy, concerns about fertility decline, and strong social welfare systems tend to be ahead of Canada in creating policies to assist parents and to help people to work and have families at the same time. Until this country has an effective national child-care strategy, it will continue to be difficult for women to both work and have families. In Western Europe, family policy tends to be sharply focused, with clear objectives and goals. For example, in Sweden, the focus is on achieving gender equality in work and society and on the protection of children, so that cohabitation and divorce are not concerns.

In Western European experiences with family, gender equality tends to be given priority, although in varying degrees. Western European family policies also generally recognize the structural linkages between the family and other major social institutions, particularly work. Significantly, though, Western European experiences with family policies aimed at increasing the birthrate have been consistently unsuccessful. Inconsistent policies, which first promote patriarchy and then greater choice for women and later return to some aspect of promoting patriarchy, seem to have negative consequences for families, particularly for women. This could also be said to characterize policies in Canada.

Policies that reduce gender inequities, thereby enhancing women's choices, tend to strengthen families too. In Sweden the policies that aim for gender equality have tended to create a more stable family background. Livia Olah (2001: 130) confirms this in a study of the factors that have an impact on parental dissolution. She shows, for example, that fathers who use parental leave have a reduced risk of marriage breakup. The more gender equality there is in a family, in economic provision, child care, and housework, the more stability there is in the family.

TOWARDS "WOMEN-FRIENDLY" CANADIAN FAMILY POLICIES

In Canada, with its rapidly diminishing social safety net, profoundly shifting labour market, and redefinitions of women as a "special-interest" group, the prospect of developing "women-friendly" family policies seems unlikely. Women's roles are being recrafted, as they were at the time of the Industrial Revolution, by state policy (or now, more properly, by the abrogation of policy) as both familial and labour market, with the two roles strongly interconnected. For example, the paid labour market is being "feminized" as more women work for pay regardless of whether or not they are mothers of preschool children, at the same time as the family is being "privatized" as more women take on greater responsibilities for the old, the young, and the ill and disabled in the face of health-care, social-service, and child-care support cuts (Armstrong and Armstrong 2002; McDaniel 1997c; McDaniel and Tepperman 2006). Nonetheless, it is important not to lose track of the ideal of "women-friendly" family policies or to lose hope in preparing and lobbying for their development.

"Women-friendly" family policies for Canadians should consider issues of basic, and growing, inequities and polarities in Canadian society. Families, more than any other social institution, determine the life chances of children, and increasingly of women. In Canada the chances of experiencing a low income are greatly reduced if women put off marriage and childbirth, thus enabling a more complete education. The likelihood of marrying and having children later is in turn strongly correlated to growing up in a family with highly educated and wealthy parents (Statistics Canada 1998b, 2001c). Family policies, widely defined as including socio-economic policies, must, then, address basic inequities among Canadians, including inequities based on class, ethnicity, region, gender, and physical ability. Family policies, in the very least, must acknowledge that families are becoming more unequal in Canada and that individuals within families are disadvantaged by these inequities. The implementation of pay equity and the elimination of workplace discriminations, including sexual harassment (see McDaniel 1997b), are essential components of "women-friendly" family policies.

Bashing and trashing of women on social assistance as abusers of the system, as lazy, or as bad or inadequate mothers have become commonplace facets of neo-liberal political policies (see Swanson 2001; Baker 2005). With drastic cuts to social assistance, which are most deep in Alberta, Ontario, New Brunswick, and British Columbia, women with sole responsibility for dependent children are finding it harder to live, work, and find suitable shelter. In Ontario, the 1995 changes to social assistance led to more than one thousand people being cut off — 86 percent of them female, and 76 percent of those being single mothers. This state abuse occurred, in part, through a redefinition of eligibility that changed the meaning of "spouse," part of a reassertion of the traditional family model. Meanwhile the work of poor women in the home and with their children was made invisible, and the reality of their lives, particularly those fleeing abuse, was ignored (Mosher 2000). Social assistance is often the vital and only link between poor women and society. We should take immediate steps to resist the damaging policies and labels and to give dignity to women on social assistance, as well as facilitate realistic entry, or re-entry, into the labour force with a sense of choice rather than punishment. It is important that women be defined not solely or primarily by family status or by their, often temporary, reliance on social assistance.

Reproductive issues are a central dimension of "women-friendly" family policies. In many circles, a concern about the low birthrate in Canada is at the heart of the family policy debate, particularly in Quebec. Yet the low Canadian birthrate is far from unique in the Western world. Since the nineteenth century most industrial countries have seen a long-term decline in birthrates. Perhaps the higher birthrate in the post–Second World War period was the anomaly, after which the long-term decline resumed. If this is the case, it is unlikely that any policy interventions, no matter how carefully thought out, will have much impact on the birthrate in the long run.

Of course, reproduction involves issues other than birthrate. Reproductive choice is vital — both to having a child when desired and to avoiding pregnancy when a child is not wanted. Without reproductive choices, women cannot participate equally in society. In Canada today, new challenges to reproductive rights are being raised as biological fathers, sometimes with the encouragement of their parents or "men's rights" groups, take legal steps to control ex-girlfriends' or ex-wives' attempts to seek abortions or rights to give a baby up for adoption. Laws and policies remain to be written on these challenging issues, as well as to govern "surrogate" motherhood, "in vitro" fertilization, embryo transplants, cloning, and the other new reproductive technologies. The recommendations of the Royal Commission on Reproductive Technologies of 1992 were only implemented in small part in 2002, with most of the recommendations still not touched by 2007.

Aging is an issue centrally important to "women-friendly" family policies, for a number of reasons. Women outlive men by a considerable margin and are thus more often left without a spouse to care for them during their last years (McDaniel 1992b, 1997c). Women also have limited access to pensions, other than the basic Canada or Quebec pensions, if they have spent their adult lives as homemakers (Abu-Laban and

McDaniel 1997; Gee and McDaniel 1991) or have had intermittent labour force participation. Women, additionally, are more often expected to care for ill or disabled relatives rather than, or in addition to, spending their time in the paid labour force (McDaniel 1992a, 1995, 1997a, 1997b, 1997c; Connidis 1989). This expectation creates stress and the potential for burnout for women caught in what has come to be called the "caregiving crunch." These stresses become exacerbated in an uncertain climate of health-care reform, amid regular reports of threats to services (Martin-Matthews 2001). Employers and state policies seldom acknowledge the legitimacy of caring for aging relatives.

Child care, which appeared on the federal policy agenda of the Liberal government only in 2005, had long not received the attention it deserved as a central family policy issue. Women who work outside the home, as well as women who work at home, increasingly need access to quality child care. In a 2006 survey of business executives in Canada (Pitts 2006), 64 percent of the executives saw child-care policy as linked to productivity. In 1996–97, according to Statistics Canada data, less than one-third (29 percent) of preschool children who received non-parental care were in licensed or regulated child care (Johnson, Lero, and Rooney 2001). By 2000–01, of the half of all children aged six months to five years who were in some kind of child care, half of them were in a child-care centre (Statistics Canada 2005a). The minority Harper government of 2006 turned back the national child-care strategy, including the previous government's promises for increases in the numbers of child-care centres. It opted instead for giving all parents of preschool children $1,200, of which a significant amount would be "clawed back" through taxes.

Women will differentially bear the costs of social and economic responsibility for child care in the home and at the same time work in the paid labour market. The Canadian National Child Care Study (Lero et al. 1992) highlighted the extent of the need for child care, not only so that women can work and contribute to their families' economic well-being and that of the country, but also for the benefit of their children as well. The survey of Canadian business executives also highlighted the need for child care as a key element in achieving economic prosperity. Countries that include family policies as part of labour policy recognize the centrality of a national, universally funded child-care system as family market policy (Baker 1995, 2005; Pitts 2006).

Alberta provides an interesting example of the relationship between child care and labour markets. It appears that Alberta women have left the labour force to look after their children full-time, because it is the only province where the number of children aged five and under increased after 1999. But, while the province had more infants, it has also had the smallest share of children in day care (Statistics Canada 2006c). If the participation rate of women with young children in Alberta had risen in tandem with that of Quebec, thirty thousand more women would have been in the labour forces in 2005. In Alberta's red-hot labour market, this increase

> Canada's child tax benefits programs are no substitute for a comprehensive, national child-care policy that would benefit the economy, families, women, and children.

in the labour force would have boosted the employment rate for people between the ages of fifteen and sixty-four by a full percentage point — a considerable gain given Alberta's unemployment rate (Statistics Canada 2006c). Canada's child tax benefits programs are no substitute for a comprehensive, national child-care policy that would benefit the economy, families, women, and children.

Violence against women in families, including abuse of elderly women, has yet to be treated with the seriousness it deserves (see chapter 2 here for more on this subject). Family policies that are "women friendly" should have the eradication of family violence as a central tenet.

Family poverty is a continuing problem in Canada — a function of the continuing gender gap in pay and opportunity combined with the persistent expectation that men will support women in families and share their social status with them. Once the marital bond is severed, women often tumble quickly into poverty, along with their children. Women with dependent children and those who are old have long comprised the greatest proportion of the poor (Cohen 1997; McDaniel 1992b). In 1997, more than half (56 percent) of female-headed lone-parent families with children under eighteen fell below the low-income cut-off line (Drolet and Morissette 2000). By 2001, although the numbers of lone mothers (and fathers too) had risen, so too had their real earnings (Statistics Canada 2005b). Some 34 percent of lone-parent families, mainly lone-mother families, lived in poverty in 2000 — a figure that is down from 38 percent in 1999 (Statistics Canada 2002a) but still very high. In 2000, 868,000 children under age eighteen lived below the low-income cut-off, representing 12.5 percent of all children (Statistics Canada 2002a). This finding marks a twenty-year low, but that will be little consolation to those almost 900,000 children experiencing poverty. Child poverty began to emerge as a policy concern in Canada in the late 1990s, and is also a growing concern as the effects of childhood poverty in producing problems in adulthood become better known.

The monumental changes experienced in Canada in the past few decades o — the globalization of markets under NAFTA and other free-trade agreements, the restructuring of the workplace and of work, resulting in "McJobs" and more involuntary part-time work, and government programs fixated on deficit and debt reduction — have added to family poverty and gender inequities. That jobs may be becoming "feminized" in the new workplace does not mean that women or families benefit. Rather, equality is being gained by reducing everyone's incomes — although big business profits and the incomes of their top executives do not seem to be suffering.

Immigrant families pose particular challenges to the development of "women friendly" family policies for Canadians. Two concerns are paramount: 1) dependency relations that are incorporated into immigration entry status; and 2) the sponsored entry status of many immigrant women, which hinders them in gaining access to government programs to promote integration and provide social services (Arnopoulos 1979; Côté, Kerisit, and Côté 2001; Estable 1986; Seward and McDade 1988). In addition, immigrant women tend to be defined by immigration policy mainly as family members, so that any labour force skills they have are overlooked in the immigration assessment (Albanese 2005). Immigrant families are too often characterized by immigration policy as having only one central wage-earner, the husband. Policies that encourage the importation of domestic workers but at the same time deny entry to those women's families are guilty of discriminating against women.

Aboriginal family issues are also central to the development of family policies for Canadians. To ensure that policies support and help strengthen First Nations traditions and family life, we need to develop an understanding of the inappropriateness of Western models and assumptions that have little connection to the more holistic worldviews of most First Nations peoples (Albanese 2005; Status of Women Canada 2000). Many First Nations people argue that the breakdown in traditional Aboriginal families is a key factor in the social problems that they are grappling with (Albanese 2005: 124). Family policies, for example, often fail to understand that while the overall birthrate in Canada is declining, First Nations people are experiencing high birthrates. Family policies designed for other Canadians discourage the traditional adoption practices of the Inuit. The recommendations of a lengthy, costly, and by all accounts, excellent Royal Commission on Aboriginal Peoples report in 1996 remain to be enacted a decade after its publication.

Policies must also help to preserve ethnic diversity in families, while including sensitive attention to issues of gender justice. For example, policy-makers and advocates must not presume that violence against women is a "cultural" expression, nor should cultural practices such as female genital mutilation be permitted in Canada under the label of tolerance of cultural practices or diversity (see Levine 1999). Many immigrant women facing domestic violence may face language and cultural barriers to reporting, which place these women at increased risk (Albanese 2005).

Disabled women and families with a disabled person should receive careful attention, so that family policies can more specifically meet their special needs. Most essentially, the life choices of women with disabilities and of family members with disabilities could be enhanced by the creation of a social environment in which people are valued for their contributions rather than for their physical abilities. Policy should also pay attention to the mothers of children with disabilities; they put in long hours of care, concern, and worry without the benefit of government programs to support them.

Created or "voluntary" families are a growing segment of the population. These created families come in array of forms: relatives through various marriages that break down though the family connections continue; friends and neighbours who are close and help out; volunteers helping in family situations (such as big sisters or big brothers); foster or temporary care; voluntary grandparents; groups of friends living together or supporting each other as a family; and extended families, among others. Studies of aging people reveal the importance of "fictive kin" — long-term friends who offer assistance of various types to an older person in need (Connidis 1989; McDaniel 2005). In a study of HIV/AIDS families, Gina Wong-Wylie and Marianne Doherty-Poirier (1997) found an immensely diverse and widely cast network of people to whom the HIV/AIDS survivor relates as family.

In targeting families with specific needs, multiple identities, and multiple communities may matter. For example, gender might be as important to the situation of a woman immigrant as immigration status or ethnicity. The same might be true of a disabled woman, of a mother, or of a disabled child. Social science, no matter how well done, is not capable of ferreting out the specific needs of groups unless their own views can be heard and translated into policy and programs. It is crucial, therefore, to get input from members of interest groups themselves before we design policies on their behalf.

GUIDELINES FOR THE BUILDING OF FAMILY POLICY

Families as part of society benefit from the same changes that individuals, women and men, value. Gilbert Steiner (1981: 195) suggests, in this vein, that "peace, full employment, income support, access to health care, convenient transportation, safe good housing, clean air and water, and good schools [are] more conducive to strengthening family life than their opposites." This is consistent with the important finding of the *Second Report on the Health of Canadians* (Canada, Health Canada 1999) that access to decent income is the single most important factor in achieving and maintaining good health. It is also consistent with the 1991 House of Commons report on child poverty (*Globe and Mail* 1991: A18) and the United Nations Children's Fund (1992) report on child poverty, which links child poverty to gender inequities. The social and the familial are central to individual and societal well-being (McDaniel and Tepperman 2006; McDaniel 1997b).

Family policies, like families themselves, should be seen in plurals rather than singulars. There is no single family form, nor can there be a single family policy. It cannot be assumed that policy-makers are starting with a "fresh slate" when family policy per se is on the agenda. Many existing policies have consequences, both good and bad, for families and for women in families. Considerable danger exists in attempting to "rationalize" existing policies, in that this process could penalize women who have benefited from these policies in the past. Yet policies that have been found to damage, and even destroy, families and women in families must be rethought and lessons taken. Family policies, both new and old, ought to be enabling to families rather than providing negative sanctions. Family policies should work for the interests of women and not pit them against the interests of families, or other so-called special interest groups.

What may be most enabling to women in families is the reduction of social inequalities and the creation of better environments and opportunities for women. Family policies should explicitly recognize and reward different and diverse ways of being familial. Attempting to reinforce one family form over others will only harm people and undermine alternative ways of caring. For example, the increased reliance of older Canadians on "fictive kin" should be encouraged rather than undermined. Recognition could be accorded to alternative ways of being familial, provided that there are supports for all kinds of caring

Advocacy, both outside and within government, on behalf of groups of women with different needs is important to the development and implementation of family policies. As part of the process of developing family policies for those with special needs, the people involved should be widely and openly consulted as to what they see as being in their best interests. Family policies must respect differences among families and women and different needs and resources. Women should not be subsumed either explicitly or implicitly for "the good of the family" or "the good of society," as it seems family policy is now doing once again at the federal level and in several provinces.

While family policies should work towards greater equality between men and women in the family, the workplace, and society, policy-makers must not assume that men and women have equal resources or opportunities, in families or elsewhere, when they do not. In divorce and custody situations, for example, we cannot assume that women have the same opportunities to be self-supporting as men do. Policies based on outmoded assumptions or unrealistic models of either family or society will not work. Rather, family policies have to be built on a realistic assessment of what families actually are today, including women's changing societal and family roles. Policies should be solidly based on the best social science research. Before it is relied on for building family policies, however, research should be carefully examined for possible biases.

Family policies for Canadians should build on existing knowledge of what will work, with realistic incentives to encourage the kind of outcomes seen as desirable. For example, given what is known about the costs of raising a child to adulthood, any payment scheme to encourage births will most likely not meet with long-term success.

One particular bias that should be avoided is the assumption that family is private and a retreat from the public world of work. Family is work, particularly for women, and family policies should acknowledge this fact of life. Family policies should acknowledge the negative aspects of family life, such as violence, child abuse, and sexual abuse, and should not shrink from punishing those who engage in these behaviours. Family policies should try to root out the causes of these behaviours and, in whatever way possible, attempt to build a society that discourages violence. In Canada the research on family violence is excellent and growing.

Family policies must acknowledge the continuing nature of family change and its close relationship to other societal changes. No policies for families that limit themselves to one definition of family will be effective. Family policies that set out to prevent social change, or to turn back the clock on social change, will be doomed from the start. Family policies should work for social change, and for a better society for Canadians, including Canadian women.

GLOSSARY OF KEY TERMS

Alienation: A separation of individuals from control over their life and what they produce. The term became important for sociology through the work of Karl Marx (1818–83), who argued that, in the capitalist workplace, individuals are separated from ownership, control, and direction over their work. Individuals are also alienated from others, as social relations are changed into economic relations.

Empowerment: The possibility for an individual or group to act on their own behalf and to determine their own existence.

Family/families: For many years sociologists relied on a definition of family that depended on sharing a household or on "relatedness" by blood or marriage. Because this excludes many social groupings that could be considered families, sociologists (as well as policy organizations such as the United Nations and the Vanier Institute of the Family) now tend to define families by what they do: emotional, financial, and material support for each other, care of each other, transmitting cultural values, and serving as a resource for personal development.

Ideology: A linked set of ideas and beliefs that work to uphold and justify an existing or desired arrangement of power, authority, wealth, and/or status in a society.

Pro-natalist: Supporting an increase in population growth by attempting to raise the number of births.

Social institution: A pattern of interaction that is repeated, and sanctioned, in a society. Institutions typically have a standardized organization, although what this organization is varies cross-culturally. Examples of social institutions are family, education, and religion.

Socialization: The process of interaction and communication through which people learn the norms of their society so that they can be functioning members; it enables the transmission of cultural ideas between generations.

QUESTIONS FOR DISCUSSION

1. Some critics suggest that there is a "disjuncture" between the world that women experience and the world that male social scientists write about. Does this difference exist? If it does, discuss changes in social science research that could help to close the gap.
2. There are at least two generally opposing perspectives on the family: the family in crisis and the feminist perspective. Yet they do have some common themes. Discuss these oppositions and commonalities and how they could be used in developing new family policy.
3. Countries in Western Europe and North America show distinct differences in family policy. What are some of the factors that may have led to the differences in policy across nations?

4. What do you think is the most pressing issue facing Canadian family policy-makers today? Explain why you believe this issue is particularly important and how Canadian family policy should be adjusted to deal with it.

WEBSITES OF INTEREST

The Vanier Institute of the Family. <www.vifamily.ca/>.
The Family Network of the Canadian Policy Research Networks. <www.cprn.org /en/network.cfm?network=1>.
EGALE Canada. <www.egale.ca/index.asp?lang=E>.
Canadian Council on Social Development. <www.ccsd.ca>.
The Family and Work Institute. <www.familiesandwork.org>.

NOTE

I gratefully acknowledge readers' suggestions for revisions to this fourth edition chapter.

Chapter 12

PRIVATE INTERESTS AT PUBLIC EXPENSE
Transforming Higher Education in Canada

Claire Polster

With the exception, perhaps, of health care, there are few things that Canadians value more than public education. Our education system has traditionally been successful in enabling students simultaneously to develop their individual personalities and potential, to prepare to make a living, and to become thoughtful citizens who help to shape the nature and future of their society, and it has done this with an impressive degree of efficiency and equity (Robertson 2005: 6). While Canadians' commitment to education has remained at historically high levels (see, for example, Livingstone and Hart 2005), the nature of our public system has been quietly and gradually changing in recent years. Rather than being publicly supported for public purposes, education is becoming privatized, both in the sense that it is increasingly seen and treated as an individual rather than a social responsibility and in the sense that it is progressively shaped by and oriented to market values and practices rather than public or collective ones.

This privatization of Canadian education is visible at all levels of the system. It is reflected in the frequent knocks on our doors by youngsters selling chocolates or collecting empty bottles to help purchase the "extras" — and, increasingly, the basics — that their schools can no longer afford due to cuts in public

---

"You Should Know This"

- In 1990 government operating grants provided 79.7 percent of university operating revenues and student tuition provided 16.9 percent. By 2003 government grants provided 58.6 percent of operating revenues, and tuition provided 34.2 percent.
- Between 1993 and 2004, average undergraduate tuition fees more than doubled, from $2,000 to over $4,000. Between 1990 and 2003, medical school fees climbed by 320 percent; for law school, 217 percent; for dental programs, 400 percent.
- After graduate and professional fees were deregulated in Ontario, the participation rates of low-income families at the University of Western Ontario were cut in half.
- An analysis of cancer drug studies found that those funded by the pharmaceutical industry were nearly eight times less likely to reach unfavourable conclusions than were similar studies funded by non-profit organizations.
- In 1995 the University of British Columbia awarded a grant to develop Web Course Tools for students and faculty. Two years later, the project was launched commercially as "WebCT," and today the enterprise has accounts with 1,494 institutions in fifty-seven countries. Instead of supporting the university, profits now flow to private investors.
- In 1997 the University of Toronto signed a donor agreement with Nortel to set up the Nortel Institute of Telecommunications. In exchange for $8 million, Nortel was involved in the selection of two research chairs and three junior tenure-track positions. The agreement included an undisclosed intellectual property rights clause.

Sources: CAUT 2003a: 1, 2005a; CFS 2005; Washburn 2005: 84; CCPA 2005: 24; Graham 2000: 25.

---

funding. It is manifested in the ubiquitous advertising on school walls, bathroom stalls, and vending machines, and in the many kinds of deals and arrangements (such as the Wal-Mart adopt-a-school and Campbell's labels

> Education is increasingly seen and treated as an individual rather than a social responsibility and shaped by and oriented to market values and practices.

programs) forged between cash strapped schools and wealthy corporations seeking invaluable publicity and opportunities to grow their customer bases. Privatization is also evident in our schools' adoption of a growing number of principles and practices that predominate in the private sector. These range from the centralization of administrative control and the contracting out of janitorial, food, and other services to the growing use of standardized testing and other performance measures, and even the establishment by some school districts of private businesses as a means of generating additional funds (Kuehn 2003; Shaker 1998; Froese-Germain et al. 2006).

It is at the level of the university, however, where the privatization process is most clear and advanced. As numerous analysts have observed, a university education in Canada is increasingly regarded and treated as a private rather than public good, much less as a citizenship right (Turk 2000b). As well, our universities are progressively seeing themselves as, and operating as and/or with, businesses in the research, teaching, and other work that they do.

This chapter focuses on the nature and implications of the ongoing privatization of Canada's universities. It does this in order to highlight some of the main ways in which public education in our country is being transformed and to address what this means for our citizens and our nation. My main argument is that we can and should resist the privatization of our universities in particular and of our public education system more generally. For although this process may provide benefits to some individuals and corporations, it does not serve the majority interest. Indeed, it may ultimately undermine even the interests of its advocates.

"Traditional" or mainstream analyses frequently assert that the privatization of Canadian higher education is a natural or inevitable development that is sweeping across public institutions and *cannot* be stopped.[1] Alternatively, or at the same time, these analyses maintain that privatization is a beneficial development that *should not* be stopped. Proponents of privatization argue that running our universities more as businesses increases their overall efficiency and effectiveness, which in turn serves the interests of those who work and learn within them as well as the taxpayers who fund them. They also argue that aligning universities' research and other operations more closely with the needs of the private sector enhances national economic competitiveness and thereby helps sustain our citizenry's high quality of life.

By contrast, I would argue that privatization is the consequence of human agency, that is, of intentional human decision and action. As such, it is neither natural nor inevitable: it is produced by people and can therefore be altered — even reversed — by them. Indeed, resisting privatization is not simply possible, but desirable. In a variety of ways, privatization transforms the internal operations of our universities in ways that compromise the interests of many of those who work and learn within them. Further, given that this process leads universities to prioritize private needs and interests at the expense of those of the general public, it not only fails to enhance our collective well-being, but also harms it.

THE PRIVATIZATION OF CANADIAN HIGHER EDUCATION

In its simplest form, the term "privatization" describes the process through which a resource or service is moved out of the public or collective sphere and into the private sphere, generally through sale. Thus, for example, in the 1980s and 1990s, the federal and provincial governments of Canada privatized many firms that had been state-owned and run — including de Havilland Aircraft, Teleglobe Canada, Canadair, CN Hotels, Air Canada, Petro-Canada, the Potash Corporation of Saskatchewan, and B.C. Ferries — selling them to private interests, sometimes at rock-bottom prices (Padova 2005). In the case of Canadian education in general, and higher education more particularly, however, privatization is not this straightforward. Rather than being a matter of selling off education (or otherwise transferring it) to private corporations, the relationship is much more complex: our universities are increasingly influenced by and oriented to the needs of the private sector (as well as some wealthy individuals), all the while being funded largely by the public.[2] In other words, rather than being subject to an outright sale to the private sector, the uses and benefits of university resources are being progressively ceded to private interests at the public's expense.

The term privatization also applies to a second, related development within Canadian universities: the progressive cultivation and normalization of an individualistic, self-serving ethic as opposed to a collective, public ethic. As our universities become more market-driven, those who work and learn within them are encouraged and/or compelled to place their private interests over and above collective interests — which include the interests of their peers, of their academic departments or faculties, and even of the broader community that the university is charged to serve.

Taken together, these two general trends and the myriad dynamics that bring them into being are changing what Canadian universities do and what they fundamentally are. From public-serving institutions that meet a wide variety of social needs in a plurality of ways, our universities are becoming private-serving institutions in which people increasingly orient themselves towards their own needs and interests and those of well-resourced organizations and individuals. This transformation not only jeopardizes the real and perceived value of our institutions of higher learning, but also poses significant threats to the well-being of many if not all Canadians, both now and in the future.

> From public-serving institutions that meet a wide variety of social needs in a plurality of ways, our universities are becoming private-serving institutions in which people orient themselves towards their own needs and interests and towards those of well-resourced organizations and individuals.

In my analysis of this transformation — which for reasons of space focuses on only three areas or functions of the university (academic research, governance, and teaching), and on only some of the interactions between them — a primary analytic tool is the sphere of social relations: those ongoing courses or patterns of human activity through which people produce a given feature of the social world — in this case, the university — in its particular shape or form (Smith 1987; Campbell and Gregor 2002). One way of conceptualizing this analysis is to see it as tracking the reconstruction of the various pathways through which key players in higher education (university administrators, academics, students, and the broader community outside of the university) are brought into contact with one another. As old pathways are dismantled and as key players are brought together (or kept apart) for new purposes and/or in new ways, both their own roles and the roles of the university as a whole begin to shift in a new direction.

UNIVERSITY RESEARCH

A useful entry point into the subject of privatization of Canada's universities is to examine the transformation of their knowledge production — or research — function. Prior to the 1980s relatively little research collaboration occurred between Canadian academics and members of the private sector. While some academics did various forms of research and other work (such as consulting) for corporations, such alliances were relatively few in number and kind, and they were held in relatively low priority if not esteem in most universities (Naimark 2004: 54–55). For the most part, university research tended to be conducted by academics and with academics in response to emerging problems and dynamics within their fields of inquiry and often in the service of the broader community. The privatization and commercialization of university research were rare.[3] Rather, research results tended to be widely disseminated and/or freely shared both within the academic community and beyond (Tudiver 1999: 11).

Since the 1980s, due to a number of factors, including government cuts to university operating budgets and concerns about Canada's competitiveness in the global, knowledge-based economy, research alliances between academics and the private sector have been strongly promoted, supported, and rewarded on most if not all Canadian university campuses, becoming in the process a widespread phenomenon. These alliances take on a great diversity of forms, ranging from small-scale research contracts to collaborative research centres, institutes, and networks, technology transfer offices, and "innovation" or "smart" parks, etc.[4] While the kinds of university/industry research alliances are varied, they generally involve corporate partners footing a portion of the bill for some academic research. In exchange for this funding, the partner may shape the topic of the research and some of the conditions under which it proceeds. It is increasingly common for the research partner to also acquire intellectual property rights to some or all of the research results.

In a variety of ways, these research partnerships with industry collectively and cumulatively help transform our universities from public-serving into private-serving institutions. First, they alter both the process through which research decisions are made and the kinds of research done in the university. As opposed to being shaped by the professional judgments and choices of autonomous academics, research decisions are increasingly made by well resourced parties external to the university. Further, rather than being directed at serving the public interest, these research projects are designed to meet the partners' particular interests, which may or may not also serve, and may even conflict with, the collective good (such as when technological innovations cause job loss or environmental harm). More than simply allowing corporate sponsors to command disproportionate shares of academics' time, energies, and talents in the short term, and to do so at a small fraction of their real costs, such alliances also help skew the general scientific research agenda towards industry needs and interests in the long term. As the research needs of other social groups (particularly those who cannot afford to sponsor academic research) are neglected in favour of the needs of paying clients, academics' capacities and willingness to meet those other needs may decline and/or fail to get passed on to the next generation of Canadian researchers. Indeed, this trend is already appearing in some fields. In biology, for example, the shift towards the lucrative field of molecular biology is eroding other approaches, such as organismic approaches to biology, which can offer citizens less costly and more environmentally friendly solutions to various problems such as pest control (Press and Washburn 2000: 50).

As well as changing the kinds of research that our universities do, alliances with industry are transforming how academic research is done. Whereas university research has traditionally been an open, collaborative, and collective activity, these partnerships are helping to convert it into a more closed and competitive business-like affair. For example, academics working with or for industry partners are routinely obliged to sign secrecy agreements, prohibiting them from discussing, much less sharing, their research with colleagues until, and sometimes even after, the associated intellectual property rights have been secured. According to a 1997 survey by Harvard researcher David Blumenthal, 58 percent of companies that sponsor academic research require researchers to delay the release of results for six months or more (Bollier 2002: 142). Academics involved in partnerships with industry may also be compelled to work with very short time lines and with an eye to profitability as opposed to being free to pursue all the promising research avenues that emerge. In addition to their effects on the particular professors involved in research alliances with corporations, these market-driven norms and practices spill over into the broader academic enterprise. In a variety of ways, they further erode the collective

> Instead of a public good that is shared freely, academic research is increasingly becoming the private property of university research sponsors.

nature of academic science (such as when colleagues who are not working for industry keep research results secret as a defensive measure) as well as the many social benefits that flow from that work (including less costly, more efficient, and higher quality knowledge production) (Atkinson-Grosjean 2006: 23–28).

Finally, research alliances with business transform the ways in which, and conditions under which, academic research is accessed and used. Instead of a public good that is shared freely with all researchers and others who can use it, the research produced in these alliances is increasingly becoming the private property of research partners. If and when research results are made available to other academics or members of the public, it is more often through some kind of commercial transaction, such as paying a licensing fee or direct purchase. Needless to say, the privatization and commercialization of academic research render it far less accessible to most academics and citizens, who must now pay for previously free knowledge, often at the very high prices that stem from monopoly conditions. This was the case, for example, with the discovery by researchers at the University of Utah of an important human gene responsible for breast cancer. Rather than making this discovery freely available to other scientists, the Utah researchers patented it and granted monopoly rights to Myriad Genetics Inc., which hoarded the gene and restricted other scientists from using it (Washburn 2005: xi). This form of privatization also serves to transform university administrators' and academics' perceptions of their own interests and how they respond to those interests.

In recent years, spurred on by the efforts of federal and provincial governments, as well as their growing entrepreneurial expertise gained from involvement with the private sector, university administrators have come to realize that they not only need to serve the research needs of paying clients, but are also in a position to exploit the fruits of academic research on their own. As a result, they have pursued a range of entrepreneurial activities based on their academics' research, which include establishing commercial development offices, selling ringside seats to leading-edge research, setting up spin-off companies, and licensing valuable intellectual property, and the like. Such initiatives are not small-scale ventures that are peripheral to the activities of universities. Rather, they are complex undertakings that are consuming more and more of the available money, effort, time, and other resources of a university (see, for example, Read 2003). Administrators' growing involvement in entrepreneurial activities further entrenches private-sector values and practices within our public universities. It also leads universities to prioritize their own interests over and above those of the general public. Indeed, one might argue that it is producing a reversal in the relationship between our universities and the broader community. For instead of using public funds to serve public purposes, our universities are using increasing shares of public funds to finance private ventures aimed at enriching themselves.

The university's greater involvement in entrepreneurial activities also has an impact on individual academics, transforming their professional interests and either enticing or compelling them to prioritize those new interests. For example, as universities share the spoils of business initiatives with those researchers who produce profitable knowledge, some academics have an unprecedented opportunity to become rich from their research. This gives them greater incentive to pursue lucrative research questions and areas, which are not always the most scientifically valuable or socially useful ones. A classic example of this is the growing attention, within the medical field, to the relatively minor but highly profitable "lifestyle" concerns of wealthy people, such as erectile dysfunction, and the marked inattention to the more widespread and serious diseases of the poor, such as malaria and tuberculosis (Mahood 2005).

The growing importance of corporate partnerships and commercialization to universities is leading administrators to reward academics involved in these activities in a number of other ways, both formal (such as through the tenure and promotion process) and informal (by according them greater institutional prestige and influence). This reward system encourages faculty (especially newer and untenured faculty) to become involved in privately oriented research activities instead of publicly oriented projects. Indeed, academics who refrain from allying with private partners, and particularly from privatizing their research results, are not only forgoing the benefits that accrue to those who are involved in these activities, but may also be compromising their advancement and perhaps even their position within the university. It is also not uncommon for faculty who criticize the university's involvement in business ventures as a conflict of interest or a betrayal of its public-service mission to face various forms of sanction within the institution, ranging from mild disapproval to harassment and even job loss (for a discussion of one such case, see CAUT 2003b). In actively supporting the public's interest, then, academics may end up jeopardizing their private interests. This problem makes it progressively difficult for academics to sustain a public serving ethic.

In general, many of these changes interact with and reinforce one another to strengthen the ties that pull the university away from a public-serving orientation and towards a private-serving role. For instance, the university's involvement in partnerships with industry facilitates and promotes involvement in business ventures of its own, and promotes and facilitates even more partnership with industry.

UNIVERSITY GOVERNANCE

In the post–Second World War period, universities were run as collegial and democratic institutions (sometimes more in theory than in practice). At all levels of the university, academic decisions were made collectively, by professors, through established collegial structures and processes, such as those of academic senates and faculty councils. While administrators, who were relatively few in number, had substantial power in the institution, they tended to see themselves as, and to act as, leaders of the collegium. They saw their job as facilitating and supporting academics' work and protecting the university's autonomy from undue outside influences on the part of government and others. Particularly in response to their activism in the 1960s, students were also afforded considerable opportunity to have significant input into academic affairs (such as through designated seats on departmental, faculty, and university-wide committees). Further, while only a small number of people from outside the university were able to directly participate in academic governance (such as through university senates and boards of governors), the university's relatively autonomous and democratic nature resulted in a high degree of responsiveness to a variety of social constituencies and of accountability to the wider community (Newson and Buchbinder 1988: cha. 3; Cameron 1991: cha. 7; Tudiver 1999: cha. 4).

Beginning with cutbacks in government funding for universities in the 1970s, and continuing with corporate research alliances and universities' involvement in knowledge businesses of their own, the nature of Canadian university governance began to change. These (and other) developments led to a significant increase in the size of academic administrations, and especially of research administrations. They also led to a substantial change in the nature and practice of administration. Rather than being leaders of collegial and democratic universities, administrators began to see themselves as, and to act as, the managers of these increasingly complex organizations and of those who work and learn within them.[5] As a result they attempted to centralize as much power as possible and to adopt a range of the values and practices that predominate in the business world, thereby rendering the universities more like private-sector institutions and more amenable to the desires and demands of the private sector (Newson 1992).

University administrators have been able, for instance, to centralize power by progressively bypassing collegial bodies and making more decisions either on their own or through hand-picked advisory committees. Such actions are often legitimized by the need to capture fleeting commercial and other opportunities that presumably can be lost if decision-making gets "bogged down in democracy." Administrators have also centralized power by replacing long-standing collegial processes with various "consultative" exercises (frequently conducted online), that offer a more limited — and malleable — form of academic participation. Another approach is to define more and more issues as being purely administrative and thus not within the purview of the broader collegium. For example, administrators could forge deals that afford monopolies on campus to providers of various products, from soft drinks to software — making arrangements that have significant impacts on the general campus environment.

Perhaps most troubling is the growing amount of secrecy pervading university operations. Instead of being open to academic (and public) scrutiny and deliberation, more and more research

> More and more research and other agreements between university administrators and external partners are being made and kept under the cloak of secrecy.

and other agreements (including monopoly sales agreements) between university administrators and external partners are being made and kept under the cloak of secrecy. This practice, which is frequently justified by the need to protect partners' proprietary information, very clearly sacrifices academic tradition and community interests to the desires and demands of particular individuals and corporations (Newson and Polster 2001: 59).

University administrators are changing university operations in other ways that render them more like corporations. One significant aspect of this transformation is the adoption of private-sector practices, such as the use of performance indicators of various kinds, which serve to reduce professors' autonomy and increase managerial scrutiny and control (Bruneau and Savage 2002). A more general feature in decision-making related to a growing number of university issues, is the progressive displacement of academic considerations by economic criteria, ranging from who is hired and rewarded, and how resources are allocated to various academic units, to what research areas are and are not prioritized. This shift was starkly reflected in a recent hiring of a dean: a participant in the process stated that "as long as he brings in $20 million, the rest doesn't matter" (Polster forthcoming). Another subtle but equally powerful change is the importing into universities of corporate language in which presidents are "CEOs," faculty members and staff are "human resources," and students are "clients" (Turk 2000a: 6). More than merely new forms of address, such terms imply and help to institutionalize very different kinds of roles for, and relationships between, those who work and learn in the university.

The university is not simply being run more *as* a business. To an unprecedented degree, it is being run *by* members of the private sector and other wealthy individuals. The phenomenon of private sponsors gaining greater say over what academic research is done and how it is done appears not only in the context of isolated research projects, but also in the context of larger units and institutions on campus, such as university/industry research centres, networks, and institutes, over which corporate partners command considerable authority. Increasingly, private sponsors are being granted extraordinary say over other academic matters as well. It is not uncommon for them to be given a hand in hiring and curricular decisions, and even voting positions on university committees, in exchange for donations in cash or in kind. Such was case when the mere loan of some high-end equipment gave Sony Classical Production a seat on the curriculum committee of McGill University's Faculty of Music (Shaker 1999: 3). (For additional examples, see Graham 2000; Shaker 1999.) This change in academic governance is facilitated by, and reinforces in turn, the other changes in university administration. For instance, as members of the collegium and the general public are progressively excluded from university decision-making processes, it becomes more difficult to challenge both the particular actions and the broader cultural transformation of the university that render it more open to corporate influence and control.

As is the case with academic research, changes in the social relations of academic governance also serve to alter the interests of those within the university and to encourage them to prioritize their personal well-being over the common good. For example, these changes are reducing the payoff that academics get from participating in university governance, given that important decisions are less frequently being made within established collegial bodies and that university service is progressively less valued and rewarded (particularly in relation to activities that generate income for the institution) in the context of academic performance review. As a result, many professors are opting to minimize if not abandon their university service work in favour of their research and teaching work, which may be more personally and professionally rewarding (Newson and Polster 2001: 69–70). While this retreat from collegialism may serve academics' immediate individual interests, it undermines the collective interest and ultimately the public interest — because among other factors, it reduces, in the short run, the efficacy of those academics who remain committed to preserving our universities as democratic institutions and, in the long run, the number of academics who are familiar with and committed to this vision.[6]

The changing social relations of academic governance are also leading some faculty and others, such as lower-level administrators, to alter the ways in which they participate in the process, so that rather than seeing themselves as members of a collective pursuing common goals, they act more as individual agents pursuing their private goals. For instance, as university planning decisions are increasingly being made outside of collegial bodies, academics, department heads, and/or deans are far less able to collectively negotiate positions and policies that serve the majority interest. As such, many of them are attempting to informally influence planning processes — if and when the planning has a direct effect on them — as individuals (or small groups) advocating only for their particular needs. This is especially clear in decisions about which areas the universities and/or faculties will target as "strategic priorities." Rather than insisting that such decisions be made collectively in order to serve the general interests of the institution or faculty, more and more members of the academy are working "behind the scenes" to ensure that their own areas get prioritized, regardless of the effect that this may have elsewhere on their institutions and colleagues (Polster forthcoming). This strategy leads others to follow suit, if only to ensure that their interests are not compromised. Thus the collective well-being is progressively subordinated to individuals' well-being, and academic solidarity and power vis-à-vis increasingly managerial senior administrations are further fragmented and diminished.

These changes in university governance and academic research, then, interact in various ways that promote and reinforce privatization. The centralization of power by academic administrators facilitates the establishment of university/industry research alliances and the commercialization of academic research. In turn, the commercialization encourages — indeed, compels — administrators to run universities more as businesses by curbing collegialism, transparency, and other long-standing academic traditions and values (Newson 2005: 10). These changes also contribute to and, in turn, are reinforced by changes in the social relations of Canadian university teaching.

UNIVERSITY TEACHING

Teaching was at the heart of the postwar university. While professors were expected to contribute to knowledge production and academic governance, their first priority, based on a common understanding, was teaching students (Pocklington and Tupper 2002: 11). As a result, most university courses were taught by full-time faculty members. Relatively small class sizes promoted a high degree of interaction between professors and students, and among students themselves. By the 1960s, with the dramatic expansion of Canada's university system, higher education had progressively come to be seen as a citizenship right, rather than a privilege of the rich. Tuition and other fees were kept low and student grants and loans were made widely available to ensure that higher education was affordable and accessible to all qualified Canadians (Axelrod 1982; Rounce 1999).

Beginning in the 1970s, and continuing on a relatively consistent basis since, governments have been reducing the funding provided to universities for operating costs, which include teaching costs (see, for example, CAUT 1999, 2005b).[7] At the same time, and in part to make up for cuts in government support, universities have entered into a variety of private initiatives that are, nonetheless, frequently very costly to the institution. To participate in corporate research alliances, for example, universities need to spend significant funds developing proposals, attracting partners, building labs, and purchasing equipment. They also need to support a growing cadre of administrators and other specialists (including high-priced lawyers) to help broker and negotiate complex agreements, monitor them, and resolve inevitable conflicts. To cope with the rising costs in a context of diminished operating revenues, university administrators have adopted a number of strategies related to university teaching. These strategies serve to further privatize Canadian higher education and erode its public-serving nature.

One strategy is simply to substantially reduce teaching costs (CAUT 1999). Thus, across most if not all Canadian campuses, class sizes have swelled, library holdings have diminished, classroom and other facilities have deteriorated, and courses and programs have been slashed, particularly in the humanities and arts.[8] Universities have also upped their use of part-time and graduate student instructors,[9] who are paid far less than full-time faculty and receive far fewer benefits and opportunities for professional development (Tudiver 1999: 163–64). These kinds of arrangements both stem from and contribute to the growing influence of private-sector approaches within the university, leading in particular to the displacement of academic values by economic criteria or bottom-line thinking.

> Class sizes have swelled, library holdings have diminished, classroom and other facilities have deteriorated, and courses and programs have been slashed, particularly in the humanities and arts.

In addition to reducing the resources invested in teaching, university administrators have opted to increase tuition and other student fees. According to the Canadian Federation of Students (CFS 2005), in the space of ten years average undergraduate tuition fees more than doubled, going from $2,000 in 1993–94 to over $4,000 in 2003–04.[10] This option privatizes higher education in the sense that it becomes more of an individual and less of a social or collective responsibility; universities become increasingly inaccessible to growing numbers of Canadians. The option also privatizes education in the sense that many students have to work longer hours to finance their schooling and thus have less time to socialize or get involved in other campus activities (CAUT 2003a). Their own university education, as well as that of their peers, becomes an increasingly isolated or private rather than communal experience — a kind of privatization exacerbated for, and by, the growing numbers of students who are taking some, or all, of their courses online.

As they have developed their entrepreneurial acumen and expertise, administrators have come to regard university teaching not simply as a cost that needs to be managed, but as an untapped money-making opportunity. They are thus becoming involved in a variety of lucrative teaching ventures, ranging from providing exclusive "boutique" programs (such as executive M.B.A. degrees that run in the tens of thousands of dollars per year), to developing and/or delivering courses for private companies, to hosting foreign programs on Canadian campuses for a cut of the profits (see, for example, Day 2006). To capitalize on the huge commercial opportunities opening up in the international education market, they have expanded the profitable courses and programs offered to foreign students (both through distance education and various partnership agreements with foreign institutions), and more aggressively recruited foreign students, who pay increasingly exorbitant, differentiated fees. According to the CFS (2004), "In 2002, average graduate tuition fees for international students reached $10,841, more than double the already high fees paid by Canadian citizens. At some universities, students pay up to $26,000 a year in tuition fees."

These kinds of initiatives serve to further erode the quality of education provided to the general student body, as they divert university resources and efforts towards more valued "clients," whether they are the students who pay substantially higher fees for their education or the private partners whose education ventures make money for the university. They also further erode both public values, such as equity in, and access to, higher education, and public-serving practices, such as providing openness and accountability in university affairs.[11]

Then, too, while our universities are becoming more businesslike in relation to the education they provide, they are also becoming more businesslike with regard to the students they serve. They are investing growing amounts of time and resources in branding, advertising, and other marketing activities aimed at attracting greater numbers (and different kinds) of students. They are making greater use of technology and standardized procedures and protocols to manage student affairs. They are adopting the widespread use of teaching evaluations, student exit surveys, and other instruments to assess and improve "customer service" and satisfaction (Newson 2005). These and other such measures divert precious resources away from the practice of teaching and towards the corporate services that promote and manage teaching, further eroding public education. They also reflect, and help entrench, a different relationship between the university and its students: as opposed to participating members of an educational community, students are seen and treated more and more as isolated consumers who purchase various services from the institution.

The changing relations of university teaching also transform the interests of those within the academy and encourage them to place their private well-being over and above that of the collective. In the case of students, reduced opportunities to work together to meaningfully shape university education are leading them to act on, and for, their individual interests. Thus, for example, rather than allying with their peers to improve the quality of education for all, high-achieving students — for whom universities are competing — are entering into more frequent and aggressive negotiations with academic institutions to secure the best possible terms and conditions for their education only (Alphonso 2006a; Reich 2001: 203–204). More generally, as students are progressively treated as customers, many of them are orienting to their education as customers, expecting teaching practices and decisions — particularly those surrounding grades — to please them. This trend is evident in the growing number of accounts of students challenging evaluations of their work and even demanding A's for their courses "because they paid for them" (Alphonso 2006b: A3; Newson 2005: 35–36). In a context in which administratively imposed performance indicators, such as standardized student evaluation forms, play a greater role in academics' performance reviews, some faculty members (particularly part-time and untenured faculty) find themselves pressured to prioritize their own interests over students' interests by tailoring their teaching expectations and standards to conform with their customers' demands (Churchill 2006: C1). In so doing, these faculty members also compromise the interests of colleagues who opt to resist this pressure, as well as compromising the interests of the public, which is harmed in a variety of ways by the reduction in the quality of higher education.

POWER

In general, the ongoing privatization of higher education — and all education — in Canada serves to entrench and intensify inequality within our society. It does this, in part, by shifting resources and power upwards, concentrating them in the hands of those who already have resources and power. For example, as tuition fees (and especially fees for professional and elite programs) escalate, privileged youth and adults are comprising a growing share of the university student population (CFS n.d.) They are also more able to take better advantage of their educational opportunities than are their less affluent peers. Similarly, as universities become more involved in research partnerships and business ventures of various kinds, the institution's research resources and results are progressively being made available to those who can afford to pay for them, to the detriment of those who cannot.

> The ongoing privatization of education serves to entrench and intensify inequality within our society.

In addition to greater access to the university's resources, wealthy citizens and corporations are gaining greater control over the direction of the institution as a whole. As administrators run universities more and more like corporations, they are closing down the spaces for members of the academic community and the broader community to have input into university affairs. At the same time they are either offering or acceding to expanded opportunities for members of the private sector and other well-resourced individuals to shape academic decisions and decision-making processes. Not only does privatization thus undermine the redistributive function of public higher education (its ability to level inequalities by transferring resources from the wealthy to the poor), but it also serves to reverse that function. Rather than the rich subsidizing the educational and research needs of people with more limited financial resources, the general public is increasingly subsidizing the rich, paying the lion's share of the costs of the university's teaching and research resources — which people in general are progressively less able to use and over which they are losing control.[12]

The upwards shift of university resources serves to entrench and intensify inequalities in our society in a multiplicity of ways. As fewer disadvantaged students — and, increasingly, middle-class students — are able or willing to shoulder the huge financial burdens of higher education, the relative advantages of the wealthy stand to increase.[13] This advantage takes hold especially in the global, knowledge-based economy in which higher education plays a pivotal role in individuals' (and in the collective's) prosperity and quality of life. Further, as corporations and some individuals gain greater access to university research resources and results, they are able to sustain and expand their advantages in relation both to their competitors and to consumers. For instance, companies that obtain broad patents on important academic discoveries can stifle competition, pre-empt the development of alternative products and processes, and thus charge high monopoly prices for their products (Washburn 2005; Shulman 1999). The upwards shift of control over the university further reinforces inequalities in our society, as it provides well-resourced parties with "an inside track" into university policy and decision-making, a position they can use to privilege, and perpetuate, both their particular interests and their collective, class interests. Given that transparency and accountability in university affairs are being reduced

> As our universities become more influenced by and oriented to corporate needs, the knowledge produced becomes progressively instrumental and narrow, and thus less critical and diverse.

at the same time, wealthy individuals and corporations are able to advance their agendas with an unprecedented lack of scrutiny and a high degree of impunity.

Privatization does not simply further privilege the privileged. It simultaneously harms the majority of our citizens, and particularly disadvantaged citizens, by diminishing various resources that enable them not only to resist increasingly unequal power relations in our society but also to otherwise enhance the quality of their lives. For instance, as our universities become more fully influenced by and oriented to corporate needs, the knowledge produced becomes progressively instrumental and narrow, and thus less critical and diverse. This tendency limits the opportunities for those within the university and for the population at large to question and critique the status quo. It also deprives both those inside and outside universities of the knowledge necessary to transform their world in ways that more closely conform to their needs and interests. Thus, for example, as universities have become more involved in research and entrepreneurial ventures with agribusiness and pharmaceutical companies, it has become more difficult — both scientifically and politically — for those within all parts of the institution (and thus for those outside of it) to question and challenge the assumptions and implications of genetic engineering and the curative approach to health. The suppression in 2003 and thereafter by the University of Manitoba of a graduate student's film on genetically modified crops, which portrayed Monsanto — a powerful multinational corporation with strong research and other links to the university — in a negative light provides a powerful illustration of this difficulty (see Sanders 2005; chapter 14 here; for additional examples, see Schafer 2005; Washburn 2005). At the same time, universities are developing and disseminating relatively little alternative knowledge, such as knowledge of organic farming or of holistic approaches to illness prevention, that citizens can draw upon — even were they so inclined — to better serve their own needs and enhance the collective well-being.

The privatization of higher education also erodes important skills that enable citizens to achieve greater equality and advance the public interest. For instance, when Canada's universities were run more openly and communally, they served as important training grounds for democracy. Many civic leaders cut their political teeth on university politics, and many more citizens developed not only a sense of their right to become actively involved in public institutions as well as the skills and savvy to do so effectively during their university years (for a Canadian example, see Pitsula 2006: chas. 12, 13; the movie *Berkeley in the Sixties* provides a vivid U.S. example). As universities progressively limit the opportunities for students and others to participate in academic affairs, and instead compel and entice them to engage with the institution as isolated consumers or employees, they rob people of important opportunities to acquire and hone democratic sensibilities and capacities that are key to achieving positive change within both the institution and the broader society. (For an interesting exploration of this issue, see Brule 2004.)

Perhaps most troubling is that privatization undermines, both within the university and outside of it, various values and commitments that inspire and reinforce efforts to promote social equality and justice, such as a concern for the common good. The university deals a serious blow to the common good in and through its involvement in the privatization and commercialization of knowledge, which not only leads it to make withdrawals from our common stock of knowledge without depositing much in return, but also makes it more difficult for others to replenish our rapidly diminishing pool of free knowledge or our "knowledge commons" (Washburn 2005; Shulman 1999). To an alarming degree, growing numbers of university administrators and academics are even betraying the common good by knowingly jeopardizing citizens' well-being in the pursuit of profit — a trend that has become all too evident through the growing number of scandals and lawsuits in which universities have become embroiled. (For a thorough and chilling account of many of these, including the wrongful death of Jesse Gelsinger in the United States and the sagas of doctors Nancy Olivieri and David Healy, who were penalized for putting the interests of patients above those of university corporate partners in Canada, see Washburn 2005.)[14]

Our universities are failing to nurture the common good in a host of other ways. Academic administrators and others are restricting the opportunities for members of the university community to raise and defend the public interest in the context of institutional decision-making and policy-making. They are also reducing the resources and rewards provided to those involved in communally oriented programs and projects in the university, and suppressing and penalizing various forms of resistance to privatization that students and staff undertake in defence of the collective good. At the same time, many people in universities are promoting greater individualism and competitiveness in a myriad of ways, such as when they bestow honours and privileges on academics who privately profit from their research, and when they encourage — and even help train — graduate and some undergraduate students to do the same.

> The more that the corporate perspective is taken for granted, the more the pursuit of private interests is placed above question — and is even redefined as the primary means of achieving the common good.

Perhaps the greatest threat to the common good is the progressive normalization of the corporate perspective within the university. The more that this perspective is taken for granted and passed on by those who work and learn in the institution, the more the pursuit of private interests is placed above question — and is even redefined as the primary means of achieving the common good.

While the privatization of higher education serves the interests of the privileged at the expense of the majority of citizens, oddly enough it also fundamentally undermines the interests of the privileged, in a number of ways. Although wealthy students are getting more education, and superior education, relative to others, the overall quality of their educational experience is declining not only through the growing homogeneity, isolation, and competitiveness within the student body, but also because of the university's progressive orientation to education as a business and to students as an income source. Similarly, while particular corporations may derive immediate benefits from research alliances, privatization harms the longer term interests of the corporate sector as a whole. It erodes many of the features of academic research — such as its open and collaborative nature and the ability to engage in the curiosity-driven inquiries that are more frequently the source of significant scientific breakthroughs — that enhance the quality of research as well as its actual and potential economic contributions (Polster 1994: cha. 7; Atkinson-Grosjean 2006: 23–28). More generally, as the privatization of the university helps to enrich privileged individuals and organizations, it simultaneously impoverishes (and imperils) the larger social and natural contexts that they inhabit. Although wealth and power can insulate the privileged from some of the harmful effects of this result, ultimately the only way of dealing with these problems is through collective solutions — but then, of course, privatization impedes the development of these solutions in various ways, both directly and indirectly.

Although the university, as an institution, seems to benefit from privatization in that it gains new capacities to generate funds as well as new allies and support (particularly from within the corporate sector), it too may be seriously harmed by this process. As our universities fundamentally change what they are and what they do, and as more citizens come to understand what this means for their personal and collective well-being, public support for these institutions is likely to wane. Given that the public is still the major funder and supporter of the university, this diminishing support bodes ill for the future of the institution. A lack of public support will render the university far more vulnerable to the needs and demands of wealthy individuals and corporations, whose ability not simply to influence, but also to exploit, the university will increase in proportion to the public's abandonment of the institution.

While the implications of these trends are thus very serious and troubling, we need to remember that the privatization of higher education in Canada is a continuing process and is by no means completed. The university is indeed becoming more privately oriented in all of its aspects and activities, but there are still many sites and individuals within the academy that remain dedicated to serving and promoting the public interest. A growing number of opportunities, both within and outside of the university, offer possibilities for generating and mobilizing resistance to the privatization of higher education.

RESISTANCE

In spite of (or perhaps because of) the isolating and disempowering effects of privatization, various groups around the country have taken a number of steps to expose, and oppose, it in recent years. One of the most active of these groups is Canadian students. Through their local, regional, and national organizations, many students have launched actions to resist specific impacts of privatization and the more general process itself. These actions include campaigns to oppose tuition hikes and monopoly deals between universities and corporations (most notably those involving Coke and Pepsi), as well as efforts, such as the Corporate Free Campus project[15] at the University of Toronto, to educate students and others about the general nature and implications of the privatization of Canadian higher education (CCPA 2005: cha. 1).

> Various groups around the country have taken steps to expose, and oppose, privatization in recent years. One of the most active of these groups is Canadian students.

Many faculty have also resisted privatization. Both individually and collectively (such as through the collective bargaining process and in the context of faculty strikes, such as the York University strike in spring 1997, the longest academic staff strike in English Canada), they have opposed various developments, including the growing use of performance measures, increases in class sizes, and the greater emphasis on income-generating activities, that erode the quality of their own working lives and of the education, research, and other forms of service they can offer to the public. In addition to working within their own organizations, students and faculty have collaborated with one another and with various public-interest groups to raise awareness about privatization and to mount opposition to initiatives that entrench and advance it. Campaigns were waged, for example against a 1991 bid to establish a private International Space University on the York University campus[16] (Saunders 1992), a 2004 plan to redevelop the old Varsity Stadium site at the University of Toronto (Salterrae 2004), and a plan to establish a privately funded college on the campus of Simon Fraser University (McCuaig 2006). The York University and Varsity Stadium projects were defeated due to collective action. Beyond their direct and immediate impacts, efforts such as these help to build alliances and solidarity as well as valuable knowledge and experience that can inspire and strengthen future efforts to oppose privatization. Thus, whether they win or lose particular struggles, those involved in these forms of resistance make an important contribution to preserving public higher education in our country.

While these forms of opposition are extremely important, other approaches could also be adopted to enhance resistance. Rather than simply reacting to various initiatives and practices that promote privatization, opponents of the process might proactively establish alternative initiatives and practices that model the kind of public-serving university they hope to preserve and revitalize. One example would be to establish equivalents of the Dutch science shops on Canadian campuses. Science shops are university institutions that make academic resources and expertise available to local citizens groups in order to resolve various problems or serve other needs. They address a broad spectrum of issues ranging from investigating and helping to remedy various kinds of environmental contamination in local neighbourhoods to conducting feasibility studies and helping to produce detailed plans for local development projects (Sclove 1995).[17] Two key principles of science shops are that the groups involved do not pay for the research done for them and any results that emerge from research projects are kept in the public domain. The presence on our campuses of such institutions could challenge, and interrupt, many of the assumptions and practices associated with privatization, such as the desirability of commercializing academic knowledge and the privileging of the research needs of paying clients. Equally if not more importantly, science shops could help sustain and rejuvenate a progressive and public-serving vision for the university. They could also help to create conditions to realize this vision, by revitalizing or instilling a public service ethic in both academics and students, and by encouraging all citizens (especially those with little power) to see and treat the university as a collective resource that they are entitled to use and that should, and can, be responsive and accountable to them.

Another approach to strengthening resistance is to organize a number of broad and co-ordinated national campaigns, each of which highlights one selected aspect of the privatization process. This approach allows opponents of privatization to concentrate their resources all at once and on the same issue, rather than diffusing them on a multiplicity of isolated actions across the country. The best candidates for these campaigns are the aspects of the university's privatization that are most deeply intertwined with other aspects (because pulling on these threads is likely to cause other issues to unravel as well). They are also those aspects of privatization that speak to deeply held and widely shared values and concerns and are thus able to interest and mobilize a large cross-section of the Canadian population.

One such issue around which a national campaign could be built is the privatization and commercialization of academic research. The university's involvement in intellectual property connects with a number of other aspects of privatization, including the skewing of academic research towards industrial needs and interests, greater secrecy and managerialism in the university, rising tuition fees, and the university's growing involvement in various conflicts of interest and scandals. Because this issue is so deeply enmeshed in the privatization process, it cannot be easily dismissed, nor can it be resolved through simple or technical measures (such as guidelines or regulations) that would leave privatization essentially intact. A second advantage of building a campaign around this issue is that it touches on widespread and deeply felt concerns within our society and could thus help mobilize and unite a broad coalition of support. Within the university, it could help bring together students who are suffering from intolerable debt loads, academics whose access to increasingly expensive research materials is being reduced, and members of departments and faculties that are being penalized for their inability or unwillingness to engage in private knowledge production. It could also bring together a wide range of groups outside the university — people who have more general concerns about the privatization of the commons of knowledge, including farmers, health professionals, Aboriginal people, artists, and even a growing number of corporate leaders and entrepreneurs (Shulman 1999; Bollier 2002). A campaign like this would not only stand a good chance of succeeding, but also enhance the chances of success of subsequent campaigns against the privatization of higher education.[18] At the same time such campaigns could help strengthen efforts to oppose privatization at other levels of the education system and perhaps within other valued public institutions, such as the Canadian health-care system.

Opponents of privatization might also focus more of their efforts on outside developments that are contributing to changes within the university.[19] Much of the impetus for the privatization of the university has come from government, particularly the federal government. Beginning in the mid-1970s and intensifying since then, the federal government's conception of the university has shifted from a resource for social development to an instrument of economic competitiveness (Polster 1994: cha. 2). This shift has led politicians to reduce the basic operating funds that they provide to universities and to directly and indirectly encourage the schools to ally with the corporate sector and become involved in entrepreneurial initiatives of their own. To a large extent, this shift in the government's conception and treatment of the university has stemmed from a shift in the nature of government itself. Rather than producing university policy in-house, the government has progressively been ceding responsibility for higher education policy-making to unelected and unaccountable advisory bodies, such as the Advisory Council on Science and Technology, which are dominated by corporate and academic executives and those who are supportive of their interests. Not surprisingly, these groups have used the opportunity to advance and institutionalize visions and policies for the university that serve their particular needs rather than those of the broader society (Polster 1994).

As part of the effort to resist the privatization of the university, citizens might, then, also resist the privatization of government. They might work to ensure that those elected by the public (along with other public servants) produce policy for the public, and that they do so in a way that is transparent, accountable, and responsive to a broad range of social interests and needs. This strategy could go a long way towards undercutting many of the conditions that sustain privatization in the university and elsewhere. In so doing, it would reduce and ease the work that opponents of privatization have to do and further enhance the effectiveness of their resistance.

GLOSSARY OF KEY TERMS

Privatization: Most simply, privatization involves the transfer of assets or services from the government to the private sector. It can also involve the incorporation into public bodies of values and practices that predominate in the private sector as well as the production of a range of partnerships between public and private bodies.

Commercialization: The process through which a product is introduced into the marketplace. The commercialization of academic research means that knowledge produced in whole or in part with public funds is not made freely available to the public, but is accessible only to those who are able and willing to pay for it.

Social relations: Ongoing courses of human activity in and through which aspects of society (such as higher education) are given their particular shape and form. As social relations change, old options and possibilities for social action may be closed down, while others are opened up.

Intellectual property rights: IPRs legally establish monopoly protection for creative works such as writing (copyright), inventions (patents), and identifiers (trademarks). IPRs effectively extract ideas and other forms of knowledge from the knowledge commons or the public domain, that is, that pool of freely available knowledge to which we may all contribute and from which we may all draw.

Academic collegialism: Refers to the values and practices in and through which academics collectively govern the university. Examples of key collegial structures include university senates and faculty councils.

Dutch science shops: Bodies on many university campuses that provide research services, often free of charge, to help local groups address issues of concern such as environmental contamination and community economic development.

QUESTIONS FOR DISCUSSION

1. What impact has rising tuition had on your own experience at university and on the experience of your peers?
2. How are students involved in shaping policy at your university? How has this changed from the past, and how might the situation be improved in the future?
3. What kinds of university/industry alliances exist at your institution, and what kinds of business ventures is your university involved in? How do these affect the teaching and research at your university?
4. What other forms of privatization are visible at your university (for example, corporate advertising on campus)? What are their impacts on the general university environment?

5. What actions have been taken by people at your university to draw attention to the issue of privatization? What further actions could be taken?
6. How do you feel about making university free for all qualified students? Why?
7. Some people argue that all knowledge produced in public universities should remain in the public domain (freely accessible to all). What is your position on this and why?
8. Proponents of university/industry alliances argue that promoting economic competitiveness is the highest form of public service that the university can provide. What is your response to this assertion?
9. In what ways is privatization at other levels of the education system similar to and different from privatization at the level of the university? What are the main benefits and harms of privatization at these other levels of the system?

WEBSITES OF INTEREST

Canadian Association of University Teachers. <www.caut.ca>.
Canadian Centre for Policy Alternatives (see the Education Project). <www.policyalternatives.ca>.
Canadian Federation of Students. <www.cfs-fcee.ca>.
British Columbia Teachers Federation. <www.bctf.ca>.
Forum on Privatization and the Public Domain. <www.forumonpublicdomain.ca>.
Living Knowledge. <www.scienceshops.ca>.
University Watch. <www.uwatch.ca>.

NOTES

1. These analyses can be found in government reports on higher education, such as those produced in the context of the national innovation strategy. See <www.innovationstrategy.gc.ca>.
2. Although an increase in private and for-profit higher education has occurred in Canada in recent years <www.cfs-fcee.ca/html/english/campaigns/private.php>, the vast majority of Canada's universities are still public.
3. The privatization and commercialization of academic research involve converting the knowledge produced in the university (which is always either fully or partially publicly funded) into private, intellectual property and exploiting that property to generate profit.
4. There is no central list that includes all of these research partnerships in Canada, much less tracks their growth over time. However, several agencies, such as Industry Canada and the national research granting councils, do discuss (and, in some cases, track the growth of) some of these alliances in documents such as annual reports. Various analysts of higher education have also addressed the growth of these alliances in more general terms. For one example, see Tudiver 1999: cha. 3.
5. This trend has been exacerbated as growing numbers of non-academics have been hired as university administrators.
6. In abandoning university governance, academics also undermine their longer term private interests. For as managerial and private power becomes progressively less contested and

contestable, academics become increasingly subject to others' priorities and demands in all aspects of their work, including their research and teaching work.

7.   The dynamics of higher education funding in Canada are complex, but it is important to note that at the same time that the federal government has been reducing support for university operating costs — in absolute or relative terms — it has also, especially in recent years, been dramatically increasing the support provided to universities for academic research, and particularly for industrially oriented and partnership research — which in turn has contributed to certain aspects and consequences of privatization.

8.   Comprehensive data on the impacts of reduced investment in university education is difficult to find. One excellent, though dated, source on the impacts on Ontario universities is the Ontario Federation of Students' report *Cut to the Bone II: System Failure* (Orchard and Famula 1992). For other accounts of the impacts of reduced investment in university teaching, see the Canadian Centre for Policy Alternatives' "Missing Pieces" series and other publications of that organization. For example, according to Howard Woodhouse, at the same time that the University of Saskatchewan contributed $7.3 million to the Canadian Light Source (which will be used to commercialize research at the university), "130 faculty positions had been lost, staff drastically reduced, library holdings slashed, and buildings were literally falling down" (Woodhouse 2003).

9.   Data on part-time instructors is rare. However, in 2000 a Statistics Canada study noted that from 1992/93 to 1997/98 the number of full-time faculty in Canada decreased by 9.6 percent whereas the numbers of part-time faculty increased in almost all provinces. For example, in Western Canada, the number of part-time faculty rose by 13.5 percent and a significant 43.7 percent in full-time teaching equivalence (Statistics Canada 2000).

10.   The increases have been even more dramatic in professional programs. According to the Canadian Association of University Teachers (CAUT 2003a: 1), "Medical fees, adjusted for inflation, climbed 320 percent between 1990 and 2003. Tuition for law school rose 217 percent while dental programs charged students an incredible 400 percent more in 2003 than in 1990."

11.   Universities generate funds in many other ways, including exclusive marketing deals and allowing companies to advertise on campus. While these forms of privatization do not generally have an impact on course content, they do affect the broader lessons that students learn, both indirectly and directly, such as when criticism of their university's corporate sponsors is discouraged if not penalized on campus (Newson and Polster 2001: 73).

12.   The careful reader might question this comment, given that wealthy students and research sponsors are themselves paying a larger share of the costs of the education and research resources to which they are gaining access. While this is true, it is also true that the bulk of the costs of these resources is still paid by the general public in the form of direct and indirect government support to universities. For example, although the proportion of university operating costs paid by students increased from 16.9 percent to 34.2 percent from 1990 to 2003, the share of these costs paid by the public remained consistently higher, at 79.7 percent and 58.6 percent respectively (CAUT 2005a: 3). Many right-wing authors have used the "reverse subsidy" argument to support calls for greater privatization in higher education and elsewhere. ("Why should the poor continue to pay for resources that the rich disproportionately take advantage of?") However, an equally feasible, more just, and ultimately more productive solution would be to reverse privatization and to increase public access to public resources, such as by dramatically reducing, and eventually eliminating,

university tuition fees.

13. Privatization also intensifies other inequalities, such as those of gender, race, and dis/ability. For example, given that women tend to earn substantially less than men, even with equivalent education credentials (CFS 2003), they are less able, and may become less willing, to assume the heavy burdens associated with higher education.

14. Beyond the specific harms incurred by the particular individuals involved, cases such as these more fundamentally undermine the common good in that they erode the actual and perceived reliability and trustworthiness of our academic institutions. This development threatens to leave our society without a disinterested source of expertise to which we can turn for assessments or advice on important social, economic, and political questions and thus poses serious risks to our individual and collective well-being both now and in the future.

15. According to a Canadian Centre for Policy Alternatives (2005: 19) report, "The Anti-Corporate Rule Action Group of OPIRG Toronto began the Corporate-Free Campus project in 1998 to expose, challenge, and build alternatives to corporate connections at U of T. As part of the project, tours of campus examine corporate involvement within particular buildings, and the campus was put 'under construction' to work toward corporate-free zones."

16. The bid to establish the International Space University (ISU) on the York University campus was submitted, in secret, by the Centre of Excellence on Space and Terrestrial Science, which was located on the York campus and to which a large number of York faculty were cross-appointed. After the bid was leaked to the public, members of the university community and of a wide variety of public interest groups organized to oppose the project, for a number of reasons: the institution would be a private university — a first for Canada at the time; it would charge $25,000 in tuition fees; it would be parasitic on York student programs, library, and computer facilities; it would divert a substantial amount of government money from the public higher education system (the provincial and federal governments committed millions of public dollars to the ISU); and it would in various ways support and strengthen the U.S. military-industrial complex. After a broad-based and creative campaign by opponents of the bid, the ISU chose to locate elsewhere. For more details on the bid and the campaign, see Saunders 1992.

17. For more information on these institutions, see the website of Living Knowledge, the international science shop network <www.scienceshops.org>.

18. Broad and co-ordinated national campaigns could be organized around a number of other issues, such as the erosion of democratic control over the university and the mismanagement of public resources that stems from increasingly intense competition both within and between universities. And in addition to establishing science shops, many other proactive initiatives could be pursued, such as creating free universities in our cities (Collins 2003) and integrating universities into local and regional community economic development projects (Polster 2000).

19. Student organizations and others have addressed some of these issues, particularly cuts in government transfers to universities; but other more fundamental transformations in higher education policy and policy-making also need to be addressed.

Chapter Thirteen

HEALTH CARE "REFORM"
Privatization and Its Impact on Women

Handwritten margin note: Oct 14th — provide 80% of services → majority who use HC.

Pat Armstrong

Health care is undoubtedly an issue for all Canadians. An overwhelming majority of Canadians identify health-care reform as their primary concern, and in poll after poll Medicare shows up as Canada's most popular social program. But health is also, in great part, a women's issue (Armstrong and Armstrong 2001; Grant et al. 2004). Women are particularly concerned about health-care reforms, and this is because they not only account for the majority of those who use the system but also provide 80 percent of the services that make up the health-care system; and with women providing most of the care, what happens to women as care providers has an impact on all Canadians.

As one study put it, "Ask a Canadian what distinguishes Canada from the United States and likely as not she will take out her health insurance card" (Myles and Pierson 1997: 13, quoted in O'Connor, Orloff, and Shaver 1999: 5). Health care has been a shining example of a universal program that has worked to reduce inequalities in access to care. As Julia O'Connor, Ann Shola Orloff, and Sheila Shaver (1999: 5–6) put it, "No Canadian woman will go without pre-natal care, nor will she face harsh trade-offs between welfare with health coverage for her children and paid work with no benefits — as is so common for poor, and many working class, American women." Public health care has also provided women with decent paid work while relieving some of the pressure to

"You Should Know This"
- While 59 percent of those employed in cleaning and cooking in health care have full-time jobs, only 47 percent have full-time jobs when they do this work in other industries.
- Four out of five paid health-care workers are women, as are four of five unpaid personal-care providers.
- Wait times for hip and knee replacements have not increased over the last five years while the number of operations has grown significantly.
- In 2003–04, seven out of eight people with hip fractures had surgery within two days of being admitted to a hospital.
- Drugs account for 16 percent of health expenditures, doctors 13 percent and hospitals 30 percent.
- In 2004 private payments represented just over 60 percent of Canada's total drug costs, compared to an average of just under 40 percent for industrialized countries as a whole.
- Although the number of doctors per person has not changed since 1990, the number of nurses per person has declined from eleven to ten. This number is still higher than the average for industrialized countries and about the same as Germany and Japan.
- Provincial/territorial governments' share of health expenditures declined from 71 per cent in 1975 to 64 percent in 2003.
- In 1998 governments spent the most on health care for those aged fifteen to forty-four years, while the second largest share went to those of ages forty-five to sixty-five. They spent the least on those under fifteen and over eighty-five.

provide unpaid care at home. At the same time, however, welfare states have reinforced women's responsibility for care and taken over only some of the caring work. Indeed, the "social organization of caring structures women's opportunities and can impose significant costs and consequences" (Baines, Evans, and Neysmith 1998: 4)

Today fundamental transformations in Canada's public system are undermining both women's access to care and women's work in care, and in public debates very little attention is being paid to the impact of these changes on women. These transformations are mainly a factor of privatization, if we understand privatization in social as well as economic terms. Privatization of health care refers to several different policy initiatives that limit the role of the public sector and define health care as a private responsibility. The initiatives include shifting the burden of payment to individuals; opening health-service delivery to for-profit providers; moving care from public institutions to community-based organizations and private households; transferring care work from public-sector health-care workers to unpaid caregivers; and adopting the management strategies of private-sector businesses, applying market rules to health-service delivery, and treating health care as a market good.

These multiple forms of privatization have both different and combined consequences for access to care and the kind of care that Canadians receive. Some, such as the move to adopt business practices within the public system, are difficult to see. Others, such as the sale of hospitals to for-profit firms, are more obvious, although the consequences of such policies may be less clear. By exploring the consequences of these different forms of privatization for women, I hope to make visible not only the gendered impact of reforms but also the implications for men and the country as a whole.

MAKING A WELFARE STATE: HEALTH CARE CANADIAN-STYLE

What started in a single Prairie province a few years after the Second World War had become, by the end of the 1960s, a national health insurance system that demonstrated to Canadians how a public system could work (see Armstrong, Armstrong, and Fegan 1998). The social-democratic government in Saskatchewan introduced first a government insurance scheme to pay for hospital care and then a similar plan to pay for necessary medical care provided by doctors. Although health care is primarily a provincial responsibility, the federal government was able to promote public payment on a national scale by offering to fund half the costs of all medically necessary hospital and doctor care. The promise was contingent on provinces conforming to what have come to be called the five principles of the *Canada Health Act*: universality, accessibility, comprehensiveness, portability, and public administration. The *Act* clearly states that citizens have the right to care based on medical rather than financial need. The impulse was both democratic and financial, and it derived from pressure not only from workers' organizations and women's community groups but also from some provincial and local governments.

When hospital insurance was introduced, most hospitals were owned by either charitable organizations or local governments. When medical insurance was introduced, most doctors were in private practice charging fee-for-service. The public health plan did little to change these arrangements, in part because the power of those offering the services was firmly entrenched. Although the Royal Commission that led to the establishment of the national insurance scheme recommended that the plan be extended to home and long-term care, dental services, and drugs, the federal government focused on doctors and hospitals and thus limited the five principles to these services. For-profit insurance companies — companies that had held only a minority of the market — were left covering extras such as private rooms and dental care. They were prohibited from covering services paid for under the public plan.

Like the National Health Service (NHS) in Britain, the plan covers specific services rather than specific groups of people. But unlike the NHS, in Canada the services are not all publicly provided, patients are free to visit any doctor or hospital they choose, and when services are part of the public plan there is no option of paying for those services privately. The *Canada Health Act* prohibits user fees, or what in other countries are often called co-payments or deductibles.

From the beginning, then, Canada's public-health system was a mixture of the private and public. For doctors the system is one of public payment for private practice, and for hospitals it is often public payment for private, albeit non-profit, provision. Yet insurance companies were prevented from entering the public field, and doctors had to opt in fully to the public plan and negotiate fees with their provincial authorities. There is considerable provincial variation, given that there are multiple ways of conforming to the *Act's* five principles of universality, accessibility, comprehensiveness, portability, and public administration. The variation is even greater when it comes to services, such as home care and long-term care, that are not clearly protected under the *Canada Health Act*.

With its private provision, the Canadian system is not "socialist" in any ordinary sense of that term. Still, the concept of universality, or "everybody in, nobody out," does promote the idea of collective responsibility and shared risk. Accessibility, or the provision of services on equal terms and conditions without financial or other obstacles, means services for all according to need rather than ability to pay. Comprehensiveness, despite in practice being the weakest of the five principles, at least makes possible democratic debate and planning over the allocation and integration of health-care resources. Portability has the effect of eliminating concern over basic health-care coverage on the part of labour force workers and those dependent on them, because it means that the coverage is organized by province, not by employer. The public administration of each province's single-payer scheme prevents private insurers from enriching and empowering themselves in this huge potential market. In practice, this principle also demonstrates that the public sector can be efficient and effective (see National Forum on Health 1997).

DEVELOPING CARE FOR WOMEN

National health insurance has had a particularly profound impact on women. The enormous expansion of hospital services has resulted in a significantly increased demand for labour. While men have traditionally dominated the medical profession, women fill eight out of ten jobs in paid care (Canadian Institute for Health Information 2002). In the early years of the public system, the wages and conditions of work reflected the limited power of this traditional women's work. Since then a number of factors have contributed to the growing strength of the health-care labour force. Struggles inside and outside the sector have gained women the right to remain employed after they marry and after they become pregnant. The portability provision is particularly important for women, whose paid employment is more likely than men's to be precarious (Armstrong and Laxer 2006; Vosko 2000). Greater access to publicly funded health services means that fewer women are tied to the home by the need to provide care for family members. Women have come together in large workplaces, and they have been able to remain at or return to the same work after their children reach school age, which means they have been able to organize effectively in unions and professional organizations. Their struggles have been aided by the state's inability to "run away" (a tendency common among for-profit firms), by the state's international commitments to human rights, by labour shortages, by booming economies, and by pressure on the state to act like a model employer. Although some legislation, such as that concerning equal pay for work of equal value, applies only to the public sector in many provinces, at least health care as provided under the *Canada Health Act* is defined as public sector. Labour legislation has also made it easier to organize in this sector, as has the impact of the women's movement.

The health sector has been important as well in providing more equal opportunities for women. It has offered decent jobs to women of colour and women who are recent immigrants. Indeed, women from visible minority groups and immigrant populations are better represented here than in any other sector. This partly reflects immigration rules that give preference to those who can fill jobs with high demand, and partly the ideas about what work immigrants can do. But it also reflects the employment equity programs in place in the public sector. Those programs represent a victory for women's groups as well as the workings of a liberal welfare state philosophy. There has also been a trend towards more equal distribution within medicine. When women successfully broke the enrollment quota system that privileged men in medical schools, they rushed in large numbers into medical training. Although women still constitute a minority of practising physicians and surgeons, they form a majority in many medical schools.

None of this is to suggest that things have been perfect and perfectly harmonious in women's health-care work. Sharp differences among recognized skills and in conditions remain within what is a hierarchically organized, gendered, and racially segregated service. Many Registered Nurses define themselves as professionals rather than workers. As a result they have failed to join the labour centrals in several provinces precisely because they have not seen themselves as unionists. Many of the immigrants who do find health-care work are not in jobs that match their credentials, and people of colour and immigrants remain clustered at the bottom of the pyramid (Das Gupta 1996: 97–116). Several unions are involved in the sector — and even in specific workplaces, often representing workers employed in the same kind of job. Hospital workers have fared better than those employed in other health services, and more of these other workers are still without union protection. Such divisions among women can limit their strength, leaving them vulnerable to neo-liberal strategies. Nevertheless, health care provides jobs for 13 percent of the country's employed women, at significantly higher pay than offered for most women's work, and with better conditions than those found in much of the private sector (Armstrong and Laxer 2006; Statistics Canada 2005a).

In addition to being the overwhelming majority of health-care providers, women also make up the majority of health-care recipients, primarily because of their role in reproduction, the medicalization of their bodies, and their greater longevity. In areas such as long-term care, they account for as much as 80 percent of the clientele. The national health insurance plan has made care much more accessible for women, both because care services have been greatly expanded and because no charges are applied to care defined as medically necessary. The absence of charges means that women, who form the majority of the poor, are no longer denied care on the basis of ability to pay and no longer have to face means tests to receive care. Equally important, the system has reduced the differences in the quality of care that women receive. Everyone, in theory at least, is serviced by the same providers and at the same facilities. As a result, the quality is more uniform across classes, races, and genders.

> In addition to being the overwhelming majority of health-care providers, women also make up the majority of health-care recipients.

This is not to say that all differences have disappeared or that the care we have is necessarily appropriate. Aboriginal peoples, for example, are still quite poorly served by the system. The federal funding, combined with the principles that the provinces must respect to secure this funding, has helped to reduce differences among provinces, but many regional differences remain. Rural women and Northern women frequently have difficulty getting specialist care. Language barriers often limit women's access to care, as does a lack of cultural sensitivity in the design and delivery of many services.

Male medical dominance has been a powerful motivator for the women's health movement. The dominance has been reinforced by a public system that, as Canadian medical historian Malcolm Taylor (1987) put it, gave the doctors a blank cheque. Indeed, funding concentrated on hospitals and physicians has contributed to the overmedicalization of many women's ills. By introducing hospital and then physician insurance, on conditions favourable to the doctors, governments reinforced the medical model. The sources of illness were increasingly viewed as being exclusively biological, and the practice of medicine was defined in strictly scientific terms. The body was regarded in engineering terms as a collection of parts to be fixed or cured, and the authority of the physician was strengthened (Armstrong and Armstrong 2002: cha. 2). Still, unlike fields, such as dental care, that were not covered by the *Canada Health Act*, universal access to hospital and physician services undoubtedly improved with public funding, reducing the class differences among women.

In short, in Gosta Esping-Andersen's sense of the term, Canada "decommodified" hospital and medical services and did so in ways that had many benefits for women, mitigating to some extent the impact of class in both care work and care access (Esping-Andersen 1990). At the same time, from the perspectives of households and especially of the women within them, the public-health system "commodified" these services by providing them as part of the paid, public-sector economy. This public provision meant not only support for care work done in the home but also less state intrusion into households and women's personal lives. It also meant less decommodified care work in the home. Current developments in Canada can be understood only when analysis includes these varied, and contradictory, forms.

FROM THE WELFARE STATE TO THE
MANAGERIAL STATE: BUILDING FOR SALE

At the federal level, new notions of public management have held sway for more than a decade. Like many other states, the Canadian federal state set about reinventing government (Osborne and Gaebler 1993) along market-oriented lines. As Prime Minister Jean Chrétien (quoted in Thomas 1996: 46) put it in the mid-1990s, the country needed "smarter and more affordable government," which meant, among other things, privatization and downloading. The federal government of the 1990s established a new model for itself as employer, shifting to for-profit strategies and contracted services. In health care the federal government did not have many services to privatize, and it faced an electorate committed to public care. Still, it took steps that contributed significantly to what has been called "privatization by stealth" (Battle 1993) — a kind of privatization that is often difficult to see or identify, and thus more difficult to debate and resist.

The process began when the government altered its funding support by offering provinces room to tax as a substitute for some of the cash previously provided to them for health care. Next, the amount of the remaining cash transfers was reduced, and then not only reduced further but also combined with education and welfare support into a lump sum payment called the Canada Health and Social Transfer (now called the Canada Social Transfer). As a result, it is no longer possible to tell how much the federal government contributes to health care, even though the provinces often try to make this calculation for political reasons. It has thus become much more difficult for the federal government to use funding as means of enforcing the five principles of the *Canada Health Act*, even if it can be assumed that it wants to do so. More recently, the federal government significantly increased funding and suggested that this new money go to several areas, including home care. However, no enforcement mechanisms were attached and no efforts have been made to use old ones.

At the provincial and territorial level, where the main constitutional responsibility for health care rests, governments also began to take steps that had the effect of privatizing health care. Services in all the forms identified by Paul Starr (1990) — activities, assets, costs, and control — are being privatized, shifted to the for-profit sector. What Starr leaves out, however, is the transfer of the responsibility for both cost and care onto individuals in ways that have a profound impact on women — the same decommodification that Esping-Andersen left out of his analysis. He also left out the impact on women, an impact that changes to some extent based on how we understand privatization and its forms.

PRIVATIZING COSTS

Under the *Canada Health Act* of 1984, provinces are required to provide universal coverage for all medically necessary hospital and physicians' services. Extra-billing for these services is prohibited. However, there is no such prohibition against fees in other areas such as long-term care and home care. Few jurisdictions cover what are often called complementary and alternative therapies under their provincial plans.

In response to federal government reductions in federal cash transfers for health care, education, and social services, provinces and territories introduced major cuts in health spending and new means of increasing revenues. They cut back services or increased various forms of private payment such as user fees, deductibles, and co-payments in areas not covered by the *Act*. In some cases, provinces delisted certain health services by removing them from coverage under the public health insurance system. In other cases, they failed to cover new therapies. Most provinces redefined hospital care to exclude many people and shorten stays for others. They also moved people from hospitals into long-term care facilities and home care, where fees could be charged.

This shift to private payment became obvious in the data on health expenditures. During the 1990s, the amount that governments spent per person on health care went down in real terms. By the end of the century Canada was spending just over 9 percent of its Gross Domestic Product on health care. With the recent new money, it had increased to just over 1 percent by 2005. Some 30 percent of that money was coming from private sources, representing a significant increase in the private share over the last decade even though there was a slight decline as public spending increased in the last couple of years (Canadian Institute for Health Information 2005). Canadians are now paying more for private health expenditures, including prescription drugs, eye care, dental care, home care, long-term care, and non-physicians' services. Some of this is paid for by private insurance, while the rest comes directly out of pocket.

Much of the increase in expenditures can be attributed to drug costs. In 1975 drugs accounted for just over 8 percent of health expenditures. By 2003 drugs ac-

> Much of the increase in expenditures can be attributed to drug costs. In 1975 drugs accounted for just over 8 percent of health expenditures. By 2003 drugs accounted for 16 percent. Canadians now spend more on drugs than on doctors.

counted for 16 percent (Canadian Institute for Health Information 2005). Canadians now spend more on drugs than on doctors. This is partly a result of the move out of hospitals, where drug costs are covered. Several jurisdictions have public drugs plans, but user fees have been added and increased, and many Canadians have no coverage at all. Equally important, Canada's decision to give drug manufacturers twenty years' patent protection has contributed to rising prices just as more and more care is drug dependent (Lexchin 2001).

Some of the increase in private costs results from new definitions of services. Hospitals have been redefined to include only the most acute care. This redefinition is particularly important in determining not only who stays in a hospital but also whether patients pay fees when they do stay there. Under the Ontario regulations, a charge to the patient for accommodation is allowed if, in the opinion of the attending physician, the patient requires chronic care and is more or less permanently resident in the institution (Ontario, *Health Insurance Act*, Regulations 552: section 10(1)). The *Public Hospitals Act* further requires municipalities to pay a daily rate for indigent people admitted to hospitals who are declared by the attending physical "not to require continued medical and skilled nursing care in a hospital but only [require] custodial care." The Act allows hospitals to refuse admission to "any person who merely requires custodial care" (Ontario, *Public Hospitals Act*: sections 21, 22). This allows the province to get around the federal legislation requiring coverage for all medically necessary care. Medicare covers medications and supplies used by hospital patients, but when patients are discharged from the hospital or receive treatment at home, they often have to purchase these same medications and supplies. This condition represents a transfer of costs from the public sector to private health expenditures. Once they make this shift to other services, patients can be charged fees as well.

Both women and men are hurt by these government cutbacks and rising private expenditures, although women bear more of the burden because they use the system more than men do. Moreover, women and men do not have the same financial resources to cope with these changes. Women, on average, earn less than men, have lower incomes, and are more likely to live in poverty. Poverty is particularly the case in old age, and with women living longer than men, there are many more poor old women. Women are also less likely than men to have supplementary health insurance coverage through paid employment. Immigrant women and women of colour, who are disproportionately concentrated in precarious employment, are more unlikely than other women to have such coverage (Armstrong and Laxer 2006; Vosko 2000). As a result, women face greater financial barriers when health-care costs are privatized.

This form of privatization means that women must pay a higher proportion of their smaller incomes on care and that more of them go without food or electricity so that they can pay for care (Bernier and Dallaire 1997: 143). It also means that more women go without necessary care. A Quebec study found that, with added fees, the use of medication dropped among seniors and welfare recipients, the majority of whom are women: "The decline in use of essential drugs had negative effects on the health of the most vulnerable groups and increased their use of health services" (Bernier and Dallaire 1997: 143).

Private payment schemes limit access to those who can afford to pay, and further disadvantage women. As a result, differences in access are emerging among women as well as between women and men. There is, however, at least one bright spot. Several provinces have moved in recent years to license and fund midwives. In addition, a growing body of literature demonstrates that health-care costs are not out of control and that public care is the only sustainable option (Evans 2003).

> Private payment schemes limit access to those who can afford to pay, and further disadvantage women.

PRIVATIZATION THROUGH DEINSTITUTIONALIZATION

During the 1990s one of the cornerstones of health-care reform was the shift from institutional to home and community-based care. In the process, more responsibility for care was shifted out of the public system and access to care was reduced.

Hospitals have been a primary focus of health reform for several reasons. First, they comprise the single largest item in provincial/territorial health-care budgets (Canadian Institute for Health Information 2005). Labour costs account for most of the spending on institutions. Although the female-dominated workforce once did much of the labour as unpaid trainees or as very low-paid employees, the unionization of almost all the women employed in hospitals significantly improved both pay and conditions of work (Perspectives on Labour and Income 2005). Not surprisingly, then, various governments bent on reducing costs looked to hospitals and their labour force.

Second, hospitals are explicitly covered by the *Canada Health Act*. Setting out the conditions for federal funding, the *Act* lists a wide range of services, tests, technologies, drugs, and care work that is to be provided without fees within hospitals. As long as patients stay in the hospital, they are not individually responsible for the cost of necessary care. Private insurance is prohibited for insured care, but private insurers may cover costs not paid by the public insurance scheme. In order to lower the level of public expenditures, reformers have thus sought to limit admission to and reduce the time spent in hospital. They have also developed much more stringent definitions of hospitals and of the necessary care provided within them.

The third reason for the focus on hospitals is that new technologies, drugs, and techniques have created conditions for the transformation of hospital care. Some of this new technology, such as magnetic resonance imaging, is expensive to purchase and operate, increasing costs and making it beyond the reach of many hospitals. Some aspects, such as microscopic surgery, make it possible to reduce recovery time. Some, such as portable dialysis machines, mean that services previously provided in-hospital can be transferred to the home. Combined with the pressure to cut overall public expenditure, these new approaches have contributed to shortened patient stays and the move to day surgery and out-patient services.

Fourth, hospitals appear to the reformers to be quite similar to large, private-sector corporations. Strategies developed for large corporations therefore seem to offer appropriate models for hospital reform, especially when such models seem to increase efficiency and effectiveness defined in monetary terms.[1] The imitation of corporate strategies is evident in the centralization of hospital services through amalgamation, and so too are the limitations. Barbara Markham and Jonathan Lomas (1995: 24–35) argue that there is no empirical evidence to demonstrate economic efficiency, quality, or human resource gains with multi-hospitals, and some evidence to suggest that costs will increase, flexibility and responsiveness to individual patients' needs will decline, and relationships with employees will deteriorate.

Hospital reform is not simply driven by costs and corporate models, though. It is also guided by various assumptions and critiques of the system. The title of a report prepared for the federal/provincial/territorial deputy ministers of health summed up a central theme: "When Less Is Better" (Health Services Utilization Task Force 1994). It is a theme echoed in the Ontario deputy ministers' report, which argues that hospitals tend often to be dangerous and uncomfortable places that should be avoided as much as possible in the interests of health. This approach fits well with the moves to shorten patient stays, deinstitutionalize, downsize, and bring care closer to home. It also fits well with feminist critiques of an illness system focused on treatment and the medicalization of life processes such as birthing. Feminists, too, have often supported a move to community and home, resisting the medicalization associated with hospital stays and the medical control they implied. Women's groups, government planners, and various research organizations maintain that much of the care provided is ineffective in promoting health. Indeed, feminist critiques have been used to justify moves that are implemented in ways that contradict the objectives that feminists were seeking in the move away from the medicalization of care.

Increasingly, reformers have also been arguing that we cannot afford the demands created by an aging population and thus far the need to move more responsibility for care to the individual. Undoubtedly the seniors population is increasing and the majority of the elderly are women. In 1998, "57% of all people aged 65 and over, and 70% aged 85 and older, were female" (Lindsay 1999: 24). However, most of these seniors — 93 percent of them in 1996 — lived in their own homes, even though more than a third of the elderly women lived alone. These seniors are mainly looking after themselves, often with assistance from their female relatives, although a significant proportion also help others (Lindsay 1999). Equally important, the research available indicates that the rising costs related to the growing number of senior women are at least as much a result of medicalization as they are of ill health (Chappell 1992: 171–75). As Morris L. Barer, Robert Evans, and Clyde Hertzman (1995: 218) explain regarding aging in

British Columbia, "The common rhetoric which portrays the health care system as struggling to respond to the overwhelming 'needs' created by demographic changes (and therefore obviously requiring more resources) serves to divert attention away from the real question: Why are elderly people getting so much more health care?" Given that most of the elderly are women, the additional question is why are senior women receiving so much medical treatment and what does it have to do with being a woman, or a woman from a particular group?

In sum, hospitals have been targeted not only because they provide expensive, guaranteed public services. They have also been a focus of concern because they seem to be the most amenable to new strategies taken from the private sector and because they have been criticized by a wide range of groups, including those taking women's perspectives. Hospital restructuring reflects all these influences.

In redefining hospitals as being restricted to the most acute care, governments have moved more complex care to long-term care facilities that once primarily housed the frail elderly. Some mental-health facilities have also been closed, and the most complex cases have also been sent to long-term care facilities. Some care has been shifted to community organizations. Many patients have been sent home, where less care is provided under public services and more care is an individual responsibility.

The shift out of institutions has important consequences for women. For one thing the shift reduces their access to care. Fewer services are available, and services for women in particular may be defined out of public care. Some hospital closures have been resisted on the grounds that they would reduce women's access to services, for example.

In the case of Pembroke Civic Hospital in Ontario, a Canadian Charter of Rights and Freedoms challenge argued that the closure of the hospital would leave only a Catholic hospital to serve the area and, as a consequence, would restrict access to health services involving sexuality and reproduction, particularly abortion. The court rejected this argument. The judge maintained that one physician gave evidence that he had never experienced interference in carrying out his medical responsibilities related to sexuality and that abortion had not been provided in either hospital for the last fourteen years. On the basis of this evidence, the judge concluded that the "closure of the Civic will have no impact on the current access of Pembroke residents to abortions services" and that other claims "around reproductive health issues" were "generally unsubstantiated" (*Pembroke Civic Hospital and Lowe v. Health Services Restructuring Commission* 1997: 11). Women's groups did not have the resources to appeal the decision. The Catholic hospital is now the only hospital servicing the community.

In Toronto, Wellesley Hospital launched a court appeal against the order closing it down and transferring services to St. Michael's Hospital. Located in the city core, Wellesley had served many of the most marginalized women in the community and had also been one of the pioneers in de-emphasizing the medical model in normal births and in welcoming midwives with admitting privileges. The Charter challenge to its closure argued that the rights of patients, particularly homosexuals and women seeking birth control, would be violated because those patients would have to obtain treatment at a Catholic hospital. The hospital was not successful in the challenge, and the services were transferred. St. Michael's "moved swiftly to halt all abortions and vasectomies and restrict other birth control procedures at the former Wellesley hospital site" (Daly 1998: A1).

Protests were somewhat more successful in the case of Women's College Hospital in Toronto. The Health Services Restructuring Commission ordered Women's College closed and the services transferred to the Sunnybrook Health Sciences Centre, a hospital originally established to serve war veterans and located in the northeast area of the city. The Friends of Women's College, a group representing providers and patients, fought a long battle to defend the hospital's control of its services. According to the hospital's submission to the Commission, the concerns related to three main areas: "the loss of governance and its likely impact on a dedicated focus on women's health; the need for experienced leadership in province-wide initiatives, namely the Women's Health Council; and the preservation of academic women's health programming in the downtown core" (Women's College Hospital 1997: 1). The long battle was to some extent at least resolved by a private member's bill that kept Women's College's downtown site open as an ambulatory centre, with its own governing board. Even when services are maintained in amalgamated sites, however, women still have to travel further for care, and much of their care is submerged into other priorities. In 2006 the Ontario government announced it would once more make Women's College an independent institution and would renew the downtown cite for ambulatory care. It was a victory for those who had long struggled to create a care place for women, albeit one that limits the extent of the services they can provide. Sunnybrook will handle medicalized maternity care, for example.

Significantly, when the Commission charged with reforms ordered the Pembroke General Hospital to develop a plan to ensure representation on the governing board, it included the "cultural, linguistic, religious and socio-economic makeup of the community," but not gender. To a large extent, women's concerns have been at best ignored.

The shift to an intensified emphasis on acute cases also means a decline in care within institutions. Even if women are successful in entering care facilities for services, they find fewer people available to provide the care. Moreover, there has been little effort to accommodate the new care needs in long-term facilities either through training or through an increase in the number of providers. Ontario went even further, removing the requirement that there be a minimum of 2.2 hours of care and at least one Registered Nurse at work at all times in these facilities (Armstrong and Jansen 2000). And there has been even less effort made to ensure training and enough providers for care in the home or community. Shorter hospital stays have also reduced the amount of time available for patient education. Yet this is even more important when patients are sent home "quicker and sicker" to look after themselves.

These reforms have a particularly sharp impact on women, given that women form the overwhelming majority of those in care facilities and the majority of those needing care at home. Moreover, research suggests that women who need home care get less public care than do their male counterparts (Morris 2001). Care in the home is also not necessarily a switch to a safe haven, as femi-

> These reforms have a particularly sharp impact on women, given that women form the overwhelming majority of those in care facilities and the majority of those needing care at home.

nists have long made clear. Violence and isolation are obvious problems. Less obvious are the problems of making homes healthy places for work and care. The disposal of hazardous waste is just one example. Another is the danger involved in lifting and moving sick people without help.

The shift out of institutions also brings job loss and a deterioration in the jobs that remain. As one study found, "Between 1994 and 1996, 85 per cent of Canadian hospitals reduced their workforce by more than 10 per cent" (Wagner and Rondeau 2000: iv), and new jobs in community care did not make up for job loss in the institutional sector (Kazanjian 2000: 6). Not surprisingly, with job reduction has come lower employee satisfaction and conflict among those who remain, which, again, means women. The workers feel responsible and are held responsible for care under deteriorating conditions, in part at least because they are women (Armstrong et al. 2000). The consequences of these managerial strategies are obvious in the high rates of illness and injury, especially among nurses and assisting occupations. "There are high burnout rates, feelings of job insecurity especially among less experienced nurses, and work-family conflict," the Canadian Institute for Health Information (2001: 87) pointed out. Hospitals also pay better wages, and thus the shift of care to other facilities means lower incomes as well. With new money, new evidence, and new pressure from nurses, some rehiring has taken place. At the same time, those doing the cooking, cleaning, laundry, and dietary and clerical work in care have seen their jobs deteriorate further (Armstrong, Armstrong, and Scott-Dixon 2005; Cohen and Cohen 2004).

PRIVATIZATION THROUGH FOR-PROFIT DELIVERY

Reductions in government services allow for-profit firms to fill the gaps. Canada now has for-profit laboratories, for-profit cataract surgery, for-profit dialysis, for-profit cancer care, and for-profit home care. All of these services have been justified as compensating for inadequacies in the system — inadequacies created by government cutbacks.

Some of these procedures and services are covered under the public health insurance system, but others must be paid for privately. In some circumstances, the facilities have charged patients additional fees, over and above the fees covered by Medicare, even though these charges are a violation of the *Canada Health Act* prohibition of extra-billing. The Alberta government has introduced legislation that would allow private, for-profit hospitals to offer services and receive payment under Medicare, while Quebec has simply allowed the practice to happen.

In some provinces, private for-profit nursing homes and private for-profit home-care companies are involved in the delivery of health services. Private, for-profit companies have also received contracts to provide various non-medical services in health-care facilities. Management, cleaning, kitchen and maintenance services, and purchasing and facilities management have all been contracted out, increasingly to multinational corporations that have little to do with care. Indeed, these services have been redefined as hotel services, contradicting both what we know about the road back to good health and the way in which these workers define themselves (Armstrong, Armstrong, and Scott-Dixon 2005; Cohen and Cohen 2004; Ontario Public Service Employees' Union 1998: 6). Managers often make the decision to contract out certain services based on the assumption that private companies are more efficient and can provide the same services at reduced costs. However, substantial evidence suggests that for-profit services are often of poorer quality, more costly, and subsidized by lowering workers' wages (National Union of Provincial and General Employees 1997).

The shift to long-term care and home care is also increasingly a shift to for-profit delivery. The public purse often pays for at least part of the care costs in long-term facilities, but giant international corporations provide more and more of this care. Home-care programs that include nursing, homemaking, meal preparation, personal care, and other services are, in some places, delivered by the public health-care system. In other places, private, for-profit home-care companies have contracts with the government to provide these services. Here too privatization is justified as being more efficient and effective, but there is little evidence to support this claim. In Manitoba, for example, after some home-care delivery was offered to a major U.S. corporation, "The privatization of parts of the home care system was abandoned after it was found that none of the private corporations who bid on the contract could deliver the volume of services at or below the expenditure level provided by the public system" (Willson and Howard 2001: 228).

> Privatization is justified as being more efficient and effective, but there is little evidence to support this claim.

In addition to contracting out services, encouraging private companies to fill the gaps, and shifting more care to areas already privatized, governments have promoted public-private partnerships. Operating in these partnerships means operating like the private sector. Many of the processes formerly open to public scrutiny become confidential business processes. There is no evidence that this secrecy leads to improved services, lower costs, or even less government debt (Canadian Union of Public Employees 2001).

This shift to private care has consequences for women much like those resulting from privatizing costs and responsibility. Their access to care is reduced as costs rise and differences among women in both access and employment increase. When services are contracted out to private companies, these businesses often attempt to protect their profit margins by employing non-unionized workers at lower rates of pay. Women working as nursing home aides, hospital cleaners, and food service workers have seen their work privatized and their wages drop along with their job security. Meanwhile, as more of the funding goes to for-profit organizations that claim the need for confidentiality and as more of the services are contracted to foreign firms, women find it more difficult to influence how public money is spent on care.

PRIVATIZATION THROUGH MANAGEMENT

Along with a shift to for-profit delivery has come the adoption of for-profit methods in managing health-care reform. It has become increasingly difficult to distinguish public-sector employment from employment in the for-profit sector as governments emphasize market strategies and business practices.

Indeed, from the 1990s, hospital reform was defined primarily as a management issue. Some hospitals have hired managerial consultants to manage or to advise on management, while others have purchased software and other aids from the private sector to provide the basis for new managerial approaches. What they have in common is a reliance on people trained mainly as managers rather than as providers (Armstrong and Armstrong 2002: cha. 4). And these managers are often trained for management in the private sector and use techniques developed in that sector (Armstrong et al. 1997). For example, in his book on how to manage hospitals in the 1990s, the then president of St. Joseph's Hospital in London, Ontario, explained that the management techniques he was promoting had been tried in Motorola, Xerox, and Federal Express but were untried in health care (Hassen 1993). The authors of *Reinventing Hospitals* describe how "The Mississauga hospital adopted the model of change that has taken the business world by storm by successfully transforming several large corporations: reengineering" (Cybulski et al. 1997: 9).

These new managers have fundamentally reorganized hospital work. Hierarchies have been flattened, leading to a significant decrease in management positions held by Registered Nurses, one of the few areas with a high proportion of female managers (Baumgart 1997). Some providers initially supported this move, assuming that there would be more participation in decision-making, but experience has led to concerns that flattened hierarchies do the reverse. The Ontario Nursing Task Force noted that, as a result, "The ability of nurses to be fully integrated into the decision-making process on matters that affect health care consumers has been diminished." It recommended opportunities to participate in a meaningful way at all levels of the organization (Ontario 1999). Similarly, the mainly female non-nursing staff has also found that the promise of participation was never fulfilled. Instead, the choices of these other hospital staff members were increasingly restricted by the new processes that replaced the old hierarchies dominated by nursing and medical staff (Armstrong et al. 1997).

This lack of choice is linked to new management systems designed to measure, redistribute, and regulate work within the hospital in the same ways introduced at Motorola or other private-sector workplaces. As in the case of flattened hierarchies, many health-care workers initially welcomed the introduction of patient classification schemes, clinical care pathways, and other workload and work process measures (Choiniere 1993). These measurement techniques seemed to offer the possibilities of greater independence, relief from tasks inappropriate to training, and demonstrating the actual work done each day. Instead, they have tended to result in increased workloads, reduced individual control over work, and both deskilling and multi-tasking (Armstrong et al. 1994, 1997). In the name of reducing costs and maximizing efficiency, health-care administrators have raised patient/staff ratios, reorganized health services, shifted personnel, reassigned duties to less skilled workers, and increased the use of casual workers. Cost-cutting measures are changing the pace and organization of work. These changes have often been introduced without consultation with front-line health-care workers. During the 1990s, nurses and other workers in the health-care system have repeatedly raised concerns over understaffing, heavier workloads, and increased levels of stress and injury in the workplace.

One study of the period 1994 to 1996 found an increase in nursing services per patient combined with a decrease in support services, although the data are based on "a crude estimate" that assumes all patients receive and need the same hours of care (O'Brien-Pallas, Baumann, and Lochhass-Gerlach 1998: 41). The report cautions that these figures were prepared before the largest decline in nursing personnel and they fail to take into account the medical and nursing complexity of patients, the impact of fewer nurse managers, and the casualization of labour. By the end of the 1990s, according to the Canadian Institute for Health Information (2002: 87), "only 52 per cent of nurses had full-time jobs and casual employment was more common here than in any other sector." Furthermore, "There are high burnout rates, feelings of job insecurity especially among less experienced nurses, and work-family conflicts." A 2006 study concludes that a key to what is now defined as a nursing shortage is "reasonable workloads, supportive management, flexible work schedules, safe environments, and opportunities to perform to the full scope of their practice" (Priest 2006:2). In other words, although the data suggest adequate nursing levels, a more detailed analysis reveals problems for both patients and providers. What the data do make clear is that support staff, who are disproportionately immigrant and visible minority women, have lost jobs and those remaining do more with less (Armstrong, Armstrong, and Scott-Dixon 2005).

There has been a variety of responses to the new managerial practices. Some groups have sought to refine the measurement tools, trying to make those aspects of care work that are central to women's concerns both visible and valued. Others have argued that the measures have built-in values that cannot be eliminated by adding more variables, and that alternative methods are required, ones that take the professional judgment of providers into account. There are important debates taking place about the significance of credentials and of scope of practice rules relating to various professions. These debates often pit women against women with, for example, RNs and Licensed Practical Nurses (LPNs) disagreeing about who can do what. The new management theories tend to reject limitations on who can do what, proposing to divide work into easily learned tasks that can be assigned to those with the least training. The Nursing Task Force supported higher credentials for nurses, and women's groups have supported the transfer of certain practices from physicians to midwives and nurse practitioners.

This increased emphasis on measuring patient outcomes and identifying the most efficient treatments could help to reduce unnecessary procedures and improve care. However, the methods used to measure patient outcomes and define effective treatments seldom include the kinds of care and support that women providers define as being important to health and well-being. The focus is usually on tasks, costs, waste, discharge, and the short term. The care involved in the work is hard to measure and quality is difficult to see, especially over a limited period. Many of the skills, and much of the effort, are invisible not only because they are difficult to measure but also because they are associated with women's natural abilities.

At the same time as business practices have been applied to public work, market strategies have been applied to the system. The most obvious example is home care in Ontario. The government now requires that home-care services be commissioned under a managed competition model. While the traditional non-profit provider organizations are allowed to enter the competition, the competitive process encourages them to operate like for-profit ones. Moreover, the bidding process creates enormous job insecurity, even among those employers willing to hire full-time. Meanwhile, governments are removing, or limiting, regulations such as employment and pay equity, in the name of market efficiency.

As the public sector becomes more like the private sector, the gains that women made as employees in the public sector are disappearing. Their commodified care work is no longer very easy to distinguish from work in other sectors. Women struggle to make up the care deficit created by these strategies, and this struggle has increasingly obvious consequences for their health. It is also obvious in care for the patients, who are increasingly expected to take responsibility for their own health (Armstrong et al. 2001).

PRIVATIZATION THROUGH HOME CARE

Increasingly, health-care reforms are sending more care, and more complex care, home. Cost-cutting strategies, combined with new developments in medical techniques, mean that people are sent home from institutions quicker and sicker — or they are not sent into institutions at all. It is now possible to give oxygen and intravenous injections at home, as well as to provide a host of other treatments that could once only be carried out in a hospital. And it is cheaper for the public system, at least in the short term, to have care provided at home. It is cheaper because when people are sent home for care, both the care work and the care costs are shifted away from the public system (Grant et al. 2004).

In addition, more people have chronic diseases, and new diseases, such as HIV/AIDS, have appeared. People with severe disabilities are living longer. Most of them live at home, and many need considerable care. A higher proportion of the population is elderly. Again, women, forming the majority of the elderly as well as a significant proportion of younger people with health problems, are more likely than their male counterparts to have their care needs unmet. The public system has not moved to increase services in response to these changing demands, and instead has left more care in household or community hands.

Shifting care from institutions to private households thus primarily transfers care work from paid female health-care workers to unpaid female caregivers.

Care in the home is women's work. In addition to providing almost all (80 percent) of the paid home care, women also provide a similar proportion of the unpaid personal care for the elderly and those of all ages with long-term disabilities or short-term illnesses. Moreover, women make up a majority of the volunteers in the community who do personal care work. Home-care programs are based on the assumption that caregiving is a family responsibility and that women are available to take on caregiving roles. Access to home-care services is often limited to those who have exhausted the caregiving capacity of family members. Shifting care from institutions to private households thus primarily transfers care work from paid female health-care workers to unpaid female caregivers. The very process reinforces women's responsibility for such work.

Women are more likely than men to provide personal care and offer emotional support. Men's contribution is more likely to be concentrated in care management, household maintenance, shopping, and transportation. In other words, women are more likely to provide the care that is required daily, care that has little if any flexibility based on time, while men provide care that can be more easily planned and organized around paid work. Men are more likely than women to get paid help when they provide care, based on the twin assumptions that men must do their paid jobs and that men lack the skills necessary for the work. Yet women provide, and are expected to provide, unpaid care even when they have jobs in the labour market; and many of them do not have the skills required to provide the complicated care work now done at home (Morris 2001; Armstrong et al. 2001).

Although women are much more likely than men to be "conscripted" into unpaid care, there are differences among women in terms of the care they provide and the choices they have about providing care. In the kinds and amounts of care women provide, income, education, and geographical location matter at least as much as cultural traditions do. The poorer a women is, the fewer choices she has. The more rural her location, the more hours of care she provides. Caregivers in immigrant and visible minority communities often face racism and language and cultural barriers in their search for support. Aboriginal women are frequently disadvantaged and poorly served. Lesbians and gay caregivers also experience discrimination in their efforts to provide care. Mothers of children with disabilities account for 96 percent of the primary caregiving in their households, clearly indicating that care work is not equally distributed.

Women are also paid to provide a range of services in the home. Nurses, therapists, homemakers, and care aides are most likely to be women. Many are immigrants. It is not uncommon for these women to have obtained medical or nursing education in their countries of origin, education that is not recognized in Canada. As a result, they bring an impressive range of skills to their job, but those skills are not acknowledged in their job titles or pay.

There is nothing new about women doing the bulk of paid and unpaid caregiving. What is new is the kind of care provided at home, the number of people cared for at home, and the small number of people in households available to give care. Also new is the much greater participation of women in the paid labour force. Most women are now doing paid work, and taking employment for the same reasons that men do. Only a minority of them have the possibility of staying home full-time. As a result fewer people are left in the home to provide care, and even fewer who have the skills required to provide the kind of care being sent home. Birth rates have declined, and even though children tend to remain dependent on their parents much longer than in the past, most offspring live away from the family home once they reach adulthood. Although rising housing costs and policies such as immigration rules that require families to support dependants are contributing to a small growth in families sharing households, most homes house no more than three or four people, and many have only one occupant.

Significantly, though, the care being sent home is not care being sent back home. The kinds of complicated care now provided at home were never provided there in the past. Thus households in general, and women in particular, are facing new care demands. Health-care reforms mean more and different work at home for women (Armstrong and Kits 2001). This work, too, can be dangerous to women's health. Home can provide supportive environments for giving and receiving care, a place where people can be surrounded by their familiar things and retain some control over their lives. Much depends on the nature of their health-care needs, on the nature of their households, and on the nature of supports available.

For paid providers, working in a home can mean independence and variety in their work. But it can also mean isolation, working without the kind of equipment or support that makes work safe, and continually facing unfamiliar conditions that make care difficult to provide. It can mean facing the risk of violence or other abuse. Health and safety standards are more difficult to establish or apply in the home. In addition, working in a home means dealing with the often conflicting demands of family and friends. Those who provide care in the home are usually paid less than their counterparts who work in hospitals or long-term care facilities. They are less likely to be protected by a union, or to have benefit packages. Fewer have formal training. Many of them work on a casual basis and have to travel long distances between homes without being paid during that time. The increasing emphasis on cost-cutting means that they have less time for each visit and less control over their work.

Unpaid providers often gain considerable satisfaction from providing care at home, but they face many of the same adverse conditions as paid providers. They have the additional stress of juggling other household demands and, frequently, of providing intimate care for family members. Daughters do not often find it easy to change their father's diapers, and their father may reject this care as well. Even fewer of them have training for the job, and care demands may create conflicts with both paid providers and other unpaid ones. Perhaps most importantly, because there is no or little public support available, unpaid caregivers usually have no control over when, for how long, and whether they provide care.

Those receiving care can experience a loss of control if supports are denied, or if the care provided fails to reflect their culture and individual needs. Both paid and unpaid providers may invade their privacy, and hospital equipment squeezed into their home may not only make it unfamiliar but also dangerous. The danger can be increased by the difficulty of maintaining a clean environment, and of getting access to food that is suitable for the ill or disabled person, or by problems with the disposal of medical waste and by isolation. Moreover, cost-cutting strategies can mean that those needing care seldom have the same caregiver over time and instead face a parade of changing individuals, each of whom is a stranger with a somewhat different way of providing care.

The focus in health-care reforms has been on financial costs. The advocates assume that home care reduces public costs, primarily because much of the care cost and care work is shifted to the individuals and households and because providers who are paid from the public purse are paid less than those in facilities. Surprisingly little research has been done to test this assumption, especially research that looks at long-term private and public costs.

Research has, however, been done that shows the costs are especially high for women if we consider both financial and health costs. For women, unpaid caregiving can mean career interruption, time lost from work, income decline, and a shift to part-time work or even job loss. These costs are felt far into the future in terms of low or no pensions and a loss of social contacts and satisfaction from paid work. But many of the costs are more difficult to measure or see.

The physical demands of care, especially combined with little training or supports and time pressures, can lead to exhaustion and frequent injury, as well as headaches, chronic diseases, and a greater vulnerability to

> The costs are especially high for women if we consider both financial and health costs. For women, unpaid caregiving can mean career interruption, time lost from work, income decline, and a shift to part-time work or even job loss.

illness. Conflicts often arise with paid caregivers, and among the unpaid ones, frequently disrupting support networks. Female unpaid caregivers report feeling guilt: about being healthy, about not understanding the illness, about not making the right choice for those receiving care, about feeling trapped (Blakley and Jaffe 1999). The guilt is compounded by their role as confidante and decision-maker, and by cultural and other pressures that assume that women who care about someone must care for them. They suffer from depression and stress. The pressures are particularly acute for those unable to afford private support services or get public ones because of eligibility rules or their geographical location.

Those receiving care face obvious and less obvious costs as well. Drugs and equipment provided in facilities are seldom paid for by public home-care services. Renovations are often required, as well as special supplies. Public home-care services and eligibility criteria vary considerably from jurisdiction to jurisdiction, but most charge some fees for at least some of the services they provide. Recipients too frequently feel guilt, both about using the public system and about depending on the daughters, mothers and spouses, or, less frequently, sons and friends. Moreover, care by untrained providers or restricted hours of paid services can mean that they receive less than adequate care. The consequence can be a deterioration in health that leads to a long-term care facility, and thus greater public costs. Caregiving and care receiving also have benefits and rewards; but these rewards and benefits are hard to realize in the absence of support, relief, and choice about giving or receiving care.

In addition, more care work and care costs sent home necessarily mean greater inequality among those who give and receive care, because those with money are better able to pay for care. Home care is not clearly covered by the *Canada Health Act* principles that require universal access, and thus it is possible to introduce means tests, user fees, and eligibility requirements that also contribute to inequality. Privatization through home care carries enormous costs for women in terms of time, health, and control. It also increases differences among women in terms of both choice and care.

CONCLUSION

Canada has never had a fully developed public health-care system. Public services have been concentrated in doctor and hospital care, with other services covered to varying degrees in the different provincial/territorial jurisdictions. Still, the public system has provided Canadians in general and women in particular with decent paid employment and better, more equal access to care, even as it continued to reinforce their responsibilities for other aspects of care work.

Privatization has changed all of this. Care costs, care work, and care responsibility have been privatized. At the same time more care delivery has been shifted to the for-profit sector, and the public sector that remains now operates more like a business. Inequalities in access to care and in the nature of care work have increased, and this is especially the case for the women. The shift has not proved to either decrease costs through increased efficiency or improve the quality of care as promised. At the same time, all care providers face deteriorating conditions for work, and care recipients face deteriorating conditions for care. Given that most of those giving and receiving care are women, women are losing the most ground in this privatization process, and some women are losing much more than other women.

Women have been resisting these incursions into public care. Paid providers have gone on strike to defend care as well as their own working conditions. Unpaid providers are becoming increasingly vocal and organized.

Women have been resisting these incursions into public care. Paid providers have gone on strike to defend care as well as their own working conditions. Nurses' strikes across the country have helped to limit the introduction of business practices, and some unions, such as the Hospital Employees Union in British Columbia, have sought to limit privatization of delivery through their contract negotiations. Unpaid providers are becoming increasingly vocal and organized. Patients have been demanding access to care. One patient successfully convinced a narrow majority of the Supreme Court that care was being denied by long waiting times. In response the Court, in what has come to be known as the Chaouli decision, told the Quebec government that it must provide timely care or allow citizens the right to buy private insurance. But many know that the private payment alternative would be a mistake for Canada, as did three out of seven judges deciding the Chaouli case.

As the evidence of privatization by stealth becomes increasingly clear, women are becoming increasingly evident in their protests. The kind of public care they envisage can be seen in the 2001 Charlottetown Declaration on the Right to Care, which begins by stating: "Canadian society has a collective responsibility to ensure universal entitlement to public care throughout life without discrimination as to gender, ability, age, physical location, sexual orientation, socio-economic and family status or ethnocultural origin. The right to care is a fundamental human right."

The publication ends by making it clear that "these rights to care must be viewed through a lens that recognizes the importance of gender analysis, diversity, interdependence between paid and unpaid care, and linkages among social, medical and economic programs."[2]

GLOSSARY OF KEY TERMS

Privatization: The process of moving from a public to a private system. Privatization can happen within the public system as well as outside it. It can involve a range of tangible and visible changes, such as the sale of a hospital or the granting of a contract to a for-profit firm. It can also involve intangible and less visible changes, such as the shifting of responsibility for health to the individual in terms of the dominant ideology.

Commodification: The process of a good or service becoming part of the market and exchanged for money.

Care deficit: These days most of the emphasis is on financial deficits; that is, on money. The term "care deficits" refers to the failure to provide the conditions for the provision of adequate care and is intended to emphasize not only its importance but also that this failure results in other kinds of costs.

Decommodification: The process of a good or service that was once exchanged for money being provided without financial transfers.

The *Canada Health Act*: Federal legislation setting out the five principles that provincial/territorial governments must follow if they are to receive federal funding for health care: accessible, universal, comprehensive, portable, and publicly administered.

Delisting: The process of removing some services or procedures from coverage under the public health system.

Privatization by stealth: The process of shifting care to the for-profit sector or household in ways that are difficult for the public to see or prevent.

QUESTIONS FOR DISCUSSION

1. Are some forms of privatization beneficial in terms of equal access to services?
2. What does it mean for women as a group and for different groups of women if there are fees for health-care services?
3. Can we organize health-care work in the same way that we organize car production? If not, why not?
4. How can privatization be made more visible?
5. What should the role of care providers be in developing and administering health-care delivery? Should different kinds of providers play different roles?
6. Should unpaid care providers be trained, tested, and regulated?
7. Are ancillary workers in health care health-care workers? What are the implications, for the organization of work, of how we define this work?

WEBSITES OF INTEREST

Canadian Women's Health Network. <www.cwhn.ca>.
Canadian Centre for Policy Alternatives. <www.policyalternatives.ca>.
Canadian Health Coalition. <www.chc.ca>.
Canadian Institute for Health Information. <www.cihi.ca>.
Canadian Health Services Research Foundation. <www.chsrf.ca>.
Romanow Commission on the Future of Health Care in Canada. <www.healthcommission.ca>.

NOTES

In exploring the various forms of privatization and their consequences for women, this chapter draws heavily on research brought together in *Exposing Privatization: Women and Health Care Reform in Canada* (Armstrong et al. 2001). The National Coordinating Group on Health Care Reform and Women, a group crossing the Centres of Excellence for Women's Health, commissioned the articles in that collection, which detail how reforms are played out in different ways within provincial jurisdictions and what this means for women in different locations. The themes are drawn out here; the specifics can be found in that text. The original version of this paper was presented at the Third International Congress on Women's Work and Health, June 2–5, 2002, Stockholm, Sweden.

1. See, for example, Hassen 1993. For the contrary view, see Henry Mintzberg 1989, esp. cha.

10. Mintzberg observed that we now have the cult of measurable efficiency in health care. "We're starting to find out what we lost, but it took years to find out. They knew what they were saving instantly" (quoted in Swift 1999: 19).

2. The National Coordinating Group on Health Care Reform and Women website <www.cewh-cesf.ca/healthreform> shows the declaration from the National Think Tank on Gender and Unpaid Caregiving held in Charlottetown, November 8–10, 2001. This declaration was signed by forty-six of the fifty-five participants.

Chapter Fourteen

POWER AND THE POLITICS OF SUSTAINABILITY

Block 1912 Collective

For generations, Canadians have depended on the export of natural resources — a seemingly limitless supply of fish, fur, gas, minerals, oil, timber, water, and wheat — for economic prosperity. Debate over the control and benefit of those exports has shaped Canadian politics. Yet over the last forty years, as exploitation outpaced natural regeneration or depleted non-renewable resources, new political questions about the future and social and ecological sustainability emerged. Since the election of the minority Conservative government in January 2006, continuing disputes over the meaning of sustainable development have become more obvious and more sharply divided — that is, disputes over the means and extent to which Canadians should restrict economic growth in order to protect the planet.

Sustainable development, popularized in *Our Common Future* — the 1987 Report of the World Commission on Environment and Development (WCED) — is widely defined as "development that meets the needs of the present without compromising the ability of future

"You Should Know This"
- Genetically modified canola is a major crop on the Canadian Prairies.
- In 2003 humanity's ecological "overshoot" was 25 percent — it now takes about one year and three months for the Earth to regenerate what we use in a single year.
- Half the world's original forest cover of some 7.5 billion acres (3 billion hectares) has been destroyed in the last forty years; only 20 percent of what remains is undisturbed by human activity.
- The United States, with 4 percent of the world's population, emits nearly a quarter of all greenhouse gases. Canada's per capita emissions are second-highest.
- The amount of carbon dioxide in the atmosphere today is higher than at any time in the past 420,000 years.
- 1998 was the warmest year on record since records began in 1861; the 1990s were the warmest decade in the past 1,000 years.
- According to the WHO, by 2030 between 6 percent and 8 percent of the global population will be directly affected by climate-related disasters.
- As of January 5, 2007, it would be only 6,934 days until the Harper government's *Clean Air Act*, proposed in November 2006, sets national air-quality standards targets.

Sources: <www.footprintnetwork.org/>; Godrej 2006: 87, 106; <www.cmmgreens.blogspot.com>.

generations to meet their own needs" (WCED 1987: 8). The report's authors called for "limits to material growth" and moral concern by resource-rich countries to share their wealth with poor countries. The document's impact was limited, however, by equally powerful and contradictory messages equating sustainable development with "more rapid economic growth" to alleviate "the strains on the rural environment of developing countries," increase "productivity and consumption standards," and diversify export-dependent economies (Rees 1990: 1; Richardson, Sherman, and Gismondi 1993: 49).

In 1992 at the United Nations Earth Summit in Rio, representatives of industrialized and developing countries, non-governmental organizations, and social movements debated comparative and normative reasons to restrict economic growth, protect biodiversity, and re-distribute economic wealth and environmental capital. They explored practising the precautionary principle, establishing rights for other species, and protecting and regulating the use of common properties such as oceans and the atmosphere. Ironically, while government and business embraced sustainable development in the early 1990s, many in the environmental movement rejected the term, fearing its meaning had been co-opted. "The goal of sustainable development," one critic argued, "is viewed by some economists and business groups as being merely to preserve the environment to the extent that it is necessary for the maintenance of the economic system" (Beder 1993b). Since Rio, an all-out contest to influence the meaning and use of sustainability has taken place among corporations, social movements, planners, scientists, and citizen activists. By 2002, the year of the U.N. Earth Summit on Sustainability in Johannesburg, and a decade after Rio, differences between corporate visions of sustainability and those of environmental organizations, social movements, and poor countries of the south had become even sharper. In the years after Johannesburg, the lines of confrontation only hardened.

> Disputes over the meaning of sustainable development have become more obvious and more sharply divided — that is, disputes over the means and extent to which Canadians should restrict economic growth in order to protect the planet.

While many employ the concept of sustainable development as a means of working to change the way the economy works, others use the concept to justify our economic ways. Yet sustainability is about both meaning and consequence. As a number of Canadian stories show, today's growth patterns cannot be sustained. Collapsed fisheries, unsustainable cities, the emergence of genetically modified organisms in our food, overconsumption, large-scale disturbance of forest ecosystems by logging, and oil, gas, mining, and hydroelectric projects have radically changed ways of life, ways of production, and ecosystems. Environmental historian J.R. McNeill (2000: 3) argues in *Something New under the Sun* that the twentieth century "is the first time in human history that we have altered ecosystems with such intensity, on such scale and with such speed." Knocking ecosystems apart to extract single elements for production or consumption, introducing labour-displacing technologies, and taxing the ability of local and global ecosystems to absorb and break down pollution and waste products are weakening the regenerative capacity of the planet. Struggles for livelihood and sustainability — whether in fishing or logging communities on the East and West coasts, in one-industry towns and Native communities in Northern Canada, or in congested urban centres — affect populations in an uneven, unjust, gendered, and spatial manner and reveal an underlying crisis of the biosphere.

> Struggles for livelihood and sustainability affect populations in an uneven, unjust, gendered, and spatial manner and reveal an underlying crisis of the biosphere.

However, dramatic consequences and crises rarely bring closure to unsustainable practices. Instead, the right to define sustainability — the contest for meaning — resurfaces. Claims by the victims — the unemployed fisher, the resident living near toxic dumps, the family farmer, the urban consumer, the concerned citizen — directly confront industry and government counterclaims that disempower or explain away victim views, insisting instead that their specialists know best, and that sustainability can only be achieved through economic growth. Both industry and consumers appear even less sympathetic to requests from ecologists and deep green thinkers to preserve nature for its intrinsic worth — that is, to put nature ahead of human interests and human uses (see, for example, *The Green Web* n.d.). Even then, we must not lose sight of the crisis of sustainability as an eco-social issue. Resolving that crisis means addressing its social origins (Johnson, Gismondi, and Goodman 2006: 13–35).

> We must not lose sight of the crisis of sustainability as an eco-social crisis.

CANADIAN THEORIES

Concerns regarding the sustainability of development in Canada predate the publication of *Our Common Future* by several decades. Historically Canada's wealth was defined by its frontier economies — the crops, energy, fish, minerals, and timber extracted from Prairie provinces, rural segments of the Atlantic provinces, and the North. Resource-dependent towns in Canada followed boom and bust cycles as commodity prices fluctuated, mines were exhausted, forests were depleted, and frontiers shifted (Elliott 1981). Social analysts focused not solely on mining and timber towns, but also on Canada's agrarian struggles, which spurred some of the most significant twentieth-century protest movements (Brym 1978; Skogstad 1980). Less documented were other contradictions of development such as regulatory apathy, industrial pollution, and a racism that destroyed the social fabric of Native communities (Shkilnyk 1985). Contemporary research examines the contribution of informal economies to rural survival (Felt and Sinclair 1992) and whether tourism and service-based industry offer sustainable alternatives to global agro-industry (Epp and Whitson 2001).

In the mid-1970s the Berger Commission into the ecological and social impacts of gas exploitation in the Beaufort Sea and the proposed Mackenzie Valley Pipeline heard concerns about justice and Aboriginal rights similar to those expressed in *Our Common Future*. Justice Thomas Berger went into Native communities, held informal discussions using translators, and integrated indigenous perspectives into the Commission's call for a moratorium on development. Berger emphasized the distinctiveness of white and Native societies and the indigenous peoples' dependence on the land for identity, food, and the future. Weighing social and cultural impacts alongside biophysical impacts, the Berger Commission became

> Weighing social and cultural impacts alongside biophysical impacts, the Berger Commission became a democratic prototype for public involvement against which subsequent Canadian public inquiries would be compared.

a democratic prototype for public involvement against which subsequent Canadian public inquiries would be compared (Berger 1988). A generation later, approval of the James Bay hydroelectric projects and diamond mining in the Arctic have undermined Berger's legacy of Aboriginal justice, democratic public participation, and concern for ecological sustainability (CEAA 1996; Wismer 1996; McCutcheon 1991).

Over the years the concept of sustainability has wandered ambiguously between two theoretical paradigms about the society-nature relationship. Literature on Canadian natural resource economies and the politics of sustainability reflects this chronology of paradigms, from limits to growth arguments by staples theorists and political economists who had suggested that human communities are defined by their natural environments, to social constructionist accounts of how nature is imagined as resource or ecosystem and how political actors frame environmental conflicts. These two paradigms take different emphases in their interpretation of sustainability.

Harold Innis, in his classic descriptions of the Canadian fur trade (1956) and cod industry (1978), asserted that the geographic and biophysical characteristics of particular staple products shaped settlement, employment, transportation, communication, and political systems in Canada. Staples theorists also noted a persistent flow of surplus from resource-rich hinterlands to urban centres and found that these national and foreign centres held market and state power over the hinterlands (Dunk 1991). Describing a society-nature relationship that directly countered Frederick Jackson Turner's romantic images of the American frontier, staples theory is both influential and, perhaps, the most criticized theory of civilization's relationship to the natural environment. Today, despite Canada's relative prosperity and power in the world economy, Paul Ciccantell (2001) argues that its resource-provider role continues, in particular in the provision of raw materials to U.S corporations. Some fear that fresh water will be Canada's next staple export (Barlow and Clarke 2002; Biro 2002; Speake and Gismondi 2005).

A half-century after his death, Innis's work also influences environmental sociology and political ecology, which attribute environmental crisis to the expansionist tendencies of capitalism (Schnaiberg and Gould 1994; O'Connor 1994). Elements of staples theory have informed studies of Canadian farm labour policy (Shields 1992) and forest development (Pratt and Urquhart 1994; Marchak 1983, 1995). The propensity of capitalism to expand and speed up manufacturing has been called "the treadmill of production" (Gould, Schnaiberg, and Weinberg 1996). Ownership of production not only concentrates in fewer hands — breaking apart old economic and social relations, and increasingly deskilling labour and displacing workers with machines — but with each increase in the crop yield, wood pulp, or fish catch, nature's ability to regenerate renewable resources, absorb industrial pollution, and mitigate ecological disturbances decreases.

Social constructionism, on the other hand, examines discourses about nature, environmental problems and risks associated with economic development. Social constructionism analyses definitions of the situation as shaped by powerful groups and interests in society — corporations, scientists, the media, interest groups, politicians — and the ability of each group to define reality in ways that are accepted as true (Birmingham

1998) or that render certain landscapes and communities expendable (Braun 2002). Social constructionists ask how claims are presented to persuade audiences of a problem; what claims-making style is used — legal, scientific, moral, for instance; what is the identity of the claims-maker; and how power and authority are used to legitimate and "construct environmental problems" (Hannigan 1995: 34–35).

Geographer Noel Castree (2004) offers insights into how landscapes and notions of "local resources" are constructed differently by whites and Aboriginal peoples; Sandra Patano and Anders Sandberg (2005) set out to show how discourses frame and legitimate both resource exploitation and the protest against gravel quarrying on the Niagara escarpment; Lori Hanson (2001) studies myths of settler individualism in Alberta and rancher antipathy to government regulations in Canada's West to explain apathetic attitudes towards loss of agricultural land to rural subdivisions and acreages; and S. Harris Ali's (2002) study of the Hamilton, Ont., plastics fire contrasts the claims by government officials, technological experts, environmentalists, and lay people to show how technical experts control public debate about environmental risk. Not everyone agrees with these approaches. Sociologist Raymond Murphy (2002) uses analytical techniques from social construction theory in his study of the Montreal ice-storm disaster, but cautions us that nature is real, and *that reality* sometimes overwhelms our social frameworks in ways that need to be accounted for.

Both theoretical approaches are useful. The staples approach is helpful because of its attention to land and ecological systems as key aspects in social analysis. Its traditional political economy emphasis proves less critical sometimes, however, given its tendency to geographical determinism. We find that what works better is a combination approach that places staples and hinterland and metropolis within a critical political ecology context. Combining a macroanalysis of states, ecosystems, corporations, and social classes with the framing and deconstruction of language, meaning, and authority regarding those same issues promises an effective approach to examining power, resistance, and the politics of nature and sustainability.

Thus, while in many regions across Canada the lives of citizens continue to be defined by the economics and politics of resource extraction, long-standing debates over resource extraction should now be located within contemporary analyzes of the globalization of capitalism, and the impacts of that process on local conflicts over control of land, resources, wealth, and issues of livelihood. In urban spaces across Canada, issues of sustainable cities, global warming, pollution risks, urban congestion, green consumerism, and genetically modified foods have entered public discourses, bringing new questions of the meaning of sustainability into debate and instigating confrontation among citizens, governments, and corporations. Although often initiated through the participation of urban residents in local democratic struggles, in nearly every instance such issues inevitably jump scales from local to global, as people develop a consciousness of ecological and social justice in a globalizing world. Here again, we see strength in a dual approach that draws insight from critical political ecology and grounds these struggles over meaning and discourse within political and economic contexts.

ECOLOGICAL EXHAUSTION AND SOCIAL CRISIS:
THE COLLAPSE OF THE ATLANTIC FISHERIES

The fishing boat, nets bursting with catch, symbolizes an almost patriotic confidence in Canadian nature as abundant and never-ending. Such impressions of plenty have shaped Canadian attitudes, values, and uses of natural resources over the last two centuries. The closure of the Northern cod fishery in Newfoundland in 1992–93 challenged forever the idea of nature as cornucopia. Nevertheless, many Canadians continue to ignore the lessons.

A common property resource, owned by no one, the East Coast fisheries began to change in the 1960s as large national and foreign trawlers, factory freezer ships, and dragger ships took large amounts of cod — estimated at some eight million tonnes between 1960 and 1975 — from the deepwater breeding grounds of the Grand Banks, altering the capacity of the fish population to reproduce and the ecosystem's ability to recover. In this open-access context, the federal government in 1977 extended Canadian territorial waters from 12 miles to 200 miles across the Grand Banks. Nevertheless, overfishing continued. When the fish catch and fish stocks declined further, the government declared a moratorium in 1992, throwing 30,000 to 40,000 men and women of the inshore fisheries communities into unemployment and increasing despair. As sociologists Craig Palmer and Peter Sinclair (1997: 1) explain, the "ecological crisis has produced a social crisis."

The titles of books analyzing the collapse of the Atlantic fisheries — *The Oceans Are Emptying*; *When the Fish Are Gone*; *Strip Mining the Sea* — capture the intensity, scale, and speed of destruction by an economic activity operating within ecological processes. Taking a political economy perspective, these authors attribute the collapse to government optimism about fish-stock growth and regulatory models, and to the treadmill of production that exerted market pressures on fishers (Craig and Sinclair 1997; Rogers 1995). William Rees (1999: 26) explains the ecological consequences

"The trophic relationship of industrial economies to their host environments remains that of parasite to host — the former gains vitality at the expense of the vitality and regenerative capacity of the latter."

of this economic pressure on the fisheries: "The trophic relationship of industrial economies to their host environments remains that of parasite to host — the former gains vitality at the expense of the vitality and regenerative capacity of the latter."

Taking an analogy from banking, ecologists maintained that resource users were drawing down the principal instead of living off the annual interest (depleting natural capital stocks instead of consuming only a percentage of the annual growth). In fisheries, forestry, and agriculture, analysts use concepts such as quotas, annual allowable cut, and sustainable yield to make assessments of the annual growth and sustainable use of resource stocks — that is, they make claims about how much exploitation of nature can occur without upsetting ecological balance. But the natural capital metaphor, while useful, is limited because it depends on the authority of scientists to establish quotas or annual allowable cuts, to identify the amount of principal and the interest rate, and to predict how much exploitation is sustainable; and scientists face many competing social pressures.

In the case of the Atlantic fisheries, federal and local politicians, industrial fishing firms, consultant scientists, small fishers, field scientists, and managers within the Department of Fisheries and Oceans (DFO) often disagreed on the scientific facts and did not share values related to conservation and community. Local fishers, small-scale inshore fishers in particular, argued that scientists overcalculated the fish stocks. The miscalculations allowed for increased quotas and resulted in excessive fishing, which threw the ecosystem into imbalance. *In Fishing for Truth*, Alan Christopher Finlayson cautions that it was not a simple case of scientific error that led to the collapse. Developing a social construction analysis of the science of Northern cod stock assessment, he questions the "epistemological authority of science," scientists' allegiance to objective, neutral empirical methods, and scientists' claims to be above politics. Finlayson argues, "Social processes had significant input into the creation of scientific knowledge claims" and resulted in "interpretive flexibility" of data (Finlayson 1994: 70, 81, 150). Exposing not only pressure from politicians, but also factions, personalities, and battles among DFO scientists, he found that scientists put personal interests ahead of the public good, practised a kind of tribal warfare, and privatized and did not share data. They accepted evidence provided by large fisheries corporations and rejected counter-evidence provided by inshore fishers. Similar patterns of resource overexploitation and "interpretive flexibility" can be identified still today in concerns being expressed about the possible collapse of the West Coast Canadian fishery (Peterson, Wood, and Gardner 2005).

Knowledge and power can shape data, facts, policies, and scientific models about resources and eco-social risks. In other Canadian resource disputes, a local knowledge of ecosystems — including ethno-ecological and traditional knowledge of Aboriginal and local users — has acted as a check on the biases of expert knowledge. This leaves the way open to alternative resource management practices that draw on community values of reciprocity between human and non-human life, and it brings with it a sense of scale and an emphasis on conservation of resources (Neis and Felt 2000; Walter 1994). Controversy over the use of traditional ecological knowledge in ecosystem management confirms its democratic promise, and the threat it poses to industrial and professional environmental knowledge brokers (Robinson and Kassam 1998; Goldman 1998; Barsh 2000). Recent fisheries studies suggest using a mix of science, local knowledge, ecocentric values, and ethics as part of a management approach to more just fisheries that protect ecosystems and human communities (Coward, Ommer, and Pitcher 2000).

BIOTECHNOLOGY, FOOD, AND THE ENVIRONMENT

Corporate influence over the science of food biotechnology is also raising issues of democracy and sustainability. "Biotechnology" is broadly defined as the use of biological processes of microbes, and of plants or animal cells, for the benefit of humans (ERS 2006; also see Kumbamu 2006). Biotechnology is expected to develop into one of the key technologies in the twenty-first century (Halal, Kull, and Leffmann 2000) and will have an impact on human health, livestock, fisheries, crops, foods, forestry, environmental engineering, and energy (Coates, Mahaffie, and Hines 2000). Genetically modified organisms (GMOs) are the product of genetic engineering, in which genes of a living cell are altered or moved. Advocates of genetic engineering emphasize its potential benefits; critics warn of negative impacts on human health, biological diversity, and ecological balance.

As of 2002, the U.S. Department of Agriculture had approved fifty-three genetically modified foods, including corn, rice, canola, cantaloupe, sugar beet, soybean, tomato, flax, potato, cotton, radicchio, squash, papaya, and oilseed rape (OFAS 2005). These foods are genetically altered to make crops resistant to certain pests and herbicides, to delay food decay, and to create sterility. Inserting a gene segment of an insect, for example, is believed to generate a protein in the food that creates resistance to pests. Similarly, herbicide resistance allows spraying to kill unwanted competitor plants without damaging the crop. Genetic modification can also add desired nutrients to food crops. Golden rice, a new type of rice with beta-carotene, is intended to save many people in developing countries from blindness caused by vitamin A deficiency (Nash 2001).

Monsanto, a leader in genetic engineering, argues that biotechnology holds promise for consumers seeking quality, safety, and taste in their food choices; for farmers seeking new methods to improve their productivity and profitability; and for governments and non-governmental public advocates seeking to alleviate poverty, ensure environmental quality, preserve biodiversity, and promote health and food safety (Monsanto Imagine n.d.). Biotechnology is also promoted as being critical in preventing world hunger, protecting agricultural land from soil erosion, and slowing water depletion (FAO 2000). The corporations that develop and apply GMOs are the primary promoters of biotechnology, with support from the U.S. government and the World Trade Organization, both of which protect corporate monopolies rather than indigenous plants and genetic information. Monsanto asserts that biotechnology research continues the human quest to improve plants and animals. Other support for GMOs and GM foods includes academics and scientists as well as institutions established by the biotechnology industry (Carlson 2001). One study by the U.S. Food and Drug Administration (Fernandez-Cornejo and McBride 2000) compared yield and pesticide usage for GM crops and concluded that GM crops are cost-effective, yet it did not calculate for possible long-term harms to human health or the environment.

According to the editors of *The Ecologist* (1998: 251), Monsanto "has been quick to stifle any debate that might threaten" its interests, including delaying a special issue of *The Ecologist* devoted to examining Monsanto's practices. Other critics question Monsanto's claims to be serving the public good: "The push for patents on genes is not about encouraging scientific endeavour and pushing the frontiers of medical knowledge. It is about ring-fencing knowledge. It is about privatizing the very basis of life" (Simpson, Hildyard, and Sexton 1997: 12). Monsanto's influence has crept onto at least one Canadian university campus. Monsanto is a major investor in the University of Manitoba's new biotechnology research centre called Smartpark. Some critics see the long reach of Monsanto and its lawyers lurking behind the three-year effort by the University of Manitoba (2003–06) to block the public release of the documentary film *Seeds of Change* by two U. of M. researchers, Ian Mauro and Stephane McLachlan (Sanders 2005). The movie takes a critical look at the use of Monsanto's chemical pesticide Roundup and other seed biotechnologies in farming.[1]

GMOs and GM foods are not without other problems: potentially they could reduce genetic diversity worldwide; transfer genetic changes to plant relatives to create superweeds; possibly develop strains of pests resistant to genetically engineered protections; unintentional damage could occur to beneficial insects, or there could be possible allergic reactions (Altieri 2000; Bocking 2000). GM canola is a major crop on the Canadian Prairies. Recently, through cross-pollination, non-GM canola acquired herbicide resistance and spread across fields, making it difficult to control in fields not intended for canola. Control will most likely require more potent herbicides. One canola producer says, "I'm not anti-technology. But… science is working against us…. It may be necessary to use a lot more potentially more harmful chemicals to kill this monster…. And I will never be able to grow an organic crop… for the future, I will never be able to effectively use Roundup for my weed control" (*Globe and Mail*, July 15, 2000). Monsanto's Roundup is the herbicide most commonly used by farmers. The spread of herbicide-resistant canola through natural cross-pollination is making prairie fields unfit for organic farming, even where GM seeds were not planted.

The social construction, presentation, and framing of GMOs by political and corporate proponents tend to silence public opinion (Anderson 2001), but an anti-GMO movement is on the rise (Reisner 2001). One poll showed U.S. citizens becoming aware of the uncertainties and problems (Shanahan, Scheufele, and Lee 2001). Critics point to the inadequacy of state regulation (Gaivoronskaia and Solem 1999) and the deeper problem of capitalist organization of food production and distribution (Magdoff, Foster, and Buttel 2000). Greenpeace Canada has developed a green list of non-GMO foods and a red list of foods potentially contaminated with GMOs. The red list identifies products containing soy, corn, canola, potatoes, and their derivatives from manufacturers that do not guarantee non-GMO ingredients and have not ensured that the products are made with non-GMO ingredients.[2] The most vocal critics of GMOs are from the European Union, Japan, Australia, and New Zealand. Resistance against biotechnology companies is less strong among those countries dependent on the U.S.-controlled system of trade and investment under the IMF/World Bank Structural Adjustment Programs. A global anti-GMO movement has rallied under the banner "Say No to GMOs" and promotes a much more critical approach to the entire question (www.saynotogmos.org). Brewster Kneen (1999: 8) echoes this sentiment: "The fact that we do not really know what the long-term consequences of genetic engineering will be, and are not prepared to move slowly and take the time to find out, means that a grand experiment is taking place, and the outcome is anyone's guess."

CANADIAN FORESTS AND THE CANADIAN FORESTRY INDUSTRY

Logs, lumber, and pulp and paper have been Canadian staple exports and sources of jobs and national wealth for centuries. In Canada, 402.9 million hectares are classified as Forest Land (Canadian Council of Forest Ministers 2001). Some 94 percent of this forest land (71 percent provincial and 23 percent federal) is Crown land, that is, publicly owned (Natural Resource Canada 2001), much of it managed by foreign and national corporations. Our forests are no longer seen solely as a source of national economic development, however. The emergence of an environmental movement in the 1960s started what Jeremy Wilson (1998) calls the war in the woods between a pro-development coalition of logging companies and governments on one side, and critics concerned about the exhaustion of timber and the damage to complex forest ecosystems on the other. As forest companies accelerate the harvesting of forests for economic gain, environmental organizations (see May 1998) have been posing the question: Will forest ecosystems collapse like the Atlantic fisheries? Civil resistance has taken many forms, including blockades, boycotts, and public hearings.

The economic benefits of logging have nonetheless overridden most concerns about the negative impacts of clear-cut logging or pulp mill pollution, with development often framed in terms of "jobs versus the environment" — a trade-off those living in forest-based communities are hard-pressed to accept. Still, many forest-based communities are beginning to question the economic benefits of industrial forestry, which until now has been largely taken for granted. In the years between 2003 and 2006 alone, eighty-nine pulp and lumber mills across the country — previously thought of as permanent fixtures of forest-community life — have closed (Nadeau 2006). As a result, 14,809 forest-community residents lost their jobs, and they have few equivalent alternative job opportunities to choose from.[3] Can forestry companies use science to reform and adapt their logging to sustainable forestry practices for the sake of both the forests and the communities that depend on them? Or are the claims of forest industry scientists no more reliable than the science of the Northern cod fisheries? And what is the role of the public in these issues?

According to 2001 census data, 352 heavily timber-dependent communities and 953 moderately dependent communities exist in Canada (Parkins 2006), representing over 750,000 jobs in the forest industry (although that was before more recent layoffs). Forested regions are also home to over one million Aboriginal inhabitants, who have traditionally used the forests as a source of livelihood for centuries. These communities represent a range of local voices, reflecting different definitions of development, preferred scales of use, and temporal visions. Aboriginal and non-Aboriginal inhabitants alike not only have values that must be accommodated in forest management planning, but also harbour a wealth of local knowledge about the forest ecosystem that has until recently been largely ignored in Western-science-dominated discussions regarding forest sustainability. This clash of knowledges remains a contentious feature of forest management (Reid, Teamey, and Dillon 2002). Individuals with local knowledge or traditional ecological knowledge of the forest often doubt the integrity of government and forest industry scientists, and question technocratic forest management models. Likewise, Western-trained scientists have difficulty integrating traditional knowledge into their own scientific worldviews. We have also become more aware in recent years of the importance of Canadian forests to global ecosystems: forests act as carbon sinks that absorb greenhouse gases and decrease global warming; they are sources of water retention and groundwater preservation as well as of oxygen; they provide homes for other species; and they represent complex ecosystems valuable in themselves. These new scientific findings have reinvigorated forest advocacy organizations, encouraging Canadians outside remote forest communities to express concern about the uses of publicly owned forests. Pressure has been mounting from citizens and groups critical of industrial forest companies' use of clear-cutting, biocides, and introduced tree species, among other concerns.

Certainly, talk of a "new paradigm" in forest management has increased, premised on the notion of sustainability. But definitions of forest sustainability vary. Many argue that the corporate vision has been limited to economic sustainability. Critics see the new ecosystem-based forestry promoted by corporations, designed to "mimic nature," as inconsequential, because the forest industries continue to increase production and expand into previously untouched forest regions — a process Wilson (1998) character-izes as "talk and log." Many corporations, on the other hand, argue that their abilities to practise sustainable forestry have been restricted by government's interest in investment and jobs, and a restrictive regulatory regime replete with jurisdictional overlap. This argument does have a certain resonance. In many instances tensions exist between levels of government, given the federal responsibility for First Nations reserves and national parks, interprovincial issues, and conflicts among the rights of provinces and those of corporations to exploit lands and forests. One level of government is pitted against another, allowing courts to overturn provincial approvals.

Other critics demand a more comprehensive vision for sustainability, for integrat-ing ecological sustainability, socio-cultural sustainability, and economic sustainability (see, for example, Hart 1999). But questions regarding the ability to simultaneously manage for multiple values — timber, non-timber forest products, and habitat to name just a few — remain unresolved. Persistent conflicts reflect differently held values of the nature of limits, and attitudes towards growth and conservation. Still other conflicts occur between notions of sustainability based on anthropocentric world views, which put human needs first, and deep ecology and left-biocentrism perspectives, which put nature first (see, for example, the Greenweb website).

Attempts to resolve these conflicts have increasingly taken on the guise of stake-holder approaches to decision-making. Strongly promoted by the forest industry, these initiatives appear to be inclusive, yet studies show that the processes involved tend to be narrowly defined according to management frames of responsibility (Cragg and Greenbaum 2002), and non-representative (Parkins, Stedman, and McFarlane 2001). Those with the power to define the issues have the power to frame the discussions.

Within stakeholder processes, the dominant voices and visions of industry and government most often overpower other voices and alternative visions. Does this leave spaces of contention for the multiple voices of resistance (Gismondi 1997; Tilly 2000)? Finally, even stakeholder processes with the best of intentions limit the ability of the vast majority of citizens to decide the fate of their publicly owned forests; increased reliance on such forums has clear implications for democracy (see Orton 1997, for example).

Alternative participation models are emerging. Communities such as Revelstoke, B.C., are attempting to define their own visions of sustainable forestry. In Robson Valley, B.C., citizens are identifying community sustainability indicators to help monitor their progress, and in Saskatchewan, the Meadow Lake Tribal Council moved from "stakeholders" to "shareholders" in an attempt to alter the power balance. The federal model-forest initiative builds partnerships among Native peoples, industry, local communities, non-governmental organizations, and all levels of government. In ten regions of the country, model forests are generating innovative, sustainable methods of logging and managing forest use. Whether the model-forest method is significant remains controversial; whether this model partnership actually redistributes power and enables democratic decision-making is open to question (Natural Resources Canada 2003; Sinclair and Smith 1999; Parkins, Varghese, and Stedman 2001). Community forests, model forests, and sustainable woodlot movements all strive to alter the dominant milieus through institutional reform.

Some Canadian organizations have turned to purchasing land and using legal conventions such as conservation easements to prevent destructive agricultural, industrial, or urban use and conserve ecological integrity (Southern Alberta Land Trust 2002). Forest certification is another approach, which uses market pressure and public demand to encourage good forest management practices. To be approved under the Canadian Forest Certification program, a company must prove that its forest practices "meet a high standard for environmental protection"; promote forest-dependent cultures and communities; involve local people in forest management decisions; respect and recognize First Nations' rights; ensure worker safety and welfare; and develop opportunities for small producers and manufacturers (Forest Stewardship Council–Canada website). Certification has been an attempt by the forest industry to meet consumer preferences, especially in the European Union. Suspicious of certification and forest industry motives, the Taiga Rescue Network, a global coalition of groups and individuals across the boreal forest, poses the question "sustainability for whom?" and proposes a combination of community-defined certification and community forest models (Meek 2001).

Reading past the rhetoric and propaganda in the debate about Canada's forests, issues of political power become clearer, as does the indispensability of forest ecosystems. Yet not all observers are optimistic. Fen Montaigne (2002), in a study of the management of the boreal forest, argues that logging rates in the boreal forest of Canada remain unsustainable, and asserts that hopes for the sustainability of the forest have emerged too late, especially as industry continues to control, and counter, all moves by conservationists and environmentalists (see also Dubois 1995; Urquhart 2001).

ENVIRONMENTAL JUSTICE

The question "sustainability for whom?" draws our attention to issues of social and environmental justice — an important component of sustainable development. Environmental justice promotes a fundamental belief that "no group of people, including racial, ethnic, or socio-economic groups, should bear a disproportionate share of negative environmental consequences" (EPA, quoted in Bullard and Johnson 2000). Feminist studies also identify the overrepresentation of poor women in ecologically fragile and polluted areas (Dwivedi et al. 2001: 241).

The Environmental Justice Movement began in predominantly Black communities of the Southern United States and was further popularized with the successful activism of the residents of Love Canal — a site of severe chemical contamination — in New York State in the late 1970s (Gibbs 1998). In U.S. sociological and epidemiological studies, researchers found that polluting industries, landfills, and incinerators are often located in proximity to minority and low-income communities, exposing local residents to dangerous levels of toxics in air, water, or soil (Mohai 1990; Bullard and Johnson 2000). A report by the Commission for Racial Justice concluded that the racial makeup of a community is the best predictor of the locations of toxic waste sites in the United States (United Church of Christ 1987).

Canada has its own history of toxic waste sites, and according to Mining Watch and the Sierra Club of Canada, our government does not have an inventory, or even a reliable estimate, of the number of them (Mining Watch Canada and Sierra Club of Canada 2001; Sierra Club 2003). One of the worst hazardous waste sites in North America is the Sydney tar ponds, an area the size of three city blocks located on Cape Breton Island, N.S. Over the last century, coke and steel production in Sydney left more than a million tonnes of contaminated soil, sediment, and chemical waste, 40,000 tonnes of which are PCBs (polychlorinated biphenyls), in that area. At the heart of the tar ponds disaster were the coke ovens of the Sydney Steel Co. — large chambers where coal was heated, and which released toxic wastes, including benzene, kerosene, and naphthalene into a nearby brook connected to an estuary that flows into Sydney Harbour. About 26,000 people live within 1.5 kilometres of the tar ponds (CBC News Online 2004; Environment Canada 1998).

Many of the health effects of the Sydney tar ponds are still unknown. Some residents have reported an "orange goo" seeping into their cellars and basements; others have said that when it rains, puddles in the area turn fluorescent green. Those who live near the ponds report massive headaches, nosebleeds, and serious breathing problems. Today Sydney has one of the highest rates of cancer, birth defects, and miscarriages in Canada (CBC News Online 2004). Although steps have been taken to clean up the tar ponds, controversy has raged for years about the best method of doing the work. A report by a review panel, completed in July 2006, approved a plan from the Sydney Tar Ponds Agency to incinerate 45,000 tonnes of PCB-contaminated sludge on site. Much of the remaining material will be treated, then capped and landscaped. The cleanup project, expected to take eight years, will cost $400 million, funded jointly by the governments of Canada and Nova Scotia.

Canada's resource-driven economy continuously expands the frontiers of exploration and resource-extraction to geographical locations that are more distant, more environmentally sensitive, and often occupied and subject to land claims by Aboriginal peoples. Unlike environmental justice issues in the United States, Canada's environmental justice conflicts are spatially driven, determined by the location of resources. By its very nature, resource extraction takes place wherever the resources are located. Now that more proximate resources are dwindling, the search for more and new resources penetrates further into the remote areas and icy barrens of Canada's North.

Diamond mining in the Northwest Territories, for example, and the negotiations on the $7.5 billion Mackenzie Gas Project — designed to develop three major industrial gas fields north of Inuvik and build two pipelines to carry natural gas to Southern markets — have complex environmental and social consequences (Bielawski 2003; Caron 2005). Negotiation processes with First Nations and environmental impact assessments grapple with a set of questions that are becoming increasingly salient, not only in Canada, but also in other parts of the world, where the requirements and desires of modern societies necessitate a deeper and more intrusive reach into nature, and in doing so disrupt traditional and more holistic ways of sustainable living.

Government and industry promote resource developments in the North as "tremendous opportunities" (NRTEE 2002: xvii). Contrary to the 1970s, when Justice Berger advised the placing of a ten-year moratorium on Northern resource development to allow for the settlement of Native land claims, today many land claims have been settled. But many are not, and the presence of "third party interests," such as mines and pipelines, may very well jeopardize future settlements and aspirations to First Nations' self-government.

Canada's Aboriginal peoples are torn between their desire to retain their traditional culture, languages, and way of life and the opportunities to participate in resource development. "One sentiment echoed by many Aboriginal people captures their essential environmental ethic when faced with development: 'We want our diamonds and natural gas — but we want our caribou too'" (NRTEE 2002: 9). What will be left of the caribou, fish, muskrats, and wild berries when the non-renewable resources are gone and the oil, gas, and mining companies have moved on? Will the results be the same as that of previous legacies of resource extraction activities, where most of the benefits flowed south, with only environmental damage and social and cultural dislocation left behind?

CONSUMPTION, THE ENVIRONMENT, AND SOCIAL JUSTICE

The power and politics of sustainable development are nowhere more obvious than in consumption. "Shopping is good," says a Hudson's Bay Company slogan. In the United States, after the events of 9/11, President George W. Bush urged Americans to go shopping in order to get back to living a normal life. Given that two-thirds of the

Gross National Product of industrialized countries depends on consumer spending (Buchholz and Rosenthal 1998: 226), economic growth requires an ever-increasing consumption of material goods and services. Proponents of economic growth claim that even environmental problems can be solved by consumerism because affluence increases public pressure for environmental protection and makes capital available for the development of environmentally benign technologies.

Yet high consumption models of economic growth threaten the environment. In the past fifty years, more resources have been consumed than in all previous years combined (Buchholz and Rosenthal 1998: 226). This increase in resource consumption is distributed unevenly: the richest 20 percent of the world's population account for 86 percent of global consumption, and the poorest 20 percent account for only 1.3 percent (United Nations Development Program 1998). Agenda 21, the program of action adopted at the 1992 United Nations Earth Summit, found that "the excessive demands and unsustainable lifestyles among the richer segments" placed immense stress on the environment, at the same time as the basic needs of much of humanity were not being met (United Nations Conference on Environment and Development 1992).

Whether, and to what extent, economic growth should be encouraged or restricted to attain sustainable and equitable development is linked to how the notion of progress is socially constructed and defined. Economic progress, its growth or decline, is measured in Gross National Product, the value of all goods and services produced by citizens and corporations in a country over one year. GNP measures all monetary activity — whether positive or destructive — like a calculator that can only add and not subtract (Cobb 1993). When the massive Exxon Valdez oil spill occurred in 1989, for example, clean-up expenditures increased the GNP, but there was no mechanism to deduct the destruction of wildlife and ecosystems.

Furthermore, increased income, which increases the ability to consume, does not necessarily increase the level of human well-being. Life expectancy, infant survival, and literacy rates rise rapidly with per capita income up to about U.S.$8,000, but at higher income levels remain unchanged (World Bank 1993: Figure 1.9; Woollard and Ostry 2000: 22). Beyond the economic focus on GNP, the United Nations' Human Development Index measures longevity, knowledge, and a decent standard of living, three dimensions of human development. According to the Human Development Report produced by the U.N. Development Programme (1998: iii):

> Consumption clearly contributes to human development when it enlarges the capabilities and enriches the lives of people without adversely affecting the well-being of others and when it is as fair to future generations as it is to the present ones and when it encourages lively, creative individuals and communities. But the links are often broken and when they are, consumption patterns and trends are inimical to human development. Today's consumption is undermining the environmental resource base. It is exacerbating inequalities. And the dynamics of the consumption–poverty–inequality–environment nexus are accelerating....

For more than a billion of the world's poor people increased consumption is a vital necessity and a basic right.

Is increased consumption possible within ecological limits? If everyone consumed natural resources and emitted carbon dioxide at the same rate as the average American, Canadian, German, or French citizen, the world population would need at least two other planets like Earth. In the mid-1970s, the total environmental impact of consumption on planetary resources began to exceed the Earth's capacity for regeneration; by 1990, consumption surpassed capacity by 30 percent (Wackernagel and Rees 1996; Rees 2000). Mathis Wackernagel and William Rees (1996: 5) developed the concept of the "ecological footprint" to calculate the land and water area (usually expressed in hectares per person) necessary to sustain current levels of resource consumption and to assimilate wastes discharged by a population. Thus, if the ecologically productive land were distributed equally among the world's population today, each person would get 1.5 hectares. This finding does not take into account the space needed by other species. Yet by the mid-1990s the ecological footprint of an average Canadian was nearly 4.3 hectares. Canadians (and populations in northern industrialized countries) appropriate three times their fair share of available productive space.[4]

Between 1970 and 1997 the global ecological footprint increased by 50 percent, a rise of about 1.5 percent per year (WWF 2000), which means that resource consumption in industrialized countries would have to decline by a factor of ten within the next fifty years to reach a sustainable level (Sachs, Loske, and Linz 1998: x). A child born in the United States or Canada will consume, on average, ten times the resources and produce ten times the waste and pollution as will a child born in Bangladesh or Bolivia (Stern et al. 1997: vii). Such First World privilege makes calls for population control in the Third World appear to be racist and contrary to ecological justice and sustainability. Certainly, technological efficiency will reduce some resource consumption; but the World Resources Institute has found, "Resource efficiency gains brought about by the rise of e-commerce and the shift from heavy industries toward knowledge- and service-based industries have been more than offset by the tremendous scale of economic growth and consumer choices that favor energy- and material-intensive lifestyles" (World Resources Institute 2000).

Faith in technology, innovation, and the possibility of substitution marks the First World approach to overcoming environmental impacts from consumption. Ecological modernization theory, a leading perspective in environmental management, is increasingly being adopted by government administrations and industry. Central to this perspective is the belief that production processes and consumption can be restructured towards ecological goals. This is to be done by replacing environmentally damaging technologies, developing clean production processes, and supporting microelectronic and gene technologies. It also involves socially constructing nature as simply part of the market (and letting the market price the uncosted services and resources of nature used in production and waste assimilation) in order to make alternative ecologically benign technologies competitive and feasible (Spaargaren 1999; Spaargaren and Mol 1992). Criticized as technologically deterministic, ecological modernization proponents look to technologies, processes, and materials that have yet to be developed or invented as solutions, and they downplay the possibility of problems created by untested technologies. Advocates of ecological modernization are silent on the role of government regulation, time lags in environmental risks and problems, and the possible irreversibility of environmental degradation and pollution. Nor does ecological modernization consider the ethics of off-loading environmental damage on the countries that produce exports. In an age of global production, consumers of these exports may not generate the necessary market or political signals to change the conditions of production in another country.

For affluent countries, the organizational behaviour of corporations and governments cause the bulk of environmentally significant consumption of energy and materials, and water and air pollution (Stern et al. 1997). In Alberta, for example, lack of regulatory control of water use results in industry and agriculture consuming 78 percent of all water used in the province. In most industrialized countries, municipal waste accounts for less than 5 percent of daily waste totals — a small fraction of the waste produced by industrial processes, marketing, distribution, infrastructure, and public provisioning (Stern et al. 1997). In response to criticism, businesses have increasingly promoted corporate social responsibility as their green mantra, a tendency that one critic says is tantamount to "the fox guarding the chicken coop" (Lock 2006).

Power and politics control decisions about what is produced, how, and for whom. Governments and industry can easily ignore consumer demands for products that are long-lasting, easily repaired, or recycled. In the First World most materials are used once and then discarded (Gardner and Sampat 1998: 146); production facilities are designed for new, not recycled, materials. Industry has little economic incentive to reduce consumption. In Canada, for example, in the 1990s the manufacturers' tax rates for products made with recycled materials averaged 27 percent compared to 24 percent for those made with new materials, resulting in a $367 million disadvantage to the recycling industry (Gardner and Sampat 1998: 31).

Although blame for overconsumption and pollution often falls on the individual consumer, it does so, as Dennis Soron argues, in a way that narrows our understanding of how best to confront the ecological crisis. For Soron (2006: 237), individual consumers are not the only ones who consume, and this recognition requires us to re-

> Although blame for overconsumption and pollution often falls on the individual consumer, it does so in a way that narrows our understanding of how best to confront the ecological crisis.

politicize consumption and focus our examination on the power structures, government policies, and industry practices that foster inequitable and unsustainable development: "placing a much greater emphasis upon *producer* as opposed to *consumer* responsibility" and "transforming ourselves from ambivalent consumers of the world that exists into active creators of better worlds that might be."

KYOTO AND CLIMATE CHANGE

Northern regions will be seriously affected by climate change as hot days increase, water quality and quantity declines, new conflicts arise over resources, and more. While climate change will lead to some improvement in the growing season and shorter winters for many Canadians, overall we will encounter new problems. Our vulnerability will differ by geographic location (for example, rising sea levels at coastal cities) and social location (inner-city poor and seniors will suffer more from longer, hotter summers). Each geographic region and social sector of Canadian society will have different abilities to adapt to the challenges as climate and ecosystems change.

The people of the developing Southern countries of the globe — the most vulnerable and poorest regions of the world — will be least able to adapt to future changes. Reducing greenhouse emissions that cause global warming is one approach that Canadians have discussed as a means of acting in a just manner that meets our global obligations, as a developed nation, to poor countries.[5]

Canada announced its ratification of the Kyoto Protocol on December 17, 2002, with strong parliamentary support. Rather than a source of closure, though, Canada's ratification only served to escalate heated national debates around our responsibility for mitigating climate change. As of 2003, Canada's total greenhouse gas emissions were 740 million tonnes (up from 596 million tones in 1990, and well above our Kyoto target of 570.76 million tonnes). Critics argue that Canada's emissions represent only around 2 percent of the global total, and therefore we should not compromise our economy by attempting to comply with Kyoto, particularly when emissions from other nations such as China and India continue to grow. Kyoto supporters counter that per capita, at 23.5 tonnes per Canadian as of 2003, we are the third-highest producer of greenhouse gases in the world, producing slightly more than do citizens of the United States. Further, they argue that compliance with Kyoto will not be as detrimental to our economy as anti-Kyoto critics allege, and that, using existing technologies, Canadians are capable of even deeper reductions than the cuts mandated by the Kyoto Protocol (David Suzuki Foundation 2006).

In nearly all of the political discussions, Canada's neo-liberal, export-based economic policies continue to dominate. Kyoto supporters try to convince Canadians that implementing Kyoto will not hamper our economy, and detractors suggest otherwise. This centring of the debate on "economic harm" may itself be damaging to the long-term project of climate change mitigation. Basically it ensures that concerns for the economy will come first, and proposed methods for reducing emissions will be limited to voluntary, individualistic approaches, or yet-to-be-developed technological improvements. As Soron (2004: 64) notes "Given that any effort to tackle the mounting problem of global warming presupposes significant changes in our material social practices, the basic message is that environmental measures adopted by the state must be made to conform with current economic prerogatives, even at the cost of rendering them effectively useless."

Many federal government programs established by the Liberal government in the early years of the decade, designed to move Canada towards the Kyoto objectives, were dismantled by the minority Conservative government elected in 2006. That government's action plan assigned 75 percent of the responsibility for achieving emission reductions to individuals, when individuals are responsible for just 23 percent of Canada's emissions (Pembina Institute 2005). This strategy of placing undue, and probably unrealizable responsibility, onto Canadian citizens, would have the expressed effect of alleviating the burden on industrial producers. Although they are now responsible for nearly half of our emissions, industrial polluters would be required to reduce emissions by just 14 percent in the Conservative Party's plan. Soron's argument appeared to be coming true.

Is this simply a case of poor leadership? There may be deeper structural reasons for our weak stance on climate change. Our options are limited due to Canada's position as a semi-peripheral, or middle-power, country in the global political-economic system. While we share the economic productivity and comfortable quality of life of the globally dominant nations, our ability to continue to do so is directly dependent upon our good standing with the dominant nations, and the United States in particular. Our economic dependence thus spills into the realm of politics — our political position on Kyoto must not deviate too far from that of the United States, and our politicians are likely to avoid any effort to implement domestic policies — whether in health care, education, or the environment — that will seriously undermine our ability to attract U.S. investors or the export of Canadian products to our major trading partner, the United States.

Given our federalist governing structure, even though the federal government signed the Kyoto Protocol it is in large part up to the provinces and territories to ensure that we meet the objectives of the agreement, because they have jurisdiction over most activities associated with greenhouse gas emissions. According to a report by the David Suzuki Foundation (2005), the efforts on the part of the provinces and territories to reduce emissions have been mixed, but generally poor.

Even though Canadian citizens have shown strong popular support for Kyoto, climate change has tended not to rank very high on political agendas, at least until very recently. Social scientists studying this disconnect between the concern expressed by scientists, and the seeming lack of concern among most non-scientists, have focused on the impact of the framing of political debates, and how the frames set in place subsequently shape how we view certain issues. Particularly when it comes to issues that are complex and ambiguous, people find it difficult to see the relationship between those issues and their everyday lives. This disconnect has made the issue of climate change especially vulnerable to the multiple interpretations that result from the framing.

Alberta's position on climate change provides a clear example of an organized effort to frame the debate. In an effort to solicit support for its own, anti-Kyoto position, the Alberta government under Premier Ralph Klein paid for numerous newspaper advertisements and public-opinion surveys during the Kyoto negotiations. It encouraged citizens, and the prime minister, to support a "Made in Canada" alternative. The central feature of oil-rich Alberta's *alternative* is its focus on *the intensity* of greenhouse gas emissions relative to Gross Domestic Product, that is, on the proportion of emissions for each unit of economic output. According to Alberta's position, if the goal is reduction in intensity per GDP, then growth is purportedly not threatened; Alberta and Canada can continue to grow so long as the intensity of emissions declines. Critics disagree, arguing that a reduction in intensity can be achieved while the gross output of greenhouse gases continues to grow.

CONCLUSION

How are Canadians to respond? Canadians must face ecological reality and change the definition of sustainability. Given that most Canadians now live in cities, new research into urban political ecology and the politics of sustainable cities promises change. For students on campuses across Canada, the push for greener university systems, buildings, food services, and grounds opens a space for an ecological politics that goes beyond classroom discussion and into their daily lives. Regardless of location, Canadians must fight to restructure the economy, decommodify daily life, and repay the ecological debt to nature, to poorer countries, and to future generations. Although the first set of responses might be defined as sustainability, only the second requires humans to recognize their obligations as cohabitants of the Earth. They can do this locally by organizing politically to demand a sustainable economy, nationally through democratic control of the state, and internationally through adoption of fair trade and gaining control over transnational corporations.

GLOSSARY OF KEY TERMS

Political ecology: Critically assesses the ecological consequences of political and economic actions; examines power and the distribution of positive and negative economic and ecological impacts; and considers the interests of future generations, other species, and the function of non-marketed (unpaid for) environmental services in economies.

Ecological footprint: A measure of the "load" imposed by a given population on nature. It represents the land area necessary to sustain current levels of resource consumption, including the amount of nature required to assimilate wastes discharged because of consumption processes by that population.

Ecological modernization: A theory proposing that incremental reforms to existing industrial and political systems can bring about ecological sustainability. Considered a technocentric ideology by its critics, it assumes that ecological problems can be resolved by technological ingenuity and that natural limits can be overcome without threatening current ways of economic life.

Environmental risk: A level of uncertainty about consequences to the health of the environment because of a social, political, or technological decision. Who makes decisions in the face of uncertainty is an issue of power and democracy. Originally focused on health risks to humans from pollution and environmental degradation, contemporary risk debate includes other values such as risks to heritage, way of life, biodiversity, and ecosystem integrity — that is, risks created by the human manipulation of nature in which the outcome is uncertain.

Staples theory: Explains how the geographic and biophysical qualities of different staple goods shaped settlement, employment, transportation, communication, and political systems in Canada.

Ecocentrism: Critical of anthropocentric or human first perspectives, it draws on values that do not emanate from human beings but from ecosystems and argues that decisions should be based not on human privilege, but on taking the well-being of the ecosystem as a whole as a point of reference.

Biotechnology: Not a single technology, it draws from recombinant DNA technology, monoclonal antibody production, and cell tissue culture. Biotechnology involves separating genetic code that contains required information from the DNA in cells and manipulating and recombining that information with genes of another living organism to produce a new, desired product. "Genetically modified" (GM), "genetically engineered" (GE), and "transgenic" are often used interchangeably to describe products that have been developed using modern biotechnology.

Environmental justice: Is linked to environmental racism, but it is broader in its claims, extending from the rights of peoples of colour and Aboriginal peoples to be free from ecosystem degradation and exploitation in their home places, to discussion of global inequalities in the use of the global commons and global sinks such as oceans, groundwater, and airsheds; or consumptive inequities in ecological footprint between nations and regions of the world (North and South), or inequities between global classes of peoples across nations; up to and including biocentric arguments in defence of the rights of ecosystems and other species against human greed and expansion.

Social constructionism: Argues that we can't observe the natural world outside of social constructs, which become the lens that people use to consider environmental issues and problems. To see how issues are framed — that is, how certain facts and understandings become emphasized (while others are silenced) — requires an analysis of power and resistance.

QUESTIONS FOR DISCUSSION

1. Identify the strengths and weaknesses of a social constructionist approach to environmental issues. Critically assess these strengths and weaknesses for a politics of resistance. Use examples of a current green issue.

2. How might a critical political ecology approach move Canadians towards thinking about consumerism as an issue of production? What are the implications for activism and politics?

3. Could we use the environmental footprint tool to generate a discussion of environmental justice issues? How so? Where would you take the analysis?

4. Power and resistance sometimes require us to jump scales from the local to the global. One good example is the fair trade movement. Can you think of others? Discuss.

5. Identify the food security issues associated with GMOs.

6. How might Canadians build a politics of sustainability around the food security issue?

7. Could global climate change be effectively addressed with a local, bottom-up approach? Why or why not?

8. How are power inequities across nations illustrated in international negotiations on the Kyoto Protocol?

9. How does the prospect of absolute scarcity pose challenges for sustainable development?

WEBSITES OF INTEREST

Boreal Forest Network. <www.borealnet.org/main.html>.
Canadian Environmental Organizations. <www.alternativesjournal.ca/linkcan.htm>.
David Suzuki Foundation. <www.davidsuzuki.org/>.
Friends of the Earth. <www.foe.co.uk/>.
Greenpeace Canada. <www.greenpeace.ca>.
Redefining Progress. <www.rprogress.org/projects/gpi/>.
Sierra Club. <www.sierraclub.org/>.
The Genetic Engineering Network. <www.dmac.co.uk/gen.html>.
Woman's Environmental Network. <www.gn.apc.org/wen>.
World Watch. <www.worldwatch.org/>.

NOTES

1. See the *Seeds of Change* website for film clips <http://seedsofchangefilm.org/>.

2. In Canada, GM and non-GMO crops are not required to be segregated; therefore, unless a manufacturer guarantees a non-GMO source, it will probably contain GMOs. Visit the "Shoppers Guide to GMO-Free Food" website, available at <www.greenpeace.ca/e/campaign/gmo/gmoguide /html/guide.html>.

3. Often the loss of jobs is explained by corporations as a combination of cost pressures resulting from competition by modern offshore mills or from the need to retrofit to meet

new, more stringent Canadian environmental regulations, or both. But a good deal of the pressure is caused by corporate profitability concerns and global corporate consolidation.

4. To calculate your personal ecological footprint, see <www.lead.org/leadnet/footprint /intro.htm>.

5. For a visual overview of global warming and other human impacts on the globe, see U.N. Environmental Programme 2005.

Chapter Fifteen

CRIME AS A SOCIAL PROBLEM
From Definition to Reality

Les Samuelson

In *The Rich Get Richer and the Poor Get Prison* (2007), Jeffrey Reiman critically evaluates the implicit ideology of the criminal justice system, noting that any such system conveys a subtle yet powerful message in support of established institutions. It does this, he says, primarily by concentrating on individual wrongdoers:

> To look only at individual criminality is to close one's eyes to social injustice and to close one's ears to the question of whether our social institutions have exploited or violated the individual. *Justice is a two-way street — but criminal justice is a one-way street.* Individuals owe obligations to their fellow citizens because their fellow citizens owe obligations to them. Criminal justice focuses on the first and looks away from the second. *Thus, by focusing on individual responsibility for crime, the criminal justice system literally acquits the existing social order of any charge of injustice!* (Reiman 2007: 176)

"You Should Know This"
- Advertising executive Paul Coffin was sentenced to eighteen months in prison for defrauding the federal government of $1.5 million in the so-called Quebec sponsorship scandal.
- White-collar crime is costly, both financially and physically to Canadians: for example, sales of worthless stocks reap an average of $6 billion annually for unscrupulous stockbrokers.
- Enron investors were defrauded of US$63 billion by CEO Kenneth Lay.
- Aboriginal women in prison have a high rate of suicide — a suicide by an Aboriginal woman at P4W in February 1991 was the fourth in a sixteen-month period.
- In 1927 an amendment to the Indian Act (1876) made it illegal for Aboriginal people to form any national political organization.
- The healing lodge at Maple Creek, Saskatchewan, for federally sentenced Aboriginal women opened on October 1995. It is an important "holistic" step towards changing dismal judicial and social realities for Aboriginal women.

Reiman focuses upon the "evils of the social order" that accrue from major inequalities of economic power in society — that is, he looks at how working-class individuals are prosecuted differently than upper-class people or corporations for causing physical or economic harms.

However, as critical criminological analyses have repeatedly emphasized over the past three decades, our society is also characterized by massive inequalities of power and social position based upon race and gender. Thus, a range of these analyses focus on how legal practices reinforce not only class-based inequalities but also the patriarchal subjugation of women. In addition, since the early 1990s in Canada a constellation of critical Aboriginal justice commission reports and initiatives have pushed the issue of post-colonial social justice for Aboriginal peoples into the spotlight. These inequalities also generate differences of involvement and treatment within our criminal justice system, from the definition of crime to the responses of criminal justice personnel to offenders and victims. Certain individuals and groups are not born more "criminal" than any others, but the life conditions they face may vary greatly. Thus, for critical criminologists, a central "justice" concern is with how underlying social inequalities and processes operate to bring oppressed people into the criminal justice system, while privileged individuals — if dealt with at all — tend to be treated leniently.

CLASS

The class-biased nature of law has two basic dimensions. One dimension involves acts that are either defined in legislation as crime or are controlled through regulatory law. The second dimension involves the justice system's differential processing of working-class and professional-class individuals and corporations for "criminal acts."

Critical criminologists, following a political economy approach, hold that a relatively small group of individuals control much of the wealth and political power in our society. While not necessarily acting in unison, this elite is able to influence the political-legal process so that both criminal and regulatory law does not treat seriously the social, economic, and physical harms inflicted upon society by the process of capital accumulation. By contrast, the crimes committed by working-class people, which are frequently a result of their life circumstances, are prosecuted more severely under the law; incarceration is often the end product.

> Generally, both criminal and regulatory law does not treat seriously the social, economic, and physical harms inflicted upon society by the process of capital accumulation.

As Harry Glasbeek (2002: 118) has aptly noted on corporate deviance and the fancy footwork of the criminal law, "Corporate actors regularly and repeatedly violate our standards of moral and legal behaviour, do much more physical and economic harm than any other violators of these standards, and continue to be treated as upright members of our society, giving meaning to Clarence Darrow's aphorism that most people classified as criminals are 'persons with predatory instincts without sufficient capital to form a corporation.'" While succinct, unfortunately, this is not a new observation.

The pioneering Canadian research in this area (Goff and Reasons 1978) established the state's failure to define as "corporate crime" those behaviours that have economic and physical costs, to individuals, society, and the environment, far exceeding the costs of street crime (Gordon and Coneybeer 1995; Snider 1994a). Corporate crime, or "suite crime," is defined as "crime" committed by a corporate official in the pursuit of organizational goals, usually profit. These acts are illegal under either criminal or regulatory law — or would be if the state applied the criterion of economic and physical harm to society. This criterion is ostensibly the core element in the prohibitions and punishments of the Canadian Criminal Code.

Critical criminologists essentially agree that the costs to society of corporate crime far exceed those of street crime. Colin Goff (2001) tackles this issue via a related, but not identical, concept, white-collar crime. Generally speaking, people within the criminal justice system use the term to describe

> The annual Canadian losses due to such crimes as embezzlement, computer crime, commercial fraud, unnecessary auto repairs, unneeded home improvements, price-fixing, illegal corporate mergers, false advertising, and other business crimes are staggering.

crimes of fraud and injury that are carried out during the course of a (seemingly) legitimate occupation. White-collar crime is costly — both financially and physically — to Canadians. Ian Gomme (2007: 304–306) offers some critical observations on this concern. As he notes, business crime that is known and makes its way into official records represents only the tip of the iceberg; the annual Canadian losses due to such crimes as embezzlement, computer crime, commercial fraud, unnecessary auto repairs, unneeded home improvements, price-fixing, illegal corporate mergers, false advertising, and other business crimes are staggering. The accounting firm of Ernst and Young estimates the costs of white-collar crime in Canada at $20 billion (Gomme 2007: 306). In the United States in the early 1990s, Laureen Snider (1994a: 276) pointed out, in any given year "all the street crime" in the country was "estimated to cost around $4 billion, much less than 5% of the average take from corporate crime." The North American Securities Administrators Association has estimated that in the United States around $1 million per hour are lost in securities fraud through companies issuing false statements about earnings. Moreover, sales of worthless stocks reap an average of $6 billion per year for unscrupulous stockbrokers (Fishman, cited in Snider 2002). The big losers in these stock swindles and securities frauds are the general public and the proverbial average investors.

Consider the $63 billion investors fraud orchestrated by Enron CEO Kenneth Lay. Enron started as a profitable pipeline company delivering natural gas. But Lay and his senior executives wanted much greater, quick profits (Hagan 2004: 495). To keep the company growing, Enron executives began to use illegal financial measures to make it appear that profits were continuing to increase. As John Hagan (2004: 495) notes, "Enron developed what can only be described as a culture of greed." This truly enormous "culture of greed" had help from many of Wall Street's big "respectable" players. Hagan (2004: 496) highlights the greed and collusion:

> Executives were not content with the millions of dollars they had taken from the company. As the illegal schemes began to unravel and the company began to slide into bankruptcy, Enron paid $681 million to 140 top executives, including $67 million to CEO Kenneth Lay, who continued to encourage employees and members of the public to buy Enron stock even as he and his executives stripped the company of much of its remaining capital....

While Enron executives must take most of the blame for the company's demise, they had help from the managers of other large corporations. The Arthur Andersen accounting firm, one of the world's largest, allowed Enron's many lapses of legal and ethical standards to slip by its auditors in order to help it obtain lucrative consulting contracts with Enron. Many of Wall Street's largest banks and brokerage firms collaborated with Enron in order to profit from stock commissions, consulting contracts, and interest from loans.

When it comes to corporate human harms, Gomme (2007: 306) cautions that we need to develop a "critical eye":

> Many Canadians perceive business crime solely as property crime and see its costs entirely in economic terms. The result is an inclination to view commercial crime as a less serious problem than street crime. Street crime raises images of interpersonal violence, while suite crime does not. This is a grave misperception — business crime is frequently violent. The volume of assaults and murders in Canada pales in comparison with the number of injuries, debilitating and life-threatening diseases, and deaths attributable to business enterprises and professions engaging in unsafe practices, marketing dangerous products, violating workplace safety regulations, and polluting the air, the water, and the land. Death in the workplace ranks third, after heart disease and cancer, as a major killer of Canadians.

Yet, as Frank Schmalleger (2007: 42) notes, in 2004 some 16,137 murders came to the attention of police departments across the United States. In that country two workers are killed by jobs versus one by murder — a ratio that is probably roughly true also for Canada. Even these figures most likely underestimate the seriousness of corporate violence, as Piers Beirne and James Messerschmidt (2006: 204) conclude: "We are actually safer in the street than indoors; the evidence presented here suggests that we are safer almost anywhere than in the workplace."

Who is to blame here? Is all this physical injury just accidents? Gomme (2007: 306) cites earlier Canadian research that estimated that 40 percent of industrial "accidents" were a result of working conditions that were both unsafe and prohibited under existing law. About 25 percent of working conditions, while not illegal, are dangerous nonetheless. Yet, these violations and harms are not pursued with the same vigour as street crime injuries. As Snider (2002) concludes, "Nowhere in criminology is the role of power and class more obvious than in the creation and enforcement of laws against corporate crime."

This issue can be vividly, and sadly, foregrounded in recent multiple-death industrial events in Canada. To classify these industrial deaths as "accidents," as is generally the case, completely obscures the context within which they occur. John McMullan and Stephen Smith's (1997) analysis of the 1982 Ocean Ranger oil-rig tragedy, which cost eighty-four lives, puts the case more clearly. According to the conclusions of the official investigation itself, "Intervention could have offset design flaws and overcome lax shipping classifications, inadequate seaworthy standards and poor marine training of staff and prevented the disaster" (quoted in McMullan and Smith 1997: 62). I grew up in St. John's, Nfld., the supply depot for this rig. Local people working on the rig had nicknamed the rig the "Ocean Danger" because of its poor safety standards and operation. But jobs were in short supply on the East Coast, and for some of the local people the job on the Ocean Ranger was their last.

In 1992 the Westray mine explosion in Nova Scotia claimed twenty-six lives and also was no accident. "Initial investigations suggest the existence of careless management, unsafe working conditions that included explosively high levels of methane and coal dust, outdated equipment and a remarkably lax and inept regulations and enforcement system," McMullan and Smith (1997: 62) point out. They then add, "Sadly, further evidence shows that both federal and provincial governments overruled their own officials who had warned them against opening the mine for health and safety reasons, and then covered up their roles in the disaster."

Glasbeek (2002: 121) notes that by the time of the Westray mine explosion, the overseeing ministry had compiled a staggering record of fifty-two breaches of the health and safety standards. These breaches never led to any prosecutions under the occupational health and safety legislation that had been so flagrantly disregarded. The RCMP did lay two charges under the Criminal Code, but the charges were eventually dropped. No one was ever convicted of any wrongdoing in the non-accidental death of twenty-six people.

Government complicity of this type is not unique. From the start of the marketing of the Dalkon Shield in North America in 1971, women reported severe problems with the intrauterine device. These problems were largely ignored, and by 1974 the Dalkon Shield had killed seventeen women and infected and injured another two hundred thousand (McMullan 1992: 15). But the shield was not removed from the so-called marketplace. Instead corporate executives of A.H. Robins dumped several million unsterilized units in bulk packages onto foreign Third World markets — distributed by the U.S. Agency for International Development's Office of Population. Costing only twenty-five cents to produce (Sherrill, cited in McMullan 1992: 13) these several-million IUDs were sold for $4.35, which still provided a good profit for A.H. Robins. The company stated its justification: "that any contraceptive device was better than none, especially since birth rates were so high in third world countries" (McMullan 1992: 15).

Glasbeek (2002: 124–25) provides a seldom-seen, damming "indictment" of corporate killing as "business as usual." In "a rather famous statement — famous because it was so unrepresentative" of judges in corporate crime cases, Judge Miles Lord, who presided over the Dalkon/A.H. Robins civil litigation, wrote:

> It is not enough to say, "I did not know," "It was not me," "Look elsewhere." Time and again, each of you has used this kind of argument in refusing to

acknowledge your responsibility and in pretending to the world that the chief officers and directors of your gigantic multinational corporation have no responsibility for its acts and omissions....You have taken the bottom line as your guiding beacon and the low road as your route....You, in essence, pay nothing out of your own pockets to settle these cases.

Glassbeek notes that despite "this much published judicial indignation, neither the corporation nor any of its managers were ever charged," let alone convicted of a criminal offence. He adds (2002: 124–25):

Indeed, the civic leaders of Richmond, Virginia, the headquarters of A.H. Robbins, threw a banquet for E. Clairborne Robbins Sr., one of the men excoriated by Judge Lord. At the banquet, after much praise from the dignitaries, one of the top people behind the Dalkon Shield evildoing was given the Great American Tradition Award by his civic peers.

A similar pattern played out in the pharmaceutical industry:

Hoffman-La Roche, a giant pharmaceutical corporation, pleaded guilty to conspiring with other corporations (some, such as Hoffman-La Roche, BASF, and Rhone-Poulenc, were giants; others, such as Canada's Chinook Group, were relative minnows) to fix the prices of vitamins in several parts of the world. The conspiracy was hatched in 1990 and lasted until 1999.... In Canada during the decade of cheating, the conspirators sold products for $668 million. Vitamins were sold for 30 per cent more than a competitive market would have allowed; there was an illegal profit of just something less than $200 million. Hoffman-La Roche Canada paid a fine of $48 million of the total fines of $88 million imposed in Canada on the various conspirators. The former vice-president of Chinook, the major Canadian participant, was given a nine-month conditional sentence. He was to be allowed to serve his time in the community, rather than in prison; he was to perform fifty hours of community service. Given that he had retired, he presumably had enough time on his hands to meet this requirement without much pain. (Glasbeek 2002: 121–23)

Compare this to the "poor person" crime of welfare fraud. In a 1993 case, a mother of two, who had failed to declare that a male cohabitated with her, received $17,425 in welfare payments. She was sentenced to four months imprisonment. Glasbeek (2002: 123) adds:

A study of welfare fraud documented that 80 per cent of all persons convicted of welfare fraud of this type were given jail sentences. In contrast, another study shows that "prison" is imposed in 4 percent of all tax evasion cases, even though the amounts stolen vastly exceed those stolen by welfare abusers.

Unemployment benefit frauds reveal the same pattern: the rate of incarceration is twice that experienced by tax evaders. In June 2001 a medical practitioner convicted of fraud for overbilling the publicly funded health-care system by just under a million dollars — money used for luxury trips to Germany, Italy, California, and New Zealand and stay in five-star hotels with his partner — was sentenced to a conditional sentence of two years, to be served not in jail, but in the community. The medical disciplinary board added to the sentence by suspending his ability to bill the health-care system for a short length of time. The harshly dealt-with practitioner appealed the medical disciplinary board's decision.

Corporate disregard for the health and safety of workers and consumers — coupled with extremely lax government control and sanctioning of corporate lawlessness — appears to be the basic cause of corporate injuries, deaths, and fraud. While there has since been a move to harsher penalties, even when charges are forthcoming most corporate officials and corporations generally experience few economic, social, or legal penalties. As many analysts point out, this is largely because of the class bias of criminal law.

In the first place, corporate harmfulness is often not even defined as criminal. Most often, costly and harmful corporate behaviour, when classified as illegal, falls within regulatory law rather than under the Criminal Code, where most street crime is placed. This distinction is often made on the basis of legal notions of culpability, which were established to prosecute individual offenders for street crime but not corporations or corporate officials for industry-related killings. In Canada prior to 1941, according to McMullan, corporations were immune to any criminal liability because they were deemed to have no minds of their own. There was little progress in this area until the late 1970s and early 1980s when cases heard before the Supreme Court of Canada, such as *Sault Ste. Marie* (1978), *The Canadian Dredge and Dock Co. Ltd.* (1985), and *Southam Inc. v. Hunter* (1983), began to fit corporate offenders into an individualist model of liability, evidence, procedure, and sanction (McMullan 1992: 80).

McMullan (1992) also notes the dispute and confusion existing over whether the Canadian Charter of Rights and Freedoms under sections 7 and 1(d) are meant to enforce relatively rigid *mens rea* (guilty mind) requirements for the prosecution of corporate offenders. In Canada, to get a Criminal Code conviction the Crown must prove beyond a reasonable doubt the "blameworthiness." The law refers to "the guilty mind, the wrongful intention" — a necessary element in establishing criminal conduct (Simon Verdun-Jones 2007: 66). Decisions at the provincial appeal court level have generally muted the penalty in corporate prosecutions by eliminating incarceration.

McMullan (1992: 80–81) also states that in the *Irwin Toy Ltd.* case the Supreme Court of Canada ruled that a corporation's economic rights were not protected by section 7 of the Charter, as are the "life, liberty or security of the person." While the matter is still up in the air, Canadian judicial history suggests that Canadian courts have not been inclined to extend the scope of corporate criminal proceedings to include the illegal acts or omissions of a corporation's agents or employees. In addition to the problem of *mens rea*, corporations have been almost exclusively prosecuted for regulatory violations — such as those governing health and safety — and not for the consequences of those violations (Reasons, Ross, and Patterson 1986; McMullan 1992). For example, a company would be fined for not installing safety bolts in a construction crane, but not prosecuted for the death of several workers who were below the crane when it collapsed (as in one case in Western Canada). Corporations have frequent and vociferous input into the regulations governing them, generally under the guise of being enlisted to co-operate in creating "workable laws." The result is a lax system of regulation.

A notable example of this corporate co-optation of law is the matter of workers' compensation schemes. While the programs improved the lot of workers in some ways, injured workers lost all rights of prosecution of or compensation from corporations covered by the scheme. The compensation boards are the only source of redress and appeal (Reasons, Ross, and Patterson 1986: 124; for a more recent discussion of workers' compensation, see Tucker 2006.

Two further dimensions of legal regulation — or, more specifically, the lack thereof — are responsible for the high cost to society of corporate crime. Corporations are often able to avoid prosecution for illegal activity, and even when they are prosecuted, the penalty tends to be an inconsequential fine levied against the corporation, and the ruling does not usually single out individual corporate decision-makers legally or publicly. Even when the court does name individual corporate offenders, the penalties, both legal and social, are usually only nominal.

Snider (2002: 224) notes that the 1999 investigation of insider stock trading in Canada was carried out by a newspaper, not the securities commission: "Some [corporate] insiders were making fortunes... [but] until this was publicized, neither the Ontario Securities commission nor the Toronto Stock Exchange had taken any... action." Unfortunately, even with much public fanfare about tightening regulations around corporate governance and stock trading, the Canadian government "crackdown" on corporate misbehaviour has followed the lead of the U.S. *Sarbanes-Oxley Act* — the main concern is not with the losses suffered by "the proverbial average citizen" but with the threat that these activities present to the markets (*National Post* Oct. 11, 2002; see also Neu and Green 2005: cha. 11).

These conditions reflect a major class bias in the application of criminal, regulatory, and social justice. It should not be hard to understand why Edwin Sutherland (1977) found, in his pioneering work on corporate crime, that 90 percent of the seventy largest U.S. corporations were habitual offenders, with an average of fourteen convictions per corporation (see also Clinard and Yeager 1980). John Hagan (1992: 465) reports that more than half of Canada's largest corporations have been recidivists (convicted more than once), with an average of 3.2 decisions against them.

Perhaps we need punitive corporate "three strikes and you're out" legislation. Canada has seen fit to "innovatively" get tough on street crime in the past decade, with tough amendments to the Criminal Code and sentencing practices. At least the lenient attitude towards corporate crime and white-collar criminals is hardening, socially and judicially, as power confronts resistance. Opinion polls reveal that popular thinking and sentiment are in favour of tougher laws, regulations, and sanctions regarding corporate misconduct. In some instances judicial decisions have emphasized corporate responsibility for harmful acts. For example, a *Toronto Star* article of June 9, 2000, noted that the operations manager of a waterfront oil recycling company was jailed for ninety days. He admitted that the company, knowingly and fraudulently, spilled hazardous chemical waste into Toronto harbour (Gomme 2007: 327). Finally, there have been proposals to break down both the individual and organizational inducements to corporate crime and the traditional defences for it, through the creation of a culture that does not tolerate corporate crime. The proposed solutions include: "shaming and positive repentance, new legal tools and controls, corporate accountability and restructuring, new forms of penalty and criminal sanctioning, and the application of countervailing force against corporate crime" (McMullan 1992: 118).

In the mid 1990s, it appeared that at least in some respects the rich would not always get richer while the poor get prison. Snider (1994a: 278) stated, "Pro-regulatory pressure groups (for example, environmental activities, 'green' politicians trying to eliminate chemicals from farmers' fields, unionists working to secure stronger health and safety laws in the workplace, and feminists working to control the pharmaceutical industry) are absolutely central to the regulatory process." The pressure these groups exert, she added, provides the crucial leverage that forces the state to direct at least some attention to the area of corporate crime.

Some eight years later Snider (2002: 231) was much more pessimistic about what she termed the "corporate counter-revolution," whereby corporate marauding is receiving very little attention and political-legal action:

> Government's obligation to help the marginalized and desperate has disappeared, but its obligation to punish the powerless has been reinforced — incarceration rates for crimes of individuals increased throughout the 1990s, even though crime rates were falling (Canada 2000; Cayley 1998; Christie 1993). By decriminalizing and deregulating profitable corporate acts that were once seen as corporate crime, and by downsizing regulatory agencies and cutting regulatory staff, governments at all levels have been quick to shed their historic responsibility to protect citizens from corporate excess, fraud, and abuse of power.

Two recent events in Canada highlight these concerns. In the "wake" of the Gomery inquiry Paul Coffin, a Montreal ad executive, pleaded guilty to defrauding Canadian taxpayers of $1.5 million in the Quebec sponsorship scandal. The Crown asked for a thirty-four-month federal prison term. The judge, in line with Coffin's views, ordered a speaking tour to lecture business students on "ethics." This was part of his two years less a day conditional sentence with no jail time (*National Post* 2005). The Crown later appealed Coffin's sentence, and he was eventually sentenced to eighteen months in prison.

Health Canada reprimanded, suspended, and ultimately fired three research doctors who went public (whistleblowing) about their drug safety concerns.

In September 2004 the Canadian Association of University Teachers *Bulletin* (CAUT 2004:A3) told of the firing, in July, of three doctors who were Government of Canada scientists:

> A leading health policy advocate has described them as "the last few scientists at Health Canada really looking out for health safety." Perhaps it's time for the rest of us to take notice of what's going on in the bowels of the agency charged with protecting our well-being.
>
> The three scientists went public with allegations that pressure tactics had been used against them by the Bureau of Veterinary Drugs in an attempt to compel them to approve the use of certain antibiotics and hormones.
>
> Subsequently reprimanded and suspended by Health Canada, the scientists appealed to the Federal Court and were found to have acted in the public interest by alerting the wider community (through the media) to their safety concerns. Now they have been fired.

RACE

In white settler societies, Aboriginal peoples and people of colour are overrepresented in their criminal justice systems. Canada, Australia, and the United States all have similar experiences (Samuelson 1995). This is not some accident of history, or the result of a pathology of "lawlessness" among non-white people. The overrepresentation of Aboriginal people in the Canadian justice system is but one legacy of the destruction and dislocation of indigenous peoples that took place under European colonialism.

The European colonial political and economic subjugation of territories around the world has been rapidly diminishing. However, it is largely the white colonial population of European origin — and not the original inhabitants of these relatively new nations — who are enjoying freedom from colonialism and its concomitant exploitation and oppression. Essentially, indigenous peoples are still treated as a colonial population, and

In white settler societies, Aboriginal peoples and people of colour are overrepresented in their criminal justice systems. Canada, Australia, and the United States all have similar experiences.

Canada has been no exception. After all, Canada has kept a good number of its "Indians" in concentration camps, known as reserves, for over 150 years and has regulated their behaviour in all aspects of their lives. Getting this colonialist fact recognized and changed in our ostensibly post-colonialist era is apparently much harder to do in Canada than in the international arena.

Mary Ellen Turpel/Aki-kwe (1992) notes that Canada and Canadians like to think of itself and themselves as strong supporters of international rights, ready to contribute troops under the United Nations banner if need be to places like Bosnia, Kuwait, Afghanistan, and Iraq; but that Canada has become increasingly marginalized when the subject of indigenous rights is raised

Canada has been found in violation of international human rights standards by the U.N. Human Rights Committee for it's treatment of Aboriginal People.

in international political circles. For example, as director of the Canadian Institute for Human Rights and Democratic Development, Ed Broadbent remarked in the early 1990s that he would be in a particularly difficult position when he raised questions about human rights abuses in other countries because "These countries will be saying to me: what about Aboriginal rights in Canada?" Canada, Turpel (1992: 80) points out, "has been found in violation of international human rights standards on two separate occasions by the United Nations Human Rights Committee because of its treatment of Aboriginal peoples. As James Waldram (1994: 53) aptly notes, in 1990 the Canadian government sent 1,500 armed troops to the Gulf War in Kuwait. But it also sent over 3,000 troops to Mohawk lands in Eastern Canada after armed Mohawks blocked a gravel road to protest the expansion of a golf course by the neighbouring non-Aboriginal town of Oka.

Ed Broadbent's concerns in the early 1990s over Canada's poor record of Aboriginal human rights are echoed, more aptly blasted, by a 2005 United Nations Fifth Review of Canada's compliance with the International Covenant on Civil and Political Rights. The web-released report cited Canada as drawing severe criticism from the United Nations Human Rights Committee (FAFIA/AFAI website). The Committee was particularly concerned about Canada's treatment of women prisoners, many of whom are Aboriginal. The U.N. committee directed Canada to fully implement the recommendations of the Canadian Human Rights Commission and to report back to them in one year. The U.N. is losing patience with Canada's long-standing abuses of the rights of Aboriginal women. In particular, the Human Rights Committee emphasized the need to remove male staff from direct contact with women prisoners, to limit the use of segregation, and to establish immediately an independent external redress and adjudication body for federally sentenced prisoners.

As Tim Hartnagel (2000: 109–10) notes, the overrepresentation of Aboriginal people in the justice system holds for nearly all categories of offenders, all types of institutions, and all regions of the country, albeit not equally. One of the few statistical updates on Aboriginal overrepresentation came in 2003 from Julian Roberts and Ronald Melchers (2003: 211), who present data on provincial custodial sentenced admissions for Aboriginal and non-Aboriginal offenders since 1978 — the first year, they say, when national statistics including the ethnicity of offender were published. They pay particular attention in their analyses to recent trends, during a period in which Parliament and the Supreme Court have tried to address the problem. Parliament has done so by statutory recognition of the unique nature of the Aboriginal offender, such as the experiences and consequences of colonialism. In 1996 it passed section 718.2(e) of the Criminal Code, which gave special consideration to the circumstances of Aboriginal offenders. The Supreme Court, in 1999, upheld those new provisions in *R. v. Gladue*; its ruling affirmed its remedial purpose in attempting to reduce the high rate of Aboriginal incarceration. Unfortunately, Roberts and Melchers (2003: 212) state, "The findings suggest that little progress has been made in reducing the number of Aboriginal sentenced admissions over the past few decades."

The data present a bleak picture, and recent studies indicate that the overrepresentation of Aboriginal peoples in the justice system will continue to increase rapidly, especially in Western Canada, in tandem with their population's recovery from colonialism's near-devastation of their lives in the early part of this century.

Justice on Trial, an Alberta (1991: 8–17) report, provides a worst-case scenario of what could happen in western Canada if the still colonialist-based trends of the criminal justice system continue:

> Projections indicate that by the year 2011, Aboriginal offenders will account for 18,552 (38.5%) of all admissions to federal and provincial correctional centres in Alberta, compared to 29.5% of all such offenders in 1989. The Aboriginal offender admission population is expected to increase by 69.1% from 10,968 in

Table 15.1 Provincial Variation in Aboriginal Sentences Admissions to Custody, 1978–79 and 2000–01*

Province/Territory	% Aboriginal admissions to custody, 1978–79	% Aboriginal admissions to custody, 2000–01
Saskatchewan	61%	76%
Yukon	51%	72%
Manitoba	50%	64%
Alberta	26%	39%
British Columbia	15%	20%
Ontario	9%	9%
Nova Scotia	–	7%
Newfoundland and Labrador	3%	7%
Quebec	1%	2%
Prince Edward Island	3%	1%
Provincial/territorial total	16%	19%

Source: Canadian Centre for Justice Statistics. Adult Correctional Survey, * excludes Nunavut; New Brunswick and Northwest Territories data are not available. (As cited in Roberts and Melcher 2003.)

1989 to 18,552 in 2011, compared to a 13.3% increase for the non-Aboriginal population.

The cautionary views of the *Alberta Justice on Trial* report are supported by a much more recent statement by Curt Griffiths (2004: 188). Despite a concerted effort over the past two decades to address the specific needs of Aboriginal peoples and to reduce their overrepresentation in the justice system, Griffiths notes, their incarceration rates remain high: "It is predicted that the number of Aboriginal inmates will *double* in the coming years" (emphasis added).

On October 17, 2006, the minority Conservative government led by Stephen Harper introduced its "three strikes legislation" in the House of Commons. Minister of Justice Vic Toews announced that third-time violent/sexual offenders would automatically be categorized as "dangerous offenders" and be liable to indefinite prison sentences. The Crown would not have to prove the case; the onus would be on the accused to prove otherwise. As one newspaper report (*StarPhoenix* [Saskatoon] Oct. 18, 2006) concluded, this bill, Bill C-27, would hit Native offenders the hardest, leaving them with "no hope." The news was appropriately juxtaposed with a report from Canada's correctional investigator released just a day earlier. Correctional Investigator Howard Sapers called the treatment of Aboriginal Peoples in the federal justice system a "national disgrace." Overall the federal inmate population went down 12.5 percent between 1996 and 2004, and during the same period our national crime rate in general also went down. But during the same period the number of First Nations people in federal institutions increased by 21.7 percent, a 34 percent difference between non-Aboriginal and Aboriginal inmates. The numbers of Aboriginal women in prison increased by "a staggering 74.2 percent."

The *StarPhoenix* article ended by noting, with some conscience and historical clarity: "It is a world where a population that the Canadian government institutionalized and traumatized through the residential school system would be further disadvantaged." Ironically, the article notes, it was a non-Native man born in Ontario, Peter Whitmore, who came to be the "Poster boy" for the new legislation. Whitmore's act of abducting and sexually assaulting two children is undoubtedly a heinous offence, but it is the Native offender who seemed likely to pay the most individually and collectively if Bill C-27 were to go through.

While women in general constitute a pronounced minority in the justice system, Aboriginal women are the most disproportionately represented group in both provincial and

> Aboriginal women are among the most neglected, abused, and overincarcerated people in Canada.

federal institutions.[1] The best estimates tell us that although Aboriginal women made up 3 percent of the population of women in Canada, in 2001–02 they accounted for between 20 and 23 percent of female provincial and territorial inmates, and 16 to 20 percent of federal female inmates. Aboriginal males made up 8 percent of provincial and territorial inmates and 14 percent of federal inmates (Statistics Canada 2001b:

11; Winterdyk 2006: 395). This overrepresentation had the greatest concentrations in Western Canada. At one point in the 1980s, about 83 percent of the inmates of the Pine Grove Provincial Prison for women in northern Saskatchewan were Aboriginal (Daubney 1988). In the 1990s, and continuing today, the proportion of Aboriginal inmates in that institution has consistently been well over 90 percent.

Aboriginal women not only enter the justice system with more frequency than do both non-Aboriginal women and Aboriginal men, but also enter it early in life. A study by the Ontario Native Women's Association (cited in LaPrairie 1987: 104) found that 37 percent of the Aboriginal women interviewed in Ontario provincial correctional institutions were twenty years of age or younger; 52 percent were first arrested between the ages of fourteen and seventeen; and 18 percent were even younger when first arrested. In addition, 55 percent had been incarcerated one to three times previously, 40 percent had been arrested fifteen times or more, and 21 percent had seventeen prior incarcerations. Aboriginal females are thus driven up the one-way street of criminal justice early in life and often frequently, although usually for less than thirty days (Daubney 1988: 221).

Aboriginal women are treated far from leniently by the justice system. In the context of their overrepresentation in jails, John Winterdyk (2006: 395) notes, "they make up some 50 percent of women classified as maximum-security prisoners, yet about 58 percent of them are charged with minor assaults and only 13 percent are charged with serious assaults."

To fully understand Aboriginal women's overinvolvement in the justice system, and their (discriminatory) high-risk classifications, we must consider the kinds of lives that they often experience. Carol LaPrairie (1996: 36) notes Ontario research that found alcohol abuse, unemployment, and poor living conditions associated with the arrest and incarceration of Aboriginal women. Most of the women had dependants but no steady employment. The *Report of the Task Force on Federally Sentenced Women*, LaPrairie adds, found that 69 percent of individuals interviewed reported experiences of childhood violence, rape, regular sexual abuse, the witnessing of a murder, and watching their mothers repeatedly beaten. Nearly 90 percent had alcohol and drug problems (LaPrairie 1996: 37). These data are consistent with those from Western Canada (Daubney 1988), and have not significantly changed since the 1990s (Griffiths (2004: 187–88).

To make matters worse, when they are incarcerated Aboriginal women face additional factors that impede "healing instead of rage." As Terry Wotherspoon and Vic Satzewich (1993: 198) pointed out in the early 1990s, these factors were including "severely inadequate prison facilities and programs, cultural and gender-biased assessment standards, failure to acknowledge and treat the realities of aboriginal women's abusive life histories, and unsympathetic prison regimes." Unfortunately, over a decade later, not much had changed in that regard. According to the findings of the Elizabeth Fry Society, many Aboriginal women continue to experience abusive lives, often plagued with substance abuse (Winterdyk 2006: 396). Aboriginal women are regularly denied services for women and access to specific programs designed for Aboriginal offenders — that is, Aboriginal female offenders continue to be marginalized. The Healing Lodge for federally sentenced Aboriginal women in Maple Creek, Saskatchewan, is an important example of an attempt by Corrections Canada and Aboriginal peoples to change these dismal judicial and social realities.

Why does this overincarceration exist in the first place? The statistics themselves don't really provide an answer to this question; in fact, they could be taken to indicate that there are factors (or in the new corrections language, risks) within Aboriginal people themselves that propel them towards illegal and anti-social behaviour. A critical analysis, though, would offer another explanation: that the conditions are the result of prejudice and discrimination among Canadians generally and criminal justice personnel in particular.

The overinvolvement of Canadian Aboriginal peoples in crime and with the justice system, and the resistance of Aboriginal peoples to that experience, take place within this political, social, and economic context. An overinvolvement in crime is but one of the social problems generated by the relatively "passive genocide" perpetrated against Aboriginal peoples, largely under the rhetoric and guise of "assimilation." As the final report of the Royal Commission on Aboriginal Peoples (1996c: 5–7) clearly recognized, the involvement of Aboriginal peoples with the justice system tends to indicate the existence of "social" rather than "criminal" problems. The most central social problems in the area of crime and its treatment are the ones that society creates for Aboriginal individuals — not those created by any individual criminal pathology. Put simply, the problem is racism.

The frequent public perception of Aboriginal people as "drunks," "lazy," and "criminal" has long confused symptoms with the underlying causes of these social problems (Hylton 1982: 125). Confusing symptom with cause is convenient, because it allows for a one-way street of criminal justice policies and programs that address the "problem of crime" without seriously challenging the status quo of the Canadian political economy. Like most systems of domination, this condition depends on the development, by people in power, of strong ideologies and typifications that justify their control over subject populations. This was certainly true historically in Canada, and unfortunately it has now re-emerged in modern form. A 1997 poll of Canadians confirmed a general backlash of attitudes towards "Indian," Inuit, and Métis people. Conveniently and blindly ignoring historical and current realities, almost half of Canadians believe Aboriginals have an equal or better standard of living than the average citizen. Some 40 percent believe that Natives "have only themselves to blame for their problems" (*StarPhoenix* 1997).

A 2003 poll shows a similar negative picture: nearly two-thirds of Saskatchewan people indicated that they were in favour of doing away with Aboriginal treaty rights. Nationally, the poll found that 42 percent of Canadians had the same view. On the issue of Aboriginal land claims, the poll found that half of all Canadians believed "fewer or none" of the hundreds of such claims or deals were valid. In response to this poll, Nancy Pine, a spokesperson for Phil Fontaine and the National Assembly of First Nations, concluded that there is significant body of opinion that is out of sync with the constitutional reality of this country: "Treaty rights, land rights and even self government have been constitutionalized since 1987 and have been repeatedly upheld by the courts" (*StarPhoenix* 2003).

Geoffrey York's book *The Dispossessed: Life and Death in Native Canada* provides a sad historical and telling modern picture of the often racist treatment of Aboriginal peoples. York (1990) reports on a study of capital murder cases from 1926 to 1957 (capital punishment by hanging ended in 1962 in Canada), which found that the risk of execution for an anglo-Canadian who killed a white person was 21 percent, whereas an "Indian" who killed a white person in the same circumstances had a 96 percent risk of execution. Research discovered memos from Indian Affairs bureaucrats recommending that "Indian" offenders be executed because Native peoples needed "special deterrence" (York 1990: 157). In our "modern" day, York notes the differential charging of Aboriginal people by police for relatively minor public-order offences. Research done in Regina "found that 30 percent of the Indians arrested for drunkenness were charged and sent to court. By contrast only 11 percent of non-Natives were charged and sent to court" (York 1990: 149). York's concerns about overcharging were vociferously repeated by the Aboriginal Justice Inquiry of Manitoba (AJI). A large part of the overpolicing of Aboriginal peoples, the inquiry stated, must be blamed on persisting stereotypical racist attitudes and actions directed against them (AJI 1991: 595).

The problem of racism in policing has emerged as an important concern. A key dimension of this concern is the relatively high number of killings by police of Blacks and Aboriginals in questionable circumstances, adding fuel to the fire that has long raged about racism in policing (Forcese 1992). Scott Wortley (2002) and Carl James (2002) have since taken up this concern in their work. As James (2002:303) notes in the conclusion of an article entitled "Armed and Dangerous! Racializing Suspects, Suspecting Race":

> Agua Benjamin (2002) contends that the discourse of the media around po-lice shootings has "demonized and criminalized Blacks and exonerated white police officers." This discourse contributes to the "acceptance" of shootings by police "as justifiable homicide," acts that are "mainly engendered by Blacks themselves" and as such are "mainly a Black problem." This discourse, Benjamin asserts, is part of the social and legal banishment of Black people. This is evident not only in the media's racist images of Blacks (including those of leadership positions, whom the media discredit), but also in the "absence and negation of their concerns and issues," withholding of their "democratic rights and en-titlement," and their physical removal from the society through incarceration and deportations. All of these practices have become so normalized within institutions and in society generally that they operate in ways that make the general public believe that Black victims are indeed responsible for their own

deaths; consequently, concerns that would lead to collective action, including protest and resistance, are never taken up.

Commissions have been struck to evaluate this problem, but the poor record of implementation of Aboriginal justice initiatives does not bode well for eliminating racist views among police and putting curbs (such as independent review boards) on police practice. Dennis Forcese's (1992) anecdotal data highlight notable incidents of "highly questionable" police shootings, especially in Quebec and Ontario. However, the outcry within the Aboriginal community over the unjustified 1995 shooting of Dudley George, an Aboriginal man, by police at an Ipperwash protest and the subsequent initial finding of no guilt on police are not anecdotal. Nor is the 2006 inquiry into the Ipperwash incident and the shooting of Dudley George, an unarmed peaceful protester. A concern of the inquiry, apart from racist police action, was: Did the police receive a provincial "political directive" to direct them to "deal" with the incident? The incident recalls the memo uncovered by York to the effect that Indians needed "special deterrence." Consider the following web-released article on the Ipperwash inquiry and incident:

> "Probe hears talk of getting an 'army'; Police comments taped at Ipperwash"

> Forest, Ont. —Provincial police officers involved in the Ipperwash standoff talked the night before the shooting of an aboriginal protester about amassing an "army" to "do" the park occupiers, according to a recorded conversation heard yesterday at a public inquiry.
>   In the latest of a number of obscenity-laden audiotapes that have been made public at the judicial inquiry into the 1995 police shooting of Dudley George, Sergeant Stan Korosek, the leader of an emergency response team, can barely contain his contempt for occupiers of the provincial park during a conversation with Constable Wayde Jacklin.
>   "Their day will fucking come," Sgt. Korosek tells Constable Jacklin on the recording made at 11:30 p.m. on Sept. 5, 1995. "I was talking to Mark Wright tonight. We're going to amass a fucking army, a real fucking army to do these fuckers big time, but I don't want to talk about it because I'll get all hyped up." (*Globe and Mail* 2006d)

Unfortunately, but notably, the city of Saskatoon has consistently appeared in Amnesty International's annual list of human rights abuses, a list of torture, killings, and persecution around the world. The organization's 300-page report of May 2001 described in detail allegations that two Saskatoon police officers had dumped three Aboriginal men outside of the city in the previous winter. The report cited allegations of "patterns of police abuse against First Nation men in Saskatoon" (*StarPhoenix* 2001a).

> Darrel Night says he was driven by police in January 2000 to a field near the Queen Elizabeth power plant and abandoned in freezing conditions. It's also suspected the same thing happened to aboriginal men Rodney Naistus and Lawrence Wegner, whose bodies were found in the area on Jan. 29 and Feb. 3. Neither of the men were wearing jackets. (*StarPhoenix* 2001a: A1)

The Crown subsequently laid charges against two Saskatoon police officers, who were both fifteen-year veterans, not rookies. They were charged with unlawful confinement and assault. They were convicted and sentenced to eight months jail time — but they did four months. The 1990 similar freezing death of Neil Stonechild resulted in yet another inquiry. A witness, Jason Roy, stated that he saw Stonechild in the back of a police car on the night in question. He was shouting, Roy testified, "They gonna kill me." While the two constables involved denied the charges, the inquiry concluded, based on the police's own records, that they did have Neil Stonechild in their custody the night he died. Both officers were fired by police chief Sabo two weeks after the report's release. The police chief also eventually lost his job. On March 3, 2006, the Saskatoon Board of Police Commissioners announced that his contract would not be renewed after August 2006.

In Saskatchewan, the province with the greatest overrepresentation of Aboriginal people in incarceration, the life circumstances of Aboriginal youth are a particular concern. Saskatchewan had 941 court cases for youth per 10,000 youth — compared to the national average of 417 cases per 10,000 (*StarPhoenix*, May 31, 2001: A3). Vice-Chief Lawrence Joseph of the Saskatoon police stated that Aboriginal youth comprise the majority of young people in court: "It's a cycle of many things, such as a complicated lifestyle where two cultures clash. The other things are symptoms of the past, alcoholism, abuse of drugs, just about killing a culture by churches and by governments, and dismantling the extended family units" (*StarPhoenix*, May 31, 2001: A3). Don Meikle, a street outreach co-ordinator with Egadz Youth Centre, said at the same time that the courts were also seeing more and more young people with addictions and mental health issues.

The discussion of how to develop more appropriate criminal and social justice programs, which would be reflective of both the past and present cultural and structural conditions of Aboriginal peoples, began to receive attention in the justice system in the mid-1970s (Ekstedt and Griffiths 1988), but exploded in the 1990s. Various reports emphasize the need for Aboriginal self-determination, the resolution of land claims, and the reconstruction of a viable modern Aboriginal society within Canada as the most fundamental "justice" concerns. Piecemeal reforms that are not part of this larger initiative, however well-meaning they may be, achieve little substantial success. Unfortunately, the lack of implementation of Aboriginal commission recommendations from the mid-1970s (Ekstedt and Griffiths 1988) has continued in recent years. The Royal Commission on Aboriginal Peoples (RCAP) roundtable (1993) and final (1996c) justice reports noted that some modest reforms had occurred. However, the opening chapter of the roundtable report (RCAP 1993: 37) documented that most of the rec-ommendations made in the recent justice inquiries had not been addressed, especially proposals that required substantial restructuring and transfer of control to Aboriginal peoples. Post-colonial justice is in important respects being rationed out to Aboriginal peoples.

The RCAP (1996c: 82–128) final justice report laid out seven basic areas of Aboriginal initiatives and steps by non-Aboriginal governments/justice agencies to be more re-sponsive to Aboriginal peoples' experiences and needs:

1. **Aboriginal policing**. Until the early 1970s policing services to Aboriginal com-munities were largely carried out by the RCMP as part of its role in enforcing the *Indian Act*. The early 1970s saw the beginning of Band policing, which was expanded substantially in 1978 in Quebec (Amerindian Police Council) and Manitoba (Dakota Ojibway Tribal Council). In 1992 the federal government announced a policy of transferring all on-reserve policing to Bands by about the year 2000 — but by 2003 some reserves still did not have Band-controlled policing; some still had policing by the RCMP with some Band input.

2. **Indigenization**. This initiative attempts to make the system less alienating with-out substantially changing the structure and control of the criminal justice system, and/or Aboriginal overinvolvement, at least directly. It is a favoured government response in terms of money spent on Aboriginal justice initiatives, up to 90 percent (RCAP 1996: 93). There are three main venues: Aboriginal justice of the peace and judges; Aboriginal court workers; and cultural awareness programs/training for justice personnel.

3. *Indian Act* **"provisions" for on-reserve justice initiatives**. Sections of the *Indian Act* (s.81, s.83) provide for Band bylaws, but are restricted by the requirement of Minister of Indian Affairs approval. Section 107 of the *Indian Act* is utilized to replace the "Indian agent" with on-reserve courts. This practice is especially active in Mohawk communities at Kahnawaké and Akwesasne.

4. **Diversion programs and related activities**. These are alternatives for justice system processing. Guilt/innocence is generally replaced by an admission of "respon-sibility." Diversion, either before or after a charge is laid, is one option to jail. With diversion there is no criminal record. Diversion has been active at different times across the country from Nova Scotia (at Shubenacadie) to Toronto (Aboriginal Legal Services of Toronto) and the Yukon (Kwanlin Dun Justice Project, Whitehorse).

5. **Elders panels and sentencing circles**. These sprang originally from the far North, to replace "fly-in suitcase" punitive justice. These initiatives played a role in an especially seminal case, *R. v. Moses*. In elders panels, elders or community lead-ers sit with the judge and advise on sentencing openly or privately. In sentencing circles, accused, victim, family, and community members sit in the circle to discuss the case/sentence; the judge has the final say. The criterion for sentencing circle was set out in *R. v. Alaku*.

6. **Young offender initiatives**. The *Young Offenders Act* (YOA) was passed in 1982 to replace the *Juvenile Delinquents Act* (1908). The YOA (contrary to popular myth) is very punitive in terms of incarceration for youth, especially Aboriginal youth. Moreover, the *Youth Criminal Justice Act*, which has recently replaced the YOA, is predicted to be even more punitive than its predecessor (see Schissel 2002; Alvi 2002). Canada is looking to possibly emulate New Zealand family group conferencing (FGC), which is based on Maori restorative justice. FGC has seen about a 50 percent decline in youth custody, and notably 90 percent of police are satisfied with the FGC process.

7. **Aboriginal initiatives in prison**. This initiative focuses on holistic healing. Increasingly, Aboriginal prisoners maintain their right to participation in spiritual and healing ceremonies, as an existing right under s.35 of the *Constitution Act 1982* and under the Charter of Rights and Freedoms. In response, 1992 legislation by Parliament obligates Correctional Services Canada (CSC) to provide programs designed to meet Aboriginal offender needs. Changing the old CSC is very difficult, but in the 1990s a new holistic healing facility opened near Edmonton for federally sentenced Aboriginal men; this is in addition to Maple Creek for federally sentenced Aboriginal women (see LaPrairie 1996).

Justice system reforms can be notable and lead to a greater empowering of Aboriginal peoples, but some stark life facts for Aboriginal people still exist. According to United Nations studies, Canada has the highest standard of living in the world, but the living conditions of its Aboriginal people rank just sixty-third in the list of nations (*StarPhoenix* 2001b). In his response to the Amnesty International report on the Saskatoon police, Vice-Chief Joseph stated, "All issues, from justice to socio-economic conditions, must be addressed immediately" (*StarPhoenix* May 31, 2001b: A8).

GENDER

Historically, criminology, even critical analyses that link social inequalities, justice, and social change, almost entirely ignored women. For example, Taylor, Walton, and Young's 1973 groundbreaking book *The New Criminology* did not contain one word about women (Gregory 1986). An analysis of Canadian criminal justice (Griffiths and Verdun-Jones 1994) devotes only about 7 out of 660 pages to discussing women and justice. Still, gender has emerged as a rapidly growing component of criminology and socio-legal studies (see Chesney-Lind and Bloom 1997; Dobash and Dobash 1995; Comack and Balfour 2004).

> Historically, criminology, even critical analyses that link social inequalities, justice, and social change, almost entirely ignored women.

Any existing concern with gender and justice has been grounded in mainstream criminology, liberal feminism, and radical feminism. Each of these streams has its own central focus, which has resulted in a set of relatively disparate debates. Fortunately, a more promising comprehensive, theoretical, analytical, and policy-based socialist-feminist perspective has emerged. As Elizabeth Comack (1992: 156) states, "Socialist feminists focus on the interconnection between capitalism (class) and patriarchy (gender) and the manner in which class and gender relations are manifested in the productive and reproductive spheres of society." In addition, Comack (like other writers) notes that the structure of inequality in Canadian society includes racism as well. One of the most recent, and succinct, reviews of critical feminist theory is by Carolyn Brooks (2002). As she states (2002: 45):

> The last century has witnessed three distinctive waves of feminism. The first wave, early in the twentieth century, was characterized by women's struggles for basic rights, such as the right to vote; the second wave was both ideological and political — an attempt to understand the bases of women's oppression, as well as continuing the struggle for equality and justice. Third-wave feminists (starting in the 1990s) are those who argue that there is no one universal oppression of women — that women's experiences vary according to their race, class, global location, and human agency.

Within criminology the starting point for analyses of women and crime tends to be grounded in a mainstream criminological concern with the causes of crime. This approach usually emphasizes the generally low rate of female involvement in crime relative to men (Hagan 1985; Hartnagel 2004). For example, in 1995 women accounted for only 12.2 percent of all adults charged with violent crimes in Canada; even their property crime involvement rate — about 23 percent of all offenders — still indicated a reasonably large gender gap (Statistics Canada 1996). By 2002 the number of women charged with violent crime had increased to 16 percent, while property crime remained at 23 percent (Hartnagel 2004: 128).

The increases in female criminality in recent decades have caused the greatest stir. Recent data show that from 1968 to 2000 the rate for all Criminal Code offences increased by 43 percent for males and 184 percent for females (Hartnagel 2004). As early as the mid-1970s, Canada was said to be witnessing the rise of the "new female criminal," apparently a result of the encroachment of liberated women on a traditional male preserve (Adler 1975). Social roles for women were said to be changing, with women achieving greater equality of involvement not only in society generally, but also in the criminal justice system. This has been dubbed the "converging role thesis." In summarizing this literature, Hartnagel (1992) points out that a 1969 report by the Canadian Committee on Corrections found that 80 percent of the increase in the female crime rate from 1960 to 1966 was primarily due to convictions of women for simple theft. A major review of studies on gender differences in crime (Smith and Visher 1980) came to a similar conclusion. Hartnagel (2000) states that 77 percent of the increase from 1968 to 1996 in women charged with Criminal Code offences was for non-violent crime. From 1968 to 2000 the proportion of all women charged for violent crime increased from 10 percent to 26 percent (Hartnagel 2004: 130). Increases in female violent crime, and female gangs, are receiving considerable media and academic analysis, but, as Hartnagel (2004: 130) notes, "the highest rates for women charged continue to be for less serious thefts of property."

It would seem safe to conclude that "female experiences are not moving beyond traditional roles, either legitimate or illegitimate" (Steffensmeier, quoted in Hartnagel 1996: 110). As Holly Johnson and Karen Rodgers (1993: 98) note, women's involvement in crime

> is consistent with their traditional roles as consumers, and increasingly, as low income, semi-skilled, sole support providers for their families. In keeping with the rapid increase in female-headed households and the stresses associated with poverty, greater numbers of women are being charged with shoplifting, cheque forging and welfare fraud.

Comack (2002: 174) reiterates this view. Comack's (1996a, 1996b, 2002) analyses of women in conflict with the law have found very similar relationships between the everyday conflicts and dilemmas of women and their troubles with the law.

While role convergence and a less "chivalrous" or "paternalistic" (see Chunn and Gavigan 1995) judicial system cannot totally be ruled out as factors in women's involvement in crime, a more fruitful explanation would lie elsewhere. Continuing extensive female job ghettoization, the feminization of poverty (Johnson and Rodgers 1993; Broad 2000: chas. 2, 3; for the United States, see Gimenez 1991), and the development of a youth consumer market frequently directed at teenage females (Greenberg 1977) are more basic to the understanding of female patterns and rates of involvement in crime.

Little seems to have changed positively for many women in the past decades. Griffiths (2004: 187) notes that most women serving sentences in federal and provincial territorial corrections are from marginalized backgrounds: "Their past and current situations are likely to include poverty, histories of abuse, long term drug and alcohol dependency, responsibilities for primary care of children, limited educational attainment, and few opportunities to obtain adequately paid work." Sadly, virtually every critical observer concurs that prison still only teaches women at best to "do their time," medicated if necessary. More likely, prisons only add another bitter layer to their life experiences and do not deal with their underlying problems and issues (Boritch 2002). Reincarceration is thus too often a reality, and a push to move them up the "high-risk" carceral scale of inmate classification, usually with added debilitation not rehabilitation.

The justice system's treatment of women who have been the victims of crime has also been the object of considerable critical scrutiny in the past three decades. The main areas of concern have been the system's biases, injustices, and ineffectiveness in dealing with women who have been the victims of domestic violence and sexual assault, a central concern of radical, critical analytic feminists (Comack 2004). However, as Dawn

Currie and Brian MacLean (1992) and Carolyn Brooks (2002) correctly point out, in recent decades academic research and writing on domestic violence mushroomed, along very fractioned lines. (See chapter 2 here for an outline of key debates in the analysis of domestic violence.)

DOMESTIC VIOLENCE

Domestic violence, almost always against women, occurs in a large number of Canadian families. The early research in this area by Linda MacLeod (1980) estimated, for example, that at least 10 percent of women in Canada were battered by their partners each year. Unlike street crime, where victim and offender are overconcentrated in the lower socio-economic level of society, this violence is spread across all social classes. Ruth Mann (2003: 41) updates these data. She notes that, overall in Canada in 1991, 87 percent of 27,000 domestic assault charges were laid against men. That same year, 77 percent of eighty-eight homicides involving an opposite-sex spousal or dating partner resulted in the death of a woman. More data from the Violence-Against-Women Survey found that 25 percent of Canadian women over the age of sixteen had experienced violence from a current or postmarital partner (Comack 1996b: 155). Moreover, in 1995 a woman was six times more likely to be killed by a spouse than by a stranger (Statistics Canada 1996).

Past police policy in Canada frequently emphasized minimal intervention on the part of police (Burris and Jaffe 1983). In a 1983 study Burris and Jaffe found that police laid assault charges in only 3 percent of all family-violence cases, even though 20 percent of the victims were advised to seek medical treatment and 60 percent were told to lay their own charges. In the early 1980s criminal justice and especially police policy in this area underwent a significant change (Burris and Jaffe 1983). The police force in London, Ont., was one of the first in Canada to correct this judicial neglect of violence against women. In May 1981 the London police force instituted a policy encouraging officers to lay assault charges in cases of domestic violence. Officers were told that they did not have to witness the assault — they only needed to have reasonable and probable grounds to believe that an assault had occurred (for example, injury serious enough for them to advise a woman to seek medical attention). This was followed by a similar initiative in Manitoba. The changes in police practice in Manitoba not only led to a dramatic increase in charges laid but also to equally dramatic increases in convictions for spousal abuse and in the development of treatment programs for batterers; and to a change in the attitudes of Crown prosecutors to abuse cases (see Ursel 1998).

The problem of the victims' reluctance to press charges is frequently cited as a reason for police non-intervention in domestic violence. Under the new Ontario policy, the number of private informations — where the victims had to press charges themselves — dropped substantially, from forty-six to thirteen. This change was all the more important given that police-laid charges were more likely to go to criminal court and end in guilty verdicts than were charges pressed through family courts, and the police charges took only about three-quarters of the time to reach their final disposition (Burris and Jaffe 1983). Feminists had philosophical problems with this in that it was tantamount to taking power out of the woman's hands to decide her own future and handing power over to the state.

In line with this initiative — and the data from the controversial 1981–82 Minneapolis policing experiment, which found a recidivism rate of 19 percent for arrested abusers compared to a rate of 35 percent for cases dealt with by mediation only (Currie and MacLean 1992) — in 1983 a national directive (so-called "zero tolerance" for domestic abuse) encouraged police to lay charges in wife-battering cases.[2] Canada was the first country to adopt such a nationwide directive. As Comack (1992) notes, police training was upgraded to stress sensitive intervention in wife assault cases, and several provinces — such as Manitoba — have established specialized courts to deal with domestic violence (Ursel 1998; Prairie Research Associates 1994).

The end product of these initiatives is that the courts began to deal with increasing numbers of abusive men. Comack (1996b: 156) states, "In the province of Manitoba alone, for example, the number of individuals (approximately 96 percent of whom were men) charged with spousal assault increased from 1136 in 1983 to 2779 in 1990." Moreover, as Linda MacLeod (1987) stated in her second report for the Canadian Advisory Council on the Status of Women, the number of transition houses providing shelter for battered women more than tripled, from 85 in 1982 to 264 in 1987. Mann (2003: 41) provides a more recent observation and data. She notes that, intervention services aimed at alleviating or eliminating domestic violence against women included an expansive and still growing battered women's shelter system. From April 1, 1999 to March 31, 2000, 57,200 women and children were admitted to 448 shelters. Is this good news? Maybe and maybe not, as we shall see shortly.

Much criticism and controversy exist over the "success" of these initiatives. Dawn Currie (1990) and Currie, Brian MacLean, and Dragon Milovanovic (1992) point out serious concerns about how the current focus on violence against

Much criticism and controversy exist over the "success" of zero-tolerance initiatives.

women can feed into a reactionary law and order lobby (see also MacLeod 1987). Interwoven here is the concern that this "institutionalization" of women's issues fails to deal with the unequal distribution of societal resources and power. Currie, MacLean, and Milovanovic (1992: 29) frame the problem well: "Within a discourse that concerns legal rights, police protection, and criminal justice, this issue is transformed into a technical matter that can be safely met within the current system without any significant changes in relations of power [between men and women]." Comack and Balfour (2004) provide a more recent critique of zero tolerance.

However, as Jane Ursel (1998) argues about the experiences of the battered women's movement and the Winnipeg Family-Violence Court, the positive dimensions of state-sponsored approaches to domestic violence must be recognized. She acknowledges: "Not all actors and agencies in the field will share the analysis of patriarchy common to the founders of the battered women's movement" (Ursel 1991: 285; see also Rock 1986: 218). Nonetheless, she does find an element of encouragement: "It has been demonstrated that, as a result of state involvement, the number of services for wife abuse victims increased tenfold from 1982 to 1990" (Ursel 1991: 283). Still, Comack (1996b: 158) directs us to the continued importance of radical transformation in our society, when she writes of the Montreal massacre at the École Polytéchnique:

> While the murder of fourteen women in Montreal has understandably received the attention and publicity it deserves, it is also noteworthy that the violence that women encounter at the hands of men has become "routine." In August 1990 alone, eleven women in Montreal were killed by their male partners, many of them estranged. Yet, two of every three women going to a shelter in Montreal are turned away because of lack of space.

As Mann points out in chapter 2 of this book (see n. 6; citing Taylor-Butts 2005), in March 2004 58,486 women and 36,840 children were admitted to 473 shelters and transition houses in Canada — and on April 14 of that year 93 of these shelters turned 221 women and 112 children away. Almost three-quarters of these women were fleeing "intimate abuse."

SEXUAL ASSAULT

Not surprisingly, patterns of and responses to sexual assault mirror those regarding domestic violence. Research in the 1980s estimated that one in four Canadian women would be sexually assaulted, yet what is most noteworthy is that only 38 percent of an estimated 17,300 sexual assaults, overwhelmingly against females, were reported to police. While a third of the victims of sexual assault cited fear of revenge by the offender, 43 percent cited the attitude of the police or courts as the reason for not reporting the incident (Canada, Solicitor General 1985). As Comack (1996b: 157) notes, an important distinction must be made between law as legislation and law as practice. Sexually assaulted women generally have long been more afraid of the additional suffering and humiliation that the justice system was likely to inflict on them than they are of reprisals by the offender. The conviction of only a small fraction of rapists has done little to reassure victims of sexual assault (Snider 1991: 252).

Efforts have been made in Canada to reduce the trauma visited upon sexually assaulted women. A 1983 reform to the Criminal Code abolished the legal charge of rape, as well as the separate charges of indecent assault male and indecent assault female. Contrary to much public concern and fear over girls being sexually molested, before 1983 the maximum penalty for indecent assault on a female was only half that for indecent assault on a male (five versus ten years). In a male-dominated criminal justice system, it was apparently much less deviant for offenders (generally males) to sexually molest girls than boys.

In place of the rape law, the federal government created three levels of sexual assault based upon the degree of violence. The intent was to reduce the stigma of rape (and, hence, increase reporting by victims) and to emphasize, as many academics and feminists had strenuously contended, that rape was primarily a violent act of male domination in sexual form. The old rape prohibition was, moreover, primarily a paternalistic form of social control against females, not protective legislation, because it reinforced the idea of women as the property of men (husbands, for example, were immune from criminal sanction under the old law). Not surprisingly, the charge of rape was not even in the "Offences Against the Person" section of the pre-1983 Criminal Code. Rape was in section four of the Canadian Code under "Sexual Offences, Public Morals and Disorderly Conduct."

The procedural law governing the examination of persons alleging sexual assault and the rules of evidence in such cases have also been changed. Before 1983 the testimony of the victim alleging rape had to be corroborated by other evidence. If not, the judge had to instruct the jury on the danger of convicting the accused based upon uncorroborated testimony (Brannigan 1984: 27–28). However, the judge did not have to issue any such warning in criminal trials generally — for example, if the victim was identifying an individual who had stolen her purse. As well, government abolished the "doctrine of recent complaint," which implied that if a woman reported an offence on the first reasonable opportunity, she was supposedly more "trustworthy" or "believable" in her claim than if she waited until later. The law also formally limited the extent to which the victim can be questioned about her previous sexual activity in a sexual assault trial — the so-called "rape shield provision" (Task Force on the Status of Women 1985: 109–13).

Still, much scepticism remained over the extent to which these changes would produce any significant increase in the reporting of sexual assault by females or would alter the judicial stereotyping and traumatization of sexually assaulted women. As Marni Allison (1991: 2) notes, despite the legal reforms many feminists maintained that "justice" would still be elusive for many victims of sexual violence, because "changing the content of law does not ensure that implementation of the changes will reflect the objectives of the legislature." This scepticism was apparently warranted. In August 1991 the Supreme Court of Canada, in a 7–2 decision, struck down section 246.6 of the Criminal Code, the "rape shield provision," the section instituted in the 1983 reform to prevent a victim's sexual conduct from being used to discredit her. The Supreme Court justified its 1991 ruling on the grounds that section 246.6 could deny the accused the right to a fair trial, as enshrined in sections 7 and 11(d) of the Charter. In 1992 the Canadian Parliament quickly responded with new legislation, Bill C-49, which amended the Criminal Code to clarify when "No means No" and to restrict the obtaining and admissibility of evidence on the victim's sexual conduct.

Several analysts argued that Bill C-127 (the 1983 rape law change) offered little hope that rape would diminish (Boyle 1984: Heald 1985; Snider 1985; Ruebsaat 1985; Hinch 1988). Although the new legislation attempted to address some of the inequities in the original law, the present law — especially in relation to its application — remains decidedly sexist and unjust.

This view received substantial support in the Department of Justice's 1990 evaluation of the 1983 sexual assault legislative changes. The study noted that the most substantial change came from the victims. From 1982 to 1990 the number of women coming forward to report a sexual assault climbed from 12,848 to 32,861. As for other areas of the criminal justice system, the report concluded: "It is apparent that the situation has not changed since the introduction of the new legislation. In particular, unfounded rates, rates of cases cleared by charge, and conviction rates have remained more or less constant" (Canada, Department of Justice 1990: 55). A more recent study echoes this conclusion:

> While Bill C-127 was heralded as the beginning of a new age of gender neutral jurisprudence, this study's analysis suggests that it had little or no impact on the willingness of the State to redress historical gender inequity through law…. Law reforms, although struck in good faith, may be futile when created and administered in class-biased, gender-biased, socio-economic systems. (Schissel 1996: 126)

A 1993 Statistics Canada survey found that 29 percent of ever married and common-law women had endured at least one episode of physical or sexual violence, and 39 percent of all women had been sexually assaulted after the age of sixteen — 79 percent of those by men known to them. As of 1993, an estimated four million Canadian women had been sexually assaulted. Equally disturbing, in 1993, 90 percent of sexual assaults were never reported to police (Statistics Canada, cited in Schmallenger et al. 2000). The 1999 General Social Survey found that 78 percent of sexual assaults were not reported to police. Almost half of the respondents did not report sexual assault to police because they were reluctant to get the police involved (Gomme 2007: 190). Virtually the same percentage — 18 and 19 percent — did not report the sexual assault because they believed the police would not help them or because they feared retaliation. Sadly, a report from the Canadian Centre for Justice Statistics notes that in 2003 fully 98 percent of 23,000 sexual assaults known to police are coded by police as "basic" or level 1 — which means that only 460 sexual assaults out of 23,000 are coded as being more violent than a "basic" sexual assault. The 2003 Government of Canada publication states that the country's sexual assault rate, as measured by known-to-police crimes, has declined to the lowest level since 1985. It makes no mention of the problem of victims, usually women, not reporting offences to police (Statistics Canada, 2004b: 7). Importantly, Comack (2004: 183) notes that legal case decisions in the mid-1990s, such as that in the Bishop O'Connor residential-school case of rape and sexual assault, allowed the accused's defence attorney access to otherwise confidential victim treatment and counselling records. She notes, "Women who were sexually assaulted had to decide whether they would seek counseling or initiate criminal prosecution of their assailant."

WOMEN IN PRISON

Another major concern in the area of gender is the injustices and problems faced by incarcerated women. The issues here exemplify the ideologies and social practices that are often central in the subjugation of females in patriarchal and capitalist society.

As Shelagh Berzins and Lorraine Cooper (1982: 401) note: "An historical review of the treatment of the federal female offender in Canada reveals a mixture of neglect, outright barbarism and well-meaning paternalism" (see also Boritch 2002; Carey 1996). Female offenders have been contradictorily portrayed as "poor and unfortunate" women in need of protection and as "scheming temptresses who are lazy and worthless" (Cooper 1993: 33). Currie (1986) would probably challenge the "well-meaning" dimension of paternalism; at most, it reflects a "helping" attitude that masks the social control and subjugation of women. Put succinctly and accurately, "Prison, as a microcosm of society, reflects all those inequalities which discriminate against women, be their source historical, social or administrative convenience" (Ekstedt and Griffiths 1988: 337).

Imprisoned women have expressed feelings of frustration, pain, anger, anxiety, and grief overwhelmingly associated with their everyday experiences of living inside prison. Kathleen Kendall (1993: 4) notes that women "stressed that their incarceration stripped them of control over their own lives including their schedules, activities and space," a situation reminiscent of many women's experiences of abuse prior to incarceration. In the face of all this, and despite the inhibited possibilities for independence and the punitive sanctions for displays of their autonomy on the inside, the correctional staff and the parole board still expect women to take self-determined action in "making responsible choices" to become "law-abiding citizens." As Kendall (1993) points out, "Women are caught in a paradox between what they are allowed to do and what they are told or expected to do."

> Women stress that their incarceration stripped them of control over their own lives including their schedules, activities and space — a situation reminiscent of many women's experiences of abuse prior to incarceration.

In the late 1980s Shelagh Cooper (1987) analyzed the evolution of the key institution for incarcerated women: the Federal Prison for Women (P4W) in Kingston, Ontario. P4W opened its doors in 1934, just across the road from the Kingston Penitentiary for Men, which had previously housed federally sentenced women. All federally sentenced women from across Canada were now to be gathered into a centralized institution, basically modelled after federal male penitentiaries. The management of P4W continued to be the responsibility of the male penitentiary warden. P4W had no gun towers and, unfortunately, no outside windows, recreation grounds within the enclosure, provision for outdoor exercise of any kind, or educational facilities for the female prisoners (Cooper 1987: 13).

Federal penitentiaries for men were spread across the country, but with the exception of federally sentenced women doing time in provincial institutions (through a federal-provincial agreement), until recently only the Kingston facility existed for women. The Correctional Service of Canada saw the use of one centralized federal facility for the relatively small number of women as being the most cost-effective system. Within this one facility, all federally sentenced women were housed as maximum-security prisoners, which also provided a justification for limiting the quantity and quality of programs.

It is thus not surprising that virtually every major commission investigating Canada's penal system, from the 1938 Archambault Report onward, severely criticized conditions at P4W and generally recommended its closure. They tended to conclude that the relatively small number of female prisoners should be housed in their home provinces. Indeed, as Cooper (1987) noted, since 1968 no fewer than thirteen government studies, investigations, and private-sector reports had reiterated this basic conclusion. The recalcitrance of the Canadian justice system to change is indicated by the 1979 firing of Berzins and Cooper, whose task was to improve services and programs at P4W. The two women were instrumental in producing a useful review of the existing programs at P4W; their report did not meet with the approval of the Commissioner of Corrections, although it did become public by accident.

Most condemningly, the group Women for Justice, distressed by the lack of change that had accompanied report after report, finally achieved a landmark 1981 Human Rights of Canada Commission decision. The commission ruled that the Correctional Service of Canada discriminated against female prisoners at P4W. Berzins and Cooper (1982) noted major deficiencies in facilities and programs compared to those available to federally incarcerated men.

P4W had a high suicide rate, especially for Aboriginal women, who were often incarcerated far from home. A 1990 coroner's inquest into the death of Sandra Sayer connected the suicide rate to the institution's systemic discrimination. Sayer, a twenty-four-year-old Saulteaux, was found hanging from the bars of her cell less than two months before her expected release date — which was not an unusual incident at P4W. In early February 1991 a group of female prisoners had barricaded themselves in the prison recreation room to protest the fourth Aboriginal inmate suicide in sixteen months. The prison's response was to quell the protest by use of an assault team, dogs, and tear gas (*StarPhoenix* 1991a: A15). Rather than specialized psychiatric facilities for traumatized female inmates, the prison had segregation facilities where the inmates were confined to spartan, locked cells twenty-three hours a day. They lost the comforts of their home cells — the family photographs on walls, the television, the books — at a critical time. They were stripped of their clothing and left wearing paper gowns (*StarPhoenix* 1991b: D1). These conditions were reportedly worse than those in any male institution (Berzins and Cooper 1982: 406).

The programs offered at P4W — as also in provincial jails — constituted another form of blatant discrimination (Ekstedt and Griffiths 1988). Prison programs for women repeated, and attempted to reinforce, the stereotypical social and occupational roles of women in society. The 1978 Proudfoot Commission inquiry cited working in the prison laundry and in a beauty parlour, doing kitchen work, and learning sewing as typical correctional programs for women. Berzins and Hayes noted that the epitome of education in P4W, introduced as a result of the 1981 Human Rights Commission decision, was the introduction of word processors; but women were taught keyboarding only, not programming, which only reinforced their chances of experiencing poverty on their release and hence possibly starting the criminal cycle again (Berzins and Hayes 1987: 173).

Significantly, the report by the Task Force on Federally Sentenced Women (1990), *Creating Choices*, concluded that imprisoned women are "high needs, low risk." The Task Force established five fundamental principles for women in prisons:

1. empowering women (programs to raise self-esteem);
2. providing more meaningful choices in programs and community facilities (wider range of options);
3. treating women with respect and dignity (to enhance self-respect);
4. providing a physically and emotionally supportive environment; and
5. sharing responsibility for the women's welfare among both correctional workers and members of the community (co-operation by government, correctional, and voluntary organizations and members).

The plan called for regional facilities, a healing lodge, and a community release strategy. Moreover, each of these facilities was to differ from traditional "male-oriented" corrections.

After the publication of the Task Force report, the announcement was finally made that P4W would be closed and that five new regional facilities, and a "healing centre" for Aboriginal women at Maple Creek, Sask., would be built. But change would not come easily at P4W. In April 1994 the male IERT (Institutional Emergency Response Team) from Kingston Penitentiary was sent to P4W to "quell a violent incident." The public release of the horrific, brutal institutional response to an inmate-staff confrontation, which was videotaped, resulted in a 1996 Commission of Inquiry. The final report was critical of the substantial abuse of these inmates and the violation of numerous CSC formal procedures (Canada 1996). For example: "Mace was used to subdue three of the inmates involved in the April 22nd incident. Although Correctional Service policy contains elaborate provisions with respect to decontamination following the use of mace, in this case, decontamination was limited to pouring some glasses of water over the inmates' eyes" (Canada 1996: 31). The report concluded that, overall, "nearly every step that was taken in response to this incident was at odds with the intent of the new [*Creating Choices*] initiatives" (Canada 1996: 24). More specifically, the Arbour Inquiry:

> documented the violations of the rule of law, policy, and institutional regulations in a number of areas, including the use of segregation, the use of force by the IERT, and the manner in which the women had been strip-searched and

subjected to body cavity searches. Serious concerns were raised as to whether the CSC was capable of implementing the necessary reforms to ensure that the rules of law and justice were adhered to without outside intervention and monitoring. The Arbour report also contained 14 primary recommendations relating to cross-gender staffing in correctional institutions for women, the use of force and of IERTs, the operation of segregation units, the needs of Aboriginal women in correctional institutions, ways of ensuring accountability and adherence to the rule of law among correctional personnel, and procedures of handling inmate complaints and grievances (Griffiths 2004: 182).

In December 2000 and March 2001 respectively, the Saskatchewan Elizabeth Fry Society and the National Association of Elizabeth Fry Societies filed human rights complaints. The complaints cited the Correctional Service of Canada for the "temporary" poor housing and conditions for females housed in an annex of the men's prison in Prince Albert and in the Regional Psychiatric Centre in Saskatoon. These women, many of them Aboriginal, had been "temporarily" housed in substandard, relative to the men's, facilities, since 1996. Several Aboriginal analysts, including Patricia Monture-Angus (2000) and Sky Blue Morin (1999) were critical of the post-*Creating Choices* situation of federally sentenced Aboriginal women (FSAW). Morin (1999: 8) summed up the concerns, saying that the "responsibility and obligation" of the Correctional Service of Canada to FSAW had not been fulfilled, and that the CSC had "been remiss" in not respecting the ethnic, cultural, and spiritual beliefs of FSAW. Although CSC Corporate Mission Objectives, the *Corrections and Conditional Release Act*, *Creating Choices* recommendations, and Commissioner's directives had all put forth approaches for implementing programs that would recognize Aboriginal cultural and spiritual beliefs, discrimination and racism against FSAW continued. Against these odds, FSAW have not been able to reintegrate into their home communities and society at large successfully.

CONCLUSION

To move beyond piecemeal and partial socio-legal reforms in the area of gender and social justice, we need to develop a more comprehensive theoretical, analytical, and policy-based socialist-feminist critique of our society. Currie's (1986: 237) early statement is still valid:

> What is necessary is a distinctly "feminist" criminology which can explain crime in general while studying women in particular. The goal of such an investigation should be not only to understand the involvement of women in officially recorded crime, but to understand the oppression of women, without this becoming a tool of oppression itself.

Feminist criminologists such as Brooks (2002) and Comack and Balfour (2004) argue that we need a dynamic and integrated analysis of the interrelationships between patriarchy, capitalist society, and state control of women. Critical criminologists have come to see locating racism in such an analysis as an integral part of this project as well. Still, is it likely that the unequal definition of crime and involvement and treatment of women and marginalized individuals in the justice system will be significantly reduced in the near future?

Just possibly, success will come through initiatives seeking to reduce the overuse of incarceration for relatively petty offences, changes in sexual assault laws and court procedures, and justice system programs better suited to the needs of Aboriginal and female offenders. Yet these kinds of initiatives will only partially confront the status quo in Canadian society. To reduce the prevailing inequities we need to focus on the society's structural and cultural conditions and its distribution of power — the elements that are at the centre of the problem. At this level basic changes — long promoted by radical-critical criminologists and sociologists — are difficult to achieve, because they confront the underlying, socially entrenched inequalities of life conditions and power relations.

As Jeffrey Reiman (2007) states, in order for a real "society" to exist there must be two-way-street social justice. Harry Glasbeek, an astute socio-legal analyst, puts this very well at the end of his book *Wealth by Stealth*:

> As C. Douglas Lummis argued in *Radical Democracy*, to be a democrat is not an abstraction. It is a state of being: "Democracy is a world that joins *Demos* — the people with *Krakia* — power…. It describes an ideal, not a method for achieving it…. It is a historical project… as people take it up as such and struggle for it."
>
> These proposals take up what we have learned in the previous pages about the enemy of this historical project, and they are intended to help fuel the spirit of would-be democrats as they engage in their struggles to bring together *people* and *power*, break down the corporate shield, and lay the groundwork for a humanizing transformation of our polity. (Glasbeek 2002: 283)

Only if we recover, and enrich our political lives as democratic citizens, will we be able to be effective participants in local and worldwide movements to tackle the enormous human problems we face.

GLOSSARY OF KEY TERMS

Charter of Rights and Freedoms, Section 7 and Section 1(d): Prior to 1941, corporations were immune to any criminal liability because *mens rea*, "guilty mind," could not corporately exist. Section 7 and section 1(d) of the Charter have been used to argue against this rigid *mens rea* requirement in prosecution of corporate crime.

Corporate crime/suite crime: Harmful economic, human, and environmental acts committed by corporate officials in the pursuit of organizational goals, usually profit, and generally unpunished by the state.

Critical criminology: Grounded in the Marxist concepts of social class conflict and praxis, this theory sees crime and criminal justice as reflecting and reproducing the inequalities in society. As well, it is an advocacy perspective in that the point of critical analysis is not just to study society, but to eliminate unjust social acts and inequalities.

Domestic violence: Usually violence against women by their partners. The Violence-Against-Women Survey found that 25 percent of women over sixteen years of age experience violence from a current or postmarital partner.

Ipperwash inquiry: Ontario's 2006 inquiry into the Ontario Provincial Police sniper, September 1995, shooting of Dudley George, a peaceful protester.

European colonialism: The takeover by white settlers of land belonging to Aboriginal peoples, resulting in their near-genocidal destruction, both physically and culturally.

Overrepresentation of Aboriginal People: In Western Canada, since the Second World War, Aboriginal Peoples have been incarcerated both provincially and federally far in excess of their percentage of general population.

Political economy: A form of analysis that links political and economic power. An influential study of political economy contends that wealth and political power are concentrated in the hands of a few individuals and corporations, giving them substantial political, legal, and economic control over our ostensibly democratic society.

Postcolonial justice: An alternative system of justice for Aboriginals that includes Aboriginal self-determination and resolution of land claims in conjunction with traditional healing and harmony restoration.

Prison for Women (P4W): A federal prison that opened in 1934 to house federally sentenced women. Conditions were very harsh, paternalistic, and far inferior to prisons for men. Inmate despair and suicide were thus a major problem. The prison was closed in July 2000.

QUESTIONS FOR DISCUSSION

1. Critically evaluate the truth of the statement that "criminal law and the justice system protect us from serious economic and physical harm."
2. To what extent does the Canadian justice system treat upper-class individuals more favourably than lower-class people? Is Canada a "haven" for corporate crime?

3. Was it fair to sentence Paul Coffin to lecture business students on ethics, for having committed a $1.5-million-dollar fraud? Should he be sentenced to jail time given that the Crown appealed the sentence?
4. Explain the nature of the overinvolvement of Aboriginal peoples in the justice system, and outline any signs of positive change in this area.
5. Are women treated better by the justice system than men are? Explain.
6. How likely is it that inequalities of involvement and treatment in the justice system based upon class, ethnicity, and gender will disappear in the near future? Will "law and order" criminal justice policies be a help or a hindrance to this project?

WEBSITES OF INTEREST

Aboriginal Peoples in Canada. <www.statcan.ca/english/freepub/85F0033MIE /85F0033MIE01001.pdf>.
Royal Commission on Aboriginal Peoples. <www.ainc-inac.gc.ca/ch/RCAP/in-dex_e.html>.
TR Young's Redfeather Institute. <www.tryoung.com/lectures/049te>.
National Clearinghouse on Family Violence. <www.hc-sc.gc.ca/hppb/familyvio-lence/>.

NOTES

1. Getting exact data on the actual percentage of Aboriginal individuals in the justice system is difficult, in part because racial background, based on self-identification, is not always included in justice system records.
2. See Currie and MacLean (1992) for a critique of the Minneapolis research.
3. One of the most criticized cases has been the well-known ruling in *Pappajohn v. the Queen* (1980). In this case, the controversial decision given in *Morgan* (1975) was upheld. In *Pappajohn* the Supreme Court of Canada held that an honest mistake of belief to consent was grounds for a defence to the charge of rape, whether there were reasonable grounds for a defence as permitted only in circumstances where there was evidence to support such a belief. This "honest mistake of fact" defence was allowed in *Pappajohn*, even though in the latter part of the alleged repeated raping the victim was bound to the bedposts and gagged.

REFERENCES

Aaronovitch, Sam. 1961. *The Ruling Class.* London: Lawrence and Wishart.

Abele, Frances. 1997. "Understanding What Happened Here: The Political Economy of Indigenous Peoples." In Wallace Clement (ed.), *Understanding Canada: Building on the New Canadian Political Economy.* Montreal: McGill-Queen's University Press.

Abella, Rosalie Silberman. 1984. *Equality in Employment: A Royal Commission Report.* Ottawa: Supply and Services.

Aboriginal Business Canada. 2002. *Aboriginal Entrepreneurs in Canada: Progress and Prospects.* Ottawa: Industry Canada.

Aboriginal Justice Inquiry of Manitoba. 1991. *The Justice System and Aboriginal People.* Volume 1. Winnipeg: Queen's Printer.

Abu-Laban, Sharon, and Susan A. McDaniel. 1997. "Aging, Women and Beauty Standards." In Nancy Mandel (ed.), *Feminist Issues: Race, Class and Sexuality.* Second edition. Toronto: Prentice-Hall.

Abu-Laban, Yasmin. 1998. "Welcome/stay Out: The Contradiction of Canadian Integration and Immigration Policies at the Millennium." *Canadian Ethnic Studies* 30.

Abu-Laban, Yasmin, and C. Gabriel. 2002. *Selling Diversity.* Peterborough: Broadview Press.

Abu-Laban, Yasmin, and Daiva Stasiulis. 1992. "Ethnic Pluralism Under Siege: Popular and Partisan Opposition to Multiculturalism." Canadian Public Policy 27, 4.

Adam, Barry. 1986. "The Construction of a Sociological 'Homosexual' in Canadian Textbooks." *Canadian Review of Sociology and Anthropology* 23(3).

Adam, Betty Ann. 1990. "90,000-Litre Collins Bay Spill Quickly Contained." (Saskatoon) *StarPhoenix,* January 10.

Adams, Mary Louise. 1997. *The Trouble with Normal: Postwar Youth and the Making of Heterosexuality.* Toronto: University of Toronto Press.

Adler, F. 1975. *Sisters in Crime.* New York: McGraw.

Adorno, Theodor, and Max Horkheimer. 1972. *Dialectic of Enlightenment.* New York: Seabury.

Adsett, Margaret. 2003. "Change in Political Era and Demographic Weight as Explanations of Youth 'Disenfranchisement' in Federal Elections in Canada, 1965–2000." *Journal of Youth Studies* 6, 3.

African Canadian Legal Clinic. 2001. "Brief to the Legislative Review Secretariat." Available at <www.aclc.net/submissions/immigration_refugee_policy.html>. (Accessed on June 15, 2006.)

Albanese, Patrizia. 2005. "Ethnic Families." In Maureen Baker (ed.). *Families: Changing Trends in Canada,* Fifth edition. Toronto: McGraw-Hill Ryerson.

_____. 2006. "Small Town, Big Benefits: The Ripple Effect of $7/Day Child Care." *Canadian Review of Sociology and Anthropology* 43, 2.

Alberta. 1991. *Justice on Trial.* Edmonton: Task Force on the Criminal Justice System and Its Impact on the Indian and Metis People of Alberta.

_____. 2005. *The Government of Alberta's First Nations Consultation Policy on Land Management and Resource Development.* Edmonton: Government of Alberta.

Alexander, Priscilla. 1987. "Prostitutes Are Being Scapegoated for Heterosexual AIDS." In Frederique Delacoste and Priscilla Alexander (eds.), *Sex Work: Writings by Women in the Sex*

Industry. London: Virago.

Ali, Tariq, and Susan Watkins. 1998. *1968: Marching in the Streets*. London: Bloomsbury.

Alier, Juan Martinez. 1998. "From Political Economy to Political Ecology." In Ramachandra Guha and Juan Martinez Alier (eds.), *Varieties of Environmentalism: Essays North and South*. Delhi: Oxford University Press.

Allison, Marni. 1991. "Judicious Judgements? Examining the Impact of Sexual Assault Legislation on Judicial Definitions of Sexual violence." In Les Samuelson and Bernard Schissel (eds.), *Criminal Justice Sentencing Issues and Reform*. Toronto: Garamond.

Alphonso, Caroline. 2006a. "In Academia, the Early Bird Gets to Learn." *Globe and Mail*, January 27, A3.

_____. 2006b. "Among Brazen Undergrads, A is for Aggressive." *Globe and Mail*, May 1, A3.

Altieri, Miguel A. 2000. "Ecological Impacts of Industrial Agriculture and the Possibilities for Truly Sustainable Farming." In Fred Magdoff, John Bellamy Foster, and Frederick H. Buttel (eds.), *Hungry for Profit: The Agribusiness Threat to Farmers, Food, and the Environment*. New York: Monthly Review.

Alvi, Shahid. 2002. "Socio-economic Conditions and Youth Crime." In Bernard Schissal and Carolyn Brooks (eds.), *Marginality and Condemnation: An Introduction to Critical Criminology*. Halifax, Fernwood.

Ambert, Anne-Marie. 2005. "Same-Sex Couples and Same-Sex-Parent Families: Relationships, Parenting, and Issues of Marriage." Contemporary Family Trends Series report. Ottawa: Vanier Institute of the Family.

Amit-Talai, Vered. 1996. "The Minority Circuit: Identity Politics and Professionalization of Ethnic Activism." In Vered Amit-Talai and Caroline Knowles (eds.), *Re-Situating Identities: The Politics of Race, Ethnicity, Culture*. Peterborough: Broadview.

Anderson, Kay. 1991. *Vancouver's Chinatown: Racial Discourse in Canada, 1875–1980*. Montreal: McGill-Queen's University Press.

Anderson, Kristin L., and Debra Umberson. 2001. "Gendering Violence Masculinity and Power in Men's Accounts of Domestic Violence." *Gender and Society* 15.

Anderson, Paul Nicholas. 2001. "The GE Debate: What Is at Risk When Risk Is Defined for Us?" *Capitalism, Nature, Socialism* 12, 1.

Anderson, Robert B. 1995. "The Business of the First Nations in Saskatchewan: A Contingency Perspective." *Canadian Journal of Native Studies* 15.

_____. 1999. *Economic Development Among the Aboriginal Peoples in Canada: The Hope for the Future*. Toronto: Captus Press.

Anderson, S., and J. Cavanagh. 1996. *The Top 200: The Rise of Global Corporate Power*. Washington, DC: Report of the Institute for Policy Studies.

Andrew, Caroline. 1984. "Women and the Welfare State." *Canadian Journal of Political Science* 17, 4.

Ang, Ien. 1985. *Watching Dallas: Soap Opera and the Melodramatic Imagination*. New York: Methuen.

Angel-Ajani, A. 2003. "A question of dangerous races?" *Punishment and Society* 5.

Annan, Kofi. 2000. "The Politics of Globalization." In P. O'Meara, H.D. Mehlinger, and M. Krain (eds.), *Globalization and the Challenges of a New Century: A Reader*. Bloomington: Indiana University Press.

Antony, Wayne, and Les Samuelson (eds.). 1998. *Power and Resistance: Critical Thinking about Canadian Social Issues*. Second edition. Halifax: Fernwood.

Antonyshyn, Patricia, B. Lee, and Alex Merrill. 1988. "Marching for Women's Lives: The Campaign for Free-Standing Abortion Clinics in Ontario." In Frank Cunningham et al. (eds.), *Social Movements/Social Change*. Toronto: Between the Lines.

Armstrong, Pat. 1997. "The Promise and the Price: New Work Organizations in Ontario Hospitals." In Pat Armstrong et al., (eds.) *Medical Alert: New Work Organizations in Health Care*. Toronto: Garamond.

Armstrong, Pat, Carol Amaratunga, Jacqueline Bernier, Karen Grant, Ann Pederson, and Kay Willson. 2001. *Exposing Privatization: Women and Health Care Reform in Canada*. Toronto: Garamond.

Armstrong, Pat, and Hugh Armstrong. 1990. *Theorizing Women's Work*. Toronto: Garamond.

_____. 2001. *The Double Ghetto: Canadian Women and their Segregated Work*. Third edition. Toronto: Oxford University Press.

_____. 2002. *Wasting Away: The Undermining of Canadian Health Care*. Toronto: Oxford University Press.

Armstrong, Pat, Hugh Armstrong, Ivy Lynn Bourgeault, Jacqueline Choiniere, and Eric Mykhalovskiy. 2000. *Heal Thyself. Managing Health Care Reform*. Toronto: Garamond.

Armstrong, Pat, Hugh Armstrong, Jacqueline Choiniere, Eric Mykhalovskiy, and Jerry White. 1997. *Medical Alert: New Work Organizations in Health Care*. Toronto: Garamond.

_____. 1999. *Managing Reform, Managing Care: Perspectives from B.C. Nurses*. Ottawa: Carleton University and National Federation of Nurses Unions.

Armstrong, Pat, Hugh Armstrong and Krista Scott Dixon. 2005. *Critical to Care: Women and Ancillary Work in Health Care*. Toronto: National Networks on Environments and Women's Health.

Armstrong, Pat, Hugh Armstrong, and Claudia Fegan. 1998. *Universal Health Care: What the United States Can Learn from the Canadian Experience*. New York: New Press.

Armstrong, Pat, Jacqueline Choiniere, Gina Feldberg, and Jerry White. 1994. Take Care: Warning Signals for Canada's Health System. Toronto: Garamond.

Armstrong, Pat, and Irene Jansen. 2000. "Assessing the Impact of Restructuring and Work Reorganization in Long-term Care." Available at <www.yorku.ca/nnewh/avital/search.php>. Toronto, July. (accessed January 30, 2007).

Armstrong, Pat, and Olga Kits. 2001. *One Hundred Years of Caregiving*. Ottawa: Law Commission of Canada, unpublished.

Armstrong, Pat, and Kate Laxer. 2006. "Mapping Precariousness in the Canadian Health Industry: Privatization, Ancillary Work and Women's Health." In Leah Vosko (ed.), *Precarious Employment: Understanding Labour Market Insecurity in Canada*. Montreal: McGill-Queens' University Press.

Armstrong, Robin. 1999. Geographic Patterns of Socio-Economic Well-being of First Nations Communities (Catalogue 21-0060XIE). Ottawa: Statistics Canada.

Arnopoulos, Sheila. 1979. *Problems of Immigrant Women in the Canadian Labour Force*. Ottawa: Canadian Advisory Council on the Status of Women.

Arrighi, G. 1994. *The Long Twentieth Century*. New York: Verso.

_____. 1997. "Globalization, State Sovereignty, and the 'Endless Accumulation of Capital.'" Revised version of a paper presented at the Conference on States and Sovereignty in the World Economy. University of California, Irvine, February 21–23.

Artz, Sibylle. 1998. *Sex, Power, and the Violent School Girl*. Toronto, ON: Trifolium Books.

Aston, Cory, and Valerie Pottie Bunge. 2005. "Family Homicide-Suicides." In K. AuCoin (ed.),

Family Violence in Canada: A Statistics Profile 2005. Ottawa: Canadian Centre for Justice Statistics. Available at <www.statcan.ca/english/freepub/85-224-XIE/85-224-XIE2005000.pdf>. (Accessed on July 4, 2006.)

Atkinson-Grosjean, Janet. 2006. *Public Science, Private Interests: Culture and Commerce in Canada's Networks of Centres of Excellence.* Toronto: University of Toronto Press.

Aubry, Jack. 1997. "Tax Dollars Spent on Native Bands Not Controlled Enough, Many Say." *Edmonton Journal,* June 20, A7.

AuCoin, Kathy. 2005. "Stalking — Criminal Harassment." In K. AuCoin (ed.), *Family Violence in Canada: A Statistical Profile 2005.* Ottawa: Canadian Centre for Justice Statistics. Available at <www.statcan.ca/english/freepub/85-224-XIE/85-224-XIE2005000.pdf>. (Accessed on July 4, 2006.)

Avery, D. 1995. *Reluctant Host: Canada's Response to Immigrant Workers 1896–1994.* Toronto: McClelland and Stewart.

Axelrod, Paul. 1982. *Scholars and Dollars: Politics, Economics, and the Universities of Ontario 1945–1980.* Toronto: University of Toronto Press.

Axworthy, Thomas S., and Pierre Elliott Trudeau. 1992. *Towards a Just Society.* Toronto: Penguin.

Backhouse, Constance B. 1992. "Married Women's Property Law in Nineteenth-Century Canada." In B. Bradbury (ed.), *Canadian Family History.* Mississauga: Copp Clark Pitman.

Bahdi, R. 2003. "No Exit: Racial Profiling and Canada's War Against Terrorism." *Osgoode Hall Law Journal* 41.

Bailey, Sue. 2006. "Tory Bill Raises Age of Consent from 14 to 16." *Toronto Star,* June 23, A4.

Bain, Peter, and Phil Taylor. 2000. "Entrapped by the 'Electronic Panopticon'? Worker Resistance in the Call Centre." *New Technology, Work, and Employment* 15, 1.

Baines, Carol T., Patricia M. Evans, and Sheila M. Neysmith. 1998. "Women's Caring: Work Expanding, State Contracting." In Carol T. Baines, Patricia M. Evans, and Sheila M. Neysmith (eds.), *Women's Caring: Feminist Perspectives on Social Welfare.* Toronto: Oxford University Press.

Baker, Maureen. 1990. "The Perpetuation of Misleading Family Models in Social Policy: Implications for Women." *Canadian Review of Social Work* Summer.

_____. 1995. *Canadian Family Policies: Cross-National Comparisons.* Toronto: University of Toronto Press.

_____. 1997. "Parental Benefits Policies and The Gendered Division of Labour." *Social Service Review* 71, 1.

_____. 2005. "Families, the State and Family Policies." In Maureen Baker (ed.), *Families: Changing Trends in Canada.* Fifth edition. Toronto: McGraw-Hill Ryerson.

Bala, Nicholas. 1999. "A Report from Canada's 'Gender War Zone': Reforming the Child-Related Provisions of the Divorce Act." *Canadian Journal of Family Law* 16, 2.

Balaam, David, and Michael Veseth. 2005a. "Transnational Corporations: In the Hurricane's Eye." In D. Balaam and M. Veseth (eds.), *Introduction to International Political Economy.* Upper Saddle River, NJ: Pearson, Prentice Hall.

_____. 2005b. *Introduction to International Political Economy.* Upper Saddle River, NJ: Pearson, Prentice Hall.

Banks, Cara, and L. Gerlach. 2001. "The Greatest Threat Against Women Yet." *Briarpatch* March

Bannerji, Himani, 1994, "Writing India: Doing Ideology." *Left History* 2, 2 (Fall).

_____. 1995a. "But Who Speaks for Us? Experience and Agency in Conventional Feminist Paradigms." In Himani Bannerji, *Thinking Through: Essays on Feminism, Marxism, and Anti-Racism*. Toronto: Women's.

_____. 1995b. "Introducing Racism: Notes Towards an Anti-Racist Feminism." In Himani Bannerji, *Thinking Through: Essays on Feminism, Marxism, and Anti-Racism*. Toronto: Women's.

_____. 1995c. "Beyond the Ruling Category to What Actually Happens: Notes on James Mill's Historiography in The History of British India." In Marie Campbell and Ann Manicom (eds.), *Knowledge, Experience, and Ruling Relations: Studies in the Social Organization of Knowledge*. Toronto: University of Toronto Press.

_____. 2000a. "The Paradox of Diversity: The Construction of a Multicultural Canada and 'Women Of Colour.'" *Women's Studies International Forum* 23.

_____. 2000b. *The Dark Side of the Nation, Essays on Multiculturalism, Nationalism and Gender*. Toronto: Canadian Scholar's Press.

Barer, Morris L., Robert Evans, and Clyde Hertzman. 1995. "Avalanche or Glacier? Health Care and the Demographic Rhetoric." *Canadian Journal on Aging* 14, 2.

Barkan, Elezar. 1993. *The Retreat of Scientific Racism*. London: Cambridge University Press.

Barlow, Maude. 2005. *Too Close for Comfort: Canada's Future Within Fortress North America*. Toronto: McClelland and Stewart.

Barlow, Maude, and Tony Clarke. 2002. *Blue Gold: The Fight to Stop the Corporate Theft of the World's Water*. New York: New Press.

Barndt, Deborah. 1999. *Women Working the NAFTA Food Chain: Women, Food and Globalization*. Toronto: Sumach Press.

Barnholden, Patrick. 1999. "Does the 'Straight' Jacket of the Family Fit You?" *New Socialist* 4, 3 (July–August).

Barrett, Michèle. 1980. *Women's Oppression Today: Problems in Marxist Feminist Analysis*. London: Verso.

Barron, F. Laurie. 1984. "A Summary of Federal Indian Policy in the Canadian West, 1867–1984." *Native Studies Review* 1.

Barron, F. Laurie, and Joseph Garcea (eds.). 1999. *Urban Indian Reserves: Forging New Relationships in Saskatchewan*. Saskatoon: Purich Publishing.

Barsh, Russel Lawrence. 2000. "Taking Indigenous Science Seriously." In Stephen Bocking (ed.), *Biodiversity in Canada: Ecology, Ideas, and Action*. Peterborough, ON: Broadview.

Bartholl, Timo. 2005. "What is the RRG-Network?" Obtained by Daniel Morrison from Timo Bartholl via email through the RRGN (Global Resistance Network) listserv. February 22.

Bashi, V. 2004. "Globalized Anti-Blackness: Transnationalizing Western Immigration Law, Policy And Practice." *Ethnic and Racial Studies* 27.

Basinger, Jeanine. 1993. *A Woman's View: How Hollywood Spoke to Women, 1930–1960*. Hanover, CT: Wesleyan University Press.

Battle, Ken. 1996. *Precarious Labour Market Fuels Rising Poverty*. Ottawa: Caledon Institute, December.

_____. 1999a. *Poverty Eases Slightly*. Ottawa: Caledon Institute, April.

_____. 1999b. "The National Child Benefit: Best Thing Since Medicare or New Poor Law." In Douglas Durst, (ed.). *Canada's National Child Benefit: Phoenix or Fizzle?* Halifax: Fernwood.

Bauer, W. 1999. "The New Arrivals: Migrants, Refugees Or Frauds?" *Behind the Headlines* 57, 12.

Baumgart, Alice. 1997. "Hospital Reform and Nursing Labour Market Trends Across Canada." *Medical Care* 35, 10 (supplement).

Baumol, William J., Alan S. Blinder, and William M. Scarth. 1994. *Economics: Principles and Policy (Macroeconomics)*. Toronto: Harcourt Brace.

Beattie, Karen. 2005a. "Spousal Homicides." In K. AuCoin (ed.), *Family Violence in Canada: A Statistics Profile 2005*. Ottawa: Canadian Centre for Justice Statistics. Available at <www. statcan.ca/english/freepub/85-224-XIE/85-224-XIE2005000.pdf>. (Accessed on July 4, 2006.)

_____. 2005b. "Family Violence Against Children and Youth." In K. AuCoin (ed.), *Family Violence in Canada: A Statistics Profile 2005*. Ottawa: Canadian Centre for Justice Statistics. Available at <www.statcan.ca/english/freepub/85-224-XIE/85-224-XIE2005000.pdf>. (Accessed on July 4, 2006.)

Beckley, Tom. 1999. "Public Involvement in Natural Resource Management in the Foothills Model Forest." Unpublished manuscript, prepared for Foothills Model Forest, Hinton, Alberta.

Beder, Sharon. 1993a. *The Nature of Sustainable Development*. Newham, Australia: Scribe.

_____. 1993b. "Sustainable Development and the Need for Technological Change." Available at <http://www.uow.edu.au/arts/sts/sbeder/esd/21C.html>. (Accessed January 29, 2007.)

Beirne, Piers, and James Messerschimdt. 2006. *Criminology*. Los Angeles: Roxbury.

Beisel, D. 1994. "Looking for Enemies, 1990–1994." *Journal of Psychohistory* 22, 1.

Bell, Joel. 1992. "Canadian Industrial Policy in a Changing World." In Thomas S. Axworthy and Pierre Elliott Trudeau, *Towards a Just Society*. Toronto: Penguin.

Bell, Laurie (ed.). 1987. *Good Girls, Bad Girls: Sex Trade Workers and Feminists Face to Face*. Toronto: Women's.

Bell, Shannon. 1997. "On ne peut pas voir l'image [The Image Cannot Be Seen]." In Brenda Cossman, Shannon Bell, Lise Gotell and Becki L. Ross (eds.), *Bad Attitudes On Trial: Pornography, Feminism, and the Butler Decision*. Toronto: University of Toronto Press.

Bello, Walden. 1996. "Structural Adjustment Programs: 'Success' for Whom?" In J. Mander and E. Goldsmith (eds.), *The Case Against the Global Economy*. San Francisco: Sierra Club Books.

Beneria, L., and M. Roldan 1987. *The Crossroads of Class and Gender: Industrial Homework, Subcontracting, and Household Dynamics in Mexico City*. Chicago: University of Chicago Press.

Bennett, Tony, Colin Mercer, and Janet Woolacott (eds). 1986. *Popular Culture and Social Relations*. Philadelphia: Open University Press.

Berger, Peter. 1963. *Invitation to Sociology*. New York: Penguin.

Berger, Thomas A. 1988. *Northern Frontier, Northern Homeland: The Report of the Mackenzie Valley Pipeline Inquiry*. Revised edition. Toronto: Douglas & McIntyre.

Berner, Boel (ed.). 1997. *Gendered Practices: Feminist Studies of Technology and Society*. Linkoping, Sweden: Depsrtment of Technology and Social Change.

Berner, Boel, and Ulf Mellström. 1997. "Looking for Mister Engineer: Understanding Masculinity and Technology at two Fin de Siécles." In Boel Berner (ed.), *Gendered Practices: Feminist Studies of Technology and Society* Linkoping, Sweden: Department of Technology and Social Change.

Bernier, Jocelyne, and Marlène Dallaire. 1997. "What Price have Women Paid for Health Care

Reform? The Situation in Quebec." In Pat Armstrong et al. (eds.), *Medical Alert: New Work Organizations in Health Care*. Toronto: Garamond.

Berns, Nancy. 2001. "Degendering the Problem and Gendering the Blame: Political Discourse on Women and Violence." *Gender and Society* 15, 2.

_____. 2004. *Framing the Victim: Domestic Violence, Media, and Social Problems*. New York: Aldine de Gruyter.

Bertoia, Carl, and Janice Drakich. 1993. "The Fathers' Rights Movement: Contradictions in Rhetoric and Practice." *Journal of Family Issues* 4.

Berube, Alan. 19990. *Coming Out Under Fire: The History of Gay Men and Women in World War Two*. New York: Free Press.

Berzins. L., and S. Cooper. 1982. "The Political Economy of Correctional Planning for Women: The Case of the Bankrupt Bureaucracy." *Canadian Journal of Criminology* 24.

Berzins L., and B. Hayes. 1987. "The Diaries of Two Change Agents." In E. Adelberg and C. Currie (eds.), *Too Few to Count: Canadian Women in Conflict with the Law*. Vancouver: Press Gang.

Bhabha, J. 2005. "Trafficking, Smuggling and Human Rights." *Migration Information Source* March.

Bhatia, Aditi. 2006. "Critical Discourse Analysis of Political Press Conferences." *Discourse & Society* 17.

Bianchi, Suzanne. 1999. "Feminization and Juvenilization of Poverty: Trends, Relative Risks, Causes and Consequences." *Annual Review of Sociology* 25.

Bielawski, Ellen. 2003. *Rogue Diamonds: Northern Riches on Dene Land*. Vancouver, Toronto: Douglas & McIntyre.

Birmingham, Kate. 1998. "A Noisy Road or Noisy Resident? A Demonstration of the Utility of Social Constructionism for Analyzing Environmental Problems." *The Sociological Review* 46, 3.

Biro, Andrew. 2002. "Wet Dreams: Ideology and the Debates over Canadian Water Exports." *Capitalism, Nature Socialism* 13, 4.

Black, Debra. 2006. "Age of Consent Uproar, Will Law Protect Kids… or 'Criminalize' Teenage Sex?" *Toronto Star*, June 19, A1 and A15.

Black, Errol, and Lisa Shaw. 2000. "The Case for a Strong Minimum Wage Policy." In Jim Silver (ed.), *Solutions That Work: Fighting Poverty in Winnipeg*. Halifax and Winnipeg: Fernwood and Canadian Centre for policy Alternatives–Manitoba.

Blakley, B.M., and S. Jaffe. 1999. "Coping as a Rural Caregiver: The Impact of Health Care Reforms on Rural Women Informal Caregivers." Available at <www.pwhce.ca/copingRuralCaregiver.htm> (accessed on January 30, 2007)

Bland, Lucy, and Laura Doan (eds.). 1998a. *Sexology Uncensored, The Documents of Sexual Science*. Chicago: University of Chicago Press.

_____. (eds.). 1998b. *Sexology in Culture, Labelling Bodies and Desires*. Chicago: University of Chicago Press.

Blank, Rebecca. 1997. *It Takes a Nation: A New Agenda for Fighting Poverty*. Princeton: Princeton University Press.

Block, Fred. 1977. "The Ruling Class Does Not Rule." *Socialist Register* May–June.

Bocking, Stephen (ed.). 2000. *Biodiversity in Canada: Ecology, Ideas, and Action*. Peterborough, ON: Broadview Press.

Bollier, David. 2002. *Silent Theft: The Private Plunder of Our Common Wealth*. New York:

Routledge.

Bologh, Roslyn Wallach. 1979. *Dialectical Phenomenology: Marx's Method.* Boston: Routledge and Kegan Paul.

Boonzaier, Floretta, and Cheryl De La Rey. 2003. "'He's a Man, and I'm a Woman': Cultural Constructions of Masculinity and Femininity in South African Women's Narratives of Violence." *Violence Against Women* 9.

Boris, E., and E. Prugl (eds.). 1996. *Home Workers in Global Perspective: Invisible Perspective.* New York: Routledge.

Boritch, Helen. 2002. "Women in Prison in Canada." In Bernard Schissel and Carolyn Brooks (eds.), *Marginality and Condemnation: An Introduction to Critical Criminology.* Black Point, NS: Fernwood Publishing.

Bouchard, Pierrette, Isabelle Boily, and Marie-Claude Proulx. 2003. *School Success by Gender: A Catalyst for the Masculinist Discourse.* Ottawa: Status of Women Canada. Available at <www. swc-cfc.gc.ca/pubs/pubspr/0662882857/200303_0662882857_e.pdf>. (Accessed on July 12, 2006.)

Boyd, Monica. 1990. "Immigrant Women: Language and Socioeconomic Inequalities and Policy Issues." In Shiva Halli, Frank Trovato and Leo Driedger (eds.), *Ethnic Demography: Canadian Immigrant, Racial and Cultural Variations.* Ottawa: Carleton University Press.

_____. 1992. "Gender, Visible Minority and Immigrant Earnings Inequality: Reassessing an Employment Equity Premise." In Vic Satzewich (ed.), *Deconstructing a Nation: Immigration, Multiculturalism and Racism in '90s Canada.* Halifax: Fernwood Publishing.

_____. 2004. "Gender Inequality: Economic and Political Aspects." In R.J. Brym (ed.), *New Society: Sociology For The 21st Century.* Fourth edition. Toronto: Nelson.

Boyd, Monica, and Susan A. McDaniel. 1996. "Gender Inequality in Canadian Policy Context: A Mosaic of Approaches." *World Review of Sociology (Revista de Sociologia)* 3.

Boyd, Susan B., and Claire F.L. Young. 2002. "Who Influences Family Law Reform? Discourses on Motherhood and Fatherhood in Legislative Reform Debates in Canada." *Studies in Law, Politics, and Society* 26.

Boyer, Robert. 1996. "State and Market: A New Engagement for the Twenty-First Century." In Robert Boyer and Daniel Drache (eds.), *States Against Markets: The Limits of Globalization.* London: Routledge.

Boyer, Robert, and Daniel Drache. 1996. *States Against Markets: The Limits of Globalization.* London: Routledge.

Boyle, Christine. 1984. *Sexual Assault.* Toronto: Carswell.

Bradshaw, Y.W., and M. Wallace. 1996. *Global Inequalities.* Thousand Oaks, CA: Pine Forge Press.

Brah, A. 1996. *Cartographies of Diaspora: Contesting Identities.* New York: Routledge.

Braithwaite, John, and Kathleen Daly. 1995. "Masculinities, Violence and Communication Control." In M. Valverde, L. MacLeod, and K. Johnson (eds.), *Wife Assault and the Canadian Criminal Justice System.* Toronto: Centre of Criminology, University of Toronto.

Brandt, Allan. 1985. *No Magic Bullet.* New York: Oxford University Press.

Brannigan, A. 1984. *Crimes, Courts and Corrections.* Toronto: Holt.

Bratton, Jacky, Jim Cook, and Christine Gledhill. 1994. *Melodrama: Stage, Picture, Screen.* London: British Film Institute.

Braun, B. 2002. *The Intemperate Rainforest: Nature, Culture and Power on Canada's West Coast.* Minneapolis: University of Minnesota Press.

Braun, D. 1991. *The Rich Get Richer: The Rise of Income Inequality in the United States and the World.* Chicago: Nelson-Hall Publishers.

Braungart, R., and M. Braungart. 1989. "Les Générations Politiqes." In J. Crête and P. Favre (eds.), *Générations et Politiques.* Paris et Quebec: Economica et PUL.

Braverman, Harry. 1974. *Labor and Monopoly Capital: The Degradation of Work in the Twentieth Century.* New York: Monthly Review Press.

Breines, Wini and Linda Gordon. 1983. "The New Scholarship on Family Violence." *Signs* 8, 3: 490–531.

Brinig, Margaret. 2000. *From Contract to Covenant: Beyond the Law and Economics of the Family.* Cambridge, MA: Harvard University Press.

Briskin, L. 1999. "Autonomy, Diversity, and Integration: Union's Women's Separate Organizing in North America and Western Europe in the Context of Restructuring and Globalization." *Women's Studies International Forum* 22, 5.

British Columbia. 1997. *Protection of Aboriginal Rights.* Victoria: Ministry of Forests.

Broad, Dave. 1995. "Globalization, Free Trade and Canadian Labour." *Capital and Class* 21, 2.

_____. 2000. *Hollow Work, Hollow Society: Globalization and the Casual Labour Problem in Canada.* Black Point, NS: Fernwood Publishing.

_____. 2006 "Where's the Work? Labour Market Trends in the New Economy." In Dave Broad and Wayne Antony (eds.), *Capitalism Rebooted? Work and Welfare in the New Economy.* Black Point, NS: Fernwood Publishing.

Broad, Dave, and Wayne Antony (eds.). 1999. *Citizens or Consumers? Social Policy in a Market Society.* Halifax: Fernwood Publishing.

_____. (eds.) 2006. *Capitalism Rebooted? Work and Welfare in the New Economy.* Black Point, NS: Fernwood Publishing.

Brock, Deborah R. 1989a. "Regulating Prostitution/Policing Prostitutes: Some Canadian Examples, 1970–1989." Unpublished Ph.D. thesis. Toronto: Department of Education, University of Toronto.

_____. 1989b. "Prostitutes Are Scapegoats in the AIDS Panic." *Resources for Feminist Research* 18, 2.

_____. 1991. "Talkin' 'Bout a Revelation: Feminist Popular Discourse on Sexual Abuse." *Canadian Woman Studies* 12, 1.

_____. 1998. *Making Work, Making Trouble, Prostitution as a Social Problem.* Toronto: University of Toronto Press.

_____. Ed. 2003. *Making Normal, Social Regulation in Canada.* Scarborough, ON: Thomson/Nelson.

Brock, Deborah R., and Gary Kinsman. 1986. "Patriarchal Relations Ignored: An Analysis and Critique of the Badgley Report on Sexual Offenses Against Children and Youths." In John Lowman, Margaret Jackson, T. Palys and Shelley Gavigan (eds.), *Regulating Sex: An Anthology of Commentaries on the Badgley and Fraser Reports.* Burnaby, BC: School of Criminology, Simon Fraser University.

Brock, Deborah, and Valerie Scott. 1999, "Getting Angry, Getting Organized: The Formation of the Canadian Organization for the Rights of Prostitutes." *Fireweed* 65 (Fall).

Brodie, Janine (ed.). 1996a. *Women and Canadian Public Policy.* Toronto: Harcourt Brace.

_____. 1996b. "New State Forms, New Political Spaces." In Robert Boyer and Daniel Drache (eds.), *States against Markets: The Limits of Globalization.* London: Routledge.

_____. 2001. *Reinventing Canada: Politics in the 21st Century.* Toronto: University of Toronto

Press.

Bronski, Michael. 1992. "Magic and AIDS: Presumed Innocent." *Z Magazine* January.

Brooks, Carolyn. 2002. "New Directions in Critical Criminology." In Bernard Schissel and Carolyn Brooks (eds.), *Marginality and Condemnation: An Introduction to Critical Criminology.* Black Point, NS: Fernwood Publishing.

Brown, Dave. 2001a. "Men Challenge 'Bible' of Violence Against Women: A Toronto Inquest Will Question the Validity of a Standard Reference Book." *Ottawa Citizen* December 4.

_____. 2001b. "Burying the Ghosts of a Violent Past: Husband in Wheelchair Became Focus of Wife's Rage." *Ottawa Citizen* 5 December.

_____. 2001c. "'I Learned It's a System That Doesn't Listen': Wife Still Terrified by Threats from Family Violence Specialists." *Ottawa Citizen* December 6.

_____. 2001d. "Turning Domestic Violence Into a Religion: Inquest an Epic Social Debate." *Ottawa Citizen* December 7.

_____. 2001e. "Cult of the Domestic-Violence Industry: Where Are the Great Numbers of Victims We Hear About?" *Ottawa Citizen* December 8.

_____. 2002. "Recommendation 53: Electronic Shackles." *Ottawa Citizen* February 16.

Browne, Paul Leduc. 2000. *Unsafe Practices: Restructuring and Privatization in Ontario Health Care.* Ottawa: Canadian Centre for Policy Alternatives.

Browning, Andrea. 2006. Interviewed by Daniel Morrison, June 6.

Browning, James. 1984. *Stopping the Violence: Canadian Programmes for Assaulting Men.* Ottawa: Health and Welfare Canada.

Brownlee, Jamie. 2005. *Ruling Canada: Corporate Cohesion and Democracy.* Black Point, NS: Fernwood Publishing.

Brule, Elizabeth. 2004. "Going to Market: Neo-Liberalism and the Social Construction of the University Student as Autonomous Consumer." In Marilee Reimer (ed.), *Inside Corporate U: Women in the Academy Speak Out.* Toronto: Sumach Press.

Bruneau, William, and Donald Savage. 2002. *Counting Out the Scholars: The Case Against Performance Indicators in Higher Education.* Toronto: James Lorimer.

Brunell, Dorval, and Christian Deblock. 1992. "Economic Blocs and the Challenge of the North American Free Trade Agreement." In Stephen J. Randall et al. (eds.), *North America Without Borders?* Calgary: University of Calgary.

Brush, Lisa D. 1990. "Violent Acts and Injurious Outcomes in Married Couples: Methodological Issues in the National Survey of Families and Households." *Gender and Society* 4, 1.

Bryce, Jo. 2001. "The Technological Transformation of Leisure." *Social Science Computer Review* 19, 1.

Brym, Robert J. 1978. "Regional Social Structure and Agrarian Radicalism in Canada: Alberta, Saskatchewan and New Brunswick." *Canadian Review of Sociology and Anthropology* 15, 3.

Brzozowski, Jodi-Anne. 2004. "Spousal Violence." In J.A. Brzozowski (ed.), *Family Violence in Canada: A Statistical Profile 2004.* Ottawa: Canadian Centre for Justice Statistics. Available at <www.statcan.ca/english/freepub/85-224-XIE/85-224-XIE2004000.pdf>. (Accessed on July 4, 2006.)

Buchholz, Rogene A., and Sandra B. Rosenthal. 1998. "Toward an Ethics of Consumption: Rethinking the Nature of Growth." In Laura Westra and Patricia H. Werhane (eds.), *The Business of Consumption: Environmental Ethics and the Global Economy.* New York: Rowman and Littlefield.

Buchignani, N., and D. Indra. 1999. "Vanishing Acts: Illegal Immigration in Canada as a Sometimes

Social Issue." In D. Haines and K. Rosenblum (eds.), *Illegal Immigration in America.* Westport, CT: Greenwood Press.

Buckman, Greg. 2004. *Globalization: Tame it or Scrap it?* Black Point, NS: Fernwood Publishing.

Bulbeck, Chilla. 1998. *Re-Orienting Western Feminisms: Women's Diversity in Post-colonial World.* Cambridge: Cambridge U Press.

Bullard, Robert D., and Glenn S. Johnson. 2000. "Environmental Justice: Grassroots Activism and Its Impact on Public Policy Decision Making." *Journal of Social Issues* 56, 3.

Bunge, Valerie Pottie. 2000. "Spousal Violence." In V.P. Bunge and D. Locke (eds.), *Family Violence in Canada: A Statistical Profile 2000.* Ottawa: Canadian Centre for Justice Statistics. Available at <www.statcan.ca/english/freepub/85-224-XIE/0000085-224-XIE.pdf>. (Accessed on July 4, 2006.)

Burbach, R. 2001. *Globalization and Post Modern Politics: From Zapatistas to High Tech Robber Barons.* London: Pluto.

Burkie, Stacie. 2001. "Marriage in 1901 Canada: An Ecological Perspective." *Journal of Family History* 26, 2.

Burris, C., and P. Jaffe. 1983. "Wife Abuse as a Crime: The Impact of Police Laying Charges." *Canadian Journal of Criminology* 25.

Burstyn, Varda. 1985. "Masculine Domination and the State." In Varda Burstyn and Dorothy Smith (eds.), *Women, Class, Family and the State.* Toronto: Garamond.

Butler, Judith. 1990. "Lana's 'Imitation': Melodramatic Repetition and the Gender Performative." *Genders* 9.

Byars, Jackie. 1991. *All That Hollywood Allows: Rereading Gender in 1950s Melodrama.* Chapel Hill: University of North Carolina Press.

Calder v. A.G. British Columbia. 1973. D.L.R. (3rd). 145. (Supreme Court of Canada).

Caledon Institute of Social Policy. 1995. *Critical Commentaries on the Social Security Review.* Ottawa: Caledon Institute of Social Policy.

Calliou, Brian. 2005. "The Culture of Leadership: North American Indigenous Leadership in a Changing Economy." In Duane Champagne, Karen Jo Torjesen, and Susan Steiner (eds.), *Indigenous Peoples and the Modern State.* Walnut Creek, CA: AltaMira Press.

Cameron, David. 1991. *More than An Academic Question: Universities, Government and Public Policy in Canada.* Halifax: Institute for Research on Public Policy.

Camino, Linda, and Shepherd Zeldin. 2002. "From Periphery to Center: Pathways for Youth Civic Engagement in the Day-to-Day Life of Communities." *Applied Developmental Science* 6, 4.

Campaign 2000. 2005. *Decision Time for Canada: Let's Make Poverty History, 2005 Report Card on Child Poverty in Canada.* Toronto: Campaign 2000.

Campbell, B. 1990. "In the Image of the Eagle: Remaking Canada Under Free Trade." *Canadian Dimension* 24, 2.

_____. 2001. *False Promise: Canada in the Free Trade Era.* Briefing Paper. Washington, DC: Economic Policy Institute.

Campbell, Bruce. 2006. "Record Shows 'Free Trade' Detrimental For Most Canadians." *CCPA Monitor* July/August.

Campbell, C. 2000. *Betrayal and Deceit: The Politics of Canadian Immigration.* Vancouver: Jasmine Books.

Campbell, Jacquelyn C. 2005. "Assessing Dangerousness in Domestic Violence Cases: History, Challenges, and Opportunities." *Criminology and Public Policy* 4.

REFERENCES

Campbell, Marie, and Frances Gregor. 2002. *Mapping Social Relations: A Primer in Doing Institutional Ethnography*. Aurora, ON: Garamond Press.

Campbell, Robert M. 1987. *Grand Illusions: The Politics of the Keynesian Experience in Canada, 1945–75*. Peterborough, ON: Broadview.

Campement Jeunesses du Québec. 2003a. "Commentaires sur le processus de com munication du CO." Available at <www.campementjeunesses.org/?q=node/view/26>. (Accessed on May 7, 2006.)

_____. 2003b. "Qu'est-ce que le Campement?" Available at <www.campementjeunesses. org/?q=node/view/31>. (Accessed on May 2006.)

_____ 2004a. "Campement Québécois de la Jeunesse." From a computer disc, internal to and belonging to organizers of the Campement Québécois de la Jeuneese, titled: "Mouvance FSM: Campement Québécois de la Jeuneese 13 au 23 aout 2004."

_____. 2004b. "Origines due Campement Jeunesses — janvier 2003." From a computer disc titled: "Mouvance FSM: Campement Québécois de la Jeuneese 13 au 23 aout 2004."

_____. 2004c. "Perspectives 2003–2004: Construire et vivre ensemble notre espace!" From a computer disc titled: "Mouvance FSM: Campement Québécois de la Jeuneese 13 au 23 aout 2004."

Campey, John, Tim McCaskell, John Miller, and Vanessa Russell. 1994. "Opening the Classroom Closet: Dealing with Sexual Orientation at the Toronto Board of Education." In Susan Prentice (ed.), *Sex in Schools: Canadian Education and Sexual Regulation*. Toronto: Our Schools/Our Selves.

Canada. 1984. *Report of the Committee on Sexual Offences against Children and Youth* (The Badgley Report). Ottawa: Supply and Services.

_____. 1996. *Commission of Inquiry into Certain Events at the Prison for Women in Kingston*. Ottawa: Public Works and Government Services.

_____. 2001. *Overview of DIAND Education Program Data*. Ottawa: Indian Affairs and Northern Development.

Canada Employment and Immigration. 1993. *Unemployment Statistics, 1993*. Ottawa: Supply and Services.

Canada Employment and Immigration Advisory Council. 1986. *Achieving Health for All: A Framework for Health Promotion*. Ottawa: Supply and Services.

_____. 1987. *Workers with Family Responsibilities in a Changing Society: Who Cares?* Ottawa: Supply and Services.

Canada. Department of Finance. 2005. *The Budget Plan 2005* (Catalogue no. F1-23/2005-3E). Ottawa: Department of Finance.

_____. 2006a. "Federal Transfers to Provinces and Territories: Canada Social Transfers." October 2006. Available at <www.fin.gc.ca/FEDPROV /chte.html>. (Accessed on October 28, 2006.)

_____. 2006b. "Where Your Tax dollar Goes." Available at <www.fin.gc.ca/taxdollar/text/html/ pamphlet_e.html>. (Accessed on October 31, 2006.)

Canada, Department of Foreign Affairs. 2001. *Opening Doors to the World: Canada's International Market Access Priorities 2001*. Ottawa: Department of Foreign Affairs and International Trade.

Canada, Department of Justice. 1990. *Sexual Assault Legislation in Canada: An Evaluation-Overview*. Ottawa: Supply and Services.

Canada, Health and Welfare. 1986. *Achieving Health for All: A Framework for Health Promotion*.

Ottawa: Supply and Services.

Canada, Health Canada. 1999. *Toward a Healthy Future: Second Report on the Health of Canadians.* Ottawa.

Canada, House of Commons Debates. 1989. November 7: 5640.

Canada, Human Resources Development Canada. Childcare Resource and Research Unit. 2000. "Early Childhood Care and Education in Canada: Provinces and Territories, 1998." Ottawa: Human Resources Development Canada.

Canada, Indian and Northern Affairs. 1980. *Indian Conditions: A Survey.* Ottawa: Supply and Services.

_____. 1989. *INAC Population Projections of Registered Indians Based on Adjusted Indian Registry, Band Support and Capital Management and Quantitative Analysis and Socio-Demographic Research.* Ottawa: Supply and Services.

Canada, Joint Committees Senate and House of Commons (SJC). 36th Parliament, 1st Session. 1998. "The Meetings of the Special Joint Committee on Child Custody and Access, December 11, 1997 to November 2, 1998." Available at <www.parl.gc.ca/InfoCom/PubDocument. asp ?DocumentID=1032728andLanguage=E>. (Accessed on April 5, 2004.)

Canada, Solicitor General. 1985. "Female Victims of Crime." Canadian Urban Victimization Survey. Ottawa: Supply and Services.

Canada, Status of Women Canada. 2000. "Aboriginal Women's Roundtable on Gender Equality." Ottawa: Status of Women Canada.

Canadian AIDS Society. 1991. "Homophobia, Heterosexism and AIDS, Creating a More Effective Response to AIDS." Ottawa: Supply and Services.

Canadian Association of Food Banks. 2004. *Hunger Count.* Toronto: Canadian Association of Food Banks.

Canadian Association of University Teachers (CAUT). 1999. "Not in the Public Interest — University Finance in Canada 1972–1998." *CAUT Education Review* 1, 3.

_____. 2003a. "University Tuition Fees in Canada, 2003." *CAUT Education Review* 5, 1.

_____. 2003b. *Report of the CAUT AF&T Committee Into Complaints Raised by Professor David Noble Against Simon Fraser University Regarding Alleged Infringements of Academic Freedom.* Ottawa: CAUT.

_____. 2004. "The Perils of Whistle-Blowing." *CAUT Bulletin* September.

_____. 2005a. "Paying the Price: The Case For Lowering Tuition Fees in Canada." *CAUT Education Review* 7, 1.

_____. 2005b. "Financing Canada's Universities and Colleges." *CAUT Education Review* 7, 2.

Canadian Broadcasting Corporation (CBC). 2001. "'Banns' may sidestep ban on gay marriages." January 12.

Canadian Centre for Policy Alternatives (CCPA). 1997. *CCPA Education Monitor.* Ottawa: Canadian Centre for Policy Alternatives.

_____. 2005. *Challenging McWorld II.* Ottawa: CCPA.

_____. 2005. *Alternative Federal Budget 2005: It's Time.* Ottawa: CCPA.

Canadian Charter of Rights and Freedoms. Being Part II of The Constitution Act, 1982.

Canadian Council for Refugees (CCR). 2000. "A Hundred Years of Immigration to Canada 1900–1999: A Chronology Focusing on Refugees and Discrimination." Available at <www. web.net/~ccr/history.html>. (Accessed on June 12, 2006.)

_____. 2001. "Bill C-11 Brief." Available at <www.web.net/~ccr/c-11.html>. (Accessed on August 31, 2006.)

Canadian Council of Forest Ministers. 2001. "Quick Fact." Available at <nfi.cfs.nrcan.gc.ca/canfi/data/area-small_e.html>. (Accessed January 29, 2007.)

Canadian Council on Social Development (CCSD). 1992. "Countdown '92: Campaign 2000 Child Poverty Indicator Report." Ottawa: CCSD.

_____. 1994. "Countdown '94: Campaign 2000 Child Poverty Indicator Report." Ottawa: CCSD.

_____. 1996. *Maintaining a National Social Safety Net: Recommendations on the Canada Health and Social Transfer, Position Statement.* Ottawa: CCSD.

_____. 1998. *The Progress of Canada's Children 1998.* Ottawa: CCSD.

Canadian Environmental Assessment Agency (CEAA). 1996. "The NWT Diamond Mines." Report of the Environmental Assessment Panel. Ottawa: Minister of Supply and Services.

Canadian Federation of Students (CFS). 2003. "Equal Minds, Equal Education." *CFS Fact Sheet* 9, 4.

_____. 2004. "Differential Tuition Fees for International Students." *CFS Fact Sheet* 10, 11.

_____. 2005. "Tuition Fees in Canada: A Pan-Canadian Perspective on Educational User Fees." *CFS Fact Sheet* 11, 1.

_____. N.d. "Tuition Fees and Funding." Available at <cfs-fcee.ca/html/English/campaigns/background.php>. (Accessed on December 30, 2006.)

Canadian Feminist Alliance for International Action (FAFIA). 2005. Press Release: *UN Human Rights Committee Blasts Canada.* Nov. 3. Available at <http://www.fafia-afai.org/en/node/64>. (Accessed on October 26, 2006.)

Canadian HIV/AIDS Legal Network. 2004. "Criminal Law, HIV Exposure and HIV Disclosure." From *Disclosure of HIV Status After Cuerrier* (Toronto). Available at <www.aidslaw.ca/Maincontent/issues/criminallaw /OBAOresources/Chapter03.pdf>. (Accessed on June 23, 2006.)

_____. 2005. *Sex, Work, Rights: Reforming Canadian Criminal Laws On Prostitution.* Toronto. Available at <http://www.aidslaw.ca/Maincontent/issues/sexwork/SWreport.pdf>. (Accessed on June 23, 2006.)

Canadian Institute for Health Information. 2001. *National Health Expenditure Trends 1975–2001.* Ottawa: Canadian Institute for Health Information.

_____. 2002. *Canada's Health Care Providers.* Ottawa: Canadian Institute for Health Information.

_____. 2005. *National Health Expenditure Trends 1975–2005.* Ottawa: Canadian Institute for Health Information.

Canadian Labour Congress. 2003. *Falling Unemployment Insurance Protection for Canada's Unemployed.* Ottawa: Canadian Labour Congress.

Canadian Panel on Violence Against Women. 1993. *Changing the Landscape: Ending the Violence-Achieving Equality.* Ottawa: Minister of Supply and Services Canada.

Canadian Press. 2001. "Tories Spending $26M On Women's Shelters: Figure Less Than Half Amount Demanded By Women's Groups." *Toronto Star,* August 7.

_____. 2001. "UN Rights Report Criticizes Canada For Treating Migrants Like Criminals." April 12.

Canadian Public Health Association and Health Canada. 1994. Workshop on "A National Vision and Goals for Child and Youth Health in Canada." Halifax.

Canadian Union of Public Employees (CUPE). 2001. "On Public Private Partnerships for Health Care." *The CUPE Facts* November.

Capek, Stella M. 1993. "The 'Environmental Justice' Frame: A Conceptual Discussion and an Application." *Social Problems* 40, 1.

Carey, Carolyn. 1996. "Punishment and Control of Women in Prison: The Punishment of Privation." In Bernard Schissel and Linda Mahood (eds.), *Social Control in Canada: A Reader in the Social Construction of Deviance*. Toronto: Oxford University Press.

Carlat, Lewis. 1998. "A Cleanser for the Mind: Marketing Radio Receivers for the American Home, 1922–1932." In Roger Horowitz and Arwen Mohun (eds.), *His and Hers: Gender, Consumption and* Technology. Charlottesville: University Press of Virginia.

Carlson, Elof Axel. 2001. "Genetically Altered Organisms: When the Old Becomes the New." *Dissent* Winter.

Caron, Guy. 2005. "Going South: Controversial Pipeline Will have Disastrous Environmental Consequences and Could Threaten Canada's Energy Security." *Canadian Perspectives* Autumn.

Carr, M., M. Alter Chen, and J. Tate. 2000. "Global Home-based Workers." *Feminist Economics* 6, 3.

Carrington, Kerry. 1998. "Postmodernism and Feminist Criminologies: Fragmenting the Criminological Subject." In P. Walton and J. Young (eds.), *The New Criminology Revisited*. New York: St. Martins Press.

Carroll, W., and J. Beaton. 2000. "Globalization, Neo-Liberalism and the Changing Face of Corporate Hegemony in Higher Education." *Studies in Political Economy* 62 (Summer).

Carter, Sarah. 1990. *Lost Harvests: Prairie Indian Reserve Farmers and Government Policy*. Montreal: McGill-Queens University Press.

Cassell, Jay. 1987. *The Secret Plague: Venereal Disease in Canada, 1838–1939*. Toronto: University of Toronto Press.

Castells, M. 1996. *The Information Age: Economy and Society and Culture*. Oxford: Blackwell.

Castree, Noel. 2004 "Differential Geographies: Place, Indigenous Rights and 'Local' Resources." *Political Geography* 23.

Cavanagh, John, and Jerry Manders (eds.). 2004. *Alternatives to Economic Globalization: A Better World is Possible*. San Francisco: BK Publishers.

Cavell, Stanley. 1996. *Contesting Tears: The Hollywood Melodrama of the Unknown Woman*. Chicago: University of Chicago Press.

CBC News Online. 2004. "Tracking the Tar Ponds." May 6. Available at <www.cbc.ca/news/ background/tarponds/>. (Accessed on September 20, 2006.)

CBC Online. 1999a. "Officials Recommend Migrants Remain in Custody." September 2. Available at <www.cbc.ca/story/canada/national/1999/09/02/migrants990902.html>. (Accessed on September 7, 2006.)

_____. 1999b. "Department Seeks More Teeth to Detain Migrants." September 23. Available at <www.cbc.ca/story/canada/national/1999/09/23/migrant990923.html>. (Accessed on September 7, 2006.)

_____. 1999c. "Chinese Migrants Denied Due Process, Critics Charge." November 5. Available at <www.cbc.ca/story/canada/national/1999/11/05/migrants991105.html>. (Accessed on September 7, 2006.)

Centre For Social Justice Team. 1998. *Resources For Awareness and Action: Exposing the Facts of Corporate Rule*. Toronto: Centre For Social Justice.

Chang, Jen, et al. 2001. *Resist!: A Grassroots Collection of Stories, Poetry, Photos and Analyses from the Quebec City FTAA Protests and Beyond*. Black Point, NS: Fernwood Publishing.

Chapin, Vince. 1995. "Knowledge at Work: Human-Centred Machining Technology." In Christopher Schenk and John Anderson (eds.), *Re/Shaping Work: Union Responses to Technological Change*. Don Mills: Ontario Federation of Labour Technological Adjustment Programme.

Chapman, Ian, Don McCaskill, and David Newhouse. 1991. "Management in Contemporary Aboriginal Organizations." *Canadian Journal of Native Studies* 11, 2.

Chappell, Nina. 1992. *Social Support and Aging*. Toronto: Butterworths.

_____. 1999. "Health Care Reform: Implications for Seniors." *Journal of Aging Studies* 11, 3.

Chase-Dunn, C. 1994. "Technology and the Changing Logic of World System." In R. Palan and B. Gills (eds.), *The State-Global Divide: A Neo-Structural Agenda in International Relations*. Boulder, CO: Lynne Rienner Publishing.

Chauncey, George. 2004. *Why Marriage? The History Shaping Today's Debate Over Gay Equality*. Cambridge, MA: Basic Books/Perseus Books.

Chesley, Laurie, Donna MacAulay, and Janice Ristock. 1998. *Abuse in Lesbian Relationships: Information and Resources*. Ottawa: Health Canada. Available at <www.phac-aspc.gc.ca/ncfv-cnivf/familyviolence/pdfs/lesbianabuse.pdf>. (AccessED on July 12, 2006.)

Chesney-Lind, M., and B. Bloom. 1997. "Feminist Criminology: Thinking About Women and Crime." In B. MacLean and D. Milovanovic (eds.), *Thinking Critically about Crime*. Vancouver: Collective.

Choiniere, Jacqueline A. 1993. "A Case Study Examination of Nurses and Patient Information Technology." In Pat Armstrong, Jacqueline Choiniere and Elaine Day (eds.), *Vital Signs: Nursing in Transition*. Toronto: Garamond.

Chossudovsky, M. 1998. *The Globalization of Poverty: Impacts of IMF and World Bank Reforms*. London: Zed Books.

Christie, N. 1986. "Suitable Enemies." In H. Bianchi and R. van Swaaningen (eds.), *Abolitionism: Towards a Non-Repressive Approach to Crime*. Amsterdam: Free University Press.

Chunn, D., and S. Gavigan. 1995. "Women, Crime and Criminal Justice in Canada." In M. Jackson and C. Griffiths (eds.), *Canadian Criminology*. Toronto: Harcourt Brace.

Churchill, Louise. 2006. "Professor Goodgrade." *The Chronicle of Higher Education* 52 (25) February 24, C1.

Ciccantell, Paul. 2001. "NAFTA and the Reconstruction of U.S. Hegemony: The Raw Materials Foundations of Economic Competitiveness." *Canadian Journal of Sociology* 26, 1.

Citizens For Public Justice. 2001. "Too Many Missing Pieces: A Brief In Response To Bill C-11." Available at <cpj.ca/index.html>. (Accessed on August 31, 2006.)

Citizenship and Immigration Canada (CIC). 2001a. *Facts and Figures 2000: Immigration Overview*. Ottawa: Minister of Public Works and Government Services.

_____. 2001b. "Bill C-11 — Immigration and Refugee Protection Act: Overview." Available at <www.cic.gc.ca/english/irpa/c11-overview.html>. (Accessed on June 14, 2006.)

_____. 2005. "Facts and Figures 2005." Available at <http://www.cic.gc.ca/english/pub/facts2005/overview/01.html>. (Accessed on September 14, 2006.)

_____. 2006. "New Permanent Residents." The Monitor, 1. Available at <http://www.cic.gc.ca/english/monitor/issue12/02-immigrants.html>. (Accessed on September 14, 2006.)

Clairman, Cara L. 1993. "First Nations and Environmental Groups in Ontario's Parks — Conflict or Cooperation?" *Canadian Native Law Reporter* 1.

Clarke, Tony. 1997. *Silent Coup: Confronting The Big Business Takeover of Canada*. Ottawa and Toronto: CCPA and Lorimer.

_____. 2001. "Confronting McWorld." *Canadian Dimension* 35, 2.

Cleland, Charles E. 1990. "Indian Treaties and American Myths: Roots of Social Conflicts over Treaty Rights." *Native Studies Review* 6.

Cleverdon, Catharine. 1950. *The Woman Suffrage Movement in Canada*. Toronto: University of Toronto Press.

Clinard, M., and P. Yeager. 1980. *Corporate Crime*. New York: Free.

Coalition for a Just Immigration and Refugee Policy. 2001 "Position Paper on Bill C-11." Toronto.

Coates, Joseph F., John B. Mahaffie, and Andy Hines. 2000. "The Promise of Genetics." In Patrick O'Meara, Howard D. Mehlinger, and Matthew Krain (eds.), *Globalization and the Challenges of a New Century: A Reader*. Bloomington and Indianapolis: Indiana University Press.

Cobb, Chris. 1999. "'Anti-male' Booklets Pulled by Ontario." *Ottawa Citizen*, February 9.

Cobb, Clifford W. 1993. *The Green National Product: A Proposed Index of Sustainable Economic Welfare*. Lanham, MY: University Press of America.

Coburn, D. 1999. "Phases of Capitalism, Welfare States, Medical Dominance, and Health Care in Ontario." *International Journal of Health Services* 29, 4.

Cohen, Erminie Joy, with Angela Pelten. 1997. *Sounding the Alarm: Poverty in Canada*. Ottawa: Senate of Canada.

Cohen, Leah. 1983. *Affirmative Action in Canada: Ten Years After*. Ottawa: Secretary of State.

Cohen, Marjorie Griffin, and Marcy Cohen. 2004. *A Return to Wage Discrimination. Pay Equity Losses Through Privatization in Health Care*. Vancouver: Canadian Centre for Policy Alternatives

Cohen, Stan. 1972. Folk Devils and Moral Panics. London: MacGibbon and Kee.

Collins, Michael. 2003. "The People's Free University: Counteracting the Innovation Agenda on Campus and Model for Lifelong Learning." *Saskatchewan Notes* 2 (9).

Collins, Richard, et al. (eds.). 1986. *Media, Culture and Society: A Critical Reader*. London: Sage.

Coltrane, Scott, and Neal Hickman. 1992. "The Rhetoric of Rights and Needs: Moral Discourse in the Reform of Child Custody and Child Support Laws." *Social Problems* 39.

Comack, Elizabeth. 1992. "Women and Crime." In R. Linden (ed.), *Criminology: A Canadian Perspective*. Second edition. Toronto: Harcourt Brace.

_____. 1996a. *Women in Trouble: Connecting Women's Abuse Histories to Their Conflicts with the Law*. Halifax: Fernwood.

_____. 1996b. "Women and Crime." In R. Linden (ed.), *Criminology: A Canadian Perspective*. Third edition. Toronto: Harcourt Brace.

_____. 1999. "Producing Feminist Knowledge: Lessons From Women In Trouble." *Theoretical Criminology* 3, 3.

_____. 2004. "Feminism and Criminology." In Rick Linden (ed.), *Criminology: A Canadian Perspective*. Toronto: Thomson-Nelson.

Comack, Elizabeth, and Gillian Belfour. 2004. *The Power to Criminalize: Violence, Inequality and the Law*. Black Point, NS: Fernwood Publishing.

Commission for Racial Justice. 1987. *Toxic Waste and Race*. New York: United Church of Christ.

Community Inquiry into Inner City Revitalization. 1990. *Final Report*. Winnipeg: Urban Futures Group.

Connell, R.W. 1990. "The State, Gender and Sexual Politics." *Theory and Society* 19.

_____. 2002. "On Hegemonic Masculinity and Violence: Response to Jefferson and Hall."

Theoretical Criminology 6, 1.

Connidis, Ingrid. 1989. *Family Ties and Aging.* Toronto: Butterworths.

Conway, Janet. 2003. "Civil Resistance and the 'Diversity of Tactics' in the Anti-Globalization Movement: Problems of Violence, Silence, and Solidarity in Activist Politics." *Osgoode Hall Law Journal* 41, 2 & 3 (Summer).

_____. 2004. *Identity, Place, Knowledge: Social Movements Contesting Globalization.* Black Point, NS: Fernwood Publishing.

Cook, David A. 1996. *A History of Narrative Film.* New York: W.W. Norton.

Cooke, Katie. 1984. *Images of Indians Held by Non-Indians: A Review of Current Research.* Ottawa: Indian and Northern Affairs.

Coole, Diana. 1988. *Women in Political Theory.* Boulder, CO: Harvester Wheatsheaf.

Coolican, Murray. 1986. "Living Treaties, Lasting Agreements: Report of the Task Force to Review Comprehensive Land Claims Policy, 1985." Ottawa: Indian and Northern Affairs.

Cooper, Shelagh. 1987. "The Evolution of the Federal Women's Prison." In E. Adelberg and C. Currie (eds.), *Too Few to Count: Canadian Women in Conflict with the Law.* Vancouver: Press Gang.

Cornell, Stephen, and Joseph Kalt. 1990. "Pathways from Poverty: Economic Development and Institution-Building on American Indian Reservations." *American Indian Culture and Research Journal* 14.

Cornia, G., Richard Jolly, and Frances Stewart (eds.). 1987. *Adjustment with a Human Face.* Oxford: Oxford Clarendon Press.

Corrigan, Philip. 1981. "On Moral Regulation: Some Preliminary Remarks." *Sociological Review* 29, 2.

Corrigan, Philip, and Derek Sayer. 1985. *The Great Arch: English State Formation as Cultural Revolution.* Oxford: Blackwell.

Costanza, Robert, and Herman E. Daly. 1992. "Natural Capital and Sustainable Development." *Conservation Biology* 6, 1.

Côté, Andrée, Michèle Kérisit, and Marie-Louise Côté. 2001. *Sponsorship… For Better or Worse: The Impact of Sponsorship on the Equality Rights of Immigrant Women.* Ottawa: Status of Women Canada.

Cottrell, Barbara. 2003. *Parent Abuse: The Abuse of Parents by Their Teenage Children — Overview Paper.* Ottawa: National Clearinghouse on Family Violence. Available at <www.phac-aspc.gc.ca/ncfv-cnivf/familyviolence/pdfs/2003parentabuse_e.pdf>. (Accessed on July 4, 2006.)

Courchene, Thomas J. 1996. "Globalization, Free Trade and the Canadian Political Economy." In Raymond M. Hebert (ed.), *Re(Defining) Canada: A Prospective Look at our Country in the 21st Century.* Winnipeg: Presses Universitaires de Saint-Boniface.

Coward, Harold, Rosemary Ommer, and Tony Pitcher (eds.). 2000. *Just Fish: Ethics and Canadian Marine Fisheries.* St. John's, NF: Institute of Social and Economic Research.

Cragg, Wesley, and Alan Greenbaum. 2002. "Reasoning about Responsibilities: Mining Company Managers and What Stakeholders Are Owed." *Journal of Business Ethics* 39, 3.

Crawley, Brenda. 1988. "Black Families in a Neo-Conservative Era." *Family Relations* 37, 4.

Crean, Susan. 1988. *In The Name of The Fathers: The Story Behind Child Custody.* Toronto: Amanita Publication.

Creese, G. 1992. "The Politics of Refugees in Canada." In V. Satzewich (ed.), *Deconstructing A Nation.* Halifax: Fernwood Publishing.

Crepeau, F., and E. Jimenez. 2004. "Foreigners and the Right to Justice in the Aftermath of

9/11." *International Journal of Law and Psychiatry* 27.

Crepeau, F., and D. Nakache. 2006. "Controlling Irregular Migration in Canada." *IRPP Choices* 12, 1.

Cressey, Gordon. 1987. "Feeling the Strain: How Chronic Underfunding Is Causing Tension Between Labour and Voluntary Agencies." *The Public Employee* Winter (6/7).

CRIAW (Canadian Institute for the Advancement of Women). 2005. *Fact Sheet: Women and Poverty.* Available at <www.criaw-icref.ca/indexframe_e.htm>. (Accessed on February 9, 2006.)

Crimp, Douglas (ed.). 1988. *AIDS, Cultural Analysis, Cultural Activism.* Cambridge, MA: MIT Press.

Crompton, R., and N. Le Feuvre. 1996. "Paid Employment and the Changing System of Gender Relations: A Cross-National Comparision." *Sociology* 30, 3.

Crossman, Brenda. 2006. "Harm Is the New Indecency Test, Supreme Court Okays Sex Clubs, Orgies." *Xtra!* (Toronto), Jan. 5, p. 9.

Crow, Barbara, and Graham Longford. 2000. "Digital Restructuring: Gender, Class, and Citizenship in the Information Society in Canada." *Citizenship Studies* 4, 2.

Crozier, M., S.P. Huntington, and J. Watanuki. 1975. *The Crisis of Democracy, Report on the Governability of Democracies to the Trilateral Commission.* New York: New York University Press.

Currie, D., and B. MacLean (eds.). 1992. *The Administration of Justice.* Saskatoon: Social Research Unit, Department of Sociology, University of Saskatchewan.

Currie, D., B. MacLean, and D. Milovanovic. 1992. "Three Traditions of Critical Justice Inquiry: Class, Gender, and Discourse." In D. Currie and B. MacLean (eds.), *Rethinking the Administration of Justice.* Halifax: Fernwood Publishing.

Currie, Dawn. 1986. "Female Criminality: A Crisis in Feminist Theory." In B. MacLean (ed.), *The Political Economy of Crime.* Scarborough, ON: Prentice-Hall.

_____. 1990. "Battered Women and the State: From a Failure of Theory to a Theory of Failure." *Journal of Human Justice* 1, 2.

Cybulski, Nancy, Jo-anne Marr, Isabel Milton, and Dalton Truthwaite. 1997. *Reinventing Hospitals: On Target for the 21st Century.* Toronto: McLeod.

D'Emilio, John. 1983. "Capitalism and Gay Identity." In Ann Snitow, Christine Stansell and Sharon Thompson (eds.), *Powers of Desire: The Politics of Sexuality.* New York: Monthly Review.

Da Gama Santos, M. 1985. "The Impact of Adjustment Programmes on Women in Developing Countries." *Public Enterprise* 5, 3.

Dahl, Robert. 1967. *Pluralist Democracy in the United States.* Chicago: Rand.

_____. 1972. *Democracy in the United States.* Chicago: Rand.

Daly, Rita. 1998. "Abortions Banned in Wellesley Takeover," *Toronto Star* April 10, A1.

Danylewycz, Marta. 1987. *Taking the Veil: An Alternative to Marriage, Motherhood and Spinisterhood in Quebec, 1984–1920.* Toronto: McClelland and Stewart.

Das Gupta, Tania. 1996. "Anti-Black Racism in Nursing in Ontario." *Studies in Political Economy* 51 (Fall).

Daubney, D. 1988. *Taking Responsibility: Report of the Standing Committee on Justice and Solicitor General on Aspects of Corrections.* Ottawa: Supply and Services.

Dauvergne, Mia. 2005. "Homicide in Canada, 2004." *Juristat* 25.

_____. 2006. "Family-Related Homicides Against Children And Youth." In L. Ogrodnik (ed.), *Family Violence in Canada: A Statistical Profile 2006.* Ottawa: Canadian Centre for Justice Statistics. Available at <www.phac-aspc.gc.ca/ncfv-cnivf/familyviolence/pdfs/85-224-

XIE2006000.pdf>. (Accessed on July 12, 2006.)

Dauvergne, Mia, and Holly Johnson. 2001. "Children Witnessing Family Violence." *Juristat* 21, 6.

Davergne, C. 2004. "Soverignty, Migration and the Rule of Law in Global Times." *Modern Law Review* 67.

David Suzuki Foundation. 2005. "All over the Map: A Comparison of Provincial Climate Change Plans." Available at <www.davidsuzuki.org/files/climate/Ontario/All_Over_the_Map.pdf>. (Accessed on September 25, 2006.)

_____. 2006. "Kyoto Protocal." Available at <www.davidsuzuki.org/Climate_Change/Kyoto>. (Accessed on September 25, 2006.)

Davin, Anna. 1978. "Imperialism and Motherhood." *History Workshop* 5.

Dawson, Myrna. 2001. *Examination of Declining Intimate Partner Homicide Rates: A Literature Review.* Ottawa: Department of Justice Canada.

Day, Richard J.F. 2005. *Gramsci Is Dead: Anarchist Currents in the Newest Social Movements.* Toronto: Between the Lines.

Day, Terence. 2006. "Private For-Profit College to Open at SFU." Available at <http://www.universityaffairs.ca/issues/2006/may/for_profit_college_01.html>. (Accessed January 29, 2007.)

De Carli, Ana Paula. 2005. Speaker at "Youth Camps Around the World – Creative Resistance Is Alive": Workshop held as part of Intercontinental Youth Camp 2005 on January 25 at the Action Centre: Caracol Intergalaktica in Parque de Harmonia, Porto Alegre, Brazil. Translation by Eduardo Sanchez.

de Certeau, Michel. 1984. *The Practice of Everyday Life.* Berkeley: University of California Press.

De Goede, Marieke. 1996. "Ideology in the US Welfare Debate: Neo-Liberal Representations of Poverty." *Discourse and Society* 7, 3.

De Santa Ana, J. (ed.). 1998. *Sustainability and Globalization.* Geneva: World Council of Churches (WCC).

DeKeseredy, Walter S. 1995. "Enhancing the Quality of Survey Data on Woman Abuse: Examples from a National Canadian Study." *Violence Against Women* 1, 2.

_____. 1999. "Tactics of the Antifeminist Backlash against Canadian National Woman Abuse Surveys." *Violence Against Women* 5.

DeKeseredy, Walter S., Shahid Alvi, Martin D. Schwartz, and Barbara Perry. 1999. "Violence Against and the Harassment of Women in Canadian Public Housing: An Exploratory Study." *Canadian Journal of Sociology and Anthropology* 36, 4.

Delacoste, Frederique, and Priscilla Alexander (eds.). 1987. *Sex Work: Writings by Women in the Sex Industry.* London: Virago.

Delage, Benoit. 2002. "Results From the Survey of Self-employment in Canada" *Human Resources Development Canada.* Ottawa: Human Resources and Development Canada.

Delisle, Andrew. 1984. "How We Regained Control over Our Lives and Territories: The Kahnewake Story." In Leroy Little Bear, Menno Boldt and J. Anthony Long (eds.), *Pathways to Self-Determination: Canadian Indians and the Canadian State.* Toronto: University of Toronto Press.

Dench, J. 2004. "Consequences on Citizenship, Immigration and Refugee Policies in Canada." Presentation at the Forum of the International Civil Liberties Monitoring Group, Ottawa.

Denis, Claude. 1996. "Rights and Spirit Dancing: Aboriginal Peoples Versus the Canadian State." In Jonathan Hart and Richard W. Bauman (eds.), *Explorations in Difference: Law Culture and Politics*. Toronto: University of Toronto Press.

Dent, J. 2002. "No Right of Appeal: Bill C-11, Criminality, and the Human Rights of Permanent Residents Facing Deportation." *Queen's Law Journal* 27.

Department of Foreign Affairs and International Trade (DFAIT). 2004. "Canada's Actions against Terrorism Since September 11." Available at <www.dfait-maeci.gc.ca/anti-terrorism/canadaactions-en.asp>. (Accessed on June 13, 2006.)

Department of Justice. 2005. "Dating Violence: A Fact Sheet from the Department of Justice Canada." *Family Violence*. Available at <canada.justice.gc.ca/en/ps/fm/datingfs.html#head2>. (Accessed on November 4, 2005.)

Desmarais, Annette. 2007. *La Via Campesina: Globalization and The Power of Peasants*. Black Point, NS: Fernwood Publishing.

Doane, Mary Ann. 1987. *The Desire to Desire: The Woman's Film of the 1940s*. Bloomington: Indiana University Press.

Dobash, R. Emerson, and Russell P. Dobash. 1979. *Violence Against Wives: A Case Against Patriarchy*. New York: Free Press.

_____. 1992. *Women, Violence and Social Change*. New York and London: Routledge.

_____. 1998. *Rethinking Violence Against Women*. Thousand Oaks, CA: Sage.

Dobash, Russell P., and R. Emerson Dobash. 1995. "Reflections On Findings From The Violence Against Women Survey." *Canadian Journal of Criminology* 37, 3.

_____. 2004. "Women's Violence to Men in Intimate Relationships: Working on a Puzzle." *British Journal of Criminology* 4.

Dobash, Russell P., R. Emerson Dobash, Kate Cavanagh, and Ruth Lewis. 1998. "Separate and Intersecting Realities." *Violence Against Women* 4, 4.

Dobash, Russell P., R.E. Dobash, Margo Wilson, and Martin Daly. 1992. "The Myth of Sexual Symmetry in Marital Violence." *Social Problems* 39, 1.

Dobbin, M. 1998. *The Myth of the Good Corporate Citizen: Democracy Under the Rule of Big Business*. Toronto: Stoddart Publishing.

_____. 1999. *Ten Tax Myths*. Vancouver: Canadian Centre for Policy Alternatives-BC.

Dobrowolsky, Alexandra, and Jane Jenson. 2004. "Shifting Representations of Citizenship: Canadian Politics of 'Women' and 'Children.'" *Social Politics* 11.

Dodds, Felix. 2002. "Reforming the International Institutions." In F. Dodds (ed.), *Earth Summit 2002: A New Deal*. London; Sterling, VA: Earthscan.

Domhoff, G. William. 1967. *Who Rules America?* Englewood Cliffs: Prentice-Hall.

Dominick, B. 2001. "Thoughts on the Anti-Capitalist Globalization Movement." *Z Magazine* (August).

Doob, Anthony N. 1995. "Understanding the Attacks on Statistics Canada's Violence Against Women Survey." In M. Valverde, L. MacLeod, and K. Johnson (eds.), *Wife Assault and the Canadian Criminal Justice System*. Toronto: Centre of Criminology, University of Toronto.

Doucet, Andrea. 2000. "'There's a Huge Gulf between Me as a Male Carer and Women': Gender, Domestic Responsibility, and the Community as an Institutional Arena." *Community, Work and Family* 3, 2.

Doyle, Kegan, and Dany Lacombe. 2003. "Moral Panic and Child Pornography: The Case of Robin Sharpe." In Deborah Brock (ed.), *Making Normal: Social Regulation in Canada*. Toronto: Thomson/Nelson.

Drolet, Marie, and Rene Morissette. 2000. "To What Extent are Canadians Exposed to Low Income?" Ottawa: Statistics Canada (Catalogue 11F0019MIE2000146).

Drost, Helmar. 1995. "The Aboriginal-White Unemployment Gap in Canada's Urban Labour Market." Market Solutions for Native Poverty: Social Policy for the Third Solitude. Toronto: C.D. Howe Institute.

Drover, Glen. 2004. *Women's Income and Poverty in Canada Revisited.* Toronto: Canadian Association of Social Workers.

Dubois, Pierre. 1995. *Les vrais maîtres de la forêt québécoise.* Montréal: Écosociété.

Duffy, Ann. 1988. "Struggling with Power: Feminist Critiques of Family Inequality." In Nancy Mandell and Ann Duffy (eds.), *Reconstructing the Canadian Family: Feminist Perspectives.* Toronto: Butterworths.

Dufour, Christian. 1992. "A Little History, Excerpt from Le Défi Québécois." In William Dodge (ed.), *Boundaries of Identity.* Toronto: Lester.

Duncan, Greg, et al. 1984. *Years of Poverty, Years of Plenty.* Ann Arbor, MI: Institute for Social Research, University of Michigan.

Dunk, Thomas (ed.). 1991. *Social Relations in Resource Hinterlands.* Thunder Bay, ON: Centre for Northern Studies, Lakehead University.

Dupuis, Jean. 2005. "The Evolution of Federal Government Finances, 1983–2003." *Library of Parliament.* (PRB 05-40E). Ottawa.

Durham, Lord. 1902. *The Report of the Earl of Durham.* London: Methuen.

During, Simon. 1994. *The Cultural Studies Reader.* London: Routledge.

Durkheim, Emile. 1933. *The Rules of Sociological Method.* New York: Free Press.

Durst, Douglas (ed.). 1999. *Canada's National Child Benefit: Phoenix or Fizzle?* Halifax: Fernwood Publishing.

Dutton, Donald G. 1994. "The Origin and Structure of the Abusive Personality." *Journal of Personality Disorders* 8, 3.

_____. 1999. "Traumatic Origins of Intimate Rage." *Aggression and Violent Behavior* 4, 4.

Dutton, Donald G., and Tonia L. Nicholls. 2005. "The Gender Paradigm in Domestic Violence Research and Theory: Part 1 — The Conflict of Theory and Data." *Aggression and Violent Behavior* 10.

Dwivedi, O.P., Patrick Kyba, Peter Stoett, and Rebecca Tiessen. 2001. *Sustainable Development in Canada: National and International Perspectives.* Peterborough, ON: Broadview Press.

Dyck, Noel. 1985. *Indigenous People and the Nation-State: Fourth World Politics in Canada, Australia and Norway.* St. John's, NF: Memorial University of Newfoundland.

Dye, T.R. 1983. *Who is Running America? The Reagan Years.* Englewood Cliffs, NJ: Prentice Hall.

Dyer, Richard. 1985. "Entertainment and Utopia." In Bill Nichols (ed.), *Movies and Methods: Volume II.* Berkeley, Los Angeles, London: University of California Press.

Dyer-Witheford, Nick. 1999. *Cyber-Marx: Cycles and Circuits of Struggle in High-Tech Capitalism.* Chicago: University of Illinois Press.

Ecologist. 1998. "An Open Letter to Robert Shapiro, Chief Executive Officer of Monsanto." *The Ecologist* 28, 5 (September/October).

Economic Council of Canada. 1991. *New Faces in the Crowd: Economic and Social Impacts of Immigration.* Ottawa: Economic Council of Canada, Study No. 22-171.

Economic Research Service (ERS), U.S. Department of Agriculture. 2006. "Agriculture Biotechnology Glossary." Briefing Rooms. Available at <www.ers.usda.gov/Briefing/

Biotechnology/glossary.htm>. (Accessed January 29, 2007.)

Economist. 2000. "Anti-Capitalist Protests: Angry and Effective." September 23.

Ecumenical Coalition for Economic Justice. 1996. *Promises To Keep, Miles To Go: An Examination of Canada's Record in the International Year for the Eradication of Poverty.* Toronto: Ecumenical Coalition for Economic Justice.

Edgar, Patti. 2000. "Woman Must Vacate Home for Her Own Safety." *Edmonton Journal,* August 4: B5.

Edwards, Peter. 2003. *One Dead Indian: The Premier, the Police and the Ipperwash Crisis.* Toronto: McClelland & Stewart.

Ehrenreich, Barbara. 1989. *Fear of Falling.* New York: Harper Collins.

Eichler, M. 1988. *Families in Canada Today: Recent Changes and their Policy Consequences.* Second edition. Toronto: Gage.

_____. 1990. "The Limits of Family Law Reform on the Privatization of Female and Child Poverty." *Canadian Family Law Quarterly* 7, 1.

_____. 1991a. "Human Rights and the New Reproductive Technologies: Individual or Collective Choices?" Unpublished manuscript.

_____. 1991b. "Family Change and Social Policy." In Jean E. Veevers (ed.), *Continuity and Change in Marriage and Family.* Toronto: Holt.

_____. 2005. "Biases in Family Literature." In Maureen Baker (ed.), *Families: Changing Trends in Canada.* Fifth edition. Toronto: McGraw-Hill Ryerson.

EKOS Research Associates. 2002. "Public Attitudes Towards Family Violence: A Syndicated Study, Final Report." Ottawa: EKOS Research Associates. Available at <www.ekos.com/media/files/family31may02.pdf>. (Accessed on July 12, 2006.)

Ekstedt, J., and C. Griffiths. 1988. *Corrections in Canada.* Toronto: Butterworths.

Elias, Peter Douglas. 1990. "Wage Labour, Aboriginal Relations, and the Cree of the Churchill River Basin, Saskatchewan. *Native Studies Review* 6.

Elliot, Patricia, and Nancy Mandell. 1995. "Feminist Theories." In Nancy Mandell (ed.), *Feminist Issues.* Scarborough, ON: Prentice-Hall.

Elliott, John. 1981. *The Sociology of Natural Resources.* Toronto: Butterworths.

Ellis, Desmond. 2000. "Credit the Economy for a Big Drop in Attacks." *Globe and Mail,* July 27.

Ellwood, Wayne. 2002. *The No-Nonsense Guide to Globalization.* Toronto: Between the Lines.

_____. 2006. *The No-Nonsense Guide to Globalization.* New Edition. Toronto: Between the Lines

Elson, D. (ed.). 1991. *Male Bias in the Development Process.* London: Macmillan.

Enloe, Cynthia. 2004. *The Curious Feminist: Searching for Women in a New Age of Empire.* Berkeley: University of California Press.

Environment Canada. 1998. "Cleaning Up the Toxic Tar Ponds." *Let's Talk Green* 8, 6.

Epp, Roger, and Dave Whitson. 2001. *Writing Off the Rural West: Globalization, Governments and the Transformation of Rural Life.* Edmonton: University of Alberta Press and Parkland Institute.

Epstein, Steven, 1996. *Impure Science, AIDS, Activism, and the Politics of Knowledge.* Berkeley, Los Angeles, London: University of California Press.

Esping-Andersen, Gosta. 1990. *The Three Worlds of Welfare Capitalism.* New Jersey: Princeton University Press.

Estable, Alma. 1986. *Immigrant Women in Canada: Current Issues.* Ottawa: Canada Advisory Council on the Status of Women.

Evans, James, Gideon Kunda, and Stephen R. Barley. 2004. "Beach Time, Bridge Time, and Billable Hours: The Temporal Structure of Technical Contracting." *Administrative Science Quarterly* 49.

Evans, Mitchell, B. Stephen McBride, and John Shields. 1998. "National Governance Versus Globalization: Canadian Democracy in Question." *Socialist Studies Bulletin* 54 (October–December).

Evans, Robert. 2003. *Political Wolves and Economic Sheep: The Sustainability of National Health Insurance in Canada.* Vancouver: University of British Columbia Centre for Health Services and Policy Research.

Evenson, Brad, and Carol Milstone. 1999. "Women Emerge As Aggressors In Alberta Survey." *National Post* July 19.

Evetts, Julia. 1994. "Women and Career in Engineering: Continuity and Change in the Organisation." *Work, Employment and Society* 8, 1 (March).

Faderman, Lillian. 1981. *Surpassing the Love of Men: Romantic Friendships and Love between Women from the Renaissance to the Present.* New York: William Morrow.

_____. 1991. *Odd Girls and Twilight Lovers: A History of Lesbian Life in Twentieth-Century America.* New York: Columbia University Press.

Faith, Karlene. 1993. *Unruly Women: The Politics of Confinement and Resistance.* Vancouver: Press Gang.

Family Violence Prevention Unit. 2002. "The Family Violence Initiative: Year Five Report. Ottawa: National Clearinghouse on Family Violence. Available at <www.phac-aspc.gc.ca/ncfv-cnivf/familyviolence/maleabus_e.html>. (Accessed on July 12, 2006.)

Faux, J. 2001. *NAFTA at Seven: Its Impact on Workers in all Three Nations.* Briefing Paper. Washington, DC: Economic Policy Institute.

Federal-Provincial-Territorial Ministries Responsible for Justice. 2006. *Spousal Abuse Policies and Legislation: Final Report of the Ad Hoc Federal-Provincial-Territorial Working Group Reviewing Spousal Abuse Policies and Legislation.* Ottawa Department of Justice Canada. Available at <www.phac-aspc.gc.ca/ncfv-cnivf/familyviolence/pdfs/spousal_e.pdf>. (Accessed on July 12, 2006.)

Federal-Provincial-Territorial Ministries Responsible for the Status of Women. 2002. *Assessing Violence Against Women: A Statistical Profile.* Ottawa: Status of Women Canada. Available at <www.swc-cfc.gc.ca/pubs/0662331664/200212_0662331664_e.pdf>. (Accessed on July 12, 2006.)

Fedorowycz, Orest. 2000. "Homicide in Canada—1999." *Juristat* 20, 9.

_____. 2001. "Homicide in Canada—2000." *Juristat* 21, 9.

Fekete, John. 1994. *Moral Panic: Biopolitics Rising.* Montreal, PQ: R. Davies Publishing.

Fekete, L. 2004. "Anti-Muslim Racism and the European Security State." *Race and Class* 46.

Felt, Lawrence F., and Peter R. Sinclair. 1992. "'Everyone Does It': Unpaid Work in a Rural Peripheral Region." *Work, Employment and Society* 6, 1.

Ferguson, Ann. 1989. *Blood At the Root: Motherhood, Sexuality and Male Dominance.* London: Pandora.

Fernandez-Cornejo, Jorge, and William D. McBride. 2002. "Adoption of Bioengineered Crops." Agricultural Economic Report No. AER810, May. Washington, DC: Economic Research Service (ERS), U.S. Department of Agriculture. Available at <www.ers.usda.gov/publications/aer810/>. (Accessed on January 29, 2007.)

Ferraro, Kathleen J. 2001. "Woman Battering: More Than a Family Problem." In C.M. Renzetti and L. Goodstein (eds.), *Women, Crime, and Criminal Justice*. Los Angeles: Roxbury Publishing Company.

Ferree, Myra Marx. 2004. "Assessing the Science: Key Issues for Research on Violence Against Women." DAAD Center for German and European Studies. September 23. Available at <www.cahrv.uni-osnabrueck.de/conference/Ferree.pdf>. (Accessed on July 12, 2006.)

Ferri, Elsa. 1992. "Research and Policy on the Lone Parent Family in Britain: An Overview." Research and Policy Workshop on the Single Parent Family. March 18–21, Lake Louise, Alberta.

Fiebert, Martin S. 2005. "References Examining Assaults by Women on their Spouses or Male Partners: An Annotated Bibliography." Available at <www.csulb.edu/~mfiebert /assault. htm>. (Accessed on July 4, 2006.)

Field, Connie. 1980. *The Life and Times of Rosie the Riveter*. Franklin Lakes, NJ: Clarity Educational Productions.

Fillion, Kate. 1989. "The Day Care Decision." *Saturday Night* January.

Finlayson, Alan Christopher. 1994. *Fishing for Truth: A Sociological Analysis of Northern Cod Stock Assessments from 1977 to 1990*. St. John's, NF: Institute of Social and Economic Research.

Finn, Ed. 2006. "'Free Trade' clearly a Disaster, but How Do we Free ourselves?" *CCPA Monitor* July/August.

First Nations Gazette. 1997. Volume 1, Number 1. Saskatoon: Native Law Centre, University of Saskatchewan.

Fisk, R. 2006. "Has Racism Invaded Canada?" Available at <counterpunch.org/fisk06122006. html>. (Accessed on June 13, 2006.)

Fiske, John. 1989. *Understanding Popular Culture*. Boston: Unwin Hyman.

Flax, Jane. 1992. "The End of Innocence." In J. Butler and J.W. Scott (eds.), *Feminists Theorize the Political*. New York, NY: Routledge.

Fleras, Augie. 1993. "From 'Culture' to 'Equality': Multiculturalism as Ideology and Policy." In James Curtis et al. (eds.), *Social Inequality in Canada: Patterns, Problems, Policies*. Scarborough, ON: Prentice-Hall.

Fleras, Augie, and Jean Leonard Elliott. 1996. *Unequal Relations: An Introduction to Race, Ethnic and Aboriginal Dynamics in Canada*. Toronto: Prentice.

Flood, Colleen M., T. Sullivan, N. Roos, S. Lewis, and T. Noseworthy. 2006. "Health Care and Wealth Care Cannot Co-exist under Medicare." *CCPA Monitor* July/August .

Flynn, Clifton P. 1990. "Relationship Violence by Women: Issues and Implications." *Family Relations* 39, 2.

Food and Agriculture Organization (FOA) of the United Nations. 2000. "Biotechonology in Food and Agriculture." Available at <http://www.fao.org/biotech/stat.asp>. (?when accessed?)

Forcese, D. 1992. *Policing Canadian Society*. Scarborough, ON: Prentice-Hall.

Forest Stewardship Council-Canada. n.d. "Forests Certified Against FSC's Standards Must Meet All of the FSC's Ten Principles, Three of Which Deal Directly with Community and Worker Rights." Available at <www.fsccanada.org/People.htm>. (Accessed on October 16, 2006.)

Foucault, Michel. 1980a. *History of Sexuality, Volume One, An Introduction*. New York: Vintage.

_____. 1980b. *Power/Knowledge: Selected Interviews and Other Writings 1972–1977*. Edited by Colin Gordon. New York: Pantheon.

_____. 1985. *The Use of Pleasure, The History of Sexuality, Volume Two*. New York: Pantheon.

_____. 1988. *The Care of the Self, The History of Sexuality, Volume Three*. New York: Vintage.

Fox, Bonnie. 1988. "Conceptualizing Patriarchy." *Canadian Review of Sociology and Anthropology* 25, 2.

Francke, Linda B. 1978. *The Ambivalence of Abortion*. New York: Random.

Frank, A.G. 1978. *World Accumulation, 1492–1789*. New York: Monthly Review Press.

Frank, Blye. 1987. "Hegemonic Heterosexual Masculinity." *Studies in Political Economy* 24.

_____. 1992. "Hegemonic Heterosexual Masculinity: Sports, Looks and a Woman, That's What Every Guy Needs to Be Masculine." In Violence and Social Control in the Home, Workplace, Community and Institutions. ISER Conference papers, No. 3, ISER. St. John's, NF: Memorial University of Newfoundland.

Franklin, Tim. 2006. "Criminal Law and HIV Transmission/Exposure: Five New Cases." HIV/AIDS and Law Review, "HIV/AIDS in the Courts Canada" section, V. 11, No. 1, April. Available at <www.aidslaw.ca/Maincontent/otherdocs/Newsletter/vol11no12006/issue.htm>. (Accessed June 23, 2006.)

Franklin, Ursula. 1999. *The Real World of Technology*. CBC Massey Lectures Series. Toronto: Anansi.

Fraser Institute. 2006. *Annual Report*. Available at <www.fraserinstitute.ca/about/reports.asp?tnav=2&scnav=3>. (Accessed November 6, 2006.)

Fraser, Nancy. 1987. "Women, Welfare and the Politics of Need Interpretation." *Hypatia: A Journal of Feminist Philosophy* 2, 1.

Freedman, Estelle. 1987. "'Uncontrolled Desires': The Response to the Sexual Psychopath, 1920–1960." *Journal of American History* 74.

Freeman, Carla. 2000. *High Tech and High Heels in the Global Economy: Women, Work, and Pink-Collar Identities in the Caribbean*. Durham, NC: Duke University Press.

Frehill, Lisa. 2004. "The Gendered Construction of the Engineering Profession in the United States, 1893–1920." *Men and Masculinities* 6, 4 (April).

Frideres, James. 1988. "The Political Economy of Natives in Canadian Society." In James Frideres, *Native Peoples in Canada: Contemporary Conflicts*. Scarborough, ON: Prentice.

_____. 1991. "Indian Economic Development: Innovations and Obstructions." In John W. Friesen (ed.), *The Cultural Maze: Complex Questions on Native Destiny in Western Canada*. Calgary: Detselig.

_____. 1996. "Canada's Changing Immigration Policy: Implications for Asian Immigrants." *Asian and Pacific Migration Journal* 5.

Friedman, Milton, and Walter W. Heller. 1969. *Monetary vs. Fiscal Policy*. New York: Norton.

Friesen, Gerald. 1987. *The Canadian Prairies: A History*. Toronto: University of Toronto Press.

Froese-Germain, Bernie, and Colleen Hawkey, Alec Larose, Patricia McAdie, Erika Shaker. 2006. *Commercialism in Canadian Schools: Who's Calling the Shots?* Ottawa: CCPA.

Fudge, Judy, and Glasbeek, Harry. 1997. "A Challenge to the Inevitability of Globalization: The Logic of Repositioning the State as the Terrain of Contest." In Jay Drydyk and Peter Penz (eds.), *Global Justice, Global Democracy*. Winnipeg/Halifax: Society for Socialist Studies/Fernwood Publishing.

Gadd, David. 2000. "Masculinities, Violence and Defended Psychosocial Subjects." *Theoretical Criminology*, 4, 4.

Gaffield, Chad. 1988. "Wage Labour, Industrialization, and the Origins of the Modern Family." In Maureen Baker (ed.), *The Family: Changing Trends in Canada*. Toronto: McGraw.

Gaivoronskaia, Galina, and Knut Erik Solem. 1999. "Science, Consumers and Safety Evaluation of Food Produced by Biotechnology." *Sosiologisk-tidsskrift* 7, 4.

Galabuzi, Grace-Edward. 2001. *Canada's Creeping Economic Apartheid: The Economic Segregation and Social Marginalisation of Racialised Groups.* Toronto: Centre for Social Justice.

_____. 2006. *Canada's Economic Apartheid: The Social Exclusion of Racialized Groups in the New Century.* Toronto: Canadian Scholar's Press.

Gallant. Paul. 2002a. "Pussy Palace Triumph." *Xtra* February 7.

_____. 2002b. "Impact? What Impact? Pussy Palace Verdict Befuddles Cops." *Xtra* February 21.

Galloway, D. 1997. *Immigration Law.* Concord, ON: Irwin.

Galt, Virginia. 2005. "Falling in Love (With Work) All Over Again." *Globe and Mail* November 23, C1.

Garbarino, James. 1996. "A Vision of Family Policy for the 21st Century." *Journal of Social Issues* 52, 3.

Garcia y Griego, M. 1994. "Canada: Flexibility and Control in Immigration and Refugee Policy." In W. Cornelius, P. Martin, and J. Hollifield (eds.), *Controlling Immigration: A Global Perspective.* Stanford: Stanford University Press.

Gardner, Gary, and Payal Sampat. 1998. "Mind over Matter: Recasting the Role of Materials in our Lives." *World Watch Paper* 144. Washington, DC: World Watch Institute.

Gauthier, Madeleine. 2003. "The Inadequacy of Concepts: The Rise of Youth Interest in Civic Participation in Quebec." *Journal of Youth Studies* 6, 3.

Gavanas, Anna. 2004. "Domesticating Masculinity and Masculinizing Domesticity in Contemporary U.S. Fatherhood Politics." *Social Politics* 11.

Gee, Ellen, and Susan A. McDaniel. 1991. "Pension Politics and Challenges: Retirement Policy Implications." *Canadian Public Policy* 17, 4.

Gelbspan, Ross. 2004. *Boiling Point: How Politicians, Big Oil and Coal, Journalists, and Activists Are Fueling the Climate Crisis — And What We Can Do to Avert Disaster.* New York: Basic Books.

Geller, G. 1987. "Young Women in Conflict with the Law." In E. Adelberg and C. Currie (eds.), *Too Few to Count: Canadian Women in Conflict with the Law.* Vancouver: Press Gang.

Gelles, Richard J., and Donileen R. Loseke. 1993. "Conclusion: Social Problems, Social Policy, and Controversies on Family Violence." In R.J. Gelles and D.R. Loseke (eds.), *Current Controversies on Family Violence.* Newbury Park: Sage Publications.

Gelles, Richard J., and Murray A. Straus. 1988. *Intimate Violence: The Definitive Study of the Causes and Consequences of Abuse in the American Family.* New York: Simon and Schuster.

George, Malcolm J. 1994. "Riding the Donkey Backwards: Men as the Unacceptable Victims of Marital Violence." *Journal of Men's Studies* 3.

George, S. 2001. "Democracy at the Barricades." *Le Monde Diplomatique* (August).

George, S., and Fabrizio Sabelli. 1994. *Faith and Credit: The World Bank's Secular Empire.* London: Penguin.

Getting Landed Project. 2002. "Protecting the Unprotected: Submission to the House of Commons Standing Committee on Citizenship and Immigration" Available at <www.cpj.ca/getting_landed>. (Accessed on June 15, 2006.)

Ghorayshi, P. 2002. "Continuity, Despite Changes: Working Canadian Women." In V. Dhruvarajan and J. Vicker (eds.), *Gender, Race, and Nation: A Global Perspective.* Toronto: University of Toronto Press.

Gibbs, Lois. 1998. *Love Canal: The Story Continues.* Gabriola Island, BC: New Society.

Giddens, Anthony. 1984. *The Constitution of Society.* Cambridge: Polity.

REFERENCES

_____. 1996. *Introduction to Sociology.* New York: Norton.

_____. 1999. *Globalization.* London: Cambridge University.

Giese, Rachel. 1994. "Lesbian Chic: I Feel Pretty and Witty and Gay." *Border/Lines* 32 (Spring).

Gimenez, Martha E. 1991. "The Feminisation of Poverty: Myth or Reality?" *Social Justice* 17, 3.

Gindin, Sam. 2002. "Social Justice and Globalization: Are They Compatible?" *Monthly Review* 54, 2.

Gismondi, Michael. 1997. "Sociology and Environmental Impact Assessment." *Canadian Journal of Sociology* 22, 4.

Glasbeek, Harry. 2002. *Wealth by Stealth: Corporate Crime, Corporate Law and the Perversion of Democracy.* Toronto: Between the Lines.

Gleason, Mona. 1999. *Normalizing the Ideal: Psychology, Schooling and the Family in Postwar Canada.* Toronto: University of Toronto Press.

Gledhill, Christine. 1987. *Home is Where the Heart Is: Studies in Melodrama and the Woman's Film.* London: British Film Institute.

_____. 1988. "Pleasurable Negotiations." In E. Deidre Pribram (ed.), *Female Spectators: Looking at Film and Television.* London: Verso.

Globe and Mail. 1990a. "Lead Damage Long-Term, Study Says." January 12.

_____. 1990b. "Abortion Law Would Force Women To Lie, CMA Says." February 7.

_____. 1991. "Attacking the Core of Child Poverty." Editorial. December 16, A18.

_____. 1995. "Penitentiaries Close to Overcrowding Crisis." February 6, A6.

_____. 1997a. "The Gay Household." June 28, A6.

_____. 1997b. "Gay Rights and Alberta Just Don't Mix." July 25, A2.

_____. 2000 "Herbicide Resistance Is Out of Control Say Canola Farmers." Available at <http://www.tao.ca/~ban/700MSherbicideresistance.htm>. (Accessed on July 15, 2002).

_____. 2006a. "Hundreds Protest Canadian Immigration Laws." May 29.

_____. 2006b. "The Evening When All Hell Broke Loose." June 6.

_____. 2006c. "Terrorism Cases Strikingly Similar." June 10.

_____. 2006d. "Probe Hears Talk of Getting an "Army.'" March 23. Available at <www.the-globeandmail.com/servlet/Page/document/v4/sub/MarketingPage?user_URLhttp://theglobeandmail.com%2Fservlet%2Fstory%2FLAC.20060322.IPPER22%2FTPStory%2F%3Fquery%#Dprobe>. (Accessed October 13, 2006.)

Goar, Carol. 2002. "Enlightened Decision by Judicial Council." *Toronto Star*, May 18.

Goff, C., and C. Reasons. 1978. *Corporate Crime in Canada.* Scarborough, ON: Prentice.

Goldberg, David. 1990. "The Social Formation of Racist Discourse." In David Golberg (ed.), *Anatomy of Racism.* Minneapolis: University of Minnesota Press.

Goldman, Michael (ed.). 1998. *Privatizing Nature: Political Struggles for the Global Commons.* New Brunswick, NJ: Rutgers University Press.

Gomberg, T. 2001. "Silenced by a Plastic Bullet: His Throat Crushed, Eric Laferriere Wants Justice for the Pain He's Suffered." *FTAA News.* Available at <www.greenspiration.org/environ/articles/SilentBullet.htm> (accessed on January 31, 2007).

Gomery, Douglas. 1998. "Hollywood as Industry." In John Hill and Pamela Church Gibson (eds.), *The Oxford Guide to Film Studies.* Oxford: Oxford University Press.

Gomme, Ian. 2007. *The Shadow Line: Deviance and Crime in Canada.* Toronto:

Gordon, R., and I. Coneybeer. 1995. "Corporate Crime." In M. Jackson and C. Griffiths (eds.),

441

Canadian Criminology. Toronto: Harcourt Brace.

Gornick, Janet, and Marcia Meyers. 2001. "Support for Working Families: What the United States can Learn from Europe." *American Prospect* 12, 1.

Gould, Kenneth, Allan Schnaiberg, and Adam Weinberg. 1996. *Local Environmental Struggles: Citizen Activism in the Treadmill of Production.* Cambridge: Cambridge University Press.

Gould, Stephen Jay. 1981. *The Mismeasure of Man.* New York: Norton.

Graham, William. 2000. "Academic Freedom or Commercial License." In James Turk (ed.), *The Corporate Campus: Commercialization and the Dangers to Canada's Colleges and Universities.* Toronto: James Lorimer.

Gramsci, Antonio. 1971. *Selections from the Prison Notebooks.* New York: International.

Grant, Karen, Carol Amaratunga, Pat Armstrong, Madeline Bosco, Ann Pederson and Kay Willson (eds.). 2004. *Caring For/Caring About: Women, Home Care and Unpaid Caregiving.* Aurora, ON: Garamond.

Green, Karen. 1996. *Family Violence in Aboriginal Communities: An Aboriginal Perspective — Overview Paper.* Ottawa: National Clearinghouse on Family Violence. Available at <www.phac-aspc.gc.ca/ncfv-cnivf/familyviolence/html/fvabor_e.html>. (Accessed on July 12, 2006.)

Green Party of Canada. n.d. "Youth Voters Day Fun Facts." Available at <www.greenparty.ca/index.php?module=pagemaster&PAGE_user_op=view_page&PAGE_id=55>. (Accessed on October 31, 2006.)

Green Web. "Left Biocentrism Primer." Available at <home.ca.inter.net/~greenweb/gw-hp.htm>. (Accessed on January 29, 2007.)

_____. "The Sable Gas Project." Green Web Bulletin #62. Available at <home.ca.inter.net/~greenweb/GW62Sable.html>. (Accessed on October 9, 2006.)

_____. n.d. "The Green Web: An Introduction." Home page of the Green Web. Available at <home.ca.inter.net/~greenweb/lbprimer.htm>. (Accessed January 29, 2007.)

Greenberg, D. 1977. "Delinquency and the Age-Structure of Society." *Contemporary Crises* 1.

Greenberg, David F. 1988. *The Construction of Homosexuality.* Chicago: University of Chicago Press.

Greenblat, Cathy S. 1983. "A Hit is a Hit is a Hit... Or is it? Approval and Tolerance of the Use of Physical Force by Spouses." In D. Finkelhor, R.J. Gelles, G.T. Hotaling, and M.A. Straus (eds.), *The Dark Side of Families: Current Family Violence Research.* Beverly Hills: Sage Publications.

Gregory, J. 1986. "Sex, Class and Crime: Towards a Non-sexist Criminology." In B. MacLean (ed.), *The Political Economy of Crime.* Scarborough, ON: Prentice.

Griffin, Cohen, M. 1996. "Democracy and the Future of Nations: Challenges for Disadvantaged Women and Minorities." In R. Boyer and D. Drache (eds.), *States Against Markets: The Limits of Globalization.* London: Routledge.

Griffiths, C., and S. Verdun-Jones. 1994. *Canadian Criminal Justice.* Second edition. Toronto: Harcourt Brace.

Griffiths, Curt. 2004. *Canadian Corrections.* Toronto: Thomson-Nelson.

Gulig, Anthony G. 1994. "Rights and Resources: A Comparison of Native/Government Resource Relations in the Treaty Ten and Lake Superior Chippewa Ceded Territory." Paper presented at the 1994 Canadian Historical Association Meeting, University of Calgary, May.

Gunderson, Morley, and Douglas Hyatt. 1996. "Health Sector Human Resources in Ontario: Results from the HSTAP's Survey." Unpublished mimeo. Toronto, June 17.

Hagan, J. 1985. *Modern Criminology.* Toronto: McGraw.

_____. 1992. "White Collar and Corporate Crime." In R. Linden (ed.), *Criminology: A Canadian Perspective*. Second edition. Toronto: Harcourt Brace.

_____. 2004. "Corporate and White-Collar Crime." In Rick Linden (ed.) *Criminology: A Canadian Perspective*. Fourth edition. Toronto: Thomson-Nelson.

Haigh, R., and J. Smith 1998. "Return of the Chancellor's Foot? Discretion in Permanent Resident Deportation Appeals Under the *Immigration Act*." *Osgoode Hall Law Journal* 36.

Halal, William E., Michael D. Kull, and Ann Leffmann. 2000. "Emerging Technologies: What's Ahead for 2001–2030." In Patrick O'Meara, Howard D. Mehlinger and Matthew Krain (eds.), *Globalization and the Challenges of a New Century: A Reader*. Bloomington and Indianapolis: Indiana University Press.

Halifax Chronicle-Herald. 1988. "AIDS Fiend Strikes Again." September 19.

Hall, Steve. 2002. "Daubing the Drudges of Fury: Men, Violence and the Piety of the 'Hegemonic Masculinity' Thesis." *Theoretical Criminology* 6, 1.

Hall, Stuart. 1990. *Culture, Media, Language*. London: Unwin Hyman.

Hamberger, L. Kevin, Jeffrey M. Lohr, and Dennis B. Bonge. 1994. "The Intended Function of Domestic Violence Is Different for Arrested Male and Female Perpetrators." *Family Violence and Sexual Assault Bulletin* 10.

Hamberger, L. Kevin, Jeffrey M. Lohr, Dennis Bonge, and David F. Tolin. 1997. "An Empirical Classification of Motivations for Domestic Violence." *Violence Against Women* 3, 4.

Hamberger, L. Kevin, and T. Potente. 1996. "Counseling Heterosexual Women Arrested for Domestic Violence: Implications for Theory and Practice." In L.K. Hamberger and C. Renzetti (eds.), *Domestic Partner Abuse*. New York: Springer.

Hannigan, John. 1995. *Environmental Sociology: A Social Constructionist Perspective*. New York: Routledge.

Hanson, L. 2001. "The Disappearance of the Open West: Individualism in the Midst of Agricultural Restructuring." In Roger Epp and Dave Whitson (eds.), *Writing Off the Rural West: Globalization, Governments, and the Transformation of Rural Communities*. Edmonton: University of Alberta Press and Parkland Institute.

Harder, Sandra. 1994. *Violence Against Women: The Canadian Panel's Final Report*. Ottawa: Parliamentary Research Branch. Available at <dsp-psd.pwgsc.gc.ca/Collection-R/LoPBdP/MR/mr122-e.htm>. (Accessed on January 29, 2007).

Harris, George. 1986. "Fathers and Fetuses." *Ethics* 96.

Harris, Michael. 1999. *Lament for an Ocean: The Collapse of the Atlantic Cod Fishery—A True Crime Story*. Toronto: McClelland and Stewart.

Harrison, Rachel, and Frank Mort. 1980. "Patriarchal Aspects of Nineteenth-Century State Formation." In Philip Corrigan (ed.), *Capitalism, State Formation and Marxist Theory*. London, Melbourne, New York: Quartet.

Harriss, John. 2001. "Globalization and World's Poor: Institutions, Inequality and Justice." *Economic Political Weekly* June 9.

Hart, Maureen. 1999. *Guide to Sustainable Community Indicators*. Second edition. North Andover, MA: Hart Environmental Data.

Hartnagel, T. 1996. "Correlates of Criminal Behaviour." In R. Linden (ed.), *Criminology: A Canadian Perspective*. Third edition. Toronto: Harcourt Brace.

_____. 2000. "Correlates of Criminal Behaviour." In R. Linden (ed.), *Criminology: A Canadian Perspective*. Fourth edition. Toronto: Harcourt Brace Canada.

_____. 2004. "Correlates of Criminal Behavior." In Rick Linden (ed.), *Criminology: A Canadian*

Perspective. Toronto: Thomson-Nelson.

Harvey, D. 1989. *The Condition of Postmodernity.* Cambridge, MA: Blackwell.

_____. 1995. "Globalization in Question." *Rethinking Marxism* 8, 4.

Hassan-Gordon, T. 1996. "Canada's Immigration Policy — Detention and Deportation of Non-Europeans." Available at <www.hartford-hwp.com/archives/44/032.html>. (Accessed on June 11, 2006.)

Hassen, Philip. 1993. *Rx for Hospitals: New Hope for Medicare in the Nineties.* Toronto: Stoddart.

Havemann, Paul. 1989. "Law, State and Canada's Indigenous People: Pacification by Coercion and Consent." In Tullio Caputo et al. (eds.), *Law and Society: A Critical Perspective.* Toronto: Harcourt Brace.

Heald, S. 1985. "Social Change and Legal Ideology: A Critique of the New Sexual Assault Legislation." *Canadian Criminology Forum* 7.

Health Services Utilization Task Force. 1994. *When Less Is Better: Using Canada's Hospitals Efficiently.* Ottawa: Health Services Utilization Task Force.

Heath, Melanie. 2003. "Soft-Boiled Masculinity: Renegotiating Gender and Racial Ideologies in the Promise Keepers Movement." *Gender & Society* 17.

Heidensohn, Frances. 1997. "Gender and Crime." In M.R. Morgan and R. Reiner (eds.), *The Oxford Handbook of Criminology.* Second edition. New York: Oxford University Press.

Held, David. 1995. *Democracy and the Global Order: From the Modern State to Cosmopolitan Governance.* Cambridge: Polity Press.

Held, David, and Anthony McGrew. 2000. "The Great Globalization Debate." In D. Held and A. McGrew (eds.), *The Global Transformations Readers: An Introduction to Globalization Debate.* London: Polity Press.

Hemmings, Susan. 1980. "Horrific Practices: How Lesbians Were Presented in the Newspapers of 1978." In Gay Left Collective (ed.), *Homosexuality: Power and Politics.* New York: Allison and Busby.

Hennessy, Rosemary. 2000. *Profit and Pleasure, Sexual Identities in Late Capitalism.* New York and London: Routledge.

Herman, Didi. 1992. "'Sociologically Speaking': Law, Sexuality and Social Change." In Dawn H. Currie and Brian D. MacLean (eds.), *Re-Thinking the Administration of Justice.* Halifax: Fernwood.

_____. 1994. *Rights of Passage: Struggles for Lesbian and Gay Legal Equality.* Toronto: University of Toronto Press.

Hewitt-White, Caitlin. 2001a. "Direct Action Against Poverty: Feminist Reflections on the Ontario Coalition Against Poverty." *Canadian Women's Studies/Les Cahiers de la Femme* 20, 3.

_____. 2001b. "Women Talking About Sexism in the Anti-Globalization Movement." In Jen Chang, et al (eds.), *Resist! A Grassroots Collection of Stories, Poetry, Photos and Analyses from the Quebec City FTAA Protests and Beyond.* Black Point, NS: Fernwood Publishing. (?volume 20? Is that right?)

Heywood, Leslie, and Jennifer Drake. 1997. *Third Wave Agenda: Being Feminist, Doing Feminism.* Minneapolis: University of Minnesota Press.

Hiebert, D. 2003. "A Borderless World: Dream or Nightmare?" *ACME* 2, 188.

High, Steven. 1996. "Native Wage Labour and Independent Production During the 'Era of Irrelevance.'" *Labour/La Travail* 37

Hinch, R. 1988. "Inconsistencies and Contradictions in Canada's Sexual Assault Law." *Canadian*

Public Policy 14, 3.

Hintjens, H.M. 1992. "Immigration and Citizenship Debates: Reflections on Ten Common Themes." *International Migration* 30.

Hirst, P., and G. Thompson. 1999. *Globalization in Question: The International Economy and the Possibilities of Governance.* Cambridge: Polity Press.

Hoggart, Richard. 1957. *The Uses of Literacy.* Harmondsworth: Penguin.

Holloway, John. 2002. *Change the World Without Taking Power.* London: Pluto.

Holloway, John, and Sol Picciotto (eds.). 1979. *State and Capital.* London: Edward Arnold.

Holmes, Mark, and Colleen Lundy. 1990. "Group Work for Abusive Men: A Profeminist Response." *Canada's Mental Health* 38, 4.

Homer, Brian, and Colleen O'Neill (eds.). 2004. *Native Pathways: American Indian Culture and Economic Development in the Twentieth Century.* Boulder, CO: University of Colorado Press.

hooks, bell. 1992. "Selling Hot Pussy: Representations of Black Female Sexuality in the Cultural Marketplace." In bell hooks, *Black Looks: Race and Representation.* Toronto: Between the Lines.

Hotaling, Gerald T., Murray A. Straus, and Alan J. Lincoln. 1989. "Intrafamily Violence, and Crime and Violence Outside the Family." In L. Ohlin and M. Tonry (eds.), *Family Violence.* Chicago: University of Chicago Press.

Houtart, F. 2001. "Alternative to the Neoliberal Model." In F. Houtart and F. Polet (eds.), *The Other Davos: Globalization of Resistance to the World Economic System.* London: Zed Books.

Houtart, F., and F. Polet (eds.). 2001. *The Other Davos: Globalization of Resistance to the World Economic System.* London: Zed Books.

Howard-Hassmann, Rhoda. 1999. "'Canadian' as an Ethnic Category: Implications for Multiculturalism and National Unity." *Canadian Public Policy* 25, 4.

Hudson, D.R. 1990. "Fraser River Fisheries: Anthropology, the State, and First Nations." *Native Studies Review* 6.

Hufbauer, G.C., and K.A. Elliot. 1994. *Measuring the Cost of Protection in the United States.* Washington, DC: Institute for International Economics. (?which initials go with which author's names?)

Human Genome Project (HGP). 1995. "Understanding Our Genetic Inheritance. The U.S. Human Genome Project. The First Five Years: Fiscal Years 1991–1995" Available at <www.ornl.gov/sci/techresources/Human_Genome/project/5yrplan/summary.shtml>. (Accessed January 29, 2007.)

Human Resources Development Canada (HRDC). 1998. "Construction of a Preliminary Market Basket Measure of Poverty." Report by the Federal/Provincial/Territorial Working Group on Social Development Research and Information. Ottawa: Human Resources and Development Canada.

Hunter, Susan, and Kevin M. Leyden. 1995. "Beyond NIMBY: Explaining Opposition to Hazardous Waste Facilities." *Policy Studies Journal* 23, 4.

Huws, Ursula. 2003. *The Making of a Cybertariat: Virtual Work in a Real World.* New York: Monthly Review Press.

Hwang, Pauline. 2001. "Anti-Racist Organizing: Reflecting on Lessons from Quebec City." In Jen Chang, et al. *Resist!: A Grassroots Collection of Stories, Poetry, Photos and Analyses from the Quebec City FTAA Protests and Beyond.* Halifax: Fernwood Publishing.

Hylton, J. 1982. "The Native Offender in Saskatchewan: Some Implications for Crime Prevention Programming." *Canadian Journal of Criminology* 24.

Ibrahim, M. 2005. "The Securitization of Migration: A Racial Discourse." *International Migration* 43.

Illich, Ivan. 1981. *Shadow Work*. Boston: M. Boyars.

Indian Affairs and Northern Development (DIAND). 2001. *Basic Departmental Data, 2000*. Ottawa: Departmental Statistics Section, Information Quality and Research Directorate, Information Management Branch.

Industry Canada. 2004. Aboriginal Entrepreneurs in Canada. Ottawa: Industry Canada. Available at <strategis.ic.gc.ca/epic/site/abc-eac.nsf/en/ab00313e.html>. (Accessed on January 2, 2007.)

Innis, Harold A. 1956. *The Fur Trade in Canada: An Introduction to Canadian Economic History*. Revised edition. Toronto: University of Toronto Press.

_____. 1978. *The Cod Fisheries: The History of an International Economy*. Revised edition. Toronto: University of Toronto Press.

Intercontinental Youth Camp 2003 Camp Organizing Committee (COA). 2003. "Intercontinental Youth Camp: The Registration is Open until January 10." Available at <www.forumsocial-mundial.org.br/dinamic.php?pagina=juventude_fsm2003_in>. (Accessed on November 19, 2004.)

Intercontinental Youth Camp 2004 Youth Assembly 2003-2004. Available at <www.wsfindia.org/youthforum/aboutus.php>. (Accessed June 15, 2006.)

Intercontinental Youth Camp 2005 Camp Organizing Committee (COA) 2004-2005. Available at <english.acampamentofsm.org>. (Accessed November 5, 2005.)

Jackson, Andrew. 2000. *Falling Behind: The State of Working Canada, 2000*. Ottawa: Canadian Centre for Policy Alternatives.

_____. 2005. "Better Educated, Badly Paid and Underemployed: A Statistical Picture of Young Workers in Canada." *CLC Research Paper #33*. Ottawa: Canadian Labour Congress.

Jackson, Andrew, and Sylvain Schetagne. 2003. "Solidarity Forever? An Analysis of Union Density." *CLC Research Paper #25*. Ottawa: Canadian Labour Congress,

Jackson, Paul. 2004. *One of the Boys, Homosexuality in the Military during World War II*. Montreal and Kingston: McGill-Queen's University Press)

Jackson, Ross. 2005. "The Ecovillage Movement." *Permaculture Magazine* 40. Available at <www.permaculture.co.uk>. (Accessed on April 10, 2006.)

Jacobs, Lea. 1993. "The Woman's Picture and the Poetics of Melodrama." *Camera Obscura* 31.

Jacobson, Neil S., and John M. Gottman. 1998. *When Men Batter Women: New Insights into Ending Abusive Relationships*. New York: Simon and Schuster.

Jacobson, Neil S., John M. Gottman, Jennifer Waltz, Regina Rushe, Julia C. Babcock, and Amy Holtzworth-Munroe. 1994. "Affect, Verbal Content, and Psychophysiology in the Arguments of Couples With a Violent Husband." *Journal of Consulting and Clinical Psychology* 62, 5.

Jacoby, Russell. 1971. "Towards a Critique of Automatic Marxism: The Politics of Philosophy from Lukacs to the Frankfurt School." *Telos* 10 (Winter).

Jaffe, Peter G., and Claire V. Crooks. 2004. "Partner Violence and Child Custody Cases: A Cross-National Comparison of Legal Reforms and Issues." *Violence Against Women* 10.

Jagose, Annamarie. 1996. *Queer Theory, An Introduction*. New York: New York University Press.

Jakubowski, L. 1997. *Immigration and the Legalization of Racism*. Halifax: Fernwood Publishing.

James, Carl. 2002. "'Armed and Dangerous!': Racializing Suspects, Suspecting Race." In Bernard Schissel and Carolyn Brooks (eds.), *Marginality and Condemnation: An Introduction to Critical Criminology*. Halifax: Fernwood Publishing.

REFERENCES

Jamieson, Wanda. 2004. *Family Violence Initiative, Performance Report 2002–2003 and 2003–2004.* Ottawa: National Clearinghouse on Family Violence. Available at <www.phac-aspc.gc.ca/ ncfvcnivf/familyviolence/html/2004fviperformance /fviperformance_e.html>. (Accessed on July 12, 2006.)

Janoff, Douglas Victor. 2005. *Pink Blood, Homophobic Violence in Canada.* Toronto: University of Toronto Press.

Janz, Teresa. 2000. "The Evolution and Diversity of Relationships in Canadian Families." Ottawa: Law Commission of Canada.

Jawara, Fatoumata, and Aileen Kwa. 2003. "The Devil You Know: An Introduction to the WTO." In F. Jawara and A. Kwa (eds.), *Behind the Scenes at the WTO: The Real World of International Trade Negotiations.* London: Zed Books.

Jefferson, Tony. 1997. "Masculinities and Crimes." In M.R. Morgan and R. Reiner (eds.), *The Oxford Handbook of Criminology.* Second edition. New York: Oxford University Press.

_____. 2002. "Subordinating Hegemonic Masculinity." *Theoretical Criminology* 6, 1.

Jenson, Jane, and Sharon M. Stroick. 1992. "Gender and Reproduction, or Babies and the State." In M. Patricia Connelly and Pat Armstrong (eds.), *Feminism in Action.* Toronto: Canadian Scholars Press.

_____. 1999. "A Policy Blueprint For Canada's Children." *Reflexion, Canadian Policy Research Network* October.

Jeremy Wilson. 1998. *Talk and Log: Wilderness Politics in British Columbia.* Vancouver: UBC Press.

Jessop, Bob. 1990. State Theory: Putting the Capitalist State in its Place. University Park, PA: Pennsylvania State University Press.

_____. 1993. "Towards a Schumpeterian Workfare State? Preliminary Remarks on Post-Fordist Political Economy." *Studies in Political Economy* 40.

_____. 2001. "Capitalism, the Regulation Approach, and Critical Realism." Department of Sociology, Lancaster University, Lancaster LA1 4YN. Available at <www.lancs.ac.uk/fss/ sociology/research/resalph.htm#jessop>. (Accessed January 29, 2007.)

_____. 2003. "Narrating the Future of the National Economy and the National State? Remarks on Remapping Regulation and Reinventing Governance." Department of Sociology, Lancaster University, Lancaster LA1 4YN. Available at <www.lancs.ac.uk/fss/sociology/ research/resalph.htm#jessop>. (Accessed January 29, 2007.)

Jobidon, Odette. 1982. *Situation Report on the Current State of Race Relations in Vancouver, B.C.* Ottawa: Secretary of State.

Johnson, H., and K. Rodgers. 1993. "A Statistical Overview of Women and Crime in Canada." In E. Adelberg and C. Currie (eds.), *In Conflict with the Law: Women and the Canadian Justice System.* Vancouver: Press Gang.

Johnson, Holly. 1998. "Rethinking Survey Research on Violence against Women." In R.E. Dobash and R.P. Dobash (eds.), *Rethinking Violence Against Women.* Thousand Oaks, CA: Sage.

Johnson, Holly, and Valerie P. Bunge. 2001. "Prevalence and Consequences of Spousal Assault in Canada." *Canadian Journal of Criminology* 43, 1.

Johnson, Josee, Mike Gismondi, and James Goodman (eds.). 2006. *Nature's Revenge: Reclaiming Sustainability in an Age of Corporate Globalization.* Peterborough: Broadview Press.

Johnson, Karen, Donna Lero, and Jennifer Rooney. 2001. *Work-Life Compendium 2001.* Ottawa: Human Resources Development Canada.

Johnson, Michael P. 1995. "Patriarchal Terrorism and Common Couple Violence: Two Forms of Violence Against Women." *Journal of Marriage and the Family* 57.

Johnston, Darlene. 1993. "First Nations and Canadian Citizenship." In William Kaplan (ed.), *Belonging: The Meaning and Future of Canadian Citizenship*. Montreal: McGill-Queen's University Press.

Johnston, Ronnie, and Arthur McIvor. 2004. "Dangerous Work, Hard Men, and Broken Bodies: Masculinity in the Clydesdale Heavy Industries, 1930–1970." *Labour History Review* 69, 2.

Jones, A. 1998. "(Re)Producing Gender Cultures: Theorizing Gender in Investment Banking Recruitment." *Geoforum* 29, 4.

Juris, Jeffrey S. 2005. "Youth and the World Social Forum." Available at <http://ya.ssrc.org/transnational/Juris/pf/ posted 1/06/05>. (Accessed on April 20, 2006.)

Kaldor, M. 2000. "Civilizing Globalization? The Implications of the 'Battle in Seattle.'" *Millenium: Journal of International Studies* 29, 1.

Kalleberg, Arne L., and Cynthia Fuchs Epstein. 2001. "Introduction: Temporal Dimensions of Employment Relations." *American Behavioral Scientist* 44, 7.

Kalmuss, Debra. 1984. "The Intergenerational Transmission of Marital Aggression." *Journal of Marriage and the Family* 46.

Kamerman, Sheila B., and Alfred J. Kahn (eds.). 1978. *Family Policy: Government and Families in Fourteen Countries*. New York: Columbia University Press.

Kapashesit, Randy, and Murray Klippenstein. 1991. "Aboriginal Group Rights and Environmental Protection." *McGill Law Journal* 36.

Kaplan, E. Ann. 1983. "The Case of the Missing Mother: Maternal Issues in Vidor's *Stella Dallas*." *Heresies* 16.

Karlen, Arno. 1971. *Sexuality and Homosexuality*. New York: Norton.

Katz, Jonathan Ned. 1983. *Gay/Lesbian Almanac*. New York: Harper and Row.

_____. 1990. "The Invention of Heterosexuality." *Socialist Review* 1.

_____. 1995. *The Invention of Heterosexuality*. New York: Dutton.

Kazanjian, Arminée. 2000. *Nursing Workforce Study, Volume V: Changes in the Nursing Workforce and Policy Implications*. Vancouver: Health Human Resources Unit, Centre for Health Services and Policy Research, University of British Columbia.

Keddy, Bethany. 1992. *The Persian Gulf TV War*. Boulder, CO: Westview.

_____. 1995. *Media Culture: Cultural Studies, Identity and Politics Between the Modern and the Postmodern*. New York: Routledge.

Kelley, N., and M. Trebilcock. 1998. *The Making of the Mosaic: A History of Canadian Immigration Policy*. Toronto: University of Toronto Press.

Kellough, Gail. 1980. "From Colonialism to Economic Imperialism: The Experience of the Canadian Indian." In John Harp and John R. Hofley (eds.), *Structured Inequality in Canada*. Scarborough, ON: Prentice-Hall.

Kempadoo, Kamala, and Jo Doezema (eds.). 1998. *Global Sex Workers: Rights, Resistance and Redefinition*. New York and London: Routledge.

Kendall, Kathleen. 1993. "Creating Safe Places: Reclaiming Sacred Spaces." Paper prepared for the Seventh National Roundtable for Women in Prison Family Violence Programming in Jail and Prisons Workshop. Washington, DC.

Kennedy, Elizabeth Lapovsky, and Madeline D. Davis. 1993. *Boots of Leather, Slippers of Gold: The History of a Lesbian Community*. New York: Routledge.

Kenny, Eion. 1996. "More Illness, Fewer Resources: First Nations." *Winnipeg Free Press*, February 24.

REFERENCES

Kerstetter, S. 2002. "The Widening Income Gap: Unequal Distribution of Wealth Rampant all across Canada." *CCPA Monitor* 8, 9.

Kessler, Suzanne J. 1998. *Lessons from the Intersexed*. New Brunswick, NJ; Rutgers University Press.

Kessler, Suzanne J., and Wendy McKenna. 1978. *Gender: An Ethnomethdological Approach*. Chciago and London: University of Chicago Press.

Khayatt, Madiha Didi. 1992. *Lesbian Teachers: An Invisible Presence*. Albany: State University of New York Press.

_____. 1995. "Compulsory Heterosexuality and Lesbian Students." In Marie Campbell and Ann Manicom (eds.), *Knowledge, Experience and Ruling Relations*. Toronto: University of Toronto Press.

Khor, Martin. 1996. "Global Economy and the Third World." In J. Mander and E. Goldsmith (eds.), *The Case Against the Global Economy*. San Francisco: Sierra Club Books.

_____. 2001. *Rethinking Globalization: Critical Issues and Policy Choices*. London: Zed Books.

Kimmel, Michael S. 2002. "'Gender Symmetry' in Domestic Violence: A Substantive and Methodological Research Review." *Violence Against Women* 8.

Kingley, Jean-Pierre. 2004. "An Issue of Paramount Importance." In *Canadian Democracy: Bringing Youth Back Into the Political Process*. The CRIC papers. Montreal: Centre for Research and Information on Canada.

Kingston, Anne. 2005. "Why Women Can't Get Ahead." *Report on Business* (December).

Kinsman, Gary. 1985. "Porn/Censor Wars and the Battlefields of Sex." Issues of Censorship. Toronto: A Space.

_____. 1989. "Official Discourse as Sexual Regulation: The Social Organization of the Sexual Policing of Gay Men." Ph.D. thesis. Toronto: Department of Education, University of Toronto.

_____. 1990. "Review of David Greenberg, The Construction of Homosexuality." *Canadian Journal of Sociology* 15, 1.

_____. 1991. "'Homosexuality' Historically Reconsidered Challenges Heterosexual Hegemony." *Journal of Historical Sociology* 4, 2.

_____. 1992a. "'Restoring Confidence the Criminal Justice System': The Hughes Commission and Mass Media Coverage: Making Homosexuality a Problem." Violence and Social Control in the Home, Workplace, Community and Institutions: Papers Presented at the Twenty-sixth Annual Meeting of the Atlantic Association of Sociologists and Anthropologists. March 21–24, 1991. ISER Conference Paper No. 3. St. John's, NF: Memorial University of Newfoundland.

_____. 1992b. "Managing aids Organizing: 'Consultation,' 'Partnership,' and the National AIDS Strategy." In William K. Carroll (ed.), *Organizing Dissent: Contemporary Social Movements in Theory and Practice*. Toronto: Garamond.

_____. 1993. "'Inverts,' 'Psychopaths,' and 'Normal' Men: Historical Sociological Perspectives on Gay and Heterosexual Masculinities." In Tony Haddad (ed.), *Men and Masculinities: A Critical Anthology*. Toronto: Canadian Scholars' Press.

_____. 1995a. "'Character Weaknesses' and 'Fruit Machines': Towards an Analysis of the Anti-Homosexual Security Campaign in the Canadian Civil Service." *Labour* 35.

_____. 1995b. "The Textual Practices of Sexual Rule: Sexual Policing and Gay Men." In Marie Campbell and Ann Manicom (eds.), *Knowledge, Experience, and Ruling Relations: Studies in the Social Organization of Knowledge*. Toronto: University of Toronto Press.

_____. 1996a. *The Regulation of Desire: Homo and Hetero Sexualities*. Montreal: Black Rose.

_____. 1996b. "'Responsibility' as a Strategy of Governance: Regulating People Living with AIDS and Lesbians and Gay Men in Ontario." *Economy and Society* 25, 3.

_____. 1997. "Managing aids Organizing: 'Consultation,' 'Partnership,' and 'Responsibility' as Strategies of Regulation." In William K. Carrol (ed.), *Organizing Dissent: Contemporary Social Movements in Theory and Practice*. Second edition. Toronto: Garamond.

_____. 2000. "Constructing Gay Men and Lesbians as National Security Risks, 1950–70." In Gary Kinsman, Dieter K. Buse, and Mercedes Steedman (eds.), *Whose National Security? Canadian State Surveillance and the Creation of Enemies*. Toronto: Between the Lines.

_____. 2003a. "National Security as Moral Regulation: Making the Normal and the Deviant in the Security Campaigns Against Gay Men and Lesbians." In Deborah Brock (ed.), *Making Normal: Social Regulation in Canada* Toronto: Thomson/Nelson.

_____. 2003b. "Queerness Is Not in Our Genes: Biological Determinism Versus Social Liberation." In Deborah Brock (ed.), *Making Normal, Social Regulation in Canada*. Scarborough, ON: Thomson/Nelson.

_____. 2003c. "Don't Get Me to the Church on Time: Ending Social Discrimination Against Same-Sex and other Relationships." Summary of Brief to the Justice and Human Rights Committee Review on Questions Relating to Same-Sex Marriage, Sudbury Hearings, April 9.

_____. 2004a. "Capitalism and Industrialization." In Marc Stein et al. (eds.), *Encyclopedia of Lesbian, Gay, Bisexual, and Transgender History in America*. New York: Scribner's/Thomson.

_____. 2004b "The Canadian Cold War on Queers: Sexual Regulation and Resistance." In Richard Cavell (ed.), *Love, Hate, and Fear in Canada's Cold War*. Toronto: University of Toronto Press/Green College Thematic Series.

Kinsman, Gary, and Robert Champagne. 1986. "Refusing to Refuse the Pleasures of the Body." Review of Weeks, Sexuality and Its Discontents. *Fuse* 42 (Fall).

Kinsman, Gary, and Patrizia Gentile. 1998. "In the Interests of the State": The Anti-Gay, Anti-Lesbian National Security Campaign in Canada. Sudbury: Laurentian University.

Kirkby, Gareth. 2006. "Sex Laws/Harper Government Gives Priority to Anti-Sex Legislation." *Xtra*, Feb 8.

Kirkby, Gareth, and Krishna Rau. 2006. "Gay Groups Prepare for Battle, Age of Consent Increase will be Opposed." *Capital Xtra*, Thursday, March 23.

Kirkland, Kevin. 2004. *Abuse in Gay Male Relationships: A Discussion Paper Government of Canada*. Ottawa: National Clearinghouse on Family Violence. Available at <http://www.phac-aspc.gc.ca/ncfv-cnivf/familyviolence/pdfs/2004GayMale_e.pdf>. (Accessed on July 12, 2006.)

Kite, B. 2001. "Free Trade? Someone Always has to Pay." Available at <www.businessweek.com/bwdaily/dnflash/may2001/nf2001052_941.htm?chan=search>. (Accessed January 29, 2007.)

Klein, N. 1999. Rebels in Search of Rule. Available at <mai.flora.org/forum>. (Accessed on December 9, 2002).

_____. 2000. *No Space, No Choice, No Jobs, No Logo: Taking Aim at the Brand Bullies*. New York: Picador.

Klinger, Barbara. 1994. *Melodrama and Meaning: History, Culture, and the Films of Douglas Sirk*. Bloomington: Indiana University Press.

Kneen, Brewster. 1999. *Farmageddon: Food and the Culture of Biotechnology*. Gabriola Island, BC:

New Society Publishers.

Knight, Rolf. 1996. *Indians at Work: An Informal History of Native Indian Labour in British Columbia, 1858–1930.* Vancouver: New Star.

Kobayashi, A. 1995. "Challenging the National Dream: Gender Persecution and Canadian Immigration Law." In P. Fitzpatrick (ed.), *Nationalism, Racism and the Rule of Law.* Aldershot: Dartmouth.

Kolker, Robert. 2002. *Film, Form, and Culture.* New York: McGraw-Hill.

Kolko, J. 1988. *Restructuring the World Economy.* New York: Pantheon Books.

Kong, Rebecca, Holly Johnson, Sara Beattie, and Andrea Cardillo. 2003. "Sexual Offences in Canada." *Juristat* 23.

Korpi, Walter. 1998. "The Iceberg of Power Below the Surface: A Preface to Power Resource Theory." In Julia O'Connor and Gregg Olsen (eds.), *Power, Resource Theory, and the Welfare State.* Toronto: University of Toronto Press.

Korten, D.C. 1995. *When Corporations Rule the World.* San Francisco: Berrett-Koehler and Kumarian.

_____. 1999. *The Post Corporate World: Life After Capitalism.* Toronto: McGraw Hill.

_____. 2001. *When Corporations Rule the World.* Second edition. Bloomfield, CT: Kumerian Press.

Kowalski, Melanie. 2006. "Spousal Homicides." In L. Ogrodnik (ed.), *Family Violence in Canada: A Statistical Profile 2006.* Ottawa: Canadian Centre for Justice Statistics. Available at <www.phac-aspc.gc.ca/ncfv-cnivf/familyviolence/pdfs/85-224-XIE2006000.pdf>. (Accessed on July 4, 2006.)

Krafft-Ebing, Richard von. 1965. *Psychopathia Sexualis: A Medico-Forensic Study.* New York: Putnam.

Krauter, Joseph, and Morris Davis. 1978. *Minority Canadians: Ethnic Groups.* Toronto: Methuen.

Krueger, A.O. 1990. "Free Trade is the Best Policy." In R. Lawrence and C. Schultze (eds.), *An American Trade Strategy: Options for the 1990's.* Washington, DC: Brookings Institutions.

Kruger, E., M. Mulder, and B. Korenic. 2004. "Canada after 11 September: Security Measures and 'Preferred' Immigrants." *Mediterranean Quarterly* 15.

Kuehn, Larry. 2003. "What's Wrong With Commercialization of Public Education?" *BCTF Teacher Newsmagazine* 19, 4.

Kuhn, Annette. 1987. "Women's Genres: Melodrama, Soap Opera and Theory." In Christine Gledhill (ed.), *Home is Where the Heart Is: Studies in Melodrama and the Woman's Film.* London: British Film Institute.

Kumbamu, Ashok. 2006. "Ecological Modernization and the 'Gene Revolution': The Case Study of Bt Cotton in India." *Capitalism Nature Socialism* 17, 4.

Kunda, Gideon, Stephen R. Barley, and James Evans. 2002. "Why Do Contractors Contract? The Experience of Highly Skilled Technical Professionals in a Contingent Labor Market." *Industrial and Labor Relations Review* 55, 2 (January).

Kung, Hans. 1998. *A Global Ethic for Global Politics and Economics.* London: SCM Press.

Kurtz, Andrew Kurtz. 2002. "Repurposing the Workplace: Hegemony and the Contested Spaces of the Internet." *Cultural Logic: An Electronic Journal Of Marxist Theory and Practice* 3, 2 (Spring).

Kymlicka, Will. 1989. *Liberalism, Community and Culture.* New York: Oxford University Press.

Labelle, Micheline. 1990. "Immigration, culture et question nationale." *Cahiers de reserche soci-*

ologique 14.

Laclau, Ernesto. 1975. "The Specificity of the Political: The Poulantzas-Miliband Debate." *Economy and Society* 4.

LaFramboise, Donna. 1999. "Men and Women are Equals in Violence." *National Post,* July 10.

_____. 2000. "Violence Against Men Deserves Attention, Too." *National Post,* January 8.

Lahey, Kathleen A. 1999. *Are We 'Persons' Yet? Law and Sexuality in Canada.* Toronto: University of Toronto Press.

Lahey, Kathleen A., and Kevin Alderson. 2004. *Same-Sex Marriage, the Personal and the Political.* Toronto: Insomniac Press.

Laing, Marie. 1999. "For the Sake of the Children: Preventing Reckless New Laws." *Canadian Journal of Family Law* 16.

Lamble, Sarah. 2001. "Building Sustainable Communities of Resistance." In Jen Chang et al. (comp,), *Resist!: A Grassroots Collection of Stories, Poetry, Photos and Analyses from the Quebec City FTAA Protests and Beyond.* Halifax: Fernwood Publishing.

Land, Hilary, and Roy Parker. 1978. "United Kingdom." In Sheila B. Kamerman and Alfred J. Kahn (eds.), *Family Policy: Government and Families in Fourteen Countries.* New York: Columbia University Press.

Lang, T. 1999. "The Complexities of Globalization: The UK as a Case Study of Tensions Within the Food System and the Challenge to Food Policy." *Agriculture and Human Values* 16.

Langevin, L., and M. Belleau. 2000. "Trafficking in Women in Canada: A Critical Analysis of the Legal Framework Governing Immigrant Live-in Caregivers and Mail-Order Brides." Ottawa: Status of Women Canada. Available at <www.swc-cfc.gc.ca/pubs/pubspr/066231252X /index_e.html>. (Accessed on September 8, 2006.)

Langford Parks, Ellie. 2005. "8 Things to Know about Women and the Economy." *Making Waves* 16, 3.

LaPrairie, C. 1987. "Native Women and Crime in Canada: A Theoretical Model." In E. Adelberg and C. Currie (eds.), *Too Few to Count: Canadian Women in Conflict with the Law.* Vancouver: Press Gang.

_____. 1996. *Examining Aboriginal Corrections in Canada.* Ottawa: Supply and Services.

Larocque, Sylvain. 2006. *Gay Marriage, The Story of a Canadian Social Revolution.* Toronto: Lorimer.

Law Commission of Canada. 2001. *Beyond Conjugality, Recognizing And Supporting Close Personal Adult Relationships.* Ottawa: Law Commission of Canada.

Laybourn, Ann. 1986. "Traditional Strict Working Class Parenting: An Undervalued System." *British Journal of Social Work* 16.

Lefaucheur, Nadine, and Claude Martin. 1992. "Familles monoparentales en France: Situation et recherche." Research and Policy Workshop on the Single Parent Family. March 18–21, Lake Louise, Alberta.

Lehr, Valerie. 1999. *Queer Family Values, Debunking the Myth of the Nuclear Family.* Philadelphia: Temple University Press.

Leibowitz, Flo. 1996. "Apt Feelings, or Why 'Women's Films' Aren't Trivial." In David Bordwell and Noel Carroll (eds.), *Post-Theory: Reconstructing Film Studies.* Madison: University of Wisconsin Press.

Lengermann, Patricia Madoo, and Jill Niebrugge-Brantley. 1988. "Contemporary Feminist Theory." In George Ritzer (ed.), *Sociological Theory.* New York: Alfred A. Knopf.

Leonard, Eileen. 2003. *Women, Technology and the Myth of Progress.* New Jersey: Prentice-Hall.

REFERENCES

Lerner, Sharon. 2003. "An Orgy of Abstinence." In Suzanne Lafont (ed.), *Constructing Sexualities, Readings in Sexuality, Gender, and Culture*. Upper Saddle River, NJ: Prentice-Hall.

Lero, Donna S., A.R. Pence, M. Shields, L.M. Brockman, and H. Goldman. 1992. *Canadian National Child Care Study: Introductory Report*. (Catalogue 89-5265). Ottawa: Statistics Canada.

Levine, Alissa. 1999. "Female Genital Operations: Canadian Realities, Concerns, and Policy Recommendations." In Harold Troper and Morton Weinfield (eds.), *Ethnicity, Politics and Public Policy: Case Studies in Canadian Diversity*. Toronto: University of Toronto Press.

Lewis, Jane. 2001. "Debates and Issues Regarding Marriage and Cohabitition in the British and American Literature." *International Journal of Law, Policy and Family* 15, 1.

Lexchin, Joel. 2001. "Pharmaceuticals: Policies and Politics." In Pat Armstrong, Hugh Armstrong, and David Coburn (eds.), *Unhealthy Times: Political Economy Perspectives on Health and Care in Canada*. Toronto: Oxford University Press.

Lezubski, Darren, Jim Silver, and Errol Black. 2000. "High and Rising: The Growth of Poverty in Winnipeg's Inner City." In Jim Silver (ed.), *Solutions That Work: Fighting Poverty in Winnipeg*. Halifax and Winnipeg: Fernwood and the Canadian Centre for Policy Alternatives–Manitoba.

Li, P. 2001. "The Racial Subtext in Canada's Immigration Discourse." *Journal of International Migration and Integration* 2, 1.

_____. 2003. *Destination Canada*. Don Mills: Oxford University Press.

Lim, L. 1985. *Women Workers in Multinational Enterprises in Developing Countries*. Geneva: International Labour Organization.

Lindblom, Charles E. 1977. *Politics and Markets*. New York: Basic Books.

Lindsay, Colin. 1999. "Seniors: A Diverse Group Aging Well." *Canadian Social Trends* 52 (Spring).

Little, Bruce. 1997. "Nineties Take an Income Bite from the Middle." *Globe and Mail*, May 19.

Livingstone, David, and Doug Hart. 2005. *Public Attitudes Toward Education in Ontario 2004*. Toronto: OISE/UT.

Lock, Ineke. 2006. "Corporate Social Responsibility and Codes of Conduct: The Fox Guarding the Chicken Coop?" In J. Johnson, M. Gismondi, and J. Goodman (eds.), *Nature's Revenge*. Peterborough, Broadview Press.

Locke, Daisy. 2000. "Canada's Shelters for Abused Women, 1999–2000." *Juristat* 21, 1.

Locke, Daisy, and Ruth Code. 2001. "Family Homicide." In V.P. Bunge and D. Locke (eds.), *Family Violence in Canada: A Statistical Profile 2000*. Ottawa: Statistics Canada.

Longford, Graham, and Barbara Crow. 2003. "From the Electronic Cottage to the Silicon Sweatshop: Social Implications of Telemediated Work in Canada." In David Taras, Frits Pannekoek, and Maria Bakardjieva (eds.), *How Canadians Communicate*. Calgary: University of Calgary Press.

Loo, Tina. 1994. *Making Law, Order and Authority in British Columbia, 1821–1871*. Toronto: University of Toronto Press.

Loseke, D. 1999. *Thinking About Social Problems*. New York: Aldine de Gruyter.

Lovenduski, Joni, and Joyce Outshoorn. 1986. *The New Politics of Abortion*. London: Sage.

Lowe, Keith. 1982. *Race Relations in Metropolitan Toronto: A Situation Report*. Ottawa: Secretary of State.

Lowman, John. 1986a. "Prostitution in Vancouver: Some Notes on the Genesis of a Social Problem." *Canadian Journal of Criminology* 28, 1.

_____. 1986b. "You Can Do It, But You Cannot Do It Here: Some Comments on Proposals for Reform of Canadian Prostitution Laws." In John Lowman, Margaret Jackson, T. Palys, and Shelley Gavigan (eds.), *Regulating Sex: An Anthology of Commentaries on the Badgley and Fraser Reports*. Burnaby, BC: School of Criminology, Simon Fraser University.

_____. 2000. "Violence and the Outlaw Status of (Street) Prostitution in Canada." *Violence Against Women* 6, 9.

Lucal, Betsy. 1995. "The Problem With 'Battered Husbands.'" *Deviant Behavior* 16.

Lupri, Eugen. 2004. "Institutional Resistance to Acknowledging Intimate Male Abuse, Revised." Counter-Roundtable Conference on Domestic Violence. Calgary, Alberta, May 7. Available at <http://www.fact.on.ca/Info/dom/lupri05.htm>. (Accessed on July 12, 2006.)

Lupri, Eugen, and Elaine Grandin. 2004. *Intimate Partner Abuse Against Men*. Ottawa: National Clearinghouse on Family Violence. Available at <www.phac-aspc.gc.ca/ncfv-cnivf/familyviolence/pdfs/2004abusmn_e.pdf>. (Accessed on July 4, 2006.)

Lupton, Deborah. 1998. *The Emotional Self*. Thousand Oaks: Sage.

Luxton, Meg. 2005. "Conceptualizing 'Families': Theoretical Frameworks and Family Research." In Maureen Baker (ed.), *Families: Changing Trends in Canada*. Fifth edition. Toronto: McGraw-Hill Ryerson.

MacBride-King, Judith L. 1990. *Work and Family: Employment Challenge of the 90's*. Ottawa: Conference Board of Canada.

MacBride-King, Judith L., and Kimberley Bachmann. 1999. *Is Work-Life Balance Still an Issue for Canadians and their Employers? You Bet it is*. Ottawa: Conference Board of Canada.

MacInnes, T.R.L. 1946. "History of Indian Administration in Canada." *Canadian Journal of Economics and Political Science* 12.

MacKinnon, Shauna. 2000. "Workfare in Manitoba." In Jim Silver (ed.), *Solutions That Work: Fighting Poverty in Winnipeg*. Halifax and Winnipeg: Fernwood Publishing and the Canadian Centre for Policy Alternatives—Manitoba.

MacLeod, Linda. 1980. *Wife Battering in Canada: The Vicious Circle*. Ottawa: Canadian Advisory Council on the Status of Women.

_____. 1987. *Battered But Not Beaten: Preventing Wife Battering in Canada*. Ottawa: Canadian Advisory Council on the Status of Women.

MacLeod, Linda, and Maria Shin. 1992. *Isolated, Afraid and Forgotten. The Service Delivery Needs and Realities of Immigrant and Refugee Women Who Are Battered*. Ottawa: National Clearinghouse on Family Violence. Available at <www.phac-aspc.gc.ca/ncfv-cnivf/familyviolence/pdfs/isolatedafraid.pdf>.

MacLeod, R.C. (ed.). 1993. *Swords and Plowshares: War and Agriculture in Western Canada*. Edmonton: University of Alberta Press.

Magdoff, F. 1992. "Globalization: To What End?" In R. Miliband and L. Panitch (eds.), *Sociologist Register, 1992*. London: Merlin Press.

Magdoff, Fred, John Bellamy Foster, and Frederick H. Buttel (eds.). 2000. *Hungry for Profit: The Agribusiness Threat to Farmers, Food, and the Environment*. New York: Monthly Review Press.

Mahood, Sally. 2005. "Privatized Knowledge and the Pharmaceutical Industry." Paper presented at Free Knowledge: Creating a Knowledge Commons in Saskatchewan Conference. University of Regina, Regina, Saskatchewan, November 17–18.

Malik, W. 1982. *A Study of Race Relations in Montreal*. Ottawa: Secretary of State.

Mandell, Deena. 2002. *"Deadbeat Dads": Subjectivity and Social Construction*. Toronto: University of Toronto Press.

REFERENCES

Mandle, Jay R. 2003. *Globalization and the Poor.* Cambridge: Cambridge University Press.

Mann, Michelle. 2000. "Capitalism and the Dis-empowerment of Canadian Aboriginal Peoples." *Journal of Aboriginal Economic Development* 46.

Mann, Ruth M. 2000. *Who Owns Domestic Abuse? The Local Politics of a Social Problem.* Toronto: University of Toronto Press.

_____. 2002. "Emotionality and Social Activism: A Case Study of a Community Development Effort to Establish a Shelter for Women in Ontario." *Journal of Contemporary Ethnography* 31, 3.

_____. 2003. "Violence Against Women or Family Violence: The 'Problem' of Female Perpetration in Domestic Violence." In L. Samuelson and W. Antony (eds.), *Power and Resistance: Critical Thinking About Canadian Social Issues.* Third edition. Black Point, NS: Fernwood Publishing.

_____. 2005. "Fathers' Rights, Feminism and Canadian Divorce Law Reform: 1998–2003." *Studies in Law Politics and Society* 35.

Mann, Ruth M., Charlene Y. Senn, April Girard, and Salma Ackbar. 2007. "Community-based Interventions for At-risk Youth in Ontario under Canada's *Youth Criminal Justice Act*: A Case Study of a 'Runaway' Girl." *Canadian Journal of Criminology and Criminal Justice* 49, 1.

Mann, Susan A., Michael D. Grimes, Alice Abel Kemp, and Pamela J. Jenkins. 1997. "Paradigm Shifts in Family Sociology? Evidence from Three Decades of Family Textbooks." *Journal of Family Issues* 18, 3.

Mao, Y., et al. 1992. "Indian Reserves and Registered Indian Mortality in Canada." *Canadian Journal of Public Health* 83.

Marchak, Patricia. 1983. *Green Gold: The Forest Industry in British Columbia.* Vancouver: University of British Columbia Press.

_____. 1995. *Logging the Globe.* Montreal: McGill-Queens University Press.

Marchand, Marianne H. 2000. "Gendered Representations of the 'Global': Reading/Writing Globalization." In R. Stubbs and G. Underhill (eds.), *Political Economy and the Changing Global Order.* Toronto: Oxford University Press.

Marchi, S. 1995. "Speech: Tougher Tools For Deporting Criminals." *Canadian Speeches* 9 (August/September).

Marcuse, Herbert. 1961. *Soviet Marxism.* New York: Vintage.

Margolis, Jane, and Allan Fisher. 2001. *Unlocking the Clubhouse: Women in Computing.* Cambridge: MIT Press.

Markham, Barbara, and Jonathon Lomas. 1995. "A Review of the Multi-Hospital Arrangements Literature: Benefits, Disadvantages and Lessons for Implementation." *Health Care Management Forum* 8, 3.

Markoff, J. 1996. *Waves of Democracy: Social Movement and Political Change.* Thousand Oaks, CA: Pine Forge Press.

Markwart, A. 1992. "Custodial Sanctions under the Young Offenders Act." In R. Corrado, N. Bala, R. Linden and M. Leblanc (eds.), *Juvenile Justice in Canada.* Toronto: Butterworths.

Marshall, Katherine. 2000. "Part-Time By Choice." *Perspectives on Labour and Income.* (Catalogue no. 75-001-XIE) Ottawa: Statistics Canada.

Martens, Jens. 2005. *A Compendium of Inequality: The Human Development Report 2005.* Available at <www.globalpolicy.org/socecon/inequal/2005/10compendium.pdf>. (Accessed January 29, 2007.)

Martin, Diane. 2001. "Rescuing Kids, Cops Will Have the Right to Jail any Teen," *Xtra* November

15.

Martin-Matthews, Anne. 2001. *The Ties that Bind Aging Families*. Ottawa: Vanier Institute of the Family.

Marx, Karl. 1972a. *The Class Struggles in France*. 1850. Moscow: International.

_____. 1972b. "The Eighteenth Brumaire of Louis Bonaparte." 1852. In Robert Tucker (ed.), *The Marx–Engels Reader*. New York: Norton.

Marx, Karl, and Frederick Engels. 1952. *Manifesto of the Communist Party*. 1848. New York: International.

_____. 1970. *The German Ideology*. 1845. New York: International.

Matas, D. 1989. *Closing the Doors: The Failure of Refugee Protection*. Toronto: Summerhill.

May, Elizabeth. 1998. *At the Cutting Edge: The Crisis in Canada's Forests*. Toronto: Key Porter.

Maynard, Steven (1994) "What Colour Is Your Underwear? Class, Whiteness and Homoerotic Advertising." *Border/Lines* 32: 49.

Maytree Foundation. 2001. "Brief to the Senate Committee on Social Affairs, Science and Technology regarding Bill C-11, Immigration and Refugee Protection Act." Toronto, October, 2001. Available at <www.maytree.com/Publications&Resources/Publications /SenateBriefBillC11.htm>. (Accessed on June 14, 2006.)

McArthur, Doug. 1989. "The New Aboriginal Economic Development Institutions." In Paul Kariya (ed.), *Native Socio-Economic Development in Canada: Change, Promise and Innovation*. Toronto: Institute for Urban Studies.

McBride, Stephen. 1992. "Not Working: State, Unemployment, and Neo-Conservatism in Canada." In M. Watkins and L. Panitch (eds.), *The State and the Economic Life*. Toronto: University of Toronto Press.

McBride, Stephen, and John Shields. 1997. *Dismantling a Nation: The Transition to Corporate Rule in Canada*. Halifax: Fernwood Publishing.

McCallum, Tom. 2000. "Ontario Domestic Violence Courts Initiative." In V.P. Bunge and D. Locke (eds.), *Family Violence in Canada: A Statistical Profile 2000*. Ottawa: Statistics Canada.

McClintock, Anne (ed.). 1993. "Sex Workers and the Sex Trade Issue." *Social Text* 37.

McCuaig, Amanda. 2006. "Campus Fiasco: Campus Community Opposed to IBT Agreement." *The Peak* 22 (5) February 6.

McCutcheon, Sean. 1991. *Electric Rivers: The James Bay Project*. Montreal: Black Rose Books.

McDaniel, Susan A. 1985. "Abortion Policy in Great Britain and North America." *Atlantis: A Women's Studies Journal* 10, 2.

_____. 1990. "Towards Family Policy in Canada with Women in Mind." *Feminist Perspectives* 11. Ottawa: Canadian Research Institute for the Advancement of Women.

_____. 1992a. "Caring and Sharing: Demographic Aging, Family and the State." In Jon Hendricks and Carolyn Rosenthal (eds.), *The Remainder of Their Days: Impact of Public Policy and Older Families*. New York: Garland.

_____. 1992b. "Life Rhythms and Caring: Aging, Family and the State." 23rd Annual Sorokin Lecture. Saskatoon: University of Saskatchewan.

_____. 1995. "Families Function: Family Bridges from Past to Future." Occasional Paper Series. Paper no. 19. Vienna: United Nations.

_____. 1996. "Towards a Synthesis of Feminist and Demographic Perspectives on Fertility." *Sociological Quarterly* 37, 1.

_____. 1997a. "Caring and Sharing: Demographic Change and Shifting State Policies." In Monica Verea (ed.), *Women in North America at the End of the Millennium*. Mexico City: Universal

Naconal Antenoma de Mexico.

_____. 1997b. "Towards Healthy Families: Policy Implications." Paper no. 19. Ottawa: National Forum on Health.

_____. 1997c. "Serial Employment and Skinny Government: Reforming Caring and Sharing Among Generations." *Canadian Journal on Aging* 16, 3.

_____. 2002. "Women's Changing Relations to the State and Citizenship: Caring and Intergenerational Relations in Globalizing Western Democracies." *Canadian Review of Sociology and Anthropology* 39, 2.

_____. 2005. "The Family Lives of the Middle-Aged and Elderly in Canada." In Maureen Baker (ed.), *Families: Changing Trends in Canada*. Fifth edition. Toronto: McGraw-Hill Ryerson.

McDaniel, Susan A., and Ben Agger. 1982. *Social Problems Through Conflict and Order*. Toronto: Addison-Wesley.

McDaniel, Susan A., and Wendy Mitchinson. 1987. "Canadian Family Fictions and Realities: Past and Present." *New Quarterly* May.

McDaniel, Susan A., and Lorne Tepperman. 2002. *Close Relations: An Introduction to The Sociology of Families*. Toronto: Prentice Hall.

_____. 2006. *Close Relations: An Introduction to Sociology of Families*. Third edition. Don Mills, Ontario: Pearson.

McDonald, Lynn, and April Collins. 2000. *Abuse and Neglect of Older Adults: A Discussion Paper*. Ottawa: National Clearinghouse on Family Violence. Available at <www.phac-aspc. gc.ca/ncfv-cnivf/familyviolence/pdfs/Abuse%20and%20Neglect.pdf>. (Accessed on July 4, 2006.)

McElroy, Wendy. 2003. "Gender Issues Impacted by Masculinists." *The Independent Institute*. Available at <www.independent.org/tii/news/030603McElroy.html>. (Accessed on July 12, 2006.)

McFarlane, Judith, Pamela Willson, Ann Malecha, and Dorothy Lemmy. 2000. "Intimate Partner Violence: A Gender Comparison." *Journal of Interpersonal Violence* 15, 2.

McIlroy, Anne. 1998. "Child Custody, The Great Divide." *Globe and Mail* December 5.

McIntosh, Mary. 1978. "The State and the Oppression of Women." In Annette Kuhn and Anne Marie Wolpe (eds.), *Feminism and Materialism: Women and Modes of Production*. London: Routledge and Kegan Paul.

McKie, Linda, Sophia Bowlby, and Susan Gregory. 2001. "Gender, Caring and Employment in Great Britain." *Journal of Social Policy* 30, 2.

McLanahan, Sara, and Irwin Garfinkel. 1992. "Single Motherhood in the United States: Growth, Problems and Policies." Research and Policy Workshop on the Single Parent Family. March 18–21, Lake Louise, Alberta.

McLaughlin, Janice. 1999. "Gendering Occupational Identities and IT in the Retail Sector." *New Technology, Work, and Employment* 14, 2.

McMahon, Martha, and Ellen Pence. 2003. "Making Social Change: Reflections on Individual and Institutional Advocacy with Women Arrested for Domestic Violence." *Violence Against Women* 9.

McMillan, Alan. 1988. *Native Peoples and Cultures of Canada: An Anthropological Overview*. Vancouver: Douglas and McIntyre.

McMullan, J. 1992. *Beyond the Limits of the Law: Corporate Crime and Law and Order*. Halifax: Fernwood Publishing.

McMullan, J., and Stephen Smith. 1997. "Toxic Steel: State-Corporate Crime and the

Contamination of the Environment." In John McMullan et al, *Crimes, Laws and Communities.* Halifax: Fernwood Publishing.

McNally, David. 2002. *Another World is Possible: Globalization and Anti-Capitalism.* Winnipeg: Arbeiter Ring.

McNeely, R.L., and G. Robinson-Simpson. 1987. "The Truth About Domestic Violence: A Falsely Framed Issue." *Social Work* 32.

McNeill, John R. 2000. *Something New Under the Sun: An Environmental History of the Twentieth-Century World.* London: W.W. Norton.

McQuaig, L. 1998. "Grabbing the Bear by the Horns: The Global Economy is in Serious Meltdown." *This Magazine* 32, 3.

_____. 1999. "Globalization, Women and the Assault on Equality: What We Need is a Dose of Democratic Viagra." *Kinesis* (March).

Medcalf, Linda. 1978. *Law and Identity: Lawyers, Native Americans and Legal Practice.* Beverly Hills: Sage.

Meek, Chandra. 2001 "'Sustainability for Whom?'—Certification and Communities in the Boreal Region." Taiga Rescue Network. Available at <www.taigarescue.org/en//index.php?sub=2&cat=65>. (Accessed January 29, 2007.)

Mellström, Ulf. 2003. *Masculinity, Power and Technology: A Malaysian Ethnography.* Aldershot, UK: Ashgate.

Mensah, Joseph. 1982. *Situation Report on the State of Race Relations in Halifax.* Ottawa: Secretary of State.

Menzies, Heather. 1996. *Whose Brave New World? The Information Highway and the New Economy.* Toronto: Between the Lines.

_____. 1997. "Telework, Shadow Work: The Privatization of Work in the New Digital Economy." *Studies in Political Economy* 53.

_____. 2005. *No Time: Stress and the Crisis of Modern Life.* Vancouver: Douglas & McIntyre.

Mercer, Kobena, and Isaac Julien. 1988. "Race, Sexual Politics and Black Masculinity." In Rowena Chapman and Jonathan Rutherford (eds.), *Male Order: Unwrapping Masculinity.* London: Lawrence and Wishart.

Merriam, Charles E. 1964. *Political Power.* New York: Free.

Messer, Ellen, and Kathryn May. 1988. *Back Rooms: Voices from the Illegal Abortion Era.* New York: St. Martin's.

Messerschmidt, James W. 1993. *Masculinities and Crime.* Boston: Rowman and Littlefield.

_____. 1997. *Crime as Structured Action.* Thousand Oaks, CA: Sage.

_____. 2000. "Becoming 'Real Men': Adolescent Masculinity Challenges and Sexual Violence." *Men and Masculinities* 2, 3.

Messner, Michael A. 1998. "The Limits of 'The Male Sex Role': An Analysis of the Men's Liberation and Men's Rights Movements' Discourse." *Gender & Society* 12.

Meyer, J. 1996. "The Changing Cultural Content of the Nation State." In G. Steinmetz (ed.), *New Approaches to the State in the Social Sciences.* Ithaca: Cornell University Press.

Micheletti, Michele, and Dietlind Stolle. 2005. "The Market as an Arena for Transnational Politics." Available at <ya.ssrc.org/transnational/Micheletti_Stolle/> (Accessed: 30 January 2007.)

Mihorean, Karen. 2005. "Trends in Self-Reported Spousal Violence." In K. AuCoin (ed.), *Family Violence in Canada: A Statistical Profile 2005.* Ottawa: Canadian Centre for Justice Statistics. Available at <www.statcan.ca/english/freepub/85-224-XIE/85-224-XIE2005000.pdf>. (Accessed on July 4, 2006.)

_____. 2006. "Factors Related to Reporting Spousal Violence to Police." In L. Ogrodnik (ed.), *Family Violence in Canada: A Statistical Profile 2006*. Ottawa: Canadian Centre for Justice Statistics. Available at <www.phac-aspc.gc.ca/ncfv-cnivf/familyviolence/pdfs/85-224-XIE2006000.pdf>. (Accessed on July 4, 2006.)

Milan, Anne. 2005. "Willing to Participate: Political Engagement of Young Adults." *Canadian Social Trends* Ottawa: Statistics Canada (Catalogue No. 11–008, Winter).

Miles, Robert. 1989. *Racism*. London: Routledge.

Miles, Robert, and John Solomos. 1987. "Migration and the State in Britain: A Historical Overview." In C. Husband (ed.), *Race in Britain: Continuity and Change*. London: Hutchinson.

Miliband, Ralph. 1973a. "Poulantzas and the Capitalist State." *New Left Review* 82 (November/December).

_____. 1973b. *The State in Capitalist Society*. London: Quartet.

_____. 1977. *Marxism and Politics*. Oxford: Oxford University Press.

Millar, Melanie Stewart. 1998. *Cracking the Gender Code: Who Rules the Wired World?* Toronto: Second Story Press.

Miller, Daniel. 2003. "Living with New (Ideals of) Technology." In Christina Garsen and Helena Wulff (eds.), *New Technologies at Work: People, Screens and Social Virtuality*. Oxford: Berg.

Miller, J. 2005. "African Immigrant Damnation Syndrome: The Case of Charles Ssenyonga." *Sexuality Research & Social Policy: Journal of NSERC* 2, 2: 31–50.

Miller, J.R. 1989. *Skyscrapers Hide the Heavens: A History of Indian–White Relations in Canada*. Toronto: University of Toronto Press.

_____. 1991. "Owen Glendower, Hotspur and Canadian Policy." In J.R. Miller (ed.), *Sweet Promises: A Reader on Indian–White Relations in Canada*. Toronto: University of Toronto Press.

Miller, Jody. 2001. *One Of The Guys: Girls, Gangs, and Gender*. New York: Oxford University Press.

Miller, S., and S. Sharif. 1995. "Domestic Violence — The Way Men's Advocate's See It." *Family Guardian Journal* 2.

Miller, Susan L., Carol Gregory, and Lee Ann Iovanni. 2005. "One Size Fits All? A Gender-Neutral Approach to a Gender-Specific Problem: Contrasting Batterer Treatment Programs for Male and Female Offenders." *Criminal Justice Policy Review* 16.

Miller, Susan L., and Michelle L. Meloy. 2006. "Women's Use of Force: Voices of Women Arrested for Domestic Violence." *Violence Against Women* 12.

Milloy, John S. 1983. "The Early Indian Acts: Development Strategy and Constitutional Change." In Ian Getty and Antoine Lussier (eds.), *As Long as the Sun Shines and Water Flows*. Vancouver: University of British Columbia Press.

Mills, C. Wright. 1959. *The Sociological Imagination*. New York: Oxford University Press.

Mimoto, H., and P. Cross. 1991. "The Growth of the Federal Debt." *Canadian Economic Observer* June.

Mining Watch Canada and The Sierra Club of Canada. 2001. *TOXICanada: 13 Good Reasons to Establish a Clean Canada Fund*. Available at <www.sierraclub.ca/national/postings/toxi-canada-july-2001.pdf>. (Access on September 20, 2006.)

Mintzberg, Henry. 1989. *Mintzberg on Management*. New York: Free Press.

Mitchell, Bruce, and Dianne Draper. 2001. "Environmental Justice Considerations in Canada." *Canadian Geographer* 45, 1.

Modleski, Tania. 1984. "Time and Desire in the Woman's Film." *Cinema Journal* 23, 3.

Moffitt, Terrie E., Richard W. Robins, and Avshalom Caspi. 2001. "A Couples Analysis of Partner Abuse With Implications for Abuse-Prevention Policy." *Criminology and Public Policy* 1, 1.

Mohai, Paul. 1990. "Black Environmentalism." *Social Science Quarterly* 71.

Monahan, Patrick. 1987. *Politics and the Constitution: The Charter, Federalism and the Supreme Court of Canada.* Toronto: Carswell.

Monbiot, G. 2001. "How to Rule the World: Rich G-8 Nations Should be Displaced by Global Democracy." *CCPA Monitor* 8, 5.

Monsanto Imagine. *Biotech Knowledge Centre.* Available at <www.biotechknowledge.monsanto. com/>. (Accessed November 1, 2006.)

Montagu, Ashley. 1972. *Statement on Race.* London: Oxford University Press.

Montaigne, Fen. 2002. "Great Northern Forest." *National Geographic* June.

Monture-Angus, Patricia. 2000. "Aboriginal Women and Correctional Practice: Reflections on the Task Force on Federally Sentenced Women." In Kelly Hannah-Moffat and Margaret Shaw (ed.), *An Ideal Prison? Critical Essays on Women's Imprisonment in Canada.* Halifax: Fernwood Publishing.

Moodley, Kogila. 1983. "Canadian Multiculturalism as Ideology." *Ethnic and Racial Studies* 6, 3.

Morin, Sky Blue. 1999. Federally Sentenced Women in Maximum Security: What Happened to the Promises of "Creating Choices"? Ottawa: Correctional Service of Canada. Available at <www.csc-scc.gc.ca/text/prgrm/fsw/skyblue/toce_e.shtml>. (Accessed January 29, 2007.)

Morris, Marika. 2001. *Gender-Sensitive Home and Community Care and Caregiving Research: A Synthesis Paper.* Ottawa: Women's Health Bureau, Health Canada.

Morrison, Daniel. 2006. "Intercontinental Youth Camp 2001–2005: Linking Open Space Activism, the World Social Forum, and Imaginaries for Alternative Worlds." Unpublished M.A. thesis, International Development Studies, Dalhousie University, Halifax, Nova Scotia. Also available from NIGD News and Notes, "The WSF and Political Agency," Issue 08/06. Available at <www.nigd.org/nan/archived-news-and-notes/the-wsf-and-political-agency>. (Accessed November 13, 2006.)

Morrison, J., and B. Crosland. 2001. "The Trafficking and Smuggling of Refugees: The End Game of European Asylum Policy?" *Independent Expert Report/UNHCR Working Paper* 38. Available at <www.unhcr.org/cgi-bin/texis/vtx/doclist?page=research&id=3bbc18ed5>. (Accessed on September 28, 2006.)

Morrow, Marina, Olena Hankivsky, and Colleen Varcoe. 2004. "Women and Violence: The Effects of Dismantling the Welfare State." *Critical Social Policy* 24.

Morse, Barbara J. 1995. "Beyond the Conflict Tactics Scale: Assessing Gender Differences in Partner Violence." *Violence and Victims* 10, 4.

Mosher, Janet. 2000. "Welfare Reform: Exposing the Veneer of the State's Concern for Abused Women." In Sheila Neysmith (ed.), *Restructuring Caring Labour: Discourse, State Practice and Everyday Life.* Toronto: Oxford University Press.

_____. Forthcoming. "Welfare Fraudsters and Tax Evaders: The State's Selective Invocation of Criminality." In C. Brooks and B. Schissel (eds.), *Marginality and Condemnation.* Second edition. Black Point, NS: Fernwood Publishing.

Mouffe, Chantal. 1997. *The Return of the Political.* London: Verso.

Mulvey, Laura. 1975. "Visual Pleasure and Narrative Cinema." *Screen* 16, 3.

Murphy, C. 1994. *International Organization and Industrial Change: Global Governance Since 1850.*

New York: Oxford.

Murphy, Raymond. 2002, "The Internalisation of Autonomous Nature into Society." *The Sociological Review* 50.

Mykhalovskiy, Eric, Liza McCoy, Eric Bresalier. 2004. "Compliance/Adherence HIV/AIDS and the Critique of Medical Power." *Critical Public Health* 12, 1.

Mykhalovskiy, Eric, and George Smith. 1994. *Hooking Up to Social Services: A Report on the Barriers People Living With HIV/AIDS Face Accessing Social Services*. Toronto: Community AIDS Treatment Information Exchange/Ontario Institute for Studies in Education.

Myles, John, G. Picot, and T. Wannell. 1988. "Wages and Jobs in the 1980s: Changing Youth Wages and the Declining Middle." Research paper no. 17. Ottawa: Statistics Canada.

Myles, John, and Paul Pierson. 1997. "Friedman's Revenge: The Reform of 'Liberal' Welfare States in Canada and the United States." *Politics and Society* 25, 4.

Nadeau, Mary-Jo. 2002–03. "Towards 'a Peaceful Solution': NAC and the Politics of Engagement." *Canadian Woman Studies/les Cahiers de la Femme* 22, 2 (Fall–Winter): 48–55.

Nadeau, Solange. 2006. "Mill Closures and Curtailments in the Canadian Forest Industry Since January 2003." Unpublished Report. Canadian Forest Service. Ottawa: Natural Resources Canada, Ottawa.

Naimark, Arnold. 2004. "Universities and Industry in Canada: An Evolving Relationship." In Paul Axelrod (ed.), *Knowledge Matters: Essays In Honour of Bernard J. Shapiro*. Montreal and Kingston: McGill-Queen's University Press.

Namaste, Viviane. 2000. *Invisible Lives: The Erasure of Transsexual and Transgendered People*. Chicago: University of Chicago Press.

Nash, J., and M. Fernandez-Kelly (eds.). 1983. *Women, Men and the International Division of Labour*. Albany: SUNY Press.

Nash, Madeleine. 2001. "Grains of Hope." In Robert M. Jackson (ed.), *Annual Editions Global Issues 1/2*. Guilford, Connecticut: McGraw-Hill/Dushkin.

National Action Committee on the Status of Women (NAC). 1988. *Smoke and Mirrors? Or a National Child Care Strategy?* Ottawa: NAC.

National Association of Women and the Law (NAWL). 1989. "A Response to Crimes Against the Foetus." The Law Reform Commission of Canada's Working Paper No. 58. Ottawa: NAWL Working Group on Health and Reproductive Issues

_____. 2001. "Brief on the Proposed Immigration and Refugee Protection Act (Bill C-11)." Available at <www.nawl.ca/ns/en/publications.html>. (Accessed on June 15, 2006.)

_____. 2006. "Update: Immigration and Refugee Protection Act and Women." Available at <www.nawl.ca/ns/en/is-irl.html#update>. (Accessed on June 14, 2006.)

National Clearinghouse on Family Violence. 2004a. *Transition Houses and Shelters for Abused Women in Canada*. Ottawa: National Clearinghouse on Family Violence. Available at <www.phac-aspc.gc.ca/ncfv-cnivf/familyviolence/pdfs/2004Women_e.pdf>. (Accessed on July 12, 2006.)

_____. 2004b. *Directory of Services and Programs for Abused Men in Canada*. Ottawa: Health Canada. Available at <www.phac-aspc.gc.ca/ncfv-cnivf/familyviolence/pdfs/2004abusmn_e.pdf>. (Accessed on July 12, 2006.)

_____. 2004c. *Directory of Services and Programs Addressing the Needs of Older Adult Victims of Violence in Canada*. Ottawa: National Clearinghouse for Family Violence. Available at <http://www.phac-aspc.gc.ca/ncfv-cnivf/familyviolence/pdfs/2004Seniors_e.pdf>. (Accessed on July 12, 2006.)

National Council of Welfare (NCW). 1975. *Poor Kids: A Report By The National Council of Welfare on Children in Poverty in Canada.* Ottawa: National Council of Welfare.

_____. 1987. *Progress Against Poverty.* Revised Edition. Ottawa: National Council of Welfare.

_____. 1996. *Poverty Profile 1995.* Ottawa: National Council of Welfare.

_____. 1997. *Child Benefits: A Small Step Forward.* Ottawa: National Council of Welfare.

_____. 1998. *Poverty Profile 1996.* Ottawa: National Council of Welfare.

_____. 1998/99. "A New Poverty Line: Yes, No or Maybe?" A Discussion Paper from the National Council of Welfare. Winter. Ottawa: National Council of Welfare.

_____. 1999. *Poverty Profile 1997.* Ottawa: National Council of Welfare.

_____. 2000. *Poverty Profile 1998.* Ottawa: National Council of Welfare.

_____. 2006. *Poverty Profile 2002 and 2003.* Ottawa: National Council of Welfare.

National Forum on Health. 1997. "Canada Health Action: Building on the Legacy, Volume I. The Final Report of the National Forum on Health." Ottawa: Department of Public Works and Government Services.

National Post. 2005. "$1.5 M in AD Fraud, No Jail: Sponsorship Scandals' Coffin Sentenced to Speak on Ethics." September 20, 1.

National Union of Provincial and General Employees. 1997. "Medical Lab Services: Private vs. Public Delivery Systems." Nepean, ON: National Union of Provincial and General Employees, May.

Natural Resources Canada. 2003. "National Forest Strategy 2003-2008: A Sustainable Forest-The Canadian Commitment." Available at <nfsc.forest.ca/strategies/strategy5.html> (Accessed January 30, 2007

_____. 2001. "Profiles Across a Nation" Available at <http://www.nrcan.gc.ca/cfs-scf/national/what-quoi/sof/sof01/profiles_e.html>. (Accessed January 29, 2007.)

Nayer, Baldev R. 2003. "Economic Globalization and Its Advance: From Shallow to Deep Integration." *Economic Political Weekly* November 8.

Neale, Jonathan. 2001. "You Are the G8, We Are the 6 Billion." *Leftturn* September.

_____. 2002. *You Are G8, We Are 6 Billion: The Truth Behind the Genoa Protests.* London: Fusion Press.

Neidig, Peter H., and Dale H. Friedman. 1985. *Spouse Abuse: A Treatment Program for Couples.* Champaign: Research Press Company.

Neis, Barbara, and Lawrence Felt. 2000. *Finding Our Sea Legs: Linking Fishery People and Their Knowledge with Science and Management.* St. John's, NF: Institute for Social and Economic Research Books.

Nelson, Adie. 2006. *Gender in Canada.* Toronto: Pearson

Nelson, Adie, and Barrie Robinson. 2002. *Gender in Canada.* Second edition. Toronto: Prentice-Hall.

Nelson, E., and A. Fleras. 1995. *Canadian Social Problems.* Englewood Cliffs, NJ: Prentice Hall.

Nett, Emily. 1981. "Canadian Families in Socio-Historical Perspective." *Canadian Journal of Sociology* 6, 3.

Neu, Dean, and Duncan Green. 2005. *Truth or Profit: The Business Ethics of Public Accounting.* Black Point, NS: Fernwood Publishing.

Newhouse, David R. 1993. "Modern Aboriginal Economies: Capitalism with an Aboriginal Face." In Royal Commission on Aboriginal Peoples, Sharing the Harvest: The Road to Self Reliance. Ottawa: Supply and Services.

Newson, Janice. 1992. "The Decline of Faculty Influence: Confronting the Effects of the

Corporate Agenda." In William Carroll et al. (eds.), *Fragile Truths: 25 Years of Sociology and Anthropology in Canada*. Ottawa: Carleton University Press.

_____. 2005. "The University on the Ground: Reflections on Canadian Experience". Paper presented at CEDESP Conference on the Impact of Research on Public Policy on Higher Education, Rincon, Puerto Rico, June 2–3.

Newson, Janice, and Howard Buchbinder. 1988. *The University Means Business*. Toronto: Garamond Press.

Newson, Janice, and Claire Polster. 2001. "Reclaiming Our Centre: Towards a Robust Defense of Academic Autonomy." *Science Studies* 14, 1.

Ng, Roxana. 1995. "Multiculturalism as Ideology: A Textual Analysis." In Marie Campbell and Ann Manicom (eds.), *Knowledge, Experience and Ruling Relations*. Toronto: University of Toronto Press.

_____. 1988. *The Politics of Community Services*. Toronto: Garamond.

_____. 1989. "Sexism, Racism and Canadian Nationalism." In J. Vorst et al. (eds.), *Race, Class, Gender: Bonds and Barriers*. Toronto: Between the Lines.

Ng, Roxanna, and Alma Estable. 1987. "Immigrant Women in the Labour Force: An Overview of Present Knowledge and Research Gaps." *Resources for Feminist Research* 16, 1.

Nicol, Nancy. 1994. *Gay Pride and Prejudice*. Video. (?how to get it?)

Noble, David. 1995. *Progress Without People: New Technology, Unemployment, and the Message of Resistance*. Toronto: Between the Lines Press.

Nolan, K. 2000. "Engendering Globalization: What Are the Impacts on Women?" *Chain Reaction* Autumn.

Noorani, A., and C. Wright. 1995. "They Believed the Hype: The Liberals Were Elected as 'the Friend of the Immigrant': A Year Later, They're Fanning the Flames of Crime Hysteria with their New Pals, the Tabloids and Preston Manning." *This Magazine* 28 (December/January).

Nordlinger, Eric. 1981. *On the Autonomy of the Democratic State*. Cambridge, MA: Harvard University Press.

NRTEE (National Roundtable on the Environment and the Economy). 2002. *Aboriginal Communities and Non-Renewable Resource Development*. Ottawa: Government of Canada. Available at <www.nrtee-trnee.ca/eng/Publications/HTML/SOD_Aboriginal_E.htm>. (Accessed on January 14, 2003.)

Nunes, Rodrigo. 2005. "The Intercontinental Youth Camp as the Unthought of the World Social Forum." *Ephemera: Theory and Politics in Organization* 5, 2: 277–96.

Nungessar, Lon G. 1983. *Homosexual Acts, Actors and Identities*. New York: Praeger.

O'Brien, Mary. 1981. *The Politics of Reproduction*. London: Routledge and Kegan Paul.

O'Brien, Susie, and Imre Szeman. 2004. *Popular Culture, A User's Guide*. Scarborough: Thomson/Nelson.

O'Brien-Pallas, Linda, Andrea Baumann, and Jacquelyn Lochhass-Gerlach. 1998. "Health Human Resources: A Preliminary Analysis of Nursing Personnel in Ontario." Toronto: Nursing Effectiveness, Utilization and Outcomes Research Unit.

O'Connor, James. 1974. *The Fiscal Crisis of the State*. New York: St. Martin's.

_____. 1994. "Is Sustainable Capitalism Possible?" In Martin O'Connor (ed.), *Is Capitalism Sustainable? Political Economy and the Politics of Ecology*. New York: Guilford.

_____. 1998. *Natural Causes: Essays in Ecological Marxism*. New York: Guilford.

O'Connor, Julia, and Gregg Olsen. 1998. "Understanding the Welfare State: Power Resource

Theory and Its Critics." In Julia O'Connor and Gregg Olsen (eds.), *Power Resource Theory and the Welfare State: A Critical Approach.* Toronto: University of Toronto Press.

O'Connor, Julia S., Ann Shola Orloff, and Sheila Shaver. 1999. *States, Markets, Families: Gender, Liberalism and Social Policy in Australia, Canada, Great Britain and the United States.* Cambridge: Cambridge University Press.

O'Leary, K.D., Jean Malone, and Andrea Tyree. 1994. "Physical Aggression in Early Marriage: Prerelationship and Relationship Effects." *Journal of Consulting and Clinical Psychology* 62, 3.

_____. 1996. "Physical Aggression in Intimate Relations Can Be Treated Within a Marital Context Under Certain Circumstances." *Journal of Interpersonal Violence* 11, 3.

O'Malley, Martin, and Owen Wood. 2001. "The Supreme Court and Child Porn: Saving Children or Thought Control?" CBC On Line News. Updated May, 2002.

O'Neill, Brenda. 2001. "Generational Patterns in the Political Opinions and Behaviour of Canadians: Separating the Wheat from the Chaff." *Policy Matters* 2, 5.

_____. 2004. "Youth Participation — What we Know and What we Don't Know." In *Canadian Democracy: Bringing Youth Back Into the Political Process.* The CRIC papers. Montreal: Centre for Research and Information on Canada.

O'Rand, Angela, and John Henretta. 1999. "Asynchronous Lives: The Normal Life Course and Its Variations." In Angela O'Rand and John Henretta (eds.), *Age and Inequality: Diverse Pathways Through Later Life.* Boulder, CO: Westview.

Offe, Claus. 1996. *Modernity and the State, East, West.* Cambridge, MA: MIT Press.

Office of Food Additive Safety (OFAS), Center for Food Safety and Applied Nutrition, U.S. Food and Drug Administration. 2005. "List of Completed Consultations on Bioengineered Foods" Available at <http://vm.cfsan.fda.gov/~lrd/biocon.html>. (Accessed January 29, 2007.)

Office of the Registrar of Lobbyists. 2006. "*Lobbyists Registration Act* Annual Report 2005–2006." Available at <www.orl-bdl.gc.ca/epic/internet/inlobbyist-lobbyiste.nsf/en/nx00147e. html#Anchor-Registrations-54980>. (Accessed October 30, 2006.)

Ogrodnik, Lucie. 2006. "Spousal Violence and Repeat Police Contact." In L. Ogrodnik (ed.), *Family Violence in Canada: A Statistical Profile 2006.* Ottawa: Canadian Centre for Justice Statistics. Available at <www.phac-aspc.gc.ca/ncfv-cnivf/familyviolence/pdfs/85-224-XIE2006000.pdf>. (Accessed on July 4, 2006.)

Olah, Livia Sz. 2001. "Policy Changes and Family Stability: The Swedish Case." *International Journal of Law, Policy and the Family* 15.

Oliveira, Romualdo Paz de. 2005. "Constructing the Intercontinental Youth Camp." In Steffen Bohm, Sien Sullivan, and Oscar Reyes (eds.). *Ephemera: Theory & Politics in Organization. Organisation and Politics of Social Forums* 5, 2 (May). Available at <www.ephemeraweb.org/journal/5-2/5-2pazdeoliveira.pdf>. (Accessed January 29, 2007.)

Ontario. 1998. *Public Hospitals Act.* Revised statutes of Ontario, 1990, Chapter P.40, as amended to 1997, 30 September 1998, sections 21 and 22.

Ontario. 1999. "Good Nursing, Good Health: An Investment in the 21st Century." Report of the Nursing Task Force. Toronto: Ontario Ministry of Health.

Ontario Public Service Employees' Union. 1998. "The Big Chill." *Our Ontario* October.

Orchard, Jeff, and Christine Famula. 1992. *Cut to the Bone II: System Failure.* Toronto: Ontario Federation of Students.

Orton, David. 1998. "Environmental Hearings and Existential Dilemmas: The Sable Gas Project." *Green Web Bulletin* 62. [Originally published as "Hearings Not for Sale: The Sable Gas

Project." *Links Magazine* 10, 3].

Osborne, David, and Ted Gaebler. 1993. *Reinventing Government: How the Entrepreneurial Spirit Is Transforming the Public Sector.* New York: Penguin.

Osterweil, Michal. 2004. "De-Centering the Forum: Is Another Critique of the Forum Possible." In Anita Anand, Arturo Escobar, Jai Sen, and Peter Waterman, (eds.), *The World Social Forum: Challenging Empires.* New Delhi: Viveka Foundation.

Osthoff, Sue. 2002. "But, Gertrude, I Beg to Differ, a Hit is Not a Hit is Not a Hit: When Battered Women are Arrested for Assaulting Their Partners." *Violence Against Women* 18.

Oxman-Martinez, J. Hanley, and L. Cheung. 2004. "Another Look at the Live-in Caregivers Program." Metropolis Research Report No. 24. Available at <im.metropolis.net/research-policy/research_content/doc/oxman-marinez%20LCP.pdf>. (Accessed on September 8, 2006.)

Padova, Allison. 2005. *Federal Commercialization in Canada.* Ottawa: Library of Parliament, Parliamentary information and Research Service, Economics Division.

Palmer, Craig, and Peter Sinclair. 1997. *When the Fish Are Gone: Ecological Disaster and Fishers in Northwest Newfoundland.* Halifax: Fernwood Publishing.

Palmer, D. 1996. "Determinants of Canadian Attitudes Toward Immigration: More Than Just Racism?" *Canadian Journal of Behavioural Science* 28.

Pancer, S. Mark, and Michael W. Pratt. 1999. "Social and Family Determinants of Community Service Involvement in Canadian Youth." In Miranda Yates and James Youniss (eds.), *Roots of Civic Identity: International Perspectives on Community Service and Activism in Youth.* Cambridge: Cambridge University Press.

Pappajohn v. The Queen. 1980. 52 Canadian Criminal Cases. Second edition. (481–515).

Parkins, John. 1999. "Contributions of Sociology to Forest Management and Policy Development." *Forestry Chronicle* 75, 4.

_____. 2006. Personal Communication. Canadian Forest Service.

Parkins, John, Rich Stedman, and Bonnie McFarlane. 2001. "Public Involvement in Forest Management and Planning: A Comparative Analysis of Attitudes and Preferences in Alberta." Information Report NOR-X-382. Edmonton, AB: Northern Forestry Centre, Canadian Forest Service.

Parkins, John, Jeji Varghese, and Richard Stedman. 2001. "Locally Defined Indicators of Community Sustainability in the Prince Albert Model Forest." Information Report NOR-X-379. Edmonton, AB: Northern Forestry Centre.

Parnell, Ted. 1976. "The Process of Economic Underdevelopment." In Ted Parnell (ed.), *Disposable Native.* Edmonton: Alberta Human Rights and Civil Liberties Association.

Parr, Joy. 1990. *The Gender of Breadwinners: Women, Men and Change in Two Industrial Towns, 1880–1950.* Toronto: University of Toronto Press.

_____. 1998. "Shopping for a Good Stove: A Parable about Gender, Design, and the Market." In Roger Horowitz and Arwen Mohun (eds.), *His and Hers: Gender, Consumption and Technology.* Charlottesville: University Press of Virginia.

Parrish, Geov. 2001. "Imagine." In Eddie Yuen, George Katsiaficas, and Daniel Burton Rose (eds.), *The Battle of Seattle: The New Challenge to Capitalist Globalization.* New York: Soft Skull Press.

Parsons, Eileen Carlton. 1998. "Black High School Females' Images of the Scientist: Expression of Culture." *Journal of Research in Science Teaching* 34, 7 (December).

Patano, Sandra, and Anders Sandberg, 2005. "Winning Back More Than Words: Power, Discourse and Quarrying on the Niagara Escarpment." *The Canadian Geographer* 49, 1.

Pateman, Carole. 1989. *The Disorder of Women*. Stanford, CA: Stanford University Press.

Patterson, Julienne. 2003. "Spousal Violence." In H. Johnson and K. AuCoin (eds.), *Family Violence in Canada: A Statistical Profile 2003*. Ottawa: Canadian Centre for Justice Statistics. Available at <www.statcan.ca/english/freepub/85-224-XIE/85-224-XIE03000.pdf>. (Accessed on July 4, 2006.)

Patton, Cindy. 1986. *Sex and Germs: The Politics of AIDS*. Montreal: Black Rose.

_____. 1990. *Inventing AIDS*. New York: Routledge.

_____. 1996. *Fatal Advice: How Safe Sex Education Went Wrong*. Durham: Duke University Press.

Pavelich, Greg, 1999. "The Bijou Raid: The Battle for Queer Space." *New Socialist* 4, 5.

Pearson, R. 1992. "Gender Issues in Industrialization." In Tom Hewitt, Hazel Johnson, and David Weild (eds.), *Industrialization and Development*. Oxford: Oxford University Press.

Pembina Institute, 2005. "Assessment by Canadian environmental leaders of the government's Kyoto implementation plan." Available at <www.pembina.org/pdf/publications/Kyoto20050413_Kyoto_Assessment_ENGO.pdf>. (Accessed on September 25, 2006.)

Pembroke Civic Hospital and Lowe v. Health Services Restructuring Commission. 1997. Ontario Divisional Court, 394/97. June 25.

Penner, Keith. 1983. "Minutes of Proceedings and Evidence." Report of the Special Committee on Indian Self-Government in Canada 40 (October 12, 20). Ottawa: House of Common Standing Committee on Indian Affairs and Northern Development.

Perelle, Robin. 2002. "No Danger to the Public, Sharpe Sentenced for Actions, not Beliefs." *Capital Xtra!* 106, June.

Persky, Stan, and John Dixon. 2001. *On Kiddie Porn, Sexual Representation, Free Speech and the Robin Thorpe Case*. Vancouver: New Star.

Perspectives on Labour and Income. 2005. "Unionization." *Perspectives on Labour and Income* 17, 3 (Autumn).

Petchesky, Rosalind Pollack. 1985. *Abortion and Woman's Choice: The State, Sexuality and Reproductive Freedom*. Boston: Northeastern University Press.

Peters, Suzanne. 1997. "Feminist Strategies for Policy and Research: The Economic and Social Dynamics of Families." In Meg Luxton (ed.), *Feminism and Families: Critical Policies and Changing Practices*. Halifax: Fernwood Publishing.

Peterson, David L., Allen Wood, and Julia Gardner. 2005. *An Assessment of Fisheries and Oceans Canada Pacific Region's Effectiveness in Meeting its Conservation Mandate*. Vancouver: David Suzuki Foundation. Available at <www.davidsuzuki.org/files/oceans/publications.aspf>. (Accessed January 29, 2007.)

Petras, James, and Henry Veltmeyer. 2001. *Globalization Unmasked: Imperialism in the 21st Century*. Black Point, NS: Fernwood Publishing.

_____. 2005. *Empire With Imperialism: The Globalizing Dynamics of Neo-Liberal Capitalism*. Black Point, NS: Fernwood Publishing.

Pettman, Jan J. 1996. "An International Political Economy of Sex." In E. Kofman and G. Youngs (eds.), *Globalization: Theory and Practice*. London: Printer.

Petty, Mary. 2005. "Social Responses to HIV: Fearing the outlaw." *Sexuality Research and Social Policy: Journal of NSRC* 2, 2: 76–88.

Pfohl, Stephen J. 1985. *Images of Deviance and Social Control: A Sociological History*. New York: McGraw.

Pilcher, Jane. 2000. "Domestic Divisions of Labour in the Twentieth Century: 'Change Slow A-Coming.'" *Work, Employment and Society* 14, 4.

Pitsula, James. 2006. *As One Who Serves*. Montreal and Kingston: McGill-Queen's University Press.

Pitts, Gordon. 2006. "The Growing Child Care Debate." *Globe and Mail* June 13: B1, B3.

Pocklington, Tom, and Allan Tupper. 2002. *No Place to Learn: Why Universities Aren't Working*. Vancouver: UBC Press.

Poirier, Lesley. 1998. "Spare 28 Hours a Week? Caregiving Still in Women's Job Description." *Canadian Women's Health Network* 1, 3. Available at <www.cwhn.ca/network-researu/1-3/spare.html>. (Accessed December 27, 2001.)

Polet, F. 2001. "Some Key Statistics." In F. Houtart and F. Polet (eds.), *The Other Davos: Globalization of Resistance to the World Economic System*. London: Zed Books.

Pollack, Shoshana, Melanie Battaglia, and Anke Allspach. 2005. *Women Charged with Domestic Violence in Toronto: The Unintended Consequences of Mandatory Charge Policies*. Toronto: Women Abuse Council of Toronto. Available at <www.womanabuse.ca/womenchargedfinal.pdf>. (Accessed on July 12, 2006.)

Polster, Claire. 1994. *Compromising Positions: The Federal Government and the Reorganization of the Social Relations of Canadian Academic Research*. Unpublished doctoral dissertation. Toronto: York University.

_____. 2000. "Shifting Gears: Rethinking Academics' Response to the Corporatization of the University." *Journal of Curriculum Theorizing* 16, 2.

_____. Forthcoming. "The Nature and Implications of the Growing Importance of Research Grants to Canadian Universities and Academics." *Higher Education*.

Postman, Neil. 1982. *The Disappearance of Childhood*. New York: Dell.

_____. 1999. *Building a Bridge to the 18th Century*. New York: Alfred Knopf.

Poulantzas, Nicos. 1972. "The Problem of the Capitalist State." In Robin Blackburn (ed.), *Ideology in Social Science*. Glasgow: Fontana Collins.

_____. 1973. *Political Power and Social Classes*. London: New Left.

_____. 1976. "The Capitalist State: A Reply to Miliband and Laclau." *New Left Review* 95 (January/February).

Powderface, Sykes. 1984. "Self-Government Means Biting the Hand that Feeds Us." In Leroy Little Bear, Menno Boldt, and J. Anthony Long (eds.), *Pathways to Self-Determination: Canadian Indians and the Canadian State*. Toronto: University of Toronto Press.

Prairie Research Associates. 1994. *Manitoba Spouse Abuse Tracking Project Final Report Volume 1*. Winnipeg: Manitoba Research and Statistics Directorate.

Pratt, Larry, and Ian Urquhart. 1994. *The Last Great Forest*. Edmonton: NeWest.

Press, Eyal, and Jennifer Washburn. 2000. "The Kept University." *Atlantic Monthly* 285, 3.

Priest, Alicia. 2006. *What's Ailing Nurses? A Discussion of the Major Issues Affecting Nursing Human Resources In Canada*. Ottawa: Canadian Health Services Research Foundation.

Pringle, Rosemary. 1997. "Feminist Theory and the World of the Social." *Current Sociology* 45, 2.

Prokosch, Mike, and Laura Raymond. 2002. *The Global Activist's Manual: Local Ways to Change the World*. New York: Thunder's Mouth Press.

Public Safety and Emergency Preparedness Canada. 2004. "Securing Canada: Laying the Groundwork for Canada's First National Security Policy." Available at <www.psepc-sppcc.gc.ca/national_security/publications_e.asp>. (Accessed on June 13, 2006.)

Pulkingham, Jane, and Gordon Ternowetsky. 1999. "Neoliberalism and Retrenchment: Employment, Universality, Safety-Net Provisions and a Collapsing Canadian Welfare State." In Dave Broad and Wayne Antony (eds.), *Citizens or Consumers? Social Policy in a Market Society*. Halifax: Fernwood Publishing.

Pupo, Norene. 1988. "Preserving Patriarchy: Women, the Family and the State." In Nancy Mandell and Ann Duffy (eds.), *Reconstructing the Canadian Family: Feminist Perspectives*. Toronto: Butterworths.

Quéniart, Anne, and Julie Jacques. 2004. "Political Involvement Among Young Women: A Qualitative Analysis." *Citizenship Studies* 8, 2 (June).

R. v. Gladue. 1999. Supreme Court Reports 688.

R. v. Morgan and others. 1975. All England Law Reports. 1: 8–15.

R. v. Sparrow. 1990. 4 Western Weekly Reports 410 (Supreme Court of Canada).

R. v. Sullivan and Lemay. 1991. 1 Supreme Court Reports 489.

Radway, Janice. 1984. *Reading the Romance: Women, Patriarchy, and Popular Culture*. Chapel Hill: University of North Carolina Press.

Randall, Stephen J., et al. (eds.). 1992. *North America Without Borders?* Calgary: University of Calgary Press.

Ranson, Gillian. 2006. "Paid and Unpaid Work: How Do Families Divide Their Labour?" In Maureen Baker (ed.), *Families: Changing Trends in Canada*. Fifth edition. Toronto: McGraw-Hill Ryerson.

Ray, A.J. 1974. *Indians in the Fur Trade: Their Role as Trappers, Hunters, and Middlemen in the Lands Southwest of Hudson Bay, 1660–1870*. Toronto: University of Toronto Press.

Raymond, Janice. 1977. *Mass-Mediated Culture*. Englewood Cliffs, NJ: Prentice.

_____. 1993. *Women as Wombs: Reproductive Technologies and the Battle Over Women's Freedom*. New York: Harper Collins.

Razack, S. 1999. "Law and the Policing of Bodies of Colour in the 1990s." *Canadian Journal of Law and Society* 14.

Read, Cathy. 2003. *Survey of Intellectual Property Commercialization in the Higher Education Sector, 2003*. Ottawa: Statistics Canada, Science, Innovation and Electronic Information Division.

Reasons, C., L. Ross, and C. Patterson. 1986. "Your Money or Your Life: Workers' Health in Canada." In S. Brickey and E. Comack (eds.), *The Social Basis of Law*. Toronto: Garamond.

Rebick, Judy. 2000. *Imagine Democracy*. Toronto: Stoddart.

Rees, William. 1990. "Sustainable Development and the Biosphere: Concepts and Principles." Paper presented to the Teilhard Studies. Vancouver, British Columbia.

_____. 1998. "Reducing the Ecological Footprint of Consumption." In Laura Westra and Patricia H. Werhane (eds.), *The Business of Consumption: Environmental Ethics and the Global Economy*. New York: Rowman and Littlefield Publishers.

_____. 1999. "Consuming the Earth: The Biophysics of Sustainability." Ecological Economics 29.

_____. 2000. "Interview." Aurora Online. Available at <aurora.icaap.org/index.php/aurora/article/view/18/29> (Accessed January 31, 2007.)

Rege, Sharmila. 2003. "More Then Just Tacking Women on the 'Macropicture': Feminist Contributions to Globalization Discourses." *Economic Political Weekly* October.

Regush, Nicholas. 1991. "Health and Welfare's National Disgrace." *Saturday Night* April.

Reich, Robert. 2001. *The Future of Success*. New York: Alfred A. Knopf.

Reid, Alan, Kelly Teamey, and Justin Dillon. 2002. "Traditional Ecological Knowledge for Learning with Sustainability in Mind." *The Trumpeter*. Available at <trumpeter.athabascau.ca/index.php/trumpet/article/view/124/136>. (Accessed January 29, 2007.)

Reiman, Jeffrey. 2007. *The Rich Get Richer and the Poor Get Prison*. Eighth edition. Boston: Pearson.

Reisner, Ann Elizabeth. 2001. "Social Movement Organizations' Reactions to Genetic Engineering in Agriculture." *American Behavioral Scientist* 44, 8.

Report of the Committee on Homosexual Offenses and Prostitution (The Wolfenden Report). 1962. London: Her Majesty's Stationary Office.

Resnick, Philip. 1990. *The Masks of Proteus: Canadian Reflections on the State*. Montreal: McGill-Queen's University Press.

Richardson, Mary, Joan Sherman, and Michael Gismondi. 1993. *Winning Back the Words: Confronting Experts in an Environmental Public Hearing*. Toronto: Garamond.

Richter, J. 2001. *Holding Corporations Accountable: Corporate Conduct, International Codes and Citizen Action*. London: Zed Books.

Riley, Del. 1984. "What Canadian Indians Want and the Difficulties in Getting It." In Leroy Little Bear, Menno Boldt, and J. Anthony Long (eds.), *Pathways to Self-Determination: Canadian Indians and the Canadian State*. Toronto: University of Toronto Press.

Ritzer, George. 2006. *McDonaldization: The Reader*. Thousand Oaks, CA: Pine Forge Press.

Roach, K. 2005. "Canada's Response to Terrorism." In V. Ramraj, M. Hor, and K. Roach (eds.), *Global Anti-terrorism Law and Policy*. Oxford: Cambridge University Press.

Roberts, B. 1998. *Whence They Came: Deportation From Canada, 1900–1935*. Ottawa: University of Ottawa.

Roberts, Bruce. 1995. "From Lean Production to Agile Manufacturing: A New Round of Quicker, Cheaper, Better." In Christopher Schenk and John Anderson (eds.), *Re/Shaping Work: Union Responses to Technological Change*. Don Mills, ON: Ontario Federation of Labour Technological Adjustment Programme.

Roberts, Julian, and Ronald Melchers. 2003. "The Incarceration of Aboriginal Offenders: Trends from 1978 to 2001." In *Canadian Journal of Criminology and Criminal Justice* 45, 2.

Roberts, Tim. 2002. *Serving Canadians: Review of Provincial and Territorial Domestic Violence Legislation and Implementation Strategies*. Ottawa: Department of Justice Canada. Available at <www.justice.gc.ca/en/ps/rs/rep/2001/rr01-4a.html >. (Accessed on July 12, 2006.)

Robertson, Heather-jane. 2005. "The Many Faces of Privatization." Paper presented at the BCTF Public Education Not for Sale II Conference. Vancouver, BC. (February 18).

Robinson, Daniel, J., and David Kimmel. 1994. "The Queer Career of Homosexual Security Vetting in Cold War Canada." *Canadian Historical Review* 75, 3.

Robinson, Mary. 2002. "Ethics, Human Rights and Globalization." Presented at the Second Global Ethic Lecture, January 21, Tubingen, Germany. Available at <www.weltethos.org/dat_eng/st_9e_xx/9e_144.htm>. (Accessed January 29, 2007.)

Robinson, Mike, and Karim-Aly S. Kassam. 1998. *Sami Potatoes: Living with Reindeer and Perestroika*. Calgary: Bayeux Arts.

Robinson, W.G. 1983. "Illegal Migrants in Canada: A Report to the Honourable Lloyd Axworthy, Minister of Employment and Immigration." Ottawa: Employment and Immigration Canada.

Rock, Paul. 1986. *A View from the Shadows*. Oxford: Clarendon.

Rodgers, Karen. 1994. "Wife Assault: The Findings of a National Survey." *Juristat* 14, 9.

Rogers, Raymond. 1995. *The Oceans Are Emptying: Fish Wars and Sustainability*. Montreal: Black Rose.

Ross, Becki L. 1995. *The House That Jill Built: A Lesbian Nation in Formation*. Toronto: University of Toronto Press.

Ross, D., K. Scott, and P. Smith. 2000. *The Canadian Fact Book of Poverty, 2000*. Ottawa: Canadian Council on Social Development.

Ross, David, and Paul Roberts. 1999. *Income and Child Well-Being: A New Perspective on the Poverty Debate*. Ottawa: Canadian Council on Social Development, May.

Rosser, Sue V. 1994. *Women's Health: Missing from U.S. Medicine*. Bloomington, IN: Indiana University Press.

Rounce, Andrea. 1999. "Student Loan Programs in Saskatchewan, Alberta and at the federal level: An Examination Using the Neo-Institutionalist Approach." Unpublished masters thesis. Regina: University of Regina.

Roussel, Louis, and Irene Thery. 1988. "Demographic Change and Family Policy Since World War II." *Journal of Family Issues* 9, 3.

Royal Commission on Aboriginal Peoples (RCAP). 1993. "Aboriginal Peoples and the Justice System: Report of the National Roundtable on Aboriginal Justice Issues." Ottawa: Supply and Services.

_____. 1995. *Accomodating the Concerns of Aboriginal People Within the Existing Justice System*. Ottawa: Supply and Services.

_____. 1996a. "Economic Development." Royal Commission on Aboriginal People. Ottawa: Supply and Services.

_____. 1996b. "Lands and Resources." Royal Commission on Aboriginal People. Vol. II: Restructuring the Relationship. Ottawa: Supply and Services.

_____. 1996c. *Bridging the Cultural Divide*. Ottawa: Supply and Services.

Royal Commission on Economic Union and Development Prospects for Canada. 1986. "Report." Ottawa: Supply and Services.

Rudner, M. 2002. "The Globalization of Terrorism: Canada's Intelligence Response to the Post-September 11 Threat Environment." *Canadian Issues* 24 (September).

Ruebsaat, Gisela. 1985. *The New Sexual Assault Offences: Emerging Legal Issues*. Ottawa: Supply and Services.

Ruspini, Elisabetta. 2001. "The Study of Women's Deprivation: How to Reveal the Gender Dimensions of Poverty." *International Journal of Social Research Methodology* 4, 2.

Russell, Ellen. 2005. "'Budget for Everyone' has a lot more for the Rich than the Poor." CCPA Monitor, April

Russell, Stuart. 1982. "The Offence of Keeping a Common Bawdy-House in Canadian Criminal Law." *Ottawa Law Review* 14, 2.

Sachs, Wolfgang, Reinhard Loske, Manfred Linz, et al. 1998. *Greening the North: A Post-Industrial Blueprint for Ecology and Equity*. London: Zed Books.

Salterrae. 2004. "Varsity Centre Crumbles: University Yields to Pressure, Tears Down Stadium Before it's even Built." October 4. Available at <www.salterrae.ca/archive/2--4/3/article1.php>. (Accessed on December 30, 2006.)

Salzinger, Leslie. 2003 *Genders in Production: Making Workers in Mexico's Global Factories*. California: University of California Press.

Samuel, John. 1990. "Third World Immigration and Multiculturalism." In S. Halli et al. (eds.), *Ethnic Demography*. Ottawa: Carleton University Press.

Samuelson, L. 1995. "Canadian Aboriginal Justice Commissions and Australia's 'Anunga Rules: Barking Up the Wrong Tree.'" *Canadian Public Policy* 21, 2.

Sanchez, Eduardo. 2005 Interviewed by Daniel Morrison, January 21.

Sanders, Jim. 2005. "Monsanto, Lawyers, Lies and Videotape: Seeds of Censorship Sown at University of Manitoba." *Canadian Dimension Magazine.* Available at <www.canadiandimension.com/articles /2005/08/30/55/>. (Accessed on October 17, 2006.)

Sanderson, Sol. 1984. "Preparations for Indian Government in Saskatchewan." In Leroy Little Bear, Menno Boldt, and J. Anthony Long (eds.), *Pathways to Self-Determination: Canadian Indians and the Canadian State.* Toronto: University of Toronto Press.

Sarlo, Christopher. 1996. *Poverty in Canada.* Second edition. Vancouver: Fraser Institute.

Satzewich, Vic. 1996. "Where's the Beef? Cattle Killing, Rations Policy and First Nations 'Criminality' in Southern Alberta, 1892–1895." *Journal of Historical Sociology* 9.

Saugeres, Lise. 2002. "Of Tractors and Men: Masculinity, Technology, and Power in a French Farming Community." *Sociologica Ruralis* 42, 2.

Saunders, Daniel G. 2002. "Are Physical Assaults by Wives and Girlfriends a Major Social Problem? A Review of the Literature." *Violence Against Women* 8.

Saunders, Doug. 1992. "Space Academy Inc: Bidding for Canada's University on the Final Frontier." *Our Schools, Our Selves* 4, 1.

Savoie, Donald J. 2000. *Aboriginal Economic Development in New Brunswick.* Moncton: Canadian Institute for Research on Regional Development.

Schafer, Arthur. 2005. "Who're Ya Gonna Call? Not the Corporate University." *Canadian Dimension* 39, 5.

Schellenberg, Grant. 1997. *The Changing Nature of Part-Time Work.* Ottawa: Canadian Council on Social Development.

Schellenberg, Grant, and David Ross. 1997. *Left Poor by the Market: A Look at Family Poverty and Earnings.* Ottawa: Canadian Council on Social Development.

Schenk, Christopher, and John Anderson (eds.). 1995 *Re-Shaping Work: Union Responses to Technological Change.* Ontario: Ontario Federation of Labour Technology Adjustment Research Programme.

Schissel, Bernard. 1996. "Law Reform and Social Change: A Time-Series Analysis of Sexual Assault in Canada." *Journal of Criminal Justice* 24, 2.

_____. 2002. "Youth Crime, Youth Justice and the Politics of Marginalization." In Bernard Schissel and Carolyn Brooks (eds.), *Marginality and Condemnation: An Introduction to Critical Criminology.* Black Point, NS: Fernwood Publishing.

Schmalleger, Frank. 2007. *Criminal Justice Today.* Upper Saddle River, NJ: Pearson-Prentice Hall.

Schmalleger, Frank, David MacAlister, Paul McKenna, and John Winterdyk. 2000. *Canadian Criminal Justice Today.* Toronto: Prentice-Hall.

Schnaiberg, Allan, and Kenneth Alan Gould. 1994. *Environment and Society: The Enduring Conflict.* New York: St. Martin's.

Schwartz, Martin D. 2000. "Methodological Issues in the Use of Survey Data for Measuring and Characterizing Violence Against Women." *Violence Against Women* 6, 8.

Schwartz, Martin D., and Walter S. DeKeseredy. 1993. "The Return of the 'Battered Husband Syndrome' Through the Typification of Women as Violent." *Crime Law and Social Change* 20.

Sclove, Richard. 1995. "Putting Science to Work in Communities." *The Chronicle of Higher*

Education 41, 29, March 31, B1–B3.

Scott, Colin H. 2001. *Aboriginal Autonomy and Development in Northern Quebec and Labrador.* Vancouver: University of British Columbia Press.

Scott, R. 2001. *NAFTA's Hidden Costs: Trade Agreements Results in Job Losses, Growing Inequality, and Wage Suppression for the United States.* Briefing Paper. Washington, DC: Economic Policy Institute.

Scott-Dixon, Krista. 2004. *Doing IT: Women Working in Information Technology.* Toronto: Sumach Press.

Sears, Alan, 2001. "Can Marriage Be Queer?" *New Socialist* 29 (March/April).

_____. 1999. "The 'Lean' State and Capitalist Restructuring: Towards a Theoretical Account," *Studies in Political Economy* 59: 91–114.

_____. 2000. "The Opening and Commodification of Gay Space, Queer in a Lean World," *Against the Current* 89, V. XV (Nov.–Dec. 2000).

_____. 2003. *Retooling the Mind Factory, Education in a Lean State.* Aurora, ON: Garamond Press.

_____. 2005. "Is There Sex After Marriage?" *New Socialist* 53 (Sept./Oct.): 38–39.

Sedgwick, Eve Kosofsky. 1990. *The Epistemology of the Closet.* Berkeley: University of California Press.

Sefa Dei, George. 1993. "The Challenges of Anti-Racist Education in Canada." *Canadian Ethnic Studies* 25, 2.

Seward, Shirley. 1990. "Immigrant Women in the Clothing Industry." In Shiva Halli, Frank Trovato, and Leo Driedger (eds.), *Ethnic Demography.* Ottawa: Carleton University Press.

Seward, Shirley, and Kathryn McDade. 1988. "A New Deal for Immigrant Women." *Policy Options* June.

Shaker, Erika. 1998. "Privatizing Schools: Democratic Choice or Market Demand?" *Education Limited* 1, 3.

_____. 1999. "The Privatization of Post-Secondary Institutions." *Education Limited* 1, 4.

Shanahan, James, Dietram Scheufele, and Eunjung Lee. 2001. "The Polls-Trends: Attitudes about Agricultural Biotechnology and Genetically Modified Organisms." *Public Opinion Quarterly* 65, 2.

Sharma, Nandita. 2002. "Open the Borders." *Fireweed: Women, Race, War, and Resistance* — Part 1 77.

_____. 2003. "No Borders Movements and the Rejection of Left Nationalism." *Canadian Dimension* 37, 3 (May/June).

Sharpe, Andrew, Duncan Cameron, and Jean-Pierre Voyer. 1988. "Unemployment: Its Nature, Costs and Causes." In Andrew Sharpe and Duncan Cameron (eds.), *Policies for Full Employment.* Ottawa: Canadian Council on Social Development.

Shaw, Margaret, and Caroline Andrew. 2005. "Engendering Crime Prevention: International Developments and the Canadian Experience." *Canadian Journal of Criminology and Criminal Justice* 47.

Shepard, Benjamin, and Ronald Hayduk. 2002. *From ACT UP to the WTO: Urban Protest and Community Building in the Era of Globalization.* London & New York: Verso.

Sherman, L., and R. Berk. 1989. "The Specific Deterrent Effects of Arrest for Domestic Assault." *American Sociological Review* 49.

Shields, John. 1992. "The Capitalist State and Farm Labour Policy." In David A. Hay and Gurcharn S. Basran (eds.), *Rural Sociology in Canada.* Toronto: Oxford University Press.

Shilts, Randy. 1987. *And the Band Played On: Politics, People and the AIDS Epidemic*. New York: St. Martin's.

Shiva, Vandana. 2000. *Poverty and Globalization*. Cambridge, UK: Cambridge University.

Shiva, Vandana, and Radha Holla-Bar. 1996. "Piracy by Patent: The Case of the Neem Tree." In J. Mander and E. Goldsmith (eds.), *The Case Against the Global Economy*. San Francisco: Sierra Club Books.

Shkilnyk, Anastasia M. 1985. *A Poison Stronger Than Love: The Destruction of an Ojibwa Community*. New Haven: Yale University Press.

Shostak, Arthur, B. (ed.). 2002. *The CyberUnion Handbook: Transforming Labor through Computer Technology*. New York: M.E. Sharpe.

Shulman, Seth. 1999. *Owning the Future*. Boston: Houghton Mifflin Company.

Sierra Club. 2003. Available at <http://www.sierraclub.ca/national/sydney-tar-ponds/> (Accessed January 31, 2007.)

Sigler, Robert T. 1989. *Domestic Violence in Context: An Assessment of Community Attitudes*. Toronto: Lexington Books.

Sillars, Les. 1997. "Hockey Pays the Price of Gay Tolerance." *Alberta Report*, January 20.

Silver, Jim. 1992. "Constitutional Change, Ideological Conflict and the Redistributive State." In James N. McCrorie and Martha MacDonald (eds.), *The Constitutional Future of the Prairie and Atlantic Regions of Canada*. Regina: Canadian Plains Research Centre.

_____ (ed.). 2000. *Solutions That Work: Fighting Poverty in Winnipeg*. Halifax and Winnipeg: Fernwood and the Canadian Centre for Policy Alternatives–Manitoba.

_____. 2002. *Building on Our Strengths: Inner City Priorities for a Renewed Tri-Level Development Agreement*. Winnipeg: Futures Group and Canadian Centre for Policy Alternatives–Manitoba.

_____. 2006. *In Their Own Voices: Urban Aboriginal Community Development*. Black Point, NS: Fernwood Publishing.

Silver, Susan, Sue Wilson, and John Shields. 2004 "Job Restructuring and Worker Displacement: Does Gender Matter?" *Canadian Women's Studies* 23, 3/4.

Simmons, A. 1998. "Globalization and Backlash Racism in the 1990s: The Case of Asian Immigration to Canada." In E. Lacquian, A. Lacquian, and T. McGee (eds.), *The Silent Debate: Asian Immigration and Racism in Canada*. Vancouver: Institute of Asian Research.

Simpson, Alan, with Nicolas Hildyard and Sarah Sexton. 1997. "No Patents on Life! A Briefing on the Proposed EU Directive on the Legal Protection of Biotechnological Inventions." *The CornerHouse* September.

Sinclair, John A., and Doreen L. Smith. 1999. "The Model Forest Program in Canada: Building Consensus on Sustainable Forest Management?" *Society and Natural Resources* 12.

Sinopoli, John. 2001. "Sex Trade Bill Forgets Queer Youth, Youth and Prostitution." *Xtra* November 15.

_____. 2002. "Thwarted From Plans, Catholic Board Says No-no to Same-sex Date." *Xtra* March 21.

Skelton, Ian. 1998. *The Shelter Shortage: New Directions for Low-Cost Housing Policy in Canada*. Winnipeg: Canadian Centre for Policy Alternatives–Manitoba.

Sklair, L. 1991. *Sociology of the Global System*. Hemel Hempstead: Harvester Wheatsheaf.

Skocpol, Theda. 1980. "Political Responses to the Capitalist Crisis: Neo-Marxist Theories of the State and the New Deal." *Politics and Society* 10, 2.

_____. 1985. "Bringing the State Back In: Strategies of Analysis in Current Research." In

Peter Evans, Dietrich Rueschemeyer, and Theda Skocpol (eds.), *Bringing the State Back In*. Cambridge: Cambridge University Press.

Skogstad, Grace. 1980. "Agrarian Protest in Alberta." *Canadian Review of Sociology and Anthropology* 17, 1.

Sloan, Pamela, and Roger Hill. 1995. *Corporate Aboriginal Relations: Best Practise Case Studies*. Toronto: Hill Sloan.

Smart, Carol. 1996. "Feminist Approaches to Criminology or Postmodern Woman Meets Atavistic Man." In M.E. McLaughlin and M. Langan (eds.), *Criminological Perspectives*. Thousand Oaks, CA: Sage.

_____. 1997. "Wishful Thinking and Harmful Tinkering? Sociological Reflections on Family Policy." *Journal of Social Policy* 26, 3.

_____. 2000. "Stories of Family Life: Cohabitation, Marriage and Social Change." *Canadian Journal of Family Law* 17, 1.

_____. 2004. "Equal Shares: Rights for Fathers or Recognition for Children?" *Critical Social Policy* 24.

Smith, Dorothy E. 1974. "The Social Construction of Documentary Reality." *Sociological Inquiry* 44, 4.

_____. 1977. "Women, the Family and Corporate Capitalism." In Marylee Stephenson (ed.), *Women in Canada*. Revised edition. Don Mills, ON: General.

_____. 1983. "No One Commits Suicide: Textual Analysis of Ideological Practices." *Human Studies* 6.

_____. 1987. *The Everyday World as Problematic: A Feminist Sociology*. Toronto: University of Toronto Press.

_____. 1990a. *The Conceptual Practices of Power: A Feminist Sociology of Knowledge*. Toronto: University of Toronto Press.

_____. 1990b. *Texts, Facts, and Femininity: Exploring the Relations of Ruling*. New York: Routledge.

_____. 1990c. "Femininity as Discourse." In Dorothy E. Smith (ed.), *Texts, Facts, and Femininity: Exploring the Relations of Ruling*. New York: Routledge.

_____. 1999. *Writing the Social: Critique, Theory, and Investigations*. Toronto: University of Toronto Press.

_____. 2005. *Institutional Ethnography: A Sociology for People*. London, New York, Toronto, Oxford: Altamira.

Smith, D., and C. Visher. 1980. "Sex and Involvement in Deviance/Crime." *American Sociological Review* 45.

Smith, George W. 1988. "Policing the Gay Community: An Inquiry into Textually-mediated Social Relations." *International Journal of the Sociology of Law* 16.

_____. 1990. "Political Activist as Ethnographer." *Social Problems* 37, 4.

_____. 1998. "The Ideology of 'Fag': Barriers to Education for Gay Students." *Sociological Quarterly* 39, 2.

_____. 2006. "Political Activist as Ethnographer." In Caelie Frampton, Gary Kinsman, Andrew Thompson, Kate Tilleczek (eds.), *Sociology for Changing the World: Social Movements/Social Research*. Black Point, NS: Fernwood Publishing.

Smith, Mel. 1995. *Our Home or Native Land?* Victoria: Crown Western.

Smith, Sandra M., and Murray A. Straus. 1995. *Understanding Partner Violence: Prevalence, Causes, Consequences, and Solutions*. Minneapolis: National Council on Family Relations.

REFERENCES

Smith, V. 2000. *Modern Tribal Development: Paths to Self-Sufficiency and Cultural Integrity in Indian Country*. New York: AltaMira Press.

Snider, Laureen. 1985. "Legal Reform and the Law: The Dangers of Abolishing Rape." *International Journal of the Sociology of Law* 4.

_____. 1988. "Commercial Crime." In V. Sacco (ed.), *Deviance: Conformity and Control in Canadian Society*. Scarborough, ON: Prentice.

_____. 1991. "The Potential of the Criminal Justice System to Promote Feminism." In Elizabeth Comack and Steve Brickey (eds.), *The Social Basis of Law*. Second edition. Toronto: Garamond.

_____. 1993. *Bad Business: Corporate Crime in Canada*. Toronto: Nelson.

_____. 1994a. "The Regulatory Dance: Understanding Reform Processes in Corporate Crime." In R. Hinch (ed.), *Readings in Critical Criminology*. Scarborough, ON: Prentice.

_____. 1994b. "Feminism, Punishment and the Potential of Empowerment." *Canadian Journal of Law and Society* 9, 1.

_____. 2002. "'But They're Not Real Criminals': Downsizing Corporate Crime." In Bernard Schissel and Carolyn Brooks (eds.), *Marginality and Condemnation: An Introduction to Critical Criminology*. Black Point, NS: Fernwood Publishing.

Sobel, David. 1995. "From Grunt Work to No Work: The Impact of Technological Change on the Building Trades." In Christopher Schenk and John Anderson (eds.), *Re/Shaping Work: Union Responses to Technological Change*. Don Mills, ON: Ontario Federation of Labour Technological Adjustment Programme.

Sobsey, Dick. 2002. *Family Violence and People with Intellectual Disabilities — Overview Paper*. Ottawa: National Clearinghouse on Family Violence. Available at <www.phac-aspc.gc.ca/ncfv-cnivf/familyviolence/pdfs/fvintellectu_e.pdf>. (Accessed on July 12, 2006.)

Social Planning Council of Winnipeg and Winnipeg Harvest. 1997. *Acceptable Living Level*. Winnipeg: Social Planning Council of Winnipeg.

Solnit, David. 2004. *Globalize Liberation: How to Uproot the System and Build a Better World*. City Lights Books.

Sorensen, Annette. 1999. "Family Decline, Poverty, and Social Exclusion: The Mediating Effects of Family Policy." *Comparative Social Research* 18.

Soron, Dennis. 2004. "The Cultural Politics of Kyoto: Lessons from the Canadian Semi-Periphery." *Capitalism, Nature, Socialism* 15, 1.

_____. 2006. "Decommodifying Daily Life: The Politics of Overconsumption." In Gordon Laxer and Dennis Soron (eds.), *Not For Sale: Decommodifying Public Life*. Peterborough: Broadview Press.

Soros, G. 2000. *Open Society: Reforming Global Capitalism*. New York: Public Affairs.

Southern Alberta Land Trust. 2002. Available at <www.salts-landtrust.org/conservingrange-lands_3.HTML#3>. (Accessed January 29, 2007.)

Spaargaren, Gert. 1999. "The Ecological Modernisation of Domestic Consumption." Available at <http://www.lancs.ac.uk/fss/sociology/esf/spaargaren.htm>. (Accessed January 31, 2007.)

Spaargaren, Gert, and Arthur P.J. Mol. 1992. "Sociology, Environment and Modernity: Ecological Modernization as a Theory of Social Change." *Society and Natural Resources* 5, 4.

Spakes, Patricia. 1983. *Family Policy and Family Impact Analysis*. Cambridge, MA: Schenkman.

Sparr, P. 1994. *Mortgaging Women's Lives: Feminist Critiques of Structural Adjustment*. London: Zed Books.

Speake, Stephen, and Mike Gismondi 2005. "Water: The Struggle to Decommodify a Human Right." In D. Davidson and K. Hatt (eds.), *Consuming Sustainability: Social Analyses of Ecological Change*. Black Point, NS: Fernwood Publishing.

Stacey, Jackie. 1994. *Star-Gazing: Hollywood Cinema and Female Spectatorship*. London: Routledge.

Stacey, William A., Lonnie R. Hazlewood, and Anson Shupe. 1994. *The Violent Couple*. Westport: Praeger.

Stafford, Ezra Hurlburt. 1898. "Perversion." *Canadian Journal of Medicine and Surgery* 3, 4.

Stafford, Jim. 2006. "Companies Hoard Billions Derived from Massive Tax Cuts." The CCPA Monitor, April.

Staiger, Janet. 1992. *Interpreting Films: Studies in the Historical Reception of American Cinema*. Princeton, NJ: Princeton University Press.

_____. 2000. *Perverse Spectators: The Practices of Film Reception*. New York: New York University Press.

Standing Committee on Citizenship and Immigration. 2001. *Hands Across the Border: Working Together at our Shared Border and Abroad to Ensure Safety, Security and Efficiency*. Ottawa: Public Works.

Standing, G. 1989. "Global Feminization Through Flexible Labour." *World Development* 17, 7.

Stanford, J. 1996. "Discipline, Insecurity and Productivity: The Economics Behind Labour Market 'Productivity.'" In Jane Pulkingham and Gordon Ternowetsky (eds.), *Remaking Canadian Social Policy: Social Security in the Late 1990s*. Halifax: Fernwood Publishing.

_____. 1998. "The Rise and Fall of Deficit-Mania: Public Sector Finances and the Attack on Social Canada." In Wayne Antony and Les Samuelson (eds.), *Power and Resistance: Critical Thinking about Canadian Social Issues*. Second edition. Halifax: Fernwood.

_____. 1999. *Paper Boom: Why Real Prosperity Requires a New Approach to Canada's Economy*. Ottawa and Toronto: Canadian Centre for Policy Alternatives and Lorimer.

_____. 2001. "Putting Globalization in its Place: Are Pro-business Policies Inevitable." *This Magazine* 34, 5.

StarPhoenix [Saskatoon]. 2003. "Majority in Sask. Opposes Treaty Rights: Report." November 27, A1.

_____. 2006. "Three Strikes bill will hit Natives." October 18, A10.

_____. 1991a. "21 Female Prisoners Charged After Riot." February 13, A15.

_____. 1991b. "Dying to Get Out of P4W." March 23, D1.

_____. 1997. "Half of Canadians Polled Believe Natives Well-Off." June 21.

_____. 2001a. "Allegations of Police Abuse Put Saskatoon on Amnesty list." May 31, A1.

_____. 2001b. "Amnesty: Group targets developing patterns." May 31, A8.

_____. 2001c. "Province has highest number of young people appearing in court." May 31, A3.

_____. 2005. "Hartwig, Senger Scapegoats for Police Problems: Lawyer." November 1, A4.

Starhawk. 2002. "Building a Diverse Movement." In *Webs of Power: Notes from the Global Uprising*. Gabriola Island, B.C.: New Society Publishers.

Starr, Amory. 2000. *Naming the Enemy: Anti-corporate Movement Confront Globalization*. London: Zed Books.

_____. 2006. *Global Revolt: A Guide to the Movements Against Globalization*. Zed Books.

Starr, Paul. 1990. "The New Life of the Liberal State: Privatization and the Restructuring of State-Society Relations." In John Waterbury and Ezra Suleiman (eds.), *Public Enterprise and*

Privatization. Boulder, CO: Westview.

Stasiulis, Daiva. 1980. "The Political Structuring of Ethnic Community Action." *Canadian Ethnic Studies* 12, 3.

_____. 1989. "Affirmative Action for Visible Minorities and the New Politics of Race in Canada." In O.P. Dwivedi et al. (eds.), *Canada 2000: Race Relations and Public Policy.* Guelph, ON: Department of Political Studies, University of Guelph.

_____. 1990. "Theorizing Connections: Gender, Race, Ethnicity and Class." In Peter Li (ed.), *Race and Ethnic Relations in Canada.* Toronto: Oxford

Statistics Canada. 1996a. *Canadian Crime Statistics.* Ottawa: Statistics Canada.

_____. 1997c. "1996 Census: Marital Status, Common-Law Unions and Families." The Daily, October 14 (Catalogue 89-553-XPB). Ottawa: Statistics Canada.

_____. 1998a. *General Social Survey on Time Use.* Ottawa: Statistics Canada.

_____. 1998b. "How Children Get Ahead in Life." Labour Markets, Social Institutions and the Future of Canada's Children. (Catalogue 89-553-XPB). Ottawa: Statistics Canada.

_____. 1999a. *Labour Force Update.* (Catalogue 71-005-XPB) Summer. Ottawa. Statistics Canada.

_____. 2000. "Part-time University Faculty." *The Daily.* August 29. Available at <www.statscan. ca/Daily/English/000830/d000830c.htm>. (Accessed on December 30, 2006.)

_____. 2001a. *Census of Population.* Ottawa: Statistics Canada.

_____. 2001b. *Aboriginal Peoples in Canada* (Catalogue No. 85 F0033M1E). Ottawa: Government of Canada.

_____. 2001c. "Participation in Postsecondary Education and Family Income." *The Daily.* December 7. Ottawa: Statistics Canada.

_____. 2002a. "Family Income 2000." *The Daily* October 30.

_____. 2002b. "The Evolution of Wealth Inequality in Canada, 1984–1999." (Catalogue 1F0019MIE). Ottawa: Statistics Canada.

_____. 2003. *Canada E-Book.* (Catalogue 11-404-XIE). Ottawa: Statistics Canada.

_____. 2004a. "Pilot Survey Of Hate Crime." June 1. Available at <www.statcan.ca /Daily/ English/040601/d040601a.htm>. (Accessed on June 14, 2006).

_____. 2004b. *Crime Statistics in Canada, 2003* (Catalogue No. 85-002-X1E, Volume 24, Number 5). Ottawa: Statistics Canada.

_____. 2004c. "Study" Immigrants Settling for Less." *The Daily,* June 23. Ottawa: Statistics Canada.

_____. 2004d. "2001 Census: Profile of Canadian families and households," Available at <www12. statcan.ca/english/census01/Products/Analytic/companion/fam/canada.cf>. (Accessed on November 30, 2005.)

_____. 2004e. Divorce. *The Daily,* 4 May. Available at <www.statcan.ca/Daily/English/040504/ d040504a.htm>. (Accessed on January 10, 2006.)

_____. 2005a. "Child Care." *The Daily* February 7.

_____. 2005b. *Perspectives on Labour and Income.* December 20.

_____. 2005c. *Women in Canada: A Gender Based Statistical Report.* Ottawa: Statistics Canada.

_____. 2005d. *Canadian Economic Observer.* "Historical Statistical Supplement 2004/05" (Catalogue no. 11-210-XIB). Ottawa: Statistics Canada

_____. 2005e. *Public Sector Statistics* (Catalogue no. 68-213). Ottawa: Statistics Canada.

_____. 2006a. *2001 Census of Canada.* Available at <www12.statcan.ca/english/census01/products /standard/themes/RetrieveProductTable.cfm?Temporal=2001&PID=57382&APATH=3

&GID=355313&METH=1&PTYPE=55440&THEME=39&FOCUS=0&AID=0&PLA
CENAME=0&PROVINCE=0&SEARCH=0&GC=0&GK=0&VID=0&FL=0&RL=0&
FREE=0>. (Accessed on June 13, 2006.)

_____. 2006b. "Women in Canada." *The Daily* March 7.

_____. 2006c. "Changing Patterns of Women in the Canadian Labour Force." *The Daily* June 15.

_____. 2006d. *Reasons For Part-Time Work By Sex And Age Group* (Catalogue no. 89FO133XIE). Ottawa: Statistics Canada.

_____. 2006e. "Canadian Internet Use Survey, 2005." *The Daily* August 15.

_____. 2006f. "Education in Canada: Raising the Standard." Available at <www12.statcan.ca/english/census01/products/analytic/companion/educ/tables/canada/eacana>. (Accessed on August 2006.)

Steger, Manfred B. 2003. *Globalization: A Very Short Introduction.* Oxford: Oxford University Press.

Steiner, Gilbert. 1981. *The Futility of Family Policy.* Washington, DC: Brookings Institution.

Steinmetz, Suzanne K. 1977. "The Battered Husband Syndrome." *Victimology* 2, 3–4.

Stern, Paul C., Thomas Dietz, Vernon W. Ruttan, Robert H. Socolow, and James L. Sweeney (eds.). 1997. *Environmentally Significant Consumption: Research Directions.* Washington, DC: National Academy Press.

Stewart, L. 2001. "Getting Spooked." *This Magazine* 34, 5.

Stone, Sharon. 1990. *Lesbians in Canada.* Toronto: Between the Lines.

Strange, C., and T. Loo. 1997. *Making Good: Law and Moral Regulation in Canada, 1867–1939.* Toronto: University of Toronto Press.

Straus, Murray A. 1979. "Measuring Intrafamily Conflict And Violence: The Conflict Tactics Scale." *Journal of Marriage and the Family* 41.

_____. 1990a. "Measuring Intra Family Conflict and Violence: The Conflict Tactics (CTS) Scales." In M.A. Straus and R.J. Gelles (eds.), *Physical Violence in American Families: Risk Factors and Adaptations to Violence in 8,145 Families.* New Brunswick and London: Transaction.

_____. 1990b. "Injury and Frequency of Assault and the Representative Sample Fallacy in Measuring Wife-Beating and Child Abuse." In M.A. Straus and R.J. Gelles (eds.), *Physical Violence in American Families: Risk Factors and Adaptations to Violence in 8,145 Families.* New Brunswick and London: Transaction.

_____. 1991. "New Theory and Old Canards About Family Violence Research." *Social Problems* 38, 2.

_____. 1993. "Physical Assault By Wives: A Major Social Problem." In R.J. Gelles and D.R. Loseke (eds.), *Current Controversies on Family Violence.* Newbury Park: Sage.

_____. 1997. "Physical Assaults by Women Partners: A Major Social Problem." In M.R. Walsh (ed.), *Women, Men, and Gender: Ongoing Debates.* New Haven: Yale University Press.

_____. 1999. "The Controversy Over Domestic Violence by Women: A Methodological, Theoretical, and Sociology of Science Analysis." In X.B. Arriaga and S. Oskamp (eds.), *Violence in Intimate Relationships.* Thousand Oaks, CA: Sage.

_____. 2006. "Future Research on Gender Symmetry in Physical Assaults on Partners." *Violence Against Women* 12, 11.

Straus, Murray A., Richard J. Gelles, and Suzanne K. Steinmetz. 1980. *Behind Closed Doors: Violence in the American Family.* Garden City: Anchor Press/Doubleday.

Straus, Murray A., Sherry L. Hamby, Sue Boney-McCoy, and David B. Sugarman. 1996. "The

Revised Conflict Tactics Scales (CTS2): Development and Preliminary Psychometric Data." *Journal of Family Issues* 17.

Stymeist, David. 1975. *Ethnics and Indians: Social Relations in a Northwestern Ontario Town.* Toronto: Peter Martin.

Sudarkasa, Niara. 1999. "African American Females as Primary Parents." In Harriette Pipes (ed.), *Family Ethnicity: Strength in Diversity.* Thousand Oaks: Sage.

Sugar, F., and L. Fox. 1989–90. "Nistum peyako sht'wawin iskwewak: Breaking Chains." *Canadian Journal of Women's Law* 3.

Sullivan, T., and K. Thompson. 1988. *Introduction to Social Problems.* New York: Macmillan.

Supreme Court of Canada. 1999. "*R. v. Marshall.*" *Canadian Native Law Reporter.* Saskatoon: University of Saskatchewan Native Law Centre.

Sutcliffe, B. 2001. *100 Ways for Seeing an Unequal World.* London: Zed Books.

Sutherland, E.H. 1977. "Crimes of Corporations." In G. Geis and R. Meier (eds.), *White-Collar Crime: Offences in Business, Politics, and the Professions.* New York: Free.

Svenson, Ken. 1978. *The Explosive Years: Indian and Metis Issues in Saskatchewan to 2001.* Regina: Indian and Native Affairs Secretariat.

Svensson, Frances. 1979. "Liberal Democracy and Group Rights: The Legacy of Individualism and Its Impact on American Indian Tribes." *Political Studies* 27.

Swan, Suzanne, and David L. Snow. 2002. "A Typology of Women's Use of Violence in Intimate Relationships." *Violence Against Women* 8, 3.

Swanson, Jean. 2001. *Poor Bashing: The Politics of Exclusion.* Toronto: Between the Lines.

Sweetman, Caroline (ed.). 1998. *Gender and Technology.* Oxfam Focus on Gender Series. Oxford, UK: Oxfam.

Swift, Jamie. 1999, "Saving the Corporate Soul." *Canadian Forum* June.

Swift, Richard. 2002. *The No-Nonsense Guide to Democracy.* Toronto: Between the Lines.

Sycamore, Matt Bernstein (Matilda). 2004. *That's Revolting! Queer Strategies for Resisting Assimilation.* Brooklyn: Soft Skull Press.

Synnott, Anthony, and David Howes. 1996. "Canada's Visible Minorities: Identity and Representation." In Vered Amit-Talai and Caroline Knowles (eds.), *Re-Situating Identities: The Politics of Race, Ethnicity, Culture.* Peterborough, ON: Broadview.

Szymanski, Albert. 1978. *The Capitalist State and the Politics of Class.* Cambridge: Winthrop.

Tabb, William K. 1997. "Globalization Is *An* Issue; The Power of Capital is *The* Issue." *Monthly Review* 49, 2.

_____. 2002. *Unequal Partners: A Primer on Globalization.* New York: New Press.

Tabi, Martin, and Stephanie Langlois. "Quality of Jobs Added in 2002." *Perspectives* (Catalogue no. 75-001-XIE) February 2003. Ottawa: Statistics Canada

Task Force on Federally Sentenced Women. 1990. *Creating Choices.* Ottawa: Correctional Service of Canada.

Task Force on the Status of Women. 1985. *A Feminist Review of Criminal Law.* Ottawa: Supply and Services.

Taylor, I., P. Walton, and J. Young. 1973. *The New Criminology: For a Social Theory of Deviance.* London: Routlege and Kegan Paul.

Taylor, Malcolm. 1987. *Health Insurance and Canadian Public Policy.* Montreal: McGill-Queen's University Press.

Taylor, P.J. 1996. *The Way the Modern World Works: World Hegemony to World Impasse.* New York: John Wiley. (?see above, Is the author's name PJ or PG?)

Taylor-Butts, Andrea. 2005. "Canada's Shelters for Abused Women, 2003/04." *Juristat* 25, 3.

Teeple, G. 2000. *Globalization and the Decline of Social Reform into the Twenty First Century.* First edition. Toronto: Garamond Press.

Teitelbaum, M., and J. Winter. 1998. *A Question of Numbers: High Migration, Low Fertility and the Politics Of National Identity.* New York: Hill and Wang.

Tennant, Paul. 1982. "Native Indian Political Organization in British Columbia 1900–1969: A Response to Internal Colonialism." *BC Studies* 3.

Tepper, Elliot. 1989. "Demographic Change and Pluralism." In O.P. Dwivedi et al., (eds.), *Canada 2000: Race Relations and Public Policy.* Guelph: Department of Political Studies, University of Guelph.

Thobani, S. 2000. "Closing Ranks: Racism And Sexism In Canada's Immigration Policy." *Race and Class* 42, 35.

Thomas. Paul G. 1996. "Visions Versus Resources in the Federal Review." In Amelita Armit and Jacques Bourgault (eds.), *Hard Choices or No Choices: Assessing Program Review.* Toronto: Institute of Public Administration of Canada.

Thompson, Kristin, and David Bordwell. 1994. *Film History: An Introduction.* New York: McGraw-Hill.

Tilly, Charles. 2000. "Spaces of Contention." *Mobilization* 5, 2.

Tjaden, Patricia, and Nancy Thoennes. 2000. "Prevalence and Consequences of Male-to-Female and Female-to-Male Partner Violence as Measured by the National Violence Against Women Survey." *Violence Against Women* 6, 2.

Toffler, Alvin. 1980. *The Third Wave.* New York: Morrow.

Tonmyr, Lil, Barbara Fallon, and Nico Trocme. 2006. "Overview of the Canadian Incidence Study of Reported Child Abuse and Neglect (CIS), 2003." In L. Ogrodnik (ed.), *Family Violence in Canada: A Statistical Profile 2006.* Ottawa: Canadian Centre for Justice Statistics. Available at <www.phac-aspc.gc.ca/ncfv-cnivf/familyviolence/pdfs/85-224-XIE2006000. pdf>. (Accessed on July 4, 2006.)

Toronto Star. 2006a. "Editorial: Our New Pioneers." March 30.

_____. 2006b. "Letter To Editor: 'Afraid Every Morning I Wake Up.'" May 28.

Totten, Mark D. 2000. *Guys, Gangs, and Girlfriend Abuse.* Peterborough: Broadview Press.

_____. 2003. "Girlfriend Abuse as a Form of Masculinity Construction among Violent, Marginal, Male Youth." *Men and Masculinities* 6.

Tough, Frank. 1985. "Challenges to the Native Economy of Northern Manitoba in the Post-Treaty Period, 1870–1900." *Native Studies Review* 1.

_____. 1992. "Regional Analysis of Indian Aggregate Income, Northern Manitoba: 1896–1935." *Canadian Journal of Native Studies* 12.

Towns, Alison, and Peter Adams. 2000. "'If I Really Loved Him Enough, He Would Be Okay': Women's Accounts Of Male Partner Violence." *Violence Against Women* 16.

Treasury Board of Canada Secretariat. 2006. "Canada's Performance Report 2005 — Annex 3 — Indicators and Additional Information." Available at <www.tbs-sct.gc.ca/report/gov-rev/05/ann304_e.asp>. (Accessed on August 2006.)

Treichler, Paula A. 1999. *How to Have Theory in an Epidemic: Cultural Chronicles of AIDS.* Durham and London: Duke University Press.

Trocme, Nico, and Nicholas Bala. 2005. "False Allegations of Abuse and Neglect When Parents Separate." *Child Abuse & Neglect* 29.

Tucker, Eric. 2006. "The Regulation of occupational Health and Safety." In Elizabeth Comack (ed.) *Locating Law: Race, Class, Gender, Sexuality Connections* 2ⁿᵈ edition. Black Point, NS: Fernwood Publishing.

Tudiver, N. 1999. *Universities For Sale: Resisting Corporate Control over Higher Education*. Toronto: Lorimer.

Turk, James. 2000a. "What Commercialization Means for Education." In James Turk (ed.), *The Corporate Campus: Commercialization and the Dangers to Canada's Colleges and Universities*. Toronto: Lormier.

_____. 2000b. *The Corporate Campus: Commercialization and the Dangers to Canada's Colleges and Universities*. Toronto: Lorimer.

Turner, William B. 2000. A Genealogy of Queer Theory. Philadelphia: Temple University Press.

Turpel, M. [Aki-Kwe]. 1992. "Further Travails of Canada's Human Rights Record: The Marshall Case." In J. Mannette (ed.), *Elusive Justice: Beyond the Marshall Inquiry*. Halifax: Fernwood Publishing.

Tutty, Leslie. 1999. *Husband Abuse: An Overview of Research and Perspectives*. Ottawa, ON: Health Canada. Available at <www.phacaspc.gc.ca/ncfvcnivf/familyviolence/pdfs/husbandenglish.pdf>. (Accessed on July 12, 2006.)

_____. 2006. *Effective Practices in Sheltering Women: Leaving Violence in Intimate Relationships, Phase II Report 2006*. Toronto: YWCA Canada. Available at <www.ywca.ca/public_eng/advocacy/Shelter/YWCA_ShelterReport_EN.pdf>. (Accessed on July 12, 2006.)

Tyyska, Vappu. 1995. "The Politics of Caring and the Welfare State: The Impact of the Women's Movement of Child Care Policy in Canada and Finland, 1960–1990." Annales Academiae Scientiarum Fennicae 277.

Umberson, Debra, Kristin Anderson, Jennifer Glick, and Adam Shapiro. 1998. "Domestic Violence, Personal Control, and Gender." *Journal of Marriage and the Family* 60, 2.

United Church of Christ, Commission for Racial Justice. 1987. T*oxic Wastes and Race in the United States: A National Report on the Racial and Socio-Economic Characteristics of Communities with Hazardous Waste Sites*. New York: United Church of Christ Commission for Racial Justice.

United Nations. 1993. Declaration on the Elimination of Violence against Women. G.A. resolution 48/104, 48 U.N. GAOR Supplement (No. 49) at 217, U.N. Doc. A/48/49. Available at <http://www1.umn.edu/humanrts/instree/e4devw.htm>. (Accessed January 29, 2007.)

_____. 1999. *Overview. United Nations Development Report*. New York: United Nations Publications.

United Nations Children's Fund. 1992. *The State of the World's Children 1992*. New York: United Nations.

_____. 2005. *Innocenti Report Card No. 6: Child Poverty in Rich Countries 2005*. Florence: UNICEF Innocenti Research Centre.

United Nations Conference on Environment and Development. 1992. "The Rio Declaration on Environment and Development." Available at <http://www.igc.org/habitat/agenda21/rio-dec.html>. (?when accessed?)

United Nations Development Program. 1995. *The Human Development Report 1995*. New York: Oxford University Press.

_____. 1998. *Human Development Report 1998*. New York: Oxford University Press.

_____. 1999. *Human Development Report 1999*. New York: Oxford University Press.

_____. 2001. *Human Development Report 2001*. New York: Oxford University Press.

_____. 2003. *Human Development Report 2003*. New York: Oxford University Press.

United Nations High Commissioner for Refugees (UNHCR). 2001. "Comments on Bill C-11: Submission to the House of Commons Standing Committee on Citizenship and Immigration." Ottawa, ON, March. Available at <www.web.ca/ccr/c11hcr.PDF>. (Accessed on September 28, 2006.)

Urquhart, Ian. 2001. "New Players, Same Game? Managing the Boreal Forest on Canada's Prairies." In Michael Howlett (ed.), *Canadian Forest Policy: Regimes, Policy Dynamics and Institutional Adaptations*. Toronto: University of Toronto Press.

Ursel, Jane. 1991. "Considering the Impact of the Battered Women's Movement on the State: The Example of Manitoba." In Elizabeth Comack and Steve Brickey (eds.), *The Social Basis of Law*. Toronto: Garamond.

_____. 1998. "Eliminating Violence Against Women: Reform or Co-optation in State Institutions." In L. Samuelson (ed.), *Power and Resistance: Critical Thinking About Canadian Social Issues*. Second edition. Halifax: Fernwood Publishing.

Usher, Peter J. 1987. "Indigenous Management Systems and the Conservation of Wildlife in the Canadian North." *Alternatives* 14, 1.

Valverde, Mariana. 1989. "Beyond Gender Dangers and Private Pleasures: Theory and Ethics in the Sex Debates." *Feminist Studies* 15, 2.

_____. 1991. *The Age of Soap, Light and Water: Moral Reform in English Canada, 1885–1925* Toronto: McClelland & Stewart.

_____. 1992. "'When the Mother of the Race is Free': Race, Reproduction, and Sexuality in First-Wave Feminism." In Franca Iacovetta and Mariana Valverde (eds.), *Gender Conflicts: New Essays in Women's History*. Toronto: University of Toronto Press.

_____. 2002. "A Pussy-positive Judgment, Women's Bathhouse Ruling Affirms Sexual Spaces." *Xtra* February 7.

Valverde, Mariana, and Lorna Weir. 1988. "The Struggles of the Immoral." *Resources for Feminist Research* 17, 3.

Van Der Gaag, Nikki. 2004. *The No-Nonsense Guide to Women's Rights.* Toronto: Between the Lines.

Van Maanen, John. 1995. "An End to Innocence: The Ethnography of Ethnography." In J. Van Maanen (ed.), *Representaton in Ethnography*. Thousand Oaks: Sage Publications.

van Oost, Ellen. 1998. "Aligning Gender and New Technology: The Case of Early Administrative Automation." In Cornelius Disco and Barend van der Meulen (eds.), *Getting New Technologies Together: Studies in Making Sociotechnical Order*. Berlin and New York: Walter de Gruyter.

Vance, Carole. 1984. "Pleasure and Danger: Towards a Politics of Sexuality." In C. Vance (ed.), *Pleasure and Danger: Female Sexuality Today*. Boston: Routledge.

Varcoe, Colleen, and Lori G Irwin. 2004. "'If I Killed You, I'd Get The Kids': Women's Survival And Protection Work With Child Custody And Access In The Context Of Woman Abuse." *Qualitative Sociology* 27.

Verdun-Jones, Simon. 2007. *Criminal Law in Canada*. Toronto: Thomson-Nelson.

Vickers, J., P. Rankin, and C. Appelle. 1993. *Politics as if Women Mattered: A Political Analysis of the National Action Committee on the Status of Women*. Toronto: University of Toronto Press.

Vosko, Leah. 2004. "Confronting the Norm: Gender and the International Regulation of Precarious Work." Ottawa: Law Commission of Canada.

_____ (ed.). 2006. *Precarious Employment: Understanding Labour Market Insecurity in Canada*. Montreal: McGill-Queen's University Press.

REFERENCES

Voyageur, Cora. 2005. "Doing Our Share: Employment and Entrepreneurship in Canada's Aboriginal Community." In Duane Champagne, Karen Jo Torjesen, and Susan Steiner (eds.), *Indigenous Peoples and the Modern State*. Walnut Creek: AltaMira Press.

Vukov, T. 2003. "Imagining Communities Through Immigration Policies." *International Journal of Cultural Studies* 6.

Wacker, Ronnie. 1994. "Strip Mining the Seas." *Sea Frontiers* 40, 3.

Wackernagel, Mathis, and William Rees. 1996. *The Ecological Footprint: Reducing Human Impact on Earth.* Vancouver: New Catalyst.

Wagner, Terry H., and Kent V. Rondeau. 2000. "Reducing the Workforce: Examining its Consequences in Health Care Organizations." *Leadership in Health Services* 13 3.

Wajcman, Judy. 1991. *Feminism Confronts Technology*. Cambridge: Polity.

_____. 2004. *Technofeminism*. UK: Polity Press.

Waldram, James B. 1994. "Canada's 'Indian Problem' and the Indian's Canada Problem." In L. Samuelson (ed.), *Power and Resistance: Critical Thinking about Canadian Social Issues*. Halifax: Fernwood Publishing.

Walker, Alan. 1991. "The Relationship Between the Family and the State in the Care of Older People." *Canadian Journal on Aging* 10, 2.

Walker, Gillian A. 1986. "The Standpoint of Women and the Dilemma of Professionalism in Action." *Resources for Feminist Research* 15, 1.

_____. 1990. *Family Violence and the Women's Movement.* Toronto: University of Toronto Press.

Walkowitz, Judith R. 1977. "The Making of an Outcast Group: Prostitutes and Working Women in Nineteenth-Century Plymouth and Southhampton." In Martha Vicinus (ed.), *A Widening Sphere: Changing Roles of Victorian Women*. Bloomington, IN: Indiana University Press.

_____. 1980a. *Prostitution and Victorian Society: Women, Class and the State*. New York: Cambridge University Press.

_____. 1980b. "The Politics of Prostitution." *Signs* 6, 1.

_____. 1983. "Male Vice and Female Virtue: Feminism and the Politics of Prostitution in Nineteenth-Century Britain." In Ann Barr Snitow, Christine Stansell, and Sharon Thompson (eds.), *Powers of Desire, The Politics of Sexuality*. New York: Monthly Review.

_____. 1992. *City of Dreadful Delight: Narratives of Sexual Danger in Late-Victorian London*. Chicago: University of Chicago Press.

Walkowitz, Judith R., and Daniel J. Walkowitz. 1973. "'We Are Not Beasts of the Field': Prostitution and the Poor in Plymouth and Southampton Under the Contagious Diseases Acts." *Feminist Studies* 1.

Wall, Glenda. 2006. "Childhood and Childrearing." In Maureen Baker (ed.), *Families: Changing Trends in Canada*. Fifth edition. Toronto: McGraw-Hill Ryerson.

Wallerstein, I. 1974. *The Modern World System*. New York: Academic Press.

Walter, Gerald R. 1994. "Defining Sustainable Communities." *International Journal of Forestry* 10, 2.

Warner, Michael. 1999. "Beyond Gay Marriage." In Michael Warner (ed.), *The Trouble with Normal: Sex, Politics and the Ethics of Queer Life*. Cambridge, MA: Harvard University Press.

Warner, Tom. 1999. "Bill 5: 'Same Sex Partner' Law." Outwards (Coalition for Lesbian and Gay Rights in Ontario) November.

_____. 2004. "Fighting the Anti-Queer Right-Wing." Gary Kinsman, interview with Tom Warner. *New Socialist* Jan./Feb.: 32–34.

Warwaruk, Jody. 2002. "Illegal Suite Leaves Sour Taste: Landlord Houses Couple in Hazardous

Converted Warehouse." *Edmonton Journal*, February 20, B1.

Washburn, Jennifer. 2005. *University Inc.: The Corporate Corruption of Higher Education.* New York: Basic Books.

Watkins, Mel. 1977. *Dene Nation: The Colony Within.* Toronto: University of Toronto Press.

Watney, Simon. 1988. "Missionary Positions: AIDS, 'Africa,' and Race." *Difference* 1, 1.

Weatherbee, Douglas. 1989. "The Social Construction of an AIDS Moral Panic in Nova Scotia Newspaper Accounts." Unpublished honours thesis. Wolfville, NS: Acadia University.

Weaver, Sally. 1985. "Federal Difficulties with Aboriginal Rights." In Menno Boldt and J. Anthony Long (eds.), *The Quest for Justice: Aboriginal Peoples and Aboriginal Rights.* Toronto: University of Toronto Press.

_____. 1990. "A New Paradigm in Canadian Indian Policy for the 1990s." *Canadian Ethnic Studies* 22.

Weber, Terry. 2006. "Ottawa Tables Bill to Raise Age of Consent to 16." *Globe and Mail*, June 23, A2.

Weeks, Jeffrey. 1985. *Sexuality and Its Discontents.* London: Routledge and Kegan Paul.

_____. 1995. *Invented Moralities: Sexual Values in an Age of Uncertainty.* New York: Columbia University Press.

Weinberg, George. 1973. *Society and the Healthy Homosexual.* New York: Anchor.

Weiner, Gerry. 1990. "Speech to Commemorate the International Day for the Elimination of Racial Discrimination." Toronto.

Weir, Lorna. 1986. "Studies in the Medicalization of Sexual Danger: Sexual Rule, Sexual Politics, 1830–1930." Unpublished Ph.D. thesis. North York, ON: Department of Social and Political Thought, York University.

Weiss, Linda. 1997. "Globalization and the Myth of the Powerless State." *New Left Review* 225.

Welton, N., and L. Wolf. 2001. *Global Uprising: Confronting the Tyrannies of the 21st Century: Stories from a New Generation of Activists.* Gabriola Island, BC: New Society Publishers.

West, Candace, and Don H. Zimmerman. 1987. "Doing Gender." *Gender & Society* 1.

West, Candace, and Sarah Fenstermaker. 1995. "Doing Difference." *Gender & Society* 9.

West, G. 1984. *Young Offenders and the State.* Toronto: Butterworths.

Wheeler, Glen. 2002. "Marc Hall's Legal Jam." *NOW*, May 16–22.

White, Julie. 1979. *Women and Unions.* Ottawa: Supply and Services.

Willhelm, Sidney. 1969. "Red Man, Black Man and White America: The Constitutional Approach to Genocide." *Catalyst* 4.

Williams, G.I., and R.H. Williams. 1995. "All We Want is Equality: Rhetorical Framing in the Fathers' Rights Movement." In J. Best (ed.), *Images of Issues.* Second edition. New York: Aldine De Gruyter.

Williams, James. 1998. "Getting Housewives the Electric Message: Gender and Energy Marketing in the Early Twentieth Century." In Roger Horowitz and Arwen Mohun (eds.), *His and Hers: Gender, Consumption, and Technology* Virginia: University Press of Virginia.

Williams, Linda. 1984. "'Something Else Besides a Mother': *Stella Dallas* and the Maternal Melodrama." *Cinema Journal* 24, 1.

Williams, Robert, Jr. 1990. *The American Indian in Western Legal Thought: The Discourses of Conquest.* New York: Oxford University Press.

Willson, Kay, and Jennifer Howard. 2001. "Missing Links: The Effects of Health Care Privatization on Women in Manitoba and Saskatchewan." In Pat Armstrong et al. (eds.), *Exposing*

REFERENCES

Privatization: Women and Health Care Reform. Toronto, ON: Garamond Press.

Wilson, Elizabeth. 1983. *What Is to Be Done about Violence against Women.* London: Penguin.

Wilson, Jeremy. 1998. *Talk and Log: Wilderness Politics in British Columbia.* Vancouver: University of British Columbia Press.

Wilson, Susannah J. 1996. *Women, Families and Work.* Fourth edition. Toronto: McGraw.

Winham, Gilbert R. 1992. "Canada, GATT, and the Future of the World Trading System." In Fred Osler Hampson and Christopher J. Maule (eds.), *A New World Order? Canada Among Nations 1992–93.* Ottawa: Carleton University Press.

Winterdyk, John. 2006. *Canadian Criminology.* Toronto: Pearson-Prentice Hall.

Winthrop, R. 2000. "The Real World After Seattle: Trade and Culture." *Practicing Anthropology* 22, 2.

Wismer, Susan. 1996. "The Nasty Game: How Environmental Assessment Is Failing Aboriginal Communities in Canada's North." *Alternatives Journal* 22, 4.

Wodak, Ruth. 2006. "Mediation Between Discourse and Society: Assessing Cognitive Approaches in CDA." *Discourse Studies* 8.

Wolfson, M., and J. Evans. 1989. *Statistics Canada's Low Income Cutoffs: Methodological Concerns and Possibilities.* Ottawa: Statistics Canada.

Women's College Hospital. 1997. "Maintaining Women's Health Values in the Context of Change." Submission to the Health Services Restructuring Commission. Available at <www.cewh-cesf.ca/healthreform>. (May 9). (?access year. Really should have a more specific address?)

Wong, Kristine. 2001. "The Showdown Before Seattle: Race, Class and the Framing of a Movement." In Eddie Yuen, George Katsiaficas and Daniel Burton Rose (eds.), *The Battle of Seattle: The New Challenge to Capitalist Globalization.* New York: Soft Skull Press.

Wong-Wylie, Gina, and Marianne Doherty-Poirier. 1997. "Created Families: Perspectives from Persons Living with HIV/AIDS." Paper presented at the Association for Research in Home Economics, Learned Societies Congress. June 8–10, St. John's, NF.

Wood, Ellen Meiksins. 1998. "Class Compacts, the Welfare State, and Epochal Shifts." *Monthly Review* 49, 8.

Woodhouse, Howard. 2003. "Commercializing Research at the University of Saskatchewan." *Saskatchewan Notes* 2, 8.

Woodsworth, Charles. 1972. *Strangers Within Our Gates.* Toronto: University of Toronto Press.

Woollard, Robert F., and Aleck S. Ostry. 2000. *Fatal Consumption: Rethinking Sustainable Development.* Vancouver: University of British Columbia Press.

World Bank. 1993. *World Development Report.* New York: World Bank.

World Commission on Environment and Development (WCED). 1987. *Our Common Future.* Oxford: Oxford University Press.

World Resources Institute (WRI). 2000. "Pollution and Waste Increasing in Five Countries Despite More Efficient Use of Resources." News Release. Available at <www.wri.org/business/newsrelease_text.cfm?NewsReleaseID=6>. (Accessed January 29, 2007.)

World Wildlife Fund (WWF). 2000. "Needed: Two More Planets." Press Release. Available at <www.panda.org/about_wwf/what_we_do/policy/news/index.cfm?uNewsID=2155>. (Accessed January 29, 2007.)

Worth H, Cindy Patton, and Diane Goldstein. 2005. "Reckless Vectors" issue of *Sexuality Research & Social Policy: Journal of NSERC* 2, 2.

Worth, H., Cindy Patton, and M. McGehee. 2005. "Legislating the Pandemic: A Global Survey of

HIV/AIDS in Criminal Law." *Sexuality Resdarch & Social Policy: Journal of NSRC* 2, 2: 15–22.

Wortley, Scot. 2002. "The Depictions of Race and Crime in the Toronto Print Media." In Bernard Schissel and Carolyn Brooks (eds.) *Marginality and Condemnation: An Introduction to Critical Criminology*. Black Point, NS: Fernwood Publishing.

Wotherspoon, Terry, and Vic Satzewich. 1993. *First Nations: Race, Class, and Gender Relations*. Scarborough, ON: Nelson.

Wright, Cynthia. 2006. "Against Illegality: Directions in Organizing by and with Non-Status People in Canada." In Caelie Frampton, Gary Kinsman, AK Thompson, and Kate Tilleczek (eds.), *Sociology for Changing the World: Social Movements/Social Research*. Black Point, NS: Fernwood Publishing.

Wu, Zheng, and Christoph M. Schimmele. 2005. "Repartnering After First Union Disruption." *Journal of Marriage and Family* 67, 1.

Wulwik, L. 1999. "Taking Action Against Corporate Globalization: Corporate Cannibalism." *Kinesis* October/November.

Wuttunee, Wanda. 2004. *Living Rhythms: Lessons in Aboriginal Economic Resilience and Vision*. Montreal: McGill-Queen's University Press.

Wynne, D., and T. Hartnagel. 1975. "Race and Plea Negotiation." *Canadian Journal of Sociology* 1.

Yalnizyan, Armine. 1998. *The Growing Gap: A Report on Growing Inequality Between Rich and Poor in Canada*. Toronto: Centre for Social Justice.

Yates, Michael D. 1994. *Longer Hours, Fewer Jobs: Employment and Unemployment in the United States*. New York: Monthly Review.

York, Geoffrey. 1990. *The Dispossessed: Life and Death in Native Canada*. Toronto: Little.

Young, Iris Marion. 1987. "Impartiality and the Civic Public: Some Implications of Feminist Critiques of Moral and Political Theory." In Seyla Benhabib and Drucilla Cornell (eds.), *Feminism as Critique*. Minneapolis: University of Minnesota Press.

Youniss, James, et al. 2002. "Youth Civic Engagement in the Twenty-First Century." *Journal of Research on Adolescence* 12, 1 (March).

Yuen, Eddie. 2001. "Introduction." In Eddie Yuen, George Katsiaficas, and Daniel Burton Rose (eds.), *The Battle of Seattle: The New Challenge to Capitalist Globalization*. New York: Soft Skull Press.

Yuen, Eddie, George Katsiaficas, and Daniel Burton Rose. 2001. *The Battle of Seattle: The New Challenge to Capitalist Globalization*. New York: Soft Skull Press.

_____. 2004. *Confronting Capitalism: Dispatches from a Global Movement*. New York: Soft Skull Press.

Zuboff, Shoshana. 1988. *In the Age of the Smart Machine: The Future of Work and Power*. New York: Basic Books.

INDEX